Books by Philip McFarland

Sojourners   1979

A House Full of Women   1960

SOJOURNERS

SOJOURNERS

Philip McFarland

ATHENEUM

New York

1979

Library of Congress Cataloging in Publication Data
McFarland, Philip James.

Sojourners.
Bibliography: p.
Includes index.
1. Irving, Washington, 1783–1859.   2. Authors,
American—19th century—Biography.   I. Title.
PS2081.M3   818'.2'09 [B]   79–63630
ISBN 0–689–11003–0

FOR PATRICIA

Why dress we up these our Inns as if they were our homes & are as careful about a few nights lodgings here as if we designed an everlasting abode. For we are but sojourners & pilgrims here, and have no fixed habitation upon earth . . .

WASHINGTON IRVING, *Tour in Scotland 1817*

WHILE PRESENTING the achievement of Washington Irving, our nation's first great man of letters, I have sought in the following narrative to recreate as well the worlds through which the wanderer Irving moved: in the United States, Britain, Germany, France, Spain, and back to America. In particular I have undertaken to reveal, more fully perhaps than would the writer of a conventional biography, some of the fascinating lives—Burr's, Scott's, Mary Shelley's, Astor's, and others'—with which Irving's was involved during a lifelong journey that took place between the end of the American Revolution and the beginning of the Civil War. But through that historical tapestry of richly contrasting design was woven, like a dark thread, the life of one as different from those on every point as they sometimes seem from each other; that foreshadowing life, of the abolitionist John Brown, I describe in these pages too.

In doing so—in evoking experiences of earlier dreamers and sufferers—and in rekindling to whatever degree the warmth of a formative past, I have been encouraged by the hope that the various sketches of Irving's worlds, friends, and contemporaries may help affirm for some readers (as they have for me) the abundant possibilities inherent in the human adventure. Armed, moreover, with an awareness of what others before us have endured and transcended, we may be better able to move with fortitude and grace into the cold reaches of the future.

P. M.

CONTENTS

---

pany—Astor & Son—The daughters—A visit with Irving in Paris—Losses—Irving goes west—His attitude toward Indians—Camp scenes—A buffalo hunt—Pawnees!—"A Tour on the Prairies"—Old man at Hell Gate—Recalling a prodigious enterprise—Irving as historian of the West—The Tonquin *sets sail—Voyage to the Pacific—Tensions aboard—End of the voyage—An expedition overland—Disaster on the Snake River—The fate of Astoria—Friends of Astor—Gerrit Smith and John Brown—Last years of a butcher's son.*

DREGS   491

Irving as Astor's executor—Tasks of old age—You should write one more book—Irving's death—His funeral—Harpers Ferry—The wagon comes to a halt.

ILLUSTRATIONS

(following page 206)

John Brown in 1856
Courtesy of The Boston Athenaeum

The Kennedy Farm

William Street, New York, in 1800
Courtesy of the Local History and Genealogy Division, The New York Public Library, Astor, Lenox and Tilden Foundations

Aaron Burr in 1802
Courtesy of The New York Historical Society, New York City

Richmond Hill
Courtesy of the Local History and Genealogy Division, The New York Public Library, Astor, Lenox and Tilden Foundations

Theodosia Burr at age 11
Courtesy of Oliver Burr Jennings

Theodosia Burr in maturity
Courtesy of The New York Historical Society, New York City

Irving during his first European tour
Courtesy of the Manuscripts and Archives Division, The New York Public Library, Astor, Lenox and Tilden Foundations

The mansion of Harman Blennerhassett
From Herbert S. Parmet and M. B. Hecht's Aaron Burr *(Macmillan, 1967)*

Aaron Burr in 1834
Courtesy of The New York Historical Society, New York City

Washington Irving about the time of *Knickerbocker's History of New York*
Courtesy of Sleepy Hollow Restorations, Tarrytown, New York

Isabella II
Courtesy of the Concord Free Public Library, Concord, Massachusetts

Madrid in the time of Isabella II
Courtesy of the Concord Free Public Library, Concord, Massachusetts

Isabella in maturity
Courtesy of Prints Division, The New York Public Library, Astor, Lenox and Tilden Foundations

Irving after his return to America
Courtesy of Sleepy Hollow Restorations, Tarrytown, New York

John Jacob Astor in 1794
Courtesy of the Collection of the New York Chamber of Commerce and Industry

Astoria in 1813
Courtesy of the Concord Free Public Library, Concord, Massachusetts

Astor in old age
Courtesy of the Collection of The New York Public Library, Astor, Lenox and Tilden Foundations

Hell Gate
Courtesy of the Manuscripts and Archives Division, The New York Public Library, Astor, Lenox and Tilden Foundations

Irving at Sunnyside
Courtesy of the Manuscripts and Archives Division, The New York Public Library, Astor, Lenox and Tilden Foundations

John Brown in May, 1859
Courtesy of the Concord Free Public Library, Concord, Massachusetts

Skirmish at Harpers Ferry
Courtesy of the Department of Defense National Archives

Maps appear on the following pages: 20–21, 104–05, 196–97, 304, 388, 432–33.

DEPARTED YEARS

The shadows of departed years . . . are gathering over me.

IRVING AT SUNNYSIDE

T H E Y   C A L L E D John Brown the Old Man, this despite his being no more than fifty-nine that summer; nor would he live to be sixty. They thought of him as old, and they thought of him as tall, although he stood no taller than five feet nine. Garrison wrote of him as a "tall, spare, farmer-like man," and Sanborn, who saw him often, described him as a "tall, slender, and commanding figure." We catch other glimpses, equally sharp, perhaps as deceptive, of "the signs of fire" in his face, a face "thin, worn, resolute." When he laughed, "he made not the slightest sound, not even a whisper or an intake of breath; but he shook all over and laughed violently. It was the most curious thing imaginable to see him, in utter silence, rock and quake with mirth."

Not that many such jocose moments were his, for here was a man obsessed; and etched more deeply in our memories than his mirthful face is the image of him at another, terrible time, near midnight before the Sabbath in a Kansas cabin, where a woman ill with measles was cowering in her sickbed, fearful for her husband who had been aroused from sleep by strangers in the room: "The old man, who seemed to be in command, looked at me, and then around at the children." At that dread instant she too perceived John Brown as "a tall, narrow-faced, elderly man," clothes soiled, a leather cravat black at his neck, a straw hat on his head. He and his little gang took the woman's husband outside. She waited fearfully, then went to the door when she thought she heard a call. All was quiet. Next morning they found Wilkinson, the proslavery settler, in the yard

among dead brush. His throat had been slit, and his head and side were
hacked open.

Four other settlers were massacred along the Pottawatomie during
that Saturday evening's grim work that lengthened into the early hours
of Sunday, May 25, 1856. Outside, the watchdogs "raged and barked
furiously," men struggled for life in the dark, cutlasses swung and
slashed, and the raiders fled on stolen horses from the Doyle cabin, from
the Harris cabin.

Three years later, though, in Maryland, during the summer and
fall of 1859, there would be mirth once more among Brown's followers
—his "flock of sheep"—when storms overhead served to liberate a score
of men from their hiding place among the wasps in the stifling attic of a
rented log farmhouse. Only in such hours, in the noise of August thunder and driving rain, could the recruits to Brown's cause, all of them
energetic and almost all under thirty, safely emerge and shout and dance
and run up and down stairs, relieving the tensions of waiting.

They were big men, cramped in that space under the sloping roof;
seven of them were over six feet tall. And almost all of them were very
far from home. Among them were a couple of Iowa Quaker boys, an ex-
army man from Connecticut, a black college student from Oberlin, a
white man down from Canada, three of Brown's own sons, a son-in-law
from the Adirondacks, and Brown's daughter Annie, fifteen years old, to
do the cooking and cleaning. Annie moved about the yard spreading
clothes on the fence to dry, like any other farm woman attending her
family. Yet much of the time she was uneasy. At any hour of day fat,
barefoot Mrs. Huffmaster might arrive with her four children, ostensibly to tend her pumpkin patch nearby. A "worse plague than the fleas,"
the woman snooped and pried. Annie would come forth from the farmhouse and, if it was mealtime, would stand gossiping in the yard while
the "invisibles," as she called them, inside in the living room were
gathering food and plates and tablecloth together and retreating silently
upstairs, making sure not to rattle their spoons.

For the neighbors must not know of the existence of this little
army. The hours of those long days of late summer and fall the recruits
passed in cleaning their Sharps' rifles or assembling pikes, weapons that
had traveled south innocuously dismantled as kitchen utensils and hoe
handles. Or the men might play checkers, while Aaron Stevens, who had
a fine baritone voice, would sing "Faded Flowers" for them. Sometimes
the eccentric Stewart Taylor mused aloud, with a strange composure, on
his own violent death that he knew to be imminent. Were they villains
or heroes, these men whose faces look somberly, bloodlessly out at us
from the paled tintypes: Will Leeman and his crony Albert Hazlett,
John Kagi, Dangerfield Newby, and the others, white and black, assembled for a purpose in that kitchen? Huddled on his low stool by

the stove, old Brown himself, shaken with the ague, would review his
plan of attack, ponder his maps and Provisional Constitution, write
more letters for funds, pore over his Bible: "So Gideon, and the hundred
men that were with him, came unto the outside of the camp in the beginning of the middle watch . . . and they cried, The sword of the
LORD and of Gideon! And they stood every man in his place round
about the camp: and all the host ran, and cried, and fled. And the
three hundred blew the trumpets, and the LORD set every man's sword
against his fellow, even throughout all the host; and the host fled . . ."

Those were the rhythms, and that was the God the old man had
known from earliest childhood—Old Testament cadences and Calvin's
awful, brooding God of wrath. From the beginning, in a stern and
humble Connecticut household at the turn of the century, Brown's father
had taught the child to fear God, and to feed that fear had often let him
feel the rod on his back that punished earthly transgressions. The boy
had had a meager enough childhood, a mother dead when he was eight,
the father restlessly on the move from Connecticut to the Western Reserve, seeking the elusive luck that his son would spend most of his own
life in search of as well. How rigorous, how bleak seems the bulk of
John Brown's quest now: a record of court trials and bankruptcy and
false starts and failures. He was married twice and had twenty children;
he tried his hand as tanner, surveyor, shepherd, wool merchant, land
speculator. He moved, from Hudson in Ohio to New Richmond in Pennsylvania, back to Franklin Mills in Ohio, to Springfield in Massachusetts, to North Elba in New York, vainly pursuing his callings. Joyless,
tireless, inept, he scraped for his livelihood through the 'twenties, the
'thirties, the 'forties. One child died of whooping cough; four in succession—Charles, Peter, Sarah, Austin—died of dysentery: "God has seen
fit to visit us with the pestilence . . . and Four of our number sleep in
the dust, and Four of us that are still living have been more or less
unwell but appear to be nearly recovered." Still more of his children
would die, though—nine in all—before he moved where his life took on
a terrific, immortal meaning at last, this time in Kansas.

One cause had always occupied that grave mind. As he had learned
of God in childhood, John Brown had also learned when a child to
loathe slavery as an abomination in the sight of the God he feared.
When hardly in his teens he had seen a black slave, about his own age,
beaten with an iron fire shovel. At that moment he had sworn "*Eternal
war* with slavery," a war that he would finally wage so fearsomely in
Kansas in the middle eighteen fifties that the whole nation, half-slave,
half-free, would soon know of him: Captain Brown, Old Brown of
Osawatomie. Five of his sons were in Kansas at the time (one would be
murdered there), where they had come in the spring of 1855 for the
golden life that the pamphlets were promising settlers of those virgin
prairies. They were coming as free-soil men to stand up against pro-

slavery ruffians, the river-bottom riffraff swarming across the border from Missouri to extend slavery by force and fraud into a fertile new territory. Before long in their midst was old Brown himself, at Black Jack, at Lawrence, on the Wakarusa, ducking grapeshot in the oaks and cottonwoods northwest of Osawatomie while twigs rained down on him, swimming the Marais des Cygnes, a "queer figure, in a broad straw hat and a white linen duster, his old coattails floating outspread upon the water and a revolver held high in each hand, over his head." And he was at Pottawatomie Creek, in the darkness after midnight that Sunday in May 1856, there with the little group bent over the water to wash their broadswords clean. Behind them, not far down the road, lay four men— Wilkinson and three others—massacred. Nearby, in the creek, lay a fifth, William Sherman, who would be found next morning with his skull split open in two places and "some of his brains" washed away. His left hand was cut off "except a little piece of skin on one side."

"And I will feed them that oppress thee with their own flesh; and they shall be drunken with their own blood, as with sweet wine." Kansas at last knew peace, and would enter the Union free; but Brown had another plan, long maturing, in another part of the field, far from the prairies. "He proposed," Colonel Forbes later wrote the New York *Herald*, "with some twenty-five to fifty (colored and white mixed), well armed and bringing a quantity of spare arms, to beat up a slave quarter in Virginia. . . ." There was more to the plan than that. He would seize a United States arsenal, arm the slaves with requisitioned weapons and those pikes he had assembled, take slaveholders as hostages, and retreat into the Alleghenies to establish a new state in which blacks would be taught "the useful and mechanical arts" and "be instructed in all the business of life." He expected, indeed, that those acts would bring on the destruction of slavery once and for all. But such a plan needed arms and dedicated, couragous men and, above all, money, for which Brown was waiting at the Kennedy farm in Maryland through the hot summer months and into the fall of 1859.

Finally in October, the signs as he read them urged action. The harvest was in, the slaves idle; the moon was near full. So Sunday morning, October 16, he mustered his men in the farmhouse living room, swore in new recruits, late arrivals—another propitious sign—and had the Provisional Constitution under which all would fight read aloud once more. There was a Bible reading too, "impressive beyond expression," one who heard it remembered, a text that spoke of our duty to free those in bondage. Then Brown left his men and went off to a neighboring Dunker church he had fallen into the habit of attending; there he was known as plain Isaac Smith from upper New York, where sharp frosts kill crops, renting the Kennedy farm down the road to see if he wanted to move to these parts for good.

Later, in the afternoon, within the close quarters of the house plans were rehearsed, final orders given, and the men left to while away what time remained to them. Some dozed; others talked low; a few bronzed their gun barrels or wrote last letters to loved ones. By eight it was dark. Now John Brown assembled his band for the third time—"Men, get on your arms"—and they went out to the wagon. It was a drizzly night, the air chill, the moon behind clouds. There were about a score of them together that autumn evening in 1859, young men eager and nervous, and one old man. Their rifles shouldered, they fell in by twos behind the wagon where the pikes had been loaded, while the old man in his battered Kansas cap climbed aboard. Then at a call the horse moved forward, starting the wagon wheels turning over the five steep, winding miles to Harpers Ferry.

Northeast of the village of Harpers Ferry, some two hundred thirty-five miles as the crow flies and twenty-five miles north of Manhattan along the east bank of the Hudson River, stands to this day Sunnyside, within the walls of which, in those same autumn months of 1859, another old man was passing his final season on earth. Contemporaries and fellow citizens of one land could hardly have been more different than were John Brown and this second old man, whose name was Washington Irving. Both men, to be sure, had grown up in the shadow of sternly devout fathers, one in Connecticut, the other in New York. Both wrote memorable prose. They would die within four days of one another. But there resemblances cease; for Brown's life foreshadowed a darkly contentious future, as Irving's reflected a more innocent past. The one man was unyielding, the other was characteristically conciliatory; the one was provincial, the other cosmopolitan; and if both expressed themselves effectively in writing, one did so by instinct, echoing biblical rhythms that were about all he knew of prose, whereas the other did so by means of a cultured taste and an easy mastery of rhetoric.

Differences continue to suggest themselves. "I have one unconquerable weakness," John Brown admitted in the final year of his life. "I have always been more afraid of being taken into an evening party of ladies and gentlemen, than of meeting a company of men with guns." But as armed men seldom threatened his poise, evening parties held no terror for Washington Irving, who during a long life moved with ease over two continents through the most accomplished societies of his time. Among his personal friends this adored American could count, as a sample, five Presidents, four foreign rulers—British, French, German, and Spanish—the novelists Scott and Dickens, the naturalist Audubon, the historians Prescott and Bancroft, the actress Fanny Kemble, the bibliographer Obadiah Rich—"honest Rich, a most obliging and good-hearted man"—that prince of publishers John Murray, the bizarre Randolph of

Roanoke, the philosopher Godwin and his daughter Mary Shelley, Aaron Burr, the poets Bryant and Longfellow, the painters Allston and Newton and Leslie, the English statesmen Russell and Peel, the Irish songster and biographer Thomas Moore, Commodore Stephen Decatur, Dolley Madison—"a fine, portly, buxom dame"—the critic Jeffrey, the theatrical producer William Dunlap, the millionaire John Jacob Astor; and among his admirers he could number virtually the entire reading public in Europe and America. "I don't believe," Senator Preston of South Carolina, another old friend, wrote Irving in this very year 1859, "I don't believe that any man, in any country, has ever had a more affectionate admiration for him than that given to you in America." And again in 1859, in the fall, appeared an article in the *Home Journal*: "Mr. Irving," it asserted, "by far the most honored man in our country, is, curiously enough, even less honored than loved."

Indeed, what other American, at any time in the nation's history, has during his life to a like degree awakened and retained the love of so many of his fellow citizens, of all parties and regions? Perhaps Franklin; certainly not Washington or Lincoln or any public figure of the twentieth century. And Irving was loved abroad as well. The young Charles Dickens could confess to him from England in 1841: "There is no living writer, and there are very few among the dead, whose approbation I should feel so proud to earn." When the two men met in New York the following year, "Washington Irving is *a great* fellow," Dickens informed his friend Forster. "We have laughed together most heartily." And later the English novelist would write of himself to Irving as "a man who loves you, and holds communion with your spirit oftener, perhaps, than any other person alive." Two decades earlier Lord Byron, after receiving a visitor in Ravenna, testified that he had "talked with him much of Irving, whose writings are my delight." The Scottish painter David Wilkie exulted over his good fortune, during a reunion in Spain, to find himself with "such a man, and such a friend, as Washington Irving." And Sir Walter Scott in Edinburgh, having repeatedly expressed "the highest opinion of Irving's productions," let it be known in the 1820s that the American was "a very great favorite" of his.

Scott, like Dickens, like Longfellow and many others, would begin by loving Irving's books, then later know the man himself and discover that love extended. "I had the pleasure of meeting Mr. Irving in Spain," Longfellow remembered in December 1859, "and found the author, whom I had loved, repeated in the man. The same playful humor; the same touches of sentiment; the same poetic atmosphere; and, what I admired still more, the entire absence of all literary jealousy, of all that mean avarice of fame, which counts what is given to another as so much taken from one's self." The traits that Longfellow mentions do characterize Irving aptly: humor, gentle feeling, diffidence. And they account

in part for his enormous popularity, as they might lead us to wonder
how so genial an individual, so casually, was able to make a mark of
such dimensions on his age.

He was a diplomat, and an able one, both in England and—for
four years as envoy extraordinary and minister plenipotentiary—in
Spain. He was a distinguished historian and biographer—only the
second American ever to be elected (and he was elected unanimously) to
the prestigious and exclusive Real Academia de Historia in Madrid. He
was an essayist and teller of tales whose success was unprecedented:
the first American, as the poet William Cullen Bryant noted, by his pen
alone to win fame—and money enough to live off what he wrote.
Irving's achievement, then, enlarged what was possible in the United
States in his time, so that others—Cooper, Hawthorne, Parkman, Bryant
himself—were encouraged by that example to persevere. Accordingly,
all American fiction, poetry, and history might reasonably be dated
(Bryant insists *should* be dated) from the publication of Washington
Irving's first internationally famous work, in 1820.

He was thus a man of consequence, more than merely a gracious
member of society, welcome guest, phrasemaker—though Irving it was
who gave us the term *Gotham* for New York, gave us Father Knickerbocker as an emblem of New York, gave us that ubiquitous phrase "the
almighty dollar" (and when criticized for doing so, explained that "no
irreverence was intended even to the dollar itself; which . . . is daily
becoming more and more an object of worship"). He gave us,
too—some fifteen years before Dickens in *Pickwick*—those descriptions
of Christmas in *The Sketch Book* that have altered a nation's customs.
For before the 1820s, in Puritan and post-Puritan America, the Christmas season had been only somberly and briefly observed. It was Irving
who first enveloped the season for English-speaking readers with the
warmth of blazing fires on fine, clear, frosty mornings, with the Christmas banquet of a boar's head decorated with lemon and rosemary, with
the climactic Wassail Bowl made of the richest and raciest wines, highly
spiced and sweetened, "roasted apples bobbing about the surface." He
gave us scenes, in short, of good cheer and innocent hilarity that still
may make old walls ring with merriment, "echoing back the joviality of
long departed years." His descriptions were read, and read widely—"Of
all American authors," it was noted authoritatively in 1853, "those of
school-books excepted, there is no one of whose books so many have been
circulated as those of Mr. Irving"; as a consequence, the spirit of his
descriptions was infused in the celebration of Christmas on both sides of
the Atlantic, not only during his own day but long after.

Irving was read, and his worlds—freshly and lovingly described
—were recreated in the lives of his readers. Those readers honored
him as they could. Packet ships bore his name. Mountains were named
after him, as well as streets and inns and banks. There were Irving

Societies and Irving Literary Institutes. In 1854, when he was seventy-one, he received a note from a neighbor that the village adjacent to his home on the Hudson was changing its name to Irvington, thereby acceding to the wishes of all the inhabitants of the community but one, that one being the ever-modest Irving himself. But perhaps the most affecting distinction of all had been bestowed upon him as long before as June 15, 1831, when this hardware merchant's son who never went to college—a writer more by chance than design—found himself in a foreign land, summoned to Oxford University. There, as he stepped forward to receive the honorary degree of Doctor of Civil Law, the English undergraduates erupted with cries of acclaim: "Diedrich Knickerbocker!" they shouted in their enthusiasm. "Rip Van Winkle!" "Ichabod Crane!"

"I have heard him say," his nephew recorded years later, "that he was quite overcome, though all the time contending with a laugh at the vociferous and saturnalian applause." We see him there, on that summer day in England long ago, most appealingly—his gowned, portly self, the laugh, the blush of embarrassment—and hear again the grateful, joyful shouts of students for this beloved foreigner in their midst. Those creations, then—of old Rip stiff in his joints, with his rusty firelock and foot-long beard, of the gallant Ichabod Crane, schoolmaster of Sleepy Hollow, with his long snipe nose, grasshopper elbows, and feet like shovels, a "scarecrow eloped from a cornfield"—those were what Irving was most loved for in his lifetime, and they remain his lasting gifts to his countrymen and to the world.

Yet he gave us other gifts: his comic *History of New York*, still a joy with its droll Dutch absurdities, that caused Scott's sides to ache with laughter and kept Coleridge up an entire night reading; his picturesque legends of the Alhambra in Spain; his books on the American West, landscapes of prairies and mountains peopled by dour Indians and trappers and carefree voyageurs; his biographies, finally, of the like-minded Oliver Goldsmith, of Christopher Columbus, of George Washington. That last was a labor of love that exacted of him a staggering price, a work first conceived when Irving was in his early forties but deferred to become the heavy capstone of his literary career, erected into place, at the end of a long life, by enfeebled hands, with only the greatest effort. The opening volume was published when its author was seventy-two. (The Life of Washington, he would say with a smile, will be the death of Irving.) Thereafter, from 1855 on, he would be primarily concerned with finishing a story that at last required four more volumes to tell. "I live only in the Revolution," he admitted to his nephew during those years of Bleeding Kansas that preceded the Civil War. "I have no other existence now—can think of nothing else."

At times he could, of course; for he did have another existence late in his career, one that has seemed singularly idyllic to those familiar with it, both then and now. "Since my return, in 1846, from my diplomatic mission to Spain," he explained in a letter to a long-silent English correspondent after the third volume of *Washington* had been published, "I have been leading a quiet life in a little rural retreat I had previously established on the banks of the Hudson, which, in fact, has been my home for twenty years past. I am in a beautiful part of the country, in an agreeable neighborhood, am on the best of terms with my neighbors, and have a house full of nieces, who almost make me as happy as if I were a married man." The correspondent to whom he was directing those words had been, as we shall discover, one of the two women in his lifetime whom Irving had passionately loved and might have married. Now, however, the Dresden years with Emily Foster were irretrievably past, and he was at Sunnyside, an old bachelor trying "not to grow rusty or fusty or crusty," as he went about making additions to his home—building a tower for guests, outhouses, a gardener's house, pruning and replanting trees to improve vistas of the river, laying out paths and raising his fruits and vegetables "at very little more than twice the market price."

Of Sunnyside—that "little old-fashioned stone mansion, all made up of gable ends, and as full of angles and corners as an old cocked hat"—the charm abides. Today a visitor finds, as did Thackeray, who, like so many others, was a guest there during Irving's lifetime, "a funny little in-and-out cottage surrounded by a little domain of lawns . . . bits of small parlors . . . a little study not much bigger than my back room." And the guides of today's visitor, sprightly and knowledgeable young ladies of whom Irving would assuredly have approved could he have seen them, crossing his green lawns in their hoop skirts, moving through a radiant summer morning toward the house still covered with wisteria and ivy and honeysuckle—the guides evoke ghosts of those nieces (Mary, Kate, Sarah, Julia) who grew up at midcentury with their father and his famous brother in these same lovely surroundings. Indeed, the niece Kate would grow ancient here, dying at last as late as 1911, in her ninety-sixth year, no doubt still full of memories, of the evening backgammon games in the parlor, of the sleigh rides and the dog Toby, and Imp, and Fanny, a pig "of peerless beauty," and of all the birds—and of her elderly uncle napping after dinner on the sofa, or emerging from his study, or lolling on the breeze-stroked piazza off the dining room that faces the Tappan Zee; for he was never tired, as he said, of sitting there in his old Voltaire chair of a long summer morning with a book in his hand, "sometimes reading, sometimes musing, and sometimes dozing, and mixing all up in a pleasant dream."

During those closing years of his life Irving occasionally made use of the new railroad that had intruded upon the serenity of Sunnyside, passing beside the Hudson with its "unearthly, infernal, and horrific alarum." He would make trips by train to Manhattan, or to Washington and Virginia, changing at Harpers Ferry, to research the enormous biography that was absorbing his thoughts. From one such excursion in his seventieth year he returned on a day in March, alighting at the station a ten minutes' walk from home. "The walk was along the railroad, in full sight of the house. I saw female forms in the porch, and I knew the spyglass was in hand. In a moment there was a waving of handkerchiefs, and a hurrying hither and thither. Never did old bachelor come to such a loving home, so gladdened by blessed womankind." He reports that after all the "kissing and crying and laughing and rejoicing" were over, he sallied out to inspect his domains, "welcomed home by my prime minister Robert, and my master of the house Thomas, and my keeper of the poultry yard, William." Everything he found to be in order: fields had been manured, trees trimmed, fences repaired and painted. "I really believe more had been done in my absence than would have been done had I been home." And his horses were in good condition: the coach horses Dandy and Billy were "as sleek as seals," while Gentleman Dick, his saddle horse, "showed manifest pleasure at seeing me; put his cheek against mine, laid his head on my shoulder, and would have nibbled at my ear had I permitted it." Elsewhere the Chinese geese and white topknot ducks "were sailing like frigates in the pond." Taffy and Tony, "two pet dogs of a dandy race, kept more for show than use, received me with well-bred though rather cool civility," in contrast to the "little terrier slut Ginger," who "bounded about me almost crazy with delight, having five little Gingers toddling at her heels, with which she had enriched me during my absence."

To such a welcome could Irving return late in life. Surely an old woman who had once been a part of the very scene would treasure to the end her own memories of so mellow a homecoming, so vivid still.

In those days visitors arrived from near and far to see the world-famous occupant of Sunnyside: not only writers like Thackeray, but such public figures as Louis Napoleon, and others less well-known; for by midcentury Sunnyside was enshrined in the public's consciousness like Wordsworth's cottage near Ambleside, like the Brownings' casa at Florence. What those visitors on the Hudson found when they arrived was a bewigged—and so dark-haired—old gentleman, dressed in old-fashioned black, wearing white stockings, a Scottish shawl, a Panama hat—a host always gracious and temperate and generous with his time. "He may be five feet six or seven inches high," one caller on a summer day in 1856 recorded; "his form rather round and full, but not corpulent; his countenance florid and slightly bronzed; his lips thick; his eyes blue or gray; his expression mild and benignant, with a slight tinge of mirthfulness; his air modest . . . his voice is not clear, but rather husky, as if catarrhal; his conversation is animated and engaging, and he appears quite as willing to hear as to speak."

But when Washington Irving did speak, the words he uttered

could evoke an age that reached back to the infancy of his country, an age that embraced worlds far beyond his country's ample boundaries. Some who heard those reminiscences would depart and publish accounts of their visit. One such the host was later moved to chide good-naturedly: "I wish . . . that I had known our conversation was likely to be recorded; I should then have tasked myself to say some wise or witty things, to be given as specimens of my *off-hand table talk*. One should always know when they are sitting for a portrait, that they may endeavor to look handsomer than themselves, and attitudinize. . . ."

So the days passed for this withered old gentleman, as he saw himself, nearing the end of an "erratic and precarious career," absorbed with his family and visitors, with the endless letters to answer, the occasional trips, and always the book: "It is now half-past twelve at night, and I am sitting here scribbling in my study, long after all the family are abed and asleep—a habit I have fallen much into of late. Indeed, I never fagged more steadily with my pen than I do at present. I have a long task in hand, which I am anxious to finish, that I may have a little leisure in the brief remnant of life that is left to me."

That on a winter night in 1852. What was left to him was seven more years of labor, of fagging long hours against ever increasing doubts of his own abilities, feeling ever increasing fears that his strength and his mind would not see him through. Then, instead of leisure when the work was done at last, what visited him left the old man shaken and pitiable, as it twisted and blackened his remnant of life remaining.

On March 15, 1859, he put the finishing touch to the final volume of *The Life of Washington*. "Thank Heaven," he reported to a friend, "my fifth volume is launched, and henceforth I give up all further tasking of the pen." On the seventeenth, in the afternoon, he rode to the home of a neighbor, a Mrs. Bartlett, to leave with her what she had earlier asked him for—the very pen with which the final words of that work had been written. But he was "sadly out of spirits." Since the preceding fall he had been tormented by asthma: breathing had become difficult, and he suffered "a sort of spasmodic affection of the stomach, which roused him whenever he was falling asleep." The complaint had taught him to dread the nights: after dinner he would find himself "horror-haunted" with the prospect of what lay ahead. His nephew, a man in his mid-fifties who would become his biographer and whose words are here quoted, had moved at Irving's request to Sunnyside about this time; with his wife, he remained to the end, helping to comfort the uncle he had worked closely with in the past and long had idolized.

Now the old gentleman was falling prey to hallucinations and bad dreams: that he had killed one of the robins outside his window, that he had still to write another huge book before he could rest, that there was—and he would start up from his bed in dismay—"some poor family he had to take care of." Nothing the nephew had ever witnessed seemed

to him more affecting than were the struggles of a beloved and courageous relative against the ravages of nerves giving way: "It was so new
to him, so opposed to his healthy and heroic nature—to the whole character of his past life—that it seemed impossible for him to yield to its
dominion."

Yet yield Irving must. April 3 was his birthday: seventy-six that
day. "A dull, cheerless morning, overcast at dawn, and raining before
seven." The dinner table had been decked with flowers, and desserts
were supplied by adoring neighbors. "All tried to be cheerful at dinner,"
the nephew tells us, though no doubt some were remembering a quite
different birthday only a year before: "a bright, beautiful, genial day"
that earlier occasion had been granted, with the usual family party assembled to honor Irving, himself "in fine spirits, serenely cheerful."
Altogether, the preceding celebration had passed off delightfully—
"nothing to mar it"—in contrast to this dinner one year later, where in
the course of the meal the old man was seized by a paroxysm of
coughing so severe that he had to leave the room, not to return. Behind
him he left loved ones grown ever more fearful that this in fact was
his final birthday; the dinner was ended, and "all rose from the table
in tears."

Before his nephew the old man would be forced in time to humili-
ate himself: "I shall have to get you to mount guard again tonight. I am
ashamed to ask it, but you cannot conceive what an abject coward this
nervousness makes of me." For relief he might smoke a medicated ciga-
rette that Dr. Peters had prescribed, or try, every four hours in a wine-
glass of water, Jonas Whitcomb's Remedy, which Dr. Oliver Wendell
Holmes had suggested during a recent visit. Yet relief came only rarely.
More often the old man was made to tremble before the door of his room
near the top of the stairs—that "haunted chamber," as he had taken to
calling it. His nephew, who slept in the porch room adjoining, was
awakened one night by low moans, indistinct. He rose and crossed the
hall. Was anything distressing his uncle? "This harassed feeling," came
the agonized answer; "these long, long, long hours till morning."

On an early summer day, out for a carriage ride, "I've always
dreaded," Irving was moved to confess, "beyond anything, becoming a
confirmed invalid, and a burden to those about me." He took to dozing on
the sofa in the parlor downstairs, among his family sewing or reading or
playing chess: "There is no arguing with these things. They are incon-
trollable. They come and go like the wind. When you are all about me
here, I can sleep quietly; but when I get to my own room, and you are all
gone, and I think all are asleep but myself, then comes over me this
strange dread again." And sometimes even during the day it assaulted
him: "Horribly nervous this morning," the devoted nephew records of
his uncle's behavior on one occasion. "Returning from a walk, I withdrew to my room, but he soon came up and knocked at my door, and

begged to be let in to be with me. Was perfectly ashamed of himself, he said, but had a horror of being alone." The two of them went down to the parlor, where the sufferer was prevailed upon to take a prescription. Then the nephew read aloud to him, as he had often done, till the old man fell asleep at last on the sofa.

Callers found him much changed. A friend stopping by late in June 1859 "thought he looked very feeble." A day in September—that same September when John Brown and his men were biding their time at the Kennedy farm in Maryland—passed starkly at Sunnyside: "Visitors abounded today—eighteen or nineteen. Mr. Irving could see no one." His symptoms had grown more disturbing; at times on waking he was bewildered, and continued so for half an hour or longer—"an uncertainty as to exactly where he was, and an idea that strange persons had been in the room—his dreams probably mingling with his waking."

Throughout the blight that had fallen on his life, however, this thoroughly civilized human being never entirely lost his sense of humor. A niece might ask him in the morning how he had rested: "So, so," Irving would reply; "I am apt to be rather *fatigued*, my dear, by my night's *rest*." Or when being read an interminable letter from a stranger proposing to call on him, the asthmatic could murmur: "Oh! if he could only give me his long wind, he should be most welcome." And against such a heart-rending outburst as this: "Good God! what shall I do—how shall I get through this day—what is to become of me?" we are grateful to hear of other moods less piercing, like one, also in that long September of 1859, on the fifteenth: "Played whist from eight to ten, after which Mr. Irving dozed awhile in his chair and then retired about eleven, quite free, apparently, from the nervous apprehensions of the night before." The nephew adds: "He was always a very poor player at whist, and cared nothing for the game, but was glad to seize on anything to keep him awake in the evening, lest any indulgence should lessen his chance of sleep for the night." About his abilities at cards, Irving himself could jest scarcely a month before his death: "I do not like to be guilty of pretension, but I must say I'm the very worst player that ever was."

In retrospect, then, those final months of Washington Irving's life, as his nephew recalled them, comprised "a strange mingling." The evenings especially, when after dinner the aged gentleman would be forced again to struggle with dread, seeking "to divert his own thoughts, or to relieve what he feared must be the weariness of those who were watching with him." Watching for what? A haunted, dwindled, and sick old man who had lived fully sat now deep into the night in order to shorten its length. Shawl gathered about him, he was feeling shame and anxiety —and gratitude to those who loved him enough to sit with him. To beguile the time they were sharing, he would reminisce. And it was odd: Never, according to his nephew, had his conversation been "more delightful." The fevers of his mind appeared to have increased its powers of recollection: so that as the little group, surrounded by darkness, lingered together in the quiet parlor at Sunnyside, all the interesting scenes of Washington Irving's long life "seemed to pass before him, a thousand anecdotes of persons and things of which you had never heard, related in the most graphic manner, and filled at times with all his old fun and humor."

YOUNG WASHINGTON IRVING & AARON BURR

Burr . . . made a mystery of everything. When I called on him, at Baltimore, in the morning, on my way to his trial, I must come again in the evening. Five or six were in the room. He would take me in one corner, and say a word or two; another in another, and so on. I met him again at Fredericksburg, and rode with him in the stage to Richmond. I could not well make out why I was sent for. . . .

IRVING AT SUNNYSIDE

New York at the end of the Revolution—Burr's background and childhood —Revolutionary service—Love and marriage—Deacon Irving's family— Pleasurable hours—The city at century's end—A rising politician—Richmond Hill—Letters to Miss Prissy—The daemon of party spirit—Jonathan Oldstyle—Irving's first voyage to Europe—Pirates—The Vice President becomes a candidate—A duel and its aftermath—Years of movement and mystery—General James Wilkinson—Landing on Blennerhassett's island— Aaron I!—Plans move forward—Fugitive—Journey to Richmond—Young John's family goes west—Salmagundi—Richmond in 1807—Wilkinson v. Burr—The trial—Irving's last interview with Burr—Verdict—Burr in exile —Return to the city—Catastrophes—Burr in old age—A final folly—What manner of man was he?

N EW YORK WAS NO CITY in 1783. It was a fire-blackened, war-weary settlement of hardly twenty thousand people (the size of modern Jamestown, North Dakota, say, or Opelika, Alabama) huddled on the southwestern tip of Manhattan Island, so small and so far southward that when young Colonel Aaron Burr, seven years earlier, had retreated with a beleaguered brigade of Revolutionary soldiers from the town limits up the island toward the Bloomingdale road, he had passed open meadows beyond which, to his left at two miles' distance on the horizon, might have been seen spires of the village of Greenwich, still a separate settlement entirely. Burr had got his troops away and to safety, leaving New York to its fate, so that from that September night in 1776 until the very end of the Revolution, the king's forces with their trulls and doxies had occupied the town, only surrendering it finally—the last bit of territory that the British held in the thirteen United States—on a memorable November afternoon in that same 1783, the year in which Washington Irving was born, there in New York, the year in which Aaron Burr, a civilian now, returned to set up his practice of law.

Burr had come down from Albany, temporarily leaving behind him a wife ten years older than he was, several stepchildren, and an infant daughter. In August his wife, whom the young man adored, had sent him a letter: "A few hours after I wrote you by Colonel Lewis, our sweet infant was taken ill, very ill. My mind and spirits have been on the rack from that moment to this. When she sleeps, I watch anxiously; when she wakes, anxious fears accompany every motion. . . . I know not whether to give her medicine or withhold it: doubt and terror are the only sensations of which I am sensible. . . ."

The words still move us, conveying anguish across two centuries that have passed since then. Yet the infant, critically ill in the year of her birth, did survive to live through a youth of amazing accomplishments and grow into an equally extraordinary maturity (when, almost certainly, she knew Washington Irving): this Theodosia, who, more than any other person, would give Burr's life meaning. "For what else," he would write her in her adolescence, "for whom else do I live?" And she could declare with equal simplicity, after becoming one of the outstanding women in the America of her day: "I had rather not live than not be the daughter of such a man."

Theodosia was still less than a year old when the family of which she was a part reassembled that autumn of 1783 in their new quarters in sight of what would become Federal Hall in New York, a few blocks from the Irving household on William Street. Burr himself was twenty-seven at the time, at the threshold of a practice that within a decade would establish him as one of the town's most successful attorneys; only Alexander Hamilton's success would rival his. But Hamilton, as John Adams said, was merely the "bastard Bratt of a Scotch Pedlar," sired in the West Indies, his ancestry confused and suspect, whereas about the elevated ancestry of Aaron Burr no doubt at all existed. For Burr had been born (a year after Hamilton), on February 6, 1756, into a family of striking cultural attainments.

His father had been one of the founders, in Newark, of the College of New Jersey, which that very year of Aaron's birth was moved to Princeton, with the elder Burr as its second president. The mother, too, had been distinguished, a woman (as one who knew her reported) of "very good Sense, of a Genteel & virtuous education, amiable in her person, of great affability & agreeableness in Conversation & a very excellent Economist." Moreover, on her mother's side she was related to the founder of Hartford, and her father was no less than the greatest of all Puritan ministers, Jonathan Edwards, a theologian reliably judged to possess the finest intellect in the English-speaking world on either side of the Atlantic during the first half of the eighteenth century.

Such parents—and such a grandfather—had Aaron Burr. At the time of his birth his mother was in her mid-twenties, keeping a diary that recounted events of family life in the vine-covered stone parsonage in Newark where both the boy and his older sister had come into being: "now I am tied hand and foot how I shall get along when I have got ½ dzn or 10 children I cant devise." And later, after the family had moved to the village of Princeton, Mrs. Burr described, September 2, 1757, in the privacy of her journal, impressions of both her children: Sally, three at the time, was "about middling on all accounts— . . . She can say some of Doct Watts verses by heart and the Lords prayer," and at

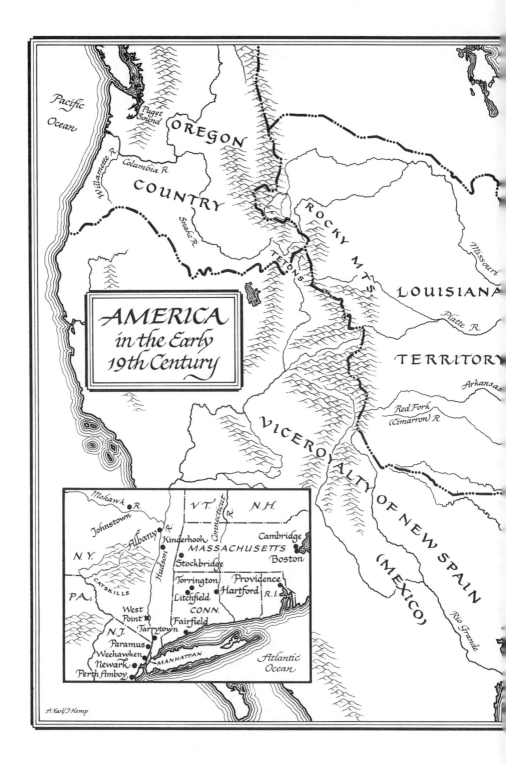

Pacific
Ocean

Puget
Sound

OREGON

Columbia R.

Willamette R.

COUNTRY

Snake R.

TETONS

ROCKY MTS.

Missouri

LOUISIANA

Platte R.

TERRITORY

Arkansas

Red Fork
(Cimarron) R.

AMERICA
in the Early
19th Century

VICEROYALTY OF NEW SPAIN

(MEXICO)

Rio Grande

Mohawk R.

Johnstown

N.Y.

Albany

Kinderhook

VT.

Connecticut R.

N.H.

Cambridge

MASSACHUSETTS
Boston

Hudson R.

Stockbridge

CATSKILLS

Torrington

Litchfield

Providence

Hartford

R.I.

PA.

West
Point

CONN.

Fairfield

N.J.

Tarrytown

Paramus

Weehawken

Newark

Perth Amboy

MANHATTAN

Atlantic
Ocean

A·Karl/J·Kemp

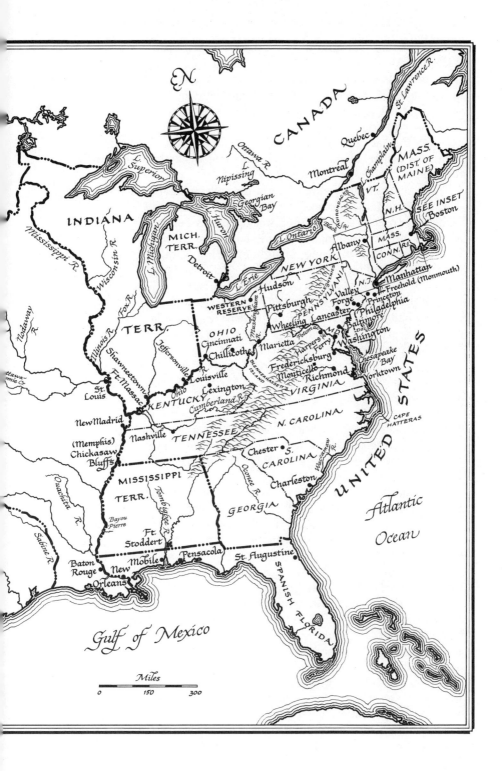

church meeting "can give a good account what Papa does there." As for Aaron, eighteen months old, he "is a little dirty Noisy Boy very different from Sally almost in every thing he begins to talk a little is very Sly and mischevious, Has more sprightliness than Sally and most say he is hand-somer, but not so good tempered he is very resolute and requires a good Governor to bring him to terms. . . ."

On the very day of that final journal entry the child's natural governor, his father, always frail, fell ill; three weeks later, overworked at forty years of age, the elder Burr was dead.

To succeed him as president of the college, his father-in-law, young Aaron's grandfather Jonathan Edwards, was summoned from the Massachusetts frontier settlement of Stockbridge, where he had for a number of years been preaching as a missionary to scarcely comprehending Housatonics and composing, in sight of their wigwams, that masterpiece of theological definition, *Freedom of the Will*. Arriving in Princeton February 16, 1758, Edwards was routinely inoculated against smallpox, but the inoculation proved excessive. Fever developed, and soon such huge pustules had formed in his throat that he was unable to swallow medicine. By spring, less than half a year after his son-in-law's death, Edwards, too, was buried in Princeton.

And still more sorrow followed. Edwards' daughter in her twenties, the elder Burr's widow and mother of Aaron, had been inoculated at the same time as her father. Although apparently recovered, so affected was she by the deaths of two so near to her that within a month of Jonathan Edwards' demise, she likewise, who had worried what she would do when she had ten children, was dead, leaving orphaned the two that she did have—the "little dirty Noisy Boy" and the girl who had Dr. Watts's verses by heart.

Young Aaron Burr, not yet two years old, and Sally were taken to Philadelphia to stay with the family of a recent graduate of the College of New Jersey, Dr. William Shippen. But the Burr children, it was thought, would live with the Shippens only briefly. In the fall of that same year, 1758, Jonathan Edwards' widow arrived to bring both home with her. Could a child make anything of the events of so grievous a time? At Philadelphia the grandmother in her turn (decades earlier, when she was a godly innocent of thirteen, Jonathan Edwards had described her in words that are famous: "She will sometimes go about from place to place, singing sweetly; and seems to be always full of joy and pleasure; and no one knows for what. She loves to be alone, walking in the fields and groves, and seems to have some one invisible always conversing with her") was fatally stricken with dysentery, so that before winter she lay dead in the cemetery in Princeton, near those three new graves of her daughter, her son-in-law, and her brilliant husband.

The children she had come for remained with the Shippens until another home could be found. In time their mother's brother, Uncle

Timothy Edwards in Stockbridge, agreed to take them in; so from 1759 onward until he entered Princeton, the child Aaron was reared by that unusual guardian, a somber and doctrinaire young man of twenty-one when he first assumed the new responsibility, adding those two to the six other relatives under fifteen years of age he was already looking after. Odd household: humorless Uncle Timothy—that old Puritan in his early twenties—waking each morning to attend to his eight wards. He dealt with them strictly, birch rod at the ready, so that what one in fact remembers of those rigorous years of Burr's childhood are images of a four-year-old gone into hiding for several days to escape his tutor, and later, at ten, the same child Aaron clinging to the topgallant masthead of a ship scheduled to sail from New York, while his uncle, having pursued the fugitive that far, was calling up terms from the deck that would coax an aspiring cabin boy to abandon his wild scheme of escape and return to the New Jersey home to which Uncle Timothy with his charges had moved by then.

Yet there was much of the Puritan about young Burr himself. He was self-disciplined and ambitious, capable even at thirteen of extraordinary application to the work at hand. That was the age at which he entered the College of New Jersey, so small in stature that he was not permitted to join the junior class, to which his attainments had entitled him. He was always determined, though. At college he studied as much as eighteen hours a day, this intense young scholar with the black eyes that burned with longings to surpass his classmates; and he altered his diet, eating lightly that his mind might remain alert under proddings of hunger. Of course he did well—such determination has a way of succeeding—and he graduated from the college an accomplished reader, writer, and speaker.

We look more closely at the commencement orator standing before his classmates in that New Jersey village on a September day in 1772. Sixteen years of age he was, no more than five feet six inches tall, which is as tall as he would ever be, possessed of the poise that comes from family and comfortable wealth (for his executor would later report that he had "inherited a handsome estate" at his father's death), the poise that arises from a winning demeanor, the poise more particularly that develops from a confidence in one's own vast abilities. The topic of his oration—ironically, considering the future those abilities would fashion for him—was "Building Castles in the Air." He spoke rapidly but well; he always spoke well and to the point, a bewitching young man of wit and grace, indifferent then as thereafter to most of the gentlemanly vices—gambling, for one, or drinking.

Indeed, Burr would have only a single private vice throughout his lifetime, abetted by those dark eyes that gazed over his classmates now and would gaze in time, hypnotically, into many a lady's eyes as well. "I wont promise for her but I am afraid them rogues eyes of your made a conquest of poor Hannahs heart—." Nor did such a letter (written in 1779) inform Burr of his first conquest; nor would Miss Hannah Pope's heart be the last surrendered to him. His executor, Matthew Davis, who became Burr's first biographer, threw up his hands in perplexity and dismay when confronting the record of such tireless promiscuities (details of which he did what he could to suppress): Burr's intrigues, Davis tells us, "were without number. His conduct most licentious. The sacred bonds of friendship were unhesitatingly violated when they operated as barriers to the indulgence of his passions. . . . And yet, by a fascinating power almost peculiar to himself, he so managed as to retain the affection, in some instances, the devotion, of his deluded victims."

Now, though, such victims and their dalliances lay in the future; for this recent graduate of the college at Princeton and grandson of Jonathan Edwards was trying, briefly, to prepare himself for the ministry. Doubtless his interests already were elsewhere. Soon he gave up the attempt, and when the British marched, in April 1775, on Lexington and Concord and the firing began that opened the Revolution, Burr was studying law at Litchfield, Connecticut, under the guidance of his brother-in-law Tapping Reeve, husband of that sister Sally of the Watts verses, now grown to womanhood.

The momentous news of hostilities in the North interrupted Burr's law studies. Bearing a letter on his behalf from John Hancock, president of the Continental Congress and a family friend, the young man set out at once for Cambridge to join Major General Washington, newly appointed commander-in-chief of the colonial forces; and for the next four years he served with outstanding success as an officer in the Revolution. Indeed, Burr was thereafter more vain about his military prowess than about any other ability he proved himself to possess over a long lifetime. He made, for example, unflinchingly, the horrendous journey north to Canada in 1775 with Benedict Arnold's pathetic band, struggling with them through the wilderness toward Quebec, surviving with a handful of others in the bitter cold north of Maine in November, involved in desperate measures to which soldiers were reduced among swamps and in dense, snow-filled forests, sharing their dwindling bits of pork and flour, alert to Indians hovering, beset by aching weariness at the fords, "sometimes climeing on all fours and at others scarcely able to see for the thickness of the bramble and small fir shrubs," rejoicing at last to eat dog, or later "a small bit of chocolate which we boiled and divided out equally by spoonfuls. . . ." Throughout, as Arnold himself testified, Burr "acted with great spirit and resolution on our fatiguing march" that opened a doomed venture. For the siege of Quebec failed, though Burr himself returned with new-won glory—returned to participate courageously in the evacuation of Manhattan Island and in the dismal autumn retreat through New Jersey in 1776 that led to a year of further reverses and at last to winter quarters at Valley Forge.

Although he mistrusted the abilities of Washington, on whose staff he had served—felt contempt for them finally—Burr as an officer behaved at Valley Forge decisively and effectively to maintain morale among the log huts and smoking camp fires. One incident lets us see him clearly. He was no more than twenty-one or -two at the time, erect, slight of build, intense, and in love with war—sent out to deal with an unruly bunch of American pickets, troublesome with their pranks and repeated false alarms of nonexistent enemy sightings that would senselessly stir up the main camp eight miles away. Burr arrived and mustered the ill-clad, surly men, then drilled them, then led them through drills again and again and yet again at all hours of day and night. Mumblings of mutiny came to his ear. Relying on the few he could trust, he secretly had cartridges removed from the weapons of the militia, then yet another time mustered them under a bright moon—this cocky young officer, armed with no more than a saber, parading before that disgruntled, disheveled band of musket-bearing roughnecks on a Pennsylvania hill-side in the glow of an early winter morning in 1778. As a signal one of the men abruptly lowered his musket and aimed directly at Burr: "Now is your time, my boys." Once more resounds that click in the explosion-less air. An instant later Burr's raised sword is slicing downward; abruptly the man's arm dangles at his side. He was ordered then to pick up the musket and resume his place in rank—left to stand there, arm half severed, blood flowing, until his officer concluded the muster that had been interrupted. At daylight the arm was amputated, and talk of mutiny ended.

And we linger over what young Burr had done—consider the cool-ness of it—remembering that the limb he sliced had borne an instant earlier a gun leveled at his own life. Far from seeing him as a cruel martinet, his men came to revere him, whether at Monmouth, where he fought (as did young Lieutenant Colonel Alexander Hamilton) to ex-haustion in 96° heat through two days in late June, or, afterward, more especially, near Tarrytown along the Westchester lines, where his skill and leadership won what seems to have been universal respect. "The troops of which he took command," recalls one who had ample oppor-tunity of observing Burr then, "were, at the time he took the command, undisciplined, negligent, and discontented. Desertions were frequent. In a few days these very men were transformed into brave and honest defenders; orderly, contented, and cheerful; confident in their own courage, and loving to adoration their commander, whom every man considered as his personal friend. . . . During the whole of this com-mand there was not a single desertion. Not a single death by sickness. Not one made prisoner by the enemy. . . . After the first ten days there was not a single instance of robbery. The whole country, under his command, enjoyed security."

Yet Burr was often ill during that period of his life. The illness—

chronic diarrhea—dated from Monmouth, where after forty-eight hours of unrelieved exertions, during which his horse had once been shot from under him, he had lain down exhausted in shade in a field on the blistering morning of the battle's end, to wake much later with the shade shifted and his body racked with sunstroke. His health henceforth was precarious until long after the war was over, and though he took leave of absence once, then resumed his duties, he was forced at last, reluctantly, to resign from the Army in the spring of 1779, before the Revolution had been won.

By then he had fallen in love with the woman who would become his wife. For this handsome, successful American Army officer still in his early twenties and already notorious as a womanizer, she seems an odd choice on paper: ten years older than he, not especially pretty, and married, since 1763, to a Colonel Jacques Prevost of His Majesty's forces stationed in the West Indies. She was, moreover, the mother of five children. All of them were living at the Hermitage, a multigabled sandstone house still standing (gloomy, boarded, decaying) in New Jersey, in what is now Hohokus, alongside the Franklin Turnpike. And it was in that home, then within the boundaries of Paramus, in the fall of 1777 that the American Colonel Burr became a frequent guest, passing over the tree-shaded lawn to be granted admittance, by this cultured wife of the English officer, to her family—her mother, her half-sister, her children.

The Tory lady's position in rebel country must have been delicate, though one is struck, in learning of the times, with the instances of personal friendship and gallantry that sometimes altered the posture of mortal enemies facing each other along the eastern seaboard. It was to Mrs. Prevost's home, for example, that Peggy Shippen Arnold fled, after the discovery of her husband's attempted betrayal of West Point in 1780. Benedict Arnold had escaped to a ship anchored in the Hudson, then to Manhattan, at that time, as through most of the Revolution, in the hands of the British. Soon after, veiled and under escort, Arnold's wife Peggy arrived late one night at the Hermitage in New Jersey. Burr saw her there—friend of his childhood, niece of the Dr. Shippen in Philadelphia with whom the orphans Aaron and Sally had been placed years before. And the sympathetic Mrs. Prevost did what she could to console the young lady, hysterically protesting her innocence of any involvement in treason. Soon Mrs. Arnold was allowed to rejoin her husband, with him to live out an unhappy life in England, leaving historians to debate whether the distraught girl at the Prevost home that autumn night in 1780 had been ignorant after all of Arnold's intentions—was truly surprised or was (as most now believe) only acting a part until delivered from behind the American lines.

Burr was out of the Army in 1779, but ill and in love with a woman he could not marry. They wrote each other through the three years that followed, while he resumed the study of law at Albany, intense and determined as always: "Made a light breakfast of tea," he was to write Mrs. Prevost, for example, on a Saturday in December 1781, "stretched myself on a blanket before the fire, fasted till evening, and then tea again. I thought, through the whole day, that if you could sit by me, and stroke my head with your little hand, it would be well; and that, when we are formally united, far from deeming a return of this disorder un malheur, I should esteem it a fortunate apology for a day of luxurious indulgence, which I should not otherwise allow myself or you."

And she to him (this during the preceding May): "Our being the subject of much inquiry, conjecture, and calumny is no more than we ought to expect. My attention to you was ever pointed enough to attract the observation of those who visited the house. Your esteem more than compensated for the worst they could say. When I am sensible I can make you and myself happy, I will readily join you to suppress their malice. But, till I am confident of *this*, I cannot think of our union."

By that time the lady was, fortuitously, a widow. And on July 6, 1782, admitted to the New York bar with the future before him, Aaron Burr, twenty-six years old, having traveled to New Jersey once more, took Theodosia Barstow Prevost to wife. The two returned together then to live in Albany, where on June 21 of the year that ended the American Revolution a girl child, also named Theodosia, was born to them. And that was the year, 1783, that the young lawyer, realizing where his future lay, journeyed south to Manhattan Island, to the battered town at its southern tip, with its commerce at a standstill and its ships idle at the docks, with the hated *Jersey* and other prison hulks still blighting the harbor, with the slums of Canvastown flourishing among charred ruins, and the hundred-years-old trees of Wall Street all gone, firewood for the winters of war. But the British would be leaving soon, at last—would have to go in the aftermath of Yorktown—and when they had left (lawyers among their Tory sympathizers disqualified already by act of the New York legislature), there would remain plenty of work to keep busy an ambitious and brilliant young attorney who happened as well to be a veteran of the American cause at Quebec, at Harlem Heights, at Valley Forge and Monmouth.

It was a time for beginnings, as Sir Guy Carleton sailed with the fleet down New York Bay to the open sea that November afternoon in 1783. Aboard were the last of the British troops and what Loyalist passengers could find room, shorn of possessions and condemned with what they could carry to set up new lives as strangers in the West Indies, Canada, or England. Behind those victims of war's chances lay confiscable land for speculators and patriot lawyers to wrangle over, in and around a town left in ruins. Piers that had fallen into decay would have to be rebuilt. Gardens needed weeding and replanting. The stench of the prison house must be cleansed from the grim sugar factory behind the small windows of which, on any summer day in years just past, could have been seen from Queen Street the gaunt faces of American prisoners of war, taking their turn to breathe unfetid air. And there were the ravages of two great fires to repair, fires that had destroyed much of the area south of what is now Exchange Place, as well as Trinity Church and most of the town west of Broadway.

But New Yorkers were exultant despite appearances, and no doubt as exultant as any, in his sedate way, was Deacon William Irving, staunch patriot, back from taking refuge in New Jersey, where—his family ill and consigned to the attic—he had for a time been forced as a rebel to quarter the hated Redcoats. The deacon returned to New York while the Revolution was still in progress, settling his wife and children again at 131 William Street. But they were to remain in that house only briefly after the war ended, moving soon (as so many moved in those restless years) to another, number 128, on the same street, between Ann and John Streets, across the way. Within the former structure the deacon's eleventh child was born, April 3, 1783. And in the latter, "the old family nest," the child grew up.

He was named Washington, a tribute his mother paid to the great general whose work she presumed had come to completion that year. The childhood haunts of Washington Irving lie now in New York's financial district, and nothing among those skyscrapers remains but street names and a plaque or two to recall the world of earlier days: town pumps and hitching posts, nearby ponds and orchards, and above the streets the frequent Dutch stepped-gable roofs of brick or timbered houses that rose three or four stories, no higher, toward the clear sky. In such a world had Deacon Irving resumed his trade—auctioneer, merchant of hardware and sugar and wines—after the struggle for independence from Britain. A native of the bleak Orkney Islands, off the northeast coast of Scotland, William Irving as a young man had gone to sea, serving as petty officer on a packet ship, armed during the Seven Years' War of the 'fifties, as it plied between Falmouth in England and the little port, once Dutch, now British, at the tip of Manhattan. In Falmouth, between such voyages, the sailor had met the only daughter of a local family, one Sarah Sanders, a pretty girl whom he married at Plymouth, not long before abandoning the sea for good in his early thirties to set up shop, in 1763, on the other side of the Atlantic, on the edge of America, at the gateway to a new world.

In a modest way the Irving business had prospered, as it continued to do during those years two decades later that immediately followed the Revolution, years in which the youngest of Sarah Irving's children was growing from infancy into an awareness first of his home, then of his little neighborhood. It was a neighborhood of shops with residences attached: saddlers, chandlers, cobblers, chairmakers. The house itself, number 128, was a triple structure, timbered, of two stories with steep roofs and a connecting passage, on a lot that extended some twenty-five feet along William Street. Within and about that house moved the numerous children: William, Jr., Ann, Peter, Catharine, Ebenezer, John, Sarah, and the adored baby, Washington himself, born with the treaty of peace that acknowledged the birth of the nation. All that progeny would grow to maturity (three others had died in infancy), and all would remain close to each other in spirit even when widely separated in fact. As for the mother, one who saw her when the author who would become world famous was still a baby remembered her as "of elegant shape, with large English features, which were permeated by an indescribable life and beauty. Her manners were full of action, and her conversational powers were of a high order." Among Washington Irving's own earliest recollections was the sound of her voice singing to him; and when he was an old man, many decades after her death in 1817, the very memory of his mother could still move him to tears.

Not so the memory of his father. A somber man was the deacon, a conscientious and God-fearing Scotch Covenanter who read the Bible aloud to his family each evening, saw that three sermons were inflicted on his offspring every Sunday, and that Thursday afternoons—the youngsters' half-school day—were consumed with the catechism. Perhaps a kind of severe relief came with regular readings from *The Pilgrim's Progress*, but the picture of paternal influence overall is gray. Decades later the mature author Irving spoke obliquely of it to his future biographer: "When I was young," he said, "I was led to think that somehow or other every thing that was pleasant was wicked."

Still, away from his father's eye the child must have had many pleasurable hours, some the more so perhaps for being tinged with wickedness. There were the escapades remembered later, precarious enough, on the steep roofs of his home, out that window, across there, then up and to the chimney to drop pebbles down and alarm the adults below. And the Highland songs his Scottish nurse Lizzie would sing to him. And battles with older brother John in the back garden, among greengages and nectarines, each boy behind his beflagged palisades hurling gravel missiles at the other. Or the fanfare when New York briefly became the capital of the new nation—parades, fireworks, and the arrival of General Washington himself, after a long and glorious journey of triumph from Mount Vernon northward, to take the oath of office as first President under the new Constitution. That was in April, 1789, and one summer day in that same year, out for a walk with her six-year-old charge, the nursemaid Lizzie spotted the tall figure of the great general inside a shop on Broadway. Undaunted she hurried the child through the door and approached his august presence: "Please, your Excellency, here's a bairn that's called after ye!" And President Washington, so his namesake and future biographer often took delight in remembering, smiled a kindly smile and rested his revered hand upon the wondering little boy's head.

But there was much else to see and hear and feel among those crowded, cry-filled streets: shops to linger before on the way to and from Mrs. Kilmaster's school, and later Benjamin Romaine's school on Partition (now Fulton) Street. There were Duncan Phyfe's furniture shop and the young German immigrant Astor's music shop on Little Dock Street, with furs for sale too, and Mr. Colgate's shop on John Street that sold soap and candles. And from time to time the child must have passed the familiar figure of dapper Attorney Burr, rising politician, striding toward his office on Nassau Street. A memorable summer day in 1788 was filled with the great parade for Hamilton, when the Constitution he had fought for was ratified, in commemoration of which a grateful citizenry dragged a vast ship bearing his name about town; and later the mobs turned out again in force, hoopla for the French minister Gênet, among which welcoming crowd was the ten-year-old Washington Irving, envying (so fiercely that he would remember the feeling the last year of his life) a feather another boy nearby wore smartly in the side of his hat. And in leisure hours the books of travel: *Sinbad the Sailor*, *Robinson Crusoe*, in his father's study a set of twenty duodecimo volumes called *The World Displayed* to pore over. And the nearby wharves: "How wistfully," he would recall later, "would I wander about the pier heads in fine weather, and watch the parting ships, bound to distant climes. With what longing eyes would I gaze after their lessening sails, and waft myself in imagination to the ends of the earth."

But maybe best of all was the theater, make-believe within a red wooden building on the north side of John Street. The young Washington Irving would attend in the early evening with an older friend (James Kirke Paulding, with whom he would be corresponding warmly when both were in their seventies), hurrying the couple of blocks to see the comedian Jefferson, say, in *Speculation*. But the family Bible-reading inexorably called him back—child seated later that same night with his brothers and sisters under the eye, in sound of the solemn voice of his deacon father. His mind, though, must have been far off, in a world of color and artifice, to which he would sometimes covertly return—one more wicked pleasure—sneaking later that same night out of his upstairs room through the window, down on the woodshed roof to the ground and into the darkness on his way to witness the afterpiece.

That house on William Street would be demolished in 1849 as the city made progress. Irving was in his sixties then, with his nephew paying the old homestead a last visit on a May day shortly before the empty rooms were reduced to rubble. Those two grown gentlemen of that later New York, by then a city, wandered among ghosts in an echoing relic of the earlier one, and the celebrated writer was led at one point to reminisce about a barber who, more than half a century before, had called regularly at the house to dress the deacon's peruke: "How well I recollect the little man, with his moist eye, as he stood before my father on this spot, wig in hand, all alive with excitement at the first tidings of the execution of Louis XVI." On this spot: present and past coalesce. "I was but nine years old, yet the scene is as freshly before me as if it were yesterday. 'Wasn't it a shame, Mr. Irving,' said he, dancing up and down, 'wasn't it a shame to put him to death? Why not let him come to this country? Only think—he might have come over here, and set up a small grocery.' . . ."

The New York that the unhappy king never served had prospered by the 1790s. Before the century was out, its population was increased almost threefold over those days, seventeen years earlier, that had seen the end of the American Revolution. Yet though perhaps as many as sixty thousand people lived in the town by 1800, a pedestrian could still start from the Battery at its southernmost tip and walk north into open country within a mile or so. And beyond, among meadows and wooded hills on the rest of the island, game for the hunt still teemed—grouse and hare and partridge. Even within the limits of the town itself there remained places secluded enough—an orchard beside Duane Street, for instance, at the rear of the Old City Hospital—where affairs of honor could be settled with flintlocks just after daybreak and nobody else the wiser.

By December 1789, not long after Washington's inaugural on the balcony of Federal Hall overlooking the cheering crowds in Wall Street, the capital of the newly constituted nation had been moved from New York to Philadelphia, that larger, more artistic, and generally more dignified community. For New York, then as now, was first of all brashly commercial, so that among the congeries of peoples collected there—West Indian planters, backwoodsmen down from Albany with their pelts, descendants of Dutch burghers, painted redskins, black slaves, English sailors—a certain crassness prevailed, along with roughhewn attitudes of live-and-let-live. There was, then, a boisterous side to New York life. As late as the end of the eighteenth century, bearbaitings and cockfights diverted the populace still, as did public whippings and executions on what was then the open common (over which City Hall looks now), raucous vaudeville and theatricals— *Darby's Return, School for Scandal, The Dead Alive*—and exhibitions like the one (in 1789) at 28 Wall Street, of "a Male and Female of the surprising species of the Ourang Outang or the Man of the Woods; . . . Monkey, Porcupine, Ant-Bear, Crocodile, Lizard, and Sword Fish; Snakes of various kinds and very extraordinary; Tame Tyger and Buffalo. . . ." All for five shillings for adults, two shillings sixpence for children. And balloon ascensions, and skating on the Collect in winter, and butchers noisily parading their sheep to market. And for the promenading dandies and belles of spring—he in a surtout, hat under arm, cane in hand—there were the pleasure gardens, one north of town near what are now Warren and Greenwich Streets, another soon after 1800 about a mile out on the Bowery Road, with lights delicately in the trees, tables where ices were served, fountains and statuary and (among shadowy arbors) swings wide enough for two.

Another New York had come into being as well, of a less numerous and still more refined population dwelling in opulence about the city, in the McComb house on lower Broadway where President Washington had lived, in the Walton house, in the Walter Franklin mansion on Cherry Street. That society of New Yorkers dining more or less exclusively with one another included the Messrs. Jay and Varick and King and Beekman and Roosevelt and Livingston, as well as a few other select families whose carriages rolled daily down crooked uneven streets among one another's addresses. And after each evening had ended and the social leaders had retired for the night, black slaves of those families (for New York would continue to sanction slavery throughout the eighteenth century) might be seen, buckets of human waste on their shoulders, filing along the same streets, dark now, on their way to the surrounding rivers.

Aaron Burr was not long in joining New York society in its leisures, to which heritage, breeding, and present prosperity fitted him with ease. For Burr had prospered since coming down from Albany, young man in his mid-twenties, to set up his law practice in the autumn of 1783. Now, ten or twelve years later, he had won a reputation as one of the two or three outstanding attorneys in this litigious town, receiving as much as £10,000—astonishing fee!—for a single case. He had prospered economically, both through such fees and in land speculation, and had prospered politically as well: state assemblyman, attorney general of the state in the late 'eighties, in the early 'nineties United States Senator to Philadelphia. That last distinction was won in an upset over esteemed old General Philip Schuyler, one of the illustrious victors at the Revolutionary battle of Saratoga—and, incidentally, father-in-law of Alexander Hamilton. Accordingly, during that period of his life Burr was away from Manhattan much of the time, tending to business in Albany or Philadelphia, leaving behind him a sizable household of stepsons, wards, tutors, servants, slaves, the adored daughter Theodosia, and an adoring wife: "I feel as though my guardian angel had forsaken me. . . . Tell me, Aaron, why do I grow every day more tenacious of thy regard? Is it possible my affection can increase? Is it because each revolving day proves thee more deserving?"

By the early 1790s Burr had acquired as well, in addition to his town house and dependents, another home, in the country to the northwest, called Richmond Hill, a mansion with impressive portico outside, filled inside with the senator's tasteful possessions—"sophas in hair cloth," "elegant Turkey carpet," "field bedstead and curtains," an "elegant traveling case of tea caddies, bottles, etc."—affluence set among spacious lawns shaded by oaks and cedars in sight of the Hudson. The hills around the estate have long been leveled, Burr's costly pond all dry, the trees removed, the ground covered with flat asphalt and brick and concrete that comprise the present downtown city blocks of Varick, King, Charlton, and MacDougal streets, but in those days the skyline of New York itself—low roofs and church spires—lay a mile and a half still farther south, and surrounding sounds of birds were delightful, and you could look above sails that dotted the sparkling Hudson and see—and when the wind was right could catch the fragrances of—buckwheat fields and orchards on the Jersey slopes.

The mansion from which such views were enjoyed had served as Washington's headquarters when Colonel Burr had first visited it as a staff officer before the Battle of Manhattan. Later, in 1789, Vice President John Adams had resided there—his wife thought it vied with "the most delicious spot I ever saw"—and when the government moved to Philadelphia Mrs. Adams might admit that her new home was a beautiful place, "but the grand and sublime I left at Richmond Hill." Burr had acquired a lease on that sublimity soon after the Adamses had vacated it, and his heart must have remained at Richmond Hill long after fortune had snatched away the home and grounds and most of those lovely possessions within.

Were they not the happiest years of his life, the years in the 'nineties at his country estate? Assuredly he was busy. A splendid law practice preoccupied him: one lucrative case, for instance, that he and Hamilton worked on together won acquittal for a certain Levi Weeks, accused of murdering a prostitute named Gulielma Sands and discarding her body in a well. Burr's practice kept him busy, and so did his speculations: huddles with wealthy young John Jacob Astor at Mrs. Keese's boardinghouse across from Trinity Yard, the deals, the borrowing (everyone who could afford to, and many who couldn't, speculated in land in those days), the profits and debts and letters: "Dear Sir" (this in 1794), "herewith will be paid you two thousand five hundred and fifty Dollars to be applied to the discharge of my larger note. I beg to know whether it will be convenient for you to allow the other to be renewed. . . ." And his political life consumed much of Burr's time too, as he led his group of Burrites, among them lads of the newly founded Society of Tammany, through the perplexing labyrinths thrown up and almost daily shifted by emergent rivals: the "monarchist" Hamilton who loathed that "contemptible hypocrite" Jefferson, and Adams who cared little for Hamilton, and Governor Clinton and his adherents in Albany, opposed to the Livingston faction—an all but impenetrable tangle of interests from which formal political parties were being fashioned. Now though, in the 'nineties, Burr's power, too, was growing, as he moved closer, if deviously, to the moment of his greatest triumph, when, in 1800, he would be a candidate, and an impressive one, for the Presidency of the United States.

Meanwhile, still other matters, besides law and politics and land speculation, were absorbing his mind. This squire of Richmond Hill had lives to manage. Letters arrived for Mrs. Burr. Philadelphia, 16th February, 1793: "You have heard me speak of a Miss Woolstonecraft, who has written something on the French revolution; she has also written a book entitled '*Vindication of the rights of Woman.*' I had heard it spoken of with a coldness little calculated to excite attention; but as I read with avidity and prepossession every thing written by a lady, I made haste to procure it, and spent the last night, almost the whole of it, in reading it. Be assured that your sex has in *her* an able advocate. It is, in my opinion, a work of genius."

That work, by a woman whom we shall know in later pages—a woman who died giving birth to Mary Shelley—was exactly what Burr would admire, advanced feminist document that it was. For he, like Mary Wollstonecraft, had the highest regard for the capabilities of the female sex—indeed, was sure that those capabilities were equal to men's, and unrealized only because of the crippling effects of inferior education to which girls were submitted in preparation for womanhood. His wife it was who had opened Burr's eyes: "It was a knowledge of your mind which first inspired me with a respect for that of your sex." And in rearing his own daughter, Theodosia, he had no intention of committing, so he said, the common "errors of education, of prejudice, and of habit": "If I could foresee that Theo. would become a *mere* fashionable woman, with all the attendant frivolity and vacuity of mind, adorned with whatever grace and allurement, I would earnestly pray God to take her forthwith hence. But I yet hope, by her, to convince the world what neither sex appear to believe—that women have souls!"

So letters from her absent papa arrived for little Miss Prissy as well, letters filled with cautions and proddings and rebuffs and corrections and encouragement. Like this one, to an eleven-year-old child: "Four pages in Lucian was a great lesson; and why, my dear Theo., can't this be done a little oftener? . . . You say nothing of writing or learning Greek verbs;—is this practice discontinued? and why? . . . Do you continue to preserve Madame De S.'s good opinion of your talents for the harp? And do you find that you converse with more facility in the French? These are interesting questions, and your answer to this will, I hope, answer fully all the questions it contains." Or this, to his daughter when she was still younger: "I rose up suddenly from the sofa, and rubbing my head—'What book shall I buy for her?' said I to myself. 'She reads so much and so rapidly that it is not easy to find proper and amusing French books for her. . . .' I went into one bookseller's shop after another. I found plenty of fairy tales and such nonsense, fit for the generality of children of nine or ten years old. 'These,' said I, 'will never do. Her understanding begins to be above such things;' but I could see nothing that I would offer with pleasure to *an intelligent, well-informed girl of nine years old.* . . ." Or these: "Your habit of stooping and bringing your shoulders forward on to your breast not only disfigures you, but is alarming on account of the injury to your health. The continuance in this vile habit will certainly produce a consumption: then farewell papa; farewell pleasure; farewell life! This is no exaggeration; no fiction to excite your apprehensions. But, setting aside this distressing consideration, I am astonished that you have no more pride in your appearance." "Never use a word which does not fully express your thoughts, or which, for any other reason, does not please you. Hunt your dictionary till you find one. Arrange a whole sentence in your mind before you write a word of it; and, whatever may be your 'hurry' (never be in a *hurry*), read over your letter slowly and carefully before you seal it." "Your being in the ballette charms me." "At present you fail most in punctuation. A very little thought will teach where the sense is complete and a full period is proper." "That 16th was really a surprising day. Three hundred and ninety-five lines, all your exercises, and all your music. Go on, my dear girl, and you will become all that I wish." " 'It was what she had long wished for, and was at a loss how to procure *it*.' Don't you see that this sentence would have been perfect and much more elegant without the last *it?* . . . By-the-by, I took the liberty to erase the redundant *it* before I showed the letter." "The following are the only mispelled words. You write *acurate* for *accurate; laudnam* for *laudanum; intirely* for *entirely;* this last word, indeed, is spelled both ways, but entirely is the most usual and the most proper." In the same letter Burr does add: "I am extremely impatient for your farther account of mamma's health. The necessity of laudanum twice a day is a very disagreeable and alarming circumstance."

For Theodosia's mother was ill that winter of 1794, more so doubtless than Burr realized, and by spring, with her absent husband unaware of the depths of her loneliness and pain, she would scrawl a note of her own to his sister Sally and Sally's husband Tapping Reeve in Litchfield: "My dear friends where are you in all my distress, that you do not come to see how I suffer—come & pray you my sufferings are not to be committed to . . . Perhaps I may see you, perhaps not—I have wrote to you many times, but I never heard from you do come, if Sally cannot—come—Reeve come I pray you, come I beg you, come . . . to your wretched."

Before the end of May the poor woman was dead, a victim of cancer. After her death, to be sure, parties at Richmond Hill would resume, and distinguished visitors would continue to call—suave Talleyrand, Louis Philippe, the Indian chief Joseph Brant: "He is a man of education," Burr would write home, "speaks and writes the English perfectly—and has seen much of Europe and America." But the hostess who received such guests was the child-woman Theodosia. Burr himself would not marry again for forty years, until the very end of his life, nor would that second marriage bring him joy. The first marriage had, though. The first marriage, the one that death ended in 1794, was—as numerous surviving letters between Aaron Burr and his wife reveal—rare indeed, rare in mutual respect and devotion. So much so that, on the basis of what followed in the years that lay before him, a stabilizing strength must have gone out of the senator's life that Sunday in May in Manhattan, when his *plus tendre amie, toujours la vôtre,* sank calmly at last into her final sleep.

Newspapers of those days, toward the end of the eighteenth century, carried little enough news in truth. Yet everyone read them. By 1800 the United States, according to a contemporary, had become "a nation of newspaper readers," purchasing those cramped pages of advertising, personal announcements, and scurrility less to find out what was happening than to enlarge, apparently, a vocabulary of all but limitless vituperation. For the papers, most of them short-lived, were in the main mouthpieces for political interests. In the capital at Philadelphia, for example, there flourished from 1791 to the end of the century Philip Freneau's *National Gazette,* friendly to Jefferson, admired by Burr; while in the same city John Fenno's even more successful *Gazette of the United States* poured out its fulsome praises for Hamilton's every act. Hamilton and Jefferson: audiences to whom such papers were addressed were fiercely if confusingly partisan. Though economic and social news of the young nation could be slighted or ignored, politics never were: "Many have complained that too small a share of our attention was given to politics," confessed the editors of the *Port Folio* after their first issue, promising in the next breath to correct the oversight from that day in early 1802 forward. And forgotten entirely was the caution twelve years before from the great Washington: "if we mean to support the Liberty and Independence which it has cost us so much blood and treasure to establish, we must drive far away the daemon of party spirit and local reproach."

That daemon was settled in now, ill-mannered, fattening itself on the rankest of charges and countercharges. And what did the vocal partisans who hurled those insults at each other stand for? In the broadest sense their differences of opinion that were responsible for all that thunderous outrage—this man an archtraitor, that one a hyena, another a cowardly Judas, a fourth a lickspittle—had formed during the final decade of the eighteenth century around two leaders, the Virginian

Thomas Jefferson and the New Yorker Alexander Hamilton. Hamilton and his supporters were of the city; Jefferson was of the country, the grass roots. Hamilton viewed human nature with suspicion: "The people are turbulent and changing; they seldom judge or determine right. . . . Take mankind in general, they are vicious, their passions may be operated upon." Jefferson, by contrast, was confident that human nature could ultimately be relied on, all men having been created "free and equal." The one advocated the virtues of nationalism, while the other extolled democracy. Accordingly, the former worked for a strong central government, whereas the latter had admired the feeble Articles of Confederation, under which America had stumbled along from crisis to crisis for nearly a decade after gaining independence; "a wonderfully perfect instrument," he had called it. And if Hamilton fought hard and successfully to establish the Constitution, strengthening the central government, it was the political philosophy of Jefferson and his supporters that was responsible for the first ten amendments to that document, protecting the rights of the individual against encroachments of the central power it strengthened. Broadly speaking, then, Hamilton's Federalists—those friends of the English—believed in rule by the upper classes; Jefferson's Republicans (who would become the Democrats of a later day)—friends of the revolutionary French—believed in rule by the masses. And in the end, the political theories both men espoused proved vital to forming the America that has survived.

Of course divisions between them were hardly that neat. Nor were their interests divided finally after a first clear cut through. For within the Federalist Party itself, factions developed. President Washington, striving to remain aloof from squabbles, nevertheless tended by temperament to favor the Federalists; and his successor John Adams was openly Federalist, hostile to France, mistrustful of the multitudes at home. Yet Adams could regard his fellow Federalist Hamilton as "the most restless, impatient, artful, indefatigable and unprincipled intriguer in the United States, if not in the world." Burr, likewise, might be a Republican of Jefferson's party, and as such could oppose those assaults against individual freedom, the Alien and Sedition Acts of President Adams' administration. But Jefferson, as early as 1797 (or so he later claimed), was already looking on Burr with "distrust"; and Burr assuredly would discover in the future reasons for mistrusting the democrat of Monticello.

Indeed, people in those early days of union still thought of themselves first as Virginians, or Marylanders, or Pennsylvanians, or New Yorkers, and only secondly as Americans. So Burr in New York, far from Carter's Mountain and Jefferson's mansion at its summit, had his own interests to develop amid a cast of conflicting characters—Hamilton himself, Clinton, the Livingstons, Jay, Yates, Schuyler, King—that further complicated the task of defining what any one man stood for. Those family names, after all, were often more important than any political label in identifying loyalties; one became a Hamiltonian, or a Clintonian, or a Burrite. And it was possible to be in principle a Federalist, sympathetic to English ways and institutions, wary of the great beast turning out in the streets to cheer and jeer and vote, and still be a Burrite, supporting a deft political leader named Aaron Burr. Just those apparently contradictory sympathies, in fact, may have been shared by the Irving family on William Street, a family of brothers and sisters the oldest of whom had by the end of the century grown to adulthood. Peter, in his late twenties in 1800, had attended Columbia College for three years, and had gone on to earn a medical degree. But he had a literary bent, too; so that soon after the new century had begun, this doctor destined never to practice medicine, this Federalist by inclination, came forth as editor of a Burrite newspaper. The *Morning Chronicle* would remain under Peter's direction a couple of years and no longer. But while he did edit it, the paper made room in its columns for the occasional pseudonymous contributions of a younger brother; and for that reason, it is in those fragile pages that are to be found the earliest published writings of Washington Irving.

"*Mr. Editor,*" the first of Washington Irving's contributions to the *Morning Chronicle* begins, "If the observations of an odd old fellow are not wholly superfluous, I would thank you to shove them into a spare corner of your paper." And the observations, less than a column in length, muse on changes in manners since the writer was young. In the old days, "how delightful to contemplate a ball-room: such bowing, such scraping, such complimenting; nothing but copperplate speeches to be heard on both sides; no walking but in minuet measure. . . ." Now, though, all is different. Today's youth "strolls round with the most vacant air; stops abruptly before such lady as he may choose to honor with his attention; entertains her with the common *slang* of the day, collected from the conversation of hostlers, footmen, porters, &c. until his string of smart sayings is run out, and then lounges off, to entertain some other fair one with the same unintelligible jargon." In short, for yesterday's young gentleman we have, alas, today's puppy; and "surely, Mr. Editor, puppyism must have arrived to a *climax:* it *must* turn; to carry it to a greater extent seems to me impossible."

The letter, published in the issue of November 15, 1802, is signed "Jonathan Oldstyle." Slight enough is its matter—a complaint no less familiar now than then. But the letter does exhibit some of the traits that would become Irving's hallmark in later years: manners for a subject, good-humored nostalgia for his tone, an observant eye, the felicitous style, the very gentle satire that avoids offense, the equally gentle verbal irony—on "honor," for example, and "entertains." At irregular intervals during the winter of 1802–3 eight other such letters followed, through the rather bland and predictable garrulity of which we gain glimpses of the New York of those times. There are ruminations on modern marriages, and three letters in succession on the theater, describing what sound assuredly like grade-school productions before grade-school audiences. For in the balcony—of the Park Theater, on Park Row between Ann and Beekman streets—are revealed the "gods," waggish, excitable, whistling and stamping and imitating animal calls, raining apple cores and peanuts and gingerbread upon spectators in the pit below, overpowering the ill-tuned sounds of the little orchestra by calling for "*Moll in the wad, Tally ho the grinders*, and several other *airs* more suited to their tastes," cheering any luckless actor with a bit role to play—a servant, say, entering on stage briefly "to move a table or snuff a candle" —or noisily "detecting those cunning dogs who peep from behind" the lowered curtain. Actors grin self-consciously over their solemner lines. Sound effects—tin thunder and the rest—get out of hand, while a battle between Tripolitan pirates and American Tars is "conducted with proper decency and decorum," the Tripolitan "very politely" giving in, "as it would be indecent to conquer in the face of an American audience." Over all, meanwhile, the candelabra strung from the ceiling drips wax indiscriminately down on the spectators' shoulders.

A last communication, of April 23, 1803, concerns the then flourishing custom of dueling. "Judge my surprize, Mr. Editor, on reading" in the *Morning Chronicle* "an act of our legislature, pronouncing any citizen of this state who shall send, bear, or accept a challenge, either verbal or written, disqualified from holding any office of honor or confidence, or of voting at any election within this state. . . ." What a catastrophe: "a damper for the mettlesome youths of the age"! So the last spark of chivalric fire has been extinguished. For the writer can recall "the genuine politeness and polished ceremony with which duels were conducted in my youthful days . . . A challenge was worded with the most particular complaisance; and one that I have still in my possession, ends with the words, '*your friend and affectionate servant Nicholas Stubbs.*'" Moreover, "when the parties met on the field, the same decorum was observed; they pulled off their hats" and "wished one another a good day," so that from start to finish "every thing was conducted in a well-bred, gentlemanly manner." To be sure, "our young men fight ninety-nine times out of a hundred, through *fear* of being branded with the epithet of *coward;* and since they fight to please the world," Oldstyle concludes, wouldn't the legislature—instead of depriving duelists of the vote—be better advised to license such contests with a newly created Blood and Thunder Office, advertise them in advance, and let the world "attend and judge in person" of the conduct of the antagonists? This "would in some degree, be reviving the *spectacles* of antiquity, when the populace were regaled with the combats of gladiators"—thereby forming, like the local bull- and bear-baits, yet another "valuable addition to the list of our refined amusements."

The nine letters—on dueling, marriage, dandyism, the theater— which Irving later would regard as of so little merit that he declined to include them in his collected works, were nevertheless encouragingly received when they first appeared. Actors were duly outraged; everyone else who read them was tickled. In addition, and to his delight, hardly anyone penetrated the disguise of the "odd old fellow" who had written them—this Jonathan Oldstyle, first of Irving's many such disguises. (The very choice of pseudonym, interestingly enough, discloses something of the writer's divided nature—*Jonathan* the current designation for any country bumpkin, that simple, brash, uncouth American, whereas *Oldstyle* harked back to continental traditions, for the most part English, in which America was formed.) Few readers discovered the old scribbler's identity, though at least one did. No doubt Irving's elder brother Peter, editor of the *Morning Chronicle*, had told Aaron Burr who the pseudonymous author was. In any case, we find Burr clipping the letters to send his daughter Theodosia; of one such enclosure he explained that "it would not, perhaps, merit so high an honour as that of being perused" by Theo's eyes and touched by her "fair hands, but that it is the production of a youth of about nineteen . . ."

For Washington Irving (like Theodosia herself at the time) was nineteen when he wrote the Oldstyle letters. Looking back years later, he was to feel that he had spent the bulk of his existence before then "mewed up, during the livelong day, in that purgatory of boyhood, a school-room." Such an enclosure brought him little enough pleasure. Outside, a bobolink would sing: a bobolink beyond a window on Fulton Street! "It seemed as if the little varlet mocked at me, as he flew by in full song . . ." Indeed, the young Irving, who saw the last of his formal schooling before he was sixteen, would spend as much time as he could in the bobolink's outdoor world, exploring crooked streets and musing: "I knew every spot where a murder or robbery had been committed or a ghost seen. . . . I even journeyed one long summer's day to the summit of the most distant hill, from whence I stretched my eye over many a mile of terra incognita, and was astonished to find how vast a globe I inhabited."

He wandered, and neglected his studies. For whatever reason, though two of his older brothers did go on to Columbia College nearby (it was located then just north of where the World Trade Center rises now), Washington Irving did not, and years later as a writer would voice predictable regrets for not having continued his education beyond Mr. Josiah Henderson's male seminary on John Street. For in those surroundings he had acquired no more than what nowadays would be regarded as a reasonable grammar-school education (though as boy or man Irving was never to plummet the mysteries of spelling and punctuation). Still, years in the 1790s when he might have been extending his learning within classroom walls at Columbia were filled with much that would be of use to him later in pursuing his "literary carreer." The theater always, to stir his imagination—as pervasive through Irving's life as movies in ours—and lengthening local journeys that during those years enlarged his knowledge of the world up through hills and woods of Manhattan, gradually up the Hudson, until by 1798 it had reached far enough to include Sleepy Hollow, near Tarrytown, where his oldest brother's wife had family.

Nearer home, too, he was stretching his awarenesses. A journal from the mid-'nineties survives, by a John Anderson, then in his late teens, who knew the Irving family. Through that journal we may share days in lives long ended—one January afternoon, for example, in 1794: "Washington Irving"—he was not yet eleven—"spent the afternoon with me. Gave him some of my drawing books to look over, and presented him with a small one; play on the violin for him. He stayed to tea. Shew'd him the copy of my old journals and let him read part. Went home with him as it was dark—set a few minutes at his Papa's." Other such entries appear—visiting with Deacon Irving in his shop there in the William Street home, "setting" with Mrs. Irving and her daughter Kitty—all tending toward this, on February 7: "Miss Kitty Irving drank tea with us in the afternoon. Waited on her to Dr. Roger's lecture . . . I partly opened my mind to Miss Kitty on a subject that I have long wished to inform her of." But that young lady was destined to marry someone else, and John Anderson himself would die scarcely four years later in New York, among the stench and horrors of an epidemic of yellow fever.

It was, in fact, to escape that very plague of yellow fever, fatal to John Anderson, that Washington Irving was sent up the Hudson for his initial visit to Sleepy Hollow in 1798. He returned after the autumn frost had brought its miraculous, mysterious relief to a perplexed and grieving populace. And it was in the following year, at sixteen, that he entered the law office of Henry Masterton, resolved to prepare himself for a profession.

But Irving was not Burr. No more promising a lawyer than he was a scholar, he would not pass his bar examinations for another nine years. Meanwhile, the young man had learned to detest his apprenticeship, listlessly doing battle with his "inveterate enemies, the ponderous fathers of the law." Far more interesting to scribble—those letters that the nineteen-year-old wrote as Jonathan Oldstyle, for instance, and saw published in his brother's newspaper and heard commented on approvingly by older and graver townsmen, to whose faces his words could bring a smile. Far more interesting to travel, up the Hudson again in 1803, ostensibly on legal business with Judge Hoffman and his family, up past Albany into the very wilds of the frontier that spread to the borders of Canada and beyond.

And anyway, he was sickly. Despite—or because of?—those sometimes grueling adventures by boat and oxcart in the wilderness (to which we shall return), he was inclined toward bronchitis, with a hacking cough that seemed to threaten consumption. Accordingly, in early 1804, his older brothers concluded that Irving should, as much for his health's sake as for his enlightenment, journey to Europe. A rare privilege that was for all but the wealthiest, and the brothers were willing to pay for the venture. "It is with delight we share the world with you; and one of our greatest sources of happiness is that fortune is daily putting it in our power thus to add to the comfort and enjoyment of one so very near to us all." So this favorite of theirs, the youngest of the family, was escorted, May 19, 1804, aboard ship in New York Harbor, bound for Bordeaux.

Watching the invalid being helped up the side, the ship's captain concluded he would never survive the voyage: "There's a chap who will go overboard before we get across." And the first hours were indeed trying: "the severest moments of my departure," Irving would write, "were when I lost sight of the boat in which were my brothers who had accompanied me on board, and when the steeples of the city faded from my view." Yet soon, after the initial heartache and a day or two of seasickness, the passenger began to improve, flourished in health, in fact thrived so articulately that we see him yet, aboard the little *Rising States* in all that blue, sunstruck expanse, clambering about a swaying masthead, "going out on the main topsail yard" with white canvas slapping near his shoulder—for that was still the era of sails: not for three more years would Fulton's Folly, the *Clermont*, steam from Manhattan up the Hudson to Albany, foreshadowing the end of a purer and more leisurely passage at sea. Meanwhile, Irving's letters and journals let us experience his six weeks' crossing of the ocean by sail both ways, over to Europe in 1804, back to New York two years later, as in this vivid sight of a long morning in that world of canvas bellying, of tar smells and creaking wood: "After breakfast go to after cabin Miss B. wishes tune on flute—I play—Little Guitar & admiral sings most hideously Ladies cover their ears—Miss Bayley scolds—Eliza laughs—Miss B requests a serious sentimental tune. . . . Hard work to kill time—Deck wet—Cabin too warm—go and sit in Jolly boat over the stern and finish a volume of Virgil—return into cabin nothing to do set down & scribble this nonsense. . . ."

He would remain in Europe twenty-three months. Landing at Bordeaux June 30, 1804, he would linger there briefly before setting out across southern France, through Marseille and Nice, into Italy. Six months in Italy and Sicily, then north through Switzerland to Paris, where he would settle into four months of delight: "You will excuse the shortness and hastiness of this letter, for which I can only plead as an excuse that I am a *young man* and in *Paris*": Paris, granting "the perfect liberty of private conduct." At last, reluctantly, he would leave that world to hurry through flat ancestral lands of those phlegmatic, pipe-smoking Dutch burghers he had known along the Hudson, would hurry through Holland ("where cleanliness is almost a vice") to England, to see for the first time, October 5, 1805, at sunrise opposite Margate, a country he would only later learn to love. In London he would remain three months, dandy in "light gray coat, white embroidered vest, and colored small-clothes," before taking sail finally for America, aboard the *Remittance*, from Gravesend, in late January 1806.

Nine or ten countries he visited in all, in a Europe that Napoleon's ambition was then redrawing, rumbled with his trunks over tortuous roads in cumbersome diligences, stopped at inns with manure piled against their walls, where "dirt, noise, and insolence reigned without control," sailed dreamily in feluccas along romantic coasts: "Towards evening the breeze died away, and the men had to take to their oars. It was a bright moonlight, and the sound of a convent bell from among the mountains would now and then salute their ears, and immediately the rowers would rest on their oars, pull off their caps, and offer up their prayers." An altogether attractive young observer—aspiring lawyer, aspiring man of letters, hardly serious about either, with a zest for adventure and a nature both genial and uncomplaining: "when I cannot get a dinner to suit my taste I endeavor to get a taste to suit my dinner." He made friends easily. There was a Dr. Henry, for example, from Lancaster, Pennsylvania, whom he met first outside Bordeaux and would encounter again, coincidentally, at other places along his travels, as though Europe for an American gentleman were of domestically cozy dimensions. Dr. Henry was a jester. Traveling with Irving through southern France, he played on one occasion upon the sympathies of a group of impressionable and attractive girls who sat quilting inside a village doorway. In fluent French (for he was a gifted polyglot as well) the doctor assured the girls that his traveling companion, who had fallen to with needle in hand and was amusing them by helping them quilt, was in fact under guard, a young English officer on his way to his execution. The girls' hearts were touched; they made a great fuss over Irving, plying him with what gifts they had: fruit, wine, their benedictions. (Many, many years later, when he was over sixty but a wanderer still, Irving went out of his way to pass through that village on a journey from Paris to Madrid, peering through his carriage window for the tangible world that his memories were built on: "I believe I recognized the house; and I saw two or three old women, who might once have formed part of the merry group of girls; but I doubt whether they recognized in the stout elderly gentleman, thus rattling in his carriage through their streets, the pale young English prisoner of forty years since.")

But Dr. Henry had been helpful as well as amusing, those linguistic gifts aiding his young companion through the arduousness of European travel then: weeks-long passport problems at Nice, the quarantines. There were other friends, too, whom Irving met in Europe on this first visit, some of them friends he would keep for a lifetime—the painter Washington Allston, young Joseph Carrington Cabell, who would sit on a famous jury in Richmond and some years later would, with Jefferson, found the University of Virginia. And one evening at a dinner party in Rome, he met Madame de Staël. And everywhere were girls to look at and comment on, from the first stop onward: Bordeaux girls "torture the hair into unatural twists & ringlets and lard it over with a profusion of *ancient oil*," unlike the girls back in New York, with their ringlets "dry & elastic, that play with every zephyr." Italian girls, like the French (he knowingly records for us), are kept under such restraint that they rush into loveless marriages simply to be able to "indulge themselves with greater freedom." And he notes and grieves over the poverty in Sicily that leads fathers to relegate daughters to convents: "It is a painful sight to behold young females—endowed with all the graces of person and charms of countenance that can render a woman lovely with apparent sensibility of mind—sprightliness of manner & susceptibility of heart—shut up for-ever from the world." He does go visit them, finds at a convent in Syracuse "the most lovely girl that I have seen in Sicily," and four days later with Captain Hall, Wadsworth Baker, and Lieutenant Cargill visits a Benedictine convent where the abbess who greets them takes care "to send the handsome nuns out of sight." And during yet another such visit: "Nuns on tops of the convents talking with Baker Lieut Morris & myself—& making lascavious gestures."

Lascavious? Could Irving be using that misspelled word correctly? The rooftop image defies time. He saw other unforgettable spectacles: of Nelson's fleet in full array at the straits of Messina, two brigs, three frigates, and eleven sail-of-the-line including the flagship *Victory* (and less than a year afterward, in a London theater, Irving would be among a crowd informed of the British triumph over Napoleon's navy at Trafalgar, would hear the cheer begin that would end as suddenly, stopped by the further news that Nelson himself was dead). And there was an authentic adventure with pirates in which the young Irving participated, on the *Matilda*, not far from the island of Elba (a decade before Bonaparte's exile there would make it universally famous):

"I was sitting in the Cabin yesterday writing very tranquilly when word was brought that a sail was seen coming off towards us from the Island. The Genoese Captain after regarding it thro a Spy Glass, turned pale and said it was one of those privateers . . . A moment after she fired a Gun upon which we hoisted the American flag. Another gun was fired the ball of which passed between the main & formasts and we immediately brought to."

Alarmed, the passengers hid what valuables they could while the privateer was approaching—"about the size of one of our Staten Island ferry boats—with latine sails and two small guns in the bow. (As for us we had not even a pistol on board.)" The outlaws drew alongside. "One of them appeared to have command over the rest, he was a tall stout fellow shabbily drest, without any coat and his shirt sleeves rolld up to his elbows . . ." His crew carried rusty cutlasses and, in their waistbands, pistols and stilettos. They swarmed aboard, commanding in a babel of Italian, English, and French that sails be shortened, the ship's papers produced, cargo identified. Irving, translating their jargon French, was ordered into the pirates' own boat. "As we were going over the side the genoese Captain stopped me privately and with tears in his eyes entreated me not to leave the ship as he believed they only intended to seperate us all, that they might cut our throats the more easily."

But throats of unarmed victims could be cut as well here as there, so Irving did as the pirates ordered. "When we arrived on board the privateer," he continues in his letter to his brother, "I own my heart almost faild me." It was a villainous, scowling bunch on those strange decks, bearded, fierce-eyed. Their captain was telling "some confused contradictory story of his being employed by the health office of Leghorn. After a while he told us we might return on board with which we cheerfully complied . . ." But the *Matilda* was meanwhile being ransacked. In time the pirates came across Irving's portmanteau, "which I opened for them and the Captain rummaged it completely without finding any money"—only letters of introduction in abundance. Irving was permitted to put the letters away; "I huddled them in carelessly," he writes, revealing a mind forlorn, "as I expected never again to have the use of them . . ."

The long afternoon dragged on; the profitless search continued. But there was little cargo aboard, so finally after dickerings and petty theft—of a watch, clothes, some pipes of brandy, and two boxes of quicksilver—"about sun down to our great joy they bid us *adieu* having been on board since 11 Oclock in the morning." Then, soon after the pirates had left, the wind fell, and the *Matilda* lay becalmed nearby, its passengers all anxious lest "some of the gang—inflamed with the liquors they had taken from us, might come off in the night unknown to their leaders, and commit their depredations without fear or restraint." Uneasy himself, Irving was nevertheless so exhausted from the ordeal that he did soon fall asleep, lying in his clothes in his bunk to dream horrible dreams all night, two or three times starting up with the image of buccaneers before him again and a stiletto raised at his heart. Daybreak at last: "Happily for us a favorable wind sprung up early this morning and we had the satisfaction of leaving the island far behind us before sun rise."

That adventure occurred between Genoa and Naples. For nearly three months Irving had delayed at Genoa, joyously among newfound friends in an English home where he was always welcome, dancing, as he says, or singing, or playing blindman's bluff or battledore and shuttle-cock. Now he was on the move again, and on July 8, 1805, his brother William, seventeen years older, who had principally financed the trip, responded to his progress: "This day your letter, dated Rome, 4th April, was received, and afforded us both pleasure and mortification—pleasure to hear that your health is so completely re-established, and mortification to learn that you have determined to *gallop through Italy*. . . . all Italy, I presume, is to be scoured through, (leaving Florence on your left and Venice on your right,) in the short period of eight or nine weeks!" Then this, acutely: "Good company, I find, is the grand desideratum with you; good company made you stay eleven weeks at Genoa, where you needed not to have stayed more than two, and good company drives you through all Italy in less time than was necessary for your stay at Genoa. . . ."

Well, Irving was young, and Paris lay before him—and besides, he could be solemn on occasion, as in an earlier letter from that very Genoa in the autumn of 1804: "My fellow countrymen do not know the blessings they enjoy," he had written soberly enough to William then; "they are trifling with their felicity and are in fact *themselves* their worst enemies. I sicken when I think of our political broils, slanders & enmities and I think when I again find myself in New York I shall never meddle any more in politicks."

What had occasioned so grave a reflection? A letter from his eldest brother had just informed the innocent abroad that Alexander Hamilton, Federalist leader, on the morning of July 11, had been shot and wounded mortally by the Vice President of the United States.

Colonel Aaron Burr's life had altered significantly by the spring of 1804. Some changes seemed of a kind with his earlier attainments, as ambition, discipline, and quickness of mind brought him ever more abundantly the rewards of this world. His loves and interests had flourished. At Richmond Hill in 1801, his daughter was honeymooning, at seventeen, at the start of a happy marriage to a wealthy and attractive young South Carolina planter, Joseph Alston, in a decade or so to become governor of his home state. And within scarcely more than a year of that marriage, from Washington the colonel could write to his Theodosia, now mistress of an estate along the Waccamaw in South Carolina, what may have been his first playful mention of the grandchild on whom his thoughts would so often fix in coming years: "If you will have *Pet* or *Peet, Peter, Peter Yates, Peter Alston, Petrus Burr* (or by every other name he may be known) taught to write a good hand, and make me a present of him, I will subscribe myself your very much obliged and humble servant." The grandchild's proud name, in fact, was to be Aaron Burr Alston.

Politically, too, the years at the turn of the century had favored Burr. In part because he had labored successfully to deliver an overwhelmingly Federalist New York into the hands of the Republicans in the state elections of 1799, he was to become a leading Republican candidate for President the following year. But in those days there was, officially, no "ticket" of President and running mate for which electors balloted. Rather, votes were cast for the two candidates thought most qualified regardless of party loyalties. That way, so the Founding Fathers had reasoned (innocent that political parties would form at all), whoever was Vice President would be the man judged second most able in the country to occupy the office of the Presidency. Thus, in 1796, the Federalist President John Adams had for his Vice President the Republican Jefferson. And four years later it was Jefferson himself who, as candidate once more for President, found his votes tied, unprecedentedly, with those of Aaron Burr.

To settle the tie, the election went to the House of Representatives, and there, within that temporary brick structure, after thirty-five separate ballots that consumed a stormy, exhausting week from February 10 to 16, 1801, Thomas Jefferson was declared at last third President of the United States. "*Had Burr done any thing for himself,*" one of those who was a party to the balloting had said while it still was in progress, "*he would long ere this have been president.*" But it was the Virginian who, in the muddy new capital on the Potomac, took the oath of office March 4, 1801, as Chief Executive of the land; and it was Burr at his side, within the Capitol's north wing that perched on the bare crest of Jenkins Hill, to whom, that same morning, Justice John Marshall administered the oath that made him the nation's third Vice President.

What were the colonel's feelings on so historic an occasion? Was he digesting the gall of the failed intriguer, as his enemies have ever after proclaimed? Recognizing that Jefferson was in fact the popular choice, Burr before the election had not expected to win; when the electoral votes he received were tied with Jefferson's, he did not expect the tie to be resolved in his favor. That much appears clear. But "it seems to be the general opinion that Colonel Burr will be chosen President," Gouverneur Morris was writing in his diary before the event. "I state it as the opinion, not of light and fanciful but of serious and considerable men. . . ." For most Federalists and some Republicans in the House supported him. Burr, however, would do nothing in his own behalf. The previous December he had stated unequivocally that he would not "be instrumental in counteracting the wishes and the expectations of the

United States." On the other hand, he did not come forward in support of
the Virginian—did not work for Jefferson's election over his own. And
for that lapse he was not forgiven. Indeed, certain newspapers were soon
proclaiming that Burr, who in times past had found it possible to work
as well with either party, had schemed and conspired in this later instance with opponents of Jefferson to seize the Presidency from its rightful heir. Now, as always, the colonel refused to answer such charges; he
would not condescend (as he had said on another occasion) "to refute a
calumny. I leave to my actions to speak for themselves, and to my
character to confound the fictions of slander." But he should have con-
descended. For many came to believe what had not been pointedly re-
futed, and among those learning mistrust of the new Vice President was,
assuredly, Jefferson himself.

As a consequence, during this first Republican administration,
Burr's recommendations were increasingly ignored: others than his
friends were appointed supervisor of the Internal Revenue, naval officer
of the Port of New York. In his home state, meanwhile, the Clintons—
Governor George and his nephew De Witt—were wresting power from
supporters of the absent Burr, and were exercising that power further to
rob Burr of his national influence. By early 1804, accordingly, such
threats to his fortunes had provoked a response. With his political career
as Vice President languishing (men in the same office before and since
have known Burr's frustrations), he determined to return home to run
for the governor's seat that the venerable George Clinton was finally
vacating that year—vacating to become the Vice President of Jefferson's
second administration.

Burr's plan made sense. The governorship of his home state was at
that time perhaps the second most powerful elective office in America.
And there would be support for the colonel—among his Tammany followers in New York City, among members of his own Republican Party
elsewhere in the state, among many New York Federalists who found in
the Vice President the solidest counterpoise to the weight of the Virginian dynasty that was pushing the country in a direction many in the
North and East would rather not go.

Not all Federalists, to be sure, found Colonel Burr to their liking.
One in particular did not—had not for a very long while. As long before
as September 1792—more than eleven years earlier—the Federalist
Alexander Hamilton, then Secretary of the Treasury, had written of
Burr: "I feel it a religious duty to oppose his career." That duty, self-
imposed, was assumed not long after the colonel had unexpectedly defeated Hamilton's father-in-law for the United States Senate. Before
then, the two lawyers and rising politicians had seemed to thrive together amicably enough. They had first met at least as far back as the
Battle of Manhattan in 1776, had fought together at Monmouth, after
the war had argued cases together in New York, had served on commit-

tees and directories together, had often dined together. And even after 1792, the year Hamilton took his resolve to thwart Burr's further advancement, the New Yorkers remained outwardly cordial. Six years after that date they were working side by side on another law case; eleven years after that date, as late as 1803, Hamilton was once again a dinner guest at Richmond Hill: the very handsome General Hamilton, the urbane Aaron Burr sipping wine within the same four paneled walls.

But it would have been Burr's way to control his emotions, before the world to show the unruffled civility of his admired Lord Chesterfield, whatever his inner feelings. Hamilton behaved differently. The two men were similar in height, in age; both had distinguished war records; each was a most gifted lawyer. Both had, in addition, married adoring wives. And both men philandered, although the widower Burr's conquests were without number, whereas Hamilton perhaps in only one instance (with a certain Maria Reynolds) was unfaithful to his beloved wife, Eliza, who would survive him and flourish to protect his reputation into her ninety-eighth year. Both men speculated. Both lived beyond their means. And each was charming; each was ambitious; each was naturally a leader.

Yet there were contrasts between the two, and not only in ancestry. For Burr was contained, closemouthed. Politics rarely entered his many letters, and when they did, he doted like a child on ciphers that made the most innocent observations mysterious. He might request, for instance, "18 to ask 45, whether, for any reasons, 21 could be induced to vote for 6, and if he could, whether 14 would withdraw his opposition to 29, and 11 exert his influence in favor of 22." By contrast, Hamilton in those outspoken times, when intense statesmen who had helped form a nation saw any opposition as part of a plot to destroy their handiwork, was among the most outspoken of all. A brilliant man, a very great man, but (in the words of the friend chosen to deliver his eulogy, words set down on the very eve of that eulogy) "indiscreet, vain, and opinionated." The character of his fellow Federalist John Adams, for example, Hamilton publicly charged was possessed of "great and intrinsic defects"; Adams suffered from "extreme egotism," from "a vanity without bounds, and a jealousy capable of discoloring every object." Jefferson, according to the voluble Hamilton, was "tinctured with fanaticism," "crafty and persevering in his objects," "not scrupulous about the means of success, nor very mindful of truth." But Burr—Burr was "one of the worst men in the community." He was "as unprincipled and dangerous a man as any country can boast." His "friends do not insist upon his integrity. He is without doubt insolvent . . . No mortal can tell what his political principles are. . . . He has talked all around the compass. . . . The truth seems to be that he has no plan but that of getting power by any means and keeping it by all means. . . ."

So Hamilton throughout the 'nineties was doing all he could to fulfill that religious duty he had set himself of opposing the colonel's career. In 1792, largely through his rival's active interference, Burr lost an opportunity to run for governor of New York. In 1794, President Washington sought Hamilton's advice on who should be appointed ambassador to France. Others urged Burr; Washington appointed Monroe. In 1797, Burr's senatorial career ended, Hamilton's father-in-law having been named by the legislature to succeed him. In 1798, during the undeclared war with France, the willing Burr, ever vain (with reason) about his military prowess, was denied promotion in the Army at the same time that Hamilton was made major general. And in the presidential election of 1800, smarting anew from Burr's success the preceding year in delivering New York from the Federalists to the Republicans, it was Hamilton who threw all his formidable influence behind the candidate he regarded as "a contemptible hypocrite," that other Republican, Thomas Jefferson.

Burr, then, became Vice President—an office "the most insignificant that ever the mind of man contrived or his imagination conceived," so one of his predecessors, John Adams, had called it. And the new Vice President came soon to understand that any real influence, any real power lay elsewhere. That was why, in the spring of 1804, he was fighting again for a position of significance, as an independent candidate for the governorship of New York, in what was to become one of the most scurrilous and bitter elections in American history.

"Hamilton," the Vice President wrote Theodosia early in that libelous campaign, "is intriguing for any candidate who can have a chance of success against A. B." But intriguing indirectly. Direct attacks came mostly from Republican newspapers, in the pages of which, and on handbills and broadsides, the electorate could read of the independent candidate's "Abandoned Profligacy, and the Numerous Unhappy Wretches who have fallen Victims to this accomplished and but too successful Debauchee." Editor James Cheetham of the New York *American-Citizen* was promising to "tear away the veil that hides this monster, and lay open a scene of misery at which every heart must shudder." "AARON BURR is closeted with his satellites in dark divan. He is using every wicked art to promote his own election. . . . If decency would permit, I could tell such tales of all of them as would put them down for ever." Cheetham would tell this much, though: the creed of the Burrites maintained that "fornication and adultery are not crimes; and that any unmarried man or widower, before or after he is governor of the state, has a right to keep a seraglio. . . ."

In that poisoned atmosphere, void of issues, heavy with slander, in the last days of April 1804, the voting took place. Burr did carry New York City, barely, but the state went for his Republican opponent, Morgan Lewis. "The election is lost by a great majority," the defeated candidate was writing offhandedly in a letter to Theodosia of May 1, and he added: *"tant mieux."*

So much the better, and yet the loss—an effect "present and palpable"—must sharply have stung him. The first Vice President, John Adams, had gone on to become President. So had the second, Thomas Jefferson. When Jefferson became President, in 1801, his own Vice President might reasonably have looked forward in time to the same elevation. Instead, three years afterward, following a campaign of vicious attacks on his character, Burr could muse on a political career shattered, both in the nation and in his home state. Though he affected never to notice libels, he did tell a friend that "he was determined to call out the first man of any respectability concerned in the infamous publications" recently written about him. And in June he did so. He called out General Hamilton.

N York 18 June 1804

Sir

I send for your perusal a letter signed Ch. D. Cooper which, though apparently published some time ago, has but very recently come to my knowledge. Mr. Van Ness who does me the favor to deliver this, will point out to you that clause of the letter to which I particularly request your attention.

You must perceive, Sir, the Necessity of a prompt and unqualified acknowledgment or denial of the use of any expressions which could warrant the assertions of Dr. Cooper.

I have the honor to be
Your Obdt s^t
A. Burr

That cryptic and momentous note, composed at Richmond Hill, was delivered to the general in New York City about eleven in the morning of the summer day it was written, Monday morning, a new week beginning. Hamilton was surprised to receive it. He had not openly campaigned in the recent election, before then had been for several years in political retirement. But he had talked and written a great deal of late: "my animadversions on the political principles character and views of Col Burr have been extremely severe," as he himself was to concede—though not to the colonel—"and on different occasions I, in common with many others, have made very unfavorable criticisms on particular instances of the private conduct of this Gentleman." One such occasion, allegedly, was in Albany, during the campaign just ended. The general had been overheard at a dinner in a private home; Burr, he had said, was a dangerous man. He had said more: ". . . I could detail to you," one of those present had written in a letter that was published and subsequently came to the defeated candidate's notice, "a still more despicable opinion which General HAMILTON has expressed of Mr. BURR. . . ."

On precisely that clause Burr was now directing his rival to comment.

The unexpected intrusion in his life interrupted a morning that held much business for the distinguished attorney: "a variety of engagements" had been scheduled over the next two days. Accordingly, Hamilton asked Burr's emissary, Mr. Van Ness, for time to consider his reply. The request was granted, and when an answer did come, on the morning of the twenty-first, it was the colonel's turn to read—these words: "Sir, I have maturely reflected on the subject of your letter of the 18th instant; and the more I have reflected the more I have become convinced, that I could not, without manifest impropriety, make the avowal or disavowal which you seem to think necessary. . . ." An explanation followed, at some length, ingenious, evasive: "the phrase 'still more despicable' admits of infinite shades," General Hamilton elaborated, "from very light to very dark. How am I to judge of the degree intended? Or how shall I annex any precise idea to language so indefinite? . . . I trust, on more reflection, you will see the matter in the same light with me. If not, I can only regret the circumstance, and must abide the consequences. . . ."

Those consequences were nearer now. Colonel Burr was not satisfied, and his own response was prompt: "Sir, Your letter of the 20th inst. has been this day received." In it, he regretted to find nothing sincere; the question was not whether Dr. Cooper, who had made the original remark about Hamilton's still more despicable opinion of Burr, "understood the Meaning of the word or has used it according to syntax and with grammatical accuracy, but whether you have authorised their application either directly or by uttering expressions or opinions derogatory to my honor." The colonel's conclusion was ominous: "Your letter has furnished me with new reasons for requiring a definite reply."

That sentence Hamilton was perusing about noon Friday, June 22, 1804, in the presence of Burr's emissary, young Mr. Van Ness, who awaited instructions. The general was troubled. He had hoped not to have received such a letter; "it contained several offensive expressions & seemed to close the door" to all further negotiation. Indeed, no reply was possible, Hamilton felt, unless Mr. Burr would phrase his interrogation in other terms. Yet there were further exchanges, replies and counter-replies, still to be written at the southern tip of Manhattan between two men in their forties and between their seconds—Van Ness for Burr, Nathaniel Pendleton for Hamilton—while summer days passed and one life moved, as though all were normal, between the general's town house on Cedar Street and his country house eight miles northward, as another life at Richmond Hill awaited, inexorably, those consequences that the general's behavior seemed to defy. As though witnessing the motions of a grim and governed dance of two men moving with stately grace under a spell, one reads the correspondence—those formal periods, the incessant references to delicacy and propriety and decorum, the charge by Hamilton of "predetermined hostility," the insistence by Burr that he was proceeding "without sensations of hostility or wishes of revenge," the reminder that the colonel had never slandered political opponents himself, was not "capable of imitating the conduct of Mr. Hamilton, by committing secret depredations on his fame and character." Yet such covert slurs by others Burr had endured long enough: "these things must have an end." And they would end, soon, as Mr. Van Ness handed to Mr. Pendleton, at twelve o'clock Wednesday, June 27, "the Message which it is unnecessary to repeat," "the simple Message which I shall now have the honor to deliver."

The invitation had been extended, and was accepted. But at the time a circuit court was sitting, before which General Hamilton had cases to argue. In order not to cause hardship to clients, his second requested and was granted a postponement until after the court had closed, which would occur Friday or Saturday. The time and location of the duel were agreed upon, then, as July 11, the Wednesday after the weekend, in the morning at seven, at Weehawken on the Jersey shore, three miles north of town and across the Hudson.

Thus, from that morning in late June when the fateful "alternative" was accepted until the duel itself took place, two full weeks passed, during which both principals went about their normal business. Almost no one knew of what had been scheduled. Burr had told only Van Ness. Hamilton had told Rufus King and one or two others, but would not discuss particulars with them. On July 4, one week exactly before the duel, the Society of the Cincinnati was holding a patriotic dinner on Pearl Street, at the Fraunces Tavern (which still stands); both Hamilton and Burr were in attendance. The latter was subdued, "a disappointed and mortified man," one eyewitness thought him; but when the general, who seemed in cheerful spirits, sang "The Drum," Burr was observed to raise his head, gaze at the singer, and listen.

Neither, of course, could know the outcome of a morning that lay in the future. We who do know remind ourselves that not one but two men were preparing to die. It was part of the ritual—before, during, and after such a meeting—to affect unconcern. Yet the night before the duel, Tuesday evening, July 10, 1804, both men in solitude, having made their wills, were writing final letters to those they loved most in the world. Hamilton wrote to his wife Eliza, mother of his seven children. She was sleeping that night at the Grange, their country house to the north, unaware of the business on which her husband was engaged. Earlier, on the fourth, he had written a message she would receive only if "I shall first have terminated my earthly career." In that note he explained that the interview could not have been avoided "without sacrifices which would have rendered me unworthy of your esteem." Now, from Cedar Street, once more he wrote, to tell her that he had determined to expose his life without firing at his opponent. "This must increase my hazards & redoubles my pangs for you. But you had rather I should die innocent than live guilty." Should he fall, religion must be her consolation.

Afterward, when Burr was told that his rival had committed to writing on the eve of the duel his determination to hold fire, he called the act, if true, contemptible. For now though, he too was writing—to Theodosia, to her husband—from the library at Richmond Hill. To his daughter he made no mention of the forthcoming meeting, but did explain that he had lately set down his will, in which his private papers were bequeathed to her charge. His estate—"I mean, if I should die this year"—would just about pay his debts. Give his wearing apparel to his stepson Frederic. "Give him also a sword or pair of pistols." Letters were in six blue boxes in the library; burn those that would, if published, injure any person, "more particularly . . . the letters of my female correspondents." And he concluded: "I am indebted to you, my dearest Theodosia, for a very great portion of the happiness which I have enjoyed in this life. You have completely satisfied all that my heart and affections had hoped or even wished. With a little more perseverence, determination, and industry, you will obtain all that my ambition or vanity had fondly imagined. Let your son have occasion to be proud that he had a mother. Adieu. Adieu."

One more letter was written that night, to Theodosia's husband: "I have called out General Hamilton, and we meet to-morrow morning. Van Ness will give you the particulars. . . . If it should be my lot to fall . . . yet I shall live in you and your son. I commit to you all that is most dear to me—my reputation and my daughter . . ."

After a few last recommendations and requests, Burr ended. He lay down, there among the busts and portraits in the library at Richmond Hill, and was sleeping soundly when awakened at daybreak, in time to set out for the interview. About five in the morning, then, the Vice President of the United States, dressed elegantly in a coat of bombazine over black cotton pantaloons and half boots, was passing with his second and two other friends through the gates of Richmond Hill, located at what is now the corner of Spring and MacDougal Streets. The gentlemen walked west through the brightening morning until they reached the Hudson shore. There a boat was waiting for them. They boarded it, to be rowed upstream across the river in order to arrive, as had beforehand been agreed upon, first at the dueling ground. Once landed, Burr and Van Ness removed their coats and together set about trampling weeds and clearing the site of fallen branches.

Soon afterward Hamilton and Pendleton arrived by barge. What were the general's thoughts? "I was certainly desirous of avoiding this interview for the most cogent reasons," he had written the preceding evening. He was in debt, and his creditors would suffer if he fell. More particularly, "my wife and children"—the youngest was only two years old—"are extremely dear to me, and my life is of the utmost importance to them in various views." But above all, "my religious and moral principles are strongly opposed to the practice of dueling. . . ." Yet they had not always been so. Some years earlier, in 1797, it was Hamilton who had become involved in an affair of honor with thirty-nine-year-old James Monroe (later to become President), regarding his liaison with Maria Reynolds, whose urgent and amorous letters had obliged the general to admit publicly his private indiscretions. And on that occasion it had been, ironically, Aaron Burr who had intervened to reconcile the principals before the interview could occur. But since then an event had altered Hamilton's feelings, for his eldest son, Philip, not three years before, late in 1801, had been killed in a duel arising out of a political squabble—had stood, indeed, and fired and fallen on this same ledge over the Hudson toward which the barge now bearing his father was tending.

The site, located directly across from what is now Forty-second Street, was well suited for such an encounter—two small beaches hidden from each other, some natural stairs ascending, then the flat ledge itself twenty feet above water, no more than a couple of yards wide, ten or twelve yards long, jutting into the river. Whatever happened on that ledge could be neither seen from below, nor interfered with from the heights of the cliff above, heights that now hold the little tangible that remains of where that morning's meeting took place. For brought up there and placed on a platform before the American flag is a boulder on which the wounded general is supposed to have rested his head, a rock preserved when the Weehawken dueling grounds were blasted into nothingness in 1883 to make room for the West Shore Railway Yards.

In 1804, though, on a clear July morning, the steps to the ledge were still solid underfoot as Hamilton and Pendleton, leaving Dr. Hosack as agreed upon at the beach, mounted them to the clearing where Burr and his second were waiting. Formal salutations between the two parties were exchanged. The seconds measured off ten full paces, then drew lots to determine positions. Pendleton won for Hamilton, and chose the upstream spot, looking south over the sunlit river toward vessels at anchor and, off to the left, roofs of the awakening city. Burr would stand facing the cliff from which the ledge protruded. The seconds loaded the flintlocks, English weapons with barrels almost a foot long, and the adversaries took their positions.

Now Pendleton was reviewing the rules that had earlier been agreed upon. Were they clear? Both the general and the colonel answered affirmatively. Were the two gentlemen ready? A delay, while

Hamilton adjusted his spectacles. Finally, a single word signaled that the moment had come. "Present!" Within seconds two shots had sounded, two puffs of smoke rose briefly from the ledge and faded. Hamilton was lifted on his toes, was turning a little to one side, was falling forward on his face, for a bullet had ripped through his rib, his liver, his diaphragm, to lodge in a vertebra. He, too, had fired—deliberately or as a reflex?—but his shot had gone wild, striking a branch over Burr's head and to his left. His opponent, concerned, was moving toward the fallen antagonist, until Van Ness stepped between them and led Burr quickly from the scene; the duelist must not be observed by the doctor who had been called immediately from the beach below.

Face ashen, Hamilton was half-sitting on the ground, his head supported on Pendleton's arm. Now the two friends, Pendleton and Dr. Hosack, were carrying the unconscious body down to the barge at the river's edge. Once on the river, about fifty yards out, the wounded man revived; his vision was blurred, and he felt nothing in his legs. The doctor had been rubbing with spirits of hartshorn his lips, forehead, neck, wrists. "Take care of that pistol," Hamilton murmured at one point. And later: "Let Mrs. Hamilton be immediately sent for—let the event be gradually broken to her; but give her hopes." From a wharf in Manhattan the barge could be seen approaching: two men seated in the stern sheets, a body lying on the bottom. At last the wounded man was being borne, as tenderly as possible, to a friend's house on Jane Street nearby. And there, enduring pain that was all but unbearable, Hamilton was to linger in life, through the morning, the afternoon, the evening, through all that night and the following morning. Laudanum hardly helped; anodyne fomentations could hardly touch his pain. Throughout the ordeal—surgeons called into hopeless consultations, long summer hours ticking by—except for fitful naps the dying man was conscious, and his mind was clear. Only once did his marvelous composure break, when all seven of his children appeared together at the bedside. No more than an instant could he look at them, before closing his eyes and keeping them closed until the two-year-old and the others were led from the room. But he talked of them often, and of and to his wife, distracted with grief: *"Remember, my Eliza, you are a Christian."* Images and achievements would survive: young Hamilton speaking in the Fields by the liberty pole against English oppressions, Hamilton at Yorktown heroically storming the redoubt, Hamilton among the founders at Philadelphia helping to create the Constitution, Hamilton as Secretary of the Treasury penning his reports, Hamilton on his white horse haranguing the New York voters. Those would survive, but at two o'clock Thursday afternoon, July 12, 1804, thirty-one hours after a lead ball had opened his vitals ("Adieu best of wives and best of Women," he had written unsteadily before the duel, "Embrace all my darling Children for me") the patriot's eyes closed a final time, and his life—"these things must have an end"—his brilliant career, and all that sudden suffering were over.

Led down to the boat from the dueling grounds, Burr had voiced a wish to return to the man he had wounded: "I must go and speak to him." But that would have been a conclusion to this extralegal rite both useless and imprudent. Accordingly, the duelist let himself be hurried aboard the waiting boat—Van Ness, to obscure his identity, holding an umbrella over his head, under the bright sky. The boat crossed to Manhattan ahead of Hamilton's, landing at a wharf somewhat farther south, from which the colonel returned on foot to Richmond Hill. He had regained his composure by then. A neighbor encountered along the way he greeted with his usual cordiality. Within the hour, unexpectedly, a cousin from out of state dropped by Burr's home; he was shown into the library, where he joined his host at breakfast about eight. They chatted together amiably of various friends; and only later that morning, with amazement and disbelief, did the young man learn, passing among agitated crowds on Broadway—"Colonel Burr has killed General Hamilton in a duel this morning!"—of the business his breakfast companion had been about, not long before, on the other side of the Hudson.

During the Federalist leader's final hours, Burr did write a note to their mutual friend Dr. Hosack, inquiring "of the present state of Gen^1. H. and of the hopes which are entertained of his recovery." But though his own life had more than thirty years to run, he was not then or at any later time heard to express a word of remorse for his action, unless one comment uttered when he was nearly seventy may be so interpreted: "Had I read Voltaire less, and Sterne more, I might have thought the world wide enough for Hamilton and me!" Now, though, in the days immediately after the duel, Burr's conscience must have been clear. The ceremony he had just completed, however we may regard it, provided the accepted recourse for settling disputes between gentlemen then: De Witt Clinton, Henry Clay, John Randolph, Stephen Decatur, Jackson, Pitt, Wellington, many, many others were involved in duels during those years. And Burr's conduct throughout had been entirely proper. "It is not my design," Hamilton himself had written in the days before the encounter, "to affix any odium on the conduct of Col Burr, in this case." And if the general privately had determined not to fire . . . But in fact, both Burr and Van Ness maintained ever after that Hamilton had fired first. Yet if the general had determined in his own mind not to fire, that deception, as his opponent suggested, was hardly praiseworthy—and a far less courageous determination than to decline to duel altogether.

For his part, Burr had been rowed to Weehawken to shoot and get shot at. The claims of honor now being satisfied, that should have ended the matter. But it didn't. "General Hamilton died yesterday," his rival was writing Joseph Alston, Theodosia's husband, on the thirteenth. "The malignant federalists or tories, and the imbittered Clintonians, unite in endeavouring to excite public sympathy in his favour and indignation against his antagonist. Thousands of absurd falsehoods are circulated with industry." They were saying, for instance, that for three months before the interview Burr had daily been practicing his marksmanship until he could hit at ten paces a circle no larger than a dollar coin. That his cronies had been diligently combing newspapers before discovering at last, exultantly, the letter from Dr. Cooper that could justify a challenge. That Burr at the duel had worn specially woven silk underclothing to deflect bullets, and afterward, over wine, had jocularly apologized to his myrmidons for not hitting his opponent in the heart. Moreover, men of all political parties, including those recently most hostile to the Federalist Hamilton, were now joining in the outcry against his slayer, who during the days that immediately followed the interview dared not venture forth from his country home. Newspapers of the town branded him murderer. Mobs gathered to yell taunts beyond the gates of Richmond Hill. A coroner's jury was sitting; an indictment was called for. And the city's grief swelled at the funeral of the slain general, Saturday the fourteenth, which, starting from Robinson Street (now Park Place), proceeded in awesome procession to Trinity Church: horses in a cortege with Hamilton's empty boots reversed in stirrups, bells muffled, minute guns sounding, the general's older sons there on the platform, a eulogy by Gouverneur Morris from the church portico to the lamenting, resentful spectators, who had to be urged not to allow their "indignation to lead to any act which might again offend the insulted majesty of the law."

Even a week after the duel, however, that indignation was gaining strength in the city, as columns of newsprint continued worrying every detail of the interview and its consequences. A warrant—an "unexampled measure"—was being sought in New York for Burr's arrest. Another was being prepared in New Jersey, where the meeting had taken place. Van Ness had gone into hiding. Others of Burr's friends had gone to jail rather than tell what they knew of the proceedings. "The most illiberal means are practised in order to produce excitement, and, for the moment, with effect," Burr had continued in his letter to his son-in-law the day after Hamilton's death. And he had added: "I propose leaving town for a few days"—though on the eighteenth, nearly a week later, he was still writing from Richmond Hill, in a "sort of exile," which he admitted might "terminate in an actual and permanent ostracism." So he would leave after all, and did so on Saturday evening, a week and some days after the duel, moving (and now for the last time) about ten o'clock down to the river once more from his darkened hilltop house with the pond and the cedars: Burr, a servant, and a traveling companion, all muffled, five large trunks to get aboard the waiting barge that would carry passengers and baggage through the night southward past a sleeping city, lights in some windows, out the mouth of the Hudson and along the Kill van Kull to reach, at sunrise, Blazing Star Ferry on Staten Island Sound.

He was headed for Perth Amboy, where he arrived about ten. His host there was to be Commodore Thomas Truxtun, celebrated naval hero, recently retired, who that Sunday morning was working in his study when a servant announced that a gentleman wanted to see him. The commodore would wait on the gentleman in a few moments, but Mrs. Truxtun entered immediately afterward to identify the visitor as the Vice President of the United States. Not long before, Truxtun had sent an invitation to Burr to make such a visit; downstairs, Burr's servant Peter was waiting to point out the colonel's boat, a little way offshore. The commodore, a close friend of both Hamilton and his rival, promptly directed the boat to his landing place. After his night on the river Burr was asking for a "dish of good coffee," and soon he was seated at breakfast, a fugitive whose cordial reception Truxtun had later publicly to defend in the columns of a New York newspaper: "I . . . gave him a hearty welcome, as I should have done General Hamilton, had the fate of their interview been reversed."

So Burr spent that Sunday in late July of 1804 as a guest in another man's home, first of many such days at other men's tables that were to fill his wandering life for the next thirty-two months—as well as for long years afterward. But it is those months specifically, those two years and most of a third, that are to be considered now, years of movement and mystery in Burr's adventure, leading at last to the disgrace that was preparing for him March 26, 1807, as he arrived, under guard, at the Eagle Tavern in Richmond, Virginia. In the interval he was to travel thousands of miles—"think of drinking the nasty puddle-water, covered with green scum, and full of animalculae—bah!"—by foot, horse, mule, carriage, wagon, flatboat, along the Ohio, down the Mississippi, into the Spanish Floridas almost as far south as St. Augustine. Indeed, he first journeyed, in that summer of 1804, beyond Georgia into those forbidding Spanish regions, then back by canoe four hundred miles (that model of elegance in his fiftieth year seated four hundred miles in a canoe in the southern wilderness) to visit in South Carolina Theodosia and Gampy, his adored grandson—then again on the move. To Washington, to perform, in February 1805, his final substantive act as Vice President of the United States and President of the Senate, by presiding over the impeachment trial of Justice Samuel Chase.

With two indictments, one in New York and one in New Jersey, out for his arrest, would Burr have the effrontery to appear in public? To be sure, many in the South felt differently about dueling—and about

General Hamilton—than did the citizens of New Jersey and New York. Moreover, Burr's vote in the trial of the Federalist judge might be decisive; accordingly, members high in the Republican administration were going out of their way before and during the proceedings at the capital to pay heed to the Vice President. Secretary of State Madison, for example, was observed sharing his carriage with him. So Burr did appear in public, and at the trial his officiating earned praise from all sides. He was "one of the best presiding officers that ever presided over a deliberative assembly," Senator Mitchill of New York asserted flatly; and this, Burr's last public function, the colonel, as friend and foe agreed, discharged with admirable dignity and fairness. He presided, as one observer—and he not a Burr partisan—remarked, "with the dignity and impartiality of an angel, but with the rigour of a devil." Chase was acquitted, and President Jefferson's efforts to purge the courts of those Federalist appointments of his predecessor Adams thereby suffered another defeat.

When the trial ended, it fell to the Vice President, there in the Senate chamber, to open the electoral ballots and announce the executives of the new administration: Thomas Jefferson and George Clinton. And that cheerless task, performed without visible emotion, concluded a public career. To give Burr full credit, his positions on matters public and private were often, when judged from our vantage point, enlightened: opponent of slavery, advocate of more liberal bankruptcy laws, opponent of the Alien and Sedition Acts that had denied individual freedoms at the end of the Adams administration, supporter of open public debate in the Senate, vigorous advocate in private life of the rights of women. Now, though, that varied and controversial political career was ending, as the Vice President delivered on the Senate floor his extemporaneous farewell, an inspired speech some half hour in length that left none of his listeners unaffected. This house, he reminded them, was a "sanctuary; a citadel of law, of order, of liberty; and," the retiring Vice President was intoning, "if the constitution be destined to perish by the sacrilegious hands of the demagogue or the usurper, which God avert, its expiring agonies will be witnessed on this floor. . . ." He had spoken "with so much tenderness, knowledge and concern," an eyewitness reported, "that it wrought upon the sympathy of the Senators in a very uncommon manner." And then the dapper little New Yorker had bowed and departed, the door of the chamber closed firmly behind him, behind his honors and achievements, leaving him no more than a private citizen now.

"Where he is going or how he is to get through with his difficulties I know not," the same eyewitness was writing that very March day in 1805. Burr was forty-nine. Always impecunious, he had spent his inheritance on his command in the Revolution, had consumed the income from his law practice on land speculations and on the lavish indulgences of life at Richmond Hill, that sublime estate already sold to his friend John Jacob Astor to satisfy creditors. So he had no home, no money, no job. He kept, though, the sustaining devotion of his daughter, as well as considerable admiration among Southerners and Westerners. And he kept and must live with the sting of having been treated unjustly—by the President, by members of his party, by citizens of his home state, where an indictment forbade his return. Finally, he kept as well an ambition for greatness that was apparently undiminished, as he set about to persuade trusted old friends—and some new ones—of glorious uses to which his talents might yet be applied.

One old friend with whom he had already conferred was General James Wilkinson, commanding general of the Armies of the United States and first governor of the Louisiana Territory. That fabulously extensive real estate had fallen, scarcely a year earlier, all unexpectedly into the hands of the President's astonished ministers in Paris; and soon after, in the spring of 1804, at the height of his career, the official chosen to govern it was sending a cryptic note to Burr in New York: "To save time of which I need much and have but little, I propose to take a Bed with you this night, if it may be done without observation or intrusion." They met and talked. About what? Veterans of the Quebec campaign, both old friends had led lives since then to cause comment. Wilkinson's doings after 1775 had included, for example, the dishonorable appropriation as his own, during wartime, of another man's information on enemy troop dispositions; by claiming what was not his he had won advancement in rank. Later, in 1788, he had dealt clandestinely with the Spanish to deliver them Kentucky in exchange for a pension and control of trade along the Mississippi. The plot to betray his country had, in fact, fallen through, leaving Wilkinson's part in it undiscovered; so that here he was now, after Indian campaigns in the 'nineties, somehow in high favor with the current administration in Washington, a vainglorious leader whose pompous prose style suggests for us still the insincerity that was at the heart of his being. For Wilkinson's was an extraordinary case: all during these years this commanding general of the American Armies had continued secretly in the pay of the Spanish, their Number 13, pensioner of that nation whose possessions of Mexico and the Floridas bordered uneasily on the American South and West. Of course his role as a spy was unknown to Burr, remained unproven until a century after Burr's involvement with him. Accordingly, the hapless former Vice President found himself dealing in 1804 and after with what was apparently an officer honored by his government in positions of exalted responsibility, an old friend and yet (as we now know) a liar, fraud, traitor—and by no means simply the buffoon "booted to the middle—sashed to the chin—collared to the ears— whiskered to the teeth" that Washington Irving made him out to be in a widely read satire that would appear in 1809.

Hear Wilkinson for a moment, on whatever subject: "The fair fabric of our independence purchased by the best blood of our country will be prostrated, and the Goddess of Liberty will take her flight from this globe forever." "I gasconade not when I tell you that in such a cause I shall glory to give my life in the service of my country." "I perceive the plot thickens; yet all but those concerned, sleep profoundly. My God! what a situation has our country reached. Let us save it if we can." "Hurry, hurry after me, and if necessary, let us be buried together, in the ruins of the place we shall defend." And those utterances were merely from his personal correspondence, the private prose of this Wilkinson, florid and dangerous, who was insinuating himself once more into Aaron Burr's life at a critical time. Didn't the colonel's future, like that of others whose luck had run out in the East, lie westward, in those new lands beyond the Alleghenies, along the rich reaches of the Mississippi? Whatever was said between the two men, hardly a year had passed before Burr had purchased at Pittsburgh a flatboat, grand affair, sixty feet long with dining room, two bedrooms, kitchen with fireplace, glass windows, and steps to the roof with a walkway the whole length up there (all for $133.00, "and how it can be made for that sum passes my comprehension"). So now, in the spring of 1805, May days and nights in fine weather on the river, Burr was descending from Pittsburgh, down past Wheeling, down past Marietta, down the Ohio, stopping at villages along the river's edge to marvel at curious Indian mounds or at surprisingly fashionable ladies promenading along unpaved lanes, then back to the river—that great highway—to meet a friend whose boat could be tied to his as they traveled together ever deeper into the West, land of brave settlements and huge dark forests yet to be cleared, and of people far removed in fact and in feelings from the citizens of towns he had known in New England or along the Hudson. Should Burr, his traveling friend Congressman Lyon was wondering, settle down out here, where people felt he had been persecuted long enough, practice law in Nashville, say, and establish residence, then run for Congress from the West?

But maybe the voyager already had dreamed more glorious dreams than that. They were below Marietta now, drifting with the current, the boat poled away from sandbars but no other effort needed to advance on destiny. Ahead of them, windows golden in sunlight beyond acres of green lawn, lay the white mansion of Blennerhassett at the northern point of an island in the river. The colonel would stop and have a look at it, for it was something to see then. Some hundred and seventy years have washed past the place, eight miles south of Marietta, since Burr first stepped ashore, and during that time the island has shrunk in size and now stands all but deserted, property of E. I. DuPont de Nemours & Company, from whom occasionally a visitor receives permission to poke among undergrowth where yet can be discovered foundations of what was once a palatial residence in the wilderness. Harman Blennerhassett, who had it built in 1800, had come to the spot three years earlier, escaping (so he said) turmoils of endless warfare at home in Ireland. With his lovely young wife he meant to find peace deep in the New World. Two years and much money were spent clearing a part of the island, removing primeval trees, erecting wharves, laying gravel walks, building the white, two-story mansion of ten rooms, with porticoes forty feet long that joined smaller structures to right and left. One structure housed servants; the other contained Blennerhassett's library and laboratory, his telescope, his pharmacy, his violin, his instruments for experimenting with galvanism. With such tastes to gratify, husband and wife settled down. Nor was it until 1901, nearly a century after the sudden notoriety that was approaching the couple now, that a descendant revealed the real reason the Irishman had left his native country: not to flee political troubles at all but rather to avoid the consequences of having eloped with his teen-age niece Margaret, his outraged elder sister's daughter. And in her late twenties, learning on a May day in 1805 that a distinguished visitor had landed, it was that accomplished young lady, Margaret, who sent an invitation to the former Vice President of the United States to stay at the mansion for dinner.

Dark walls of the dining room, golden moldings around the high ceiling. Upstairs, behind an unobstructed view down the long lawn to the river, the sitting room held its fine carpets, gold-framed mirrors on green and gilt walls, massive furniture imported from Philadelphia, from far-off England. Blennerhassett himself was away at the time, yet it was not long before Burr was writing this credulous and apparently well-to-do immigrant, and not long before the Irishman was responding: "I hope, sir, you will not regard it indelicate in me to observe to you how highly I should be honored in being associated with you, in any contemplated enterprise you would permit me to participate in." During the months ahead they would ripen their friendship, each bent on using the other no doubt, for Blennerhassett in truth was looking for ways to enlarge a shrunken fortune, whereas Burr, as always, was in quest of funds to carry his plans to completion. Doubtless a glance around the island—its two-acre flower garden abloom, the grottoes and arbors, orchards of peaches and gooseberries, the dairy—had been enough to suggest that the master of so much rustic opulence could be useful. There was Alston, too—Burr's wealthy son-in-law—who could help. And others would hear and heed the colonel's appeal as he journeyed deeper into the West, spreading out his maps on tables in Chillicothe, in Lexington, on balconies in New Orleans, more than once at the planter Andrew Jackson's blockhouse home outside Nashville.

To his different listeners Burr told different stories. To Jackson, for instance—that implacable foe of the Spaniard, "one of those prompt, frank, ardent souls whom I love to meet"—he would have set forth, during his several visits at the Hermitage (not yet the mansion it was to become), the version of his plans that he was to write Senator Smith: "If there should be a war between the United States and Spain, I shall head a corps of volunteers and be the first to march into the Mexican provinces. If peace should be proffered, which I do not expect, I shall settle my Washita lands, and make society as pleasant as possible." For war did seem inevitable, and meanwhile, the colonel was acquiring possession of 350,000 acres of rich bottom land along the Ouachita River in what is now northern Louisiana. Money had been needed to make that purchase. More money would be needed to settle the land, and toward what ends? To act as a buffer between willful Spaniards at the mouths of the Gulf rivers and vulnerable, irascible American settlers along the courses of those same rivers farther north? Or did Burr mean to use his wide lands as a launching place, assembling forces there under the guise of settlers who would be ready to strike southward at his order, for greater glory and profit than the wilds of the Orleans Territory could ever offer? Would he strike at the lands of Moctezuma, as he must have told Jackson, wresting the fabled Mexico from its distracted motherland? Aaron I! And his daughter, his adored Theodosia, would be a princess, and her husband would be there too as prime minister, and Blennerhassett would be ambassador to England, and the boy Gampy, little Aaron Burr Alston, would grow up in a court, near a throne to which he would succeed! Such imperial schemes directed at Mexico were reported to have been uttered in other men's hearings by Burr and his daughter's family when they assembled at Blennerhassett's island in the late summer of 1806, their preparations all made at last and the eve of the grand descent down the river at hand. But in what tone did Burr phrase such schemes: solemnly or lightheartedly, among those happy, fantastic adventurers? And even if the colonel were serious about carving himself an empire larger than Bonaparte's (Aaron I: little men would dream huge dreams in a world where the career of the Corsican was prospering), a filibuster against Mexico was hardly treason against the United States; efforts to revolutionize the feebly held colonies of tyrannical Spain had preceded and would follow Burr's episode.

So the colonel's plans had moved forward: flatboats were being built on the Muskingham, and Jackson himself had taken an order to supply five boats at Clover Bottom in Tennessee, to be floated down the Cumberland to make rendezvous where it joined the Mississippi. There were salt pork on order, pack saddles and bear skins, flour, cornmeal, whiskey, and tools—axes and hoes—and weapons too, for the settler was rare who would venture West unarmed. And responding to General Wilkinson, farther downriver at St. Louis, Burr sent two friends with an encouraging message—in cipher, as so many of the colonel's letters had been since youth. "Everything internal and external favors our views," he may have exulted (though Wilkinson was later to admit having altered the letter after deciphering it). "Naval protection of England is secured

. . . and final orders are given to my friends and followers. It will be a host of choice spirits. Wilkinson shall be second to Burr only; Wilkinson shall dictate the rank and promotion of his officers. . . . Our object, my dear friend, is brought to a point so long desired. . . . it remains to be seen whether we deserve the boon."

Burr, Alexander Hamilton had written years earlier, "is of a temper bold enough to think no enterprise too hazardous and sanguine enough to think none too difficult." Was the colonel really planning to strike against Mexico, as he later insisted? Or against the Spanish Floridas, engaging his enemy first at Baton Rouge or Mobile or Pensacola? But if he was successful, did he not mean to take the western states with him, forming a country by merging a New Spain conquered with those lands through which the Ohio and Mississippi flowed? For the regions west of the Alleghenies in those very early days of union were bound often by the thinnest ties to the distant eastern seaboard. Nor did Burr's contemporaries regard it as by any means inevitable that a single nation must stretch across our continent. Under Napoleon's shadow, the immigrant Astor may even then have been dreaming of his own empire in the Northwest, and Jefferson himself could write as late as 1803 about the trans-Alleghenians: "If they see their interest in separation, why should we take side with our Atlantic rather than our Mississippi descendants? It is the elder and the younger son differing. God bless them both, and keep them in union, if it be for their good, but separate them, if it be better."

We read history poorly unless we put ourselves backward in time. No more was Burr able to envisage the continental America of the twentieth century than we may know—and adjust our own schemes to—the America of the mid-twenty-second century, as far forward in time as Burr's world lies behind us. So his band of settlers, warriors, conquerors, patriots, traitors, whatever—sixty to a hundred of them all told, and most of them as unaware as we remain of their final destination—started down the river. "The people of the country to which we are going are prepared to receive us," their leader had presumably written Wilkinson. "Their agents, now with Burr, say that if we will protect their religion, and will not subject them to a foreign Power, that in three weeks all will be settled." Catholic Mexico, then; or perhaps a strike at the Floridas. And if parts of the American West, their interests all flowing southward along the river courses in those days before railroads, should decide to join a new nation more naturally its kin than was that eastward-looking country that hugged the Atlantic seaboard beyond the blockade of the Alleghenies, why, let the West come! "It will be a host of choice spirits."

And yet Burr may have meant to strike first at New Orleans. There, three years earlier, General Wilkinson himself had stood in the Place d'Armes as his government's representative and watched the French flag ceremoniously lowered—the crowds mute, the artillery booming—and the American flag raised in its stead, a gesture on a December morning that took possession of lands stretching northward so far upriver that fifteen new states or parts of states in time would be fashioned from its wild acreage. The refined Creoles of that elegant coastal city, who in the last half century had lived under more than one master—French, then Spanish, then French again, now Americans— were hardly contented under this latest regime, without spokesmen for their interests in faraway Washington, and with a profound distaste for the frontiersmen they saw descending along the river path from northern forests with whiskey and pork and flour to sell. Those rough traders were Americans, cousins of the Americans that fate had arbitrarily set to rule over Creole families of long and noble lineage. There would have been support among such families for any plan that might free the city at the mouth of the Mississippi from domination by French, Spanish, and American alike: maybe Burr did mean first to strike at New Orleans. But if he did, such a move was treason.

"I have no project or views hostile to the interest, or tranquility, or union of the United States, or prejudicial to its government," the colonel wrote unequivocally November 27, 1806, to Governor William Henry Harrison of the Northwest Territory, "and I pledge you my honour for the truth of this declaration." He wrote as much to others, including young Henry Clay and Andrew Jackson. But the West was in turmoil nevertheless; in raising his money and promoting his schemes, the colonel had dreamed too openly to too many listeners. To be sure, "much more was to be collected from the *manner* in which certain things were said, and hints given, than from the words used"—as one informant had already written the Secretary of State at Washington. But the fear was that a thousand, five thousand men were ready to follow Burr at a signal. And General Wilkinson was writing Jefferson too, for the bemedaled officer had thought about it—and decided to turn his coat. Never mind that as late as the end of September 1806, he himself had been trying to involve a friend in "subverting the Spanish government in Mexico—be ready & join me. . . . We cannot fail of success." Or that to another he was writing of pushing the Spaniards "over the Sabine . . . *after which from* 20 *to* 30,000 *will be necessary to carry our conquests to California* and the *Isthmus of Darien . . .*" Now Wilkinson spied a chance to have it both ways. With the betrayal of Burr's plans—or what might be represented as those plans—not only would Spain reward its agent covertly for having saved her colonies, but the President, cooling of late toward the general of his armies, would be led to heap further honors on Wilkinson for vigilance in defense of the western territories. The general accordingly made his decision. To Jefferson he wrote, October 21, 1806: "although my information appears too direct and circumstantial to be fictitious, yet the magnitude of the enterprise, the desperation of the plan, and the stupendous consequences with which it seems pregnant, stagger my belief, and excite doubts of the reality, against the conviction of my senses. . . ." Thereafter details of Burr's "deep, dark and wicked conspiracy" were placed in the President's hands.

Jefferson acted. "Whereas information has been received that sundry persons . . . are conspiring & confederating together to begin . . . a military expedition or enterprise against the dominions of Spain . . . I have therefore thought fit to issue this my proclamation, warning and enjoining all faithful citizens who have been led to participate in the sd unlawful enterprise without due knolege or consideration to withdraw from the same without delay . . ."

His proclamation, and accompanying means to enforce obedience to it, moved westward while Burr's flotilla, under Blennerhassett, was descending the Ohio in mid-December, past Cincinnati, past Jeffersonville. In the sequel no thousands were rising to join the voyagers—at most only about sixty; they might have been "bound to market," so one observer of their passage downriver thought. The falls at Louisville fell behind them, and Shawneetown on the Illinois side, behind the string of flatboats, red-shirted backwoodsmen aboard, and on the decks chicken coops and pig barracks and sacks of flour and barrels of bacon, and seed ears and pumpkin slices hanging from lines to dry. Burr himself, meanwhile, had been elsewhere, in Tennessee and Kentucky defending the innocence of his intentions to some, inspiring the fainthearted among others, cajoling, wheedling, defying, protesting. Finally, however, he did join the flotilla, emerging with two boats from the wilderness at the rain-drenched mouth of the Cumberland. From there, the enlarged caravan floated on southward past Fort Massac, past New Madrid, past Chickasaw Bluffs (now Memphis), to Bayou Pierre in Mississippi Territory. And it was at Bayou Pierre, still some two hundred miles above New Orleans, that Jefferson's proclamation caught up with the colonel. He was seized and given over to trial.

Yet throughout the proceedings that followed, Burr was treated graciously, guest of a wealthy planter, dinners tendered him, southern ladies doing him honor. And the jury proved friendly; within days he had been acquitted of all charges, and the Territorial Government was even reprimanded by the jurors for having curtailed the freedom of the accused. By no means, however, was General Wilkinson (whose treachery Burr had come to realize) yet finished. He wanted his former coconspirator out of the way—no doubt wanted him dead; in that event the general's version of occurrences of the preceding months would go all but unchallenged. From New Orleans, accordingly, Wilkinson's agents, "armed with Dirks & Pistolls," were even then on their way to Bayou Pierre, with orders to "cut off the two principal leaders. . . . If you fail your expenses will be paid. If you succeed I pledge the government to you for five thousand dollars." And at their destination, though acquitted, Burr remained under detention, all illegally, and unluckily, in the hands of a staunch Jeffersonian judge.

Now the colonel's friends on the spot feared for his life. There was a lady he must bid farewell to, a certain Madelaine, "a miracle of beauty," but on a February evening he and a local companion were mounting horses to ride from Cole's Creek near Bayou Pierre southeastward, into the wilderness toward the Spanish Floridas. The border lay many miles distant, though, and the route was made longer because of bridges washed out over swollen rivers. The two men, Burr and a Major Ashley, rode in disguise: the once fashionable host of Richmond Hill now wore the old blanket coat of a riverboatman, with a battered white hat to hide his face and a scalping knife and tin cup hanging from a leather strap about him. Under a full moon they reached Wakefield, in what is now Alabama. There they would spend the night at the Hinson home; but stopping for directions, the strangers attracted the attention of a local lawyer. Those elegant boots on one, his bright eyes. The lawyer, a man named Nicholas Perkins, became suspicious. His backgammon game was left unfinished, and later that evening he was riding with the sheriff out to peer through rain into the Hinsons' kitchen. The quiet one seated in there, Perkins felt sure, was Aaron Burr. At once he set off for Ft. Stoddert to report his suspicions, and the following morning early was back with a lieutenant from the fort. Along the way the riders encountered Burr in the woods, on horseback too, heading toward the ferry that would take him across the Tombigbee.

The road to Pensacola lay on the far side of that river, but the colonel would never travel it. Again under protest he was detained, taken to Ft. Stoddert, and from there led a thousand miles overland to Richmond, Virginia. Seven rugged frontiersmen had been hired to get him east safely. The group left the fort March 5, tracking thirty miles the first day through Cherokee country along the Indian trace till they reached the Oconee River. Through the journey, that day and the many days following, Burr was treated respectfully, allowed to keep his knife and pistols, given tea and coffee and wine, at night furnished with the only tent. But the horses were belled and hobbled when the troop made camp each evening.

"My great offense," the prisoner had told his captors before setting out, "and the only one laid to my charge was a design to give you the Floridas." Yet he must tell that to others. Day followed day—one week, two weeks—as the band pushed eastward through the forests. Only when they reached South Carolina, Theodosia's home, and Gampy's, did the colonel's amiable composure give way. Until then his self-control had amazed his guards; but now, in passing a village tavern at Chester before which a group had gathered to watch dancing within, Burr, with two captors before him and two behind, suddenly leapt from his horse:

"I am Aaron Burr," he shouted, "under military arrest, and claim the protection of the civil authorities." Nor would he remount, even when ordered—"*I will not!*"—until one of his guards had forcibly lifted the little man and put him back in the saddle. None of the villagers was permitted to interfere. His captors surrounded his horse, one seizing the bridle, and the troop passed on through the settlement to resume the road that led northward.

In Washington all this while, Burr's progress had continued to interest the President. Jefferson calculated exactly the distance to be covered: the prisoner would reach Richmond, he figured, on the twenty-sixth. And so it turned out. After more than three weeks of wilderness travel, thirty-two months after his trunks had been stealthily loaded at night aboard a barge on the Hudson, Aaron Burr had come to a halt at last, delivered, that March evening in 1807, to the Eagle Tavern on Richmond's Main Street. "It seems," he wrote his daughter from within its walls next morning, "that here the business is to be tried and concluded."

Two years earlier, on May days, the now imprisoned former Vice President Burr had been descending the Ohio in his spacious flatboat with the fireplace and glass windows, moving westward beyond Marietta, beyond Blennerhassett's island, grand schemes still forming before him. And at about that time, through warm days of early summer in 1805, a party of two families of a far humbler station was likewise moving westward, but overland by ox team, from Torrington, Connecticut (no more than ten miles from the Litchfield where Burr had been studying law when the Revolution began, where his sister Sally and her husband Tapping Reeve lived their lives out). The two migrating families were bound for Hudson, a village twenty-five miles southwest of the frontier settlement of Cleveland on Lake Erie. Ohio was a wilderness then, "filled with wild beasts, & Indians." There were rattlesnakes, too, "very large; & which some of the company generally managed to kill." Among that company was a five-year-old boy, learning along the way, through southern New York and Pennsylvania and into Ohio, "to think he could accomplish *smart things* in driving the Cows; & riding the horses."

All in all, the migration to new land of an ambitious Connecticut tanner with his family and the family of a neighbor formed a happy interlude, one of the few such interludes in John Brown's tortured life, as the ox team creaked westward in 1805 toward a frontier world that would mingle a boy's awed days with Indians, would teach him to dress skins and make whip lashes, "which brought him some change at times." In the months immediately ahead, young John would become "quite a rambler in the wild new country finding birds and Squirels, & sometimes

a wild Turkeys nest." And in Hudson "he was placed in the School of
adversity." For life there would begin to take his loves from him. "You
may *laugh* when you come to read about it": a yellow marble an Indian
boy had given him (*"It took years to heal the wound"*) lost, and a
squirrel named Bobtail, lost or dead, and—loss "complete & permanent"
—his mother, dead when he was eight. He continued (so he tells us) to
pine for her for years.

A *"travelled man,"* young Washington Irving was home from
Europe at last. Aboard the *Remittance*, March 24, 1806, a year after
John Brown's family had migrated westward from Connecticut, a year
almost exactly before Burr's incarceration at Richmond, Irving had
landed at New York following sixty-four days—many of them stormy—
at sea. "The passengers," he would recall afterward of that earliest of his
crossings from England, "cracked their jokes on each other in great good
humor at first, while Mumford sat like an owl, and said nothing; but
before we landed, he became the greatest favorite of all. The familiarity
of the others led to quarrels, and then the jokes we had cracked on each
other soured on our stomachs." Finally, though, the voyage did end for
those sufferers, Mumford—Irving's New York friend met in London—
leaving the ship on his way to oblivion, and Irving stepping ashore—to
what? Crabbed and unwieldy law books awaited him, and a career he
deplored, but at least he could bring to the town, still of a handy size
at the end of Manhattan, varied and vivid memories of two years
abroad. Paris he could remember—"had caught paris by the Tail"—and
could recall the beseeching voice of the *fille de joie* in the gardens of the
Palais Royal. Would recall, too, the incomparable Mrs. Siddons performing at Covent Garden, as he no doubt would always remember St.
Peter's at Rome, where he had climbed to the very top of the dome,
clung to the huge cross up there "as firmly as the strictest Catholic," and
been amazed on returning to earth at how high he had ventured and how
small that same cross looked. He would remember the very speech of the
bootblacks pursuing him for his trade in southern France— "Monsieur,
monsieur, G—d dam, G—d dam son de bish son de bish"—and
the look of the bandit Musso on his way to execution in Genoa,
viewed by multitudes peering from every window and thronging the
streets, with Irving among the crowds at the city gate to get "a tolerable
view of him as he passed. He appeared to be about five feet 8 inches
stout & well set . . . about 26 years of age. . . . Two priests attended him." Memories would linger as well of the wretched poor in
Sicily; a bone thrown to a dog had been snatched up by a woman and
given to her children. And the beggars surrounding his carriage in
whatever village it paused—beggars everywhere, in fact: in church be-
sieging "an honest Catholic while at prayers" and worrying him "for an

half hour till his torpid charity was fairly forced to exert itself." Might remember that stormy night's crossing from Palermo, Irving in his greatcoat in the captain's hammock, seasickness all about him: "An old woman laid near me who I believe calld on every saint in the calendar. after every cascade she would call a new one. Oh bellissima madre di christi. Oh santissimo Francesco Oh bellissima Santa Rosalia oh mea carissima santissima Rosalia. The saints however manifested their assistance in no other manner than in helping her to discharge the contents of her stomach which I believe it took the whole night to do." Poignant scenes and amusing ones: at a provincial French hotel he had been asked to surrender his room to the Engineer General of the Department and his wife—dignitary who, having stopped there in the past, desired the quarters now inadvertently given to a foreigner. The *grand homme* "ought to be well accomodated." But Irving had had the last word: as he reminded the landlady, he was an American gentleman, "& of course considered myself *equal at least*, to any engineer general in France and would not give up my room to him if he was to come with all his engines & lay seige to it but that I would have no objection to give a part of my room to the engineer's *lady. . . .*"

Those were all memories now—Genoa, Paris, London, the roads and seas that join them—as Irving, home once more, resumed the task of making himself a lawyer. His efforts were uninspired. These seem perhaps the years in his life—two years, from 1806 to 1808—when he appeals least to the Puritan in our nature. He acts so young—this twenty-four-year-old. Nor does the gaiety conveyed by his letters of the time travel well over the many decades that have elapsed since then. His abundant slang has grown hoary, and his attitude is too frequently mannered in those epistles, shallow and supercilious. To be sure, no slang ages well, and what gifted youth has not lifted his eyebrows at the inferior world about him? Yet the effect is hardly more attractive for being dressed in the high cravat, tailcoat, and pale pantaloons of the early eighteen hundreds: "I shook hands with the mob—whom my heart abhorreth"; "If those chaps in Philadelphia don't treat you better, cut and run; and, foregad, we'll hear the cocks crow in New York for three mornings at least"; "I absolutely shudder with horror—think what miseries I suffer—me to whom a pun is an abomination . . ."

Of course the portrait such phrases sketch must remain incomplete: no more than a hint of what the real man was. He was, then and always, fine company. Handsome, clever, this favorite of his family was also rather idle—beau, diner, theatergoer, one of the Nine Worthies devoted for the most part to enjoying themselves. The worthies included among others Henry Brevoort, James Kirke Paulding, Henry Ogden, and Gouverneur Kemble, and they would meet at Dyde's or some porterhouse for "blackguard suppers" together, or on weekends would retire to a rambling home on the Passaic, north of Newark, that Kemble had inherited from an uncle. Cockloft Hall they called the place—full of antique furniture and dusty family portraits—and there they would have their roisterous times, these self-styled Lads of Kilkenny. No doubt among the least of their dissipations was the leapfrog on the lawn that one of their number recorded—grown men out there cavorting about, and the Puritan frowns: so much talent being squandered. Yet Irving was no Puritan—was a pleasure-loving New Yorker who never warmed to Yankee ways—and if he was capable of extraordinary labors at times in his life, he could idle too, without a hint of remorse, and enjoy himself, as he did now. "Who would have thought," many years later, in his mid-sixties, he wrote to the still surviving Kemble, who had made note of the leapfrog, "that we should ever have lived to be two such respectable old gentlemen!"

Rather idle he was, then, during that couple of years. Yet not altogether so. The law remained to be mastered. Finally, nearly a decade after undertaking the task, this clerk submitted his knowledge to examination. Later he would suggest his own modest qualifications by telling the story of the two examiners commenting on a particularly feeble candidate: "Martin," one had ventured, "I think he knows a *little* law." To which the other had replied, "Make it stronger, Jo; d——d little." The same could have been said of Irving; nevertheless, the applicant did pass, somehow, and was admitted to the New York bar, November 21, 1806—Washington Irving, Attorney at Law and Public Notary. Early the following year he moved into the law office of his brother John at 3 Wall Street.

Little endures of that career amid what he would call in another connection "the technical rubbish, and dull routine of a lawyer's office," and in truth, Irving never prided himself on any litigious gifts. Personal reasons, as we shall see, would urge him soon to struggle for professional respectability. But now, hardly a month after being admitted to practice, he and one or two others of the Lads of Kilkenny—Paulding in particular—were up to something more diverting than any will or contract. They were about to publish a magazine, to be called *Salmagundi*. "As every body knows, or ought to know, what a Salmagundi is," so they would begin, "we shall spare ourselves the trouble of an explanation—besides, we despise trouble as we do every thing that is low and mean, and hold the man who would incur it unnecessarily, as an object worthy our highest pity and contempt. . . ."

What a salmagundi is, by the way, is a strongly seasoned appetizer made of raw chopped meat, pickled herrings, oil, vinegar, and cayenne pepper; it goes well with beer. The purpose of this *Salmagundi*, served up in twenty irregular installments from Saturday, January 24, 1807, to Monday, January 25, 1808, was announced at the start: "Our intention is simply to instruct the young, reform the old, correct the town and castigate the age." But mostly the purpose was to be appetizing, and this the odd-sized little magazine managed with high success. One holds its yellowed sheets and imagines the thrill it brought its perpetrators new: eighteen pages or so in each issue, about four by six inches in size. Succeeding numbers were gobbled up ever more readily—as many as eight hundred copies of the fourth issue were sold in a city of no more than eighty thousand people—and what the purchasers savored were the whim-whams of Launcelot Langstaff and other oddly named scribblers, each of whom contributed articles to successive efforts. Fashions were surveyed skeptically by Anthony Evergreen, Gent.; the theater was the province of William Wizard, Esq.; political matters were commented on by the visiting Arab Mustapha Rub-a-dub Keli Khan, writing bemused letters home to his slave driver; and there were humorous poems from the mill of Pindar Cockloft (in reality Irving's eldest brother, William —"the man I most loved on earth"—he who had made possible the two years of travel in Europe). Langstaff himself wrote "from my elbow-chair" on whatever he chose, and in those contributions is found, presumably, Washington Irving's hand most frequently at work. But all is hidden behind the absurd pseudonyms—that was part of the jest, to overhear the town guessing at the identity of its gentle correctors—and so uniform in tone and style are the various parts of the publication that exactly who wrote what will doubtless never be sorted out. In any case, the result of these joint and convivial efforts, frankly derived from such eighteenth-century English periodical publications as *The Spectator* of Addison and Steele and Goldsmith's *The Citizen of the World*, was impressive. Then and in the years ahead scores of imitators of *Salmagundi* sprang up and flourished in cities all along the eastern seaboard, while during its own year-long lifetime the magazine was widely talked about, laughed over, and occasionally even criticized: "From one end of the town to another," complained a relocated (and somewhat humorless) New Englander during its vogue, "all is nonsense and 'Salmagund.' America has never produced great literature—her products have been scrub oaks, at best. We should, then, encourage every native sapling; but when, like *Salmagundi*, it turns out to be a *bramble*, and pricks and scratches everything within its reach, we naturally ask, why it encumbereth the ground."

That was a minority viewpoint certainly, even though the insouciant authors themselves professed to have overheard other objections along the way. In the very first number, for instance, Anthony Evergreen had sported with the prevalence of red in place of the more demure white as a fashionable color, alluding at the same time to the Republican President's notoriously casual dress: "I was, however, much pleased to see that red maintains its ground against all other colors, because red is the color of mr. Jefferson's******, Tom Paine's nose, and my slippers." To which impertinent observation (the discreet stars mask "breeches"), one attentive and fictitious judge, Ichabod Fungus by name, is made to respond in the second number. Fungus "listened to our work with the most frigid gravity—every now and then gave a mysterious shrug—a *humph*—or a screw of the mouth; and on being asked his opinion at the conclusion, said, he did not know what to think of it; he hoped it did not mean any thing against the Government—that no lurking treason was couched in all this talk. These were dangerous times—times of plot and conspiracy;—he did not at all like those stars after mr. Jefferson's name, they had an air of concealment."

The date of that comment was Wednesday, February 4, 1807, when the second number of *Salmagundi* appeared for sale in what was about to be called for the first time, in that very issue, Gotham. On the same day in February but far from New York, in Mississippi Territory, had begun one of the several legal ordeals to which Colonel Aaron Burr had been and would be subjected, this one resulting in his acquittal by a civil court of all charges against him, his detention despite that exoneration, his subsequent escape toward the Floridas, his apprehension on horseback near Wakefield, and the long trip under guard overland by late March that brought him to await trial at last in Richmond.

Now, in May, as spring advances, Washington Irving has abruptly interrupted his anonymous labors on *Salmagundi*. His colleagues will continue publishing the little magazine in his absence, and he will send material back to them, but Irving is traveling south, for reasons somewhat obscure. Perhaps he has been retained by friends of the former Vice President—to offer legal advice, or more likely to compose articles on Burr's behalf for the New York papers. In any case, May 13, 1807, he writes from Fredericksburg, Virginia: "I did not so much as dream of this jaunt four and twenty hours before my departure . . . but having got into this part of the world I shall spend some time in visiting my virginia friends, tending Burrs trial &c &c . . ."

In the capital of Virginia he lingered two months, and no wonder: "I have been treated in the most polite and hospitable manner by the most distinguished persons of the place—those friendly to Colonel Burr and those opposed to him." So Irving wrote while still there. "I am absolutely enchanted with Richmond, and like it more and more every day. The society is polished, sociable, and extremely hospitable, and there is a great variety of distinguished characters assembled on this occasion, which gives a strong degree of interest to passing incidents." Indeed, during that spring and summer of 1807, Richmond was the most exciting place in America. From there, day after sweltering day, came news that crowded even Napoleon's doings off front pages of the Charleston *Courier*, the Baltimore *Federal Gazette*, the Philadelphia *Aurora*, the New Orleans *Courrier de la Louisiane*. For in that hillside town the crime of treason was being defined, with the life of one of America's most celebrated citizens hanging on the definition.

The atmosphere was unforgettable. Ordinarily no more than 5,000 people lived on the slopes of Richmond and down by the river, and of those as many as half were black slaves. Now, however, with the town swollen to twice its usual size, every room in every inn and boarding-house was filled. Private families fitted up spare rooms for guests, and the overflow slept in wagons or tents down beside the James or simply out under the stars. For the visitors were of all types, and from every-where in the nation. Gentlemen of the old style in powdered hair, small clothes, boots and silk stockings, had come down from New York and Philadelphia and Baltimore, as had those dressed in the new French fashions of top hats and shoes and pantaloons. And they crowded as spectators together during the day into the bare, shabby hall of the House of Delegates side by side with frontiersmen with long hair flow-ing free, with deerskin jackets and coarse woolen trousers and the smell of the wild about them. Within the hall wooden benches had been ar-ranged in curved rows, with boxes of sand for tobacco chewers to aim at; but those sandboxes were among the few adornments to ease the lot of the curious multitudes returning morning after morning—the lucky ones getting inside the doors in all that heat—to hear arguments and orations that sometimes lasted all day, sometimes lasted two days, as the trial stretched through May, through June, through the scorching afternoons of July and August, through September, and into October.

From Fredericksburg, May 13—already a month and a half after Burr's arraignment in a back room of the Eagle Tavern—Irving had written a New York friend: "tomorrow I set off for Richmond." And as an old man he recalled that youthful journey in company with the ac-cused Burr himself, for the colonel had been out on bail in early May until the twenty-second, when the circuit court would convene: "I . . . rode with him in the stage to Richmond. I could not well make out why I was sent for. From some sounding of his, I suspected he wanted me to write for the press in his behalf, but I put a veto on that."

Maybe Irving did decline to serve Burr's interests, although it later became customary for the world-renowned author (as for others whose years have led them away from their youthful enthusiasms) to make the least of his early infatuation with a disgraced politician. His letters of the time, though, testify to the fascination that the defendant on trial for his life exerted over a twenty-four-year-old New York jour-nalist. "I am very much mistaken," that journalist wrote while attending the hearing, "if the most underhand and ungenerous measures have not been observed towards him." Burr, however, Irving went on admiringly, "retains his serenity and self-possession unshaken, and wears the same aspect in all times and situations."

That extraordinary self-possession, often noted throughout Burr's lifetime, would be taxed to the utmost in the weeks ahead. The great majority of spectators were hostile, here in the supremely popular Thomas Jefferson's own state and prepared by Jefferson's own words: "it has almost been considered as culpable," Irving wrote of the prisoner at the time, "to evince towards him the least sympathy or support." The jury itself was composed of fourteen Republicans and no more than two Federalists, only the latter assumed to be other than subservient to the President's desires, which were well known. The traitor must pay for his treason. "Burr is on his way to Richmond for trial," Jefferson had observed in late March, "and if the judges do not discharge him before it is possible to collect the testimony from Maine to New Orleans, there can be no doubt where his history will end." Moreover, after Burr's arrival and throughout the proceedings, couriers would be speeding the hundred miles between Richmond and Washington and back again, keeping the Chief Executive informed of every development in the hearing and trial, and returning with personal counsel to Chief Prosecutor George Hay for conducting the government's case.

For Jefferson was committed to destroying Burr once and for all. Aaron Burr, he had announced flatly in his message to Congress January 22, 1807, is "the principal actor, whose guilt is placed beyond question." (And former President John Adams, in retirement at Quincy, had noted promptly upon hearing of that judgment, "If his guilt is as clear as the Noon day Sun, the first Magistrate ought not to have pronounced it so before a Jury had tryed him.") Jefferson had determined that, as for Burr, the halter should "get its due," and he possessed all the resources of the government to bring about that doleful outcome.

Yet if the President was after Burr, he was equally determined that the circuit judge sitting at Burr's trial should be rendered harmless to the present administration, one way or another. For that judge, owing to the simpler judicial system of the time, was in addition the Chief Justice of the United States, one of those midnight appointees in the final hours of the preceding administration, President Adams' Secretary of State elevated for life to the Supreme Court, a Federalist, though a Virginian like Jefferson, even a relative—third cousin once removed—but Jefferson's enemy for all that.

Like Burr himself, Mr. Justice John Marshall had been a valorous officer in the Revolution; like Burr he had been at Valley Forge, had fought at Monmouth. Since then, General Marshall's career had continued to flourish: in a profitable law practice at Richmond, as emissary of his government to negotiate with France, as a successful candidate— at President Washington's urging—for the federal House of Representatives, as Adams' Secretary of State, and now, since 1801, as Chief Justice of the United States, a position he would hold for thirty-four years, during which time, in a series of fundamental decisions, he would fashion the highest tribunal into the powerful instrument it remains. Some years before the trial of Burr, for instance, Justice Marshall had established, in February 1803, in the case of Marbury *v.* Madison, that the Supreme Court may pass upon the constitutionality of any bill that Congress enacts into law. That was the kind of ruling that seemed to the President usurpation: "The Federalists have retired into the judiciary as a stronghold," Jefferson had already written a friend, "and from that battery all the works of republicanism are to be broken down and erased." It must not be. So Marshall, who six years earlier at Federal City had administered the oath of office to his relative and political enemy, was now in a sense on trial as well. During his sitting in judgment on Burr, any irregularities, any lapses, any grounds whatsoever for reforming the judiciary would be seized upon. As the President had already clutched at pretexts to impeach two other Federalist judges (including Justice Chase, over whose trial Burr as Vice President had presided), so he would reach for any new opportunity to rid the judiciary of another active opponent of Republicanism, and this the most powerful and effective of the lot.

That Marshall was presiding at all over this trial was an accident of fate. In those days Supreme Court justices, less burdened than now, served as well on circuit courts—often a grueling arrangement that involved comfortless travel over long distances but that at least did allow, for instance, Mr. Justice Marshall himself to spend part of each year at home in Richmond, where he had lived from young manhood, and where his beautiful brick house on the then fashionable Shockoe Hill, behind the state capitol, is still lovingly cared for. Burr's crime, the prosecution had charged, was treason, the only crime specifically defined in the Constitution (by those Founding Fathers whom precedent in English law would have permitted to be disemboweled alive as traitors if Britain had triumphed in their recent Revolution). Treason, according to the Constitution, is committed when a citizen adheres to enemies of the United States, "giving them Aid and Comfort." But in 1806, and through the years surrounding Burr's western adventure, America was at peace with the world. Or it may be committed—and this is the only other way—by levying war against the United States itself. Such an act, so the prosecution maintained, had occurred on Blennerhassett's island in December 1806. The island, in those years before the creation of West Virginia, was a part of Wood County, Virginia, so that a crime allegedly committed there would be tried in the court of the Fifth Circuit and District of Virginia, which met at Richmond, and over which the Chief Justice presided.

Chance, then, had brought them together once more—the immaculate and polished little colonel from New York and the gangling, slovenly judge from Virginia—as they had been together, the then Vice President and the newly appointed Chief Justice, in muddy Washington on Jefferson's inaugural day. Once more crowds were gathered, this time in Richmond, pushing, shoving, gaping in the hall of the House of Delegates. One young man was climbing on the massive lock of the courtroom door to peer over heads of other spectators; he was Winfield Scott, who, some forty years later, would march into Mexico City in the van of a conquering American army, as Colonel Burr was conceding here that he had been longing to do. Now young Scott, stretching to see, would have beheld the judge in robes on the dais, above the accused and his counsel at a table in the oval clearing, spectators crowded on benches all around them and most of those already convinced of the prisoner's guilt. "Aaron Burr," they were toasting in the taverns in the evenings after court adjourned: "May his treachery to his country exalt him to the scaffold, and hemp be his escort to the republic of dust and ashes." And yet with all that tension and all that hostility, the two calmest people in the courtroom, as many remarked, seemed to be the same coarse-featured, kindly judge—image of integrity—and Burr himself, dressed faultlessly in black silk with hair powdered and impeccably queued. He looked, Scott from his perch on the door lock thought, "as composed, as immovable, as one of Canova's living marbles."

How could the prisoner manage such serenity? Even the Chief Justice was reported to have commented privately that "it would be difficult or dangerous for a jury to venture to acquit Burr, however innocent they might think him." Yet Burr must already have realized that his case could not depend on winning a jury's sympathy; it would be won on law or not at all. For in addition to local sentiment against him, the prosecution was scouring the country for witnesses: two hundred people and more were involved officially with the trial before it was over. But one witness summoned by the State was never called to the stand. His opinions he made sure were heard nevertheless, repeatedly, after-noons on the steps of a grocery store within earshot of Capitol Square. Andrew Jackson, first citizen of Tennessee, spoke out publicly in defense of the accused: "I am more convinced than ever," he was writing a friend during the hearing, "that treason never was intended by Burr." And of the trial: "I am sorry to say that this thing has . . . assumed the shape of a political persecution." With such opinions he defied listeners gathered around him on the steps of the store in this Republican town. Moreover, there was an air about the Indian fighter and frontiersman, who, like the colonel, had killed his man, that allowed him to speak those opinions to frowning crowds unmolested.

Others, too, more covertly, felt sympathy for the accused and expressed it in quieter ways. By July Burr was lodged not uncomfortably in the new penitentiary, outside town on one of Richmond's seven hills. And to those quarters gifts began to arrive: calf's foot jelly, fresh butter, apricots, pineapples, lemons. They came from the ladies of the capital, for "not a lady I believe in Richmond," so Washington Irving observed, "whatever may be her husbands sentiments on the subject, but what would rejoice on seeing Col Burr at liberty."

This was the mood then, during the weeks that Irving was spending in Richmond, through late May, June, and into July. While free on bail before the grand jury had convened, Burr had journeyed to Washington to seek certain documents necessary, so he maintained, for his defense. Denied them, he had returned to the scene of his hearing; by prearrangement Irving had shared the stage with him on that journey. Then, on a day in June, the accused, continuing to take a major part in the conduct of his own defense, had risen in court and requested that a subpoena be served on the President of the United States, possessor of those very documents on which a life might depend. Most important among the papers sought was the letter in cipher that the colonel had written to General Wilkinson the preceding summer, the contents of which, deciphered by Wilkinson himself—and perhaps inaccurately—formed the basis of the government's charges against the accused, charges of treason that the President had publicly addressed to Congress and the American people.

Burr's unprecedented demand, made with characteristic calm, caused a sensation. The Chief Justice, as was his custom throughout the hearing and the trial that followed, deferred a ruling until the next morning, after adjournment at four retiring to his home to study and ponder and set down in writing that evening what he would pronounce when court reconvened the following day. Exhausting routine! "The most unpleasant case which has ever been brought before a Judge in this or perhaps any other country, which affected to be governed by laws." So Marshall himself would write a friend when it was all over. Now, though, his lucubrations led him to conclude that, despite the doctrine of separation of powers, the subpoena against the President must be issued: "Might I be permitted to utter one sentiment, with respect to myself," he added next day in delivering his opinion, "it would be to deplore, most earnestly, the occasion which should compel me to look back on any part of my official conduct with so much self-reproach as I should feel, could I declare, on the information now possessed, that the accused is not entitled to the letter in question, if it should be really important to him."

Jefferson fumed. How could the Chief Executive fulfill his responsibilities if he were at the beck and call of every circuit judge in the land? Making his way over wilderness roads from courthouse to courthouse, while the nation's affairs were left unattended . . . Yet Aaron Burr was on trial for his life. In time a compromise was reached: the President remained in Washington, but the contents of the letter by

Burr that General Wilkinson had deciphered and sent to the Executive Mansion were made available to the court. The defense had scored its point.

And through all this time where was the prosecution's star witness, that same rotund Wilkinson who for weeks had been reported on his way from New Orleans to testify? The state could develop its case no further without him. "Day after day," writes Washington Irving from the scene in June, "have we been disappointed by the non-arrival of the magnanimous Wilkinson; day after day have fresh murmurs and complaints been uttered; and day after day are we told that the next mail will probably bring his noble self, or at least some accounts when he may be expected. We are now enjoying a kind of suspension of hostilities," he continues airily, "the grand jury having been dismissed the day before yesterday for five or six days, that they might go home, see their wives, get their clothes washed, and flog their negroes. As yet we are not even on the threshold of a trial; and, if the great hero of the South does not arrive, it is a chance if we have any trial this term."

But while he was waiting with the rest of the town, the young New Yorker must have been enjoying himself. Ensconced in the Swan, best hotel in Richmond, he could look from the porch over his cigar smoke to the capitol building across Broad Street, where the hearing was being delayed, and be reminded agreeably of his European tour. For President Jefferson had based his design of that structure (which still stands, considerably enlarged) on the Maison Carrée in Nîmes, in southern France, to which classical temple the traveler Irving had been drawn three years earlier: "the most perfect roman remain I have yet seen," he had recorded conscientiously in his vellum journal August 17, 1804. And "I have been two or three times more to look at the *Maison Carrée. . . .*"

Richmond held another vivid reminder of those happy travels through Europe in the person of Joseph Carrington Cabell, one of the jurors at the hearing, whom Irving had met first in Naples on a rainy March morning in 1805. The two young men had become great friends, sharing a carriage to Rome, then on together through northern Italy, Switzerland, eastern France, and into Paris. Now Cabell, who had "lately married one of the finest & richest girls" in Virginia (and whose brother was governor of the state), was entering a career that would lead him in a few years to found, with Jefferson, the University of Virginia and become its rector. This summer, though, the juror and his friend from European days might under the gaze of the bartender Lovell in the barroom of the Swan reminisce, if they chose, about that early spring night when the two of them, Irving and Cabell both, were almost asphyxiated by sulphurous fumes beneath a bright moon at the top of Vesuvius; or remember the carriage ride through Alsace, Irving dozing while Cabell flirted with a pretty French traveler: "in the midst of his courtship I awoke. I kept my eyes shut for some time listening to his fine speeches to which the damsel pretended to turn a cold ear at length my disposition to laugh became so strong that I had to awake completely and interrupt one of the most amiable conversations that ever took place in a Dilligence. C——— tried in vain to induce me to sleep again." Or the two might have recalled the landlady in Troyes who threw a fit one May afternoon in 1805 because Cabell, ill and exhausted from a day's travel, had dared lie down on a bed in the sitting room without ordering anything: "She snatchd the pillow from under poor C———s head before he was well awake and began abusing him with the utmost volubility. He immediately quit the house with expressions of the utmost comtempt. . . ."

Past and present alike would have offered them much to talk about. ("The countenance of an old fellow traveller," Irving would write some years later, "always brings up the recollection of a thousand pleasant scenes, odd adventures, and excellent jokes.") The town while it waited held other distractions as well, for the ladies of Richmond had early decided that Irving was "an *interesting young man*"—a demanding role for him to play in hot weather: "you must of course be fond of moonlight walks—and rides at day break, and red hot strolls in the middle of the day (Farenheits Thermom. 98½ in the shade) and 'Melting hot—hissing hot' tea parties—and what is worse they expect you to talk sentiment and act Romeo, & Sir Charles and King pepin all the while." Well, the sociable New Yorker could handle all that well enough, and how else should he sound but weary of it when writing—as he was—to one of the belles left back home on the tip of Manhattan?

Meanwhile, would Wilkinson ever arrive? Supporters of Burr, who were increasing in number as the colonel's composure and impeccable conduct won converts to his cause, were beginning to think not. General Jackson for one "does not scruple to say that W is a pensioner of Spain to his knowledge and that he will not dare to show his face here." Friends of the prosecution, on the other hand, still in the great majority, were certain that the prisoner himself would bolt justice at Wilkinson's first heavy tread on Richmond soil. In the event, the general did arrive at last, June 10, by sea from New Orleans, and the accused was there to see this former friend and present betrayer bring himself to court, only a little less resplendent than he had appeared in Washington three years before astride a blooded mare, his saddlecloth a leopard skin with claws dangling, his boots in golden stirrups and spurred with gold, his corpulent form clothed and epauletted in that elaborate major general's uniform of his own designing. Aides accompanied him impressively, then as here at Richmond.

Irving beheld it all, and to his friend Paulding, busy back home with *Salmagundi*, wrote of Wilkinson's arrival at court: "The first interview between him and Burr was highly interesting, and I secured a good place to witness it. Burr was seated with his back to the entrance, facing the judge, and conversing with one of his counsel. Wilkinson strutted into Court, and took his stand in a parallel line with Burr on his right hand. Here he stood for a moment swelling like a turkey cock, and bracing himself up for the encounter of Burr's eye. The latter did not take any notice of him until the judge directed the clerk to swear Gen. Wilkinson; at the mention of the name Burr turned his head, looked him full in the face with one of his piercing regards, swept his eye over his whole person from head to foot, as if to scan its dimensions, and then coolly resumed his former position, and went on conversing with his counsel as tranquilly as ever. The whole look was over in an instant, but it was an admirable one. There was no appearance of study or constraint in it; no affectation of disdain or defiance; a slight expression of contempt played over his countenance, such as you would show on regarding any person to whom you were indifferent, but whom you considered mean and contemptible. . . ."

Wilkinson, to be sure, had seen things differently. "I saluted the Bench," the general wrote President Jefferson grandiosely of that same encounter, "& in spite of myself my Eyes darted a flash of indignation at the little Traitor. . . . This Lyon hearted Eagle Eyed Hero, sinking under the weight of conscious guilt, with haggard Eye, made an Effort to meet the indignant salutation of outraged Honor, but it was in vain, his audacity failed Him, He averted his face, grew pale, & affected passion to conceal his perturbation." Yet if Wilkinson was satisfied with his own demeanor in court, he was not pleased with the sentiments he encountered in and out of the courtroom. "To my astonishment I found the traitor vindicated and myself condemned by a mass of wealth, character, influence and talents. Merciful God, what a spectacle did I behold. . . ."

Because support for Burr was increasing. Each morning admirers in ever larger numbers—as many as a hundred, even two hundred gentlemen—would mount the hill outside of town to escort their hero from the penitentiary to the courtroom, the immaculate little colonel, having spent another evening "busy, busy, busy," now striding in the morning along Broad Street, surrounded by admirers, at the start of a new day. "Burr lives in great style," the hapless Blennerhassett, on trial as well, would record from Richmond in August, "and sees much company within his gratings, where it is as difficult to get an audience as if he really were an Emperor."

Aaron I! By August Wilkinson had long completed his testimony before the grand jury, although he had "such a mighty mass of *words* to deliver himself of," as Irving wrote drily in late June, "that he claims at least two days more to discharge the wondrous cargo." And when he was done, the general had made so bad an impression that he narrowly escaped indictment himself. "The most finished scoundrel that ever lived," John Randolph, foreman of the jury, concluded privately. "The only man that I ever saw who was from the bark to the very core a villain." But on the general's testimony conviction of Burr depended. He got off then, by what Randolph confessed to a friend was a technicality: "The mammoth of iniquity escaped,—not that any man pretended to think him innocent, but upon certain wire-drawn distinctions that I will not pester you with."

The grand jury brought in its indictments at last, in late June. Five more summer weeks passed before the trial itself could begin, a trial to prove that Aaron Burr, owing allegiance to the United States, "not having the fear of God before his eyes, nor weighing the duty of his said allegiance, but being moved and seduced by the instigation of the devil," at Blennerhassett's island on December 10, 1806, "with force and arms, unlawfully, falsely, maliciously and traitorously did compass, imagine and intend to raise and levy war, insurrection and rebellion against the said United States." A new jury had to be impaneled, and witnesses were called once more, as testimony unfolded through August and into September. How, the defense demanded to know, could Burr be guilty of treason when he was not even on Blennerhassett's island, when he was far off in Frankfort, Kentucky, that December night that lanterns had signaled across the Ohio and muskets in the hands of a few of some thirty adventurers had allegedly been raised on the wharf against the authority of the United States in the person of General Edward Tupper of the Ohio militia? Why would the prosecution not call Tupper himself to the stand? But Burr was guilty of *constructive* treason—treason by construction of the law—so the state asserted. His agents on the island had acted under his direction as surely as if he had stood among them. Yet where were the two witnesses to the overt act, as required by the Constitution? That would come in time; first the prosecution meant to proceed chronologically to demonstrate the colonel's perfidy, starting as far back as his visit to Pittsburgh in April 1805. Witnesses would show—But the defense objected. An overt act against the government had first to be established. In the absence of proof of such an act, all other evidence against the defendant was collateral, and thus inadmissible: "would it not be absurd to go into evidence to shew that the *act* was committed with a treasonable *intent*, without any testimony to prove that the act was committed at all?" Only those witnesses whose testimony could establish such an act should be allowed to take the stand. Still, before it was over General Wilkinson did strut forth to testify again, and to admit on cross-examination that he had indeed tampered with Burr's cipher letter. To the stand likewise, among others, was called the respected Commodore Truxtun, with whom Burr had stayed when he fled New York after the duel, and to whom the colonel had offered command of the naval forces he would direct, should war break out, against the Vice Royalty of New Spain off Vera Cruz. Burr, questioning the witness: "Did you ever hear me express any intention or sentiment respecting a division of the Union?" And Truxtun testified, impressively: "We were very intimate. There seemed to be no reserve on your part. I never heard you speak of a division of the Union."

Where was the treason in what Burr had done? The colonel, the defense argued, would have settled his Ouachita lands and moved against Mexico only in the likely event of war with Spain. And again, how convict Burr, who had been crucially absent, of any treason without first convicting Blennerhassett, present on the island the night the overt act was allegedly committed?

Precedents were cited back and forth: Lady Lisle, widow of a regicide; the Duke of Cumberland after the Battle of Culloden; Flora Macdonald, who had aided in the escape of Bonnie Prince Charlie. Speeches filled the close air of the courtroom. Burr's brilliant, bibulous counsel Luther Martin (that "unprincipled & impudent federal bulldog," as Jefferson called him) had earlier growled: "The president has undertaken to prejudge my client by declaring, that 'Of his guilt there can be no doubt.' He has assumed to himself the knowledge of the Supreme Being himself, and pretended to search the heart of my highly respected friend. He has proclaimed him a traitor in the face of that country, which has rewarded him. He has let slip the dogs of war, the hell-hounds of persecution. . . ." Now, also on Burr's behalf, John Wickham pleaded with a dazzling display of erudition, through an oration that took two days to deliver.

For the prosecution William Wirt answered at comparable length, memorably evoking the earlier bliss of innocent Harman Blennerhassett, he who (as a friend testified) "had every kind of sense but common sense," and who even now was sweating in his penitentiary quarters of an evening, burning muriatic acid to cleanse the noisome air. Wirt for the prosecution:

". . . Who is Blennerhassett? A native of Ireland, a man of letters, who fled from the storms of his own country to find quiet in ours. . . . But he carried with him taste and science and wealth; and lo, the desert smiled! Possessing himself of a beautiful island in the Ohio, he rears upon it a palace and decorates it with every romantic embellishment of fancy. A shrubbery, that Shenstone might have envied, blooms around him. Music, that might have charmed Calypso and her nymphs, is his. . . . And to crown the enchantment of the scene, a wife, who is said to be lovely even beyond her sex and graced with every accomplishment that can render it irresistible, had blessed him with her love and made him the father of several children. . . . Such was the state of Eden when the serpent entered its bowers. . . ."

In late July the ophidian Burr to whom Wirt was referring had sent for his daughter, Theodosia: "If absent, you will suffer great solicitude. In my presence you will feel none, whatever may be the *malice* or the *power* of my enemies. . . ." And she had come—and promptly charmed Richmond by her address, winning new supporters for her father. Yet how could she bear the strain, she whose health had been precarious ever since the birth of her only son five years earlier? In answer, "it afflicts me, indeed, to think that you should have suffered so much from sympathy with the imagined state of my feelings," she wrote one inquiring friend, "for the knowledge of my father's innocence, my ineffable contempt for his enemies, and the elevation of his mind have kept me above any sensations bordering on depression. Indeed, my father, so far from accepting of sympathy, has continually animated all around him. . . . Since my residence here, of which some days and a night were passed in the penitentiary, our little family circle has been a scene of uninterrupted gayety. . . ."

Despite the animation, however, and the hopeful evenings, not all was triumph for the beleaguered colonel during those drawn-out proceedings. The jury verdict on the charge of high treason was delivered at last in late August. By then Washington Irving had been nearly two months gone from Richmond, had in fact left before Theodosia's arrival. But the day before his departure he had ridden the mile and a half out of town to the building of "bolts & bars & massy walls" where the prisoner was confined. Writing after that interview from the Washington parlor of the brother of the Van Ness who had served as the colonel's second in the duel with Hamilton, Irving noted that "Burr seemed in lower spirits than formerly; he was composed & collected as usual; but there was not the same cheerfulness that I have hitherto remarked." For only a few moments had the visitor remained in the cell. The colonel "had a bad cold, which I supposed was occasioned by the dampness of his chamber which had been lately white-washed. I bid him farewell with a heavy heart, and he expressed with peculiar warmth & feeling, his sense of the interest I had taken in his fate—I never felt in a more melancholy mood than when I rode from his solitary prison—such is the last interview I had with poor Burr—and I shall never forget it."

It would prove indeed to be their final meeting. Though Irving wrote those words in July 1807, soon after the prison visit and with many years of life remaining to both men, henceforth their worlds would diverge. No record survives to indicate that either ever saw the other again.

Monday, March 30, 1807, in the Eagle Tavern in Richmond, a warrant had been served on Aaron Burr. Three months later, on June 24, he had been, with Harman Blennerhassett, indicted on two counts, of treason and high misdemeanor. On the first count the jury delivered its verdict in late August. Burr was found not guilty. In September he was tried again, this time on the second count, of violating an act of

1794 that makes it a high misdeameanor to wage war against any nation with which the United States is at peace. On this charge, too, of hostile acts against Carlos IV of Spain, the jury in late October brought in a verdict of not guilty.

Having failed to convict Burr in a Virginia court, the government would decline further prosecution of him elsewhere, or of Blennerhassett or any of the others implicated in the western adventure. It was clearly a victory for the defendants; nor would the colonel's astonishing buoyancy allow him to doubt about the future. "I visited Burr this morning," the amazed Blennerhassett noted incredulously in his journal September 13, a Sunday evening near the end of the seven months' ordeal. "He is as gay as usual, and as busy in speculations on reorganizing his projects for action as if he had never suffered the least interruption." And those projects were on his mind when, free to take up his life once more, the colonel at last left Richmond in late October, as did Blennerhassett, who traveled as far as Baltimore in company with their victorious counsel, Luther Martin. In that Maryland city, incidentally, could be experienced one specimen of Republican outrage in the aftermath of the trial, as effigies of those three men and a fourth—Chief Justice John Marshall—were hanged from a gibbet on Gallows Hill before a howling mob. Blennerhassett, warned and in hiding, peered down through an attic window on a part of the torch-lit frenzy, a parading multitude "of about fifteen hundred," heard the shouting and the Rogue's March played on fife and drum in the street below. Did the Irishman, crouching in an alien garret over the rabble's menace, not bemoan once more his first encounter along the Ohio with Aaron Burr?

Declining to witness the gallows spectacle, the former Vice President had already set out on his way to Philadelphia. Blennerhassett, for his part, would rejoin his wife in time, but henceforth the years of his life—and of hers—would be in contrast to happy days on their island Eden downriver from Marietta. A little luck might visit them for a while on a plantation along the Mississippi near Bayou Pierre, but debts would dog them constantly now, and the War of 1812 would destroy the value of the cotton crop they had managed by then to get under cultivation. Afterward, sordid years of depending on relatives, in Canada, back in England, finally on Guernsey in the English Channel. One of Blennerhassett's sons became a drunkard—"I firmly believe he has no longer the power to refrain from drink"—another proved retarded. Having resorted in desperation to blackmail on both sides of the Atlantic (on neither side successfully), the Irishman died at last, island-bound, on Guernsey, in 1831. His wife survived him eleven years, dying impoverished, obscure, in New York City, long after the mansion those two romantics had erected so hopefully, beautiful and unexpected at the head of an island in the Ohio, had burned to the ground, destroyed on a late winter day in 1811 by careless intruders seeking shelter with their candles among dry hemp stored within its walls.

Others of the principal actors at the Burr trial were affected by the war that followed with England a year after that lesser conflagration, and by distracting tensions between that country and America that had preceded the conflict. General Wilkinson's involvement with Spain had been scrutinized during and after Burr's trial, but the Spanish governor of West Florida, Vizente Folch, had spirited all incriminating documents off to Havana, confident, as he wrote the general, "that before the United States will be in a state to conquer that capital, You, I, Jefferson, Madison, with all the secretaries of the different departments . . . will have made many marches on the trip to the other world." In Havana, buried in the archives, the documents remained until the end of the century, when in what was by then the newly independent Republic of Cuba scholars at last gained access to them to establish beyond doubt the treachery of the commanding general of the American Armies in those early years of the nation. By then Wilkinson himself—all that bombast and beefy posturing—had long been stilled, having endured one more opportunity during his lifetime to demonstrate his military ineptitude, against Canada at the St. Lawrence frontier in 1814, and having somehow survived the indignity of a court of inquiry into charges of neglect of duty, drunkenness, and conduct unbecoming an officer. By the end of the war this charmed schemer had been once more acquitted, and thus honorably discharged. His final years were spent in Mexico, dabbling in Texas land speculations, collecting claims for foreign creditors, serving as representative of the American Bible Society! He died—"I was prompted by that pure patriotism which has always influenced my conduct and my character, which I trust will never be tarnished"; "Posterity will do justice to my name and service"—he died in Mexico City in 1825.

Probably John Marshall, another major actor in the drama at Richmond, escaped impeachment for his conduct of the Burr trial only because of those same turbulent and absorbing relations with England that would result in Jefferson's policy of embargo inaugurated late in 1807, preface to war four and a half years later. Whatever accounts for his survival, Marshall did remain on the Supreme Court for more than a quarter of a century after his ruling for Burr in Richmond that was to be regarded by some as the only major blemish on a distinguished career and, by others, as his finest and fairest single achievement. By the time of his death, in Philadelphia in 1835, when the Liberty Bell rang out its final knell, Mr. Justice Marshall had been granted the respect and love of all those partisans whose leaders he had outlived—model of fairness, humility, patience, compassion, a patriot endearingly ungainly, Lincolnesque before Lincoln, unmartyred.

As for the principal of that famous trial, a number of years equal to Marshall's lay yet before his almost exact contemporary Aaron Burr. From Baltimore in early November 1807, Burr had journeyed to Philadelphia, then to New York, where he was still under indictment for having earlier issued the challenge to Hamilton. In Manhattan he secreted himself with friends who helped him assemble passage money for Europe. On the other side of the Atlantic he would be beyond reach of his creditors; and there, while at home hostile feelings toward him were cooling, he might still find ways to make real his dreams of empire: "X," as he referred to them in cipher, his conquest of Mexico. Toward that goal, under the alias of H. E. Edwards, he boarded the packet *Clarissa Anne* at the Narrows one late spring afternoon in 1808. In quarters on Stone Street that morning at ten, a relative, muffled, using the name Mary Ann Edwards, had visited him for the last time; the lady was his daughter, Theodosia.

"June 1, 1808 . . . At 4 p.m., left in a skiff, with a man and a boy. . . ." Thus, at the outset of his exile, Burr begins a journal that he will continue through the entire four years he remains in Europe. A remarkable document of nearly a thousand pages, it reveals as does no other surviving source the man himself, moving among streets and about lodgings in London, Edinburgh, Stockholm, Hamburg, Paris, Amsterdam. Ten months Burr spent in Great Britain, befriended, housed through much of that time, and warmly admired by the philosopher Jeremy Bentham. He was welcomed often in the home of another philosopher, William Godwin, and in the quarters of Charles Lamb—"He is a writer, and lives with a maiden sister, also *literaire*, in a fourth story." During his stay in Scotland Burr became friends with Walter Scott and the critic Jeffrey and Henry Mackenzie. Later, at Weimar, he moved through that distinguished court with ease, and was taken to meet Wieland and Goethe. The journal is filled, in fact, with names of the noble and illustrious of five countries who delighted in the companionship of this urbane American: "At 10 to *la* Princesse Caroline," for example: this on January 3, 1810, at Weimar, "a very lovely, interesting woman. Υ: M'lle *la* Baronne de Knebel, Madame *la* Baronne de Stein, . . . To *le* Baron de Schrade, where ½ hour. . . ." And so on through much of the exile.

Yet the journal is far more than a catalogue of distinguished names. It contains, distinctly uttered, the intimate voice of a man sharing as much as he can of his whole life with the absent woman he loves most in the world. "But again and again I remind you that this Journal is only a memorandum to talk from. The most interesting and amusing incidents are not noted at all, because I am sure to remember them." Similarly, December 3, 1808, he writes of declining an invitation in order to remain in his tavern room near London, "being more at my ease to smoke my segar and tell little T. what I have been about. But," he adds, "I don't tell ½ nor ¼. These are only notes to write from. Afraid to write *out*."

He does tell little Theodosia a great deal, however, and not only about the notable people he is meeting, though they of course would interest the highly cultured wife of the southern planter and legislator. He tells her, too, and in a tone invariably free from self-pity, about his frustrations: his hopes for "X" are not to be realized. Almost simultaneously with Burr's arrival in England in the summer of 1808, Napoleon has put his brother Joseph Bonaparte on the throne of Spain. France thereafter will be unwilling to entertain any schemes designed to dismember the New World empire, whereas England, supporting the deposed government, will for its own reasons share that reluctance. Not only is Burr rebuffed, then, at Whitehall, but he is finally expelled from England, doubtless at the urging either of the administration in Washington or of the Spanish *junta*, then a British ally. At 35 James Street, April 4, 1809: "Having a confused presentiment that something was wrong, packed up my papers and clothes with intent to go out and seek other lodgings. At 1 o'clock came in, without knocking, four coarse-looking men, who said they had a state warrant for seizing me and my papers. . . . They took possession of my trunks. . . ."

In time his belongings were restored to Colonel Burr, but he would have to leave the country, this shorn object of mistrust and vindictiveness. Aaron I he might have been, and yet we discover him now under the thumb even of his landlady at a tavern on the corner of Oxford and Swallow streets in London: "Tobacco interdicted; but I ventured to smoke my pipe up chimney, with a window open." He might have been Aaron I, and we find him instead, cheerfully enough, packed in with others on his way to Sweden, a May morning in 1809: "I took possession of the long boat. Made a sort of lounging place, where, with an umbrella, I read much at my ease; taking no notice of any one, not even *les dames*." But Theodosia would be amused. "My territories were invaded yesterday by Madame D. Reads remarkably well, and is indefatigable. Read to me all M'lle Wollstonecraft's 'Tour through Sweden' . . ."

Yes, he would tell his daughter all he could, about the raging toothache in Altona, all the more dismaying "as the tooth is the most important one of the few I have left." About the lodgings in Frankfurt: "My rooms are so small and the ceiling so low, that when the stove is heated I am suffocated, the hot air being above; while my head is in an oven, my feet are in an ice-house." About the autumnal nocturne in Amsterdam: "Spent the night in flea-hunting. Had great luck. Killed five; but the friends and relations of the deceased revenged themselves on me most cruelly. From my head to my heels, there is not a square inch free of flea-marks. . . ."

He had been attacked earlier as well, in Germany on a November evening in 1809, and set that down in the journal too: "the lip which was bitten by a venomous animal on Friday last has swollen, and is very painful. I did not mention it before, because the origin of the thing is so ridiculous that I wished to hush it up; for the bite was given in a paroxysm of great good humour." That animal, female and two-legged, was only one of scores, of hundreds whom Burr encountered in his travels. And he set them all down. Three different women in one day, in Stockholm, June 13, 1809: "Had scarcely got out of bed when *la Hanoverienne* mentioned on Saturday came in. Being unable to communicate anything by the ear, we tried, successfully, all the other senses. Passed an hour. After breakfast, *ma bel Mar.* came in to try to settle that affair of the broken glass. *Je voud. mieux* that her vis. had been defd. till tom. *mais el. est si jolie*"—I would have preferred that her visit had been deferred until tomorrow, but she is so pretty. And at two "came in Carolin. *C'est trop!*"—It's too much. He fell asleep at three and slept two hours.

At the time of that afternoon nap he was in his fifty-fourth year. Throughout the journal Burr is ruthlessly honest about this need for what he calls *muse*—his euphemism, French slang denoting the beginning of rutting time among animals. In Paris, December 8, 1810, this devotee of Chesterfield writes, "For some days past, and more particularly to-day, I have been in a state of irritability very unusual. Answer brusque and rapid. Say things almost rude; even to the good Valkenaer I was unkind, and not always civil to Albert'a. Can you imagine from what this arises? The want of *mus*. . . ." His "*rencontres*" or "accidents," for which he would pay even when money was lacking for food, for coal for a fire in his rooms, are recorded, in bastard French, sprinkled with abbreviations, as either good, or bad, or fat, or voluptuous, or whatever—and their price is included. In Copenhagen, two *rencontres* in a day, the first on a stroll: "*mus. mauv.* 1 d."—bad *muse*, one dollar; and at his lodging "*ll. de ch. gro. pas mauv. mus. encore*"—fat chambermaid, not bad, muse again. Sometimes he was repentant of these hasty street encounters (he might have been Aaron I, might by now have been former President Burr)—in the same city, October 25, 1809: "In walking . . . a *renc.*; 2 r.d.; *passab.* How unnecessary and how silly!" And the following day he records, "Sat up till 1 last evening, being a little out of humor with one Gamp; made some pious resolutions. . . ."

But resolutions were more easily made than kept. The respectable as well as the less so enticed him. In mid-May 1811, he finds his numbered seat within a diligence already occupied by a fat, well-dressed, ill-looking Flemish burgher. Very well, Burr will ride outside in the curricle. But at a stopping place the other passenger within wonders if the seat beside her isn't really his. She is a woman of about twenty-five. "*Mais entrez donc. Prenez votre place*"—come inside and claim your seat, she is soon scolding Burr, by now, incidentally, the possessor of new teeth made for him in Paris. Madame, he answers, "*je n'aime pas ces discussions*"—I don't like quarreling over such things. Absurd, she replies, kick the rascal out: "*Folie! Chassez cet cochon.*" So Burr with his numbered ticket takes the seat beside her, and the Fleming returning to the diligence must ride outside. Thus the voyagers within proceed to Rotterdam, chatting pleasantly: the lady turns out to be "the wife of a *c. d. noble*, who enjoys a place of some consequence under the present government." Arrived at where they are to change coaches, they may hurry and make the next stage; or they may, so the driver tells them, catch one tomorrow. The lady chooses to delay. Soon she and Burr are seeking an inn. The one they find is crowded. A single room their landlord shows them, with two beds. "I," Burr records with sly economy, "like a booby, said: '*Il faut une autre chambre.*' There was no other. Looked at Madame to see what was to be done. 'This will do.' Supper in our room." And he adds mischievously, "*Hiatus valde deflendus*"—a gap exceedingly to be lamented—before resuming with his further travels of the following morning.

Why does he set such intimacies down? "It was his theory," we are reminded by the colonel's close friend Matthew Davis (who knew the daughter Theodosia well), "that female education should in no respect differ from that of young men; and that, between parent and child, there should be the same frankness and candour of demeanour and conversation as between two friends of equal age. The theory may have been most unfounded; and yet he may be excused for adhering to it, when he saw before him, produced by it, or in spite of it, such a model of purity, intelligence, and loveliness as *Theodosia Burr Alston.*"

Davis seems not to exaggerate; his exalted opinion of Theodosia is confirmed repeatedly by others who knew her. A truly remarkable woman she must have been; and during his prolonged absence in Europe, it was the memory of her and the longing for reunion with her and her son that sustained Aaron Burr even when his schemes had all come untangled, when he was made to wake at last from those dreams of recovered power. "X is abandoned!" she writes her father at the end of October 1808. "This certainly was inevitable, but I cannot part with what has so long lain near my heart, and not feel some regret, some sorrow. No doubt there are many other roads to happiness, but this appeared so perfectly suitable to you, so complete a remuneration for all the past . . ."

Thereafter, she and her son are Burr's sole support—his reason for life—during his enforced and extended exile. Even at the start of his wanderings, on a November night in London: "Strolled and *pensant a T. et tous mes petits plans*"—thinking of Theo and all my little plans. At Jeremy Bentham's quarters at Queen's Square Place: "B. always goes to bed at 11, at which hour, of course, I come down to my room. Wrote to you, and for you, and about you, till 2." Again, "Roved about for two hours, ruminating on this sort of non-existence and on you." People he sees remind him of his daughter. In Edinburgh: "M'lle Erskine, daughter of the late Chancellor—the form, the eyes, the hair, and manner of Theodosia." He longs for letters: "The sight of your handwriting would make a jubilee in my heart." The letters do come. From New York, in October 1808: "I shall certainly remain here this winter," she writes, "but my situation will not have the charms we supposed. Indeed, I find that your presence threw a lustre on everything around you. Everything is gayer, more elegant, more pleasant where you are." One letter, in January 1809, will be hand-delivered by Washington Irving's brother: "Dr. P. Irving, who takes this, will give you more satisfactory intelligence. . . ." And Theodosia adds: "Do not be unhappy about me. Irving will tell you that I am quite plump. . . ." Her father plans a restorative trip to England for her. Their hopes are high, then the plans fall through. He is in Sweden now. And it is there, at Göteborg after a five months' silence while mail has been delayed, that he receives the long, revealing letter from Theodosia, written from Rocky River Springs, South Carolina, August 1, 1809, within the pages of which is the unforgettable tribute that follows her acknowledgment of "all the accumulated difficulties which already pour in upon us"—money exhausted, health enfeebled, friends faithless, exile prolonged, enemies keeping hostilities alive on both sides of the water—"and which would absolutely overwhelm any other being than yourself. Indeed, I witness your extraordinary fortitude with new wonder at every new misfortune. Often, after reflecting on this subject," Theodosia goes on in what must have delighted a father's spent spirit, "you appear to me so superior, so elevated above all other men; I contemplate you with such a strange mixture of humility, admiration, reverence, love, and pride, that very little superstition would be necessary to make me worship you as a superior being: such enthusiasm does your character excite in me. When I afterward revert to myself, how insignificant do my best qualities appear. My vanity would be greater if I had not been placed so near you; and yet my pride is our relationship. I had rather not live than not be the daughter of such a man. . . ."

Has any parent ever received a more moving tribute, more perfectly expressed? It made Burr "happy, very happy," of course; "I can only thank you, most cordially thank you." And is not their relationship a marvel? He cherishes Theo's portrait, sets it up in rooms of inns when he stops overnight on his travels, packs it with care. "Done, even the picture; all, all packed, ready for starting at sunrise. I bid you *bon soir* a dozen times before I shut you up in that dark case. I can never do it without regret. It seems as if I were burying you *alive*." He is jogging along pebbled roads in Denmark, in a wickerwork wagon behind four black horses: "The picture has come on my lap. I could not bear to see you bouncing about at the bottom of the wagon." And he daydreams.

"Let me see, how are you now employed? Probably at breakfast, with Gampy asking you an hundred of questions about—God knows!"

Germany, where "among the great number of Americans . . . all are hostile to A. B.—all." Then, at last, after many delays, Paris. Money is constantly a worry. Often Burr walks, on legs weakened by fasting, to save coach fare; he shivers through winter evenings to save the cost of a fire in his dreary rooms at No. 7, rue du Croissant. Having arrived in the French capital February 16, 1810, he is fated to remain there two years, at first with the life-sustaining hope that he might through Napoleon somehow yet return to power. He notes which evening the Emperor attends the opera, attempts unsuccessfully to see him, to communicate with him by letter. Though now, as always, Burr has a few loyal friends who admire and help him, he continues proudly to hide from them the extent of his wants. Throughout his exile gratuitous cruelties have been borne—mail denied, his trunks confiscated, his movements under constant surveillance. And now, in Paris, abandoning finally all other longings except to return to America, he encounters a further cruelty. The American consul empowered to issue the passport that will permit the exile to make such a voyage home is unluckily the Alexander MacRae who was an attorney for the prosecution of the treason trial at Richmond. Letters, delays, evasions, further rebuffs. Burr purchases, meanwhile, his little gifts for when he may depart. Paris, September 6: Went out "at 9 to a bookstore in St. Honoré, where bought for you and Gamp to the amount of 16,10—just 3 dollars. I mean to buy you about fifty plays of those written since '88. . . . Yesterday, no, it was Tuesday, the weather changed, and it is now so cold that I should be glad of a fire; but to that there are great objections; for what would become of the fifty plays, and of something, I won't tell what, which I meditate to buy for Gampillo, that will make his little heart kick?" For months past, and in several countries, he has been amassing a medal collection for his grandson—of great events in history, for example, and of Charles XII of Sweden as a boy. "What running I have had about that little rascal's medals." And when at last, through the intervention of friends, Burr is given that to which all along he has been legally entitled—the passport that lets him travel to Holland to take ship for home—he longs even in Amsterdam, June 14, 1811, to return to Paris briefly "to buy Gampy some beautiful marbles, and you some silk stockings, and father a pail to water his horses on the road. . . ." And "there is your watch which I have ordered, and one for Gampy, if I can squeeze out the money; and some books, and some garden-seeds."

But money will have to be squeezed out for other uses. In September he is still in Amsterdam, though booked on one of the rare ships that may venture to pierce the British blockade of the Continent. Yet "money must be raised or the voyage given up. So, after turning it over, and looking at it, and opening it, and putting it to my ear like a baby, and kissing it, and begging you a thousand pardons out loud, your dear, little beautiful watch was—was sold. I do assure you—but you know how sorry I was. If my clothes had been saleable, they would have gone first, that's sure. But, heighho! when I get rich I will buy you a prettier one."

That same day, September 12, he pays a ship's captain 480 guilders, raising the money in part by selling those medals he has for three years been meticulously collecting for his grandson. Now "we shall certainly—certainly! that's a word which should not be used here—yet it seems we shall go." And at last they are underway: "My windows look over the ocean, that ocean which separates me from all that is dear. . . . I am never weary of looking at it. There seems to be no obstacle between us, and I almost fancy I see you and Gampy, with the sheep about the door, and he 'driving the great ram with a little stick.'"

Ahead of Burr, however, lies yet a distressing, enforced delay in England, through that fall and winter, before he can resume his odyssey again, toward Boston. He sets it all down as that penultimate voyage unfolds: an insolent steward thrashed by the captain, the abandoned ship they pass, the iceberg—"a perpendicular rock of alabaster or white marble, of an elevation of not less than 250 feet"—and in mid-Atlantic on an April night in 1812, "the full moon now traversing a cloudless sky. . . ."

The little *Aurora* reached Boston on an unseasonable early May morning, with snow falling. Burr would delay in lodgings there almost a month, under the name of Mr. Arnot, raising a bit of money by selling some books to President Kirkland at Harvard, waiting for word from New York about how his return might be received. "Thanks to Dr. Smith's wig and my huge whiskers if I have not been recognized." His creditors, friends in New York reassured him, would not be vindictive. Accordingly, just before midnight, May 29, 1812, the returning exile boarded the sloop *Rose*. We see him in that night's dark glow, and feel a little of what he must have been feeling: "The tide would not serve till 1. I agreed to keep watch till that hour, and then wake the Captain. The sloop lay at the end of the long wharf, and I passed the hour walking on the wharf or sitting on the timber, ruminating on *things to come*, and talking with you and Gampillo. It was a beautiful, clear, mild moonlight night. A light breeze at N., just what we wanted, sprung up. At 1 we made sail. . . ."

For New York. Down the Connecticut coast, a stop at Fairfield, town Burr had known in his childhood, on down then, to Hell Gate finally, on a June evening, about eleven o'clock, with a voice hailing the ship from Manhattan itself. Burr landed and made his way through those dark cobbled streets to the home of his friend Sam Swartwout. And "here I am," so he concludes the amazing journal kept solely for his daughter's pleasure, "in possession of Sam.'s room in Stone street, in the city of New York, on this 8th day of June, *anno dom.* 1812, just four years since we parted at this very place."

Aaron Burr had returned to the city and resumed the practice of law at Nassau Street, a New York newspaper announced in late June 1812, some days after the exile had disembarked from the *Rose* and been rowed ashore near midnight to find his way to Sam Swartwout's. War with England had broken out that same month, so that the quarrelsome had a whole nation on which to vent their animosities; and meanwhile, friends of the colonel had rallied to his support. Hundreds stopped by his office to wish him well that first day he resumed practice. An awesome reputation as an attorney would serve him still; even those who scorned him as a man might value and pay for his advice in matters of law. So he would satisfy his creditors finally, would have money to visit his daughter again, soon would be beaming proudly over his grandson. He wrote with hopes abounding.

Then this, without warning, in reply:

> Seashore (S.C.), July 12, 1812
>
> A few miserable days past, my dear father, and your late letters would have gladdened my soul; and even now I rejoice at their contents as much as it is possible for me to rejoice at anything; but there is no more joy for me; the world is a blank. I have lost my boy. My child is gone for ever. He expired on the 30th of June.
>
> My head is not sufficiently collected to say anything further. May Heaven, by other blessings, make you some amends for the noble grandson you have lost.
>
> THEODOSIA.

Without warning: a letter she had written as late as May 16 had contained the news that "Gamp. is well; his little soul warms at the sound of your name." Throughout the years in Europe letters that father and daughter had exchanged rarely neglected to mention the boy, then learning Latin, the boy with whom the delighted grandfather had spent happy months from the time at Washington soon after his birth to the weeks at Richmond that preceded the exile, the boy dead now in his eleventh year.

The grandfather's desolation may be imagined as he wrote helplessly from New York to console his daughter, bereft and far away. "Alas! my dear father, I do live, but how does it happen?" she answered at last, a month to the day after the stark note that told of her only child's fate. "Of what am I formed that I live, and why? . . . You talk of consolation. Ah! you know not what you have lost. I think Omnipotence could give me no equivalent for my boy; no, none—none." But in her grief she felt one longing. "I wish to see you, and will leave this as soon as possible, though not so soon as you propose. I could not go alone by land, for our coachman is a great drunkard, and requires the presence of a master; and my husband is obliged to wait for a military court of inquiry." Alston was governor of his state at the time, and brigadier general in the state militia. "When we do go, he thinks of going by water, but is not determined. . . ."

The departure was delayed after all until December, and in the event, Alston remained behind, coping with duties he could not forsake. But he did see his wife aboard the schooner *Patriot* at Winyah Bay, December 30, 1812, saw her bound for New York, where the society of her father, it was hoped, would restore the enfeebled health of a grieving lady not yet thirty years of age.

Burr awaited the ship's arrival. Each morning he would walk down to the Battery and out to the end of the pier, looking past anchored craft that lay in the harbor. Ships did arrive, specks growing as they neared from the horizon, but he did not see the ship he waited for. Morning followed morning (perhaps she had not left home on schedule) until more than two weeks had passed, two weeks of a voyage that should have consumed five days. Then ("How has expectation darkened into anxiety—anxiety into dread and dread into despair") finally what did arrive was this anguished scrawl from Theodosia's husband:

"Gracious God! Is my wife, too, taken from me? I do not know why I write, but I feel that I am miserable. . . ."

Neither Mrs. Alston nor any of the other passengers aboard the *Patriot* were seen or heard from again. Nor was the ship recovered. Despite rumors and a deathbed confession years later by a derelict who professed to have been among the pirate crew witnessing the last moments of the governor's wife as she proudly walked the plank to her doom, it is assumed that she met her death in fact in a storm raging off Cape Hatteras as the new year 1813 began.

Whatever its cause, her loss was a blow that her husband, for one, could scarcely survive. Three more years he lingered in life, visiting, when he could bear it, the country estate that he and Theodosia had shared, was indeed at the Oaks when Burr's letter confirming his loss was received: "It was there, in the chamber of my wife, where every thing was disposed as usual; with the clothes, the books, the playthings of my boy around me, that I sustained this second shock. . . ." In 1816, not yet forty years old but "too much alone," as he himself said, "too entirely unconnected with the world, to take much interest in any thing," Alston followed his wife to the grave—hers in water, his in his native earth.

Behind him was left a sealed letter in a trunk that the grief-stricken husband had never found courage to open; the letter Theodosia had written some years earlier, in 1805, in a mood of despondency when an illness had seemed to bring near the end of her earthly content. "Death is not welcome to me," that stilled voice speaks there movingly once more. "I confess it is ever dreaded. You have made me too fond of life. Adieu, then, thou kind, thou tender husband. . . . You are away, I wished to hold you fast, and prevented you from going this morning. But He who is wisdom itself ordains events; we must submit to them. Least of all should I murmur. I, on whom so many blessings have been showered— whose days have been numbered by bounties—who have had such a husband, such a child, and such a father. Oh pardon me, my God, if I regret leaving these. . . ."

In dying when she did, Theodosia abandoned the world where her father would go on existing more than two decades longer: twenty-three more years of life, gamely pursued. It was never Burr's way to complain. "At some other time," he did write Alston late in 1815, "I may give you, in detail, a sketch of the sad period which has elapsed since my return." But the sketch was postponed and forgotten. "For the present, it will suffice to say that my business affords me a decent support." His law practice did prosper, and his schemes in time revived, though on a scale much reduced. Those schemes would keep creditors, whose names might change, hovering about him till the end of his days. Meanwhile, he became again a pedestrian traversing Nassau Street, Wall Street, Broadway, where at its intersection with Fulton Street one child when later grown to womanhood remembered having him pointed out by her father: "Do you see that queer little old man? That's Aaron Burr. I want you to remember I showed you Aaron Burr. Some people think him the wickedest person in all the world, but I do not think that." The object of their attention, buying a taffy apple from a street vendor, was wearing a blue coat with standing collar, a buff vest, dark trousers, and had a shell comb in his powdered hair. Another child when grown would recall playing marbles in the dirt on Reade Street before the door that held the somber brass knocker bearing Aaron Burr's name; the boy had "vaguely heard that some terrible old man, whom nobody would speak to, lived there all alone." In fact, the old man did still venture into society on occasion, but when he did in these late years, he addressed only those who addressed him first, ignoring stares and impertinences, unresponsive to slights. Henry Clay, a friend of years before, refused publicly to shake his hand, and Burr accepted the incivility without comment. Madame, he had said about another potential unpleasantness, "*je n'aime pas ces discussions*"—I don't like quarreling over such things.

Near the end of his life, still vigorous (for at his death in his eighty-first year Aaron Burr left a will that provided for support of an illegitimate child two years old at the time), near the end the colonel engaged briefly in the folly of another marriage, four decades after his first, happy one. This time he married the widow of the merchant Stephen Jumel, reputedly the wealthiest woman in Manhattan. Over the years rumors had connected the flamboyant Eliza with gallants of an earlier New York, and it had even been whispered that Hamilton and Burr had rowed to Weehawken that July morning so long before not as political enemies but as rivals for her love. "The celebrated Col. Burr was married on Monday evening to the equally celebrated Mrs. Jumel," former mayor Philip Hone noted dryly in his diary July 3, 1833. "It is benevolent in her to keep the old man in his latter days. One good turn deserves another."

By then, Eliza Bowen had reached sixty more or less, when she and Burr, then seventy-seven, were joined in wedlock at the Jumel mansion that still stands, on the low brow of the highest hill in Manhattan, at 160th Street and Edgecombe Avenue. The marriage was a disaster. "I dont see him any more," the new Mrs. Burr, encountered in the street a year later, told William Dunlap. "He got 13,000 dollars of my property, and spent it all or gave it away & had money to buy him a dinner. I had a new Carriage & pair of horses cost me 1000 dollars he took them & sold them for 500." A dismal coda. Their divorce was made final September 14, 1836, the very day that Colonel Burr, old at last, bedridden, paralytic, died in the upstairs bedroom of a boardinghouse on Staten Island.

Yet the memory of him—as a living person, dark-eyed, courteous, full of grace—survived even into our own century. As late as 1900, one old lady could still recall being entertained at play as a child of five or six by the former Vice President of the United States. "I once knew Aaron Burr"—and her eyes shone brightly when she spoke of their friendship. Her father had been lecturing at West Point, and the then elderly Burr, doubtless on legal business, had been staying at the same hotel through a number of days. "We children could hardly wait until we were dressed for the afternoon, when we made straight for the piazza, where our hero was sure to be waiting for us. We had, what was rare at that time for children, a little wicker carriage, and after we were seated in it, Col. Burr, acting as horse, would run nimbly up and down the long piazza, or through the wide corridors with us, amidst shrieks of delighted laughter from all the little spectators. How I wish I could remember what he talked of, for though he was taciturn when men were near, when he was with women and children his mirth bubbled freely and spontaneously, notwithstanding the trouble the years had brought him. Ah, what a man! Who shall now say what he was?"

Gallant soldier, devious, erratically effective political leader, demanding and adoring father, debt-ridden, ever generous, credulous and crafty, the "little dirty Noisy Boy very different from Sally" grew into a brilliant lawyer, a charming host, and "as unprincipled and dangerous a man"—so one of his enemies thought—"as any country can boast." Few neglected to voice opinions of him. "Burr," said Andrew Jackson, "is as far from a fool as ever I saw, and yet he is as easily fooled as any man I ever knew." "Burr's life, take it all together, was," according to John Quincy Adams, "such as in any country of sound morals his friends would be desirous of burying in profound oblivion." "His figure and form," Madame Jumel remembered wistfully thirty years after his death, "had been fashioned in the model of the Graces. He was a combined model of Mars and Apollo." "I find," wrote Theodosia of the living Burr in his absence, "that your presence threw a lustre on everything around you. Everything is gayer, more elegant, more pleasant where you are." "Aaron Burr," they had toasted in the taverns once: "May his treachery to his country exalt him to the scaffold, and hemp be his escort to the republic of dust and ashes." "I consider him as a man so fallen, so shorn of the power to do national injury"—this from young Washington Irving—"that I feel no sensation remaining but compassion for him."

"I am not a libertine; I am not a murderer; I am not a traitor. I never broke a promise to a woman in my life. I did not intend to kill Hamilton and did not shoot first. I never got within ten thousand leagues of a wish to break up the United States by a separatist or a secessionist movement, though I did hope to establish an empire in Mexico and to become its emperor."

And an old lady surviving into our century, eyes still kindled by her memory of a privileged friendship amid distant laughter on the piazza at West Point, repeated the question that one of her listeners would record for us to overhear:

"Who indeed shall say what manner of man he was?"

THE GREAT UNKNOWN
& GEOFFREY CRAYON, GENT.

I never felt such a consciousness of happiness as when under his roof. I awoke in the morning, and said to myself, "Now I know I'm to be happy. I know I have an unfailing treat before me."

IRVING AT SUNNYSIDE, OF HIS VISIT
WITH SCOTT AT ABBOTSFORD

A P O S T C H A I S E from Selkirk, some four or five miles westward, rattled up to the gates of Abbotsford at an early hour that Saturday morning in the late summer of 1817. The noise it made brought out the dogs, all kinds of hunting dogs; one black greyhound leapt on a hewn boulder in the courtyard and began barking his heart out, as though leading the chorus, while the sole occupant of the chaise, up at the road, sat nervously awaiting the delivery of the message that his driver was carrying down the gravel walk. What the traveler gazed at while he lingered he would remember the rest of his life: descending walkway, dogs in clamorous greeting, courtyard with building stones piled about, the "snug gentleman's cottage" covered with vines and scaffolding, and over the doorway a great pair of elk's antlers that gave to the whole the appearance of a lodge. Beyond the house green fields sloped gently down in the distance to the River Tweed—more lovely stream than river, so it appeared to this observer from a New World of vaster perspectives.

Meandering like the Tweed itself, the road that had led Washington Irving, now thirty-four years old, from Richmond in Virginia in 1807, across a decade exactly, to the gates of a cottage being transformed in Scotland in 1817, had seemed as often as not to wander without purpose, had tarried awhile in uncertain sunlight, once had penetrated the gloomiest shadows. Irving was a businessman now, of necessity, and though he had written nothing of note in eight long years, he was by this time also the most famous author in America. That fame, to be sure, told more about the paucity of America's imaginative literature early in its history than it did about the dimensions of her best-known author's achievement. For what supported Irving's reputation were only those slight and easily forgotten Oldstyle Letters by a boy of nineteen, the more substantial and much more popular *Salmagundi* (in part composed while Burr's treason trial was in progress), and, finally, one other comic work that had grown out of *Salmagundi* soon afterward. That last, finished as long ago as 1809, a couple of years after the Burr trial ended, was called *A History of New York, from the Beginning of the World to the End of the Dutch Dynasty*. No less than that. Like Irving's earlier writings, this one, too—by far his most impressive work to date—had appeared under a pseudonym, Diedrich Knickerbocker. And it was *Knickerbocker's History of New York* that was to make its author a welcome guest, in his mid-thirties, within the cottage in Scotland before which his postchaise was halted now.

Inside that cottage, Walter Scott, poet, antiquary, critic, sheriff of Selkirkshire, suspected author of certain anonymous novels that had begun appearing within the last two or three years to wondrous public acclaim, was at breakfast with his family. Breakfasts in the Scott household tended to be substantial. That morning there may have been—there often was—a venison pasty, collared eels, reindeer tongue, beef slabs, cold sheep's head, ham, and kippered salmon. There were assuredly rolls and white bread and bannocks of barley meal and plenty of porridge. For beverages there would have been tea and coffee and chocolate, as well as flagons of ale and claret on the sideboard. And it was from such a feast—breakfast was his favorite meal—that Walter Scott was to be called forth to greet still another of his numerous visitors from near and far. Yet one who was later told it by a young lady at the table that morning assures us, "Scott's family well remember the delight with which he received this announcement" of the unexpected arrival of the American author whom he had never met. The host "sallied forth instantly, dogs and children after him as usual, to greet the guest, and conduct him in person from the highway to the door."

Irving watched the Scotsman emerge. "I knew him at once," he recorded years later, "by the descriptions I had read and heard, and the likenesses that had been published of him. He was tall, and of a large and powerful frame. His dress was simple, and almost rustic. An old green shooting-coat, with a dog-whistle at the buttonhole, brown linen pantaloons, stout shoes that tied at the ankles, and a white hat that had evidently seen service. He came limping up the gravel walk, aiding himself by a stout walking-staff, but moving rapidly and with vigor." Even before reaching the gate Scott had boomed out welcome to Abbotsford, and at the chaise he grasped Irving warmly by the hand.

"Come, drive down, drive down to the house; ye're just in time for breakfast . . ."

But Irving's written message, delivered along with the letter of

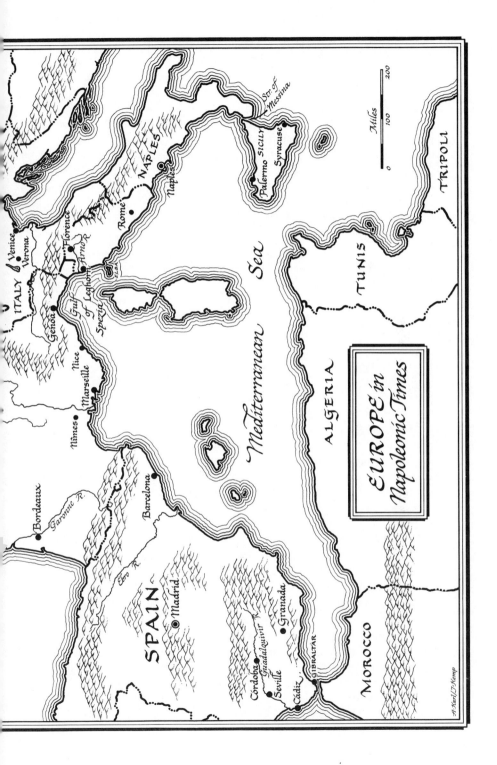

EUROPE in
Napoleonic Times

Mediterranean Sea

ITALY
Venice
Verona
Genoa
Nice
Marseille
Nîmes
Florence
Arno R.
Rome
Elba
Gulf of Spezia
Leghorn
NAPLES
Naples
Palermo SICILY
Str. of Messina
Syracuse
TRIPOLI

TUNIS

ALGERIA

MOROCCO
GIBRALTAR
Cádiz
Seville
Córdoba
Guadalquivir R.
Granada
SPAIN
Madrid
Ebro R.
Barcelona
Garonne R.
Bordeaux

Miles
0   100   200

A. Karl/J. Kemp

introduction from a mutual friend, had explained that he was on his way
to view the nearby ruins of Melrose Abbey; would it be agreeable, he
had written, for Mr. Scott to receive a visitor later that morning? Anyway, the traveler had already breakfasted before setting out. Yet Scott
was insistent. "Hout, man," he cried, "a ride in the keen air of the Scotch
hills is warrant enough for a second breakfast." Afterwards there would
be plenty of time to see the Abbey.

"I was accordingly whirled to the portal of the cottage," Irving
remembered, "and in a few moments found myself seated at the breakfast table." Seated at breakfast with his idol, one of the two most famous
poets then living in the English-speaking world, author of *The Lay of
the Last Minstrel*, of *Marmion*, of *The Lady of the Lake*. Like thousands of others, the American knew whole passages from each of those
poems by heart. Seated at breakfast with Walter Scott and his family:
his wife, his two sons, his two daughters. Irving's heart was "in a glow"
with so cordial a welcome. "You must not think," Scott was chiding him
good-humoredly, "our neighborhood is to be read in a morning, like a
newspaper. It takes several days of study for an observant traveller that
has a relish for auld world trumpery. . . ." His words contained an
invitation: what was to have been a brief morning visit was to grow
into the four happiest days of Washington Irving's long life.

For the most part he owed those days, as has been mentioned, to
The History of New York.

Having left Richmond in the summer of 1807, with Burr's treason
trial still in progress, the young journalist Irving had made his leisurely
way back to Manhattan to resume his position among the genial brother-
hood of the Lads of Kilkenny, those Nine Worthies a couple of whose
anonymous literary efforts would continue to emerge periodically
throughout that fall of 1807 to form successive numbers of the abid-
ingly popular *Salmagundi*. And such amusing satires on foibles of New
York society, by Irving and his friend Paulding, might have gone on
longer; "Launcelot Langstaff" and the rest of that outrageous company
of fictitious contributors seemed as the year 1807 ended to have by no
means exhausted their inspiration. Abruptly, however, in late January
1808, the series came to a stop.

The reason for the sudden termination of so successful an enterprise had to do with a quarrel over money between authors and publisher, but one outcome was that Irving, with a demonstrated knack for
writing humorously, was left with no obvious means of exercising it.
What to do with his energies? His legal career had languished (although as an old man defending that meager career, he liked to joke
somewhat imprecisely and with eyes twinkling, "I was one of the counsel
for Burr, and Burr was acquitted"). The law repelled him, but what else

could he do? Within three months of the abortive demise of *Salmagundi*, he and his elder brother Peter—the same who had earlier edited the Burrite *Morning Chronicle*—had settled on an answer. They determined to have some harmless fun at the expense of a work, then receiving attention, by a pedantic fellow citizen of their town: "Our idea was, to parody a small hand-book which had recently appeared, entitled 'A Picture of New York.' Like that, our work was to begin with an historical sketch; to be followed by notices of the customs, manners, and institutions of the city; written in a serio-comic vein, and treating local errors, follies, and abuses with good-humored satire."

What was envisaged, then, was much like *Salmagundi* extended. But what in time appeared was something different. Dr. Samuel Mitchill's brief *A Picture of New York* had opened with a solemnly bookish consideration of the original aborigines of the island. The brothers Irving would go that one better; they would start right back with the beginning of the world. And to provide the right flavor, both had soon buried themselves among dusty tomes of the local historical society; "we laid all kinds of works under contribution for trite citations, relevant, or irrelevant, to give it the proper air of learned research." Yet the labor, begun in high spirits, took time. Months passed, while their mountain of erudition grew. And then Peter's fate directed him back to Europe, so that his younger brother was left to pursue the undertaking alone.

"I now altered the plan of the work," Irving later explained. "I determined that what had been originally intended as an introductory sketch, should comprise the whole work, and form a comic history of the city." *Salmagundi* had exposed the New York of the present; the work in hand would reveal the New York of the past.

And so it did, unforgettably. Twenty-two months elapsed between the inception of the book and its publication, and during those months Washington Irving sustained the most grievous hurt of his life; but somehow, in December 1809, appeared from his pen the rollicking annals of the fictitious Diedrich Knickerbocker. "It took with the public," the author himself confessed, "& gave me celebrity, as an original work was something remarkable & uncommon in America. I was noticed caressed & for a time elated by the popularity I gained."

Three or four years afterward, one of Irving's friends traveling in Europe happened during a visit in Edinburgh to give a copy of the second American edition of *Knickerbocker's History* to the poet Walter Scott. In that way, by chance, this provincial success reached even overseas, in those days when European readers ordinarily paid no attention whatever to literary labors of the former colonials. "I beg you to accept my best thanks," Scott was soon writing enthusiastically to the donor of Irving's volume, Henry Brevoort, "for the uncommon degree of entertainment which I have received from the most excellently jocose history of New York." These last few evenings in the spring of 1813 Scott had been reading the annals "aloud to Mrs. S. and two ladies who are our guests, and our sides have been absolutely sore with laughing." Heady praise indeed, of the work of an unknown American from the most successful writer in the world! "You must understand his words literally," Irving's friend Brevoort insisted in passing the praise along, "for he is too honest and too sincere a man to compliment any person."

To our tastes as well, a hundred and sixty-five years and more after their first appearance, the annals that brought Scott joy retain much of their tang. Modern critics have called *Knickerbocker's History* "our first remarkable piece of comic literature," "full of warm, breathing life," "so distinctive in its imagination and humour that it is difficult to class," "one of the most valuable assets"—even now—"of our national literature," an achievement that "deservedly belongs among the most admired books of all American literature." But—better than admiration—the book on page after page can still awaken delight, as it records the preposterous doings of those pipe-smoking Dutchmen who governed Manhattan in the middle of the seventeenth century. Some of us may find a little labored the opening portion, elaborately footnoted, "containing divers ingenious theories and philosophic speculations concerning the creation and population of the world, as connected with the history of New York." But as soon as Hendrick Hudson appears on the scene, jerking up his breeches as he barks out his orders, his voice sounding "not unlike the brattling of a tin trumpet," a cavalcade begins that blunders its inept, endearing way through to the final chapter. Never mind that the Dutch rulers of New Amsterdam in actuality were cruel autocrats who routinely resorted to torture and massacre; in these pages they become transmuted, endowed with a comic life—Wouter Van Twiller, William the Testy, the pegleg Peter Stuyvesant—within a world where little more than dates and place names may be confidently relied upon. No matter; the world that Irving has created is possessed of its own integrity, as colorful, as funny, and finally as sane in its attitudes as those not dissimilar worlds that Irving's admirer Charles Dickens, inspired in part by the New Yorker, was to start creating from frequently sordid materials a quarter of a century afterward.

Within Irving's legendary universe of Dutchmen in sugarloaf hats and brimstone breeches lay, however, another world, real enough, that his original readers would have had no trouble recognizing. As allusions to Ike's grin and mangled syntax and penchant for golf, to LBJ's belly scar and barbecues, to Nixon's ski nose, beetling brow, and expletives deleted, to Ford's stumbles and Carter's pieties would be promptly discovered today however they were disguised, so New Yorkers of 1809 would not fail to identify, say, Irving's treatment of the historical but shadowy Governor William Kieft, whose fretful reign is described in hilarious detail—William the Testy, sage of Saardam, in his corduroy smallclothes, mounting his "tall raw-boned charger" to trot out to his rural retreat of Dog's Misery; William with all his inventions—"carts that went before the horses; weather-cocks that turned against the wind"—who sought to conquer by proclamation, who declared an embargo on trade with the neighboring Yankees, "ordering the Dutch burghers on the frontiers to buy none of their pacing horses, measly pork, apple sweetmeats, Weathersfield onions, or wooden bowls, and to furnish them with no supplies of gin, gingerbread, or sourkrout"; William whose stumbling-block was "the fatal word economy, . . . according to which the cheapest plan of defence was insisted upon as the best," and whose wrath against the nation's foe, "though quick to rise, was quick to evaporate. He was a perfect brush-heap in a blaze, snapping and crackling for a time, and then ending in smoke."

Which of Irving's American contemporaries was so dull to political affairs that he would not have seen Thomas Jefferson in all that? And what reader in 1809 would not have recognized the general who enjoyed William the Testy's favor, the valiant Van Poffenburgh, so "embroidered with lace and tinsel, that he seemed to have as much brass without, as nature had stored away within"? About this Van Poffenburgh, forever prating of his honor, whose bulk proceeded not "from his being fat, but windy; being blown up by a prodigious conviction of his own importance," rumors intimated "that he had in reality a treacherous understanding" with the enemies of the Dutch to the south of New Amsterdam, "that he had long been in the practice of privately communicating with the Swedes; together with divers hints about 'secret service money.'" And in recognizing in that portrait General James Wilkinson, Spanish pensioner and betrayer of Burr, would Irving's first readers have had any difficulty seeing something of General Washington in the old soldier Peter Stuyvesant, accused by his domestic enemies "of being highly aristocratical," who put an end to party strife and who ended his own days in dignified retirement? Did they not remember the vanished Federalist era under John Adams when they read of the Golden Reign of Wouter Van Twiller—"Ah blissful, and never to be forgotten age!"—and was it Burr himself they thought of when they encountered "one Peter Minuits or Minnewits, a renegade Dutchman, formerly in the service of their High Mightinesses; but who now declared himself governor of all the surrounding country, to which was given the name of the province of NEW SWEDEN"?

Of course most of the book at that level will escape the modern reader, as it did certain readers even then. "I am sensible," wrote Walter Scott to Brevoort in 1813, "that as a stranger to American parties and politics, I must lose much of the concealed satire of the piece, but I must own that looking at the simple and obvious meaning only, I have never read any thing so closely resembling the style of Dean Swift, as the annals of Diedrich Knickerbocker."

And for us, as for Scott, the simple and obvious meaning of

Knickerbocker suffices, so filled is the book with lively incident and image. We see, for example, and revel in that golden reign of Wouter the Doubter, when "the lover with ten breeches, and the damsel with petticoats of half a score, indulged in all the innocent endearments of virtuous love without fear and without reproach; for what had that virtue to fear, which was defended by a shield of good linsey-woolseys, equal at least to the seven bull hides of the invincible Ajax?" We delight in the image of Antony Van Corlear, the Trumpeter, sent northward to parley with those Yankees who bore such names as Preserved Fish and Habakkuk Nutter and Return Strong and Determined Cock—Antony on his Flanders mare "twanging his trumpet like a very devil, so that the sweet valleys and banks of the Connecticut resounded with the warlike melody—bringing all the folks to the windows as he passed through Hartford and Pyquag, and Middletown, and all the other border towns, ogling and winking at the women, and making aërial wind-mills from the end of his nose at their husbands—and stopping occasionally in the villages to eat pumpkin-pies, dance at country frolics, and bundle with the Yankee lasses—whom he rejoiced exceedingly with his soul-stirring instrument." We smile at those Yankees, whose husbands and fathers are forever praying and making money, as well as at the Swedes and the Indians—and the Southerners, whom Irving had mischievously observed on his trip to Richmond, down in the land of "hoe-cake and bacon, mint-julep and apple-toddy." But at the heart of our pleasure caper the Dutch: the Brinkerhoffs and the Van Votens and the Van Curlets and the Bunschotens, always the Dutch, with their absurd ships modeled on "the fair forms of their countrywomen . . . full in the bows, with a pair of enormous cat-heads, a copper bottom, and withal a most prodigious poop," the Dutch with their oysterlike phlegm and their long pipes fogging the air, the Dutch dozing away their lives while their busy wives clean the parlor—then close the shutters against flies and lock the door until the revolution of time brings round the next weekly cleaning day—the Dutch with their language, which, in places like Communi-paw, continues "unadulterated by barbarous innovations; and so critically correct is the village schoolmaster in his dialect, that his reading of a Low-Dutch psalm has much the same effect on the nerves as the filing of a handsaw."

Not everyone, of course, would encounter such portraits without taking offense. One rich tapestry of the Dutch in battle, for instance, reveals those corpulent, wheezing warriors waddling about on their short legs beside the Delaware, finally joining weapons with the Swedes, who during the epic conflict are at one point punningly "pressing on their rear and applying their feet *a parte poste* of the Van Arsdales and the Van Bummels with a vigor that prodigiously accelerated their movements," although in the end the enemy is somehow bumblingly defeated, so that "Victory, in the likeness of a gigantic ox-fly, sat perched upon the cocked hat of the gallant Stuyvesant," that last, silver-legged governor of New Amsterdam.

Not every one of Irving's first readers could be expected to appreciate such humor. Bulging with farcical life, *Knickerbocker's History* did indeed offend a few, but it also achieved what its author had hoped it would: it forever embodied "the traditions of our city in an amusing form." Out of an obscure and neglected past—"I was surprised to find how few of my fellow-citizens were aware that New York had ever been called New Amsterdam, or had heard of the names of its early Dutch governors, or cared a straw about their ancient Dutch progenitors"—the book wove legend and fable, and its popularity in general was as instantaneous as it has been enduring. Before long, Knickerbocker societies, Knickerbocker insurance companies, Knickerbocker steamboats and omnibuses and bread, and even Knickerbocker ice had all become ubiquitous features of the New York of the nineteenth century.

As for those offended first readers, they got over it. "When," wrote Irving with pardonable complacency some thirty years later, "I find New Yorkers of Dutch descent priding themselves upon being 'genuine Knickerbockers,' I please myself with the persuasion that I have struck the right chord . . ."

That chord—of indulgent good-humor toward those "good old Dutch times"—sounds again and again in *The History of New York*. In vain do we search Irving's pages for some genuinely somber note. The wonder remains, then, how such a buoyant book as this could have emerged from the pen of the author in his mid-twenties, for we have his own word that during much of its composition he was "in a wretched state of doubt and self distrust," fallen deeply in love and uncertain of his future. Moreover, before the book was finished he had been plunged into black despair.

Briefly, not long after returning from his first trip to Europe he had become enamored of a young New Yorker named Matilda Hoffman. He saw the girl every day, as their love for each other grew. Then abruptly Matilda caught cold—"nothing was thought of it at first"—and within two months, after protracted suffering, was dead of consumption, April 26, 1809, in her eighteenth year. Irving's was the last face her dying eyes looked on.

Later pages will offer the story in some detail—what kind of person Matilda was, how she moved and spoke—but for now it is enough to imagine Irving's desolation in her loss: "I cannot tell you what a horrid state of mind I was in for a long time—I seemed to care for nothing." For months after her death he struggled with his grief, some of that time spent in retirement in the country, at the home near Kinderhook of his friend William Van Ness (the same Van Ness who five years earlier had acted as Burr's second in the duel with Hamilton). Irving's anguish and "dismal horror"—fear of the night, fear of being alone, dread of society, an overpowering sense of the blankness of everything—did give way at last, and "when I became more calm & collected," he wrote privately years later, "I applied myself, by way of occupation, to the finishing my work. I brought it to a close, as well as I could, and published it but the time & circumstances in which it was produced rendered me always unable to look upon it with satisfaction."

Knickerbocker satisfied others, however—so many others that the young author soon found his fame enlarged far beyond the boundaries of New York, to Boston and Philadelphia and Baltimore, and as far south as the new capital at Washington. So now, in his late twenties, he was already the foremost man of letters in the country: "Wherever I went," he recorded, "I was overwhelmed with attentions . . . and I was quite flushed with this early taste of public favour."

Why, then, did he wait so long to write more? Ten years would pass—an entire decade out of the prime of his life—before Irving again would compose at the level of *Knickerbocker*. Granted, in those days before the protection of international copyrights, American writers were in competition with the best writers of England and Scotland, whose work publishers on this side of the Atlantic could pirate for free. Under that lush imported growth, there for the taking, budding native careers in literature, requiring financial nourishment, could hardly blossom. Especially since the pragmatic Americans with a nation to build saw belles-lettres merely as an adornment—fit activity for dabbling, an amusement for idle hours, but hardly the stuff real careers were made of. Yet equally important, as Irving confessed to only one other person, in his own case there was the crippling memory of Matilda: his heart "would continually recur to what it had lost, and whenever there was a pause in the hurry of novelty & excitement I would sink into dismal dejection. For years I could not talk on the subject of this hopeless regret; I could not even mention her name; but her image was continually before me, and I dreamt of her incessantly."

Elsewhere in the same moving confession he writes, "I am growing perhaps too minute—I don't want to make any romantic story." Irving did survive his loss, among periods of apathy and aimlessness did find himself in Philadelphia "engaged every day to dine, & every evening to sup out," in Washington did don his pease blossoms and silk stockings, gird up his loins, and attend Dolley Madison's levee at the White House: Dolley "has a smile & a pleasant word for every body," but as for her husband the President—"ah! poor Jemmy! he is but a withered little apple-John." Society everywhere along the East Coast welcomed the new young literary lion, who could fashion a pun and carry on small talk with easy wit, "besides his travels which you know he makes go a great way." And back in New York some years after Matilda's death, writing to his friend Brevoort, who was absent at the time on that European tour that brought *Knickerbocker* to Walter Scott's attention, Irving showed himself able to relay gossip as cynically as the next bon vivant: one virgin left behind has become "D——d stringy," and, moreover, "has been acting very much the part of the Dog in the manger—she cannot enjoy her own chastity but seems unwilling to let any body else do it." Meanwhile, a mutual friend, Brevoort should know, has become "one of your little gluttons" about the ladies; his "eyes are greedier than his belly, and where he honestly rodgers one, he dishonours a dozen with his lascivious looks."

Irving's young life—alternately insouciant and lethargic, spirited and dull—did go on after Matilda's death. We find him on a June day in 1810 (six years after the duel between Burr and Hamilton) recalling a recent happy cruise on the Hudson to Weehawken: "We took the girls" —one was Matilda's married sister Ann—"over to Hamilton's monument yesterday, and made a very prosperous and delightful voyage." And from another retreat on the Hudson, that same summer, he is discovered having eagerly stolen off by himself with an early copy of a just published poem: "Aug 12, 1810: Seated, leaning against a rock with a wild cherry tree over my head, reading Scott's Lady of the Lake. The busy ant hurrying over the page—crickets skipping into my bosom—wind rustling among the top branches of the trees. Broad masses of shade darken the Hudson and cast the opposite shore in black."

His prosperous mercantile brothers, meanwhile—William, Ebenezer, and Peter—were doing what they could to make Irving's life easy. That might have been part of the trouble. To allow him to pursue his literary inclinations they had made him a silent partner in their business—dealers in "whitehead, glassware, Epaulets, Sword Knots, Sashes, Hardware, &c"—on condition that he not "become engaged in commerce, except so slightly as not to interfere with your other habits and pursuits." Irving's habits, alas, at this time of his life were slack: "I have suffered day after day to slip by," he was writing Brevoort in 1811, "and here I still am, in much the same mood as you are when in bed of a fine genial morning endeavouring to prolong the indolent enjoyment, to indulge in another doze, and renew those delicious half waking dreams that give one an idea of a musselmans paradise." As for his pursuits, they were about what such habits would dictate: "I have now no prospect ahead," he had written the preceding year to Matilda's stepmother, "nor scheme, nor air castle to engage my mind withal; so that it matters but little where I am . . ." He did wander to Washington, vaguely to look into government doings that might affect his brothers' business affairs, but even that minor role as an agent at large made him feel he was degenerating into "a mere animal; working among hardware and cutlery." He hacked out a brief biography of the Scottish poet Thomas Campbell—"up hill work"—for which that friend of Scott later rewarded him with a glowing letter of introduction to be presented at Abbotsford. And in Philadelphia, through 1813 and 1814, Irving worked doggedly as editor of *The Analectic*, two drudging years during which he learned certain valuable lessons: that he was no critic or reviewer and was "not ambitious of being either wise or facetious at the expense of others," that he hated the unremitting toil of such a task as this and "would never again undertake the editorship of that or of any other periodical work," but that he did have a gift for writing sketches —of the lives, for example, of the American naval heroes currently making names for themselves in the war being fought against England. To Irving, too, that war came home at last, in August 1814, after the English Vice-Admiral Sir Alexander Cochrane had sailed his fleet up Chesapeake Bay and dispatched a landing force that all but burned the city of Washington to the ground. For a time the editor's martial ardor was aroused; he became Colonel Washington Irving, aide-de-camp to Governor Tompkins in the New York State Militia.

But his service, brief and clerical on the Canadian front, was soon behind him. Early in 1815 the war was over, and Irving, done with editing and soldiering, was back in New York, at Mrs. Bradish's boardinghouse on the corner of Greenwich and Rector streets. "There is nothing so irksome," he had written to his expatriate brother Peter three years before, "as having nothing to do." Happily, in the midst of this new idleness he found among his fellow boarders Commodore Stephen Decatur, who was about to set sail, now that peace with England reigned, to chastise the Barbary pirates in the Mediterranean. Why didn't the commodore's good friend Irving come along? "I determined to do so," the author recalled some time afterward, "to break off in this way from idle habits and idle associates & fashionable dissipation, and when I returned to settle myself down to useful and honourable application."

As it happened, the naval squadron delayed its departure. Meanwhile, Napoleon escaped from Elba, throwing all Europe into agitation. Irving, restless and packed, could stand it no longer. He booked passage and sailed alone late May 1815, aboard the *Mexico*, bound not for the Mediterranean but for Liverpool. There he would see his brother Peter, and from Liverpool would journey to Birmingham to visit his sister and her family. Afterward, a tour of England, France, and Italy—maybe even to Greece for a number of months—before returning home to that life of useful and honorable application within a year or two.

In fact, he was not home in one year, or two years, or ten. Seventeen years passed before this, Irving's second visit to Europe, ended.

The desultory conflict that was known then variously as the Second War of Independence or Mr. Madison's War had begun in June 1812 (just as Aaron Burr was returning clandestinely from four years of exile abroad). It ran down finally in these early months of 1815.

During the course of that second conflict with England, a tanner's boy in Hudson, Ohio, had been led to declare his private war against a different foe. Since coming west with his family in 1805, Squire Owen Brown's young son John had shown himself to be highly impressionable, grieving for months and even years over the loss of a marble or a pet squirrel. But he had developed strength and self-reliance as well. "To be sent off through the wilderness alone to very considerable distances was particularly his delight," John Brown himself wrote many years later of the boy that he had become after arriving at Hudson, "& in this he was often indulged so that by the time he was Twelve years old he was sent off more than a Hundred Miles with companies of cattle; & he would have thought his character much injured had he been obliged to be helped in any such job. . . ."

Rugged apprenticeship for a twelve-year-old, far from the school-rooms, the decorous parlors and "fashionable dissipation" of the East. The cattle that this frontier boy was driving through lonely forests were bound for the camps of American troops assembled around Detroit to fight the War of 1812; and it was during that war with England, as Brown in middle age recalled of those years—still writing of himself in the third person—that "a circumstance occurred that in the end made him a most *determined Abolitionist:* & led him to declare, or *Swear: Eternal war* with slavery."

The boy had been staying at an inn far from home, where the landlord—"a very gentlemanly landlord since a United States Marshall" —had been much taken with him. The older man "made a great pet of John: brought him to table with his first company; & friends; called their attention to every little smart thing he *said or did:* & to the fact of his being more than a hundred miles from home with a company of cattle alone." Such treatment might have been altogether gratifying, except that this same landlord owned a slave who was about John's age, "very active, inteligent, & good feeling; & to whom John was under consider-able obligation for numerous little acts of kindness." While praise was being lavished on the white boy, the landlord was able to treat the Negro—"badly clothed, poorly fed; & *lodged in cold weather*"—with an almost casual cruelty, on occasion beating him before John's eyes "with Iron Shovels or any other thing that came first to hand."

The discrepancy acted as a revelation: it "brought John to reflect on the wretched, hopeless condition of *Fatherless & Motherless* slave *children:* for such children have neither Fathers or Mothers to protect, & provide for them." Four or five years earlier John himself had lost his mother—loss "complete & permanent"—and the anguish stayed with him in his loneliness. Now about these orphan blacks he found himself raising the question: *"is God their Father?"* And the answer he must have known, for he was certain that at least this one defenseless black slave his own age, who had felt the gentlemanly landlord's iron shovel across his vulnerable back in the inn somewhere between Hudson and Detroit, was, as compared to John himself, "fully if not more than his equal."

"I am like another being from what I was in that listless period of existence that preceded my departure from America." So to his friend Brevoort, back home in New York, an exultant Washington Irving announced soon after arriving in England. The crossing aboard the *Mexico* had been a rough one—"mewed up together for thirty days in dirty cabins"—but once landed in Liverpool, in the midst of jubilation as laurel-bedecked mail coaches thundered through the streets announcing the stupendous victory of the Allies at Waterloo, Irving's mood was transformed. "It seems as if my whole nature had changed . . . my very blood seems to flow more warm and sprightly."

Besides the triumph over Napoleon, there were personal reasons for Irving's excitement: for the first time in seven years he was seeing his brother again, that brother Peter who, in the midst of joint labors on *Knickerbocker's History*, had left for Europe in January 1809 (carrying, we recall, a letter from Theodosia Burr to her exiled father: "Do not be unhappy about me. Irving will tell you that I am quite plump. . . ."). Ever since that faraway time Peter had remained in Europe, for much of it as the English agent at Liverpool of P. & E. Irving and Company, purchasing luxury items to be sold in America. "I found him," Washington wrote brother Ebenezer—the E. of P. & E. Irving—"very comfortably situated, having handsome furnished rooms, and keeping a horse, gig, and servant, but not indulging in any extravagance or dash. He lives like a man of sense. . . ." Peter's health, to be sure, was disappointing—confined to his rooms with rheumatism, he had not been able to meet the ship on Irving's arrival—but the trappings of the life he was leading did seem agreeable, with travel and interesting friends and money enough from the export business to provide for considerable comfort.

Money enough for both brothers, in fact. Washington, after all, was a partner in the business enterprise, though a silent one; as long ago as 1810 Peter had written, "I need not repeat that I consider your attention to *esta obra*"—*Knickerbocker's History* that the older brother had deserted—"as amply performing your part in our little partnership." Accordingly, since then the three brothers—Ebenezer, Peter, and Washington—had shared the fortunes of P. & E. Irving and Company, though only two of the three were actively involved: Peter in purchasing stock in England, Ebenezer in selling that stock at a profit in America. And if the recent war had interrupted so lucrative a flow of merchandise westward, the war was over now. The future looked promising, as Peter confidently resumed his investments on credit in those English-made luxury items—glassware, sashes, whitehead, and the rest—that he was sure Americans had had to do without too long.

Joyous weeks, then, in the early summer of 1815 soon after landing: a new, intenser life for Washington Irving, reunion with Peter, the initial visit of many that would be made to Birmingham, to sister Sarah's lovely home—walled garden, marble vestibule, the happy family within: "Hal and Sally" and the four children. And travels farther afield: to London to join in public celebrations after Waterloo, from London on to Bath, to Gloucester, to Bristol, to a spell of castle hunting in Wales. At Chepstow, for instance: "Rise early and visit the ruins of the castle. . . . sit on the grass in its large court-yard, and listen to the distant bell of the village tolling for church; walls of castle overrun with ivy; various birds have made their nests in the crevices of the tower and battlements, and keep up a continual twittering. . . ."

A lyric interlude, but the vagabond had to rise at last, to return to Liverpool and putter among the ledgers of P. & E. Irving and Company. For as summer turned to fall Peter's indisposition was growing worse, alarmingly so; the older brother was, in fact, suddenly an invalid, crippled and housebound, forced to depart Liverpool in September for the waters at Harrowgate, then move painfully on to their sister's home in Birmingham. In addition, that same fall, most unluckily the experienced and knowledgeable chief clerk of the company grew ill and died, throwing matters into even worse disorder. "Perfectly ignorant of every thing about business affairs," Irving later explained, "I came in and made them teach me." He had to—there was no one else to take charge. And he found out facts that dismayed him: "It was all wrong . . . every thing was in confusion. As I began to learn the business I saw the difficulties, the breakers ahead."

Those breakers came to look ever more unavoidable, rising before this light craft in alien waters that had originally meant to chart nothing beyond a pleasure cruise of modest duration. Creditors were everywhere, and no remittances. The problems besetting the company arose mostly from Peter's earlier overconfidence: during those perilously laggard economic times he had invested on credit in goods for which, events would show, a market no longer existed in the United States; for two years and more of war had forced America to develop her own light industries. With the new peace, the New York market was glutted with English wares anyway. Moreover, even the goods of P. & E. Irving that might have been sold were, through the perversity of the weather, blocked by contrary winds from being shipped out of Liverpool. Day after day weathercocks pointed westward, and day after day freighters tarried, until finally seasonal merchandise would have to be held in storage for another whole year before it could even be offered for sale at home.

Details in those ledger books would make barren reading now, but emotions they stirred then still can be felt. For what the dry entries signified the younger Irving was coming to understand: no bright future lay before P. & E. Irving. Instead, what threatened the brothers was financial ruin.

In one of the rare references he ever allowed himself to make to two years better forgotten, Irving confessed much later that so sudden a reversal of fortune "cast me down in spirit, and altered the whole tenor of my life." It was no exaggeration. All plans for extensive travel were abandoned: "I have no intention for the present of visiting the continent," he wrote Ebenezer at the end of 1815. "I wish to see business on a regular footing before I travel for pleasure. I should otherwise have a constant load of anxiety on my mind." The new year saw him more despondent: to possess the wealth of Croesus, so he wrote January 9, 1816, "I would not again experience the anxious days and sleepless nights which have been my lot since I have taken hold of business." By April he saw himself "so much a man of business, of mere pounds shillings and pence business, that I have little leisure for writing—and when liesure does come, I find every gay thought or genteel fancy has left my unhappy brain and nothing remains but the dry rubbish of accounts." Accounts, accounts, ledgers, creditors, remittances. Creditors pressing, remittances postponed, dismal ledgers to consult, accounts, and always the creditors closing in.

Only rarely was Irving able in those wearying months to "emerge from the mud of Liverpool, and shake off the sordid cares of the Counting House" by joining his sister's family in Birmingham. "Peter continues a cripple from the rheumatism, & is confined to the house," he had written from there to Brevoort over the Christmas season of 1815; "I do not think he will be able to go abroad before spring." The prediction proved accurate; it was not before the spring of 1816, eight months after his departure to Harrowgate and Birmingham, that Peter had regained enough of his health to return to Liverpool, allowing his younger brother "to crawl out of the turmoil for a while." But the novice in business could not really escape: worldly cares, as he said, had hurried back and forth across his mind until it was worn "as bare as a market place."

Much of the anxiety that he felt was for the welfare of his family. "My own individual interests are nothing. The merest pittance would content me if I could crawl out from among these troubles and see my connections safe around me." But some of what he felt was for himself. He had loathed business—"knew nothing about it & disliked the very name"—so that this approaching ruin, among strangers in a strange land, was fraught with a special kind of humiliation. At least the calamity of Matilda's death, however overpowering, had aspects about it that were "solemn and sanctifying, it seemed while it prostrated my spirits, to purify & elevate my soul. But this was vile and sordid and humiliated me to the dust." For months and months, through 1816 and into the new year, as he labored futilely, he suffered: "I lost all appetite I scarcely slept—I went to my bed every night as to a grave. I saw the Detestable ordeal of Bankruptcy in the distance and that it was inevitable, for my name stood committed in a commercial form." And he summed up the experience feelingly: "I would not live over that dreadful term of trial to be sure of a long life of felicity."

If we wonder whether he exaggerates the horrors of such a trial, we must recall the sensibilities of this tradesman's son who prided himself on being a gentleman (his chosen pseudonyms are suggestive: Jonathan Oldstyle, *Gent.*, Launcelot Langstaff, *Esq.*). "I felt cast down—," he wrote some years afterward, "abased—I had lost my *cast* —I had always been proud of Spirit, and in my own country had been, as it were, a being of the air." Now, however, in this foreign land all was changed, encumbered: "I shut myself up from society—and would see no one. . . ."

Moreover, in the midst of the ordeal, he learned of his mother's death. She had died in New York on the ninth of April, 1817. The demise ten years earlier of Irving's father—that stern old Calvinist to whom all pleasure was wicked—had brought forth not so much as a comment; but the death of his beloved mother was altogether different. The youngest son had always been her favorite: "She talked of me to the last, and would not part with a letter which she had received a few days before from me." Her death added much to Irving's griefs in a distant country, for he had "loved her with all the affection of a son."

And yet at least she had been spared his disgrace. In the hated Liverpool he stayed through the spring and early summer of 1817, counting "the days as they lag heavily by. Nothing," he wrote at the time, "but my wish to be with Peter & relieve the loneliness of his life would induce me to remain an hour in this place." Should he go home? "I received some time since your kind letter urging my return," he wrote Brevoort that fateful spring. "I had even come to the resolution to do so immediately, but the news of my dear mothers death put an end to one strong inducement that was continually tugging at my heart, and other reasons have compelled me to relinquish the idea for the present." Brevoort himself, for one thing—like Paulding, that other Lad of Kilkenny—would soon be married; and Brevoort, related to J. J. Astor, was thriving in business, on the threshold of becoming one of the wealthiest men in New York. A humiliated Irving could hardly face his friend's success just now. But to tautly strung nerves an alternative presented itself: "The idea suddenly came to return to my pen, not so much for support, for bread & water had no terrors for me, but to reinstate myself in the worlds thoughts—to raise myself from the degradation into which I considered myself fallen. I took my resolution—threw myself a stranger into London, shut myself up and went to work."

That was in the heat of early August 1817. He worked hard, all but solitary in London in his lodgings off Trafalgar Square—and made plans to work harder. But in the midst of his labors, he did take time at last for a trip that he had had in mind for more than a year. He journeyed—the only visit he ever made there—to the country of his ancestors. Early on the twenty-first he left London aboard the smack *Lively*, bound for Berwick-on-Tweed. From that English border town he traveled overland by coach to Edinburgh, arriving in a night of heavy rain to put up at MacGregor's Hotel on Princes Street. Three days of late August in Edinburgh—"remarkably picturesque . . . Smoke rising from houses between new & old town, & lighted up by the morning sun"—then southward to Selkirk to spend a night before setting out early Saturday morning, August 30, by postchaise to visit the ruins of Melrose Abbey, which Walter Scott's *The Lay of the Last Minstrel* had made famous throughout the English-speaking world. And about four miles out of Selkirk Irving made a stop "at the gate of Abbots Ford: Mr. Scotts country residence." The American sent down his card and waited eagerly above that rabble of barking hounds, above the scaffolded cottage and the glittering Tweed, until "in a few minutes," as he was soon able to record with pride in his notebook, "Scott himself appeared limping up the hill."

Scott: "He is a sterling golden hearted old worthy," Irving was writing brother Peter from within the very walls of Abbotsford before his visit ended, "full of the joyousness of youth, with an imagination continually furnishing forth picture, and a charming simplicity of manner that puts you at ease with him in a moment." The "old worthy," in fact, had turned forty-six just two weeks earlier; that is, he was no more than twelve years Irving's senior. Hardly decrepit yet, and ahead of him still, to be written before he finally set his amazing pen down for good, lay twenty-one more novels including some of his very best, several short works of fiction, a nine-volume life of Napoleon, a history of Scotland, and page upon page of occasional prose—letters, long notes, reviews, and learned articles.

Yet Walter Scott's appearance in August of 1817 may have belied such vigor; for six months earlier, at his Edinburgh home at 39 North Castle Street, during a dinner party as his guests were lingering over the candlelit table about nine at night, he had suddenly been attacked in his stomach with a pain so exquisite that he had been forced to scream out "like a bullcalf" and stagger off to bed in agony. Though the sufferer feebly sent down word that the party should continue, his alarmed guests soon dispersed, fearful that their host might even then be on his deathbed.

It was Scott's first serious illness since childhood, but a shattering one: gallstones, for which no effective treatment existed in those days, certainly not surgery. "All sorts of remedies were applied," he wrote a friend not long afterward, "but such was the pain of the real disorder that it out-devild the doctors hollow. Even heated salt which was applied in such a state that it burnd my shirt to rags I hardly felt when applied to my stomach. At length the symptoms became inflammatory and dangerously so the seat being the diaphragm: they gave way only to very profuse bleeding and blistering which under higher assistance saved my life." But at a cost. For days the patient was exhausted: "I could neither stir for weakness and giddiness nor read for dazzling in my eyes nor listen for a whizzing sound in my ears nor even think for lack of the power of arranging my ideas. So I had a comfortless time of it for about a week." And early that summer, three or four months after the attack, Scott on a Highland pony in Charlotte Square was observed still looking like a skeleton, seated "slanting on his horse, as if unable to hold himself upright; his dress was threadbare and disordered; and his countenance, instead of its usual healthy colour, was of an olive-brown . . ."

Toward the end of that same summer, however, when Washington Irving made his visit, Walter Scott's full strength was returning under the regimen of life in the country; indeed, he had risen from what his friends feared was his deathbed to enter the years of his greatest triumphs and happiness. And if at breakfast that Saturday morning with Irving he still had to choose carefully among the dishes spread before them, avoiding "pastry fruit &c. and all that tends to acidity," he was able to fill the day that followed breakfast with his usual demanding and varied activities. The American would make his morning visit to Melrose Abbey, but with Scott's younger son, eleven-year-old Charles, as his knowledgeable guide. "I shall not be able to accompany you," the host explained, "as I have some household affairs to attend to . . ."

Nor would such a guest as Irving be tactless enough to inquire into the nature of those affairs. But did they include, the visitor surely wondered, another chapter or two to be written on the current Waverley novel? On more than one occasion Walter Scott had denied any involvement with the series of fictions that during the last three years had begun appearing anonymously and creating unprecedented excitement: *Waverley* itself in mid-1814, like a wonderful bolt from nowhere, totally unexpected, without model or prototype, and the others that soon followed, *Guy Mannering, The Antiquary, The Black Dwarf, Old Mortality,* each in turn causing a sensation, each recognized as by him who would identify himself only as "the author of *Waverley.*"

But who, if not the poet Scott, was that author, the Great Unknown, whose work was provoking endless speculation among English-speaking readers everywhere? *Aut Scotus aut Diabolus*—either Scott or the Devil: no one else alive could know so much of Scottish history, landscape, character, language, tradition—and could write the poetry the novels contained. Yet the sheriff of Selkirkshire did courteously but firmly deny any part in that astounding venture—"I am *not* the Author of *Waverley* nor in any way connected with these very successful novels" —and far from seeming engaged in the extensive desk work such productions must require, these days he apparently had plenty of leisure, after discharging his duties as sheriff here and as Principal Clerk of Session in Edinburgh, to supervise, for instance, all the complicated labor now going forward toward improving his lands by the Tweed and rebuilding his country home. Moreover, by the time Irving had returned from visiting the nearby abbey that Saturday morning in 1817, here was Scott ready for a hike, prepared to spend the afternoon unhurriedly showing his guest around his acquisitions.

The dogs came along—Maida, the inky-coated greyhound Hamlet, the spaniel Finella—and the conversation of the two men was as rambling as were the paths they followed together: about amiable peculiarities of domestic animals, about popular native songs, about their mutual friend Tom Campbell, about the stonecutters with whom the strollers pleasantly passed the time of day at the quarry, about Scott's children, then in their teens and younger, of whom the father was extremely proud, about the forested Catskills back in America and the "gray waving hills, line beyond line," here over the naked stream that was the far-famed Tweed. The emotions Scott's visitor was feeling were strong: "what touching associations were called up by the sight of Ettrick Vale, Galla Water, and the Braes of Yarrow!" For these names Irving had known not only through his host's well-loved verse. "Every turn brought to mind some household air—some almost forgotten song of the nursery, by which I had been lulled to sleep in my childhood; and with them the looks and voices of those who had sung them, and who were now no more"—voices of the Scottish nursemaid Lizzie, his sister Ann, his mother, thirty years earlier, back home on William Street.

These surroundings at Abbotsford did seem enchanted—"a little realm of romance" that had suddenly opened. And after the walk was ended Scott still had time for his guest, devoted the entire evening to him. So could this relaxed and genial laird be really the industrious author of *Waverley?* In the drawing room that also served as his study, the host was reading aloud from *Le Morte Darthur:* "It was a rich treat to hear such a work, read by such a person, and in such a place; and his appearance as he sat reading, in a large armed chair, with his favorite hound Maida at his feet, and surrounded by books and relics, and border trophies"—scimitar, broadsword, spurs from Bannockburn, Rob Roy's gun—"would have formed an admirable and most characteristic picture." Mrs. Scott sewed in a chair nearby, and from time to time Scott's daughter Sophia, then seventeen, sang at her father's request—ballads of Scotland, old Jacobite songs "in their native dialects, which gave them an additional charm."

And striving to hear again an echo of that lively young voice, one thinks of the difference between the two gentlemen listening. Scott the world-famous poet, acknowledged master of Scottish antiquity, assumed author of the most popular novels ever written, admired husband, adored father, respected public servant, beloved master and laird of an evolving estate that provided work for upwards of fifty people: "It has been a constant source of pleasure to me," Irving wrote Peter from Abbotsford, "to remark his deportment towards his family, his neighbours, his domestics, his very dogs & cats—every thing that comes within his influence seems to catch a beam of that sunshine that plays round his heart." Scott in triumph, and Irving, by contrast, heart-clouded, with family bankruptcy threatening public disgrace, with only plans and some light verbal sketches in his notebooks, with literary credentials that were moldering, supported by hardly more than one work, his comic history, now nearly a decade old! Yet amazingly, that very morning of his arrival at Abbotsford, hadn't Scott on the basis of *Knickerbocker* received him "in his ordinary dress, recognizing him as a kindred mind, with whom he had been long familiar"?

Irving's heart was too full to allow much rest that night. "The idea of being under the roof of Scott; of being on the borders of the Tweed, in the very centre of that region which had for some time past been the favorite scene of romantic fiction; and above all, the recollections of the ramble I had taken, the company in which I had taken it, and the conversation which had passed, all fermented in my mind, and nearly drove sleep from my pillow."

And when he rose next morning, early, and looked through his sunstruck lattice window and beyond the eglantine, "to my surprise Scott was already up and forth, seated on a fragment of stone, and chatting with the workmen employed on the new building. I had supposed, after the time he had wasted upon me yesterday, he would be closely occupied this morning: but he appeared like a man of leisure, who had nothing to do but bask in the sunshine and amuse himself."

During that day, as on the day before, the two writers enjoyed another long outing together, and in the afternoon Scott in Irving's company received and entertained additional visitors—"two English tourists; one a gentleman of fortune and landed estate, the other a young clergyman." And then, incredibly, yet again on the following day, which was Monday, the same leisurely hospitality prevailed. Irving "made an excursion with Scott and the young ladies"—the two daughters Sophia and Anne—"to Dryburgh Abbey. We went in an open carriage, drawn by two sleek old black horses. . . ."

Off they rode, four sojourners in their open carriage, pleasantly trundling over the gentle countryside. Their ride that Monday morning in the late summer of 1817 followed haunts that the poet had known all his life. "In one part of the drive," Irving tells us, Scott "pointed to an old border keep, or fortress, on the summit of a naked hill, several miles off, which he called Smallholm Tower, and a rocky knoll on which it stood, the 'Sandy Knowe crags.' It was a place, he said, peculiarly dear to him, from the recollections of childhood. . . ."

Today's visitor driving northwest from Kelso five miles or so through Scott's Border Country may still see Smailholm Tower brooding on the horizon, off to the left of the hamlet that shares its name. More difficult than gaining a glimpse of the tower is finding the road that guides you to it, but inquiries and patience will place you finally on a dwindling country lane that leads to a farm path and ends at last in the confines of a farmyard. A dog or two may appear, tails wagging, as you drive up—pale reflection of another, earlier arrival nearby at Abbotsford—but no host emerges either to welcome or to encumber you. From a wall box alongside the barn, following instructions, you take two huge iron keys that are chained together and then proceed alone.

The crags on which the tower stands rise about half a mile beyond the farmyard. Keys in hand, you approach on foot, over wild green grass, past a small pond and lesser outcroppings of gray stone. The tower looms before you much larger and more awesome than its photographs suggest, Norman stone rising nearly sixty feet into the air, unmarked and unattended on these windswept, bleak, and beautiful expanses.

Having climbed the rocks, you are rewarded with the view of a superb panorama. Out over moorland southward some fifteen miles at the English border lie the purple Cheviot Hills. On the right near at hand rises the three-humped landmark of the Eildon Hills; and beyond those are Dryburgh Abbey, lovely beyond description, and Ettrick Forest, and Gala Water, and—some ten miles off due west—the site of Abbotsford. From this height, as Irving remarked, Scott "may be said to have had the first look-out upon the promised land of his future glory."

Turning now from the vista to the great black entrance of the tower near at hand, you put each key in a separate hole of the lock, force the weighty old tumblers, then push the door creakingly inward.

Inside is cool and dim and still. The floor is of earth; stone stairs in one corner circle darkly up to a higher level, rather more ornate with its gigantic stone fireplace, empty where flames once leapt high. Bending down and looking up, as from the bottom of a well, you see the astonishing sky far above the chimney's opening. In this raised room, their cattle and women huddled on the earthen level beneath them, above them on the ramparts their lookouts keeping watch against the hated English, belligerent generations of Lowland warriors caroused. And still, ghosts haunt the spaces:

> Methought grim features, seam'd with scars,
> Glared through the window's rusty bars . . .

The image, of grim and glaring features that appear to linger yet, has visited other minds in other times, once filled the mind of a child no more than three years old, lying among peacefully grazing sheep on the velvet grass, days in the early 1770s, within sight of this same tower. Wattie Scott had been brought down to Sandyknowe farm, his grandfather's farm, from Edinburgh thirty miles away, in hopes that country air and country life hereabouts would help cure a mysterious illness that had befallen him some time before. He had been born healthy—"uncommonly healthy" were his words—the ninth child in his family but only the third to survive infancy, in acrid confines in College Wynd, old Edinburgh, August 15, 1771. No doubt the infant Wattie would have perished like his older brothers and sisters had his family remained in those dank third-floor rooms of his birthplace, among slops and stale air in the narrow, lightless wynd. But soon after his birth his parents—the father was a prospering lawyer—moved outside the city proper to a newly built home at George Square, and here, in far more healthful surroundings, with the air coming in fresh from the Pentland Hills and the Forth, the child flourished through the first year and a half of his life.

One night, however, when he was not yet two (as it was often told to him later), "I showed great reluctance to be caught and put to bed, and after being chased about the room, was apprehended and consigned to my dormitory with some difficulty. It was the last time I was to show such personal agility. In the morning I was discovered to be affected with the fever which often accompanies the cutting of large teeth. It held me three days. On the fourth, when they went to bathe me as usual, they discovered that I had lost the power of my right leg. . . ."

Though at the time the disease was nameless and its causes not understood, the child had been struck with infantile paralysis. In an effort to cure so sudden and perplexing an affliction, he was sent south to the country life of Sandyknowe, in Tweedsdale, and "it is here at Sandy-Knowe, in the residence of my paternal grandfather . . . that I have the first consciousness of existence." Wattie lay on the floor in the farmhouse parlor, stripped and wrapped in the still-warm hide of a sheep, in accordance with someone's suggested remedy for lameness, while his grandfather tried to get him to crawl. "I also distinctly remember the late Sir George MacDougal of Makerstoun . . . in his old fashioned military habit . . . with a small cocked hat, deeply laced, an embroidered scarlet waistcoat, and a light-coloured coat, with milk-white locks tied in a military fashion, kneeling on the ground before me, and dragging his watch along the carpet to induce me to follow it." A visitor to the farm in those days wrote of the grandmother "old Mrs Scott sitting, with her spinning-wheel, at one side of the fire, in a *clean clean* parlour; the grandfather, a good deal failed, in his elbow-chair opposite; and the little boy lying on the carpet, at the old man's feet, listening to the Bible, or whatever good book Miss Jenny was reading to them."

In that placid atmosphere Walter did thrive, though his right leg remained shrunken and useless. On fair days they sent him out with the shepherd to lie on the grass among grazing sheep near the Norman tower; "the impatience of a child soon inclined me to struggle with my infirmity, and I began by degrees to stand, to walk, and to run." He used a crutch to get about. And in that uneventful world, with no other children near, he found ample solitude to mull over the talk of adults around him. "This was during the heat of the American war, and I remember being as anxious on my uncle's weekly visits (for we heard news at no other time) to hear of the defeat of Washington, as if I had had some deep and personal cause of antipathy to him."

But others besides heroes and villains of current affairs came to people his fancies. Those others emerged from the past, that turbulent Scottish past of rapine and rebellion: Bonnie Prince Charlie and the Forty-five, the Old Pretender with his role in the doomed Stuart cause, the Covenanters and Claverhouse, Mary the lovely and luckless queen, Bruce, Wallace. What helped to give life to the past was that Scott's own blood descended from participants in those dramas, for as to his birth, "according to the prejudices of my country, it was esteemed *gentle*, as I was connected, though remotely, with ancient families both by my father's and mother's side." With the Hardens, for instance, and the Buccleuchs, and the Rutherfords, and the Swintons, all names of families that had figured large in border legend or Scottish life.

The cow-bailie of the farm, old Sandy Ormistoun, had tales to tell out of the past as well, knitting stockings under a sunny wall among the crags with the Norman tower looming:

> And still I thought that shatter'd tower
> The mightiest work of human power;
> And marvell'd as the aged hind
> With some strange tale bewitch'd my mind,
> Of forayers, who, with headlong force,
> Down from that strength had spurr'd their horse,
> Their southern rapine to renew,
> Far in the distant Cheviots blue,
> And, home returning, fill'd the hall
> With revel, wassel-rout, and brawl. . . .

In the boy's mind pebbles and shells in ranks on the farmhouse floor served to mimic those antique combats. But though under this regimen his general health was improving as his imagination awakened, the leg got no better. When he was not yet four, they sent him by sea to London, and on from there to Bath, in the company of Aunt Jenny, who had read the Bible to him at Sandyknowe. In this most beautiful of English cities the two remained a year, and yet the spa waters did the boy's leg no good either, so that the lasting benefits of the excursion were other than physical. Those benefits were nevertheless real. Scott's infant memory had taken the imprint of London, so retentively that when the mature writer revisited England's capital a quarter of a century later, he was astounded to discover how accurate were his recollections of its famous sights—the Abbey, the Tower; "I have ever since trusted more implicitly to my juvenile reminiscences." And from Bath his memory (that superb tool that could hold into full maturity not only the image of a watch dragged along a carpet before a child hardly three years old, but the exact looks of the man who dragged it) kept forever the impression of his first play, *As You Like It*, and the way that dreamlike marvel ended: "the bursts of applause, like distant thunder, and the permission afforded to clap our little hands, and add our own scream of delight to a sound so commanding." From that moment (as was true with Irving) Scott remained a lover of theater and of Shakespeare.

When, after his year in Bath, the self-styled grandame's child was brought back to Scotland, it was not to Sandyknowe, but rather to George Square in Edinburgh, where for the most part he would remain until his marriage two decades later. The atmosphere at his father's house was different from what the child had come to know. For one thing, the family had grown—there were four brothers and a sister now. "I felt the change," he wrote later, "from being a single indulged brat, to becoming a member of a large family, very severely." The father himself (not unlike Irving's) was austere: "Sabbath," as his son grown to manhood remembered, "was severely strict, and I think injudiciously so." There were, in addition, the childhood taunts at the boy's lameness; an impatient maid scolded him for his handicap as she lifted him roughly over a stile "which my brothers traversed with shout and bound. I remember the *suppressed bitterness* of the moment . . ." And a sense of inferiority to others of sound limb. And the envy.

But there were pleasures as well: reading aloud to his mother from the wonders and terrors of Pope's Homer, listening to reminiscences, always stories out of the past, that visitors went on telling, here as at Sandyknowe: "What a godsend I must have been as a boy to the old Trojans of 1745, nay 1715"—those Jacobite years of rebellion when the exiled Stuarts were striving through Scotland to regain their lost throne—"who used to frequent my father's house, and who knew as little as I did for what market I was laying up the raw material of their oft-told tales!" And there were other pleasures. In his mother's bedroom he found odd volumes of Shakespeare, whom the performance at Bath had taught him to love, "nor can I easily forget the rapture with which I sate up in my shirt reading them by the light of a fire in her apartment, until the bustle of the family rising from supper warned me it was time to creep back to my bed, where I was supposed to have been safely deposited since nine o'clock."

So his life progressed in George Square, and the boy grew tall and hardy—sandy-haired, a high forehead, somewhat slovenly in dress, strong. He was twelve years old, a satchel-bearing student at the Edinburgh High School, reading widely but without system, neglecting his studies, compensatorily scrambling over Salisbury Crags and Castle Rock, making a name of sorts for himself as a storyteller among his classmates. But at one point "my health had become rather delicate from rapid growth, and my father was easily persuaded to allow me to spend half-a-year at Kelso with my kind aunt," the doting Aunt Jenny who had accompanied him to Bath and had now moved from Sandyknowe to a small house in this market town five miles eastward.

At Kelso events occurred that were to affect the remainder of Scott's life. Here, in what the poet later called "the most beautiful, if not the most romantic village in Scotland," close to the ruined abbey, to Roxburgh Castle, to the flowing Tweed and Teviot, he developed an exultant feeling for the beauties of inhabited nature, so intense a feeling that it "has never since deserted me." Here, too, in the local school that he attended a few hours each day, he began a lifelong friendship with a classmate named James Ballantyne, son of a Kelso draper. Much would come of that friendship, which only at the very end would cool. And here in Kelso, in his aunt's garden, young Scott discovered, among his far-ranging readings of travel books, of history, of Spenser and Ossian and other poets celebrating worlds of vanished glory, one book that stunned his fancy, Bishop Percy's collection of medieval ballads, the *Reliques of Ancient Poetry*. In its pages the boy was overjoyed to find the kind of simple verse that had haunted him throughout his childhood "considered as the subject of sober research, grave commentary, and apt illustration . . ." In the shade of a huge platanus tree in the garden he became absorbed in this treasure; "the summer day sped onward so fast, that notwithstanding the sharp appetite of thirteen, I forgot the hour of dinner, was sought for with anxiety, and was still found entranced in my intellectual banquet."

Nearly forty years later Scott at the height of his powers revisited the spot where as a child he had almost missed a meal: "the huge Platanus had died, like most of its kind, in the beginning of this century," and everything else about the garden had changed for the worse. But the image remained and does remain, of a boy rapt in wonder—"nor do I believe I ever read a book . . . with half the enthusiasm"—among yew hedges and labyrinths of a garden in a Scottish village, mind filled with joy as a summer afternoon in 1783 drew to a close, in that year when Colonel Aaron Burr was coming down to Manhattan, on the other side of the Atlantic, to commence his practice of law, in that same year when the youngest son of Deacon Irving was born.

"Did I ever pass unhappy years any where?" Scott asked himself when he was in his mid-fifties. "None that I remember——." Unhappy days, unhappy weeks, even once or twice unhappy months. But no years that were unhappy "save those at the High school which I thoroughly detested on account of the confinement" (like young Irving on Fulton Street in America, mewed up the livelong day in that purgatory of boyhood, a schoolroom). "I disliked serving in my father's office too from the same hatred to restraint." As for the schooling, Scott did endure it, even as far as the University of Edinburgh. But he was much of "a roaring boy in my youth, a desperate climber, a bold rider, a deep drinker and a stout player at single stick," so that most of his vast if erratic learning was gained outside the classroom and after play, with the aid of his fabulous memory and a marvelous sense of the past. By means of wide reading, each century before his own grew to be distinct in Scott's maturing mind; each lived vividly through whatever medium he entered it—diaries, journals, wills, sermons, ballads, contracts: then and throughout a lifetime his reading devoured them all. And he was able in time to absorb with ease much that was written in German, French, Italian, Spanish, and Latin, and always for story—for what he could learn of how people behaved in times past.

But his father would have him a lawyer; what other profession was open to a gentleman? Only the military, and the young man's lameness closed that glamorous avenue of escape. So in the mid-1780s he "entered upon the dry and barren wilderness of forms and conveyances." For law's "musty arts" he cared scarcely more than Irving would in New York a few years later; though like the American, he did see the task through, and on July 11, 1792, passed the examinations that entitled him to don the long black gown of an advocate.

And he even practiced law for a while, with some success. It was by no means a bad life. Within the great outer hall of the old Scottish Parliament House, next to St. Giles Cathedral on Edinburgh's teeming High Street, he would gather each morning with other members of his profession, on the lookout for clients among that noisy, congenial throng, candles dimly lighting the crowded scene, dusty portraits brooding down from the stone walls, bewigged lawyers and judges—an occasional red velvet gown among a preponderance of black ones—conducting business together or simply gossiping and molding new friendships around the three great iron stoves when business languished. The jovial society extended itself after hours into smoky lounges and pubs about—

for claret at Bayles's, Walker's, Fortune's—or into the numerous oyster cellars for rum punch or pots of porter. And there were clubs to help fill leisure time. In this cultured town, for instance, "where the remarkable coincidence between the German language and the lowland Scottish, encouraged young men to approach this newly discovered spring of literature, a class"—Scott tells us—"was formed of six or seven intimate friends, who proposed to make themselves acquainted with the German language." The young barrister was among the group, and within a few years was translating German poetry and even seeing it in print—his first published work.

So his life was changing. "The love of Solitude was with me a passion of early youth," this famously sociable being recorded late in life, "when in my teens I used to fly from company to indulge visions and airy Castles of my own, the disposal of ideal wealth and the exercize of imaginary power. The feeling prevaild even till I was eighteen when Love and Ambition awaking with other passions threw me more into society . . ." At the time it seemed that ambition could be gratified only by laboring "hard and well" at the irksome legal profession: doing so at least rendered the young man useful to his father, whom he loved despite the sternness. On his father's behalf, for instance, Scott in the early 1790s journeyed southward some forty miles to Jedburgh, in Rox-burghshire, to obtain a brief from the Lord Justice-Clerk on circuit there. The trip was business, but it turned into pleasure.

Jedburgh is a village close to the English border, on the edge of Liddesdale, a sparsely populated region of heathery moorland, without roads, unaltered for centuries. Into that wild region the young lawyer let himself be guided by the local sheriff-substitute, in quest of ballads like the ones he had loved from childhood, ballads that had been sung in those parts from generation to generation but that even then were start-ing to fade from men's memories. The two wanderers had a marvelous time on their raid, visiting cottagers, sleeping out in the open on peat stacks, stumbling through moss hags, meeting and learning what they could from gypsies, tinkers, farm laborers. Scott "never made himsell the great man, or took ony airs in the company," the sheriff recalled years later—and even the recollection was a delight: "Ah me, sic an endless fund o' humour and drollery as he then had wi' him. Never ten yards but we were either laughing or roaring and singing." On holidays there-after for six successive years the barrister was to return to Jedburgh to journey with Sheriff Shortreed into Liddesdale in quest of more ballads, songs he adored to discover on old people's lips, hunting such rarities as others hunt game: "He was *makin' himsell* a' the time," the old Scotsman realized much later, "but he didna ken maybe what he was about till years had passed: At first he thought o' little, I dare say, but the queer-ness and the fun."

Scott's father back in Edinburgh, meanwhile, feared his son was turning into a "*gangrel scrape-gut*"—a rascally fiddler—with all that talk about ballads and ballads. Back home the young man would tarry within his cramped den on the sunk floor of his father's home in George Square, among piles of dingy books and manuscript ballads that overflowed available shelf space; on the walls hung a claymore, a war ax, a print of Prince Charlie. Scribbling, dreaming in that sanctuary: would anything ever come of all his browsing among dead words?

And he had fallen in love. Ambition and love, he tells us, were what brought him into society. There were three girls in succession. Jessie was a Kelso beauty who came to Edinburgh to tend a sick aunt; teen-age Walter would hide in the aunt's closet, among crockery, haddocks, and marmalade, until the old woman fell asleep and Jessie could escape:

> Come hither! You my closet are
> Where all my sweets are stored,
> Oh save me from your aunt's good things
> And some of yours afford.

That romance dwindled in time, to be replaced by a more potent one. On a rainy Sunday morning in 1792, as he was emerging from a service in Greyfriars Church, the nineteen-year-old Scott was moved to share his umbrella with a young lady and fellow congregationalist wearing a silk embroidered walking cape under a green mantle. Her name proved to be Williamina Belsches; she was fourteen, blue-eyed and lovely, and her family lived near and was acquainted with the Scotts, as Walter learned on their walk together from church toward George Square that same rainy Sunday. During the next five years, the girl came to dominate his thoughts. Her rank in society was considerably higher than his, but gradually the lame young barrister learned to hope, and at last came to feel that he and his "*chère adorable*" would be married.

He was mistaken. In January 1797, Williamina married the wealthy William Forbes, a banker's son whom she had only recently come to know. It was a crushing blow for Scott; at first friends feared for his reason. Before long he did get his emotions outwardly under control, but as late as thirty years afterward, the recollection of her name (so he confided to himself alone) could still agitate his heart. And though Forbes in that small, gregarious society of Edinburgh became a "kind honest friend" and aid to Scott in later days, so that the two men saw each other often, in no letter of Scott's from 1797 onward is Forbes' wife, who lived in the same town until her death in 1810, ever mentioned or alluded to.

"What a life mine has been," the great author summarized to his private journal concerning these early years. "Half educated, almost wholly neglected or left to myself—stuffing my head with most nonsensical trash and undervalued in society for a time by most of my companions—getting forward and held a bold and clever fellow, contrary to the opinion of all who thought me a mere dreamer—Brokenhearted for two years—My heart handsomely pieced again—but the crack will remain till my dying day—. . . ."

The crack had endured for at least three decades when he wrote those words, one dire Sunday night soon after half past eight, December 18, 1825. The piecing of his heart, to be sure, had been undertaken so promptly after Williamina's marriage those many years before, at the beginning of 1797, as to suggest that her disappointed lover was bitterly on the rebound. That same summer of 1797, in fact, on a trip across the border into England's Lake District, the jilted Scott had chanced to see and be struck by the beauty of a dark-haired girl on horseback. He saw her again that evening, a guest with her chaperone in the resort hotel where the visiting Scotsman was staying. And he got to know her. She was a young French lady a few months older than he was, surrounded by various admirers, one "a puny fop," another "a wordy youth trained early for a statesman's part," a third, as he seemed to Scott in amused recollection, "a walking haberdashery of feathers, lace and fur." All things came together: Charlotte Carpenter's admired beauty, Scott's own forlornness, the distant place, the time; so that before the year had ended, after a whirlwind courtship of passionate letters and poetry, the two were married, at Carlisle, Christmas Eve 1797.

This was the lady Washington Irving met and came to know at Abbotsford twenty years later, the mother of Scott's four children. To the American visitor Mrs. Scott seemed not always to understand her husband's humors, "and would now and then make a casual remark which would operate a little like a damper. Thus, one morning at breakfast, when Dominie Thompson the tutor was present, Scott was going on with great glee to relate an anecdote of the laird of Macnab, 'who, poor fellow!' premised he, 'is dead and gone—' 'Why, Mr. Scott,' exclaimed the good lady, 'Macnab's not dead, is he?' 'Faith, my dear,' replied Scott, with humorous gravity, 'if he's not dead they've done him great injustice, —for they've buried him.' " Scott's little joke "passed harmless and unnoticed by Mrs. Scott," so Irving reports, "but hit the poor Dominie just as he had raised a cup of tea to his lips, causing a burst of laughter which sent half of the contents about the table."

Others, no doubt, had a laugh at Mrs. Scott's expense—at her overdressed little form in later life, her imperishable French accent, her plump bourgeois indifference to Scott's writing—"nonsense," as she called it, that served to put rugs on the floors at Abbotsford. But she had been handsome and enticing when her husband first knew her: "In about 3 weeks," he wrote late in 1797, deliriously in love, "I think I shall wrap you in *my Tartan plaid* and call myself the happiest of human beings— O I will be so good to my little stranger and love her *so dearly*." And at the end of Charlotte's life, at the end of the long road they would journey together, Scott deeply mourned the loss of one to whom "all might be safely confided." Thus, a month after her death: "Bad dreams about poor Charlotte—woke thinking my old and inseparable friend beside me and it was only when I was fully awake that I could persuade myself that she was dark low and distant—and that my bed was widowd . . ."

His inseparable friend. Not long after their marriage they had acquired a home in the new town of Edinburgh, at 39 North Castle Street, where they were to live through all but the very end of their married life. Their home was within sight of Edinburgh Castle beyond the southern termination of the street, sprawled on its great rock above drained Nor' Loch at the western edge of the old town, to which precincts the new husband now either limped each morning during term time or rode in the Clerks' Coach to pursue his legal calling. His companions had more reason to think of him these days as "a bold and clever fellow," for he was getting ahead. His new wife received an allowance from her brother, as did he, from his father; he was earning money at the bar; and in 1799 he secured the appointment of sheriff-deputy of Selkirkshire. Not long afterward, in 1804, an uncle died and left Scott a valuable property, some thirty acres of rich land near Kelso that the new owner was not tardy in selling to add to his income. And soon, in 1806, he received yet another appointment that would become lucrative, as one of the Principal Clerks to the Court of Session, a post he held and discharged dutifully in Edinburgh for twenty-five years.

Yet with all these claims on his time—a wife, a growing family, new responsibilities—Scott had not abandoned his interest in ballads. By 1802 that lively interest would result in the publication of the first two volumes of a three-volume work that might reasonably have been expected to take a lifetime to prepare. *The Minstrelsy of the Scottish Border* preserves and brilliantly annotates some of the great folk poetry in the language, poetry that might otherwise have been lost forever. "Johnie Armstrang" and forty-two other ballads appear there in print for the first time, among the precious fruit plucked during those happy excursions Scott made through Liddesdale and Perthshire during the 1790s.

Indeed, the notes to the ballads alone—those new ones as well as other ballads already familiar but here printed in alternate versions—are enough to demonstrate Scott's iron hold on the multitudinous details of Scottish history; probably no one else alive at the time could have written so knowledgeably and comprehensively about Scotland's involved and colorful past. So the dreamer and "roaring boy" had shown himself in his early thirties to be a clever fellow indeed, more than a mere browser in old books and affable mimic and storyteller at Edinburgh dinner tables. And while he found other interests to add to these present ones as his career advanced, he went on exhibiting his impressive skills as antiquary and editor for the rest of his life. In 1808, for example, appeared his eighteen-volume edition of the Complete Works of Dryden, still after a hundred and seventy years definitive. And in 1814 appeared his nineteen-volume edition of the Life and Complete Works of Swift, on which he had been laboring for six years previous (during that period when he first came to know of *Knickerbocker's History*, ". . . so closely resembling the style of Dean Swift . . .").

For a barrister, public servant, and busy family man, such an outpouring of learned prose in his spare time might have seemed enough. But soon after the publication of the third volume of his *Minstrelsy* in 1803, Scott had begun dreaming of one more song, a lay that "the last of all the Bards" along the Scottish border might sing—*The Lay of the Last Minstrel*. He began to write it, a poem of his own now, not verse heard and recorded from other people's lips, not lines translated from German, but rather six long cantos of a narrative he himself had devised, drawing on what he knew of Scotland's past, its history and legend, conveyed in lines filled with the sound of braying war horns, with the fury of border raids, with images of a languishing golden-haired lady and a wizard entombed in the moonlit ruins of ancient Melrose Abbey, with steeds spurred and foaming-mouthed, with a goblin dwarf, combat on the moors at midnight, gory wounds from which broken lances protrude. And when it was published, this verse chronicle of border life in the sixteenth century created a sensation. At thirty-three, Scott had abruptly revealed a portion of his gifts that few could have suspected he possessed.

One who knew him, and lived in Edinburgh during those times of excitement and discovery, conceded afterward that "Walter Scott's vivacity and force had been felt since his boyhood by his comrades," but before 1805 "his power of great original conception and execution was unknown both to his friends and himself." Now, with the completed draft of *The Lay of the Last Minstrel* on his desk, the barrister ambling into print in his thirties as a poet had finally resolved to devote himself to imaginative literature. But he would hold on to his position as sheriff, and would aspire to—and soon obtain—that appointment as Clerk of Session. For "I determined," he wrote later, "that literature should be my staff, but not my crutch . . ."

Thus, in the autumn of 1806, while continuing to discharge his public duties and working on the monumental edition of Dryden, he began another long poem, which appeared two years later—to even more resounding acclaim. Any English-speaking lovers of poetry who had somehow not yet read *The Lay* assuredly read *Marmion* soon after it appeared. Now Scott's name was on everyone's lips, by means of this verse tale of treachery, with its images doleful and haunting—nuns in passage on the green sea-foam of northern waters, dungeons dank and clanking, torch-lit banquet halls, the turmoil of fateful battle at Flodden

Field. Scott's literary triumph was complete. And yet, as a contemporary noted, "his advances were like the conquests of Napoleon: each new achievement overshadowing the last." For two years after *Marmion*, the most astonishingly popular of all his poems appeared.

It was in this interval, on New Year's Day 1809, between the publication of *Marmion* and *The Lady of the Lake*, that a political exile from America then visiting Edinburgh recorded in his journal, "Called on Walter Scott," about whose "animation" Aaron Burr was soon writing his daughter Theodosia: "talks much and very agreeably. May be about forty. . . ." Scott was, in fact, thirty-seven when former Vice President Burr met him and, during frequent visits, "received civilities and hospitalities." At the time the writer was busy indeed. He had "both another Scotch poem and a *Scotch novel* on the stocks," so his printer James Ballantyne, that former school friend from Kelso, confided to the English publisher John Murray. Scott was also deeply involved in establishing a new conservative magazine to rival the popular Whig *Edinburgh Review* and in writing articles to help with its launching. In addition, he was forming a new publishing house and preparing antiquarian material for its list, all the while continuing with his legal duties in Edinburgh and Selkirkshire.

Long afterward, the lawyer-author was reminded of the hectic pace of those years, when each day was crammed with projects to perform. "Ay, it was enough to tear me to pieces," he agreed, "but there was a wonderful exhilaration about it all: my blood was kept at fever-pitch—I felt as if I could have grappled with any thing and every thing .. ." The Scotch novel that Ballantyne mentions did not soon appear in print, but the poem did, in May 1810, set in the Highlands among the craggy wilds of the Trossachs and over the remote and beautiful Loch Katrine. The spot is tamed now, tamed by Scott's pen, so that today's visitor securely walks the edge of that Highland lake along a broad asphalt path, rather too much protected by a cast-iron white railing that draws its long, obtrusive lines for miles along the lake shore. Resort hotels thrust upward over the treetops; souvenir shops cluster about the parking lot at the pier; the ferries chug back and forth from the mainland to the island where fair Ellen is supposed to have dwelled. Indeed, this dubious transformation began at once; English crowds with the newly published *Lady of the Lake* reechoing in their consciousness swarmed northward to have a look at wild Loch Katrine, and "as the book came out just before the season of excursions, every house and inn in the neighborhood was crammed with a constant succession of visitors. It is a well-ascertained fact," wrote an observer of those happenings in the early nineteenth century, "that from the date of the publication of the Lady of the Lake the post-horse duty in Scotland rose in an extraordinary degree"—and kept on rising, as a new tourist industry was born out of the verse of Walter Scott. And even those who couldn't come to see the Highlands right away longed and made plans to. Thus Washington Irving, that summer of 1810, along the sun-dappled banks of the Hudson across the Atlantic, mused with delight over the northern world of Snowden's knight and Scotland's king, while the busy ant was traversing the page in his lap that held Scott's newest, most ravishing poem.

This year, then, and the next, saw Walter Scott at the height of his influence as a poet. He was the most famous living poet in the English-speaking world, "Monarch of Parnassus," as he was called by "one of his subjects," an aristocratic young English lyricist and satirist just then launching his own career as a writer of narrative verse. In March 1812, the first two cantos of that young man's *Childe Harold's Pilgrimage* were published; and with that enormously successful work, Lord Byron, too, leapt instantly into a position of extraordinary fame— the new lion of London society—and "the reign of Scott" (again, Byron's phrase) was suddenly challenged.

It didn't matter that neither writer was eager for competition. "If they want to depose him," Byron remarked of Scott, "I only wish they would not set me up as a competitor. . . . I like the man—and admire his works to what Mr. Braham calls *Entusymusy*. All such stuff can only vex him, and do me no good." Admittedly the English poet had not always felt so generously disposed. After the *Edinburgh Review* had dealt severely with his first volume of lyrics, Byron, then hardly twenty, had a few years earlier, in 1808, responded with spirit in his *English Bards, and Scotch Reviewers*, attacking all things Scottish, including the poet who had received £1,000 for *Marmion* before a line of it was written:

> No! when the sons of song descend to trade,
> Their bays are sear, their former laurels fade,
> Let such forego the poet's sacred name,
> Who rack their brains for lucre, not for fame . . .

And so on through several additional lines that mention *Marmion* specifically and refer to a "prostituted Muse," a "hireling bard." "It is funny enough," Scott had responded privately to Southey after coming upon the lines the following year, "to see a whelp of a young Lord Byron abusing me, of whose circumstances he knows nothing, for endeavouring to scratch out a living with my pen. God help the bear, if, having little else to eat, he must not even suck his own paws. I can assure the noble imp of fame it is not my fault that I was not born to a park and £5000 a-year, as it is not his lordship's merit, although it may be his great good fortune, that he was not born to live by his literary talents or success."

So at first, around 1809, neither Byron nor the understandably irritated Scott had cared much for the other. But within three years, the older writer had learned through the publisher Murray that the English-man had suppressed his youthful satirical attack and repented of it. By then, in the spring of 1812, *Childe Harold* had appeared, "a poem of most extraordinary power," in Scott's opinion, which "may rank its author with our first poets." To Murray's efforts at peacemaking he now responded by writing Byron directly, "to put your Lordship right in the circumstances respecting the sale of Marmion, which had reached you in a distorted and misrepresented form . . ." Scott had not bargained with his publisher about the price, nor had he received any additional recom-pense for that enormously popular production. "The poem, my Lord, was *not* written upon contract for a sum of money—though it is too true that it was sold and published in a very unfinished state (which I have since regretted) to enable me to extricate myself from some engage-ments which fell suddenly upon me by the unexpected misfortunes of a very near relation. . . .

"I am sure," Scott went on in this initial letter to Byron, "your Lordship's good sense will easily put this unimportant egotism to the right account, for—though I do not know the motive would make me enter into controversy with a fair or an *unfair* literary critic—I may be well excused for a wish to clear my personal character from any tinge of mercenary or sordid feeling in the eyes of a contemporary of genius. Your Lordship will likewise permit me to add, that you would have escaped the trouble of this explanation, had I not understood that the satire alluded to had been suppressed, not to be reprinted. For in re-moving a prejudice on your Lordship's own mind, I had no intention of making any appeal by or through you to the public . . ."

The letter reveals Scott to perfection—proud, correct, respectful of genius but without a trace of fawning. Byron's reply, July 6, 1812, is equally admirable: "Sir,—I have just been honoured with your letter.— I feel sorry that you should have thought it worth while to notice the 'evil works of my nonage' as the thing is suppressed *voluntarily* & your explanation is too kind not to give me pain.—The satire was written when I was very young & very angry, & fully bent on displaying my wrath & my wit, & now I am haunted by the ghosts of my wholesale Assertions.—I cannot sufficiently thank you for your praise . . ."

And from that time on the friendship between these quite different writers was constant and heartfelt. Joanna Baillie might write Scott a few years later (not altogether accurately, as we shall see) that Byron had been sharing quarters on the banks of Lake Geneva with "a married man who has run away from this country, and a girl whom he has seduced, and that their house was anything but a respectable one." And she could press forward: "Oh! why have you endeavored to reconcile the world in some degree with that unhappy man, at the expense of having yourself perhaps considered as regarding want of all principle and the vilest corruption with an indulgent eye? Indeed, my good, my kind, my unwearied friend, this goes to my heart!" But even before such strident onslaughts Scott's loyalty to his young friend never wavered—not through the latter's divorce, or self-exile, or well-publicized scandalous life on the Continent.

For his part, an older Byron, with much behind him to have grown cynical about, would write from Genoa in 1823 to Henri Beyle (who, as Stendhal, was to compose two of the greatest of French novels) concerning a published essay that found fault with Scott: "You say that 'his character is little worthy of enthusiasm,' at the same time that you mention his productions in the manner they deserve. I have known Walter Scott long and well," Byron testified at that later time, "and in occasional situations which call forth the *real* character—and I can assure you that his character *is* worthy of admiration—that of all men he is the most *open*, the most *honourable*, the most *amiable*. With his politics I have nothing to do: they differ from mine, which renders it difficult for me to speak of them. But he is *perfectly sincere* in them: and Sincerity may be humble, but she cannot be servile. I pray you, therefore, to correct or soften that passage. You may, perhaps, attribute this officiousness of mine to a false affectation of *candour*, as I happen to be a writer also. Attribute it to what motive you please, but *believe* the *truth*. I say that Walter Scott is as nearly a thorough good man as man can be, because I *know* it by experience to be the case."

But that judgment lay a decade in the future, to be given in the year before Byron's death. Now, as for the tales in verse that were coming from Walter Scott's pen from 1813 on, they would all falter under his Lordship's shadow, however much and uncharacteristically the older poet might labor over them. *Rokeby* appeared in January of that year, a work that Scott himself in time dismissed as "pseudo-romance of pseudo-chivalry." And later in 1813, struggling with another poem, which would become *The Lord of the Isles*, Scott seemed still daunted by Lord Byron's swelling success; "James," he remarked humbly to his friend Ballantyne, "Byron hits the mark where I don't even pretend to fledge my arrow."

So the antiquary turned poet was finding his inspiration flagging. At this point in his life, in the autumn of 1813, at his newly acquired summer cottage at Abbotsford, Scott went looking one morning for fishing tackle upstairs in a lumber garret, in a cabinet that he hardly used any more. One drawer he opened in that search for lines and flies revealed a dog-eared pile of manuscript, the beginnings of a story in prose about the Stuart Rebellion of 1745 that he had started to write eight years earlier and then abandoned after a friend had read it without enthusiasm. This may have been the "Scotch novel" Ballantyne mentioned in 1809; in any case, its author had totally forgotten what had become of the manuscript in the interval. Now having unexpectedly rediscovered it, he took time to read through the pages again, then determined at least to finish what he had begun. That he did rapidly, the final two volumes of it in three weeks. The subtitle of this novel of the Forty-five hardly accorded with the time the author had let pass by: " 'Tis Fifty Years Since." He changed "fifty" to "sixty." But the title he left as it was: *Waverley*.

Scott's future son-in-law, John Lockhart, happened to be visiting a friend in George Street, Edinburgh, one warm summer afternoon in June 1814. This was some seven months after the fortuitous rediscovery of that long-lost manuscript of *Waverley*, during which time its author had been busy, as usual, with a dozen unrelated projects—articles on Drama and Chivalry for the *Encyclopaedia Britannica*, completion of his comprehensive work on Swift, which would appear during the summer, a new, long poem much on his mind, always his official duties at Parliament House. Now in June, however, during three weeks of unremitting effort, Scott had returned to his novel and was pushing it through to completion.

Nearby, in the house in George Street, young Lockhart and his friends were gathered in the library to pass the bottle around. A second bottle was uncorked, then a third. But after an hour or more of good fellowship, the party's host was seen to grow moody. Was he ill? "No," the young man answered Lockhart's question. "I shall be well enough presently, if you will only let me sit where you are, and take my chair; for there is a confounded hand in sight of me here"—out the library window looking northward—"which has often bothered me before, and now it won't let me fill my glass with a good will."

As Lockhart rose obligingly to change places, the host pointed out the offending sight, past a little garden and beyond a neighboring window in a building at right angles that would be facing Castle Street. "Since we sat down, I have been watching it—it fascinates my eye—it never stops—page after page is finished and thrown on that heap of MS., and still it goes on unwearied—and so it will be till candles are brought in, and God knows how long after that. It is the same every night—I can't stand the sight of it when I am not at my books."

"Some stupid, dogged, engrossing clerk probably," Lockhart or another guest remarked in an effort to make light of so troublesome a neighbor.

"No, boys," the host assured them, "I well know what hand it is— 'tis Walter Scott's."

And the hand wrote on, filling page after marvelous page. But the young gentlemen who watched in dismay could not know what the hand was writing, nor could any except a very few be certain of Scott's achievement even as *Waverley* appeared. For the author chose to publish his novel anonymously. He had a friend, James Ballantyne's brother, transcribe the manuscript to disguise its penmanship, then submitted it for publication to Constable & Company, just before departing indifferently on a six weeks' sea voyage around Scotland to visit the Northern Islands.

But why the secrecy? "My original motive for publishing the work anonymously," Scott wrote years later, "was the consciousness that it was an experiment on the public taste which might very probably fail . . ." Was there any reason needlessly to risk the enormous reputation he had won as a poet? "Of literary fame, whether merited or undeserved, I had already as much as might have contented a mind more ambitious than mine; and in entering into this new contest for reputation, I might be said rather to endanger what I had, than to have any considerable chance of acquiring more." So the book appeared with no author's name on the title page, left to make its way on content alone.

In fact, the impression *Waverley* made in Edinburgh, according to one who witnessed the furor, was "instant and universal." Returning from his trip to the North, Scott found the entire town talking about this stirring novel of the Forty-five. "The unexpected newness of the thing," Lord Cockburn, who was in the midst of the excitement, later recalled, "the profusion of original characters, the Scotch language, Scotch scenery, Scotch men and women, the simplicity of the writing, and the graphic force of the descriptions, all struck us with an electric shock of delight." Quickly the fame of *Waverley* swept southward to England, then overseas. Who had written it, though, this Great Unknown who soon followed his first success with successes even vaster? *Guy Mannering*, written over Christmas of that same year, was published in 1815 to louder acclaim than its predecessor. In 1816 appeared no less than three more novels by the new and prolific writer: *The Antiquary*, *The Black Dwarf*, and a masterpiece, *Old Mortality*.

But who was their author? "The speculations and conjectures, and nods and winks, and predictions and assertions were endless," Lord Cockburn tells us, "and occupied every company, and almost every two men who met and spoke in the street. It was proved by a thousand indications, each refuting the other, and all equally true in fact, that they were written by old Henry Mackenzie, and by George Cranstoun, and William Erskine, and Jeffrey, and above all by Thomas Scott, Walter's brother, a regimental paymaster, then in Canada." And meanwhile, Walter himself, coolly, courteously, and firmly went on denying authorship to those who were ill-bred enough to put the question to him point blank: "Mr. Wright, the author of *Waverley* whoever he may be, gets people to buy his books without a name; and he would be a greater fool than I think he is, were he to give a name." Or the poet might point out that though he was not the author of those celebrated prose works, obviously whoever the author was desired not to be known, and therefore would be entitled to deny authorship if asked directly—as Scott himself would do even if he were their author.

Yet why did he keep up the pretense, which after all required an effort—of duplicate proofsheets so that corrections could be transcribed in another hand, of letters answered through a third person, the Kelso childhood friend James Ballantyne ("Madame, I am desired by the Author of *Waverley* to acknowledge, in his name, . . .")? Scott explained later that it had simply been his humor, like Shylock's. (Irving, too, we remember, enjoyed the mystification of pseudonyms, and would go on using them through much of his life.) Lockhart thought the device was a way of sparing an author remarkably free of vanity those tedious, flattering conversations that otherwise would invariably turn on his work whenever he stepped into society. But for whatever reason, the mask of authorship was kept in place for many years; as late as 1825, for instance, eleven years after the first of the novels appeared, Scott on a triumphal visit to Ireland could reply publicly to a Dublin librarian who was apologizing for not yet having read *Redgauntlet*, latest success of the author of *Waverley*, "I have not happened to fall in with such a work, Doctor."

It would have been one thing to lay claim to what he had not done. To decline to acknowledge what he had so meritoriously accomplished seemed something else entirely. The printer James Ballantyne and the publisher Archibald Constable were two, however, who knew the identity of the Great Unknown very early—and who knew thus what name to write on checks that paid the author his share of profits in this grand new enterprise. For from 1814 on Scott's energies were keeping Ballantyne's presses in the Canongate humming merrily late night after night, and profits were proving to be enormous. To understand just how enormous, we should note that an artisan in the United Kingdom at about this time might make £55 a year; a miner laboring under horrifying conditions and for long hours might make as little as £40 a year; a farm hand might make £30 a year. By contrast, Scott (who, to be sure, was neither farm hand, miner, nor artisan) was paid outright £1,500 for the initial rights to *Guy Mannering*, written in six weeks, and much more came to him from subsequent editions of that same work. Later novels earned comparable rewards—for instance, another £1,500 for *Ivanhoe* in 1819, for first rights, plus half-profits, at a time when a schoolmaster might make annually £120, when a shopkeeper might feel pleased to make £150 in a year.

Scott was the first of the best-selling novelists, and his earnings still seem, in our own inflated age, impressive. They had seemed dramatic even when, years earlier in 1807, the publisher Archibald Constable had caused eyebrows to lift by generously offering £1,000 for *Marmion* sight unseen, simply on the basis of the success of *The Lay of the Last*

Minstrel. But such fees, heady enough then, would have seemed tame now to the wizard whose wells of inspiration seemed as inexhaustible as they were obviously estimable and rare. And the wizard meanwhile had discovered ways to spend the money he made.

There were the trips he loved, no fewer than fourteen of them to London during his lifetime, when London was at the distant end of comfortless roads or wearisome, long sea lanes. But Scott would travel in style, a carriage for his wife, others laden with luggage, his hounds accompanying him, and alongside the extravagant caravan ponies for the children. Wherever he went he was known: in Selkirkshire as the respected sheriff, elsewhere in Scotland as the innkeeper's friend who had all but created the tourist trade, in England as the explicator of Scottish ways who had done more than anyone else to enlarge understanding between the neighboring nations. The summer of 1815 found Scott in London attending a "snug little dinner" in his honor at Carlton House given by the plump Prince Regent, and passing down Albemarle Street or along Bond Street arm in arm with his admired and admiring fellow poet Lord Byron, each with his limp, the middle-aged, six-foot Scottish lawyer alongside the pale, handsome young English nobleman. Later that summer Scott crossed the Channel to visit Waterloo, its ground still strewn with unsalable flotsam—hats, shoes, empty cartridges—of the battle that was then scarcely six weeks into the past. Lunching at a nearby inn the traveler-historian bought his share of the more valuable leavings of rifles and swords and buttons. Then, additionally burdened, he lumbered on elatedly to Paris, now aswarm with English tourists who, for more than a quarter of a century, all during the Revolutionary and Napoleonic years, had been deprived of access to this most enchanting of cities. In so victorious an atmosphere Scott was, of course, introduced to—and delighted in the company of—that other conqueror, the Duke of Wellington.

There were travels as elaborate in later years, to Ireland, for example, where the Scotsman was received as a veritable hero—crowds gaping from shops and streetcorners wherever he ventured to go. And when he returned from such journeys, it might be either to "dear old 39," his town house on Castle Street in Edinburgh, or—more likely—now to his new and burgeoning country home along Tweedside. For as far back as the spring of 1811, the poet whose *Lady of the Lake* had appeared a year earlier had found a further use for the phenomenal profits that the poem had earned him; he had "resolved," so he wrote James Ballantyne, "to purchase a piece of ground sufficient for a cottage & a few fields." Two pieces of property were for sale along the Tweed, halfway between Melrose and Selkirk. "I have serious thoughts of purchasing one or both and I must have recourse to my pen to make the matter easy. . . ." That very summer he effected the purchase of one—a neglected farm, unfenced, undrained, with a small farmhouse, a barn, and a duck pond on it, as well as marshland, hill pastures, and a single line of fir trees newly planted. The price was high: £4,200. Clarty Hole it was called, but remembering the crossing of the Tweed that the monks of Melrose in medieval times used to make near this spot, Scott promptly changed the name to Abbotsford.

By the spring of the following year, May 1812, he and his wife and children were taking up residence there, after one more colorful journey five miles eastward along the river from Ashesteil, the country house he had previously leased from a relative over nine summers. Twenty horse-drawn wagons and carriages transported the family's accumulated belongings down the highway: "I assure your ladyship," Scott reported to a friend at the time, "that this caravan, attended by a dozen of ragged rosy peasant children, carrying fishing-rods and spears, and leading poneys, greyhounds, and spaniels, would, as it crossed the Tweed, have furnished no bad object for the pencil"—caravan of an antiquary's chattel, including old swords, lances, bows, and a family of turkeys.

Once in place, he set about immediately converting the land, planting trees—oaks and pines and larches and chestnuts—more trees and ever more trees. Relics of the past he clutched at when he could, and paid for them handsomely to put in his farmhouse—thumbscrews and border war-horns, the great wooden door of the Edinburgh Tolbooth prison, a human skull (around which at night he would sometimes wrap his neckpiece like a turban)—all those mute, moldering objects out of the past that his sensibilities could invest with such vigor and feeling. Friends shopped for him at auctions in London, and sent him what they found: rare books, for example, or "that splendid lot of ancient armour, advertised by Winstanley." And always he was ready to buy more land; by 1816, the original hundred and fifty acres that was Clarty Hole had grown to nearly a thousand, and plans were afoot to buy still more, and to alter the little farm cottage into a mansion that would house the new laird of Abbotsford in appropriate style.

Money was needed, of course, and the author made money as no author had ever made money before. In that very year 1816 appeared, in addition to three separate novels (three novels in a year!), Scott's account of his travels in Belgium and France, entitled *Paul's Letters to His Kinsfolk*, as well as a book-length History of 1814 (880 pages of duodecimo) for the *Edinburgh Annual Register*. For all these various efforts he was paid unprecedentedly well, and those earnings he meant to devote to making a dream become real in glass and stone. Accordingly, masons and carpenters and glaziers and gardeners arrived in ever increasing numbers to perform ever more elaborate, ever more expensive feats of craftsmanship, making the air at Tweedside resound with ring of chisel, slice of dibble, thud of spade.

Guests arrived too. They found the laird "Social, Joyous, full of anecdote of irrepressible good spirits." This despite his preoccupations and his serious illness of gallstones in the spring of 1817. The painter Wilkie, for instance, come to do a portrait of the guest-plagued Scott and his family in the fall of that same year, waited considerably before imposing himself on the hours of a man so busy and besieged. He was hoping to find an interlude after guests had all gone when the author might have returned to his work for a while and so be willing to spare a part of a morning for sitting. Miraculously, the guests did leave at one point, every one of them but Wilkie himself—and what Scott did was immediately make plans for an excursion to hunt hare with his good friend Laidlaw before other guests arrived: "Laidlaw, to-morrow morning we'll go across the water and take the dogs with us." In short, Wilkie discovered that his subject apparently required no time away from company, always appeared to have leisure to amble with guests among his flourishing plantations, or guide them proudly to Rhymer's Glen or the remains of the Roman camp on his land, or read to them with his deep Scottish burr in the evening, or set out with them on a whole day's outing at the start of another week, as he and his daughters were setting out with Washington Irving Monday morning, the first day of September 1817, happy in an open carriage behind black horses, bound for Dryburgh Abbey.

Of the abbey itself, most beautiful of the five great medieval abbeys that lie in ruins along the border, Irving could later recall little; it was to contain Scott's tomb in future years, and the eccentric present owner, Lord Buchan, was (so Irving remembered) in unseemly haste to claim the bard's remains, in order that an appropriate monument might be erected on the spot to the mighty Minstrel of the North. Scott, not eager to fulfill the earl's grand designs, had still before him, two years into the future in the midst of another severe illness, the added ordeal of Lord Buchan's officious presence outside his bedroom, seeking to reassure the apparently moribund sufferer of the elaborate funeral arrangements that were then pending, including a eulogy by the earl himself. On that occasion, friends would manage to bar the ridiculous man from the sick room, and Scott even had the lugubrious satisfaction of outliving him in the end. But such trials and rewards lay in the future; the first September day of 1817, Dryburgh Abbey served as the background only to delightful conversation between a Scottish host and his American guest. "This," Irving remarked many years afterward, "was to be happy. I felt happiness then."

Indeed, the joy of the entire visit at Abbotsford never diminished in his mind. In October 1858, scarcely a year before his own death, Irving in his mid-seventies was reminiscing at Sunnyside on the Hudson, comparing Scott and his fellow Caledonian, the critic Jeffrey. "Jeffrey was delightful," the old gentleman remembered, "and had *eloquent runs* in conversation; but there was a consciousness of talent with it. Scott had nothing of that. He spoke from the fulness of his mind, pouring out an incessant flow of anecdote, story, &c., with dashes of humor, and then never monopolizing, but always ready to listen to and appreciate what came from others." Forty years and more had passed without dimming the luster of what one visitor to Abbotsford had carried away: "I never felt such a consciousness of happiness as when under his roof. I awoke in the morning, and said to myself, 'Now I know I'm to be happy. I know I have an unfailing treat before me.' We would go out in the morning. Scott, with his brown pantaloons, greenish frock coat, white hat, and cane, would go stumping along. Would hear him ahead, in his gruff tones, mumbling something to himself, like the grumbling of an organ, and find it would be a snatch of minstrelsy . . ."

That deep voice, more than any abbey ruin or landscape, was the vehicle that transported Irving's happiness: Scott's burred speech with its distinctive vowel sounds of "perils" for "pearls," "fear" for "fair," "debt" for "date," "over" for "offer." Such sounds heightened the charm of the speech, but it was, after all, what Scott said that mattered to his guest and that affected the younger writer's life from those moments onward. On his second day at Abbotsford the visitor was observed by Scott's daughter Sophia to arrive at breakfast looking pale from lack of sleep; we have Irving's own admission that he had indeed slept poorly, so excited was he to find himself welcomed by, and under the very roof of, an author so admired. The two of them shared much: those strict and oversolemn Calvinistic Sabbaths of their childhoods on either side of the Atlantic that bred as a consequence an aversion throughout their respective lifetimes to tub-thumping religion; a mutual distaste for schoolrooms and other devices of confinement; a period in their young manhoods when both were wrestling with law's musty arts; a devotion to the towns of their birth in every guise—reeky Edinburgh, commercial New York—each of which cities its native writer had painted in romantic colors so unfading that they could glow brightly thereafter for every subsequent generation.

And more. The one man's works had brought tourists surging to the Trossachs; the other's would bring them scrambling over the Catskills. Each writer loved the medieval past and the world of fantasy; both were drawn to the supernatural and the picturesque. They were alike in their capacities for friendships varied and lasting. Both delighted in and excelled at mimicry; each had a sharp perception of that individualizing detail that reveals character: a turn of speech, the way spectacles sit on a nose. They shared a love of the theater. And if Irving recognized the modesty of his gifts beside the vast talents of Scott, who "could tenant half a hundred scribblers like myself on the mere skirts of his literary reputation," the American by no means merely took without giving. Already had occurred the spring evening four years earlier, in 1813, when Scott had read *Knickerbocker's History* aloud to his family, laughing till his sides ached; a few months after that memorable experience the poet had discovered his own abandoned prose manuscript in the cabinet of his lumber garret at Abbotsford and was sitting down to finish it, filling later pages of *Waverley* with comic characterizations, of Macwheeble and Cosmo Comyne Bradwardine and the others, scarcely like any found in the works of the poet Scott before that year. Was not Irving's humorous narrative one of the influences that helped a flagging poet turning to historical fiction to find his way? Indeed, after he had been writing his singularly successful stories for thirteen years, Scott himself could wonder uneasily, in his journal of May 1826, whether his just completed introductory matter to *Chronicles of the Canongate* "may be considerd as an imitation of Washington Irving."

In addition, a specific influence of the younger writer on the older seems certain: a year or so after Irving's visit, Scott began *Ivanhoe*, which contains one of the most impressive of his many characterizations, that of the Jewish maiden Rebecca; it is likely that she was inspired by his American guest's description of Rebecca Gratz, a beautiful Philadelphia friend whom Irving had long known and admired.

But if he gave in return, Irving did take from his host what he most needed just then. As one example, Scott must have talked during their visit of the richness of German legend and literature, and the nourishment his knowledge of that language had provided him. Soon afterward, Irving would begin his own study, filling pages of notebooks with irregular German verb conjugations and gender lists—"guter Wein gute Milch gutes Bier"—sheltering himself within that sturdy effort while the storms of bankruptcy were raging over his darkened world. From German sources he would draw the hint for his most famous story; to Germany he would travel and there would live in search of further inspiration, after the storm had cleared.

Scott had opened the gateway on an expanse of castle-studded and specter-haunted landscape. But he served Irving in a way still more vital. For at a time when the American had determined at last to return to his pen as a means of salvation from those years of idleness in New York that had preceded the degradation of impending financial ruin at Liverpool, at such a time when he had made his resolution to write his way back into the world's favor but was not far enough along to feel much confidence about managing so bold an undertaking, he met Scott and thus came to know one whose interests coincided with his own. What had always mattered most to Irving—legend, fantasy, the picturesque and mythical past, humor and sentiment in the present—however fragile these might seem to merchants and creditors, mattered to one other person, and that one no less than the foremost writer of his age, or so Irving with multitudes of others would have agreed at the time.

No wonder the visitor was pale that second morning at Abbotsford, after his restless night. Perhaps he would follow Scott even to writing a novel! For notes in the journal he kept in Scotland show Irving struggling with such an enterprise: *Rosalie*, it would be called, a long tale of the Alleghenies, with the catastrophe of a fire at Richmond to illumine its pages—that Richmond where the would-be novelist had lingered at Burr's trial a decade earlier. Irving's projected work never appeared—no novel ever emerged from his pen—but at least he was resolved to continue with and add to those verbal sketches that were already jotted down on other pages of the same notebook. Slight they might be, but he would go on with them. He must have told Scott of these—one about a visit to Stratford, another about Sundays in London, a third about London antiquities—and told him something of his hopes for them: to send them to be published in America, where interest in things English remained high. And with the guidance and encouragement that Irving had received in his mentor's presence, no wonder he was writing his brother Peter from Edinburgh September 6, within the week of his departure: "I left abbots ford on Wednesday morning, and never left any place with more regret. The few days that I passed there were among the most delightful of my life, and worth as many years of ordinary existence."

Moreover, his host's spirit followed the traveler as he proceeded on his way. In Edinburgh Irving dined with Scott's publisher Constable, and with Jeffrey, the critic, who had earlier assured him about the identity of the Great Unknown. Although Londoners were still doubtful, everybody in Edinburgh had made up his mind, so Jeffrey asserted: "There seems to be no doubt here," Irving had noted, "that Scott is the author. It is said that Scott has traversed over the ground of all his novels & has lived among the people, diligently drawing characters & manners." Before returning to London and Liverpool, Irving likewise would traverse the ground that had molded Scott's imagination. On a two weeks' tour of the Highlands—"by chaize, by coach, by gig, by boat, on foot and in a cart"—he visited Ellen's isle on Loch Katrine and peered into Rob Roy's cave and scaled Benledi. "My tour in the Highlands was delightful," he wrote when it was ended to the author whose achievement had inspired and hovered over it. "The weather was as fine as could be desired, and the scenery beyond my expectations." And he would return southward with an olive-green notebook full of sharp observations that let us still glimpse sights he saw in his wanderings: "Highlanders in plaids—See but one or two in kilts. small black cattle. Sheep with black faces & legs"—solemn ancestors of the sheep today's tourist sees—and "herdsmen with highland blue bonnets—plaids wrapped round them & staff under the arm. Shepherd dogs following——." He noted down the apt Scottish speech of carters and innkeepers and village girls, and from the heights of Stirling Castle that remain a breathtaking vantage point overlooking beauty, with the field of Bannockburn in sight, Irving held a moment in amber: "Long lines of mountains in the distance. fertile valley hamlets—lines of cottages—road intersecting it—forth winding thro. See horsemen traversing the road—the noise of waggons rattling away below—feeble shouts of children—sun here & then lost—then gleaming again—"

Delightful Abbotsford, delightful Highlands, delightful Stirling Castle rising above ephemeral shouts of children far below in the valley. Yet not all was delight, as other entries in the notebooks reveal. On one page he jotted down: "now & then a fit of devouring melancholy that eats into my very soul—a melancholy that corrodes the spirits & seems to rust all the springs of mental energy—character gradually impaired by melancholy—" Elsewhere, for his eyes only, of course, occurs in the same notebook: "How has my heart lost all its tune—that heart that then was all tenderness and melody . . . Misfortunes have crushed me to the earth—." Death had claimed his loves:

> Spring may bloom but she we lovd
> Neer shall feel its sweetness
> Time that once so fleetly moved
> Now hath lost its fleetness . . .

Those lines from a ballad by Thomas Moore he copied down too. Matilda was dead, and in the spring of this very year his mother's life had ended. The future held dread certainties: impending bankruptcy and public disgrace. What would he do with himself then, and how would he live? During his Scottish travels Irving's mind went back to his youth, "before I had lost a friend or experienced a disaster." And it mused morosely over his life so far: his promise as a writer remained unfulfilled; his lengthening exile from home perplexed his friends and family in New York. But "why should I go home? . . . Why return to see the changes from places in desolation . . . to knock at the doors . . . and be received by strange faces . . . to enquire for the abode of youth & gaity & content and to be led to the tombstone."

Prey of such varying moods, the wanderer would leave Scotland before the month ended and return to his solitary, uncertain work, but not before trying once more to see Walter Scott, if only briefly, on his way south. He had been urged to stop by. Yet when in late September he found his coach before the gates of Abbotsford again, and again heard the barking of his old friend Hamlet in greeting at the foot of the gravel drive, it was to discover that the laird was in Edinburgh now, at his town house. From Hawick near the border, September 23, Irving had to content himself with writing a letter: "I have been excessively disappointed in not meeting with you yesterday. It was not my intention to have intruded again on your hospitality . . . but I could not feel satisfied to leave Scotland without once more seeing you. . . . Surrounded as you are by friends among the most intelligent & illustrious, the goodwill of an individual like myself cannot be a matter of much importance yet I feel a gratification in expressing it . . ."

Whether he would ever afterward see Scott he could not know, "but wherever I go I shall bear with me the warmest wishes for the happiness of yourself & your family."

So Irving rode southward over the border to his precarious future, distance lengthening between his rattling coach and the peaceful, white-pebbled Tweed, along the banks of which Walter Scott's Abbotsford was continuing to grow—turrets and stone screens and corbels taking shape, and £10,000 that very next month agreed on as the price for the Toftfield estate that would add hundreds of acres to the laird's holdings. Visible evidence it all was—receding behind a coach for England—of a full and exhilarating life being led in these northern parts, in the midst of friends and loved ones, from whose affectionate attentions, and from his productive work, Walter Scott had already taken a moment, on the twenty-second, to write to a London correspondent: "When you see Tom Campbell tell him with my best love that I have to thank him for making me known to Mr. Washington Irving who is one of the best & pleasantest acquaintances I have made this many a day."

Mr. Washington Irving, thirty-four years old, was "a small gentleman dressed in black," so one who saw him often during those months remembered. He appeared to be a "man of a grave, indeed a melancholy aspect, of very staid manners, his kindness rather the offspring of principle and cultivated taste than of emotion. There was an unfailing air of moderation about him, his dress was punctilious, his tone of talking soft and firm and in general over subdued until a natural turn would occasionally run into humor and laughable delineation of character or events."

The melancholy aspect in that description would not be hard to account for. Back in Liverpool in early October, soon after leaving Scotland, Irving was acknowledging word from his New York friend Brevoort: "I have received your letter of Aug. 20th. and congratulate you most heartily on the happy change you are about to make in your situation." Yet the announcement of the impending marriage at home seemed to herald an end to Irving's own relationship with so close a companion, "for marriage is the grave of Bachelors intimacy," and it must have heightened the exile's sense of solitude and aimlessness. Scott's last words to him, standing by a gate at Abbotsford, resounded in his ears: "The best wish I can make you, my friend," the poet had said, laying his hand on Irving's shoulder, "is, that when you return to your own country, you may get married, and have a family of young bairns about you. If you are happy, there they are to share your happiness— and if you are otherwise—there they are to comfort you." But such connubial support would have seemed far off that fall of 1817. In late November, still in dreary, despised Liverpool, Irving was writing to another New York friend: "I long to see you all once more; but when it will be my lot, I cannot tell. My future prospects are somewhat dark and uncertain; but I hope for the best, and that I may yet find wholesome fruit springing out of trouble and adversity."

Adversity, within the offices and among the ledger books of P. & E. Irving and Company, was taking firmer, uglier shape. The struggle against it, as Irving knew, "was certainly vain, yet the disgrace must be kept off as long as possible. There it was, day after day"—so he afterward described those weeks—"work hard all day and then to bed late, a troubled sleep, for three hours perhaps, and then wake up; thump, thump, thump, at the heart comes the care. No more sleep for that night; then up and off to the coffee-house to see the wind dial; wind due east, due east, day after day, no ship can come in, payments must be made, and nowhere for remittances to come from." Money for whatever merchandise Ebenezer might have sold in New York would remain aboard vessels that contrary winds were blocking from entering the Mersey and tying up at the Liverpool piers. And always English creditors were pressing. "Then comes an invitation to a great dinner; must go to keep up appearances; sit at table half asleep; no life for any thing; stupid myself and everybody else stupid; stay there three mortal hours; then to bed with three hours of broken sleep again; and the same thing over, day after day, week after week."

At last no escape remained for the partners but to declare bankruptcy, a humiliation that he and his brother Peter steeled themselves to submit to finally as the new year 1818 began. Irving's mind, as he wrote Brevoort in late January after a first meeting before the Commissioners, "is made up to any thing that will extricate me from this loathsome entanglement in which I have so long been involved. . . . For upwards of two years have I been bowed down in spirit and harrassed by the most sordid cares—a much longer continuance of such a situation would indeed be my ruin." He was, in fact, almost benumbed to reverses by then, conning German verbs in his quarters hour after hour as he awaited the unfolding of drab legal proceedings. By mid-March, creditors of P. & E. Irving had met for the last time; the company was dissolved, and Washington Irving's ordeal as a tradesman was over.

Some time earlier the bankrupt had received a letter from a Scotsman, James Ogilvie, whom he had known in New York in the palmy days of *Salmagundi*. "The intelligence, my dear Irving, of the misfortune you have sustained has reached me," Ogilvie had written from London in July 1817, referring to the distresses that had now, eight months later, dragged to their legal end, "and as it may affect the prosperity and happiness of persons near and most dear to you, all my sympathy with your feelings was awakened. So far, however, as you are individually concerned," this prophetic voice went on, "I should deem the language of condolence a sort of mockery. I am perfectly confident that even in two years you will look back on this seeming disaster as the most fortunate incident that has befallen you."

Well, it could hardly have looked so at the time, as Irving packed and left Liverpool in defeat, June 1818, to pass some weeks with his sister's family in Birmingham. He was still relatively young, to be sure, and—as Ogilvie had written in that same vatic letter—"in possession of higher literary reputation than any of your countrymen have hitherto claimed, esteemed and beloved by all to whom you are intimately or even casually known." What he needed, his correspondent felt certain, was something to jolt him out of his indolence, and "this seemingly unfortunate incident will supply this stimulus—you will return with renovated ardor to the arena you have for a season abandoned, and in twelve months win trophies, for which, but for this incident, you would not even have contended."

Since the optimistic prediction, however, most of those twelve months had passed, and Irving was hardly a step nearer winning new trophies as he accompanied his ailing sister to a watering place near Birmingham in hopes that her health and his own enfeebled spirits might be improved. How bleak were his prospects! Memories made them bleaker. On the other side of the chasm he had crossed, mumbling his German verbs, at Liverpool, he could remember once having drawn in "new life & health hopes with the bright air of the Scotch mountains as I looked around upon the lovely landscape. I thought it could not be that a world so fair should be the appointed abode of wretchedness." Already that new life and hope seemed dissipated, so that here at Leamington with Sarah, he must have felt wretchedness in his very bones. True, another edition of *Knickerbocker's History*—that trophy from the past—was in preparation, but the sketches he had begun before the trip to Scotland last summer were as they had been then. He found it all but impossible to write—only letters and jottings as the empty days passed on.

Spring became summer. His ailing sister was restored to health, and Irving was back with her family in Birmingham. There were the children, and Sarah's husband, who had been born and reared in America, in Sleepy Hollow country, around Westchester and Tarrytown, up the Hudson a little way from Manhattan; as a boy Irving himself had explored the region with delight. In the early 1800s, having married Irving's sister, Van Wart had moved overseas to England, where in the course of a long life he would become one of the most distinguished nineteenth-century citizens of Birmingham. At this time, however, in 1818, he too was suffering in the aftermath of P. & E.

Irving's collapse, and so could understand and sympathize with the despondent moods of his visiting brother-in-law. Yet Van Wart soon had reason to feel more cheerful; he had "resumed business in a prosperous style," Irving could write Brevoort in July, "and I have no doubt of his going on well and ultimately building up a fortune."

That change in prospects would have helped lighten the tone of an evening the two men had passed together a month before. They had got to reminiscing, there at Camden Hill in the Van Wart home in Birmingham on a June evening in 1818, with Irving's empty sheets of paper awaiting him up in his room—reminiscing about the Dutch people and places back home around Sleepy Hollow, faraway land that time would have altered by now. And they found themselves laughing together into the night over matters thought forgotten, so that when the evening ended and Irving had retired, instead of getting ready for bed he sat down at the table in his room and began at last to write:

"Whoever has made a voyage up the Hudson must remember the Kaatskill mountains. They are a dismembered branch of the great Appalachian family, and are seen away to the west of the river swelling up to noble height and lording it over the surrounding country." Suddenly he was envisaging it all: "Every change of season, every change of weather, indeed every hour of the day, produces some change in the magical hues and shapes of these mountains, and they are regarded by all the good wives far and near as perfect barometers. When the weather is fair and settled they are clothed in blue and purple, and print their bold outlines on the clear evening sky; but sometimes, when the rest of the landscape is cloudless, they will gather a hood of grey vapours about their summits, which, in the last rays of the setting sun, will glow and light up like a crown of glory."

Thus he set his scene, scribbling eagerly over the pages. A village appeared there, at the foot of the mountains, smoke curling lazily upward from chimneys. He could see in his mind's eye the small yellow bricks, brought from Holland, with which the houses of the village were built, and the latticed windows, and the shingle roofs gleaming in sunlight, and the weathercocks. He peopled the village with descendants of the good old Dutch—the Derrick Van Bummels and the Nicholaus Vedders and the Brom Dutchers and the Peter Vanderdonks—who lived there still when America was a province of England. One of their number was an easygoing, henpecked idler named Rip Van Winkle.

How much of himself Irving poured into this myth that would make him immortal! Like Rip, he too had known what it was to idle, had gone squirrel shooting himself, in fact and in fancy, among witch hazel and sassafras high in the woods over the broad, sail-flecked Hudson. Like Rip, down from his mountain sleep, like all of us separated from a past we can never reclaim, Irving had gazed perplexed at time's mutations, able with Rip to ask of strangers only the heartbreaking question: Where? "Where's Nicholaus Vedder?" Silence would answer, and then a thin, piping voice: "Nicholaus Vedder! why he is dead and gone these eighteen years! There was a wooden tombstone in the church yard that used to tell all about him, but that's rotted and gone too."

And "Where's Brom Dutcher?" "Where's Van Bummel the school-master?"

Rip's heart—like Irving's, like those of all of us who have slept through our lives, or in black moods believe we have—"Rip's heart died away at hearing of these sad changes in his home and friends, and finding himself thus alone in the world—every answer puzzled him too by treating of such enormous lapses of time and of matters which he could not understand—war—Congress, Stoney Point—he had no courage to ask after any more friends, but cried out in despair, 'Does nobody here know Rip Van Winkle?' "

Who is it that can tell me who I am? Bent over his foolscap in the guest room of his sister's home in Birmingham, Irving wrote on, through the night and past the dawn that brought morning sunlight to let him put out his candle. Without having slept at all, he came down to breakfast bearing his manuscript to share with Sarah's family. "He said it had all come back to him," Van Wart remembered of that ecstatic morning; "Sleepy Hollow had awakened him from his long dull, de-sponding slumber; and then he read the first chapters of 'Rip Van Winkle.' "

The story would be polished over the following months to its present perfection. Discard the prefatory explanation and the note and digressive postscript at the end, and what remains seems unflawed: wisely humorous, profoundly true, a small, imperishable masterpiece. The germ of its inception may have been found at Abbotsford, on one of those rambles Irving made with Scott to Rhymer's Glen, where Thomas the Rhymer, centuries earlier, was supposed to have met the Queen of the Fairies and been enthralled for seven years. Or Irving more likely had encountered in his German studies this past winter and spring the story of Peter Klaus, whose mountain adventures resemble Rip's own. But the American creation is something different from any earlier ver-sion, something unique, a legitimate short story written a decade and more before Poe and Hawthorne are supposed to have invented the form, and a short story suffused with a palpable atmosphere that surrounds and infiltrates every corner of that compact universe, curling like their pipe smoke around those local old philosophers, irrelevantly wise, as-sembled on their bench before the King George Inn, reaching up to mountain heights over the woodlands that spread down to the glassy, majestic Hudson, penetrating Rip's desolate house after twenty years— "the roof fallen in, the windows shattered and the doors off the hinges"

—where an old man calls out hollowly for his children and for his wife, who had always kept it clean: "the lonely chambers rung for a moment with his voice, and then all again was silence."

That wife, termagant with the tart temper that time never mellowed and the sharp tongue that use never dulled, is but one of the several memorable characters Irving created to populate his Catskill village. There is the dapper and learned Van Bummel, the little schoolmaster who would drawl out for his cronies the contents of some obsolete newspaper that had fallen into his hands from a passing traveler; the most gigantic word in the dictionary would not daunt him, and how sagely did his listeners "deliberate upon public events some months after they had taken place." There is the patriarch and landlord Nicholaus Vedder, moving his seat at the door of the inn just sufficiently "to avoid the sun and keep in the shade of a large tree; so that the neighbours could tell the hour by his movements as accurately as by a sun dial," taciturn Vedder, who yielded his opinions to his adherents—"(for every great man has his adherents)"—by the way he puffed his pipe, vehemently when displeased, tranquilly otherwise; "and sometimes taking the pipe from his mouth and letting the fragrant vapour curl about his nose," he would nod gravely "in token of perfect approbation." There is the commander of that "most melancholy party of pleasure" high in the Catskills, the weather-beaten little old gentleman with his "high crowned hat and feather, red stockings and high heel'd shoes with roses in them," playing with his crew of the Half Moon at ninepins, drinking the magic Hollands in flagons among the ravines and waterfalls of the upper wilderness. But above all, there is Rip, thirsty soul, "one of those happy mortals of foolish, well oiled dispositions, who take the world easy, eat white bread or brown, whichever can be got with least thought or trouble, and would rather starve on a penny than work for a pound," Rip, at whom not a dog in the village would bark, who taught all the neighbor children to play marbles and fly kites, who helped the neighbor women with their chores, and on a wet rock liked to fish the day away—poor Rip doomed to sleep through the best of his life, and in doing so, once more waken us to our peril.

Irving had got him down on paper—this mythic personage of humble origins—when he left Birmingham to return to London in mid-August of 1818, armed with the same determination he had brought to this Regency capital exactly one year earlier, in the heat of another summer. This time, though, he could see his way more clearly. He had met Scott since then; he had written his story of the Catskills. Those other sketches too—of life in London and rural England, of Stratford where the immortal Shakespeare was born, of the Indians in America whom he had described earlier and might now make use of again: all of it could add up to a volume or two that his brother Ebenezer might arrange to get published back home. True, nothing was quite ready yet; autumn would be needed to finish what he had begun.

But with his labors scarcely under way, a few weeks after his arrival in London, letters came unexpectedly from that same Ebenezer, and from the eldest brother, William, that almost undid Irving's plans. These elders had of course been troubled by the plight of their adored younger brother, whom their own prosperity had often been able to help before. Now there was little enough money to share, but there were other ways they might be of assistance—indeed, might end his exile at last and bring him home in style. "Commodore Decatur informed me," William wrote happily October 24, "that he had made such arrangements, & such steps would further be made by the Navy Board, as that you will be able to obtain the office of first Clerk in the Navy Department, which is indeed similar to that of under secretary in England. The salary is equal to 2400 Dollars p^r annum, which as the Commod^{re} says, is sufficient to enable you to live in Washington like a prince." Like a prince, after all these months of grubbing from hand to mouth. Hadn't Irving himself just been musing in his essay "The Wife," on which he was working that fall: "It is not poverty so much as pretence, that harrasses a ruined man. The struggle between a proud mind and an empty purse—the keeping up a hollow shew that must soon come to an end"? Now he could end the pretense, could fill his own empty purse again, for good. To live like a prince, and back in America! "They have determined to secure the birth for you, until your answer can be obtained," William's glad tidings went on. "It is a birth highly respectable—Very comfortable in its income, light in its duties"—better and better—"and will afford you a very ample leisure to pursue the bent of your literary inclinations."

Who could ask for worthier brothers? Irving, too long absent, might book his passage home now, gather up his notebooks and sketches, and on the leisurely voyage back perhaps even finish the work he had set himself. He could step ashore at New York to the embraces of his delighted benefactors and friends, then arrange for publication of his travel notes before journeying southward to Washington to assume what earlier in his life he had coveted: a position, not demanding but eminently respectable, in public service.

Yet to his brothers' surprise and dismay, he turned down the opportunity. It was not easy to do so. "I do not wish," he tried to explain to Ebenezer, "to undertake any situation that must involve me in such a routine of duties as to prevent my attending to literary pursuits." Hadn't it been made clear, though, that this position would provide plenty of leisure for writing? Moreover, as William had urged temptingly, "you will be able to spend your days in the best of society & among the worthies of the land." But Irving explained once more, in March, more firmly: he was no politician, and had no talents for such a life. Although it grieved his brothers, who found his decision inexplicable, although it distressed him so much to grieve them that his writing hand was palsied, as he said, for weeks thereafter ("fancy, humor—all seemed to have gone from me. I had offended the best brother a man ever had; given over the chance Providence seemed to have opened . . ."), yet he stood by his refusal. And in time grew more confident: "I now wish to be left for a little while entirely to the bent of my own inclination," he reiterated forcefully to the well-meaning Ebenezer, "and not agitated by new plans for subsistence, or by entreaties to come home. My spirits are very unequal, and my mind depends upon them; and I am easily thrown into such a state of perplexity and such depression as to incapacitate me for any mental exertion." Of course he longed to be back in America! "My greatest desire is to make myself worthy of the good-will of my country, and my greatest anticipation of happiness is the return to my friends. I am living here in a retired and solitary way, and partaking in little of the gaiety of life, but I am determined not to return home until I have sent some writings before me that shall, if they have merit, make me return to the smiles, rather than skulk back to the pity of my friends."

Audacious spirit; "My pride was up—I would receive nothing as a boon granted to a ruined man—I was resolved if possible to raise myself once more by my talents, and owe nothing to compassion." In that same letter to Ebenezer, dated from London March 3, 1819, Washington Irving wrote that he was sending "by Capt. Merry, of the Rosalie, the first number of a work which I hope to be able to continue from time to time. I send it more for the purpose of showing you what I am about, as I find my declining the situation at Washington has given you chagrin."

What he was about, when published, would (to the astonishment of its author) inaugurate a brilliant success—this initial number of *The Sketch Book*, first imaginative work by any American that would reveal itself possessed of sufficient strength to leap the barrier of the Atlantic and achieve international fame.

All Britain—all Europe—would come to adore *The Sketch Book* in time. Yet Irving had not intended that it even be published outside his own country. Much of it, he assumed, would not interest Englishmen: the sketches of their cities and countryside would seem too familiar, as writings about the old Dutch ways in America, or about the American Indians, would seem irrelevant to the reading public in London.

Moreover, as he later confessed, he was "deterred by the severity with which American productions had been treated by the British press" heretofore. So he sent his first packet of five or six sketches, including "Rip Van Winkle," off to Ebenezer in New York that early March day of 1819 and returned with modest expectations to resume writing in his

London lodgings for an American public. "I feel great diffidence about this re-appearance in literature," he had confessed to his friend Brevoort at the time. "I am conscious of my imperfections——." Yet a month later, April 1, while the first package may still have been on the high seas, Irving sent off a second, containing four more sketches. A third group went off in mid-May: "I am extremely anxious to hear from you what you think of the first number—& am looking anxiously for the arrival of the next ship from N York." The fourth packet was not ready until well into the summer; he sent it off August 2. By then his anxiety was somewhat eased; he had seen a printed copy of his first number, returned from home—had held the handsome little gray-brown pamphlet in his hands and turned its ninety-three pages: *The Sketch Book of Geoffrey Crayon, Gent.* And might have already received the pleasing news from Ebenezer, who, soon after the initial pages of manuscript had arrived in America, had heard them read aloud to a circle of friends on a spring evening; at the finish the listeners had burst into spontaneous, delighted applause, moving the grateful elder brother to weep tears of joy. But would the public outside that friendly New York circle find matter to applaud with equal fervor? Irving, across the Atlantic, must wait for his answer; he would send off no more packages until he heard.

Could it have been less than agony: day following August day and no word, August turning into September and still no word? At last, by the ninth day of September the suspense was finally ended with the arrival of a bundle of reviews that Brevoort had forwarded from home. The first three numbers of *The Sketch Book* had found their readers. Irving restudied the clippings with blissful amazement: "The manner in which the work has been received," he wrote Brevoort that day, "and the eulogiums that have been passed upon it in the American papers and periodical works have completely overwhelmed me. They go far, *far* beyond my most sanguine expectations. . . . The receipt of your letters and the reading of some of these criticisms this morning have renderd me nervous for the whole day."

He was reading judgments like this: "When the first number of this beautiful work was announced, it was sufficient to induce an immediate and importunate demand, that the name of Mr. Irving was attached to it in the popular mind. With his name so much of the honor of our national literature is associated, that our pride as well as our better feelings is interested in accumulating the gifts of his genius. We had begun to reproach him with something like parsimony; to tell him that he was in debt to us; that the wealth and magnitude of his endowments were the patrimony of his country—a part of their inheritance." Hardly the language of a dissatisfied creditor; now having made a generous payment from his endowments, Irving could browse happily among the various expressions of gratitude: "We . . . notice the first number of this work . . . for the purpose of announcing its appearance, and of congratulating the American public that one of their choicest favorites has, after a long interval, again resumed the pen. It will be needless to inform any who have read the book, that it is from the pen of Mr. Irving." Geoffrey Crayon might be represented as the author of these sketches, but only Washington Irving could compose works of such humor, such fancy, such felicity of original expression, and such pure and fine moral feeling. So readers of the *Analectic* of July 1819, back in America, were being assured, and so Irving himself was learning in September as he read over the reviews that Brevoort had forwarded him. "I feel almost appalled by such success," he confessed in writing to his New York friend, "and fearful that it cannot be real—or that it is not fully merited, or that I shall not act up to the expectations that may be formed—We are whimsically constituted beings—I had got out of conceit of all that I had written, and considered it very questionable stuff—and now that it is so extravagantly bepraised I begin to feel affraid that I shall not do as well again."

Nevertheless, he would try. By late October he had sent off a fifth packet of sketches, this time of Christmas customs in rural England—images of an illumined Yule clog, of two great Christmas tapers, and mince pie, and children caroling Christmas morning, of the walk through frosty, clear air to church in the nearby village, and the walk back to Christmas dinner in the great hall beside the crackling fire, heart overflowing all the while "with generous and happy feelings"—appealing notations on passing manners that would revive them for subsequent generations of celebrants even to our own day. And in late December he sent off yet another bundle of manuscript for publication in America, this one containing a story that grew out of an idea that had occurred to him crossing with his brother Peter over Westminster Bridge a Sunday morning that autumn. Once more Irving had been reminiscing about the Dutch around Tarrytown when the outlines of a story had abruptly taken shape. Leaving Peter to continue on his way to church, he had returned to his lodgings near Portland Place and scribbled down his recollections. All the next day, foggiest of dark fall days in London, he had sat by candlelight in his second-floor room on Edward Street, writing the story out. "It is a random thing," he explained in forwarding the manuscript to Ebenezer, "suggested by recollections of scenes and stories about Tarrytown. The story is a mere whimsical band to connect descriptions of scenery, customs, manners, &c." That tale—his most famous after "Rip Van Winkle"—is of a schoolmaster and a village belle and a headless horseman: "The Legend of Sleepy Hollow."

Meanwhile, the fame of the earlier numbers from America had already reached as far as the household on Skinner Street in London of the philosopher and social theorist William Godwin. Intimate friend of Aaron Burr during his months of exile in London a decade earlier, husband of the Mary Wollstonecraft whose work on the rights of women had inspired Burr in rearing the child Theodosia, father himself of a remarkable daughter who had during the preceding year published her novel *Frankenstein*, Godwin was writing September 15, 1819, to the James Ogilvie who two years earlier had predicted this very triumph to the then despondent Irving: "You desire me to write to you my sentiments on reading the Sketch Book, No. II., and I most willingly comply with your request. Everywhere I find in it the marks of a mind of the utmost elegance and refinement, a thing as you know that I was not exactly prepared to look for in an American." Thus, even before his English debut, Irving was being stared at in the way that would come before long to annoy him thoroughly: odd, inexplicable hybrid—an American with culture. Where, in those forest wilds among redskins and tobacco spitters, could an American have acquired culture? "Each of the essays," Godwin went on about the work of this interesting phenomenon, "is entitled to its appropriate praise, and the whole is such as I scarcely know an Englishman that could have written. The author powerfully conciliates to himself our kindness and affection." Four essays constituted the number that Godwin was reading: "English Writers on America," "The Broken Heart," "The Art of Bookmaking"—"But the Essay on Rural Life in England," so he thought, "is incomparably the best. It is, I believe, all true; and one wonders, while reading, that nobody ever said this before. There is wonderful sweetness in it."

If one perceptive Englishman so enjoyed reading about his own countryside as described by an American traveler, maybe others would too. Soon the *London Literary Gazette* was publishing selections from *The Sketch Book* for its readers' delectation, and a local publisher was planning to pirate the separate numbers and bring them out as a book. In those days before international copyright laws, foreign authors could protect themselves against such unauthorized printing of their works in England only by publishing their own version in book form first. Toward that end, Irving in mid-October, no doubt diffidently, sought out the most prestigious London publisher of them all, John Murray, "the 'prince of Booksellers,' so famous for his elegant publications," in his fashionable offices at 50 Albemarle Street.

Even today the House of Murray, under a highly respected colophon, publishes from the same address. In Irving's day the firm, already half a century old, had for seven years been located in that Mayfair building; and among those whom John Murray II, the Murray of 1819, had published were Madame de Staël, Jane Austen, the poets Campbell and Crabbe and Thomas Moore, Scott himself, and—glory of the list at present—the self-exiled Byron, whose *Don Juan* was emerging that very year and causing a tremendous stir in literate society. Up the stairs that Byron and Scott—two of his heroes—had trod together, Irving now took the printed American numbers of *The Sketch Book* for Mr. Murray's consideration; the essays already published overseas as separate magazines would fill a volume, and "I had materials enough on hand for a second volume," so the American hopefully added in surrendering his work for judgment.

Two elegant octavos by Geoffrey Crayon, with the great Murray's name at the bottom of their title pages! Murray, whose *Quarterly Review* was read all over the English-speaking world, Murray who entertained each afternoon in his drawing room at Albemarle Street the most stimulating of the literate society of the city. Eagerly the foreigner awaited that exalted personage's reply, on which so much depended. "My dear Sir," came the wordy verdict at last, "I entreat you to believe that I feel truly obliged by your kind intentions towards me, and that I entertain the most unfeigned respect for your most tasteful talents." Alas, this rejection letter of 1819 went on, "If it would not suit me to engage in the publication of your present work, it is only because I do not see that scope in the nature of it which would enable me to make those satisfactory accounts between us, without which I really feel no satisfaction in engaging—but I . . . shall be most ready to attend to any future plans of yours. With much regard, I remain, dear sir, Your faithful servant, John Murray."

Even now the letter disheartens, as it disheartened Irving then. He said later that he would have given the matter up at once, here in England where the one-eyed publisher had just informed him his work lacked scope. But there remained that spurious edition about to appear from the presses of a pirate printer; at the least, Irving felt, a version of the text should be in circulation that the author himself had superintended.

He thought of Scott, and of Scott's famous publisher in Edinburgh, Mr. Archibald Constable. Two years earlier, on his trip north, the author of *Knickerbocker* had dined with Constable; accordingly, he now sent Scott by coach the printed numbers of *The Sketch Book* that had reached him from New York, and at the same time wrote to him, hinting, as he remembered, "that since I had had the pleasure of partaking of his hospitality, a reverse had taken place in my affairs which made the successful exercise of my pen all important to me; I begged him, therefore, to look over the literary articles I had forwarded to him, and, if he thought they would bear European republication, to ascertain whether Mr. Constable would be inclined to be the publisher."

The parcel went to 39 Castle Street, Scott's Edinburgh home. The letter went to Abbotsford. Scott answered at once, in a reply filled with generosity, November 17, 1819: "I was down at Kelso when your letter reached Abbotsford. I am now on my way to town, and will converse with Constable and do all in my power to forward your views; I assure you nothing will give me more pleasure." Meanwhile, his mentor wondered, would Irving be interested in assuming the editorship of a new weekly about to be launched in Edinburgh? "The appointment of the editor (for which ample funds are provided) will be £500 a year certain, with the reasonable prospect of further advantages." Scott ventured the proposal because he knew of "no man so well qualified for this important task, and perhaps because it will necessarily bring you to Edinburgh. If my proposal does not suit, you need only keep the matter secret and there is no harm done." The offer Irving's friend dated from Abbotsford on Monday, and on Tuesday he added to his letter a post-script from Edinburgh that must have misted the eyes of the joyful reader for whom it was written:

"I am just come here and have glanced over the Sketch Book; it is positively beautiful, and increases my desire to *crimp* you if it be possible." *Crimp:* procure or decoy. "Some difficulties there always are in managing such a matter, especially at the outset," Scott concludes in reference to getting Irving's new work published. "But we will obviate them as much as we possibly can."

Once more a timely opportunity was presenting itself to one who, hardly six months earlier, had written to Brevoort: "I am now at the end of my *fortune*." And once more—as he had done with the offer of an appointment in Washington—Irving declined. "My whole course of life has been desultory," he groped to explain in answer to Scott's proposal, "and I am unfitted for any periodically recurring task, or any stipulated labour of body or mind. I have no command over my talents such as they are . . . & have to watch the veerings of my mind as I would those of a weather cock." He was grateful for—and flattered by—his Scottish friend's confidence in him, but had to "keep on pretty much as I have begun, writing when I can & not when I would. . . . Should Mr Constable feel inclined to make a bargain for the wares I have at present on hand he may encourage me to further enterprize and it will be something like bargaining with a gipsy who, if you at one time buy of him a wooden bowl, may at another time bring you a Silver tankard."

What he had to sell now was assuredly golden, though he could not yet know that. He changed his mind, in fact, before hearing from Scott again. He decided "to look to no leading bookseller"—no Murray or Constable—"for a launch, but to throw my work before the public at my own risk, and let it sink or swim according to its merits." At Irving's expense, then, the obscure publisher John Miller, Burlington Arcade, London, would bring out, early in 1820, one volume of *The Sketch Book*.

This part of the story is almost, but not quite, ended. In mid-February Miller did bring out the volume, consisting of the first four numbers. But within another month, just as the unheralded book was beginning to be talked about favorably, its publisher (the vicissitudes of the literary life!) went bankrupt. By then, however, a friendly review of the work—instigated, as it happened, by Walter Scott, and written by the Lockhart who soon would be Scott's son-in-law—had appeared in the influential *Blackwood's Magazine,* and Scott himself was on his way to London, in order to receive his baronetcy. Irving's bad luck was being balanced with good: to Scott on his arrival he promptly appealed for help, "as I was sticking in the mire, and, more propitious than Hercules, he put his own shoulder to the wheel. Through his favourable representations, Murray was quickly induced to undertake the future publication of the work which he had previously declined. A further edition of the first volume was struck off and the second volume was put to press, and from that time Murray became my publisher. . . ."

At least for quite a while he did, although the relationship between Washington Irving and the House of Murray would not always be serene. "Remember, you doubted the success and declined the publication of the Sketch Book, when I offered you the materials for the first volume," an Irving nearly ten years older, and somewhat wiser, might grumble from Granada in 1829, "and it was only after it had been published in London by another bookseller & had been well received that you ventured to take it in hand." But in the joyous spring of 1820 such tempered feelings were far in the future, as the spirits of a recently bankrupt American, so often downcast, now soared skyward, during those thrilling weeks when (in his later words of gratitude, recalling favors performed on his behalf) "under the kind and cordial auspices of Sir Walter Scott, I began my literary career in Europe."

The work—in a sense, the first recognized American classic—that brilliantly opened Irving's international career is composed of thirty-two sketches, none of them long. The majority, some twenty-six, are about English scenes and customs. Of the remaining, four deal with American matters (the two Indian essays that Irving had written as editor of the *Analectic* during the War of 1812, plus "Rip" and "Sleepy Hollow"), one—"The Spectre Bridegroom"—is a German tale of the supernatural, and one is the introductory sketch of "The Voyage," which takes the reader eastward over that "vast space of waters that separates the hemispheres . . . like a blank page in existence."

At the very beginning of *The Sketch Book* stands "The Author's Account of Himself," a typically graceful statement of three pages that epitomizes Irving's virtues and appeal. On America, he explains in those pages, nature has lavished beauty more prodigally than anywhere else on earth, and if this wanderer from childhood had been merely a lover of scenery, he would not have stirred from his native land. "But Europe held forth the charms of storied and poetical association," he goes on. "My native country was full of youthful promise; Europe was rich in the accumulated treasures of age. Her very ruins told the history of times gone by, and every mouldering stone was a chronicle. I longed to wander over the scenes of renowned achievement—to tread as it were in the footsteps of antiquity—to loiter about the ruined castle—to meditate on the falling tower—to escape in short, from the common-place realities of the present, and lose myself among the shadowy grandeurs of the past."

Merely transcribing the prose stirs admiration anew for those long, languorous sentences, and reminds the transcriber of how many nineteenth-century American schoolchildren, how many present-day Europeans and Asians have learned to write English with Irving as their model.

He continues, characteristically: "I had, beside all this, an earnest desire to see the great men of the earth. We have, it is true, our great men in America—not a city but has an ample share of them. I have mingled among them in my time"—alongside Aaron Burr and others— "and been almost withered by the shade into which they cast me; for there is nothing so baleful to a small man as the shade of a great one, particularly the great man of a city. But I was anxious to see the great men of Europe; for I had read in the works of various philosophers, that all animals degenerated in America, and man among the number. A great man of Europe, thought I, must therefore be as superior to a great man of America, as a peak of the Alps to a highland of the Hudson; and in this idea I was confirmed by observing the comparative importance and swelling magnitude of many English travellers among us; who, I was assured, were very little people in their own country.—I will visit this land of wonders, thought I, and see the gigantic race from which I am degenerated. . . ."

How skillfully the modest author balances himself between opposing worlds. How cunningly he manages to rebuke those ubiquitous, ill-mannered English visitors to the United States, while exonerating Englishmen in general from blame. Of course Southey and Godwin, like so many others in the land of wonders, found themselves conciliated by so delightful a book. Moreover, among its various sketches was something for almost every taste. There was, to be sure, little that was monumental, and "not a single Glacier or Volcano" for melodramatic temperaments. But to lovers of "nooks and corners and bye places" the work offered—and certainly still offers—real pleasure. In each number Irving had taken pains to balance humor with sentiment: "Rip Van Winkle" with the lachrymose portrait of "The Wife," "The Art of Bookmaking" with what seems now the too-sticky "Broken Heart." Now too sticky, but over that last-named essay Byron in Italy shed tears: "Crayon is very good," he was writing Murray admiringly in October 1820. Eyes less cynical than Byron's, then, were certain to fill when reading such essays: of innocent love spurned, of lovely youth dead, of motherhood long-suffering and ennobled.

But it is not those conventional exercises in pathos—"The Widow and Her Son," "Rural Funerals," and the rest—that gratify our tastes, however much they may have moved Byron and other first readers for whom the book was intended. (Yet is your taste or mine better than Byron's?) Rather, what has survived a century and a half without tarnish is a handful of essays that express, forcefully and sincerely, emotions awakened by what Irving called the dilapidations of time. Nowhere else, in fact, has this familiar, fundamental theme been more eloquently expressed than in "Rip Van Winkle" and "The Boar's Head Tavern, Eastcheap" and "The Mutability of Literature" and two or three other sketches that remain as fresh as when they were written. "What then," this visitor to the ruins of Melrose reflects, for instance, about Westminster Abbey, "is to insure this pile which now towers above me from sharing the fate of mightier mausoleums? The time must come when its gilded vaults, which now spring so loftily, shall lie in rubbish beneath the feet; when . . . the wind shall whistle through the broken arches, and the owl hoot from the shattered tower— . . . Thus man passes away; his name perishes from record and recollection; his history is as a tale that is told, and his very monument becomes a ruin."

Coming at the end of an exquisite essay, the thought may move us deeply. Some of the moralizing and much of the conventional sentiment of *The Sketch Book* have dated. The moments of sincerity have not. The humor has not, nor the style at its frequent best, nor the sharp observation of customs, of character and picturesque scene. It is not a profound book: "I have attempted no lofty theme nor sought to look wise and learned," its author conceded at the start to Brevoort in New York. "I have preferred addressing myself to the feeling & fancy of the reader, more than to his judgement." Others may analyze and philosophize and instruct. "I seek only to blow a flute accompaniment in the national concert, and leave others to play the fiddle & frenchhorn."

Not a profound book, but a warm and appealing one. Of course the stated ambition proved to be more modest than what Irving accomplished. England, like America, soon took *The Sketch Book* to its heart, so much so that from then on, specimens of American literature would find themselves treated seriously abroad. "I think you are a most fortunate fellow of an author in regard to your debut amongst us in this critical age," a friend was writing Irving before the year was out, "for I have not heard of your having so much as a *nose* or a member of any kind cut up by the anatomists of literature; on the contrary, there seems to be almost a *conspiracy* to hoist you over the heads of your contemporaries." The withering pen of Francis Jeffrey, which could dismiss Wordsworth with scorn ("This will never do!"), in the pages of *The Edinburgh Review* enlisted an enormous critical influence in support of *The Sketch Book*. *The Quarterly Review* began a highly appreciative notice of the work thus: "The author before us is the best writer of English, in our estimation of that term, that America has published since the era of her independence." *The Monthly Magazine* judged the work among "the best classical writings of our own country." As for *The*

Edinburgh Magazine, and Literary Miscellany. "It proves to us distinctly that there is *mind* working in America, and that there are materials, too, for it to work upon, of a very singular and romantic kind."

Not to forget Scott's destined son-in-law Lockhart (Sophia and he were married this April of 1820): the savage Lockhart, who had been clawing viciously at the careers of the Cockney School, as, for example, "The very concubine of so impure a wretch as Leigh Hunt would to be pitied, but alas! for the wife of such a husband. For him there is no charm in simple seduction; and he gloats over it only when accompanied by adultery and incest." Or this, about Keats: "The phrenzy of the *Poems* was bad enough in its way; but it did not alarm us half as seriously as the calm, settled, imperturbable drivelling idiocy of *Endymion.*" This same snarling Lockhart (who, by the way, would become the most loving of husbands and fathers) had already in the pages of *Blackwood's* grown docile before these sketches of Irving, which were "to be classed," so he adjudged, "with the best English writings of our day." ("You will perceive," their author was informing his brother Ebenezer from London in August, "that I have dedicated my second volume to Scott; but this dedication had not been seen by Lockhart, at the time he wrote the eulogium. Should a new and complete edition of the work be published in America, I wish the dedication to be placed in the first volume.")

Should a new edition be published? Should a new edition of the Bible be published! A new edition of Shakespeare! Having prepared his own new English edition (crown octavo to sell at twelve shillings a volume), the publisher Murray, who had watched and aided the fabled careers of Scott and Byron and therefore knew of triumphs, summed up the overwhelmingly favorable reaction to his newest author's work: "Its success, considering all things, is unparalleled."

Happy Irving! "I am astonished at the success of my writings in England," he was soon confessing to that same delighted Murray, "and can hardly persuade myself that it is not all a dream. Had any one told me a few years since in America, that any thing I could write would interest such men as Gifford and Byron I should have as readily believed a fairy tale." And yet here was Gifford now, editor of the *Quarterly,* helping to make Irving welcome at the afternoon gatherings in Murray's drawing room, the redoubtable, splay-eyed Gifford near the marble fireplace under Byron's portrait, with his misshapen old body propped up on pillows, the same Gifford whose acid opinions of all pretenses at culture from America had been for long known, feared, and hated across the waters. "A small, shrivelled, deformed man of about sixty," his new American friend was already by May 1820 able to write one stay-at-home, "mild and courteous in his manners, without any of the petulance that you would be apt to expect." And Gifford, beneath those shelves of gorgeously bound volumes, was only one of many valuable acquaintances to be encountered in that "great resort of first-rate literary characters" at Albemarle Street. "Whenever I have a leisure hour I go there, and seldom fail to meet with some interesting personages. The hours of access are from two to five. It is understood to be a matter of privilege, and that you must have a general invitation from Murray. Here I frequently meet with such personages as Gifford, Campbell, Foscolo, Hallam, (author of a work on the Middle Ages,) Southey, Milman, Scott, Belzoni, &c., &c." Mr. Hallam was "a copious talker," "affable & unpretending." The huge Belzoni, explorer of Egyptian ruins, enlivened an afternoon for Irving with an account of a temple he had discovered in the side of a hill; inside were "rows of Gigantic statues, Thirty feet high, cut out of the Calcarious rock, in perfect preservation." The American listened enrapt, as to an Arabian tale. And there was Mitchell, translator of Aristophanes, who "writes those very clever & very amusing articles in the Quarterly Review on the manners of the Athenians Greek cookery &c." And the young Cohen, whose articles examine "the Superstitions & mithology of the middle ages . . ."

Indeed, Irving complained, his "circle of acquaintance" was "extending faster than I could wish." Earlier he had met Coleridge: "I was surprised by his volubility. He walked about, in his gray hair, with his right hand over his head . . . the thumb and finger of his right hand moving over his head, as if sprinkling snuff upon his crown." Now he met others: Lady Holland, Byron's former lover the scandalous Lady Caroline Lamb, the Countess of Bessborough, the Duke of Wellington. In short, our American had become (as the Miller who all too briefly had published *The Sketch Book* was remarking before the year 1820 was out) "the most fashionable fellow of the day."

We gaze at drawings of Regency London, by Malton and Rowlandson and Shepherd and others, trying to set into motion once more the frozen little figures, top-hatted gentlemen, bonneted ladies with children in hand, along the sidewalks before the sunstruck buildings of, say, Brooks's Club and Boodle's on fashionable St. James's Street, along the Pall Mall as it passes the screen of Carlton House. Dogs hold their frisking gestures on the pavement. Once more we try to jog into movement over the cobblestones of Bond Street or Whitehall frozen stanhopes and phaetons and tandems and tilburies that clattered about in the hearing of Irving as he made his excited way, among dusty throngs of foot passengers and laden carts and tramping horses, perhaps to keep another rendezvous at the York Chop House with his artist friends Newton and Leslie. That Leslie, incidentally, who in April had written his sister: "Walter Scott (now Sir Walter) is in London, and I am to have the honour, and I am sure it will be the very great pleasure, of breakfasting with him at his lodgings on Friday next. Irving, who I suspect of being a very great favourite of Scott's, is to introduce me. It is what I did not venture to ask of him, but Irving, knowing how much such an introduction would gratify me, proposed it himself. I believe we are to meet Crabbe, the poet, there." Ah yes, and "old D'Israeli is a staunch friend of mine also," Irving himself, all alive from head to toe in the post-Regency, was assuring Brevoort in May, "and I have met with some very interesting people at his house. . . ."

Into such glittering company had he now moved, the same who not three years earlier, from Liverpool, had been somberly intoning to brother William: "I have led comparatively such a lonely life for the greater part of the time that I have been in England, that my habits and notions are very much changed. For a long while past, I have lived almost entirely at home; sometimes not leaving the house for two or three days . . ." Well, his habits had changed again. The house had changed, from dirty Liverpool to London, and the times had changed too, so that the sociable, amiable bachelor was seldom to be found now in those second-floor quarters he was sharing with his brother Peter at 21 Edward Street. All had become stimulating, unreal, exhausting; it could be indulged in precisely because it would soon have to end.

Through the spring and summer of 1820 Washington Irving alternately gloried in and endured his new status in English drawing rooms. He had money now, and more would come to him. In mid-August, with the social season finally concluded, he held in his hand Murray's draft for two hundred and fifty guineas, payment for the British copyright of *The Sketch Book*. He had made his plans by then. One phase of his life was coming to a close. The night before, this uncertain conqueror of the summits of London's cultural world had ended a letter to his friend Brevoort back home: "And now my dear fellow I must take my leave—for it is midnight and I am wearied with packing trunks and making other preparations for my departure. The next you will hear from me will be from France, and after passing five years in England among genuine John Bulls it will be like entering into a New World to cross the Channel."

Of us, too, for now, Irving takes his leave—he and his brother Peter aboard ship the following evening under a summer moon between Dover and Le Havre. The date is August 18, 1820. By then the Regency had ended, for the former Prince Regent had been, as of January of this same year, transformed into King George IV, all two hundred and eighty pounds of what Irving half a decade earlier had privately referred to as "this bloated sensualist, this inflation of sack & sugar." The king was no trimmer now than then; indeed, in 1818, an eyewitness to the event reported that Prinny—the prince, as he then was—had "let loose his belly which now reaches his knees." All those pleasure parties—eclairs and cherry brandy—at the Brighton Pavilion and at Carlton House in London had done their work, those elaborate dinners that bespeak the Regency, wherein long, laden banquet tables supported down their flowered length artificial streams in beds of silver, in which glistened live goldfish swimming among china and crystal before Prinny and his cronies. There is of course much to deplore about a ruler so self-indulgent, so indifferent to the appalling plight of many of his subjects in the hard years that followed the end of the Napoleonic Wars. Yet granting his limitations, we grant too that he was a man of taste whose schemes did much to beautify London, and whose enthusiasms did much to encourage the arts. Typically, "I shall always reflect with pleasure," so he was soon observing, "on Sir Walter Scott's having been the first creation of my reign."

For within two months of the time that reign had begun in late January 1820, Scott, as we have seen, was in London to be gazetted baronet. Leslie the painter did get to meet the novelist on that occasion, the way his friend Irving had promised he would, for breakfast in lodgings at Piccadilly with a number of ladies and gentlemen, including one of the sons of Johnson's Boswell. At the time Scott "was in the full enjoyment of his high and increasing reputation," so Leslie remembered, "and he appeared to great advantage." The painter noted him well, over the profusion of a Scottish breakfast, and "as I take it for granted that the most insignificant particulars relating to such a man will be interesting to you," he was writing his sister soon afterward, "I will give you a description of his personal appearance, and even his dress. He is tall and well formed, excepting one of his ankles and foot (I think the right) which is crippled, and makes him walk very lamely. He is neither fat nor thin. His face is perfectly Scotch, and though some people think it heavy, it struck me as a very agreeable one. He never could have been handsome. His forehead," this portraitist went on, "is very high, his nose short, his upper lip long, and the lower part of his face rather fleshy. His complexion is fresh and clear, his eyes very blue, shrewd, and penetrating. I should say the predominant expression of his face is that of strong sense. His hair, which has always been very light (as well as his eyebrows and eyelashes) is now of a silvery whiteness, which makes him look somewhat older than he really is (I believe forty-six is his age)." Scott was then forty-eight. "He was dressed in a brown frock coat, blue trowsers, and had on a black cravat. His son was with him; he is a young man of eighteen or nineteen, and in the army—he does not at all resemble his father."

The hair of silvery whiteness may be accounted for by events of the preceding year, 1819, during much of which time Scott had once more been suffering acutely from gallstone attacks. They would leave him finally, but meanwhile some days of that year brought as many as eight or ten hours of uninterrupted pain, of vomiting and cramps against which neither laudanum nor calomel nor ipecacuanha nor opium nor hyoscyamus nor bleeding nor blistering availed. He took the suffering manfully: "I should be a great fool and a most ungrateful wretch to complain of such inflictions as these. My life has been," he wrote, "as fortunate perhaps as was ever lived . . . and whether pain or misfortune may lie beyond the dark curtain of futurity, I am already a sufficient debtor to the bounty of Providence to be resigned to it." But the ordeal transformed his appearance: "When I crawl out on Sybil Grey I am the very image of Death on the pale horse, lanthorn-jawd, decayd in flesh, stooping as if I meant to eat the poneys ears & unable to go above a foot-pace."

So illness, from which the author had only recently recovered, would account for the appearance that his guest Leslie described in London in the spring of 1820, just as Scott's accomplishments would explain the worshipful minuteness of that description. For in health or sickness, he had gone on writing. Amazingly, three novels had appeared that very year of suffering, 1819. One was *Ivanhoe*, and later, in Paris in October 1826, Scott himself was witnessing a French opera based on the work: "it was strange to hear anything like the words which I (then in an agony of pain with spasms in my stomach) dictated to William Laidlaw at Abbotsford now recited in a foreign tongue and for the amusement of a strange people. I little thought to have survived the completing of this novel." But he had survived, and had published that same year—1890—*The Legend of Montrose* and *The Bride of Lammermoor*, the latter one of his most disturbingly profound creations—and written all but unconsciously: "He assured me," James Ballantyne testified, "that when it was first put into his hands in a complete shape, he did not recollect one single incident, character, or conversation it contained!"

Astounding testimony! All through these years the novels kept appearing, always anonymously, almost always to enormous acclaim. The popularity of even the less successful productions of the Great Unknown, this Wizard of the North, would have been the envy of any other contemporary. They were, in fact, by far the most popular novels the world has ever known—twenty-six of them in all, including a number that work their enchantment still: *Waverley* itself and *Old Mortality* and *The Heart of Midlothian* and *Rob Roy* and still *Ivanhoe* and *Quentin Durward* and *Redgauntlet*, to name the bare minimum. What Scott succeeded in doing was to create a new literary form—the historical novel—then exemplify it many times over, in Scotland and England on the Continent, in the past that lay within memory, and the past that extended backward six and seven hundred years. Surely no other novelist, ever, has made use of a more spacious canvas, more packed with event and character. Flights through lonely bleak landscapes, challenges hurled from parapets, torch-lit riots, witches at the scaffold, battles described in all their clatter and horror, jousts, dungeon tortures, midnight assassinations—and the humor, too, in such Scottish creations (four of some eight hundred individualized creations) as Andrew Fairservice, and Dandie Dinmount, and Edie Ochiltree, and Jonathan Oldbuck, and the marvelously expressive Scottish speech of, say, wild Meg Merrilies howling out her curses, and the pathos of such moments as, for instance, in *The Heart of Midlothian* when Jeanie Deans makes her appeal to Queen Caroline to save her sister's life, or in *Rob Roy*, as Frank and the moonlit, enchanting Diana endure their farewell—so much, at the very least, is in the possession of readers of Scott. The novels may seem at first to lumber somewhat creakingly to modern, streamlined tastes; yet the best of them display workmanship altogether solid and reliable, and each has its atmosphere as enveloping as the interior of a great old coach, in which we may be assured of traveling picturesque roads, knowledgeably guided, and of reaching our destination.

And though they now may appear to move leisurely, each succeeding novel was written at full speed. *Ivanhoe* appeared in December 1819; *The Monastery* in March of 1820; *The Abbot* in September; *Kenilworth* in January 1821—with the trip to London managed as well: ". . . if there be any thing good about my poetry, or prose either, it is a hurried frankness of composition which pleases soldiers sailors and young people of bold and active disposition. I have been no sigher in shades . . ." Of course there was more good about his prose than that. The style might on occasion be lax, as his son-in-law Lockhart, editor by profession, would remind Scott: "J. G. L. kindly points out some solecisms in my stile—as *amid* for *amidst*, *scarce* for *scarcely*. *Whose* he says is the proper genitive of *which* only at such times as *which* retains its quality of impersonification. Well! I will try to remember all this. But after all I write grammar as I speak, to make my meaning known, and a solecism in point of composition like a Scotch word in speaking is indifferent to me." Style—except in the wonderful Scottish portions of his novels—might often be no more than competent, but excellences are abundant, not least the accuracy with which the author creates the various worlds that his novels recover from the past. His empathy, his omnivorous reading, and his memory all serve him well; rarely does he make the mistake of seeing the past simply as an oddly costumed present. Rather, with impressive consistency his novels clearly understand and delineate those qualities of thought and attitude that distinguish then from now.

Naturally, as creator of a successful literary form that for the first time placed fictional characters alongside historical people in a factually authentic setting, Scott inspired imitators even while he was alive. Of their efforts, he noted privately—and with typical modesty: "They may do their fooling with better grace but I like Sir Andrew Aguecheek do it more natural. They have to read old books and consult antiquarian collections to get their information—I write because I have long since read such works and possess thanks to a strong memory the information which they have to seek for." And because his imitators must rummage in old books, "this leads to a dragging in historical details by head and shoulders, so that the interest of the main piece is lost in minute descriptions of events which do not affect its progress." Not that Scott was publicly ever less than generous to his fellow writers; we have witnessed his repeated generosity to Irving. Publicly he was ever modest about the extent of his own achievement, and sincerely so: his poems were "mere cairngorms, wrought up, perhaps, with a cunning hand," but of so little consequence that his own children he discouraged from reading them. And privately, too, he was generous toward others at his own expense, as in this appealing journal entry of March 14, 1826: "Also read again and for the third time at least Miss Austen's very finely written novel of *Pride and Prejudice*. That young lady had a talent for describing the involvements and feelings and characters of ordinary life which is to me the most wonderful I ever met with. The Big Bow wow strain I can do myself like any now going but the exquisite touch which renders ordinary common-place things and characters interesting from the truth of the description and the sentiment is denied to me."

In defining his own limitations, Scott went too far, and in doing so provided hostile readers with the very terms by which to attack his achievement. Assuredly there is more to what he accomplished than a phrase like "the Big Bow wow strain" suggests. He made history live, as no writer before him had. He explored tensions between past and present that affect every generation, including our own, transformed by time into something that perhaps must be, but is so at a price—Old Town and New Town of Edinburgh, old wild clannish Scot and new North Briton of the Union, old doomed and romantic Jacobite cause and the comfortably vulgar middle-class prosperity of the Hanoverians. Both the cost and the benefits of these changes Scott recognized more clearly than most, and made many of them the basis of his successful fictions. Moreover, is there anywhere else outside those pages where the cruelty and senselessness of battle are more graphically conveyed, battle for which (in the words of Rebecca in *Ivanhoe*) "domestic love, kindly affection, peace and happiness, are so wildly bartered" just to make heroes for "ballads which vagabond minstrels sing to drunken churls over their evening ale"?

In America as well as in Britain, the influence of Scott's writing has been enormous. The antebellum American South, finding reflections of its own social order and ideals in those recovered worlds of feudalism, Jacobitism, and clannishness, yearned after every word he wrote; his works went everywhere, shaping attitudes that saw in his thrilling battle scenes more of the glory than the horror. How much the assumptions of, say, *Gone with the Wind* owe to Scott! Indeed, a traveler down the Mississippi reached Baton Rouge on an April day in 1882 and from what he saw concluded that much of what ailed the South even that late was the fault of one Edinburgh barrister. "Sir Walter Scott is probably responsible for the Capitol building," wrote Mark Twain (who, incidentally, once explained that the way to start a good library was to throw out all the books by Jane Austen); "for it is not conceivable that this little sham castle would ever have been built if he had not run the people mad, a couple of generations ago, with his mediaeval romances. The South has not yet recovered from the debilitating influence of his books. Admiration of his fantastic heroes and their grotesque 'chivalry' doings and romantic juvenilities still survives here, in an atmosphere in which is already perceptible the wholesome and practical nineteenth-century smell of cotton factories and locomotives; and traces of its inflated language and other windy humbuggeries survive along with it. . . ."

That sham castle that Mark Twain derided is gone now, replaced by Huey Long's skyscraper, and the cotton factories and locomotives— they of the wholesome smell—have given way to jet planes and diversified industry, with the language of the Compsons challenged ever more stridently by the utterances of the Snopeses. Scott would have understood the changes as well as Faulkner—seen which were necessary and beneficial, and lamented values that were lost.

Comparable changes, after all, had been transforming his own Scotland all during his lifetime, which had begun in the reeky Old Town of Edinburgh just four years after the first stone houses had been built in the New. Among those stone houses now, on Castle Street in the early 1820s, the writer was leading out his enviable maturity, each morning during term time returning over the Mound to the Old Town of his infancy to take his place in his black leather chair in Parliament House as Clerk of Session, put in his day's work there (as he did for a quarter century), before limping back home, down High Street and across North Bridge, among jostling crowds and hawkers and peddlers and ballad singers with their Scots tongue sounding in his ears. He would already have done a stint of writing early in the morning, and might correct proof in the late afternoon, and yet as Irving had remarked during this period of Scott's life, "It is only astonishing how he finds the time, with such ample exercise of the pen"—not to mention his professional duties—"to attend so much to the interests and concerns of others . . . Life passes away with him in a round of good offices and social enjoyments. Literature seems his sport rather than his labor or his ambition . . ."

One good office Scott filled in these years led a Hanoverian king for the first time to set foot on Scottish soil. *Waverley*, his own first novel, had told of the clandestine return from France to Edinburgh in 1745 of Bonnie Prince Charlie, of the exiled Scottish House of Stuart that had ruled England during most of the seventeenth century. The bold venture to assemble his followers, march southward to London, and reclaim the crown that had been wrested from the prince's grandfather ended, after a brief flurry of high expectations, near Inverness at Culloden Moor, April 16, 1746. Those stirring events of the Forty-five had occurred only a quarter of a century before Scott's own birth, so that the memory of them remained green in the hearts of elders while he matured, and while Prince Charles himself, in exile once more in Italy, was growing daily less bonnie into his flaccid, debauched old age. The memory of the Pretender over the water stayed fresh in the minds of the Hanoverians, too, who throughout the rest of the reign of George II and through the long reign of George III declined to visit their Scottish realms. Moreover, to punish the rebels further, they forbade all manifestations of Scottish nationhood: no clans could assemble, no kilts be worn, no bagpipes sound.

Now, finally, seventy-seven years after the last clamor of rebellion had been stilled, bagpipes were sounding once more north of the border, as plumed and kilted Highlanders gathered to march joyously through the streets of Edinburgh, which had been transformed to welcome the arrival of his gracious majesty George IV. The king had brought his great bulk northward at his friend Walter Scott's urging. All had been put in readiness for the distinguished visitor. Scott himself, health restored, was in charge as master of ceremonies, with tents spread over Arthur's Seat (empty now, and bracken-covered, over Edinburgh), with banners and pennons waving above the castle in the August breeze, with pibrochs sounding along Princes Street and colorful plaids visible along the heights of Salisbury Crags. In trews and the tartan of the Campbells Sir Walter had dressed himself expectantly. Alas, after all the preparations, and with the king aboard the *Royal George* anchored nearby in the Forth, the rain poured down that late summer day of 1822, so that Scott's welcome had to be extended in the midst of dismal inclemencies.

"What! Sir Walter Scott! The man in Scotland I most wish to see! Let him come up."

And there on board, this loyal subject beheld the vast expanses of his sovereign begirt in kilt, bare-kneed, ready to enter an unremittingly festive fortnight during which bands would play ceaselessly, multitudinous toasts would be offered, illustrious Scots would be knighted, banquets would be consumed, the confiscated cannon Mons Meg (at Scott's request) would be promised to be returned to the castle from London, and all the former follies of these Scottish subjects would be forgiven.

It was only one more in Scott's succession of triumphs, endearing him further to Scotsmen and Englishmen alike, as his triumphal trip to Ireland four years later would endear him to that island of the realm. In 1825, his elder son Walter, the young officer whom Leslie had seen at breakfast in London, married a Miss Jane Jobson, an heiress whose solicitudes were destined to bring her father-in-law much pleasure. Lieutenant Scott and his bride were stationed in Dublin, set up comfortably at 10 St. Stephen's Green. Scott, who had never crossed the Irish Sea and had not been abroad for a decade, would pay them a visit.

No liberator could have been more warmly received by the Irish people. Crowds followed the great writer wherever he went; colleens curtseyed as he passed, and a tumultuous audience in a Dublin theater would not allow the play to begin until Sir Walter had risen to acknowledge its cheers. In a proud ceremony Trinity College tendered him a degree. He was entertained at public dinners, and during his month's visit moved among cordial company over much of the Irish countryside. "I do not think even our Scottish hospitality can match that of Ireland," was his grateful, exhausted conclusion. "I verily believe the story of the Irish harper who condemnd his harp to the flames for want of fire wood to cook a guests supper."

And when he returned home, it was to an Abbotsford finally completed. This was on the evening of August 26, 1825. Abbotsford, twelve years in the building: he would say later that of all the grand homes he had seen in a lifetime—a lifetime that had frequently given him access to grandeur—"I have seen in my travels none I liked so well—fantastic in architecture and decoration if you please—but no real comfort sacrificed to fantasy." On this summer evening, with a month-long ovation still ringing in his ears, with his two novels (*The Betrothed* and *The Talisman*) just successfully published, with an exciting task—his monumental life of Napoleon—to begin, he might well view complacently and with a light heart his beloved material possessions to which he was returning in a fit setting at last. Abbotsford was finished—masons and glaziers and varnishers and stonecutters all gone—and he could settle down to taste pleasure among his plantations of laburnums and sweetbriers and horse chestnuts and poplars and birches and the beloved oaks. ("I promise you my oaks will outlast my laurels," he had written a friend a few years earlier, "and I pique myself more upon my compositions for manure than on any other compositions whatsoever to which I was ever accessory.") By then the laird had made the bare slopes along Tweedside bloom with thousands of trees. What had struck his earlier visitors, including Irving, was the nakedness of the surroundings; the lushness strikes us now. And the house itself, chambers of which we may yet visit, had been fashioned to contain his future years in comfort—innovative gas jets that burned all day long, the heat ducts and water closets—all surrounded by splendor. Inside and out, the past had been brought into his present; without, the Gothic bartizans and turrets and machicolations, the stone screen across the garden, the Tolbooth door; within, the corkscrew staircase, marble floors of the entrance hall, the great library forty feet long with its twenty thousand volumes bound in leather, cedarwood windows, escutcheon panes, crimson curtains, the carved-oak ceiling. And throughout the house curiosities: hair from the severed head of Charles I, Montrose's sword, a silver urn of Attic bones from Byron, cuirasses from Waterloo, suits of armor.

Visitors, who had always come, came in increasing numbers, as many as sixteen coach loads in one day. "The most wealthy of the English nobility," Ballantyne's brother wrote later, "are accustomed to entertain large parties of guests at their country mansions at certain periods of the year, such as the Christmas holidays or the commencement of the shooting season, for a few days, or a week or two perhaps, at a time; but the halls of Abbotsford, for months and months in succession, were filled with parties of noble and distinguished guests, and crowds of pampered servants, while the stables might at any time have mounted a troop of horse." Incidentally, one such servant would write of his congenial master: "All the seven years I was in his service I never seed him the least the worse of licure"—this in an age even thirstier than our own—"A most happy gentleman when all his family was around him."

Yet the mansion harbored a secret that hardly anyone suspected. To Abbotsford in the autumn of 1825 came one more of many visitors. "The house was full of company," this one recalled. "It was a beautiful moonlight night and I walked with Sir Walter to the terrace towards the Tweed. The thriving holly hedge was glistening in the moonbeams and the library which we had left was gay with brilliant light and high and happy guests—everything contributed to inspire me with admiration for Sir Walter's efforts and success and merited station and happiness and I could not refrain from expressing that sentiment. I dare say I did so as fervently as I did it sincerely: I was thunderstuck when instead of responsive acquiescence he uttered a deep sigh and said, 'I wish to God I had the means of providing adequately for poor Anne.'" Anne was his unmarried daughter. "Knowing that his life was insured, I observed that that fund was ample. He made no explanation and was silent; but I could not but feel when his misfortunes were soon afterwards disclosed, what a pang I must have inflicted,—the fund I had alluded to and all he had being absorbed in his overwhelming pecuniary ruin."

Ruin. Dread word that had haunted Irving's life some years earlier. Now all that the laird of Abbotsford had so lovingly established was to be suddenly overwhelmed. All was about to be swept from him. How could it have happened?

The story is contained in one of the most moving and inspiring works in the English language, *The Journal of Sir Walter Scott*. Like that intensely honest record that Aaron Burr kept of a brave man's spirit in torment during four years of exile onward from 1808, Scott's *Journal* lays bare a soul struggling manfully to surmount losses and pain, from shortly before disaster strikes late in 1825, to April 1832, when the enclosing body is too much weakened to go on. "Shall we," he quotes from the Book of Job, "receive good at the hand of God and not receive evil?" And it was in the midst of all the good that God's hand had bestowed on him that Scott had begun his journal—or "Gurnal . . . A hard word so spelld on Authority of Miss Scott now Mrs. Lockhart"—lightheartedly, a Sunday in late November 1825, at his town house in Edinburgh. The Irish triumph was not far behind him, and a new Waverley novel, *Woodstock*, was under way, as well as the *Life of Napoleon*. "I am enamourd of my Journal," he wrote at the start of his second long entry, on Monday. "I wish the zeal may but last." He would put into his handsome locked volume ("such as might serve for a Lady's Album") events and recollections—of Ireland, of his work and family, of his numerous friends: their visits, their stories. Thus during the remainder of November he does fill a number of pages, there in his Castle Street study, with diverting reminiscences of the poet Tom Moore and of Byron, who had died the year before, with thoughts on his son-in-law Lockhart's recent appointment as editor of Murray's *Quarterly Review* in London, with accounts of guests, of dinners out, of work and business.

December opened serenely. "Rather a blank day for the Gurnal," he notes on the second. "Correcting proofs in the morning—Court from ½ past ten till two— . . . from two till five transacting business with J. B. All seems to go smoothly. Sophia dined with us alone, Lockhart being gone to the West to bid farewell to his father and brothers. Evening spent in talking with Sophia on their future prospects. . . ."

All seemed, as he said, to be going smoothly: J. B.—Ballantyne, Scott's printer and friend since Kelso days—would be helping with manuscripts and galley sheets, deciphering the Unknown's handwriting, expunging repetitions, suggesting clarifications. On the fifth, the Lockharts set off for their new home in London. On the ninth: "Yesterday I read and wrote the whole day and evening." Then, within five days of that untroubled entry, on a Wednesday in mid-December the first hint of difficulties in the offing: "Affairs very bad in the money market in London. It must come here and I have far too many engagements not to feel it."

He would feel it in truth. Four days later he was told the worst. Sunday, December 18. "Ballantyne calld on me this morning," he wrote at the beginning of one of the longest—and most affecting—entries in the *Journal*. "My extremity is come. Cadell has received letters from London which all but positively announce the failure of Hurst and Robinson so that Constable and Coy must follow and I must go with poor James Ballantyne for company. I suppose it will involve my all. . . ." But how could it have happened? Suddenly, beset by economic troubles that are general over England, a London firm totters, and simultaneously in Edinburgh the publisher Constable and Co. and the printer

Ballantyne find themselves shoved roughly to the edge of bankruptcy. And I must go with them, Scott realizes. "This news will make sad hearts at Darnick and in the cottages of Abbotsford which I do not nourish the least hope of preserving." Lying between Abbotsford and Melrose, the village of Darnick contained many who had found work helping the laird tend his grounds and build and maintain his mansion, that mansion that was his Delilah—"and so I have often termd it—and now—the recollection of the extensive woods I have planted and the walks I have formed from which strangers must derive both the pleasure and profit . . ." The full meaning of the news from London sank in as he sat over his journal in Edinburgh that winter Sunday. "I was to have gone there on Saturday in joy and prosperity to receive my friends—my dogs will wait for me in vain—it is foolish—but the thoughts of parting from these dumb creatures"—Hamlet and Ginger and Whiskey and the others—"have moved me more than any of the painful reflections I have put down." But how could it have happened, to the most popular author in the world, and to one of the most productive? "I must end this or I shall lose the tone of mind with which men should meet distress. I find my dogs' feet on my knees—I hear them whining and seeking me everywhere. . . ." How did it happen? "For myself the magic wand of the Unknown is shivered in his grasp. He must henceforth be termd the Too well Known."

The Wizard was to be granted a reprieve, however. On that same evening: *"Half past eight.* I closed this book under the consciousness of impending ruin. I open it an hour after, thanks be to God!, with the strong hope that matters may be got over safely and honourably in a mercantile sense." In the *Journal's* prose, day by day, sometimes hour by hour, vicissitudes etch the writer's emotions urgently across the page. Yet we do Scott an injustice extracting his cries of anguish this way. To get at these heartrending feelings, pages of delight and wisdom must be passed over, pages in which examples of humor and balance and generosity are as abundant as are the quotations, cited from memory, with ease and aptness, and from far-ranging sources: Shakespeare and Burns and Chaucer and Cervantes and Milton and Fielding and the Bible and Swift and Virgil and Dr. Johnson and Butler and Voltaire and Dryden —all these and more within, for example, the first year. What a memory, what a mind he carried with him through his days and evenings. Yet now that mind was sorely tried, as the heart that had been near breaking this afternoon took in the better news that might hold it together. "When I die will the journal of these days be taken out of the Ebony cabinet at Abbotsford and read as the transient pout of a man worth £60,000 with wonder that the well seeming Baronet should ever have experienced such a hitch? Or will it be found in some obscure lodginghouse where the decayd son of chivalry has hung up his scutcheon for some 20/- a week and where one or two old friends will look grave and whisper to each other, 'poor gentleman'—'a well meaning man'—'nobody's enemy but his own'—'thought his parts could never wear out'—'family poorly left,' 'pity he took that foolish title'? Who can answer this question?"

Only time could, and time, in the midst of Scott's respite, soon brought other woes. The new year 1826 was hardly started when, on the fifth of January, sitting down to work in the early afternoon after a walk over his grounds at Abbotsford: "To my horror and surprize I could neither write nor spell but put down one word for another and wrote nonsense. I was much overpowerd at the same time and could not conceive the reason. I fell asleep however in my chair and slept for two hours. On waking my head was clearer . . ." But did this dread interval mark the start of mental decay? A few days later, when the alarm seemed to have passed, Scott confessed to a friend who had been visiting that he had felt "mortal fear," grappling alone with what must have been a mild stroke, not the last, to be sure, that he would suffer.

And soon, very soon—within a couple of weeks—came more to grapple with, nor could this next alarm be kept quiet. From Abbotsford to Edinburgh, Monday, January 16: "Came through cold roads to as cold news. Hurst and Robinson have sufferd a Bill of £1000 to come back on Constable which I suppose infers the ruin of both houses. We will soon see. . . ." From their ruin would follow Scott's own, and this time there would be no reprieve. Tuesday, the seventeenth: "James Ballantyne this morning, good honest fellow, with a visage as black as the crook. He hopes no salvation . . ." And Scott's butler later set down his recollections of those first, direful days:

"At the failure of Sir Walter I did not hear of it until the afternoon, but I see that all was not right with them, for they were sitting with millincoly countinances. Dinner was taken up the same as usual. I, taking off the cover of the tureen, Sir Walter says: 'Dalgleish, just leave us and I will ring the bell when we want you.'

"In about ten minutes the bell rings. 'Take away dinner,' nothing touched.

"As soon as dinner was down, I went out, and passing down South Castle Street, I meets a friend of Sir Walter's, he stopping me ast how the family was. I said I could scarcely answer his question with satisfaction.

" 'How is Sir Walter in spirits?'

" 'I cannot say that any of them is in good spirits.'

" 'No wonder,' says the gentleman.

" 'Pray Sir, do you know anything that has taken place?'

" 'Have you not heard of it? Sir Walter has lost seventy thousand pound.' "

Before long all the city was possessed of the astounding news. "The opening of the year 1826," one citizen reminisced much later, "will ever be sad to those who remember the thunderbolt which then fell on Edinburgh in the utterly unexpected bankruptcy of Scott, implying the ruin of Constable the bookseller, and of Ballantyne the printer. If an earthquake had swallowed half the town, it would not have produced greater astonishment, sorrow, and dismay." The two merchants were one thing: they had taken their chances. "But Sir Walter! The idea that his practical sense had so far left him as to have permitted him to dabble in trade, had never crossed our imagination." How had it happened? How? And "how humbled we felt when we saw him—the pride of us all, dashed from his lofty and honourable station, and all the fruits of his well-worked talents gone." From the city the news spread outward, south toward London, through London to Brighton, where the Earl of Dudley would soon be reading of it in his newspaper: "Scott ruined! The Author of *Waverley* ruined! Good God, let every man to whom he has given months of delight give him sixpence, and he will rise tomorrow morning richer than Rothschild!"

Yet the solution would not be that simple. At the center of the crisis, Scott himself, visited by a succession of solemn friends and advisers, was passing restless nights. "He that sleeps too long in the morning let him borrow the pillow of a debtor." This on the eighteenth, shortly after the downfall, with days to dread ahead of him. "I had of course an indifferent night of it. I wish these two days were over . . ."

He kept to his room until nine, and "this," as his butler recorded, "is not your ordinary way, however it is excusable.

"They assembled in the dining-room to breakfast. In the course of an hour the bell rings. 'Take away the things.' The same way, nothing touched."

And at noon, Lady Scott summoned Dalgleish upstairs to tell the servants that they must look out for other places.

" 'I am very sorry to hear it, but I shall not leave you.'

" 'Oh, you know we will have nothing, so we cannot pay your wages.'

" 'I don't care. I will not go.' "

Nor did the devoted butler leave the household, though no windfall occurred to provide for his wages. "We dined of course at home," Sir Walter was writing a day or two later. "A painful scene after dinner and another after supper endeavouring to convince these poor dear creatures" —Lady Scott and their daughter Anne—"that they must not look for miracles but consider the misfortune as certain and only to be lessend by patience and labour." The talk in the household, as his daughter complained, was now all of shillings and pence. *Woodstock* and *Napoleon* must be pushed forward to completion as rapidly as possible for whatever they would bring. Creditors must somehow be held at bay, a trusteeship established to deal with them. The Edinburgh home on Castle Street, where Scott had moved with his young bride Charlotte more than a quarter of a century earlier, must be put up for sale.

And in the midst of this dismal turmoil, the condition of that same Charlotte grew distressing. For some time Scott's wife had suffered from asthma and dropsy; now as spring approached, she remained longer in bed and got about more feebly when she arose. In mid-March the novelist was engaged in the melancholy task of moving from Castle Street for the last time, beset by "the confusion and chucking about of our old furniture, the stripping of walls of pictures and rooms of ornaments; the leaving a house we have so long calld our home . . ." He was clearing away papers, packing for the journey to Abbotsford: "What a strange medley of thoughts such a task produces. There lie letters which made the heart throb when received now lifeless and uninteresting as are perhaps their owners—Riddles which time has read." But never to return to Castle Street; rather, when his duties at court called him back to the city, to take up rented lodgings. "It does not mend the matter," he had already noted earlier, February 14, 1826, "that this is the first day that a ticket for sale is on my House. Poor No. 39. One gets accustomd even to stone walls and the place suited me very well. . . ." Now with the town house all but vacated, a dejected Scott set off southward at midweek, March 15, for Abbotsford, with his wife and daughter intending to follow him over the weekend.

Instead, on Sunday came "a most melancholy letter from Anne." Lady Scott's illness—the dropsy that was disfiguring her—had grown worse; her departure from Edinburgh must be delayed. Somehow she did manage her arrival at Abbotsford by the following Wednesday, looking, in fact, "better than I expected," but thereafter was "seldom able to rise till 12 or one." Through the spring she grew yet more feeble— poor circulation, malfunctioning kidneys—and when her husband was forced to return to court session in early May, she had not left her bed for a week, and "was unable to take leave of me being in a sound sleep after a very indifferent night. Perhaps it was as well—an adieu might have hurt her and nothing I could have expressd would have been worth the risk." So he stole off from his "companion of twenty nine years . . . It withers my heart to think of it and to recollect that I can hardly hope again to seek confidence and counsel from that ear to which all might be safely confided . . ."

A day not far ahead would fully justify his fears. The single entry for Monday, May 15, 1826, written alone in lodgings at Edinburgh, reads: "Received the melancholy intelligence that all is over at Abbotsford." Now he must make the solitary trip south for yet another ordeal: "I have seen her—" This after his return. "The figure I beheld is and is not my Charlotte— . . . There is the same symmetry of form though those limbs are rigid which were once so gracefully elastic—but that yellow masque with pinchd features which seems to mock life rather than emulate it, can it be the face that was once so full of lively expression?" Within the stillness of her room: "the pressure of the coffin was visible on the bed but it had been removed elsewhere— All was neat as she loved it but all was calm—calm as death. I remembered the last sight of her—she raised herself in bed and tried to turn her eyes after me and said with a sort of smile 'You all have such melancholy faces.' They were the last words I ever heard her utter . . ." He had returned to her side before leaving—that was only seven days ago—to find her in a deep sleep. "It is deeper now . . ."

Thus a man struggles to set down his grief in this year 1826 that seems cruelly endless. It did end at last, and when it did, at Abbotsford—site of grand parties in the past, with light and laughter spilling out of the paneled library over the lawn—there was yet one more small, traditional celebration of neighbors: "The Fergusons came in mass and we had all the usual appliances of mirth and good cheer. Yet our party like the Chariot wheels of Pharaoh when involved in the Red sea draggd heavily. Some of the party grow old and infirm; others thought of the absence of the hostess whose reception to her guests was always kind. We did as well as we could however." And Sir Walter Scott, for whom times had turned sour, humbly concluded his entries of that year that had altered almost everything in his life: "why should we give up the comfort of seeing our friends because they can no longer be to us or we to them what we once were to each other?"

The cause of so sudden and total a financial ruin is at best difficult to understand. The immensity of Scott's debt resulted from his expenses building and maintaining Abbotsford, from the danger-fraught system of easy credit that prevailed at the time, and above all, from the author's involving himself in trade. That involvement had been kept secret over the years from all but a very few. One as close to him, for instance, as his son-in-law Lockhart was unaware of it—and utterly shocked when the crash came. "It is easy no doubt," Scott wrote that young gentleman in extenuation when the secret could be kept no longer, "for any friend to blame me for entering into connexion in commercial matters at all. But I wish to know what I could have done better in 1806 . . . Literature was not then"—early in the century when he was beginning to write— "what poor Constable has made it and with my little capital . . . I was too glad to make commercially the means of supporting my family. I got £600 for the Lay of the Last Minstrel and—a price which made mens hairs stand on end—£1,000 for Marmion. . . ."

He could make much more by allying himself as part owner of the company that printed his books, more still as part owner also of the company that published them. These arrangements came about over the years, in secret. As long ago as 1800, Scott had been urging his school-boy friend, James Ballantyne, by then a printer, to move from Kelso to Edinburgh to establish his presses in the larger city: "It appears to me that such a plan, judiciously adopted and diligently pursued, opens a fair road to an ample fortune." Early in 1802, Scott's *Minstrelsy of the Scottish Border* had been printed, and admirably printed, by Ballantyne from Kelso; *The Lady of the Last Minstrel* he printed in Edinburgh, at his new shop in the Canongate. And thereafter the presses rolled steadily, printing (and always handsomely) *Marmion*, *The Lady of the Lake*, all those Waverley novels—in addition to legal and antiquarian material Scott guided their way. As many as 145,000 volumes of Scott's own various works of prose and poetry were coming off the presses in the year 1822 alone. And the fecund author was part owner of the printing plant. More: he had at times been part owner of the publishing house that published those works—though his involvement with both commercial enterprises was assiduously kept from the public.

All of us, of course, are prisoners of our age. In the Edinburgh in which Scott had grown up, gentlemen were not tradesmen. That was a law of nature. Gentlemen, who knew who their ancestors were, became lawyers, voted, and—however poor—associated socially only with other gentlemen. Tradesmen, by contrast, of humble antecedents, lived in the present, modestly—at that time no great fortunes had yet been made in trade—and did not vote or in any other way interfere in the management of public affairs. Such matters they left to their social betters, as they had left them for centuries—one more manifestation of the natural order of things. So it had been in Scott's childhood—when, too, was beginning, there in that very Scotland along the banks of the Clyde, the Industrial Revolution that would in the writer's maturity alter forever such hierarchies as had formed his youth. The Great Unknown, meanwhile, who enjoyed secrets, was innocently keeping this mercantile one very well: "But Sir Walter!" we have already heard Lord Cockburn exclaiming after the truth had come to light. "The idea that his practical sense had so far left him as to have permitted him to dabble in trade, had never crossed our imagination. . . ."

Yet if Scott had his secret, his publisher Constable had one too. Long before 1825, Scott's own publishing firm had blundered into financial difficulties from which his earlier publisher (that same Constable) had rescued it, though at a price—that the rival firm be dissolved. So by this date, the ominous year 1825, the author was no longer a secret partner in publishing ventures. He did, however, still make an additional profit from the printing of his books at the jointly owned

Ballantyne Press. For on May 12, 1822, some three years earlier, he had signed a fateful partnership agreement with James Ballantyne that allowed Scott a share of all profits and—unlikely prospect—made him likewise liable for a share of all debts that might attach themselves to so flourishing an industry.

Strangely enough, by 1825—and here was Constable's secret—the debts of the whole operation were staggering. How? Why? Scott when he found out was as baffled as we may be: "Constable's business seems unintelligible. No man thought the house worth less than £150,000— Constable told me when he was making his will that he was worth £80,000." But it had not been in the publisher's interest to share his true predicament with his most successful writer. That must remain secret, for the last thing Constable had wanted in straitened times was that this Wizard of the North should lose confidence and turn elsewhere for a publisher of his future volumes. "Our most productive culture," an associate had superfluously reminded Constable, "is the Author of Waverley; let us stick to him, let us dig on and dig on at that extraordinary quarry." But all the while costs were horrendous, so that that same associate was expressing misgivings about Constable's affairs as early as January 1823: "We have been so long carrying on large transactions, and all the time with an apparent strain & want of money—." The bankers, he feared, "may say to themselves—'are these men never to get easy? are all these Reviews and Encyds. & books of the Author of Waverley, about all which we have heard of such immense profits being made—are these books never to bring them home?'!!!"

More projects, and ever more ambitious ones. Earlier loans falling due. Borrowing to pay interest and extend credit. Books paid for in advance, before a word had been written. And the next book by Scott would finally clear off debts, and if not that one—then surely the one after that. Meanwhile, promises to pay, counter checks, accommodation notes extended with no funds to back them, payment for book sales delayed, more and larger publishing projects undertaken. And Scott's own debts—£20,000 or so at the crash—had gone on obliviously mounting all this while, to pay for Abbotsford and the spacious life he chose to live therein.

The crash had come. An accommodation check was returned to drawer, and there were no funds to meet it. All else followed inexorably. Suddenly, in those days before limited liability, the Author of *Waverley* was liable, and for more than merely the £20,000—merely!—that made up his personal indebtedness. Possessed of whatever resources the creditors could get at, he was technically liable for the debts of James Ballantyne & Co. as well—an additional £100,000 of debts, of which £40,000 was owed by the bankrupt Constable, whose finances by then were hideously entangled with Ballantyne's own.

The crash had come, and a dazed Scott had been forced to consider what course of action he should follow.

Three courses were open to him. He could turn over all he owned to his creditors, an action that would keep him out of jail at least, and since Abbotsford by chance had been presented to his son Walter and daughter-in-law as a wedding gift, that possession would be beyond the creditors' grasp, although they could, in order to raise the money that was owed them, make off with Scott's furniture and magnificent library and life-rent—that is, his legal right to use Abbotsford during his lifetime. Not an attractive solution. The second alternative Scott as an attorney would have recommended to any client in similar distressing circumstances: declare bankruptcy as a tradesman, pay off some fractional amount of the debt as best he could—so many pence to the pound—and discharge the obligation, however inadequately, in the eyes of the law. This, essentially, was the course the brothers Irving had followed in Liverpool eight years earlier, the course Constable would follow, the course routinely followed by insolvent enterprises right up to the present. "I might," Scott acknowledged in his journal January 24, days after the crash, "save my library, etc. by assistance of friends and bid my creditors defiance. But for this I would in a court of Honour deserve to lose my spurs for—No"—he would take the third course—"if they permit me, I will be their vassal for life and dig in the mine of my imagination to find diamonds (or what may sell for such) to make good my engagements . . ."

That same morning, January 24, he had for the first time since the disaster been obliged to appear at Parliament House in Edinburgh to discharge his court duties, "and like the man with the large nose thought everybody was thinking of me and my mishaps." Lord Cockburn, incidentally, was in the hall that morning and saw it differently: "Well do I remember his first appearance after this calamity was divulged, when he walked into Court one day in January 1826. There was no affectation, and no reality, of *facing it;* no look of indifference or defiance; but the manly and modest air of a gentleman conscious of some folly, but of perfect rectitude, and of most heroic and honourable resolutions."

And concerning Scott's behavior the witness remembered one moment in particular from that morning. "It was on that very day, I believe, that he said a very fine thing. Some of his friends offered him, or rather proposed to offer him, enough of money, as was supposed, to enable him to arrange with his creditors. He paused for a moment; and then, recollecting his powers, said proudly—'No! this right hand shall work it all off!'" Every bit of the debt, though it would come to a staggering £116,838. 11s. 3d. In our own currency the amount might approximate just under a million dollars. And yet, unwilling to borrow a penny more, the novelist signed the Trust Deed for his creditors: "I the said Sir Walter Scott have resolved to employ my time and talents on the production of such literary works as shall seem to me most likely to promote the ends I have in view, the sums arising from which works I am also desirous to devote to the payment of the debts owing by me as a Partner of the said company"—James Ballantyne & Co.—"and as an individual."

The trustees chosen to deal with this personal crisis had agreed, in light of Scott's resolution, to allow him the use of his library at Abbotsford, so that the writing might proceed. But 39 Castle Street was sold in July 1826, for £2,300, reducing the debt at least by that much: "It is worth £300 more," its former owner noted wistfully in his journal, "but I will not oppose my own opinion or convenience to good and well meant council, so farewell poor No 39." For himself, he would retrench at Abbotsford, limiting his entertaining severely, sharply limiting his purchases of books, though as his daughter Anne, with some exaggeration, told Tom Moore: "Papa is a bad hand at economising. All his great plans of retrenchment have ended in selling my horse!"

In truth, his style of living—formerly so liberal—was changed more radically than that. And he worked. Sunday, June 4, 1826: "I wrote a good task yesterday and to-day a great one, scarce stirring from the desk the whole day except a few minutes when Lady Rae calld . . ." Saturday, April 7, 1827, nearly a year later: "The same history occurs, my desk and my exercize. I am a perfect Automaton. *Bonaparte* runs in my head from 7 in the morning till ten at night without intermission. I wrote six leaves to-day and corrected four proofs." *Woodstock* was finished, and its copyright sold for £6,000; the money went to Scott's creditors. *The Life of Napoleon*, swelling to nine volumes, immediately brought another £9,000 to the creditors. *Chronicles of the Canongate* appeared, and another Waverley novel was begun: *The Fair Maid of Perth*. By the end of 1828, Scott's efforts had reduced his debt by some £35,000—that is, by about a quarter, maybe $200,000 or so in our currency—an achievement so gratifying that his creditors formally voted him their thanks; two years later they presented him with his library as an outright gift, reducing the indebtedness in so doing by an additional £3,000.

"It grieves me," Washington Irving wrote the painter David Wilkie of all these efforts, "to find that Scott is bestowing so much glorious labor to satisfy the claims of creditors, who, if I understand the affair rightly, are his creditors only by some technical construction of the law." Yet the Wizard of the North labored on. "I was thinking this morning"—Thursday, October 5, 1826—"that my time glided away in a singularly monotonous manner like one of those dark gray days which neither promises sunshine nor threatens rain, too melancholy for enjoyment, too tranquil for repining." Much of it seemed like that, though manuscript piled up, while Scott's health began paying the price for so many hours at the desk. Out for a walk on his grounds that August, "fell in with the ladies but their donkies outwalkd me—a flock of sheep afterwards outwalkd me and I begin to think on my conscience that a snail put on training might soon outwalk me. I must lay the old salve to the old sore and be thankful to be able to walk at all. . . ."

Gray much of his life seemed now, amid toil and declining health; yet one Friday evening some months later we do linger over thankfully. It meant little enough, apparently, to Scott himself, who made no entry at all in his journal for that date, February 23, 1827. Yet virtually every newspaper in Europe would soon carry columns about what went on that night in his life. The widower was in lodgings for Court Session at the time, in Edinburgh, where he had been invited to preside at a dinner to raise money for indigent actors, to be given in the Assembly Rooms in George Street. "Do you care anything about the mystery of the Waverly novels now?" Lord Meadowbank had asked him casually in the drawing room before the festivities. "Not I," Scott had answered; "the secret is too generally known." The author expected as a consequence, when the toasts went round, some jesting allusion to *Rob Roy* perhaps, but instead, before the three hundred gentlemen assembled there, the lord was rising during the course of the dinner for a more extended speech.

"I would beg leave to propose a toast," he began. "The health of one of the Patrons, a great and distinguished individual, whose name must always stand by itself, and which, in an assembly such as this, or in any other assembly of Scotsmen, must ever be received, I will not say with ordinary feelings of pleasure or of delight, but with those of rapture and enthusiasm." The name of that patron was withheld until the end, but who could it be but Scott, seated among them? And the lord was proceeding for the first time to allude publicly to what his listeners soon realized Scott must have been forewarned of and have sanctioned: ". . . the Great Unknown—the minstrel of our native land—the mighty magician who has rolled back the current of time, and conjured up before our living senses the men and the manners of days which have long passed away, stands revealed to the eyes and the hearts of his affectionate and admiring countrymen . . ." Applause had broken out and rose deafeningly, as gentlemen got to their feet, climbed on chairs and tables, called out their approval while Lord Meadowbank over the clamor continued as best he could to his conclusion: "He it is who has conferred a new reputation on our national character, and bestowed on Scotland an imperishable name, were it only by her having given birth to himself. I propose the health," he pronounced unequivocally at last, "of Sir Walter Scott."

And amid the rapturous cheers of the company at the Theatrical Fund Dinner, the silver-haired Scott was standing finally to acknowledge his open secret, that he was "the total and undivided author" of all those marvelous works from *Waverley* in 1814 on through *Woodstock* twelve years and twenty-one novels later. "Meadowbank taxd me with the novels," the modest author did mention in his journal the following evening, "and to end that farce at once I pleaded guilty. . . . I got away at ten at night." But not before leaving behind him, then once more as so often wherever he went, feelings among those who knew him of pleasure and pride and gratitude.

For five years after the dinner Scott continued to write—four more novels, a collection of short stories, a play, the nine-volume life of Napoleon, a history of Scotland, two volumes of essays, four series of *Tales of a Grandfather*, and notes to a new, uniform edition of all his works. That enormous (if uneven) achievement in five years' time. All told, his hours at the desk earned some £50,000 for his creditors—something approaching half a million dollars now—and of what he still owed, the balance his executors would be able to pay within five weeks after the author's death, by means of insurance, sales of copyrights, and additional earnings from published writings. Scott believed, in fact, in his last days that he had succeeded in making good all his obligations, and those around him let him think he had, willing enough that the proud author might find what consolation he could in fancying himself a free man at last, toward the very end of his decline.

Already by 1831 that decline was all too obvious to his friends and family. The tireless laborer over the foolscap had endured rheumatism in his one good leg and chilblains in his fingers, and near the start of the preceding year he had suffered another stroke, this time staggering into the drawing room of his Edinburgh lodgings in Shadwick Place and crumbling speechless to the floor before his horrified daughter Anne and a visitor. Scott's inarticulateness lasted ten minutes or so—but, indeed, he never really recovered from that fit in the early afternoon of February 15, 1830. Through the remainder of the year he did continue to write— almost as much as in years previous—but the quality of most of it fell sadly off. He wrote on, in 1831, through March, April. And yet to his journal, abandoned for a while and then resumed, he confided about his physical deterioration: "I only know that to live as I am just now is a gift little worth having. I think I will be in the Secret next week unless I recruit greatly."

He did recover from that sickness, well enough to be denied the secret for yet another year. "I am sure it is mere fear keeps half the world, especially if they have been blisterd bled and criticized. I have sufferd terribly, that is the truth, rather in body than in mind, and I often wish I could lie down and sleep without waking. But I will fight it out if I can. . . . My bodily strength is terribly gone, perhaps my mental too." This to his journal, confidentially, a Sunday in May 1831, on learning with mixed emotions of the suicide at Birmingham of an acquaintance and fellow sufferer. Lockhart came up from London for a visit to Abbotsford soon after. On his arrival, the first glimpse of his father-in-law seemed the most painful of all the sights he had ever beheld. "Knowing at what time I might be expected, he had been lifted on his pony, and advanced about half a mile on the Selkirk road to meet me. He moved at a footpace, with Laidlaw at one stirrup . . . Sir Walter had had his head shaved, and wore a black silk night-cap under his blue bonnet. All his garments hung loose about him; his countenance was thin and haggard, and there was an obvious distortion in the muscles of one cheek. His look, however, was placid—his eye as bright as ever—perhaps brighter than it ever was in health; he smiled with the same affectionate gentleness, and though at first it was not easy to understand everything he said, he spoke cheerfully and manfully."

This was the Scott, pitifully enfeebled from overwork, whose carriage was stoned a few days later by the mob at Jedburgh, who was spat upon from the windows of that border town. Against his family's advice he had insisted on attending the elections in that nearby community, where he meant to speak in favor of the traditionalist candidate. For although reform was in the air—and long overdue—the laird of Abbotsford was now as all his life a Tory, a believer in paternalism, personally the most generous and humane of men and the most beloved of employers—but increasingly appalled (as were Blake and Wordsworth and Carlyle and many other thinking people of his time) by what industrialism had done and was doing to the society he had loved: the contented hinds and drovers he had known in his youth of gathering ballads and living among them seemed gone, replaced, as he noted, by "the stern sullen unwashd artificers whom you see lounging sulkily along the streets of the towns in Lancashire." And though throughout his life he had included among his closest friends Whigs high and low as well as Tories, he was prematurely an old man now, outraged by the behavior of those who would stir up mobs against authority: "They have much to answer for who in gaiety of heart have brought a peaceful and virtuous population to such a pass."

He (who, though not yet sixty, had already lived too long) had gone to Jedburgh to the dismay of his family, and had been stoned and spat upon for his pains: "Burke Sir Walter!" the mobs had yelled at him—kill him as the ghoul Burke, hung for murder in Edinburgh two years earlier, had killed his victims before selling them to doctors for dissection. And although a couple of months earlier, in this same town, Scott had hurled back in disgust at a similar mob, "I regard your gabble no more than the geese on the green," now his voice was too weak to carry over the blasphemies and insults pelting him as he limped away from that abusive world that seemed a repudiation of whatever his own life had valued. He returned to Abbotsford, and not long after, in July

1831, had a falling-out with his long-standing friend James Ballantyne, desk mate in the schoolroom at Kelso nearly a half century before, his "Tom Tell-Truth" and constant supporter since then. But Ballantyne, too, had aged. The printer was full of temperance ideas now: "J. B. wishes to engage himself & I in what he calls a pledge to a temperate Society, that is to proclaim ourselves sots & intemperate fools to the whole world. He be damned—& so much for that." Moreover, this reader whose opinion Scott had always valued had recently condemned the Waverley novel currently being written: *Count Robert of Paris* should be redone. "*You*," he had informed Scott, "are of the opinion the subject is an excellent one; whereas *I* do not even know what the subject is." And the exhausted author had confided to his journal, "The blow is a stunning one I suppose for I scarcely feel it. It is singular but it comes with as little surprize as if I had a remedy ready. Yet God knows I am at sea in the dark and the vessell leaky . . ." In these desperate straits, his gifts played out, Scott entertained his old friend at Abbotsford once more, on a July evening in 1831. But worst of all for their friendship, Ballantyne, the critic and teetotaler, was ardently Whig now—all for reform. Something happened that evening—what, is not known—but the disgruntled guest left next morning early, without good-byes, and never saw Abbotsford or Scott again.

The feast of fancy was almost over. "I have had as much happiness in my time as most men, and I must not complain now." So Scott had remarked earlier to one admirer, who in turn had commented that no one could have labored harder for the happiness that had come to him. But, the tireless author had clarified, "I consider the capacity to labour as part of the happiness I have enjoyed." Now, however, the labor was killing him. To get him away from his desk his family proposed a voyage to the Mediterranean. Accordingly, in the fall of 1831 he was again—and for the next to last time—in London.

One who saw Scott then spoke of his "red-sandy complexion and straggling whiskers—slow and thick manner of speaking—and broad Scotch accent—. . . . limping very much . . . and using for support an immense thick stick; dressed in checkered black & white trousers and dark square cut coat." They had got him to London in late September 1831, away from his desk and to his son-in-law Lockhart's home, where soon after his arrival his host had sent for Washington Irving to dine with the family. A decade had passed since these two writers—the Scotsman and the American—had seen each other. Now Irving, forty-eight years old and rather more portly than formerly, was about to end his long European exile. After his nearly seventeen years of life spent in England and France and Germany and Spain, he was at last on the point of returning to New York. Meanwhile, he did share this family dinner in London with Scott, the daughters Anne and Sophia, and Sophia's husband.

"Ah! my dear fellow," Sir Walter said as Irving approached where he was seated and took him by the hand, "time has dealt lightly with you since last we met." With Scott it had dealt heavily indeed. The laird was still weary from having traveled from Edinburgh, and during dinner he could hardly take part in the conversation. "How different," Irving would remember of this sad occasion, "from the time I last dined with him, when Scott was the life of the company, all hanging on his lips; every body making way for his anecdote or story." Now, although occasionally he tried, his stories that began in the old way trailed off into incomprehensibility, and his eyes would grow dull and his head sink as he realized he had not made his meaning understood. "Irving, give Scott your arm," Lockhart said when dinner was over, and the old man—just turned sixty—clutched at the offered arm with one hand and at his cane with the other. "Ah!" he said, "the times are changed, my good fellow, since we went over the Eildon hills together. It is all nonsense to tell a man that his mind is not affected, when his body is in this state." So Irving for the last time stood beside—for the last time his hand touched—this friend of his, now gravely diminished, this fellow writer whose genius the American, like many others of his age, regarded as second only to Shakespeare's.

From London they took Scott south to the Mediterranean on a frigate that the government provided—the most popular gesture that the new king William IV would make during his brief reign. On the HMS *Barham* Scott and his family sailed southward to milder climates, and his spirits did seem to pick up for a while in sight of Gibraltar, of Algeria, of Malta, where he sat patiently behind the quarantine bar in his brown coat and trousers of check Lowland plaid. His face was mottled and inexpressive, his hands crossed passively on a shepherd's staff. Yet his mind, as the pages of his *Journal* reveal, was continuing effortfully to function: he would write one more novel, *The Siege of Malta*—"it shall be one of the best which I have written," he explained by mail to his publisher back in Edinburgh, "& will have much description & some real history." But his phenomenal memory was finally betraying him; much of what he wrote was simply remembered, all but verbatim, from a book he had read in his youth. And the work was never completed; half of it the befuddled author burned by mistake sometime during that winter in Italy, before the spring of 1832 came—before April came, when abruptly, in mid-sentence, the *Journal* that is now increasingly filled with errors breaks off. The party had entered Rome. He writes, "We slept reasonbly but on the next morning," and puts down his pen and writes no more.

He wanted to return home. He did not want to die in exile as the novelist Fielding had in Lisbon. On May 11, 1832, his party, including his son Charles and his daughter Anne, started the long journey northward by coach. Stage by stage they made their lumbering way, through Florence, Venice, Verona, over the Brenner Pass, to Innsbruck, Munich, Ulm, Frankfort (where Scott wrote the last few words—courteously declining a visit from the philosopher Schopenhauer—that he would ever write, and where he paused to browse in a bookstore and purchase a copy of Irving's *Alhambra*, just published that spring), from Frankfort to Mainz, by steamer to Cologne, then on to Nimeguen. But just before reaching that Dutch city he suffered another stroke, so that when the weary travelers arrived at London at last, on the evening of June 13, Scott was hardly conscious any longer of his surroundings. For three weeks he lingered near death in an upstairs back room in the St. James's Hotel in Jermyn Street. Yet still he hung on to consciousness, until they could get his racked body, his dazed mind back to his beloved Abbotsford. By steamship from London to Edinburgh; then on July 11, stretched out in a makeshift cot in a carriage, the moribund Scott, face pale from bleeding and plastered where the leeches had bitten, began the five-hour journey south to Tweedside. He had hardly known what was happening, but as the carriage came in sight of the Eildon hills, Lockhart, who rode with him, tells us that "he became greatly excited, and when turning himself on the couch his eye caught at length his own towers, at the distance of a mile, he sprang up with a cry of delight."

So much energy, so much vitality would not be easily quenched. "I do not intend to die a moment sooner than I can help it," he had promised three years earlier. And he held on now two months more, at first seated in his wheelchair under his plaid in the summer sunlight of his own garden and terrace. "This is sad idleness," he did say at one point to those about him soon after his return. "I shall forget what I have been thinking of, if I don't set it down now. Take me into my own room, and fetch the keys of my desk." Wheeled to his study, with ink and clean paper before him, he told Sophia, "Now give me my pen and leave me for a little to myself." But when she touched the pen to his hand, the writer's fingers could no longer close; it fell uselessly over the paper, and he whose sentences had covered so many pages sank back into the pillows of his chair, his eyes filling with tears.

Thereafter his condition grew worse and ever worse. Soon, as his amanuensis Laidlaw was explaining to a concerned friend, he had become "as helpless and requires to be attended in every respect as an infant of six months old. Of his powerful mind, which as it were shone over the civilized world, there remains only a pale and uncertain glimmering." No longer could he recognize people. This most considerate of men grew now irritable, demanding, frenzied, and delirious. In his ravings his dutiful daughters Sophia and Anne became his Goneril and Regan, he the tortured Lear. Through the halls of Abbotsford rang his screams; fourteen hours he screamed, then slept at last a drugged sleep to awake "as wild and violent as before." Of another awful interval Anne recorded, "Not withstanding immense doses of laudanum, He screamed without ceasing *Six and twenty hours*."

The end of such torment came as a mercy, by open windows of the dining room where Scott's bed had been moved, within sight and rippling sound of the Tweed, on a beautiful autumn afternoon, September 21, 1832. The sufferer grown quiet gave up at last, leaving his halls silent of that recent hideous anguish. Then, in the unaccustomed stillness there and about the grounds, ghosts that mattered to this full, completed life might begin to assemble—wife, good friends, the many visitors from near and far whose spirits seem to haunt the spot yet, and among whom we from overseas yet may feel the presence of one in particular. Above the spectral clamor of hounds in the courtyard, seated alone and nervous in his postchaise, an American author and sometime business-man waits to be welcomed by a host still in his wonderful prime, on a late August day of 1817, those fifteen years earlier—now those hundred and sixty some years ago—at the upper end of the gravel walk by the gate on the Selkirk road.

THREE WOMEN,
FRIENDS OF IRVING'S

A thousand recollections broke . . . upon my mind, of Emily Foster as I had known her at Dresden, young, and fair, and bright, and beautiful.

IRVING AT SUNNYSIDE

E M I L Y F O S T E R was born in Bedfordshire, England, in 1804, and died eighty-one years later, in Northamptonshire, in 1885. Matilda Hoffman was born in New York City in 1791, eight years after the birth of the American writer whose career we are following. She died in New York in 1809. Mary Wollstonecraft Shelley was born in a London upstairs room on a summer night in 1797. She died in 1851.

Facts, bald enough. Yet those six dates embrace lives that can be conjured before us now, more than a century later, with pleasure and benefit. And clearly, too; for much of and about those three remarkable people was written during their sojourns here that has been preserved. All were friends of—all three were warmly fond of—Washington Irving.

"Heavens! what a haphazard, schemeless life mine has been," the thirty-eight-year-old Irving was writing from London in 1820, during the first weeks that witnessed the unexampled triumph of his *Sketch Book*. "What a haphazard, schemeless life mine has been, that here I should be, at this time of life, youth slipping away, and scribbling month after month and year after year, far from home, without any means or prospect of entering into matrimony, which I absolutely believe indispensable to the happiness and even comfort of the after part of existence. . . ." The correspondent to whom he was writing so wistful a sentiment was the James Kirke Paulding with whom as a child Irving had played truant from his room on William Street to sneak down village byways to see the afterpiece at the nearby theater, the Paulding with whom he had collaborated in his young manhood to write *Salmagundi*, the same Paulding who had recently married Gertrude Kemble and was thriving in his new bliss in Washington. "Peter, who is sitting by me," Irving added in a postscript, "desires me to remember him most heartily to you and Gertrude." That was on May 27, 1820. And it was three months later, in August, that Washington Irving with his brother Peter was boarding ship at Dover to escape further lionizing by journeying to the Continent. "The next you will hear from me," he had written on the eve of his departure to Henry Brevoort, his other good friend recently married back home, "will be from France, and after passing five years in England among genuine John Bulls it will be like entering into a New World to cross the Channel."

Accordingly, fifteen years from the time he had first visited there, he was back at last in Paris, but in a city much changed. On that earlier visit, in 1805, Irving had just turned twenty-two, an American youth whose well-to-do merchant brothers were providing him with the means of making the Grand Tour. Then the theater and *filles de joie* had interested him more than did those botany lessons that his journals record his occasionally, dutifully having attended: "You will excuse the shortness and hastiness of this letter, for which I can only plead as an excuse that I am a *young man* and in *Paris*." Now, in the late summer of 1820, he was hardly young any more—and was famous, and his fame was growing. As for the city, this capital of the French was older too, having twice been conquered in the last six years, its emperor twice banished, its citizenry made to play host to his conquerors. From lodgings at No. 4, rue Mont Thabor, near the Tuileries, Irving was soon writing brother William that fall of 1820: "Either Paris or myself has changed very much since I was here before. It is by no means so gay as formerly; that is to say, the populace have a more grave and triste appearance. You see but little of the sprightliness and gaiety of manner for which the French are proverbial."

And why should those hordes of visitors from England expect otherwise? Irving himself acknowledged that the English would hardly have been gracious had the French forcibly restored the exile Charles II to his throne in 1660, then flocked to London to enjoy that city. He was writing William, incidentally, that late September day of 1820, with a more particular aim in view. Funds were needed from home to help launch brother Peter in a new enterprise, "a most promising mode of turning a small amount of money and some activity of talent and exertion to large account." On their way to Paris, the Irvings had come by Le Havre, and there had been charmed with the prospects of a steamboat on the Seine—a maiden service between populous banks clear up to Rouen.

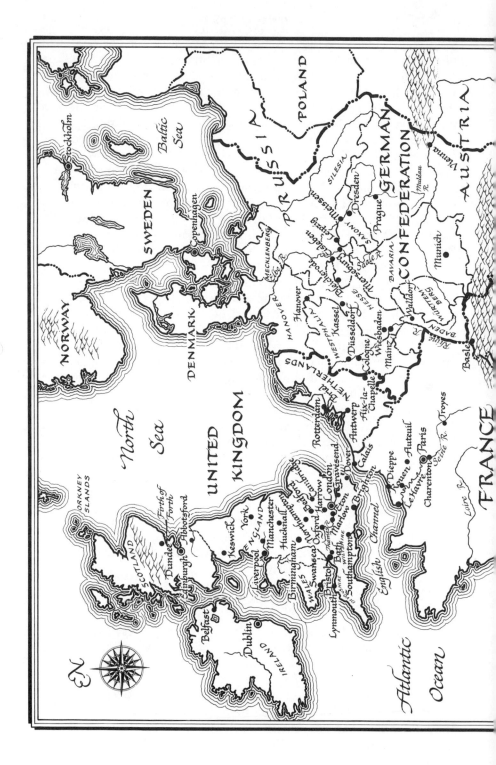

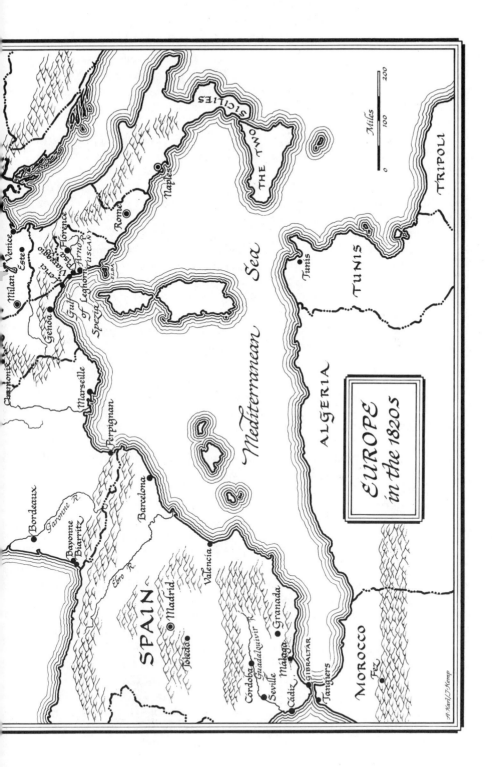

The brothers had ascended the French river with mounting excitement: "It appeared to be one of the most advantageous places possible for steam navigation, both as to procuring freight and passengers." Nor was the venture risky, "for Mr. Church, the conductor of the enterprise, had already proved his capacity by his very successful attempts on the Garonne. . . ."

The story we are telling might here have taken a different turn. This was an age of speculation and sudden wealth, as the lives of both Burr and Scott reveal. Fortunes were there to be made; William Irving himself had made one from small beginnings among the Indians in the Mohawk Valley, and notably a fortune of prodigious size had been gathered in by John Jacob Astor, whom Washington Irving would be seeing in Paris during these same months. That letter to William back home was seeking funds—$5,000, in fact—to be invested in the steamboat venture, in addition to the profits from *The Sketch Book* already invested: "I am induced to take this share in the enterprise, not from a desire of making money for myself, but to enable Peter to lay hold of what I consider the *best*, and indeed what is the *only* chance for getting into fortune's way again, that has presented since our disasters"—since those months of bankruptcy and humiliation three years earlier at Liverpool.

In the event, William declined to contribute to his youngest brother's scheme, and wisely so. Peter was doomed to linger fruitlessly about Le Havre at least for the next few years, the French themselves unwilling to invest in this newfangled intrusion on their waters. And Washington Irving in Paris would fret time away with his mind diverted by thoughts of steamboats, and with his own newly won fortune soon diminished to about where it had been before *The Sketch Book* appeared.

Autumn turned into winter. With Peter a frequent visitor, he would stay in Paris eleven months, his pen for a long time idle, his mind distracted, his accounts dwindled, even as his fame was rising to its zenith. The great Murray, who had first rejected *The Sketch Book* for publication, was now moved to write Irving from London, "I am convinced I did not half know you, and esteeming you highly as I did, certainly my esteem is doubled by my better knowledge of you"—and by those sterling sales. An English noblewoman made enquiries: Was it true, as some were whispering, that *The Sketch Book* had been written not by a savage from overseas but by the wizard in Edinburgh, Sir Walter Scott? Irving had the pleasure of laying that rumor to rest: Scott "never saw my writings until in print," he wrote from Paris; "but though he has not assisted me with his pen, yet the interest which he took in my success; the praises which he bestowed on some of the first American numbers forwarded to him; the encouragement he gave to me to go on and do more, and the countenance he gave to the first volume when republished in England have, perhaps, been more effectually serviceable than if he had revised and corrected my work page by page. He has always been to me a frank, generous, warmhearted friend, and it is one of my greatest gratifications to be able to call him such. . . ."

Additional letters besides those two called for answers and helped pass the time. One in particular, to his friend Brevoort back home, back on the island washed by the Hudson from which Irving had set sail five long years and more ago: "You urge me to return to New York—and say many ask whether I mean to renounce my country?" The jingoes were aroused in our young nation, and yammering. "For this last question I have no reply to make—and yet I will make a reply—As far as my precarious and imperfect abilities enable me, I am endeavouring to serve my country," the expatriate took care to explain. "Whatever I have written has been written with the feelings and published as the writing of an American—Is that renouncing my Country? How else am I to serve my country—by coming home and begging an office of it; which I should not have the kind of talent or the business habits requisite to fill?" His return to America, he continued on this March day in 1821, "must depend upon circumstances, not upon inclinations. I have, by patient & persevering labour of my most uncertain pen, & by catching the gleams of sunshine in my cloudy mind, managed to open to myself an avenue to some degree of profit & reputation—I value it the more highly because it is entirely independent and self created; and I must use my best endeavours to turn it to account. In remaining therefore abroad, I do it with the idea that I can best exert my talents, for the present, where I am—and that I trust will be admitted as a sufficient reply, from a man who has but his talents to feed & clothe him."

There was much good sense in the attitude. Irving's English reputation, assured by the House of Murray, had vastly enlarged his readership in America; his fame was flourishing as it simply could not have done then had he been an American writer in the United States. But his thoughts in those uncertain months were tending homeward nevertheless, and meanwhile he struggled with the task of completing another book; for the time was ripe, as he was aware, and he needed something fresh in the bookstalls to take advantage of his new fame. Tom Moore, the Irish poet and confidant of Lord Byron, had by now met this celebrated American (as Moore met everyone of consequence), and had become a close friend. December 21, 1820: "Dined with M'Kay at the *table d'hôte* at Meurice's, for the purpose of being made known to Mr. Washington Irving, the author of the work which has lately had success, the 'Sketch Book;' a good-looking and intelligent-mannered man." Within three months, "Irving called near dinner time," Moore at home with his family on the Allée des Veuves was noting in his diary; "asked him to stay and share our roast chicken with us, which he did. He has been hard at work writing lately; in the course of ten days has written about 130 pages of the size of those in the 'Sketch Book;' this is amazing rapidity. Has followed up an idea which I suggested, and taken the characters in his 'Christmas Essay,' Master Simon, &c. &c., for the purpose of making a slight thread of a story on which to string his remarks and sketches of human manners and feelings: left us at nine."

Thus, essays in *The Sketch Book*, that earlier triumph, were being developed, at Moore's suggestion, to form what Irving nervously hoped would be acceptable as a sequel: further glimpses of English country life highlighted by sentiment and some humor among the paneled walls and arborways of his fictional Bracebridge Hall. Maybe it would work, yet despite bursts of energy, Geoffrey Crayon, Gent., would have trouble seeing his new scheme through. Indeed, he was still toiling in the midst of it as he set off again across the Channel that summer, in part to witness the pageantry of George IV's coronation in London. Ever the wanderer, he had remained in France less than a year before this departure for England, where little more than a year would pass before he would yet again resume his travels on the Continent—a year containing work and illness and grief and, finally, renewed success.

Irving did witness the coronation, craned his neck with the multitudes around Westminster Abbey, then visited with Scott and other friends in London before setting out for Birmingham to finish his book in the sanctuary of his sister's home. But in Birmingham, before the end of that year 1821, he was to learn of the death of his brother William, "the man I most loved on earth," as he would write on another occasion; "one of the dismallest blows that I have ever experienced." The news quite put him out of mind for working. And there was still more to endure, a perplexing ailment in his ankles that kept him housebound, so that this writer still in his late thirties was hobbled week after week like an old man. To the artist Leslie, November 2, 1821: "I am still preyed upon by this tedious complaint, and find the eruptions on my legs worse than ever, while the general tone of my system is relaxed and ennervated by this nursing and confinement." The malady, whatever it was—something cutaneous: erysipelas?—dragged on, so that Irving's stay in Birmingham was necessarily extended. But by early 1822, back in London at last with his legs horizontal for much of each day, he was finally sending off to brother Ebenezer in New York the first volume of *Bracebridge Hall: or The Humorists, A Medley*. The second volume was not long in following; the complete work appeared that spring, almost simultaneously in England and America. "I have fagged hard to get another work under way, as I felt that a great deal depended upon it, both as to reputation and profit," the author the preceding September had written Peter, still dawdling at Le Havre. Now the manuscript was with the printer, and Irving meant—as he had promised then—to give himself a holiday.

But he was understandably apprehensive about the reception of what he had done. *The Sketch Book* had been a novelty to its enraptured English readers, written as they assumed by "a kind of demi-savage, with a feather in his hand, instead of on his head." It had been much praised—indeed, praised to extravagance, as Irving was the first to concede. The novelty was ended, however. "I must now," he wrote at the outset of *Bracebridge Hall*, "expect to bear the scrutiny of sterner criticism . . . as there is nothing for which the world is apt to punish a man more severely, than for having been over-praised. On this head, therefore, I wish to forestall the censoriousness of the reader; and I entreat he will not think the worse of me for the many injudicious things that may have been said in my commendation."

He need not have worried. Murray had already paid £1,000 sight unseen for the manuscript, and the purchase proved to be a shrewd one. Devotees of *The Sketch Book* would find little that disappointed them in its successor. We may adjudge the pages of *Bracebridge Hall* more often than not as bland—still may enjoy "Dolph Heyliger" and "The Stout Gentleman" and an additional piece here and there, but for the rest agree with one of the rare contemporary reservations expressed: "The fault of the book is that the workmanship surpasses the work. There is too much care and cost bestowed on petty objects"—on family retainers and pothering old squires whose antiquated idleness finally exasperates more than amuses. The comment just quoted is Maria Edgeworth's, but it was only one small dissonance in the general chorus of approval surrounding Irving, now giving himself his holiday in London in the spring of 1822. Most English readers, grown disenchanted by then with the mocking and cynical Lord Byron in exile, welcomed the American's genial vision so gratefully that they were coming to regard him as Byron's most appealing successor. No writer of English, in fact, had a brighter future than did Irving at that time, and all the more so after the exacting Jeffrey, arbiter whose written word from Edinburgh guided the taste of a multitude, pronounced favorably on the "singular sweetness of the composition" that was the distinguishing characteristic of this new book, as of its predecessor.

Of course so excellent, amiable, and now accessible an author would be finding his days in London full: song recitals, plays, operas, balls, dinners and more dinners, routs, levees, blue-stocking coteries, visits to country seats. The Duke of Bedford requests the pleasure. Lady Blessington requests. Lady Spencer. And on and on. By mid-June he is confiding plaintively to Brevoort: "I have not a moment to myself, and am so fatigued with company and dinner & evening parties, that I find it impossible to regain a perfect state of health, but am still troubled with lameness & inflammation in the ancles, the lingerings of my tedious malady." He must get away from England, try the baths on the Continent to see if they might help. Try Aix-la-Chapelle. "Within these two months past I have given myself up to society more than I have at any time since I have been in Europe . . . The success of my writings has given me ready access to all kinds of Society. And I have been the rounds . . ."

But he was again, as after *The Sketch Book*, getting his fill of it. "Literary success, if it has its charms has likewise its disadvantages," he confessed to another correspondent soon after; "the least notoriety takes away from a man all command of his time or person; unless he becomes absolutely rude & churlish"—which was not Irving's way. Or unless he flees. He would take his aching ankles to Germany for the baths. He had written himself out of English subject matter anyway—had now written all he would ever write about English gentry and manor life. But perhaps a German Sketch Book, full of magic, of haunted castles and wild huntsmen, of goblins and ghostly ladies and dwarfish crones with twenty rings on their fingers. Irving had been contemplating a trip to Germany for several years; Scott's interest in that fabled land had reinforced his own. Such a venture need not take long, and "when that is accomplished," he was writing to reassure Brevoort this summer of 1822, "I shall have one grand obstacle removed to my return home; and will endeavour to arrange my concerns so as once more to see my native land; which is daily becoming dearer & dearer to my imagination, as the lapse of time gives it all the charms of distance."

Meanwhile, that distance would have to be extended. Autumn 1822 found Irving in quest of health and literary inspiration, traveling from Aix-la-Chapelle up the Rhine toward Baden, his spirits lifting among new sights, his pain gradually receding in the midst of a fresh landscape of vineyards and rich plains spreading back to purple hills and peaks capped with snow. From time to time he passed through villages all but medieval beyond old gateways, rattling down "streets so lively with people—the gay colours of the womens dresses—the groups of Soldiers—costumes &c." And briefly we may leave him there: "It would amuse you to see me in a crazy, clumsy open carriage, drawn by two ragged, bony, long-tailed horses, and harnessed with old ropes and rotten strips, which are the kind of hackney vehicles in German towns. Here I sit with my legs coiled up something like a Turkish bashaw, and hold a mongrel conversation, made up of English, French, and German, with the drivers. . . ."

In Germany, too, at the end of the road that would soon lead Irving from Wiesbaden through Frankfort and Munich and Vienna to the little kingdom of Saxony, was residing at the time an English family whose life together would within weeks become familiar and increasingly important to this American traveler. As of now, to be sure, he did not know them—had no hint of their existence. Their name was Foster. In the late summer of 1820, that season of *The Sketch Book*'s first European success, the Fosters—mother and her five children—had left from London to begin an adventure of living abroad that would last three years. The father had remained at home in Bedfordshire, while his wife (who was his third wife, and about the age of Irving) brought five of the children of this large and affluent family to Dresden, near where some of their relatives had established themselves through marriage. Soon the new arrivals were settled comfortably in a wing of the massive Schloss Uebigau on the banks of the Elbe a mile below the city, and the children, guided by tutors, were pursuing their education in this German community that was celebrated throughout Europe, as much for its culture as for its architectural beauty.

There was no single Germany then. There were only German states—Prussia, Bavaria, Hanover, Mecklenburg, Wurttemberg, numerous duchies, electorates, and the like—of which the kingdom of Saxony was one small patch on the quilt. Dresden was its capital. The whole Saxon kingdom, made up of about a million people, extended over land roughly the area of Connecticut—and a lovely land it seemed to its English visitors: "the rocks, the mossy stones, the slender birches the stream sounding below, swelled by the rain . . . the fields above carpetted with anemonies, hypaticas, the plain of Dresden beyond, the domes & steeples softened by a blue haze & the distant hills speckled with villas—."

That glimpse Emily Foster, then seventeen, recorded on an early spring day in 1822, after one of numerous excursions into the hills and mountains that surround the city where she and her family were staying. Much of the life the Fosters led during those three years of voluntary exile is recoverable within the pages of this vibrant journal that the older of the daughters kept. The family had not intended to stay so long—had planned a visit of some months at the most. But the days passed, and they lingered, first in the tree-shaded wing of the palace on the right bank of the Elbe, later in the Courland Palace in the Altstadt, near the center of the old city. There were three boys in the family—Algernon, Arthur, and Morgan—ten years old and younger, in addition to the two girls in their mid to late teens, Emily and her younger sister Flora. Effortlessly the hours passed for them, and they lingered: "how many sunny days, & happy months . . ." Skating parties on the river, the city gardens, art galleries to visit, the theater, opera, sketching, in the evenings at home charades or cards or reading Dante aloud as a group, during the mornings the language study—Emily writes parts of her journal in French, parts in Italian, parts in German, all fluently enough. And for a while in the summer of 1821 her pages are filled with the bustle attendant on her father's expected arrival from Bedfordshire for a visit: new clothes to buy, gifts, plans made for his entertainment, the dragging hours preceding his coming, until finally he is with them, getting to know the rooms and tree-lined streets and new friends that make up their world now, accompanying his loved ones on those rides and picnics into the hills. Emily sets down what they see: "black clouds gathering, immense fir woods; stags browsing the moss & rubbing their noble antlers against the trunks . . ."

And even as she is writing, black clouds have begun to gather in her own life, and in that of her family. Algernon, oldest of the three boys, had been ill for some while. He was ten. During their father's stay in Dresden, the child's health grew much feebler; perhaps the visit at just that time had been urged because of his decline. In any case, the little fellow lay very sick in his bed, his mind wandering piteously through those late summer days and nights of 1821: "what a painful thing is illness in a house—Papa is constantly in tears—alas he cannot live—He says 'God's will be done'—He is very delirious, as Mama says why, why is the sweet child so tormented?"

Thus confusedly Algernon's eldest sister recorded as much as she could express of the sorrow she was feeling. The boy died, and was buried in a suburb of Dresden. Nearly two years later Washington Irving, a privileged friend, would be taken to see the stone. But as of now, the American had not yet arrived in the city, was on his way from Paris through the festive London of the king's coronation to Birmingham, with his manuscript of *Bracebridge Hall* not yet completed, during these early autumn days while an English family in Dresden was absorbing as well as it could the new emptiness that death had brought, the new absence that had to come with their father's necessary departure to return to England.

Their lives resumed more even rhythms. But the Emily of the journal is older now, and seems so. The child of sixteen bedaubing herself with sour cream to remove her freckles has grown into the attractive young lady presented in early 1822 at the Saxon court before the Princess Amelia, niece of King Frederick Augustus. Her eye is sharp: the elderly queen of that court she notices to be "highly rouged or rather *lilacced* & looks more like an old maid than the mother of a large family." There are balls to attend, and before the balls tutors to fret over, and family friends to enjoy, and beaux constantly about this blooming and witty seventeen-year-old. The Bavarian Gumppenberg, one suitor, "marched up to me with a mouthful of laughter, & burst out in bad English—'you are very pretty—I love you' he laughed & was so diverted at his own gibberish I thought he was laughing at me & was quite discomposed." Emily is coming to like this laughing young German, assigned to the Bavarian legation at the Saxon court: "we heard something of his leaving Dresden I hope not—cher G——g que tout le bien du monde vous arrive mais que ce soit ici!"—May every blessing of the world come your way, but let it be here! He compliments her on her etchings, for she is a skilled young artist. There are card games—Tippen and commerce. Epistolary novels are undertaken by the group of which these two young people are members; male friends including Gumppenberg write one letter to advance the narrative, and in answer Emily and her younger sister Flora write the next, and so through the weeks the novel grows. Or they play at bouts rimés, each one of the group composing a line of verse to a set meter and with a given rhyme but without knowing the lines that have come before or will follow. The completed, disjointed poem read aloud will provoke much laughter.

Indeed, laughter is what one seems to hear most often echoing still, however faintly now, down the long years from those few enchanted Dresden seasons. "I wonder whether the time will ever come that the names I pronounce daily will become strange to my lips—Anikeef, Rumigny, Allegri, Gumppenberg, Cicognara, Airey Campusano—I hope not—How irretrievably eternally lost is the moment but just past, as thoroughly as if Centuries were heaped upon it—." So this young lady is led to reflect after a stroll on a passing summer afternoon in the Zwinger, blooming garden on Dresden's fringes, with its grotesque statues, its orange trees, and the pretty views afforded of the city. Again, we see the group together riding into the springtime countryside, the girls inside the carriage, the gentlemen outside, hanging on: "they sung the whole way like mad." At a stop, "We climbed up a steep heathy hill, and arrived at a romantic village where we drank milk— . . . running down the steep banks holding hands . . ."

In the group, in addition to the young Bavarian, are others who find this Bedfordshire teenager very attractive. The English Captain Richard Airey does, and especially does the Italian Count Allegri: "Poor dear A——i his pale large face & honey words do him much mischief." But Allegri is ardent: "Kanikoff's party so dull that without shawls or bonnets we crept out, & walked upon the bridge, the warm fresh air about one's face & hair, the dark night, the reflected lights in the river, all was charming, but—Allegri talked *sweet*. (I think I begin to hate him,) came home & supped upon dry bones, & sour cherries" to get the sweetness out. No doubt about it, she preferred the Bavarian. On a Wednesday in June 1822: "Allegri read home of his journal to us with fear & trembling & cause thereto—we were *not* in extasies— . . . then G——g read us his journal. How very different! Such frank simplicity —it was written with such modesty, so unaffected so natural—noble generous, excellent man.—" The two suitors are, she writes, "like candle light & daylight, the Italian brilliant lively artificial, the Bavarian, natural, true, universal."

And the days pass. "Finished the bride of Lammermoor . . . ," Scott's novel that had appeared three years earlier. Of Allegri: "I remember he used so often to strike me as a great, comfortable, monk, but not pious—& when he spoke so insinuating & agreable like Rashleigh Osbaldistone in Rob Roy without his crimes—or courage." (*Rob Roy*, that novel that Scott had been writing in 1817 during Irving's visit to Abbotsford.) And the evenings in Dresden: at the opera attending Rossini's *La donna del lago*, based on the Scott poem. And in the midst of other reflections, this allusion in early 1822, to a novel that a girl hardly older than Emily had published anonymously four years before: "I do like G——g he is truly good & amiable—he entertained me delightfully—Musical soirée had all sorts of horrid ideas about poor Miss Bib—" (Madame Bibikoff, an old Russian lady with whom Emily would sing on occasion.) "She looked like a corpse painted up—Frankenstein's monster . . ."

Those appealing days and evenings pass, until from the pages that record them, one evening in particular stands out. Emily is being visited yet again by her charming Bavarian, who has been discoursing agreeably: "Friendship sees the faults, it is clairvoyant; it is only love that is blind." And the young lady unguardedly answers before considering. "Still, it is very odd," she confesses, "that after all my scrutiny I haven't been able to find faults in you." Too late she realizes how much she has revealed. In confusion she rises, starts to leave the room. "Comment Mlle Emilie, attendez ecoutez"—Wait! Listen! But she is fleeing up the stairs now, "lui aprés moi sautant trois degrés a la fois tout agité & joyeux" —with Gumppenberg after her taking three steps at a time, all excited and joyful. She does make her escape, but must come down again before long to the sitting room and bear an endless evening in company with other guests, feeling awkward in her chair under the Bavarian's enkindled gaze: "n'otoit pas ses regards, je detournois la tete de tous les cotés je bondois, je grognois, je pleurois presque, mais impossible, ses yeux etoient toujours là: de la vie je n'ai tant souffert d'embarras"—he didn't stop staring; I turned my head in every direction; I trembled, I groaned, I almost wept, but no use, his eyes were always there: never in my life have I suffered so from embarrassment.

Yet only a few more nights will pass before her admirer is called away, quite suddenly. The rumors of his departure are true. He is "*going the day after tomorrow*." On their last evening together, the moments tick by, until Gumppenberg finally moves to leave, tears in his eyes. "Comme c'est bête," he says to her, and repeats it helplessly; "comme c'est bête": how stupid it is! He kisses her hand and withdraws. If she supposes, hearing his retreating steps beyond the door, that she will never see him again, she supposes no more than what will prove true. The remainder of that night Emily comes to know her new loneliness, an intruder still with her in the morning: "I woke & could not sleep, I saw out of the window that it was wet & rainy it is absolutely dismal, what shall we do all these evenings now!—a dull walk in the evening twilight on the ramparts, a storm & lightning I wonder what

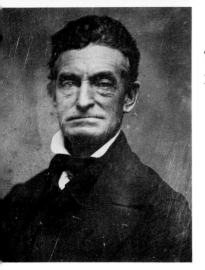

John Brown in 1856. During this same year the Pottawatomie massacres occurred in Bleeding Kansas.

The Kennedy farmhouse in Maryland. Here John Brown and his men awaited the hour for their strike against slavery at Harpers Ferry. The photograph was taken in 1974.

William Street, New York, in 1800. On this street, seventeen years earlier, Washington Irving was born.

Aaron Burr in 1802. The Vice President would fight his duel with Hamilton two years after this likeness was taken. Portrait by John Vanderlyn, a friend of both Burr and Irving.

Richmond Hill. The site of Burr's commodious home, then north of New York City, has long since been leveled, drained, bricked, paved, and asphalted.

Theodosia Burr at age eleven. Portrait by Gilbert Stuart, who painted John Jacob Astor in the same year, 1794.

Theodosia in maturity. When John Vanderlyn painted this portrait, in 1807, Burr's daughter was twenty-four, and married to Joseph Alston.

Irving during his first European tour. The engraving, after a crayon portrait by Vanderlyn, shows the young man in his early twenties, as he appeared in Paris in 1805.

The mansion of Harman Blennerhassett on the Ohio River.

Aaron Burr in 1834. The previous year Burr, already in his late seventies, had married Mme Eliza Jumel. Likeness by James Vandyck.

Washington Irving, soon after the death of Matilda Hoffman and about the time of his writing *Knickerbocker's History of New York*. Portrait by John W. Jarvis, "conceded without dissent . . . to be a faithful and admirable likeness" (P. M. Irving).

Sir Walter Scott in 1818. The novelist had met Irving during the preceding summer. Portrait by Andrew Geddes.

Smailholm Tower. Near the base of this tower the crippled Scott acquired some of his earliest impressions. The farmhouse in the foreground belonged to his grandfather. Nineteenth-century watercolor by George Manson.

Scott at home. The poet and novelist may have looked just so, in his study with a favorite dog at his feet, during Irving's visit. Painting by Sir William Allan.

Abbotsford as it appeared soon after its completion.

ing at the time of the appearance of *The
etch Book*. The author was in his late
rties, and suddenly famous on both sides of
Atlantic. The portrait, by Gilbert Stuart
wton, was done in London in the spring of
20.

Regency London. This view of the Strand was published in 1816, a year after
Irving's arrival in England.

Sir Walter Scott in 1824. The portrait, by Irving's friend David Wilkie (to whom *The Alhambra* is dedicated), reveals the aging that sickness and hard work had already inflicted on the novelist, two years before his public ruin.

Flora and Emily Foster. Emily is on the right. From a watercolor by Henry Deffel.

Matilda Hoffman. A miniature by Anson Dickinson.

poor G———g is doing! Mama saw his dog Pumperlin sitting at the door so woe begone & forlorn.—I go and draw with Mme Anikeef."

Routines continue as though nothing has happened. But luster has left those gatherings in theater and garden and drawing room. Summer is over, and autumn comes. What shall we do all these evenings now? In September a message arrives from an acquaintance traveling in Italy, where the Bavarian has gone: "Mama has had a letter from Campusano, asking me in marriage for a friend who he did not name but I know." It could only be Gumppenberg. "I felt a rush to my head—my chief sorrow is that we must now I suppose give up all hope of ever seeing him again—that very morning Du Berg called asking how, 'les amours de G———g' went on *les amours!* indeed—"

One can concoct objections that prudent elders might have urged to a marriage between the Bavarian official and this young English girl far from home. Whatever the reasons, Emily was acquiescent—and may have understood them—though her days were emptier now. Gumppenberg was removed from her life, and the cloying Allegri was in disfavor, so that she would have had both time and inclination to keep more to herself, and to muse. Perhaps to read more, too, although she was always a great reader: "I prefer reading travels where the author's sentiments are skillfully introduced," she did record during this autumn of transition; "we wish the author not to isolate himself as an object to be looked at, & admired, but as a guide to that ocean of feeling common to every heart . . ."

Such a preference would have made agreeable those sketches of sentiment common to every heart by an American writer supremely popular just at that time. And to be sure, the work of Geoffrey Crayon was known to this English family in Dresden.

Emily's mother had, during the fall, written a long, chatty letter home to Bedfordshire. In it, amid gossip and queries, this highly literate woman reported on her family's current reading. *The Sketch Book* was a work they had particularly enjoyed of late, and to end her crowded letter she had transcribed a favorite passage from the source, marking it at the bottom of the page, "Washington Irving." No room was left for her signature.

The letter miscarried. Officials opened it, noted Irving's name at the conclusion, and in their ignorance of English recalled only that the famous author was then traveling through Germany. Thus, in Vienna on a fall day in 1822, Irving was surprised to receive a fat communication assumed to be his own, but from an unknown hand and filled with praise of his writing ("He told us, afterward, that no praise had ever seemed to him so sweet, so genuine, as what he so unexpectedly found in those lines). The letter contained as well, so he learned in attempting to discover its rightful owner, news to a family in England from what was obviously some of its members living at the time in Germany. He would keep it for now with his other papers.

Meanwhile he was writing letters of his own, one to his sister in Birmingham: "I am beginning to think of leaving Vienna. I shall probably stay a week longer and then take my departure for Dresden, which will be my winter quarters. . . . There is scarcely any such thing as literary society, or I may say literary taste in Vienna. Dresden, on the contrary, is a place of taste, intellect, and literary feeling . . ." And the right place, too, to learn German, for nowhere, Irving had been led to understand, was that language more purely spoken than in Saxony.

For those reasons, at sunset on what was November 28, 1822, the American was approaching that classic little capital, that Florence of Germany, by carriage from Vienna and Prague. Fishing boats lay before him on the Elbe, the river still and rosily gleaming beneath evergreen hills that he saw as cheerful in the distance. "As the day closes," he wrote in his journal, "the full moon shines out from among clouds which gradually draw off and leave her in full splendour in a deep blue sky—fine effect as we approach Dresden—Moonshine brings out white buildings—Steeples—domes &c Enter & drive thro tall spacious streets—tho dark—open into broad moonlight Squares of fine houses—fountains, churches—put up at Hotel de Saxe—"

His mood at the moment was as cheerful as seemed those evergreen hills he had used that adjective to describe. Not three months earlier, in the course of his travels as his health was improving, he had been writing his sister, "I never was more sensible to the delicious effect of atmosphere: perhaps my very malady has made me more susceptible to influences of the kind. I feel a kind of intoxication of the heart, as I draw in the pure air of the mountains . . ." The malady in his legs was gone when he reached Dresden, where he would soon be dancing quadrilles and polonaises, this wanderer at the threshold of forty. So for the most part he was cheerful, if not entirely free (he would never be free) from effects of that depression that had visited him throughout his adulthood. Again in the journal, early in the fall on the German tour: "the leaves of past pleasures are strewn around me—the joys of youth how have they passed away—friendships faded—loves untimely fallen—hopes blighted—what fruit is there to repay this ill spent prime." Or this, in similar mood, at about the same time: "A weight rested upon my mind—there was a soreness of heart as if I had committed some hideous crime & all mankind were justly irritated agst me—I went about with a guilty look & sought to hide myself—it was not without some effort that I occasionally threw off this weight & reccollected that my only crime had been an unsuccessful attempt to please the world."

Such feelings were recurring during what Irving regarded as his own autumn of life coming on. But for now the weight of uncertainty was thrown off, as he set about establishing himself at the Hotel de Saxe, his presence soon noted by the Dresden *Abendzeitung*: "Herr Washington Irving . . . here . . . in Dresden, among us . . . busies himself tirelessly with our language . . . with whose characteristics he has been acquainted since his earlier sojourn on the Rhine, at Mainz and Vienna." Well, if not tirelessly, at least diligently: "guter Wein gute Milch gutes Bier." Soon after his arrival he had engaged a German master, and his journal records gossip gleaned from—and payments made to—more than one language teacher during his stay.

Thus established in winter quarters, intending to remain until spring opened, he could by early December write back to England with some complacency: "I have a very neat, comfortable and prettily furnished appartment on the first floor of a Hotel; it consists of a cabinet with a bed in it, and a cheerful Sitting room that looks on the finest Square—I am offered this appartment for the winter at the rate of *thirty Six Shillings* a month!—would to heavens I could get such quarters in London for any thing like the money." And from his new sanctuary he was now sallying forth to renew acquaintances—one, for instance, with the British minister, John Philip Morier, who had known Irving earlier in Washington, and who did not long delay in presenting the distinguished American to the Saxon court: "we went, by galleries & corridors to the Kings appartments," the new arrival recorded, "where we had to wait for some time in a cool saloon—when the King entered & went round the circle I was introduced & he spoke to me very flatteringly about my works—."

The theater, too, as always, attracted Irving, and it was there, between acts one evening early that month, that he was introduced to an English lady and her two teenage daughters then living in Dresden. Indeed, he sought out the introduction, something this diffident gentleman rarely did. From their Bedfordshire relative Barham Livius of the Hussars, a new friend, Irving had learned of this family named Foster, and had recognized them as the family in the letter that had earlier been misdelivered to him in Vienna. Now he entered their box at intermission with an innocent joke to play. The Fosters, seeing this dark-haired and very handsome newcomer approaching "with all the air of your old-fashioned, high bred gentleman," with his manner "full of composure and gentleness," must have been pleased to learn his name, though they were not surprised that the well-known American writer had found his way to this center of German culture. They were surprised, however— very much so—when he courteously began to ask after members of their family whom he could never have met or known of: "Have you lately heard from Miss Margaret?" She was the stepdaughter at home in England to whom Mrs. Foster's misdelivered letter had been addressed. "Mr. Foster liked his journey to the north, I hope?" But how could this stranger know about that? "And I hope poor Bessie is better?" Bessie was the stepdaughter's favorite horse, but "How did you know?—how could you tell—," cried Mrs. Foster. "Ah," answered Irving, "there's the mystery!"

It was, of course, not long being solved. The letter was produced, reread with delight, and, with an added note from the Fosters' new friend, forwarded on to its original destination. "At the play tonight," Emily, elder of the two daughters, was promptly recording, "Mr Irving the author of the Sketch book was introduced to us.—" On the nineteenth he was dining for the first time at the Fosters' home: "merely the family (Mrs F— two daughters & 2 Boys) and Col Livius—Miseries of an indulgent mistress—Best natured & worst served woman in the world—Dinner ill cooked—not done enough—Cook ill tempered & wrong headed—." The same group dined together (minus the cook) at Livius' apartment the following day, and soon the friendship was firmly established. "Mr Irving is always with us entertaining & interesting— walks in the great garden." And again Emily notes, "Mr Irving is very interesting with his stories about his handsome Indians painting & pluming themselves, & strutting up & down before their cabin doors— . . . he is neither tall nor slight, but most interesting, dark, hair of a man of genius waving, silky, & black, grey eyes full of varying feeling, & an amiable smile—."

How pleasurably the following weeks unfolded, in this precious world somehow preserved as it had been centuries earlier, like an enclave of life (so Irving remarked) contemporaneous with the Tudors, a life gratifying to the fullest his all but insatiable love of the picturesque. Monday, December 23: "In morning wrote a little at the history of an Author—walked out with Col Livius who is full of the project of private theatricals—met Trotter & Butler went together to Mrs Fosters where the Col interested the young ladies in his plan." For the colonel had directed plays in London, and if Irving would adapt some appropriate drama to suit the local talent, they might all have fun performing before the cultured English-speaking audience that could be assembled here. The new friends might well have talked more about it the following evening: "Dine at Mrs Fosters—present Mrs Foster & family— . . . Col Livius . . . Capt Morier—Mr Walter Scott"—of the Hussars, elder son of Sir Walter—"Mr Airy. Mr Williams . . . A very pleasant dinner—and a merry Christmas eve—various games—Charades Hoodmanblind &c—" On Christmas morning, "Military musick goes by the Hotel about 7 oclock. Servant with silver laced cocked hat—silver laced drab livery & long cane enters my room & announces that the Queen has put off her Court of today—½ past ten Chaunt of scholars in the streets—walkg two & two dressed in black—fine sunny weather." Christmas dinner was taken at Mr. Morier's, with young Walter Scott present again. Next morning, with the shops still closed for the holy days, "we went on the Elb—where the ladies & some of the gentlemen went in little traineaus on the Ice & were shoved along by skaeters—" A ball at the Prussian ambassador's saw the old year out. "Supper at ½ past 11—very plentiful & elegant—at 12 oclock an old watchman appeard at the door of the appartment & blew his horn—wished a happy N Year & sung a long drowsy watchmans song—great mirth. After supper more dancing & very animated . . ."

So in a whirl the year 1822 that Irving was ending in Dresden turned into the new year, which began as colorfully: "Levee of the princes & princesses to receive the congratulations of the day . . . Oceans of courtiers thro which I had to wade to get into the presence chamber—Court dresses scarlet with profusion of gold lace—½ past 12—Levee of Queen—old lady richly dressed with fine diamonds— Asked Scott when his father would come . . ." But because of Lady Scott's illness, the novelist's planned trip from Edinburgh to the Continent would not materialize. Meanwhile, Livius' amateur theatricals were going forward: rewriting of Fielding's *Tom Thumb*, rehearsals in a salon of the Fosters' leased palace. Irving would be King Arthur, Emily and Flora the ladies in waiting. January 8: "Busy in the Morng getting dresses for private theatricals—found a warehouse of Dresses kept by a Jew—ascended a narrow dark staircase to get to it—chose dresses—Hunted up a theatrical barber—lived at the top of a house—little round lively man—chose wigs—"

The dress rehearsal was performed that evening. Next morning by eleven, Irving, a carefree Thespian in fur mantle and fur cap, was riding in a droshky a mile and a half out of the city to hunt hare: "fine clear frosty morning—sunshine—glistening of spangles of frost on the snow—distant hills in frosty mist . . ." The assembled sportsmen were posted in dry ditches awaiting the game that the peasants, formed in a crescent, would be charged with driving toward them: "Sport not very good today—about 20 hares killed—I killed one." But the following day the American was out again, through pine forests to a village five miles northeast of the city, in order to observe the royal boar hunt: "Station myself by a large tree of the forest—by road side—first come one or two horsemen—Huntsmen with the four lancer dogs who are first put on the track of the boar—then Whippers in with the pack of hounds—More horsemen arrive—then King & Prince Antoine in carriage—horses led out for King & prince—They mount—The boar turned loose—passes near me—shortly after the 4 hounds let loose—King & prince Antoine & suite gallop by—they salute me as they pass—Antoine cries out *gute Morgen* . . ."

Later in the month Irving would be out once more, among trees covered with snow. Fires were crackling for warmth along the roadside, and the cold air was filled with sounds of hunting horns, of whips snapping and dogs howling and the horses bearing their green-clad riders at a gallop through the woods. For the rest, back in Dresden there were the dinners and soirées and teas and balls and masked balls and theater and opera. There were the language lessons (French lessons with Emily, Italian lessons with her mother, in addition to lessons from the gossipy German master), and efforts feebler and feebler to write, except for altering those plays that were delighting his new friends. The drama now secretly in rehearsal at the Fosters' was *Three Weeks after Marriage*, with Irving as Sir Charles Rackett and Emily as Lady Rackett. Day after day through early February the conspirators, including this make-believe man and wife, practiced their lines and gestures, although some days Irving must occupy himself in other ways. Thursday, February 13, 1823: "At Home till 1 oclock—cannonfire to give notice of breaking up of the Ice—in the river—Go to Bridge which is crowded—ice does not move—return home—dine at Cockrans—present—Werry —Capt Towers—Mr. Garforth—Price, Livius Williams

"In Evg—go to see Hamlet—sit in the Box of Baron Lowensterns —go home & take tea at Mrs Fosters & chat there till ½ past 11."

Then back to his hotel afterward, again down the two long blocks, now so familiar, from the Courland Palace, home of the Fosters, down through those tall spacious streets, under those white buildings—Steeples—domes—Squares of fine houses—fountains, churches—

They were still standing exactly one hundred and twenty-two years later, on February 13, 1945, when over those same dark streets of an open city passed the bombers. Eight hundred Lancasters of the British Bomber Command would fly over this target of baroque beauty, this architectural masterpiece hitherto undamaged, into which war refugees had swarmed on the assumption that such splendor would be spared as Oxford and Cambridge had been spared by the Luftwaffe. The Allies had already won the air war by then, but on the night of February 13, 1945, the British Bomber Command would drop on these same streets through which Irving had passed, these streets filled now with homeless civilians, 1,471 tons of high explosives, 1,175 tons of incendiaries. The United States Eighth Air Force would follow next morning—four hundred Flying Fortresses and Liberators—and on the next day two hundred more American aircraft would fly through the skies over the ruins. By then fires would have raged so closely together in those streets, would have so raised the temperature of all the air in the city, that every inflammable substance would have burst into flames. An updraft would have swept the flames along crowded avenues faster than people could flee. One hundred and thirty-five thousand victims would perish in the attacks, more than were to be killed in the bombings of Hiroshima and Nagasaki combined. And the minutes of the evening meeting of the British War Cabinet for 19 February 1945 would accurately and dispassionately record the results: the attack on Dresden four nights earlier "had practically wiped out the city."

A century and a quarter before, February 13, 1823: ". . . go home & take tea at Mrs Fosters & chat there till ½ past 11." "Mr. Irving came home with us . . . and stayed a long while talking as usual, before he wished 'good night.' " The record of that same evening is Flora's, Emily's younger sister. "He was exceedingly entertaining, and gave us a vivid description of the gatherings of the Methodists in America . . . at one of which he was present . . . Our house, he said, now seems to him *his home*. But let only one of the many visitors who frequent our house come in, he immediately buttons himself up, retires to *his recess*, sheltered by curtains and book stands, and there stays, silent and uninterested, till we are again alone, when his animation returns, his countenance, pale and languid, lights up, and he becomes again the most lively and interesting companion."

And she—this impressionable and emphatic teenager—goes on to note, amid the anecdotes and epigrams recorded from the mouth of the Fosters' new friend, "Evening after evening is spent in happy converse. Why is it that, at times, a deep shade gathers on his brow?" Almost daily Irving has been seeing the family, and a special attachment has been forming between this author nearly forty and Flora's lovely older sister, his stage wife, soon to be nineteen. After one visit Emily herself is writing in Italian in her journal about sensitive men to whom the world can never do justice. She is made deliciously melancholy, tears come to her eyes on another occasion, as he reads her "a sweet little poem on spring." And Flora, thrilled for her older sister, sets down what she observes: "Yesterday, a large party was here—De Rumignys, the French Minister, the young Countess Loos and her *fiancé* . . . in short, all good, kind-hearted people Irving has learned to like, to some extent at least. He was languid, pale, depressed beyond measure, and hardly spoke; yet he did not leave us till all the world was gone, nor, indeed, till long after. He said he would write in the morning."

And immediately afterward on the page, breathlessly: "He has written. He has confessed to my mother, as to a true and dear friend, his love for E———, and his conviction of its utter hopelessness."

Why, Mrs. Foster had asked him during one of their conversations (that she would do so suggests the intimacy that had developed between her family and their American friend), why had he never married? And in talking with him she must have wondered, too, what her younger daughter Flora had set down privately: "Why is it that, at times, a deep shade gathers on his brow?" Why, with all Irving's success, all his friends, all his charm and attractiveness, should this accomplished gentleman in the prime of his life seem often to be weighted down with melancholy, a melancholy that, as he knew and had written, could corrode the spirits and "rust all the springs of mental energy"?

Among his close friends, in addition to others from every walk of life, were three of the five most popular writers in English of the time: Scott, Moore, and Campbell. A fourth, Lord Byron, warmly admired— and was admired by—this American essayist and storyteller. The fifth writer of that select group was Irving himself. His career, then, and his associations, so resplendent after the dismal humiliations of bankruptcy at Liverpool only five years earlier, should have brought him boundless comfort, as they brought his family in England and America pride and satisfaction. Moreover, his very presence—should he entertain any doubts about his worth—inevitably delighted those lucky enough to know him, however casually. That pleasure is denied us, who have only his work and the comments of his contemporaries by which to form our acquaintance. But it was real and special. "Never beat a more kindly heart than his," Flora Foster grown into old age testified, "alive to the sorrows, but not to the faults of his friends, but doubly alive to their virtues and their goodness. Indeed, people seemed to grow more good with one so unselfish and so gentle." Her testimony would be less persuasive if it were not confirmed by so many others. The American historian George Bancroft, as an already acute young man of twenty, after an extended stay abroad had met Irving in Paris in 1821, two years before these Dresden days, and pronounced him flatly the most excellent man he had encountered in Europe. "I can almost say," the brilliant historian would remark, "that I never go away from him, without finding my better principles and feelings warmed, strengthened and purified by his eloquent conversation."

From such statements we must infer what effect the presence of Irving would have on us if he were to walk through that door, into this room. Yet despite the love and success that were this remarkable man's lot, despite the warm affection he was capable of feeling for others, he who had so often chronicled the pleasures of domesticity was living out his wandering life alone, subject to recurring fits of despondency. Why?

One obvious reason his Dresden friends found him sometimes dejected arose from his inability to get writing again. The German Sketch Book languished. "I have done nothing with my pen since I have left you! absolutely nothing!" he exclaimed from amid the distractions there in mid-March, 1823, to the artist Leslie back in England. "I have been gazing about; rather idly perhaps—but yet among fine Scenes & striking characters and I can only hope that some of them may stick to my mind, and furnish me with materials in some future fit of scribbling."

But other facts about his life could be summoned to account for his darker moods, and for his celibacy. Answering Mrs. Foster's expressions of interest and concern, Irving set down during these months, in April 1823, or perhaps a little later, and gave her to read the most revealing document he would ever write about himself. He put it personally into her hands, a manuscript of some eighteen pages, with the request that she take no copy of it, that she show it to no one outside the family, that she merely read it, then return it directly to him. After his death thirty-six years later, a consecutive portion of the manuscript, amounting to sixteen pages but missing the beginning and the end, was found locked away among Irving's private papers at Sunnyside. Locked for what he took to be good reasons: nowhere else in all his writings does this author, generally reticent about his personal feelings, allow us to look so deeply into his heart.

What survives of the manuscript begins in mid-sentence, a sentence that confesses to a disposition morbidly sensitive, easily wounded, but not embittered by suffering—and readily responsive to pleasurable impressions. "When I was very young," Irving proceeds, casting his mind backward thirty years and more to the deacon's home on William Street in the town at the tip of Manhattan, "I had an impossible flow of spirits that often went beyond my strength. Every thing was fairy land to me. As I had some quickness of parts I was intended for the Law which with us in America is the path to honour and preferment—to every thing that is distinguished in public life. I read law with a gentleman distinguished both in legal and political concerns. . . . He took a fancy to me, though a very heedless student, and made me almost an inmate of his house. . . ."

The gentleman's name was Josiah Ogden Hoffman, and his household, in fact, those many years earlier in New York, was in some ways remarkably like the home that would come to mean so much to Irving in Dresden. The judge's second wife, Maria Fenno, had been a girl scarcely older than young Irving, then nineteen. Within the Hoffman household, accordingly, was a gracious wife—Irving's contemporary, "like a sister to me"—and children that included her two stepdaughters, Ann and Matilda, both of whom were still in their early teens at the start of the law student's acquaintance with them. The year was 1802, that long-ago year of the satirical Oldstyle letters in brother Peter's Burrite *Morning Chronicle*, first venture into print of this anonymous observer of urban follies. About the Hoffman girls, "they were two lovely little beings," Irving was remembering later as he wrote to Mrs. Foster. "Ann was brilliant both as to beauty and natural talent. Matilda was a timid, shy, silent little being, and always kept by the side of her step mother; who indeed looked more like an elder sister, and acted like a most tender one. I saw a great deal of them."

They had been together—he and the Hoffmans—for two years and more before their friendship suffered an interruption. Irving's weakening health led his brothers to send him to Europe, on that restorative first visit that lasted from 1804 to 1806, and that included the boarding by pirates of the voyager's ship off Leghorn, his brush with death among suffocating fumes atop Vesuvius, his scramble to the top of the dome of St. Peter's in Rome, that first leisurely stay in Paris with its "perfect liberty of private conduct," and his initial glimpse of England.

From Europe young Irving's letters home warmly acknowledged his New York friends. "You have delighted me with the mention you made of a visit to the Hoffmans," he wrote, for example, from Genoa to his brother William late in 1804. "God bless them all—I love the whole of them . . . and have passd the happiest moments of my life in their company When you see them again give my *most affectionate* remembrances to them and assure them that I look forward to a meeting with them as one of the most delightful events providence has in store for me."

About that reunion, which would occur in the spring of 1806, an older Irving in Dresden reminisced years later in his account to Mrs. Foster. "On my return," he wrote, "I resumed my legal studies. My meeting with my little female friends was a delightful one. Ann was encreased in beauty, indeed there was an effulgence in the beauty of her countenance that struck every one." But the other change was even more remarkable: "I reccollect my meeting with Matilda as if it was yesterday. She came home from school to see me. She entered full of eagerness, yet shy from her natural timidity, from the time that had elapsed since we parted, and from the idea of my being a *travelled man*, instead of a stripling student—However what a difference the interval had made. She was but between fifteen & sixteen, just growing up, there was a softness and delicacy in her form and look . . . I thought I had never beheld any thing so lovely—"

We would behold her too, bring into life if we could the pensive little face in the miniature that remains to us. Her eyes are dark and large, her mouth small, her auburn hair severely gathered into a bun behind her ears. Motionless image, and yet she was once vivacious enough. "There Matilda come here and let me feel your arm Why Matilda you are not the same girl. You came here a puny thing and now you are a right down Country girl. It is a pleasure to feel such good solid flesh and blood. Why what have they done to you girl? You must always live in Philadelphia if you grow so fat here." So she herself had quoted for her sister's benefit the chatter of a Mrs. Hayes on a Sunday visit to Germantown in the fall of 1805. "Mr Ewing was there and we rode home with him in the evening he began with his old subject my not talking. What is the matter with the man? he expects me to talk to him and just as I am prepared to do it he begins with his 'what's the matter why do not you talk?' This frightens me and I usually shut my mouth when he comes into the room with an intention not to open it again."

But she was only fifteen then, enrolled in Philadelphia at Mrs. Greland's school; and to those close to her she had no trouble expressing her playful nature: "My love to papa and mama and all my aunts uncles grandmothers and cousins and to eliza diza de believe me your Affectionate not in love sister Matalinda dinda dinda."

In Philadelphia friends of the Hoffmans would keep the family back home in New York informed of Matilda's activities: "She went with us to the theatre on Wednesday evening and spent yesterday at Mrs. Meredith's. Her cold has quite left her and her appetite returned." And of the schoolgirl's needs: "About Christmas time"—the letter, written in February 1806, is from Rebecca Gratz to her friend Maria Hoffman—"Matilda mentioned to me that she was so badly off for frocks that she could not manage to have one clean for Sundays, as she had outgrown all her old ones. I then purchased three new ones for her, and had one or two of her old ones fitted up and lengthened. I also got her a velvet spencer and some other trifles amounting to about thirty dollars . . ."

So she was growing, this shy young lady, toward normal human enjoyments in most times and places: clothes, the theater, gossip. The daughter of the wealthy John Jacob Astor, an older Matilda back in New York was soon noting in a letter to her sister Ann, has married a "very ugly" man who "wears a shoe with the heel two inches thick . . . and to crown all he is a modern philosopher." She scribbles on about jet and bone and buttons, about Caty Ogden and Sally Gratz and Mary Fairlie, about Gertrude Kemble, who "drank tea here the day before yesterday she was quite well and desired her best love to you . . . *Washington* says he saw a beautiful girl at Coldenham whose name was Ellen. Tell her that. My love to Aunt and Uncle, tell the former her worsted cap shall be forthcoming in a short time." And she ends: "Burn this letter as soon as you have read it, I beg of you I cannot bear that such nonsense should be seen by any one."

Yet the nonsense was what her sister Ann, absent from home, would have wanted to read, bits of news about the doings and sayings of their mutual friends. Matilda may gossip without being judged giddy; Irving himself assuredly did not undervalue her. "No body knew her so well as I," he insisted years later in writing to Mrs. Foster. "I in a manner studied her excellence." For a long time he had been seeing Matilda every day, "and I became excessively attached to her. Her shyness wore off by degrees. The more I saw of her the more I had reason to admire her. Her mind seemed to unfold itself leaf by leaf, and every time to discover new sweetness."

The quality of that mind is hardly captured among schoolgirl letters that survive, any more than is her natural vivacity revealed through the one prim little miniature of her. An acquaintance who remembered her wrote of her hair not in the severe bun of her portrait, but rather playing "carelessly in the wind, and her features, though not of classic outline . . . radiant with life. Her eye was one of the finest I have ever seen—rich, deep-toned, and eloquent, speaking volumes in each varying expression . . ."

Under the influence of those eyes young Irving had come, of those dark eyes and what he felt to be her "intuitive rectitude of mind." To Mrs. Foster he was explicit: "I am not exaggerating—what I say was acknowledged by all that knew her. Her brilliant little sister used to say that people began by admiring her but ended by loving Matilda. For my part I idolized her."

She was seventeen at the time; he was twenty-five, admitted to the bar but loathing his profession. "I could study any thing else rather than Law, and had a fatal propensity to Belles lettres." *Salmagundi*, however, was abandoned, and there had been little enough money in that enterprise anyway. What prospects had he? *Knickerbocker* had secretly been started, pages of unmanageable manuscript that might never come to anything—he had lost interest in the work, his fraternal collaborator had departed for Europe, and in any case, completing and publishing it (were that even possible) would hardly support a wife and family. "I had gone on blindly, like a boy in Love, but now I began to open my eyes and be miserable. I had nothing in purse nor in expectation."

The girl's father, Judge Hoffman, intervened. He liked this young lawyer, and thought well of his abilities. Irving he would take in as a partner on probation, help him get established in the profession, so that he and Matilda might marry. The offer was generous. Accordingly, Irving "set to work with zeal to study anew, and I considered myself bound in honour not to make further advances with the daughter until I should feel satisfied with my proficiency in the Law. . . ."

But how he hated those folio volumes, that dried-out language of contracts! "It was all in vain. I had an insuperable repugnance to the study—my mind would not take hold of it." His self-doubts, his self-distrust grew, and he was wretched. In secret he scribbled at the chaotic Knickerbocker manuscript, hoping he might somehow finish it to earn a reputation that would gain him appointment to public office. "In the mean time I saw Matilda every day and that helped to distract me." Between his family's house on the corner of Ann and William Streets and the Hoffmans' welcoming home—his betrothed's home—on Greenwich Street a few blocks west, Irving made his way through that uncertain winter of 1809, in the midst of anxiety about his future, beset with the dismays of an unequal struggle.

Then one evening in February Matilda returned home from the theater complaining of another cold. "Nothing was thought of it at first, but she grew rapidly worse, and fell into a consumption." When did concern turn to alarm, alarm to dread, dread to blank certainty around the spool bed in the dimity-hung chamber on Greenwich Street? Irving was often by her side as she grew feebler and her thoughts strayed into delirium. The thin face on the pillow looked angelic; the unguarded words she uttered to him seemed overpowering: "I saw more of the beauty of her mind in that delirious state than I had ever known before." She was dying. Near the end her struggles were painful and protracted. "For three days & nights I did not leave the house & scarcely slept. I was by her when she died—all the family were assembled round her, some praying others weeping, for she was adored by them all. I was the last one she looked upon—"

Thus suddenly it was over. Her lover would have a braid of her hair, her miniature, her prayer book, but she was gone. "Died," the papers would note, "on the 24th instant, in the 18th year of her age, Miss Sarah Matilda Hoffman, daughter of Josiah Ogden Hoffman, Esq. Thus another and youthful victim is added to the ravages of that relentless and invincible enemy to earthly happiness, the *consumption*. . . ." But gone, forever. And Irving was left with all he had so abruptly been made to see, hear, feel.

"I cannot tell you what a horrid state of mind I was in for a long time—I seemed to care for nothing—the world was a blank to me—I abandoned all thoughts of the Law—I went into the country, but could not bear solitude yet could not enjoy society—There was a dismal horror continually in my mind that made me fear to be alone—I had often to get up in the night & seek the bedroom of my brother, as if the having a human being by me would relieve me from the frightful gloom of my own thoughts."

At Kinderhook he rested, at his friend Van Ness's home. Gradually, as day followed empty day, he began to try to work his way through his grief, applying himself to his manuscript history of New York, "but the despondency I had suffered for a long time in the course of this attachment, and the anguish that attended its catastrophe seemed to give a turn to my whole character, and threw some clouds into my disposition which have ever since hung about it." His work, to be sure, seems unshadowed—that brightly bubbling chronicle by "Diedrich Knickerbocker" of the colonial Dutch in Nieuw Amsterdam. Published at last, in December 1809, it promptly brought its author fame, establishing him as the leading American writer of his day, "but the time & circumstances in which it was produced rendered me always unable to look upon it with satisfaction."

Matilda was gone, and somehow *Knickerbocker* had been finished. There followed in Irving's life those years of aimlessness that we have already recounted, nearly a decade with nothing of consequence written to show for it, as he drifted about tasting his new public favor, dabbling as a silent partner in his brothers' business, serving as magazine editor for a while in Philadelphia, then as aide de camp near the end of the war with England. During those years "I was naturally susceptible and tried to form other attachments," so he wrote Mrs. Foster later, "but my heart would not hold on; it would continually recur to what it had lost; and whenever there was a pause in the hurry of novelty & excitement I would sink into dismal dejection. For years I could not talk on the subject of this hopeless regret; I could not even mention her name; but her image was continually before me, and I dreamt of her incessantly."

After the war had ended in the winter of 1815, the ex-Colonel Irving once more found himself with nothing to do. Indifferent now to literary reputation, apathetic, he determined on a second trip to Europe, "to break off in this way from idle habits and idle associates & fashionable dissipation, and when I returned to settle myself down to useful and honourable application." The trip did come to pass, but his anticipated return in a year or so would be delayed, delayed beyond those eight years that now had slipped by since his departure from New York. Now the internationally successful essayist was writing his account for Mrs. Foster in Dresden, was telling her of his arrival in Liverpool in the summer of 1815, of his brother Peter's illness there, of struggles in that cheerless city through months and months to save the family business from financial ruin. Ruin did come, "in all its bitterness & humiliation—in a strange land—among strangers." The brothers Irving finally had to declare bankruptcy, and in the aftermath of that "Detestable ordeal," the younger of them determined suddenly to return to his long-neglected pen, "to reinstate myself in the worlds thoughts—to raise myself from the degradation into which I considered myself fallen."

What came from that pen, for the most part haltingly, was *The Sketch Book*. Before and during the years when he was developing the essays that filled its pages—those years that included his visit to Scott at Abbotsford—he had not forgotten Matilda. "Mat died in April," he had written bleakly in one notebook dated as far back as 1810, a year after the event, and in a German dictionary purchased in London about 1816 he set down the awful fact once more: "M Hff died April 26, 1809 aged 17 yr 5 M." Among the entries in the journal he kept of his tour to Scotland in 1817 are several that evoke her memory, in phrasing now a hundred and sixty years old, quaintly expressed no doubt, but from the heart. In a church during his travels he was on one occasion overwhelmed by the sound of a soft voice singing the hymn "Angels Ever Bright and Fair." "I drew into a corner of the cathedral and covering my face with my hands drank in the exquisitely mournful sound. My heart felt as if it would melt within me—the recollection of Matilda—ever allied in my mind to all that is pure spiritual & seraphic in woman came stealing over my soul—I recalled all the scenes of our early attachment." And again he remembered the awful time in the room on Greenwich Street: "the agony of her death." In *The Sketch Book*, which appeared two years after the journal entry, in the essay "Rural Funerals," Irving would describe that same scene in such a way that Matilda's stepmother in New York was moved to write him, "It surprises me to see that your memory is as tenacious as mine—some things are so deeply fixed there . . ." ("The bed of death, with all its stifled griefs, its noiseless attendance, its mute, watchful assiduities." He remembered those matters, and the "pressure of the hand—the faint, faltering accents struggling in death to give one more assurance of affection—the last fond look of the glazing eye, turning upon us even from the threshold of existence!")

Those moments had happened to her, to him. Yet again, in an essay in *Bracebridge Hall*, which appeared in 1822, Matilda was in his thoughts as Irving wrote of "departed beings that I have loved as I never again shall love in this world;—that have loved me as I never again shall be loved!" The following year, to his English friend Mrs. Foster in Dresden, he would speak forthrightly. "You wonder why I am not married. I have shewn you why I was not long since—when I had sufficiently recovered from that loss, I became involved in ruin. It was not for a man broken down in the world to drag down any woman to his paltry circumstances, and I was too proud to tolerate the idea of ever mending my circumstances by matrimony. My time has now gone by . . ."

Had she wondered, too, about his bouts of despondency? His heart had borne illnesses of relatives and loved ones, deaths of loved ones—Matilda, his mother, his adored brother William. "You want to know some of the *fancies* that distress me; I will mention one as a specimen of many others. I was one evening going to a Ball at the Countess de Hohenthals. I had not slept well the night before & after dressing myself I lay down on the sopha & fell asleep. I dreamt of my poor Brother whom I had lost about eighteen months before, & whom I had not seen for years. We walked & talked together. The dream was most vivid and consistent & affecting. When I went to the Ball I was engaged to dance, I think with both Emily & Flora, I tried to dance but could not; my heart sank at the very sound of the music and I had to give up the attempt & go home. Do you want some of the *real* causes. While at Dresden I had repeated"

And as in mid-sentence it began, so in mid-sentence, tantalizingly, does this manuscript confession, unique among Irving's writings, break off.

"He has written," Emily's teenage sister Flora set down without date in her Dresden journal. "He has confessed to my mother, as to a true and dear friend, his love for E——, and his conviction of its utter hopelessness."

If this was the confession Flora meant (although its conclusion hints that the surviving fragment may have been written away from Dresden, possibly on the trip to Silesia that he would soon be making), presumably it was delivered early in April 1823: "Mr. Irving had not been to us for a day or two, but this morning he came. He had with him some sheets . . . he had been writing. He had long wished us to know every detail of his first affection." The account, according to Flora, "was left with us under a sacred promise that it should be returned to him; that no copy should be taken; and that no other eyes but ours should ever rest upon it." And because what she says, when checked against Irving's life and against other documents discovered later (notably, Emily's own journal), has proved for the most part to be accurately set down and remembered, there seems little reason to doubt her recollection here, about an account the length and contents of which she describes correctly years later, even though she confidently assumes it has long ago been destroyed.

Through the winter that led up to his confession, Irving, as we have seen, had been with the Fosters repeatedly. "They occupy part of a palace," he was explaining at a merrier time, in mid-March of that year 1823, to his brother Peter, who was still patiently awaiting the turn of fortune's wheel at Le Havre, "and in a large saloon a little theatre was fitted up, the scenery being hired from a small theatre; and the dresses from a masquerade warehouse." Inevitably such undertakings consume hours and days; the troupe of amateurs was rehearsing *Tom Thumb*, directed by the green-room veteran Colonel Barham Livius, adapted by Irving, with Irving himself as King Arthur, Mrs. Foster as Dollalolla, the girls as ladies in waiting. Next they put together an opera altered from the French by the colonel; only Livius, having written for the London theaters, took his job too seriously. As director, he was a martinet who so overmanaged matters that the production seemed in danger of faltering. "In the mean time a few of the colonel's theatrical subjects conspired to play him a trick, and get up a piece without his knowledge. We pitched upon the little comedy of *Three Weeks after Marriage* . . ." Irving adapted it: "I played the part of Sir Charles Rackett; Miss Foster, Lady Rackett . . ." They rehearsed in secret, in Mrs. Foster's drawing room, "and as especially our dramatic sovereign, Colonel Livius, was almost an inmate of the family, we were in continued risk of discovery, and had to gather together like a set of conspirators."

The evening came for the dress rehearsal of the colonel's over-directed opera: "the scenery was all prepared, the theatre lighted up, a few amateurs admitted: the colonel took his seat before the curtain, to direct the rehearsal. The curtain rose, and out walked"—not the operatic characters, but those from another play entirely, from the comedy, all "in proper costume. The little colonel was perfectly astonished, and did not recover himself before the first act was finished; it was a perfect explosion to him. . . ."

The pleasures of such a conspiracy were abundant—"You cannot imagine the amusement this little theatrical plot furnished us"—and through the winter and early spring the group would experience other satisfactions. "We are now on the point of playing *The Wonder*, which I have altered and shortened to suit the strength of the company, and to prune off objectionable parts. In this, I play the part of Don Felix, to Miss Foster's Violante. She plays charmingly," does the pretty Emily. There were costumes for her mother to trim, of pink satin and velvet, a scarf to make, and black velvet vandykes to put on, and a little pink hat and black feathers, as the delighted Emily was recording in her own journal: red and white turban, great white veil, diamonds. And parts to learn, and the bustle behind scenes while the audience was assembling, before the anticipatory hush, before the first words spoken into the silence on the lighted stage. "I have dwelt rather long on this subject," Irving told his brother, "because I know you relish matters of the kind."

The delights of one other springtime evening in Dresden shine brightly still: April 3, Irving's birthday, his fortieth, a signal occasion. During the day he had driven a few miles southwest of the city with the Fosters and Livius in order to view the picturesque gorge of Plauen Glen and dine at the Golden Lion. "Return before dark—In the Evg a small party at Mrs Fosters to keep my birthday—The Miss Fosters prepare a surprize by getting up tableaus of scenes in The Sketch Book & Brace-bridge Hall & Knickerbocker." Emily tells more about it: "The performers stood in a raised niche, framed in by dark drapery the background also dark, & the light proceeding full & strong from one point, a gauze stretched before the scene took away the reality of the look & it did as the name indicates exactly imitate a vivid painting.—The attitudes were well chosen & not a muscle stirred—"

Costumes and postures precisely recreated illustrations of Irving's work by Leslie and others; Emily herself took part in depicting a scene from *Bracebridge Hall*. "Conclude the evening by waltzing," Irving chronicled pleasantly enough, and yet the warmth that the forty-year-old and the lovely English girl of eighteen could bring each other on such an evening seems already to have been tempered. "Irving," wrote Emily about this time, "is amiable & amusing I must not yield to capricious coldness fits—" No such fits would be permitted to mar his birthday, but during other evenings she would be visited by them, and scold herself accordingly in her journal. The little English-speaking community had begun to gossip. "Party at Friesen's—that report that I am to marry 'certo signor autore'—begins to annoy me—Kleist joking about it—got up when —— appeared to leave me a tete a tete with him I was quite angry—"

She had seen the famous writer's weaknesses early enough: "M^r I—— is in want of constant excitement, & support, interest & admiration of his friends seem the very food he lives on he is easily discouraged & excited." True, and hardly a lover's estimate, however flattering might at first have been the attentions of her handsome, sophisticated foreigner.

Yet Irving himself, whatever Emily was experiencing, apparently had fallen in love. The younger sister Flora had no doubts about that, she who had shared his company, sensed his moods, observed his glances across the room. He seemed hopelessly in love in fact, distracted, idle as the weeks went by. About that love for her sister, Flora wrote, "He feels himself unable to combat it. He thinks he must try, by absence, to bring more peace to his mind. Yet he cannot bear to give up our friendship—an intercourse become so dear to him, and so necessary to his daily happiness." Even Irving's own reticent journal hints confirmation of what she surmised. Through the first weeks of April occur visits every day with the Fosters. On the ninth, "Emily very unwell." On the tenth, "Emily better." On the eleventh, "Emily in good Spirits . . . E writes in my mem. book." On the twelfth, "At about 1 Mrs Foster & the young ladies call for me in carriage—to go to Findlater to dine with Livius . . . Go to the Fosters & pass the evening writing in scrap books reading from Scrap books—reading italian—and telling ghost stories until 11 oclock." On the thirteenth, "At 3 oclock go to Mrs Fosters—take italian lesson—dine there—stay to tea—Emily unwell with headache." And then on Monday, the fourteenth of April, confirming what Flora records, "Take lesson early—endeavour to write poetry but in vain—write only one verse—determining not to dine today at Mrs F Think of leavg Dresden—lunch at 1 oclock go to Mrs F. take Italian lesson—Emily somewhat better—very pale

"Leave there about 4. Mrs F very urgent for me to stay—E looks surpd & triste—return home but do not dine . . .

"Mrs F scolds me for not staying to Dinner—"

Again, on the seventeenth, "determine to quit Dresden soon," and this as well: "E. wished to leave D for England tomorrow if possible." Scattered through these late April entries are more signs of his troubled feelings: "Am very triste—"; "talk with the girls—E in good spirits & listens delightfully"; "E looking very much better is in good spirits"; "E much better."

Among such varying moods he delayed his contemplated departure even as April became May. On the fourth of May, 1823, Emily turned nineteen: "My Birthday, that good dear nice Mr Irving sent me delightful verses the first almost he ever wrote." Good and dear and nice he might have seemed, at least on this occasion, but he was tormented too. He must leave the city, leave these friends, if only for a few weeks. "My mother encourages him to do so," Flora notes at the time, "and leads him to hope that, on his return, he will feel more cheerful and contented." Accordingly, on May 19, a last meaningful visit to the Fosters, after the many earlier ones—after the ghost stories, the scrapbooks, the walks together, the afternoons pushing the girls in the garden swing. "Our last evening with Irving—before his journey," Emily records. "Mama suspects he meant not to return, he said he had thought of it—but that he would he could not help it—We stood on the balcony by moonlight & talked of heaven.—"

"Take tea in open air," wrote Irving succinctly of the same communion. "—moonlight evg.—talk of stars &c."

The contrasting entries might hint at what kept the two apart: their ages, to be sure, and Emily's unspoken memory of the charming Bavarian whose name continues occasionally to appear in her journal; but also this talk of heaven, which Irving chose to hear differently. For beyond her wit and gaiety, her high spirits and concern for the pleasures of this world, the charming Emily possessed a strong religious sense that was crucial to her being—that would, in fact, direct her adulthood. She and Irving would talk more later of this difference between them. For now though, he was off with a traveling companion, a Dresden acquaintance named Cockburn, for a month and longer of a sojourn to Silesia and Bohemia, east and southeast of Saxony.

"We are receiving delightful letters from Irving at Prague," the girl he had left was soon noting in her journal; and so, for the most part, they must have seemed, with their agreeable chatter of fortress visiting and mountain climbing. But her absent friend's letters contained as well many signs of homesickness, much talk of headaches, of restlessness:

"The evening is now coming on. You are all seated, I suppose, in the little Pavilion. I shall lie down on the sofa, and drive away this pain by picturing you all at your occupations, and recalling the many evenings of homefelt enjoyment I have passed among you. They were the sweetest moments that I have passed in Dresden . . ." From Prague itself, May 28, to Emily's mother: "I am in truth quite spiritless and listless. My mind has been in a restless state of strife & indiscision and has sunk into almost apathy, from its exhaustion. I hope to hear from you again—I do not know when I shall leave this—I have fifty plans of what I ought to do & only one of what I should really like to do. . . ." Delightful, such a letter from Prague? Should Irving return to Paris, to England, even to America—or tamely go back to Dresden? As he agonized, he treasured word from there the way a lover would: "I thank you a thousand times, my dear Mrs Foster for your letter of Wednesday. I cannot tell You how interesting it was to me, placing the dear little circle of the pavillion So completely before my eyes. I was so impatient to read it that I would not wait till I got to my Lodgings which were distant from the post office—yet I would not read it in the bustle & confusion of the Street." A public garden was closed, but he had found a place at last, on "the grassy ramparts, and read it in quiet, with old Prague & the Moldau at my feet. I have since read it over half a dozen times, for whenever I read it, it seems to bring me among you all again." How enticing must have appeared a reunion with them in that distant sanctuary, as Irving penned his reply "in poor Cockburns room, who is quite ill with a fever and Sore throat." For the Englishman had contracted scarlet fever there in Prague, where he was being alarmingly treated by a strange doctor in an unfamiliar hotel.

His fellow traveler helped nurse him through the crisis: the vomiting, the mustard plasters, the leeches at the throat. "I have passed the night on a sopha in Cockburns room, who has had a very restless night, with a high fever . . . This has been an unlucky journey for us both . . ."

Indeed it must have seemed so as the slow hours dragged by. "You charge me," he would write Mrs. Foster in that same lengthy, time-passing letter, "with tormenting myself almost into a nervous fever because I cannot write—Do you really think me so anxious about literary reputation; or so nervous about the fleeting and fallacious popularity of a day? I have not been able to write it is true, because I have been harrassed in mind. . . ."

Little enough of comfort would Irving find in the Bohemian capital. The enforced pause lengthened there, with Cockburn bedridden through one week, through two. The doctor overtreated and overcharged—"a great Humbug"—but finally against his orders the patient was sitting up and gradually regaining strength. On June 24, nearly a month after their arrival at Prague, the two travelers were able at last to resume their journey. Accordingly they proceeded northward, although there was rain now, and a weariness with the whole adventure, and several times they lost their way. On the twenty-sixth: "Cloudy & drizzly early in morng—but clears up—Mr Cockburn feels indisposed. we determine to push for Dresden. Order Post Horses & leave Toplitz at half past 10 oclock."

Thus Irving was returning after all, tamely, wearily, happily. That same evening, "Arrive at Dresden about 8 oclock & put up at my old Quarters—Hotel de Saxe—

"Arrange dress & call on the Fosters—Find E alone seated in dusk in Saloon." Sparse is this record of a moment so appealing, so fortuitous, so longed for. "The rest of the family comes in—pass the Evg till 12 Oclock—"

Emily's journal tells more: "I had just returned from a grey twilight walk, & was sitting in the dusk when some one rushed in, I was delighted before I quite recognized Irving's voice it was him, a pair of handsome moustachios had puzzled me I was so pleased & startled I could not speak only gasp."

From so ill-starred a journey to Bohemia the moustachioed lover had come back in order to resume, if only for a little longer, his life among his friends at Dresden. But that life, that interlude at the cultured little court miraculously preserved from earlier times, was drawing to a close. Already the end of June had arrived, and since the beginning of May the Fosters had been planning their return to England, to conclude an absence of nearly three years. Would Irving—as he had talked of doing weeks earlier—accompany them on their homeward journey, at least part way?

They would set out Saturday morning, July 12, 1823, hardly more than a fortnight after their American friend's reappearance among them. The interval could not have been joyous, filled as it was with packing, with last visits to people who might never be seen again: Cockburn, Livius, Morier, Rumigny, Loewenstern. With Emily, Irving seemed subdued; privately he was led to reflect on "Love cooled down into friendshp. which is Love retired on half pay." "Fidgetty," Flora described him, as once more he filled those trunks with his belongings on the eve of departure. He would accompany the Fosters, who were finally leaving their little Pavilion, their familiar box at the opera, the gardens, friends, the grave of their son and brother. At half past nine of a summer's morning they would set out, a morning that began "cloudy with a sprinkling of rain but cleared up fine & brightly before we started."

In the lead carriage, an English barouche, Irving was to ride with Mrs. Foster and her two daughters, and in the German traveling carriage, Flora tells us, "were the three philosophers, as Irving always termed them—my two little brothers, namely, and their excellent and clever German tutor," who was going to England with the family. In their laps the ladies held bouquets of flowers, farewell remembrances from the garden of the French Count de Rumigny. Waiting maids, tearful and affectionate, had gathered at roadside for a last glimpse and smile, and a little group of friends—the count, Mr. Wherry, Colonel Livius—were there, with Livius mounting horse to escort the carriages as they rumbled at last out of town over the chaussée, occupants waving and calling good-bye at the first stage, with Dresden's "pretty domes and towers" become shapes on the landscape, almost out of view.

"Oh, Dresden, Dresden!" Washington Irving would exclaim later, "with what a mixture of pain, pleasure, fondness, and impatience I look back upon it!" As he departed now, little enough of manuscript was packed away in those trunks, little enough but memories to show for the months spent there—the language not mastered, the foolscap blank, the love felt for Emily unreturned. "I am annoyed at myself & displeased with others," she would write in the course of this very journey. "I ought to feel more gratitude for I——g's esteem & regard." And it was more often Flora or Mrs. Foster who took turns riding outside on the dickey with their friend as the carriages trundled eastward out of Saxony, through Meissen, Leipzig, Merseburg, Eisleben, on the way to Kassel. Often the roads were dreadful, the accommodations foul, but in their leisurely paced summer adventure the travelers would sing nevertheless, and read to each other, and sightsee: willows by the Saale, the forest scenery, the mountains, glens "very still & lonely—the babbling of a small stream the scream of a crow or Hawk—saw two deer stalking up a Hill side—"

On the road to Eisleben, two days after setting out, came a hail-storm and blasts of wind so forceful that the terrified horses dragged the carriage down a steep bank and capsized it, fortunately without harm to the occupants, soon "drenched to the skin but in good spirits & unhurt." In a nearby inn they found refuge and dined on "cold tongge & wine" while the carriage was being righted and repaired. Finally, though not until late in the week, they reached Bleicherode, anxious at the end of "wretched" roads, at eleven in the evening. "A small miserable town—a wedding in the place & people dancing at the Inns—no beds to be had—wandered about seeking shelter in rain—ordered Horses & de-termind to proceed—Seated ourselves near midnight on steps of Post House—servant maid brought us Bread & Beer soup from inn & we ate by the light of a lantern—" Then on in the carriage all night behind four horses, so that the following morning they reached Hesse, and that night its capital city, where Irving had planned to leave his friends and under-take a voyage alone down the Rhine. "Put up at the Konig von Preuss—a spacious & fine Hotel—appartments looking out on a circular public place—Balcony—Moonlight—Supped in the Saloon—Interesting evg E very gentle & amiable—"

So he experienced that Monday night, July 21, 1823. "We arrived at Cassel by a beautiful full moon at an excellent inn on the circular piazza," wrote Emily. "I was very out of sorts." Is the "I" Emily—and did he understand her moods so little—or Irving abbreviated, and was she being kind? They remained at Kassel two days: "I suppose Irving goes tomorrow he read us his M—S—S—." That was Wednesday eve-ning: "returned home & remained chatting and readg Ms: to ladies till near 12 oclock." But on the morrow he could not leave them. "Good Irving has given up the Rhine to go with us to Rotterdam," Emily records, and so for another five days they will all be together, making more rapid progress now across the lovely valleys of Westphalia, through Dusseldorf on the Rhine, and northward until on Sunday, July 27: "We are now in Holland."

Then Rotterdam, at half past one at night. In that city they had a last day together, the Fosters and their friend. "Tuesday, July 29: Fair weather—walked about Rotterdam—market day—streets in bustle—dined at Table d Hote—in the Evening took a walk in the avenues in vicinity of Rotterdam with the young Ladies—return." Irving's entry for that day leaves out much that Flora provides: the "dismal walk along the slimy canals of Rotterdam," the "sorting of our separate property in sketch books, memorandum ditto, umbrellas, boxes, and all the small paraphernalia that accumulate on such a journey as ours," the exchange of final gifts. "Irving was in terrible spirits. . . . We sat round, looking silently upon one another."

The steam packet would sail from Briel, twenty miles downriver, at eight in the morning. "Poor Mr I. is out of spirits," Emily had recorded at the time; "when shall we see him again soon in England I hope." He went with them now just as far as he could, those two hours to Briel with breakfast together on board the river boat.

Then from Emily this: "we were hurried pêle mêle into the steam packet—Mr Irving accompanied us down the river quite into the sea, when he was put down into the boat, as he looked up to us, so pale & melancholy I thought I never felt a more painful moment, such starts of regret, a little self-reproach & feelings too quick to analyse."

They are all dead now—all of them dead so long, who then were so alive to grief, after the last walk along the canals together, the packing, the sorting of umbrellas, the farewells at the start of separate journeys. The young ones of the party, with England and their lives before them, were growing smaller aboard as the "Steamboat goes off finely." And Irving, alone, would return to Briel, from there to empty Rotterdam— "road thro cornfields &c along a dyke—9 of us in old fashioned carriage—Comes on to rain lend my coat to lady . . ."

We may voyage both ways briefly as the distance widens into their different futures. The steamboat bearing the Fosters crossed the channel on a passage "as good as contrary winds w^d permit, but smooth as the sea was," Flora and Emily both would be "terribly ill." Emily "did not undress—and as I lay awake in my little dark dungeon, the sea growling all round, and the waves rippling almost in my ears, I felt a most nervous sense of helplessness." Abruptly, in the middle of the night, came shouts overhead on deck: "Stop her" "Stop her." Loud voices, oaths, confusions, while within the ship lay the blue-eyed girl dressed and frightened through "a heart-beating hour, till I felt to my relief by the smooth motion that we were on the river. . . ."

England. On deck next morning "no one could tell me the cause of last night's alarm," though finally Emily did glean that the ship "had nearly run down another steam packet, that tacked right across our path . . . As it was we tore off their boat & deranged their tackle." Now England lay beside them at last, as the steamboat made its way up the Thames toward London: "What with the fog, the black ugly colliers, the slimy banks of the river, farther than which the mist prevented our seeing—and some pirates hung on the shores, our feelings were as unpatriotic as possible. . . ."

Irving, meanwhile, was making his way southward, over the "strange" Dutch countryside: "mingled land & water & sky—ships gliding along fields & thro meadows—mist—." From Paris he would soon be writing his brother Peter, still as ever among steamboat schemes at Le Havre, of that leavetaking of the Fosters, "as if I had been taking leave of my own family; for they had been for nearly eight months past more like relatives than friends to me.

"I now made the best of my way for Paris," his message to Peter continues, "travelling day and night, excepting a short stay of a night and part of a day at Antwerp. I arrived here the day before yesterday and have taken lodgings in the *Hotel de Yorck, Boulevard Montmartre*. I shall now put myself *en train* for literary occupation, as it is high time for me to do something, having been so long unsettled. . . ."

Irving arrived in Paris August 3, 1823, and on that same day in London, "It is odd," Emily was writing at a lodging house on Vere Street, "that we breakfasted in this very room, this same day of the month, when we set off for the continent." Three years exactly had passed since the departure she was remembering, Dresden years that had turned the child into a woman. Now they were almost home, "in this separate world of London which seems to frown on strangers as if one were intruders, & oppress one with its mass of inhabitants." For a couple of days the Fosters would tarry in the metropolis, fidgeting about, strolling in Kensington Gardens, admiring the transformations ordered by their king—"they are really superb—rows of palaces, & beneath the colonnades shop windows that seemed fairy walls of cristal the elegant drapery of materials from every part of the world—"

But the travelers were eager to be home, at Brickhill, by Bedford, to the north at the end of those last fifty miles. "We set off at two—and were whirled in breathless speed thro' the '*pleasant fields of England*' At Coldecot as Mama looked out she began screaming & knocking about— Papa was there, she got out to join him in the gig—we got a peep & a kiss thro' the window—& were rolled on—At Bedford we alighted in a crowd—Met good old Mr Turner, & set off on foot over the hill We raced the good old man unmercifully . . ."

Breathless, the girls hurried forward, joyfully straining to see: "It was dark still we perceived the gates, the bowers of Brickhill, a light— And the dining room window arched with ivy & roses Margaret standing in it & William dear dear Margaret, we flew in mad—We then had a good supper and soon Papa & Mama arrived—"

So they were home, all together again, with trunks to open, gifts to distribute, chatter of news and recollections under the shimmering light in their own dining room. At last to bed, to rest, voices ceasing. "Sunday—What a pity rain for our first day in Brickhill Mrs Fawcett & Elinor called the latter dined with us—after dinner wet as it was we walked round the pretty gardens shrubberies & plantations—a pleasant comfortable tea"

There, at home amid comfort and pleasure, Emily ends her journal without so much as a final period: taking tea, "for life, as it were." In time, their friend Irving would visit the Fosters at Brickhill, but for now his mood on the other side of the Channel was a contrast. In his mezzanine apartment, two rooms at the Hotel de Yorck in Paris, the American that same month was feeling "wretchedly out of spirits." To Peter, August 20, he confessed: "I feel like a sailor who has once more to put to sea, and is reluctant to quit the quiet security of the shore." He knew he had to resume his literary pursuits. But already, nine days earlier, privately in his journal had appeared the first of repeated, anxious notations that would be set down through this period: "Woke at 4 oclock this morng—with a strange horror on my mind—a dread of future evil—of failure in future literary attempts—a dismal forboding that I could not drive off by any effort of reason—could not sleep again— . . ."

During this troubled interval of Irving's life, his thoughts would often journey homeward, past England across the ocean to New York: "that little spot of earth, that beautiful city and its environs, that has a perfect spell over my imagination." By this time, back in America but farther inland than Manhattan, so far away as scarcely to be within the scope of Irving's present imaginings, young John Brown of Hudson, in the Western Reserve, had sought and found a wife. Brown was in his early twenties now, with his childhood behind him. For a brief spell during that childhood he had attended the local school, to little effect: "the opportunity it afforded to wrestle, & Snow ball, & run, & jump, & knock off old seedy Wool hats," so the man himself grown older remembered, "offered to him almost the only compensation for the confinement, & restraints of school. I need not tell you that with such feeling & but little chance of going to school *at all*: he did not become much of a schollar. . . ."

For only a short time had Brown attended classes, though briefly had gone to school even as far away as Massachusetts and Connecticut, to ponder Latin texts doggedly by candlelight in hopes of becoming a divine. But the effort had inflamed his eyes, forcing him to abandon that ambition within weeks and return scarcely wiser to the Ohio frontier. "From Fifteen to Twenty years old," the mature John Brown wrote of that period, ignoring the abortive venture eastward, "he spent most of his time working at the Tanner & Curriers trade keeping Bachelors hall; & he officiateing as Cook; & for most of the time as foreman of the establishment under his Father."

The boy who "during the warm season might generally be seen *barefooted, & bareheaded:* with Buckskin Breeches suspended often with one leather strap over his shoulder but sometimes with Two"—that boy "ambitious to perform the full labour of a man" was indeed a man already, possessed of his own tannery to manage in Hudson in his late teens. By the time he was twenty he had enough to do, overseeing apprentices in his bachelors' hall, to feel moved to talk the widow Lusk and her daughter into cooking and cleaning for the establishment.

The daughter, Dianthe Lusk, was, as Brown described her, "a *remarkably plain;* but neat industrious & economical girl; of excellent character; earnest piety; & good practical common sense." At times she would retire to the surrounding woods to pray alone, this plain girl a year younger than her new employer who, on June 21, 1820, became her husband.

The household John Brown and Dianthe formed in Hudson in the early 1820s was to be an aggressively righteous one, in the midst of all that godlessness that had drifted into the Western Reserve. Among the flotsam of wrecked lives—swindlers and brutes and card sharps and counterfeiters and confidence men—that had flowed into that "Satan's sea," Brown felt, like his father, "a determination to help to build up and be a help in the seport of religion and civil Order." Those are the father Squire Owen Brown's words, and the son would testify about his own inclinations that John Brown "never attempted to dance in his life; nor did he ever learn to know *one* of a pack of *Cards,* from *another.*" Mostly he worked and prayed—"I do not believe he ever eat a meal of even Potatoes & Salt but he asked a blessing and returned thanks"—and prayed and worked and held rigorously sacred the Sabbath. Before the June wedding, Dianthe's brother Milton had been used to visiting his mother and sister at Brown's tannery on Sundays, the only day that the boy had free from work at Squire Hudson's in the village. "Brown was an austere feller, and he did n't like that; one day he said to me, 'Milton, I wish you would not make your visits here on the Sabbath.' I said, 'John, I won't come Sunday, nor any other day,' and I stayed away a long time. When Dianthe was married, I would not go to the wedding."

Their frontier marriage would produce children promptly and regularly: John Brown, Jr., in 1821, Jason in 1823, Owen in 1824. Seven in all would arrive during the decade near the start of which a surviving father of the Republic, his battles with Burr and Adams and Marshall behind him now, had been led to feel terror in his heart, had heard in his ears, at Monticello on his mountaintop, the sound of a firebell in the night. For during these years as Brown's family was growing, after the invention of Whitney's cotton gin and the second war with England, slavery was once more on the rise. In the Gulf states a prime field hand would soon be worth $1,000, and the coffles of men and women would drag their way southward from border states—Kentucky, Virginia—by the hundreds, finally by the thousands, chained together under armed guard, to be worked numbingly from daybreak to nightfall for what was left of life in the muggy heat of the cotton fields.

"When I was four or five years old," John Brown, Jr., oldest of Brown's children, remembered, "and probably no later than 1825, there came one night a fugitive slave and his wife to father's door." Brown had built a house for his family in Hudson and painted it white by then, along the route of the Underground Railroad. "They were the first colored people I had seen; and when the woman took me up on her knee and kissed me, I ran away as quick as I could and rubbed my face 'to get the black off.' " The couple were fleeing to Canada, to freedom. "Mother gave the poor creatures some supper; but they thought themselves pursued and were uneasy. Presently father heard the trampling of horses crossing a bridge on one of the main roads, half a mile off; so he took his guests out the back door and down into the swamp near the brook to hide, giving them arms to defend themselves, but returning to the house to await the event. It proved to be a false alarm; the horsemen were people of the neighborhood going to Hudson village. Father then went out into the dark wood—for it was night—and had some difficulty in finding the fugitives; finally he was guided to the spot by the sound of the man's heart throbbing for fear of capture."

Thus in the America of the 1820s, about to awaken to sounds that hardly anyone was hearing yet: a firebell in the night, heartbeats.

In Paris, the homesick Washington Irving was meanwhile enduring his own midnight terrors, of a different order, of course, but to the sufferer real and intense: "dismal feeling still hanging about me." Tuesday, August 12, 1823: "Awake between 3 & 4 with some horror of mind—read & half doze at times till near 8 when get up shave & breakfast—go to Storrows—read americ: papers—"

Homesickness was assuredly a part of his despondency, here in Paris among expatriate American acquaintances: Beasley, Colden, "Young Cooper of N York who is lame." Part too was formed no doubt from a sense of the Dresden adventure ended, the Fosters gone from his life and little enough gathered during their time together out of which to fashion the publicized German Sketch Book for which he had set out to collect material a full year earlier. During these weeks letters would come from Brickhill in Bedfordshire—home of the Fosters—and from Emily would be sent a miniature that Irving kept for the rest of his days. But the friends themselves were gone, and he who had published nothing and written little in the past year and more must now finally be about his business—most famous American author from whom much was expected. He had almost no money left, his travels and Peter's steamboat schemes having drained off the sums that Murray had paid for *The Sketch Book* and *Bracebridge Hall*. Not much money, and not enough written to risk a book. He had meant "to get into the confidence of every old woman . . . in Germany and get from her, her budget of wonderful stories"; now he was back from his travels with notebooks all but empty of usable prose. For subject matter he would have to look elsewhere: "There are such quantities of these legendary and romantic tales now littering from the press both in England and Germany," so he temporized in a letter to Peter this September, "that one must take care not to fall into the commonplace of the day. Scott's manner must likewise be widely avoided. In short, I must strike out some way of my own . . ."

But what way? His visits with American and English acquaintances would continue to help him pass the daylight hours: "Call on Bradish—talk with him about Decatur" (the commodore, Irving's friend and fellow boarder in New York eight years earlier, with whom the writer had almost sailed to the Mediterranean in the spring of 1815, was dead now, killed in a senseless duel with a fellow officer on a March morning in 1820). "Breakfast with Mr. Colden . . . Mr Livingston . . . Went to Thuilleries with Bradish—" This on Saturday, August 9, not long after his arrival in Paris—"Met the Coldens &c there had admissions to see the private appartments of the King—" And from that regal view Irving emerged to encounter by chance yet another American friend—"Returning thro palais royal met with Payne—" with whose life his for the next two years was to become entangled.

He had first met John Howard Payne back home in New York seventeen years before, in 1806. Irving had been in his early twenties then, just returned from his initial tour through Europe, with Matilda Hoffman alive, still so young that she was only beginning to awaken the interest of this *"travelled man,"* one of the Lads of Kilkenny who dined and idled in chophouses and about the poplar-lined streets of the little city. Three or four years earlier Irving had scribbled his Oldstyle Letters for brother Peter's newspaper, but he had written nothing else yet. *Salmagundi* lay ahead of him, and indeed, it was John Howard Payne, in that same year 1806, who broached the idea that would develop into the popular satirical magazine that young Irving and his cohorts soon would be producing. To Irving's friend Brevoort, Payne suggested in October a "secret history of the times"; the town was ripe for satire. "You have a field for remark before you, which, with your observation, may be rendered very luxuriant. Cooper . . . in the theatrical,—Watts in the critical,—Irving in the Literary,—Hoffman in the eloquent, and Fairlie & Livingston in the fashionable, world . . ."

The suggestion was coming from a writer himself, and a prodigy, for Payne at the time had just turned fifteen. Moreover, the boy had already written and published anonymously, at fourteen, *The Thespian Mirror,* "chiefly intended," through its several knowledgeable issues, "to promote the interests of American drama." And during the run of that creditable periodical in New York, John Howard Payne's own first play, *Julia; or the Wanderer, A Comedy in Five Acts,* had been performed, February 1806, at the Park Theater by a company of the town's leading actors. The *Morning Chronicle,* the paper that Peter Irving edited, had mincingly adjudged the fourteen-year-old playwright's comedy to be "destitute of that delicacy of which the simplicity of our manners and the purity of our morals demand a scrupulous observance." But Payne was clearly a youngster to reckon with. "Dear Sir," Brevoort in his early twenties was writing the lad at Mrs. Saltonstall's on Pearl Street, Saturday night at eight o'clock, February 1, 1806, "I did myself the pleasure of calling at your Lodgings this evening; finding you absent, I take the liberty without apologizing of addressing a line to you." Would Payne dine with him tomorrow at Thompson's, "corner of B Way & Cedar St"? Please call at noon, "as I am very desirous of having a familiar tete a tete for an hour or so before dinner, as well as to make you acquainted with a young lady who has importuned me to see you."

Such attentions, while the editor and author was scarcely into his teens. He had been born in New York in 1791, but his father, a teacher of elocution, had moved the family to Boston before the end of the century in order to become headmaster of the Berry Street Academy there. From Boston young Payne had returned to Manhattan, alone, in the autumn of 1805; his eldest brother, employed in a countinghouse on South Street, had died, and the youngster was to take his place, training to become an accountant. Gloom filled that situation, however—as much as twelve hours of bookkeeping a day, six days a week—"even more tedious than anticipated," so the new employee was writing home by December. The most junior of three or four boarders at Mrs. Saltonstall's, Payne would make his way as often as he could after work that fall to the Park Theater, for already in Boston at his father's school he had fallen in love with drama. Now, back in his New York boardinghouse one evening, "in the hours usually devoted to repose," the fourteen-year-old began and within three nights around Christmas completed the first anonymous issue of *The Thespian Mirror*, which appeared in the booksellers' stalls December 28, 1805.

Other issues would follow, thirteen in all, reviewing local talent and the vehicles that displayed it: *Spoiled Child* and *No Song, No Supper; or the Lawyer in the Sack*. The reviewer's identity became known. "The little editor of the *Thespian Mirror*," the *Port Folio* in neighboring Philadelphia reported February 4, 1806, "is almost the only topic of fashionable table talk." Before the month was out Payne had provided more to talk about. Somehow, "in the space of seven evenings," he had found time after hours at the countinghouse to write and copy out his play *Julia*, performed at the Park February 7. Within weeks of that date, Washington Irving had returned from Europe, young literate of twenty-two, and would soon have been introduced to the prodigy about whom his friend Brevoort and the rest of the town were exclaiming.

The attentions that Payne's gifts attracted included, in addition, those of earnest elder citizens, concerned for the amazing child's future and prepared to sponsor his college education. For three years, from that summer of 1806 until the late winter of 1809, Payne was accordingly off at Union College in Schenectady: "if you, sir, can reclaim this

youth and by any means whatever supplant a love of pleasure by a love
of study, you will confer a high obligation upon his friends and render
an essential service to his country . . ." Yet by February 1809 the boy
was back unreclaimed at the Park Theater to debut—a prodigy still—as
an actor, playing at seventeen the role of young Norval in John Home's
blank verse tragedy *Douglas*.

During his childhood in Boston Payne had chosen for his idol
Master Betty, a prodigy of the English theaters whose fame was
flourishing then on both sides of the Atlantic. Born in the same year as
Payne, 1791, Master Betty had first appeared as an actor in Belfast
when he was twelve. In 1804 this Tenth Wonder of the World had
moved to London to star at Covent Garden, and the town was enraptured. Critics compared him to Kemble and Siddons, even to Garrick.
Mobs crowded the theater on nights when the boy played, leaving actors
elsewhere frowning at empty houses. Pitt adjourned Parliament to allow
it to go en masse to witness Master Betty as Hamlet. The aristocracy
fussed over the Child Wonder, who was granted an audience with the
king. And across the ocean Master Betty's exact contemporary, inspired,
had made his way from Boston to New York, had studied the local
theater, written his play, and now in 1809 was beginning his own career
as an actor at the remodeled Park, on stage under the modern glass
lamps, beyond the great lobby with its two fireplaces, its mirrors, the
purple and gold dome of its refurbished ceiling.

In his new career Master Payne was a success—the first American
stage idol, The American Roscius, so called after the classical Roman
actor to whom Hamlet alludes in addressing the players at Elsinore.
Soon after being acclaimed in New York, he was on tour—the first
American, in fact, to play Hamlet, in Boston; his Ophelia was Mrs.
David Poe, whose infant son Edgar was three months old at the time.
For three years, beginning in the summer of 1809, Master Payne toured
the cities of America, acting at Providence, Philadelphia, Richmond,
Charleston, Baltimore. During that time letters of advice from his friend
Washington Irving followed him about. In November 1809, Irving was
advising the vastly popular teenager to leave Baltimore soon: "You cannot excite more attention—You cannot gain greater notoriety & applause; but you may cease to be a novelty—curiosity may become satisfied." And again: "play any thing but the idler, the spendthrift & the
little great man—I hope you are superior to all of them."

Of course Payne found himself in time at a levee at Dolley Madison's White House. Even more alluring, however, was London, that city
of a million inhabitants—ten times the size of New York—and by
1813 a group of Baltimore fans had arranged to sponsor a voyage for
the young man to England, so that he might become the first American
performer to appear on a European stage.

As with Irving two years later, Payne planned no more than a visit when he sailed from New York, but the visit grew in length until he had remained abroad twenty years. He made his debut—twenty-one years old then—in June 1813 at the Drury Lane Theatre, again as young Norval. Brevoort was there; Peter Irving was on hand: "It may be some comfort to you to know that you will have friends present on Friday. . . ." But though the young actor found roles to play in several English cities in the coming months, his success was moderate and short-lived. A reviewer in Manchester might be impressed: "This gentleman has a figure not imposing, but well-proportioned; a face almost too beautiful for a man; and a voice the clearest and most bell-like we remember ever to have heard." At least one wealthy young London lady—her husband away on an extended business trip—might offer him hospitality and friendship (and after her husband Von Harten's return, the twenty-three-year-old Emelia would write to Payne: "I blush to own it, but my feelings toward Von Harten have changed. . . . When he held me in his arms, it was your face I saw, not his"). Yet Payne, however attractive, was no longer a prodigy. Master Betty himself, after two or three years of tumultuous popularity, had already subsided into the role of fellow commoner at Christ's College, Cambridge, before living out his life obscurely in the North Shropshire Yeomanry Cavalry. Payne, too, growing older and portly now—beginning, as he said, "to *fatten* on trouble and starvation"—had soon to turn elsewhere than acting for a livelihood.

He started to assemble from various sources—adaptations and translations from the French theaters, syntheses of earlier versions on popular subjects—plays that might be performed as his own. His *Brutus*, which would be revived repeatedly throughout the nineteenth century, was such a synthesis, first produced at Drury Lane December 3, 1818, with Edmund Kean in the title role. By then Washington Irving had made his way to London, and an undated note requesting of the playwright complimentary tickets, or orders, probably refers to this new tragedy: "I mean to get Newton & Leslie to accompany me & make a party to persuade the folks not to hiss. If you can furnish us with orders—so: if not we will go at our own expense & consider ourselves at liberty to hiss as much as we please. We will call at your lodgings on our way to the theatre; if you have spare orders leave them for us. I wish to hold out no menace; but I have in my possession a cat-call; that has been of potent service in helping to damn half a score of new tragedies. . . ."

Irving forbore using his cat-call; Payne's *Brutus* thrived. But this earliest American playwright to have his works produced abroad was unlucky. Financial arrangements denied the author just profits from what he had written, whereas creditors, "who were quiet before," became clamorous after learning of his apparent good fortune. He owed them money, yet had little enough of it—now or at any time in his life: "My success has obliged me to keep myself out of view." For a year, in 1820, the American imaginatively and unprofitably managed the Musick House at Sadler's Wells, but creditors caught up with him there, obtaining judgments that put him in Fleet Prison on Ludgate Hill before that year was out.

The ordeal of the indigent manager was eased by visitors to his prison quarters—Miller the bookseller, the philosopher Godwin's eighteen-year-old son, who was a reporter for the London *Chronicle*. But the debtor's life could be cheerless: on January 9, thick fog excluded light from his life all day; on the tenth, "a death-like melancholy possessed me"; on the eighteenth, "sent shirt to pawn brokers and got enough money to buy a day's provisions and begin work on 'Thérèse.' "

That melodrama when finished was produced at Drury Lane and warmly applauded by theatergoers; Payne was free, and his most pressing creditors for the moment satisfied. He went to Paris, beyond their further reach, and there Irving—*The Sketch Book* behind him, before him *Bracebridge Hall* and Dresden—had continued his friendship with his fellow American during the interlude. April 25, 1821: "Breakfasted this morning with John Howard Payne" at his apartment on the first floor of a small house at No. 16, petit rue de St-Petre. "The morning was fine and the air soft and spring-like . . . He has a couple of canary birds, with a little perch ornamented with moss. He stands it in the window, and they fly about the garden and return to their perch for food and to rest at night."

Irving adds that "Payne is full of dramatic projects, and some that are very feasible." That report in the spring of 1821. Two years later, in May 1823, one of the projects undertaken in Paris was produced at Covent Garden: *Clari, or the Maid of Milan*, an operetta containing Payne's most famous single piece of writing, the song "Home, Sweet Home." The playwright had moved by then to a skylit apartment, No. 156, Galerie des Bons Enfans, Palais Royal. That spring of 1823 Irving was spending at Dresden with the Fosters, but by the end of the summer he had returned to Paris restless, depressed. There on Saturday, August 9, the tourist who should be writing joined a group to admire the king's private apartments at the Tuileries. Afterward, "Returning thro palais royal met with Payne—."

With the success of *Clari* not far behind him, Payne had a little more money in hand than usual as he and Irving renewed their friendship. The playwright was on the point of moving to attractive quarters in a splendid location of the city: perhaps they might share that expense? "The situation you mention on the Rue Richelieu is very central & desirable," Irving conceded, "but the price (150 fr) is rather beyond what I wished to go in the present state of my purse." Nevertheless, by early

October the expatriates were established on the top floor—"up several pairs of stairs, what you would think the garret in America"—of this genteel private hotel, not a five-minute walk from the National Library and the boulevards. To his brother Peter, Irving elaborated: "My apartments consist of bed-room, sitting-room, and dining-room, with use of kitchen and appurtenances and a cellar. Payne has furnished them very handsomely. They have a warm southern exposure, and look into a very spacious and handsome court, and being newly finished and fitted up are very complete. You would be quite charmed with them. . . ."

In these agreeable surroundings did Irving now mean to settle down to work. Earlier, in Dresden, he had already tried his hand at adapting plays for the Fosters and their friends—and been agreeably surprised, as he had written the painter Leslie at the time, to discover "this fund of Dramatic talent lurking within me." He knew the world of the theater well—had been a playgoer since earliest childhood, and numbered among his present friends Kemble, Kean, Talma, Mrs. Siddons, Pasta. Moreover, he needed money, and he felt he must "strike out some way of my own," by means of some new literary endeavor, to get it. Payne and Charles Kemble were both encouraging him to try, so that soon his mornings of that autumn of 1823 were being devoted to an anonymous collaboration. In late October: "Payne is busy upon *Azendai*, making a literal translation. I am looking over it as he translates, and making notes where there must be alterations, songs, choruses, &c. It will have to be quite re-written, as the dialogue is flimsy and pointless; still the construction will answer, and that is the main point."

The results of that collaboration—*Azendai, Richelieu, Charles II*—Payne meant to take to England, so that he might deal directly with theater managers whom he knew. Accordingly, before the end of October he had set out, using an assumed name to foil lurking creditors, and by November 7 was writing Irving from London: "Yesterday I delivered all your letters, inquired for your music, got my passport signed by Smith, dined with Leslie and Newton, got a lodging under the name of Hayward (which I am every minute forgetting), and, heartily weary, found my bed was over a livery stable, where the hackney coaches entered every hour, and in which every horse had a violent cough. I feel as if I had not slept for a month. . . ."

Nearly two years would pass after that inauspicious arrival in England before Payne returned to Paris. Irving would keep the apartment on rue Richelieu, and for a while keep on at his new literary trade: "I feel more and more that I have dramatic stuff within me," he wrote from Paris to his collaborator in London November 22. In the manuscript of the comedy *Charles II* (so he explained four days later): "The scrap of a song of capt. Copp was hastily done and does not satisfy me—it is not characteristic. I give you here another scrap to substitute in lieu of it":

> In the time of the Rump,
> As old Admiral Trump
> With his broom swept the chops of the channel,
> And his crew of Big Breeches,
> Those Dutch sons of ———

"—and let it be stopped short at the critical word, by the daughter's putting her hand upon his mouth—he need afterward only sing two or three first lines. . . ."

That play and *Richelieu* would be sold together (as Payne's) to Covent Garden, "for 200 guineas down, and copyright may double it." When the comedy was produced the following May, the putative author could report that "the points all told *amazingly. My* notion"—which, of course, was not Payne's, but Irving's—"about Copp's always trying a song, and never being able to get it out, was very effective in representation." Still later, Payne passed on the information that "Charles Lamb tells me he can't get Copp's song out of his head, and is very anxious for the rest of it. He says the *hiatus* keeps him awake o' nights."

But the song that told amazingly in production (*Charles II* remained a popular comic vehicle on the London stage for many years) illustrates why Irving's dramatic efforts ultimately amounted to little. Payne himself, in the preface to his melodrama *Thérèse*, had opined three years earlier that "permanent literary distinction" was hardly to be looked for in modern plays, where the restive audience was "too impatient to pause for poetical beauty," where the dramatist must at all times "consult the peculiarities of leading performers," where so much was gesture and pantomime in any case: "An actable play seems to derive its value from what is done, more than from what is said, but the great power of a literary work consists in what is said, and the manner of saying it."

Irving had found that out, and had found out too that the pay was poor for the effort expended. He who late in November meant to develop the dramatic stuff within him had, by the end of the following January, changed his mind. To his collaborator he explained, January 31, 1824, "I am sorry to say I cannot afford to write any more for the theatres. The experiment has satisfied me that I never should in any wise be compensated for my time and trouble. I speak not with any reference to my talents; but to the market price my productions will command in other departments of literature. If, however, the experiment should produce any material benefit to you I shall feel highly satisfied at having made it."

So Irving forswore that brief flirtation with drama. He would return to his sketches and stories. He would abandon the play conceived on Shakespeare's life—describe instead the hotel here on rue Richelieu, verbal sketches from his elevated window "of the teeming little world below me": picturesque old Frenchmen, the porter and his wife, servants gathering to gossip in the courtyard on summer evenings. Or maybe German legends and travel incidents mixed together; he tried that, but "there was a rawness about every attempt to bring it into shape. It needed time to mellow in my mind." Maybe, then, a combination of German, French, and American sketches? "Mr. H. Payne tells me he is a fellow-lodger with you at Paris," the bookseller Murray in London was meanwhile pressing him; "I cannot refrain from sending compliments to you, and of adding an inquiry as to your literary occupations, and what your publisher may be allowed to expect from you in the course of the winter. I am perfectly ready for you, and the sooner you take the field the better."

Well, how about a brief history of William the Conqueror? Even that idea occurred to the desperate Irving, but "Feel intolerably triste"— this in his journal February 12, 1824. "Cannot bring myself to write on my work—tho' near 6 weeks have elapsed without writing." To Leslie at about this time: "I am trying to get some manuscripts in order for a couple more volumes of the 'Sketch Book,' but I have been visited by a fit of sterility for this month past that throws me all aback . . ."

He couldn't make the pen move. For weeks he had been sleeping poorly—"Again a Watchful night—renderd more irksome by the intolerable howling of a dog in a neighboring yard"—and typically, after such restless episodes, he would try in vain the following morning to push forward with his manuscripts, soon abandoning the attempt ("quite out of writing mood," "Wrote half a page at Author," "cannot rouse myself to literary exertion") in order to dress and go out. In pigeon-tailed claret coat and light waistcoat, his shoes brightly polished below flesh-colored silk stockings, Irving would stroll forth to divert himself from his anxiousness by calling on friends, among whom was now Captain Thomas Medwin—"he is cousin to Mr. Shelley": Mr. Shelley, the notorious poet drowned two summers earlier in Italy. Medwin, Shelley's friend as well as cousin, also knew Byron well; he "read me a poetical letter of Shelleys giving a description of a ride near Venice with Ld Byron. . . . Drove," records Irving in his journal February 1, with Capt. Medwin "in his cabriolet to Bois de Boulongne—all Paris in motion. Long talk abt. Ld Byron. He writes at fits—has intervals when he cannot write sometimes 2 & 3 weeks. Does not revise nor correct much. writes sometimes in Bed—rises at 12 sometimes 2—" The great poet, self-exiled, was at present (so Medwin gossiped on) "very abstemious & has reduced himself quite thin—Is in excellent health."

And has intervals when he cannot write. Irving, too, was suffering his "fit of sterility." There was much to distract him. His literary reputation was now such that when he went to Galignani's to read the American newspapers, he might (like other postwar American writers in

Paris a hundred years later) be pointed out to strangers: Geoffrey Crayon, celebrated author. At breakfast one morning he was handed a letter from a young woman—"a strange Raphsodical letter—the girl evidently deranged—requesting a lock of my hair &c &c." More welcome letters came from the Fosters, about whom on at least one night in January he had had a "vivid dream"; and invitations would arrive from the Storrows, Kenney, the Guestiers. On several afternoons Irving sat to have his portrait painted. And at home the apartment chimneys smoked, requiring to be "bedevilled by the fumiste, so that I suppose they will smoke worse than ever." Payne's dog, left behind, "dirtied himself out of all toleration" and had to be exiled. And Payne's plaguey French creditors: "I never have been placed in such a situation before," Irving wrote to London at last in exasperation. "I am tenacious in money matters. I pay down for every thing, and cannot bear to have an account standing against me: much less be dunned for one. . . ." Yet the journal confirms his predicament: "Bills brot of Mr Paynes—but Decline answering them. . . ."

Then in mid-February, finally, the words on Irving's foolscap began to come. He could start to count pages: "Capt Medwin calls" on February 19, "but I continue writing—finish the story by ½ past 3, having written 23 pages since ½ past 9." In March he was able to inform Murray: "I have the materials for two volumes nearly prepared, but there will yet be a little rewriting & filling up necessary." German subjects he had abandoned altogether. One section of what he would have to show was being put together from an abortive novel worked on for years; it would resolve itself loosely into sketches of literary and theatrical life in England. A second section assembled some American stories around the theme of greed. A third presented tales of humor and mystery told "by a Nervous Gentleman." And a fourth group was developing from talks with Medwin: "The Italian Banditti." Assuredly the work would be a miscellany, but the more Irving considered what he was doing, the better he liked it. "I think the title," he confided to Murray, "will be 'Tales of a Traveller, by Geoffrey Crayon Gent.' "

One late March day the rekindled author had the pleasure, returning home to the attic apartment at No. 89, rue Richelieu from another outing, to "find letter from Murray—full of kindness & friendly profession Offers 1200 guineas for my new work in 2 vols without seeing it till in print." Ah, that was handsome, that was reassuring! Now Irving would have means to journey to England, to finish the manuscript there, to visit friends and family—the Fosters at Brickhill, his sister in Birmingham, Moore, Payne in London. And he might see the new work through the press. May 22: "packed up trunk." May 24: "left Paris . . . with Mr Mills in his carriage—rainy cold Evg." And four nights later, on Friday, May 28, 1824, he was in London once more: "Arrive at

Whitehorse cellar at ½ past 6. leave trunks there & go to Covent Garden theatre See 2d. representation of Charles 2d."

In attending that performance of the comedy he had written, the new arrival may have been accompanied not only by Payne, the author listed on the playbills, but presumably (so the best of Irving's twentieth-century biographers asserts) by a friend with whom Payne had recently become acquainted. Mrs. Shelley, widow of the drowned poet to whom Captain Medwin was related, may have been seated beside the two Americans that evening at the theater. If she was not (and Irving, to be sure, makes no mention of her presence), certainly she would be in his company in London at other times in the weeks ahead. The bachelor and the widow, writers both, could have found much to talk about, famous American author in his early forties and the twenty-six-year-old Mary Wollstonecraft Shelley, who, while still in her teens, had written *Frankenstein*. Irving had already met her celebrated father, the philosopher Godwin. Moreover, they might speak of mutual friends (Kenney and Miss Holcroft, friends from Paris whom Irving had called on in his outings from rue Richelieu over the past winter, were Mrs. Shelley's good friends too), and shared interests, and one piece of shocking news of special meaning to both, about which all literate London was then concerned: Lord Byron, who Medwin had not long before reported to Irving was in excellent health, had been learned to be dead, in Greece, at thirty-six. His body was in transit home even now. And on May 17, only days before this meeting, his memoirs, entrusted to Irving's friend Thomas Moore, had been burned, out of delicacy, page by page, in the grate in Murray's drawing room at 50 Albemarle Street.

Not two weeks after that immolation, and on the day following his attendance at the performance of *Charles II*, Irving had his own business to conduct at Albemarle Street. Soon he was able to reassure Peter, now occupying the apartment at rue Richelieu, that everything had been arranged with his publisher "in two minutes." Murray "behaved like a gentleman . . . he agreed to my terms without seeing the MSS." But "I am rejoiced," Irving added, "that I got my work ready before coming here, or I should have been full of perplexity and annoyance, as I am kept in a continual whirl. Moore is in town. I was with him a great part of the day before yesterday. . . ."

And with the poet Rogers at breakfast on Sunday, where he was entertained with further anecdotes concerning Byron and Lady Caroline Lamb. With Payne, too, Irving was occupied; the playwright "copied part of my MS. and got other parts copied by others . . ." And time had to be saved for seeing the painters Leslie and Newton, friends with whom he had been close in London four years earlier. So the whirl went on—"Called on Col Aspinwall . . . Called on Miller . . . to Epsom Races . . . called at Sothebys . . . Called at Lady Spencers . . . on Newton . . . Mills . . . Payne . . ."—in this city he now knew so well. If he meant to finish his book, he would have to escape such distractions. Accordingly, early Monday morning, June 7, Irving was aboard the Southampton coach on his way out of town, and after leisurely visits to cathedrals and manor houses along the route, he finally reached Bath, on the other side of England, one week later. The night was rainy: "go to White Lion having engaged to meet Mr Moore there. Moore not arrived." Friends everywhere; and thereafter, one instant on record in Irving's life, past as present with the future unformed: "Did not know what to do with myself—too cold to walk about—read news papers three times over—dozed & drank tea to pass away time—returnd to my room between 9 & 10 & will now go to bed."

Moore did arrive next morning, in time to introduce his American friend around Bath for a couple of days before conducting him to Sloperton Cottage in Wiltshire, eighteen miles away—"very pleasantly situated, and a delightfully arranged little retreat"—the home that the Irish poet and his family kept through some thirty-five years. There, the morning following Irving's arrival, after a good breakfast "adjournd to Moores study where I prepared a dispatch for Murray of part of the Ms: of Strange Stories." The letter to his publisher that forwarded those tales reports on one favorable judgment at least: "Moore has read a considerable part of my manuscript and gives me great encouragement by the opinion he expresses of it." Yet Irving's host had only been exercising tact. The night before, in his own journal, Moore had entered a different —not to say ominous—opinion: Irving "read me some parts of his new work 'Tales of a Traveller.' Rather tremble for its fate. . . ."

There was reason to. The American author, however, knew nothing of that; his mood in fact was improving. From Moore's he set out soon to return to Bath, and from there rode agreeably over the ninety-two miles to Birmingham, full of the pleasure of visiting his sister's family. "I have had the happiness of finding . . . every thing prospering with them. Indeed for some time past fortune seems to have been disposed to make up for the frowns with which she had visited my family; and the good accounts which I receive from those who are dear to me make this one of the serenest periods of my life." So he wrote from Birmingham to his friend Mrs. Storrow in Paris, remembering as he did other times, "when the sight of a letter would agitate me, and a footmans rap, was enough to put my nerves in a flutter . . ."

Before him, moreover, lay yet another happy reunion to anticipate, as his new volumes edged toward completion. He would visit the Fosters at Brickhill. A year almost exactly was passed since dismal farewell walks had been taken along the rank canals of Rotterdam, since Irving had followed Emily and Flora and their mother "down the river quite into the sea" to watch the departure of the steamboat for England: "as he looked up to us, so pale & melancholy," Emily Foster had written then, "I thought I never felt a more painful moment . . ."

This later moment, about nine of a summer evening, Tuesday, July 6, 1824, would have been felt differently. Irving had left the coach office in London that afternoon, Payne seeing him off, and had "passed thro Islington—Barnet—Hatfield pretty place— . . . Country very rich & fertile," to arrive at Bedford about eight thirty. There a servant and gig were waiting to take him to Brickhill. The Fosters would have been watching eagerly, behind their gothic windows; before them the lawn stretched from the entrance door past the drive to trees through which approaching vehicles might be glimpsed and heard well before arriving. When he did come, Irving "was welcomed by the family in the kindest manner"; indeed, the next morning after breakfast he wrote Peter of having arrived "last night on a visit to my kind Dresden friends, the Fosters, who have welcomed me as to my own home. I shall stay here seven or eight days at least. . . ."

At most, as it turned out. Much about the visit was pleasant—that first morning's stroll no doubt, after finishing his letter. The sky was cloudy, but "Walked in the grounds & to Bedford with Mrs Foster & Emily. . . ." On a later evening (though Emily was not beside him) "walk by moonlight round the lawn . . . before going to bed. Beautiful moonlight night—nearly full moon—perfume of the flowers & the new hay—" And in the daylight the loveliness of the place: ivy, roses, climbing clematis, the glossy-leaved periwinkle. Yet talks with the family seemed somehow to differ from those easy talks at Dresden. Mr. Foster, civic-minded magistrate, was on hand, and spoke "of making roads. Mac Adam only has 14 or 15 inches deep of broken stone." Or he spoke "of the great number of noble Palaces in the western Part of Germany . . . Wurtzburg—Stutgard &c &c. These princes must have been rich—" And all that religion in the air, all those visitors: "At Tea a Mr Mardin calls: the curate of the parish . . . a zealous clergyman." "Visitors— Mr Simeon—fellow of St Johns Cambridge & professor of theology," in company with the curate and the Reverend Mr. Tattam: "Mr Simeon very eloquent—Soft Spoken—Waxes warm and eloquent. . . . Makes a kind of volunteer sermon & then proposes prayers from brother Madan —All kneel down and pray."

Emily's sister Flora, then in her late teens, would remember that moment: the reverend cleric abruptly rising, casting round him looks of pity and hope, flinging himself into a kneeling posture with the fervent summons, "Let us pray!" Irving, Flora recalled years later, "with an impatient gesture, and almost a shudder, placed himself upon his knees . . . I still see the sort of swing of the skirts of his frock coat, as he whisked round with ill-dissembled vexation to take his position in full conclave" at that morning hour.

"You were all wound up to so high a key," the family guest did write gently to Emily some time afterward. "I was a little jarred too by the well meant but unskillful and unseasonable handling of some of the professional persons I met there." In short, Irving felt "out of tune" with the prevailing sounds of Brickhill. "If I held myself aloof in any degree—" he tried to explain to Emily, but did she who was fated to marry a minister comprehend? On a small boy's mind stern Deacon Irving had stamped impressions years before, in New York village, in the wood and brick house on William Street: "When I was a child," so the grown man wrote Emily after his visit, "religion was forced upon me before I could understand or appreciate it. I was made to swallow it whether I would or not, and that too in its most ungracious forms. I was tasked with it; thwarted with it; wearied with it in a thousand harsh and disagreeable ways. . . ."

Not only age, then, finally separated Emily Foster and Washington Irving, not only the latter's wandering life and uncertain income (from Brickhill at this very period he was hopefully writing Peter: "I feel the impulse strong on me to keep my pen moving, and am resolved not to flag nor falter until I have secured plenty of the needful to make life easy"—vain dream, but to fulfill such a purpose was he then making plans). For Emily, "If I held myself aloof in any degree," he would later try to clarify, "it was not from a want of proper feeling for religion itself . . ." Still, those ubiquitous, sanctimonious clerics hovering about the visit, as on July 14: "This morng—the Revd Mr Grimshaw & the Revd. Mr W A Ivanson called on me" there at Brickhill, from which place, on the following morning, Irving, appropriately grateful and regretful, took leave of his friends after breakfast. "Flora at parting gave me a little ms book. Drove in the Poney car to Bedford. took place in coach, fine weather & fine road—had a pleasant journey to town."

Hardly the entry of a rejected suitor. He was going back to London, manuscript almost finished, with plans to secure the needful. The Fosters he would see in the future, but now through a busy four weeks he engrossed himself in finishing business in England before returning to the Continent. The manuscript of *Tales of a Traveller* had to be altered and fattened a little—"vile Book work"—and he had schemes to propose and pursue: Murray might be talked into reissuing *Salmagundi* brought up to date, and material might be gathered for lives of the poets that Galignani would publish in Paris, lives of Rogers, of Campbell. Moreover, as always in London, other matters would claim his notice. Byron's funeral procession wound its slow, silent way on a bright morning in mid-July along Oxford Street, out Tottenham Court Road, up Highgate Hill, commencing the final journey to the family vaults at Hucknall Torkard in Nottinghamshire. And on July 17, Irving "Sat to Newton to alter my portrait. . . . Moore, Kenney, Miss Holcroft & Mrs Shelley—came in—" Again, on August 10, two or three days before his departure from London for Brighton and the Channel crossing: "Went to Haymarket" to the theater. "Private Box with Miss Holcroft— Mrs Shelley . . ."

What Irving thought of Mrs. Shelley is not on record. What that remarkable woman thought of him—her "favourite"—is, however, set down through a series of revealing letters exchanged between her and John Howard Payne in the spring and early summer of 1825. That Mrs. Shelley was remarkable is an understatement; of the many women Irving knew, she was perhaps the most extraordinary—and her life till then perhaps the most eventful.

That life had begun in a London room in the Polygon, in Somers Town, August 30, 1797. From there, on that date, the expectant mother Mary Wollstonecraft, in her late thirties, was scribbling a note to her husband in rooms nearby: "I have no doubt of seeing the animal to day; but must wait for Mrs Blenkinsop to guess at the hour—I have sent for her—Pray send me the news paper—I wish I had a novel, or some book of sheer amusement, to excite curiosity, and while away the time—Have you any thing of the kind?"

The woman about to give birth and eager to while time away was, in her own right, no ordinary person. Mary Wollstonecraft was the revolutionary author of *A Vindication of the Rights of Woman*, which Aaron Burr in Philadelphia had read and admired four years earlier, in February 1793, near the start of his political career: "You have heard me speak of a Miss Woolstonecraft . . . Be assured that your sex has in *her* an able advocate. It is, in my opinion, a work of genius."

Still touched with genius, still timely, is Mary Wollstonecraft's polemic: just under three hundred pages of a sensible defense of women's rights, written for an age when women did not yet vote, did not go to the universities, did not enter professions, rarely owned property. Indeed, women in the late eighteenth century in England were themselves all but property, and "from the respect paid to property flow, as from a poisoned fountain, most of the the evils and vices which render this world such a dreary scene to the contemplative mind." Women, wrote Mary Wollstonecraft, "may be convenient slaves, but slavery will have its constant effect, degrading the master and the abject dependent." Her book advocates not only organized physical exercise to correct prevailing female delicacy, but also coeducational day-schools and training for women in all careers and professions. Rousseau had feared that an educated woman would lose her power over men. "This," the English feminist writes, "is the very point I aim at. I do not wish them to have power over men; but over themselves."

In the year of the appearance of *A Vindication*, 1792, Mary Wollstonecraft was herself still a spinster well into her thirties. She had been a schoolteacher and a governess and had written some fiction that was scarcely noticed. But the *Vindication* brought her fame. In that same year she set off for Paris to see the Revolution up close—through months that turned to Terror—and while in Paris met an American adventurer named Gilbert Imlay, by whom she was made pregnant in the summer of 1793. Her condition became obvious: "Finding that I was observed, I told the good women, the two Mrs ———s, simply that I was with child: and let them stare! . . . nay, all the world, may know it for aught I care!" The child, a daughter named Fanny, was born in Le Havre in May 1794. Imlay, the father, fled before the year was out to London, where he took up with an actress. Mary's letters pursued him; Mary herself, despondent, rejected, was in England with her baby the following year. "Do not turn from me," she had written Imlay earlier, "for indeed I love you fondly." And before their strained reunion: "I am content to be wretched; but I will not be contemptible."

In that mood, on a rainy October night in 1795, having left little Fanny in the keeping of a nurse, Mary Wollstonecraft made her way alone to Putney Bridge, where she paid the toll of a halfpenny, and hiding briefly from sight in one of the bays over the river, climbed the flimsy wooden railing and jumped. But when she hit the black water of the Thames, her drenched clothing held her up. Painfully struggling to die, she pressed the clothes to her, while rivermen who had seen her leap got to the sodden body that had floated by then two hundred yards downstream. Thus, miserably, Mary Wollstonecraft was returned to life—and to the dreary business with Imlay. Already he had found yet another actress, with whom Mary abjectly proposed in time a ménage à trois. Eventually, though, she did get over caring for her child's father, could see him at last indifferently, so that finally her life began to improve. His own shiftless behavior had helped effect the change. Friends she had known earlier, before going to Paris, helped cure her misery too, as did new friends, among them the philosopher William Godwin, on whom Mary Wollstonecraft paid a call, uninvited and alone, at his lodgings in Somers Town the morning of April 14, 1796.

Godwin, whom Mary had met briefly twice before, was himself an interesting person: bachelor in his forties, a lapsed dissenting minister who in 1792—the same year in which *A Vindication* appeared—had been writing his own first work of consequence, *An Enquiry Concerning Political Justice*. When published the following year, *Political Justice* had established its author at once as the outstanding English radical social thinker of that politically tumultuous age, for this dry scholar had written a potentially explosive treatise.

In the pages of *Political Justice* the philosopher maintains that people when wisely educated are capable of limitless improvement. But a wise education, Godwin asserts, must be conducted solely by the lights of Truth and Reason, which, when adequately communicated, will always triumph over error. To pursue such an education, a person needs freedom from the restraints of social institutions. Government is one obstacle to freedom: good laws that it passes are unnecessary, and bad laws are invalid. Property, too, is an obstacle: a person of wealth cannot reasonably profit from his neighbor, any more than he can reasonably deny his neighbor whatever appropriate benefit is in his power to provide. Nor, incidentally, should the wealthy man expect thanks for contributing to the general good by helping his less fortunate neighbor. When such benevolence is deserved, the gratitude of the recipient is superfluous; if undeserved, gratitude is a mockery. That conviction may help explain much that would characterize Godwin's own behavior later.

One other impediment to the freedom of the individual that the philosopher deplored in *Political Justice* was marriage, which he regarded as "a system of fraud . . . the worst of all laws . . . an affair of property, and the worst of all properties." Yet on March 29, 1797, five months before the birth of Mary Shelley, he who felt that way was wed at Old St. Pancras in Somers Town to the woman who first labeled marriage "legal prostitution." "I think you the most extraordinary married pair in existence," one close to Godwin exclaimed soon afterward, and other friends of the couple were variously moved to voice outrage, amusement, and wonder.

But the brief marriage of William Godwin and Mary Wollstonecraft—each living in his own apartment in a separate building, working separately, calling separately on acquaintances, though often dining and spending their evenings together—their marriage brought them pleasure. "Men are spoilt by frankness, I believe," Mary wrote her husband in June, "yet I must tell you that I love you better than I supposed I did, when I promised to love you for ever—and I will add what will gratify your benevolence, if not your heart, that on the whole I may be termed happy."

Thus, happily, two months later, she was awaiting, in her rooms at No. 29, Polygon, Somers Town, the birth of the "animal," with Mrs. Blenkinsop, matron of Westminster Lying-in Hospital, attending. It was to have been a boy, William, but instead a girl was born, healthy enough, shortly before midnight on August 30. The baby was healthy, but the afterbirth had not come away. At two in the morning Mrs. Blenkinsop asked urgently that Dr. Poignard be sent for. He came and—excruciating and enfeebling operation—removed the afterbirth in pieces. The patient seemed to rally, so much so that Godwin was encouraged four days later to walk to Kensington bearing the good news to mutual friends.

From that excursion he returned to Somers Town to discover his wife's condition grave once more. Puppies were brought in and put to nurse to relieve the sufferer. For the rest of a grievous week her husband stayed beside her: "Dying in the evening" was his stark journal entry on the seventh, but Mary Wollstonecraft survived two full days longer. Not until the morning of September 10 did her pitiful, drawn-out struggle finally end.

"The poor children!" wrote the unlikely husband in desperation the following month. "The scepticism which perhaps sometimes leads me right in matters of speculation, is torment to me when I would attempt to direct the infant mind. I am the most unfit person for this office; she was the best qualified in the world." Fanny Imlay, then three years old, and the newborn infant Mary were given in charge to a nurse while the distraught widower tried to reclaim his poise. During the years immediately after his wife's death he edited her work, wrote an affectionate, candid memoir of her that shocked his contemporaries—and began looking for a mother for her children. More than one woman turned down his proposals, but in the spring of 1801, four years after the death of Mary, he did take another wife, a neighbor—"a Widow with green spectacles," so Charles Lamb called her—fortyish, with two small children of her own.

Jane was one of those children: the willful Jane Clairmont, four years old. Mrs. Clairmont, now Mrs. Godwin, moved her family into the Polygon and set about making changes. "That Bitch has detached Marshall from his house," Lamb was soon wailing: Marshal, who had been Godwin's kindly friend, lodger, and fellow writer for years. Southey was disgusted: "to take another wife with the picture of Mary Wollstonecroft in his house! Agh!" Francis Place called the woman an "Infernal devil," but the new Mrs. Godwin had her way. By 1807 there were five children to look after: her own two, the two by Mary Wollstonecraft, and a boy born of this second marriage. In that year Mrs. Godwin moved the household to 41 Skinner Street; there she and her husband would publish children's stories. With their warehouse next door, they set up a shop on the ground floor under the living quarters, above which was Godwin's quadrant-shaped study, windows in the arc, old books about ("Godwin," said Lamb, "you have read more books that are not worth reading than any man in England"), on the walls Opie's portrait of Mary Wollstonecraft and Northcote's fine portrait of the philosopher himself in more impressive days. In that room, using the pseudonym Edward Baldwin, the author of *Political Justice* and of the powerful novel *Caleb Williams* (written in 1794 and still in print, earliest study in English literature of the psychology of the criminal mind) now wrote his contributions to the Juvenile Library: *Outlines of English Grammar, The History of Greece. . . .*

And here at Skinner Street—duel, trial, glory behind him—Aaron Burr arrived at the start of his exile in 1808: "I have seen the two daughters"—Fanny and Mary—"of Mary Wolstoncraft. They are very fine children (the eldest no longer a child, being now fifteen) . . ." Godwin would have been interested in Burr, for a shaping force in the philosopher's earlier reflections had been the writings of Burr's grandfather, Jonathan Edwards. Still, Burr on any terms (who almost alone among his contemporaries found Mrs. Godwin "a sensible, amiable woman") would have been an agreeable visitor. He was back from the Continent four years later, at the far side of his long, impoverished exile, eager to return home at last to his reunion with Theodosia and Gamp. February 15, 1812: "Had only time to get to G.'s, where dined. In the evening, William, only *son* of W. Godwin, a lad of about 9 years old, gave his weekly lecture; having heard how Coleridge and others lectured, he would also lecture; and one of his sisters (Mary, I think) writes a lecture, which he reads from a little pulpit which they have erected for him. He went through it with great gravity and decorum. The subject was 'The Influence of Governments on the Character of the People.' After the lecture we had tea, and the girls sang and danced an hour; and at 9 came home."

Four months later, in June, the highly literate daughter Mary was departing on an extended visit to Scotland. "I daresay," wrote her father to her hosts, the Baxters, on the day of her leave-taking, "she will arrive more dead than alive, as she is extremely subject to sea-sickness, and the voyage will, not improbably, last nearly a week." He went on to prescribe for this fourteen-year-old: "I believe she has nothing of what is commonly called vices, and that she has considerable talent. . . . I am anxious that she should be brought up . . . like a philosopher, even like a cynic. It will add greatly to the strength and worth of her character." For another correspondent some months earlier Godwin had contrasted with her older half sister this girl now on her way to Dundee: "My own daughter is considerably superior in capacity to the one her mother had before. Fanny, the eldest, is of a quiet, modest, unshowy disposition, somewhat given to indolence, which is her greatest fault, but sober, observing . . . Mary, my daughter, is the reverse of her in many particulars. She is singularly bold, somewhat imperious, and active of mind. Her desire of knowledge is great, and her perseverance in everything she undertakes almost invincible. My own daughter is, I believe, very pretty . . ."

She must have been. The surviving portrait of her in middle age doesn't show it—can't show the quick smile, the liquid hazel eyes, the pure skin, the lively expressiveness—but testimony of those who saw her in youth and early womanhood confirms a beauty about Mary Godwin that could move even a philosopher to notice. A surviving golden lock of hair suggests it, too, pressed in the yellowed note she would write Hogg within three years. Now, though, she was away for her happy interlude in Scotland, as her father entertained at Skinner Street for the first time a young man with whom he had been corresponding since shortly before Burr's recent winter visit.

Indeed, Godwin had been receiving and writing letters throughout that February, following an unexpected appeal the month before:

"Keswick Cumberland January 3,"—and the unknown writer had set down "1811" on that opening page for what was already 1812— error that each New Year makes us prone to: "You will be surprised at hearing from a stranger. . . . The name of Godwin has been used to excite in me feelings of reverence and admiration . . . and from the earliest period of my knowledge of his principles I have ardently desired to share on the footing of intimacy that intellect which I have delighted to contemplate in its emanations." But until now, the stranger had assumed that his idol was one with Shakespeare and Dante and Homer. "I had enrolled your name on the list of the honorable dead. I had felt regret that the glory of your being had passed from this earth of ours.— It is not so—you still live, and I firmly believe are still planning the welfare of humankind. I have but just entered on the scene of human operations," this introductory letter went on, "yet my feelings and my reasonings correspond with what yours were." May we, the letter concluded, be friends? It was signed "Percy B. Shelley."

The nature of Godwin's prompt and sensible response to such an overture is evident in Shelley's second communication, written a week later: "You complain that the generalizing character of my letter, renders it deficient in interest; that I am not an individual to you." The young man set about remedying the fault. He was nineteen, he explained, had been at Eton and Oxford, where he had been expelled for writing a pamphlet called *The Necessity of Atheism*. His father regarded him "as a blot and defilement of his honor." There was more, about the "sublime interest of poetry, lofty and exalted atchievements, the proselytism of the world, the equalization of its inhabitants"—and, casually in the course of the letter, this arresting clarification: ". . . I am heir by entail to an estate of 6000£ per an.—"

Arresting, indeed, for Godwin's publishing affairs were approaching a crisis. He had begun without capital; paper, type, distribution costs had proved awesome, his business sense inept. "Shall I be torn to pieces and destroyed," the philosopher would find occasion to write another correspondent that same year, "merely because I am not a young man, and because I employed my youth in endeavouring with my pen to promote the welfare of my species? May I not reasonably say, come to my aid, all ye that love literature, and honest endeavours, and do not suffer me to perish . . . ?" To young Shelley, whose mind had been opened by reading *Political Justice* ("it materially influenced my character," he had just admitted, "and I rose from its perusal a wiser and a better man"), to such an intellectual debtor Godwin was writing by mid-March: "I wish to my heart you would come immediately to London . . . You cannot imagine how much all the females of my family, Mrs Godwin and three daughters, are interested in your letters and history."

By the early autumn of that year, the vegetarian Shelley had dined for the first time at Skinner Street, in company with his wife, Harriet— "the partner of my thoughts and feelings"—with whom he had eloped the year before, when she was sixteen. "We have seen the Godwins," Harriet Shelley herself was soon, enthusiastically informing an Irish friend. "Need I tell you that I love them all? . . . There is one of the daughters of that dear Mary Wolstoncroft living with him. She is 19 years of age, very plain, but very sensible. . . . There is another daughter of hers, who is now in Scotland . . ."

That other daughter was back briefly for a visit in November with her Scottish friend Christie Baxter, who as an old lady would recall meeting the Shelleys, in particular the teenage Mrs. Harriet Shelley, would recall "her beauty, her brilliant complexion and lovely hair, and the elegance of her purple satin dress." Mary's impressions on that first meeting with her father's new young friends are not known; she went back to Scotland soon after, fostering dreams among the bleak hills, innocent (as she later wrote) "that romantic woes or wonderful events would ever be my lot." At Dundee she remained until May 1814. Thus she had been away most of two years when, as a sixteen-year-old, she returned at last to Skinner Street for good.

Or so it was assumed. Shelley, of age now but with access to his funds obstructed by an indignant father, was in town again, attempting to rescue Godwin from bankruptcy by borrowing £3,000 against the fortune he seemed destined to inherit. On this second occasion what Mary thought of the young man, and what he thought of her, were soon made clear enough. Within a month of her return to London, the two were in love, violently. His marriage discordant, his wife Harriet absent and pregnant with his second child in Bath, Shelley, who had all but deified William Godwin and Mary Wollstonecraft, now on his frequent visits to Skinner Street beheld their lovely, formed daughter. Amid the ensuing tumults of that summer, he would confide to a friend in one rare moment of calm: "Every one who knows me must know that the partner of my life should be one who can feel poetry and understand philosophy. Harriet is a noble animal, but she can do neither."

Mary seemed able to do both, and more. That summer of 1814, young Thomas Jefferson Hogg accompanied his friend Shelley to Skinner Street on a memorable occasion. Godwin (who, incidentally, had been living at No. 41 rent-free on a technicality that would cost him dearly) was not at home. "Bysshe strode about the room, causing the crazy floor of the ill-built, unowned dwelling-house to shake and tremble under his impatient footsteps." While Hogg stood examining the philosopher's tomes, "the door was partially and softly opened. A thrilling voice called 'Shelley!' A thrilling voice answered 'Mary!' " Hogg's companion darted from the room, but not before a glimpse had been disclosed of "a very young female, fair and fair-headed, pale indeed, and with a piercing look, wearing a frock of tartan . . ."

She was home from Scotland—the glimpse through the half-opened door is haunting—and had already revealed herself to Godwin's intense young friend as one able to understand and feel and sympathize. "To defecate life of its misery and its evil, was the ruling passion of his soul," she would write years later of the man she had then summoned to her side; "he dedicated to it every power of his mind, every pulsation of his heart." To be sure, the evil of those times was there for all to see: "You have no idea of the distress and misery that prevails in this country," Washington Irving would be writing home from Birmingham within a year or two of that moment: "it is beyond the power of description." Yet Irving, newly arrived from America, did try to describe those conditions he found in England in 1816: "the distress of the poor . . . the absolute miseries of nature, hunger, nakedness, wretchedness of all kinds that the labouring people in this country are liable to. In the best of times they do but subsist, but in adverse times they starve. How this country is to extricate itself from its present embarrassments . . . and how the government is to quiet the multitudes that are already turbulent and clamorous, and are yet but in the beginning of their real miseries, I cannot conceive . . ."

Shelley for his part had brooded long on those same miseries. He was obsessed by them—had, as he would say himself, "a passion for reforming the world." Tyrannies of all kinds he despised, this tall, big-boned, long-haired young aristocrat with the high voice, in the rumpled clothes. Political tyranny, the tyranny of institutional religion, of parental authority, of marriage—all those customary oppressions of the individual human spirit were his enemies, and much of his brief life had been dedicated to fighting against them. He had written on behalf of and had visited the oppressed Irish. He had tried to raise money for them, and for families of executed workingmen convicted of frame-breaking, and for the liberal editor Leigh Hunt, imprisoned for libeling the gross, outrageous Prince Regent. For other then-radical causes Shelley had worked and written, in the interest of helping humankind realize what it could become if freed from the bonds of Custom.

In addition, toward that same end, he had as a teenager composed and privately printed *Queen Mab*, a poem filled with Godwinian ideas, one copy of which was now Mary's: "July 1814. This book is sacred to me, and as no other creature shall ever look into it, I may write in it what I please—yet what shall I write?—that I love the author beyond all the powers of expression, and that I am parted from him, dearest and only love—by that love we have promised to each other, although I may not be yours, I can never be another's. But I am thine, exclusively thine. . . . I remember your words: 'You are now, Mary, going to mix with many, and for a moment I shall depart, but in the solitude of your chamber I shall be with you.' Yes, you are ever with me, sacred vision. . . ."

Throughout early July tensions at Skinner Street had mounted: strained interviews, admonitions, pleadings. Sunday, June 26, Shelley had accompanied Mary and her stepsister Jane Clairmont to her mother's tomb at St. Pancras Church—then "one mile distant from London," now deep among railroads and gas works—and there, in a favorite retreat of his daughter, so Godwin later wrote a friend, "the impious idea first occurred to him of seducing her, playing the traitor to me, & deserting his wife." On July 6, Shelley completed the transaction of a sizable loan, as Godwin noted, "to rescue me from my pecuniary difficulties." That very evening "he had the madness to disclose his plans to me, & to ask my consent." The innocent philosopher, horrified by what in one sense was merely an application of his theories, promptly opposed his young benefactor "with all the energy of which I was master." Scenes ensued in which Mary was denied Shelley's company, in which Shelley threatened—even attempted—suicide. Interested friends expostulated, but to no effect. At five "in the silent summer morning," July 28, 1814, Mary and—curiously—Jane Clairmont, as though for an early walk, left 41 Skinner Street to meet Shelley's chaise at the corner of Hatton Garden nearby. Godwin woke later to find "a letter on my dressing table, informing me of what they had done."

Shelley and Mary were eloping that hot day to Dover and—the same evening—across the Channel to France.

"The contemplation of female excellence is the favorite food of my imagination," the young poet would write Hogg immediately after their escapade (as you or I might write, "I think a lot about girls"), and that may help account for why Jane Clairmont, half a year younger than Mary, came along with them. Perhaps she was needed to stiffen Mary's resolution, or maybe—as she herself explained, not altogether satisfactorily—she was along as the one member of the trio who could speak French fluently. But her mother, Godwin's pertinacious wife, was in pursuit, and caught up with the delinquents at Calais. At Dessein's Hotel, so Shelley recorded, "Captain Davison came and told us that a fat lady had arrived, who had said that I had run away with her daughter; it was Mrs. Godwin." Her own flesh and blood, not Mary, she had come for, but after deliberating, Jane "informed her that she resolved to continue with us. Mrs. Godwin departed without answering a word."

For six weeks, then, the young aristocrat just into his majority and the girls, both sixteen, wandered across the width of France, into Switzerland, down the Rhine through Germany and Holland. The adventure, unpropitiously begun, had much against it. Money was one problem. In Paris they felt imprisoned for lack of it, dealing tediously with lawyers and moneylenders; Shelley sold his "watch, chain, &c., which brought 8 napoleons 5 francs." The landscape over which they traveled east of Paris had been ravaged by the campaign just ended that had sent Napoleon to Elba. The emperor would be back, but meanwhile his country presented scenes of desolation: villages without a cow left alive, children begging, "cottages roofless, the rafters black, and the walls dilapidated." From Paris over that razed land the trio had resolved to walk to Switzerland, and for the purpose—in order to bear their portmanteau—had bought an ass that proved so feeble that Shelley ended by carrying the animal into Charenton, the girls trailing behind with a basket of provisions. Shelley himself later painfully sprained his ankle. The weather was alternately drenching and steaming, the food at the auberges and cabarets "stinking bacon, sour bread, and a few vegetables, which we were to dress for ourselves." The driver they finally hired after Troyes deserted them. (From Troyes Shelley had naively written his wife "to shew you that I do not forget you. I write to urge you to come to Switzerland, where you will at least find one firm & constant friend, to whom your interests will be always dear . . .".) Village filth was often appalling; at night the travelers would sleep on sheets thrown over straw. Toward this odd English party French people in general were "exceedingly inhospitable," even threatening. At one squalid inn, "Jane was not able to sleep all night for the rats who as she said put their cold paws on her face—she however rested on our bed which her four-footed enemies dared not invade perhaps having heard the threat that Shelley terrified the man with who said he would sleep with Jane."

Yet despite all that, the three of them were happier during those six weeks than they had ever been before: the young man limping eastward alongside two teenage girls in black silk dust-covered dresses. It was, Shelley wrote, "one of those ephemeral summers of joy and beauty of which our visible world sometimes dreams." In Paris that first evening, after a visit to the Tuileries, they "were too happy to sleep," too happy almost to eat. Later, under the shade of trees in the countryside, they would have their bread and fruit and drink their wine, "thinking of Don Quixote and Sancho." They read to each other along the way—Godwin's familiar writings, Mary Wollstonecraft's. Their eyes were filled with "delight giving scenes . . . I should take up volumes," wrote Jane, who wanted to stop and live in every village they passed, "if I were to attempt to describe all I saw——" Fields were "bright and waving with the golden harvest." Groves of poplar and white willow surrounded green meadows. Once in a wood they dozed on soft moss, under the sweet murmur of wind in the leaves. At night tranquil rivers reflected lights of cottages, hills dim beyond. And approaching Switzerland, jostled in the bottom of a rude cart, Mary lay half asleep, looking up at the stars that wove "a wild dance, as the visions of slumber invaded the domains of reality. . . ."

> Thou Friend, whose presence on my wintry heart
> Fell, like bright Spring upon some herbless plain,
> How beautiful and calm and free thou wert
> In thy young wisdom, when the mortal chain
> Of Custom thou didst burst and rend in twain,
> And walked as free as light . . .

In Switzerland, however, the trio's money gave out. There was nothing to do but return to the England that Jane had thought they were leaving for good. Accordingly, on Tuesday, August 30, they departed from Basle together by boat, descending the swollen Rhine among green islands. The date was Mary's seventeenth birthday.

Down the Rhine to Cologne, by "detestable" slow diligence through Holland (at Rotterdam "with 20 écus; make arrangements, and talk of many things, past, present, and to come"), by sail to Gravesend, then suddenly back in familiar, unfriendly London, another Tuesday, September 13, with Shelley in quest of funds, calling on one friend whose brother "treats us very ill," and then on his wife Harriet, "whilst poor Mary and Jane are left two whole hours in the coach" outside at the curb.

Twenty months in England lay ahead of them before the three young people were once more on their way to Switzerland. Early in those months their lack of funds would continue to cause troubles that intensified. The fall of 1814 accordingly became, during desperate weeks, a time of changing living quarters to escape creditors, of keeping new addresses secret, of ducking bailiffs to avoid arrest. Sundays Shelley was by law immune from his tormentors, but weekdays he would stay out of sight, scurrying among moneylenders, meeting Mary covertly at St. Paul's, at Gray's Inn Garden, at the Cross Keys in St. John Street: "For what a minute did I see you yesterday——is this the way my beloved that we are to live till the sixth in the morning I look for you and when I awake I turn to look on you—— dearest Shelley you are solitary and uncomfortable why cannot I be with you . . ."

That feverish economic distress was somewhat eased with the death, at eighty-six, of Shelley's grandfather in January 1815; now the young man was heir to a baronetcy and an estate of some £150,000. Shelley's father, however, would continue intractable through subsequent months—indeed, for as long as he had breath—unwilling to communicate with his free-thinking son except through a lawyer, but intent on preserving the family estate from that egalitarian offspring: let Shelley accept the income from, say, £100,000 for life and give up claim to the rest. The young man was allowed a year to make a decision; but at least the threat of days as miserably secretive as those of the previous November would soon be behind him for good.

Other problems abided, however, as new ones developed. The Godwins of Skinner Street had remained unappeased. *"Friday, Sept. 16 . . .* Mrs. Godwin and Fanny pay a visit to the window, but refuse to speak to Shelley when he goes out to them." Poor Fanny did try to act as mediator, in vain: Godwin declined to be reconciled at the same time that he went on pestering his daughter's lover for money. "I return your cheque," the philosopher would write Shelley in the spring of 1815, "because no consideration can induce me to utter a cheque drawn by you and containing my name. . . . I hope you will send a duplicate of it by the post which will reach me on Saturday morning. You may make it payable to Joseph Hume or James Martin or any other name in the whole directory. . . ." To such an egregious attitude Godwin's disciple —lover of his adoring daughter—did allow himself to respond rather sharply at last: "It has perpetually appeared to me to have been your especial duty to see that, so far as mankind value your good opinion, we were dealt justly by, and that a young family, innocent and benevolent and united, should not be confounded with prostitutes and seducers." Yet Shelley did send another check, payable to Mr. Hume, as he had sent checks for Godwin's benefit before—and would send checks for many months and years afterward.

Assuredly from Mary's point of view Jane Clairmont posed another set of problems. That nubile sixteen-year-old went on living with the couple after their return from the Continent (she had no place else to live), and would be gone with Shelley for long days in town while Mary, now pregnant, languished. Or the two of them would sit up, Shelley and Jane, late into the night talking of gothic matters, "of oppression and reform, of cutting squares of skin from the soldiers' backs." Thus Friday night, October 7, 1814; Mary had gone to bed at half past eight. "At 1 o'clock Shelley observes that it is the witching time of night; he inquires soon after if it is not horrible to feel the silence of night tingling in our ears . . ." At two, "awe-struck and hardly daring to breathe," they were about to part. "Shelley says to Jane 'Good night'; his hand is leaning on the table; he is conscious of an expression in his countenance which he cannot repress . . . 'How horribly you look—take your eyes off.' 'Good night' again, and Jane ran to her room. Shelley, unable to sleep, kissed Mary and prepared to sit beside her and read until morning . . ."

Suddenly, "rapid footsteps descended the stairs. Jane was there; her countenance was distorted most unnaturally by horrible dismay . . . her eyes were wide and staring, drawn almost from the sockets . . . the eyelids were forced in, and the eyeballs . . . inserted . . . in the sockets of a lifeless head." A pillow in her room that had been on the bed was an instant later, inexplicably, on a chair. "She asked me (Shelley) if I had touched her pillow (her tone was that of dreadful alarm)." Shelley calmed her, brought her into the room, and the two of them "continued to sit by the fire, at intervals engaging in awful conversation relative to the nature of these mysteries." Then, "just as the dawn was struggling with moonlight, Jane remarked in me that unutterable expression which had affected her with so much horror before; she described it as expressing a mixture of deep sadness and conscious power over her. I covered my face with my hands, and spoke to her in the most studied gentleness. It was ineffectual; her horror and agony increased even to the most dreadful convulsions. She shrieked and writhed on the floor. I ran to Mary; I communicated in few words the state of Jane. I brought her to Mary. The convulsions gradually ceased, and she slept. At daybreak we examined her apartment and found her pillow on the chair."

In Switzerland the preceding summer the travelers' journals had already taken note of Jane's "horrors"; they would be noted again, as on the following Friday: "Night comes; Jane walks in her sleep, and groans horribly, listen for two hours . . ." (Of that occasion the girl herself records: "About ½ after ten Shelley comes up & I go down & sleep with Mary because I groan—can't think what the deuce is the matter with me—'I weep yet never know why—I sigh yet feel no pain.' . . .")

Amid such disturbances their first autumn back in England passed, moving toward winter. Pregnant, impoverished, alienated from her family, resenting the unsettling presence of her stepsister, dismayed by her lover's unrestrained exultation over the birth of his legitimate son and heir by Harriet at the end of November, Mary Godwin nevertheless continued to idolize the young man with whom she had eloped. Hence she was prepared to like—and more than like—his old friend Thomas Jefferson Hogg, who reappeared in Shelley's life at about this time.

Hogg, coauthor of *The Necessity of Atheism* which had got him expelled with Shelley from Oxford, had, in 1811, made unwanted love to Harriet Shelley, not long after her elopement: "He came to Edinburgh," Shelley had written of that situation; "he saw me, he saw Harriet; he *loved* her (I use the word, because he used it; you comprehend the arbitrariness of its meaning, the different ideas it excites under different modes of application) he loved her . . . On our arrival at York he avowed it."

But Harriet, then sixteen, had resisted, despite the sophistries that Hogg had urged: " 'There is no injury to him who knows it not,' 'Why is it wrong to permit my love if it does not alienate affection.'—These failed of success"; the love of this friend for Shelley's wife had not prospered, any more than had his earlier love for Shelley's sister Elizabeth. But down from York and studying law in London three years later, he now became a part of Shelley's new life, with Mary.

January 1, 1815: "Dearest Hogg," Mary is writing from Nelson Square in the first of a series of eleven remarkable notes that have survived from that winter and spring, "As they have both"—Shelley and Jane—"left me and I am here all alone I have nothing better to do than take up my pen and say a few words to you— . . . You love me you say—I wish I could return it with the passion you deserve . . . But you know Hogg that we have known each other for so short a time and I did not think about love—so that I think that *that* also will come in time . . . There is a bright prospect before us my dear friend—lovely . . ." Three days later: "My dearest Hogg . . . Shelley & Jane are both gone out & from the number & distance of the places that they are going to I do not expect them till very late—perhaps you can come and console a solitary lady in the mean time— . . ." On the seventh: "I send you what you asked me for"—a lock of hair; bound in three ringlets, it survives with the note— ". . . I ask but for time—time which for other causes beside this—phisical causes—that must be given—Shelley will be subject to these also— . . ."

For Mary's baby was due very soon, was indeed born February 22, a female child sickly at first—as the family made still another move, from Hans Place to Arabella Road, Pimlico—though gradually it seemed to gain strength through the first week of life. Yet not even a name is recorded for it, infant who lived only eleven days and nights, until March 6, 1815:

> My dearest Hogg my baby is dead—will you come to me as soon as you can—I wish to see you—It was perfectly well when I went to bed—I awoke in the night to give it suck it appeared to be *sleeping* so quietly that I would not awake it— it was dead then but we did not find *that* out till morning— from its appearance it evidently died of convulsions—
>
> Will you come—you are so calm a creature & Shelley is afraid of a fever from the milk—for I am no longer a mother now
>
> Mary

Once or twice, through the brevity and factualness of her journal entries, amid the comings and goings, amid the record of the scores, of the hundreds of books read, Mary's grief breaks through. Monday, March 13: "Stay at home—net & think of my little dead baby this is foolish I suppose yet, when ever I am left alone to my own thoughts & do not read to divert them they always come back to the same point that I was a mother & am so no longer. Fanny comes, wet through; she dines and stays the evening; talk about many things . . ." And the following Sunday: "Dream that my little baby came to life again; that it had only been cold, and that we rubbed it before the fire, and it lived. Awake and find no baby. I think about the little thing all day. Not in good spirits. Shelley is very unwell. . . ."

By now Hogg was living with them, from March 10 to April 17—his holidays—and increasingly was Jane's presence resented (she had changed her name, by the way—no longer Jane, but Clara now): "Shelley and I go up stairs, and talk of Clara's going." Her sleeping until four in the afternoon was enough to make one Sunday morning (March 12) "very quiet . . . and happy." But not until May did they get rid of the girl, at least temporarily, when she departed to board, presumably at Shelley's expense, in Lynmouth. And on that day one journal that Mary had been keeping came to an end on a sentiment feelingly expressed: "I begin a new Journal with our regeneration."

Regeneration seems hardly too strong a word. Clara was gone at last, and old Sir Bysshe's complicated will had been disentangled enough by May to allow his grandson's major debts to be paid. Moreover, Shelley's health, which had caused Mary alarm that spring, seemed markedly, even miraculously improved. Trips from London that the two took together raised Mary's spirits as well. The affair with Hogg, of which Shelley had been informed and which he had sanctioned from the first, would soon cool; no intimate letter from Mary to Hogg survives after late April, and in June began a long separation preceding what would become her active dislike of Shelley's "dear friend" who had briefly seemed so appealing.

In relation to Shelley himself, the summer and early autumn of 1815 may have been Mary's most serene interlude. They toured Devonshire together, and in the late summer were established at Bishopsgate, twenty some miles west of London. A boating trip during that warm, dry summer to the source of the Thames bestowed on Shelley a "ruddy, healthy complexion . . . he is twice as fat as he used to be." To Hogg from Bishopsgate September 22, Shelley reported: "I have been engaged lately in the commencement of several literary plans, which if my present temper of mind endures I shall probably complete in the winter." His first major poem, *Alastor*, was one of these, written in the oak shade of Windsor Great Park, near their rented home in which was born Mary's second child, this one a healthy, beautiful boy, William, January 24, 1816.

The poem, rejected by Murray, was published the following month in a slim volume entitled *Alastor, or the Spirit of Solitude; and Other Poems*. In Shelley's mind much depended on the reception of this "first attempt to interest the best feelings of the human heart." Yet almost everywhere the work was ignored; the notice that two or three papers did take of it was unfriendly. Moreover, the indefatigable Godwin was still, as ever, plaguing his daughter's lover for money, while a Chancery suit about old Bysshe's estate—"It is altogether a most complex affair, the words of the will being equivocal to a singular degree"—was being brought to a conclusion that was not favorable to Shelley ultimately, but that did clarify terms so that he had more funds available. With means to do so, the young poet was eager to leave England. As early as February he had written Godwin: "In the course of a few weeks I shall certainly leave the neighbourhood of London, & possibly even execute my design of settling in Italy." In the event, he went to Geneva, a destination for which Mary's stepsister Clara was responsible.

Clara had returned to London from the Lynmouth retreat, which had bored her, and was now spending part of her time that winter and early spring in the dreary, debt-ridden confines of 41 Skinner Street. But by March 1816 she was after a poet of her own, a far more illustrious poet than Mary had found in Shelley. To Lord Byron himself, twenty-eight at the time and recently estranged from his wife, Clara—now calling herself Clare—had written during that month: "If a woman, whose reputation has yet remained unstained, if without either guardian or husband to control she should throw herself upon your mercy, if with a beating heart she should confess the love she has borne you many years . . . could you betray her, or would you be silent as the grave?"

The harried lord, recipient of many such offers, was silent enough for the nonce, so that Clare had to write again, in different vein, even to get a reply. But the determined and darkly handsome seventeen-year-old did persist, did manage in time to gain a private audience at 13 Piccadilly Terrace with England's most glamorous literary figure. Lord Byron, too, was on the point of abandoning his homeland in disgust, but by early April Clare had already furthered her acquaintance with him enough to introduce her stepsister: "Mary has promised to accompany me tonight. Will you be so good as to prepare your servants for the visit . . . I say this because on Thursday evening I waited nearly a quarter of an hour in your hall, which though I may overlook the disagreeableness—she, who is not in love would not." Clare added, "She has not the slightest suspicion of our connection. For pity's sake breathe not a word . . . I shall stay a few moments after her departure to receive your last instructions."

Among Byron's confidences to the girl was included his intention of settling in exile on the shores of Lake Geneva. Before the end of that April, 1816, he had departed from England, and from Dover, May 3, Shelley was writing Godwin on the eve of his own departure: "The motives which determined me to leave England & which I stated to you in a former letter have continued since that period to press on me with accumulated force. Continually detained in a situation where what I esteem a prejudice does not permit me to live on equal terms with my fellow beings I resolved to commit myself by a decided step. I therefore take Mary to Geneva . . ."

Mary, and their child William, and Clare. Thus before the end of May the two poets had met in Switzerland and become friends. They would spend that summer together, Shelley's party at a cottage on the lake's edge, Byron and his medical attendant Polidori nearby, up the hill beyond a vineyard at the grander Villa Diodati. There were sailing parties: "as we approach the shore, we are saluted by the delightful scent of flowers and new-mown grass, and the chirp of the grasshoppers, and the song of the evening birds." There were frequent visits back and forth between the two residences, and talks together, and readings late into the evening before the fire in the spacious drawing room of Byron's villa. On one such evening, with a storm over the lake beyond the windows, he was reciting Coleridge's "Christabel":

> Her silken robe, and inner vest,
> Dropt to her feet, and in full view,
> Behold! her bosom and half her side—
> Hideous, deformed, and pale of hue—

At the words the impressionable Shelley screamed, and "putting his hands to his head, ran out of the room . . ." Polidori, Byron's physician, got to him and "threw water in his face, and after gave him ether". In time Shelley recovered enough to explain to the others that he had been looking at Mary during the recital, "and suddenly thought of a woman he had heard of who had eyes instead of nipples, which taking hold of his mind, horrified him . . ."

Other evenings they talked of "the nature of the principle of life," of Dr. Darwin's experiments to vitalize vermicelli. The mood was gothic; all of them determined to write ghost stories. Byron and Shelley started promptly but soon gave theirs up. Mary, still only eighteen, wanted to write one too. Shelley would ask her from time to time whether she had begun. But no idea came, until one night in the stillness of her room, as she described it later, a nightmare intruded:

"I saw the hideous phantasm of a man stretched out, and then, on the working of some powerful engine, show signs of life, and stir with an uneasy, half vital motion. Frightful must it be; for supremely frightful would be the effect of any human endeavour to mock the stupendous mechanism of the Creator of the world. His success would terrify the artist; he would rush away from his odious handiwork, horror-stricken." Perhaps unattended the creature might perish, return to inanimateness. The remorseful artist "sleeps; but he is awakened; he opens his eyes; behold the horrid thing stands at his bedside, opening his curtains, and looking on him with yellow, watery, but speculative eyes. I opened mine in terror . . . I see them still; the very room, the dark *parquet*, the closed shutters, with the moonlight struggling through, and the sense I had that the glassy lake and the white high Alps were beyond. . . . On the morrow I announced that I had *thought of a story*."

That day Mary Godwin wrote the words that in time would begin Chapter V of the completed *Frankenstein:* "It was on a dreary night of November that I beheld the accomplishment of my toils. . . ." When published anonymously a year and a half later, her novel would achieve a far wider fame than did any work by Shelley during his lifetime. The central theme—of a monster that man has made but cannot control— continues to have meaning, increasingly so, in our technological age a hundred and sixty and more years after it was imagined and first expressed, so that the very name of Mary's fictional doctor has come to signify a mythic truth as surely as has the name of Rip Van Winkle. Through the remainder of their stay near Geneva, Mary, with Shelley's encouragement, would be developing her idea, and would be working on the book still when, at the end of August, she and Shelley and Clare— about this time having settled on the spelling Claire—and the baby William set out regretfully to return to England.

"As to all these 'mistresses,' " Byron was writing in early September to his sister, "Lord help me—I have had but one.—Now—don't scold—but what could I do?—a foolish girl—in spite of all I could say or do—would come after me . . . and I have had all the plague possible to persuade her to go back again—but at last she went." He could not, he explained, "exactly play the Stoic with a woman—who had scrambled eight hundred miles to unphilosophize" him, adding in a subsequent letter: "I forgot to tell you—that the *Demoiselle*—who returned to England from Geneva—went there to produce a new baby B. . . ."

Claire's pregnancy was part of why Shelley himself was going back to his homeland. Godwin and others of her family were not to know, however; hence, on arriving in September, she and Mary took up residence at 5 Abbey Churchyard, Bath, to await her confinement. But another reason for Shelley's return had to do with Godwin's recurrent financial crises. Fanny, in the midst of them at Skinner Street, had been writing in August to her half sister Mary at Geneva: ". . . I left it to the end of my letter to call your attention most seriously to what I said in my last letter respecting Papa's affairs. They have now a much more serious and threatening aspect than when I last wrote to you. . . . Constable"—Scott's publisher in Edinburgh—"has a promissory note to come upon papa for the £200. This £200 I told you was appropriated to Davidson and Hamilton, who had lent him £200 on his *Caleb Williams* last year . . . You seem to have forgotten Kingdon's £300 to be paid at the end of June. . . ." The philosopher's health was suffering. "He cannot sleep at night, and is indeed very unwell. This he concealed from Mamma and myself until this day. Taylor of Norwich has also come upon him again . . . ."

Galling anxieties, but Shelley was back in London now to try to help, hoping to raise money by selling at ruinous rates post-obits on his future prospects, looking also for a house where he and Mary might settle, visiting her in Bath when he could. In Mary's journal, among those endless titles of books that acknowledge a Godwinian faith in the possibilities of self-improvement, occur moments of poignant vitality: earlier, she and Shelley had been away from Geneva for a week's sojourn to the icy wastes of Chamonix, and returning Saturday, July 27, 1816, "We saw Jura and the Lake like old friends. I longed to see my pretty babe. At 9, after much inquiring and stupidity, we find the road, and alight at Diodati. We converse with Lord Byron till 12, and then go down to Chapuis, kiss our babe, and go to bed." As the total record of Thursday, September 5, on the way home to England, Shelley writes in Mary's journal, "We arrive at Havre, and wait for the packet. In the evening Willy falls out of bed, and is not hurt." That one day. Those lives. On October 6, settled at Bath, with Shelley present and writing again: "On this day Mary put her head through the door and said, 'Come and look; here's a cat eating roses . . .'"

So much sentience, before—suddenly—such entries as these, beginning three nights later, October 9, as Mary records the first of two personal calamities: "Read Curtius; finish the 'Memoirs of the Princess of Bareith'; draw. In the evening a very alarming letter comes from Fanny. Shelley goes immediately to Bristol; we sit up for him till 2 in the morning, when he returns, but brings no particular news. *Thursday*, Oct. 10.—Shelley goes again to Bristol, and obtains more certain trace. Work and read. He returns at 11 o'clock. *Friday*, Oct. 11.—He sets off to Swansea. Work and read. *Saturday*, Oct. 12.—He returns with the worst account. A miserable day. Two letters from Papa. Buy mourning, and work in the evening."

Her half sister Fanny, born on the outskirts of revolutionary Paris to Mary Wollstonecraft and Gilbert Imlay, reared in London as Godwin's child, had in the twenty-third year of her age left Skinner Street and made her way westward to the Mackworth Arms Inn in Swansea, on the southern coast of Wales. There, on October 9, alone in a rented room, she had taken a fatal dose of laudanum. "I have long determined that the best thing I could do was to put an end to the existence of a being whose birth was unfortunate, and whose life has only been a series of pain to those persons who have hurt their health in endeavouring to promote her welfare. Perhaps to hear of my death may give you pain, but you will soon have the blessing of forgetting that such a creature ever existed as——"

The signature she had torn off and burned. Her foster father, whose livelihood depended on the success of his Juvenile Library, had suffered when two of his daughters shocked respectability by eloping with a married man. His last and most faithful now threatened to envelop the family in the shame of suicide; her name she destroyed in order to spare them that shame. "Go not to Swansea," Godwin wrote Mary desperately, breaking a two years' silence between them. "We have so conducted ourselves that not one person in our home has the smallest apprehension of the truth." It was given out to those who had to know that Fanny had set forth to visit relatives in Ireland, had been taken ill en route, and had died of an "inflammatory fever"; indeed, so successfully was the truth hidden that nearly a year later, in August 1817, her own brother, on the Continent, was planning a visit to see her, inquiring of Shelley whether he and Fanny were often together.

The blow of her death to Shelley, to Mary, was severe. Both had been close to Fanny; Shelley had been innocently with her in London shortly before she undertook her lonely journey "to the spot from which I hope never to remove." The blow was severe—and it was to be followed within two months by news of a second calamity.

Since June, apparently, Shelley had not been in touch with Harriet—had not seen his wife in more than a year and a half—but now, during the autumn, as he was drawing up a will to provide for his legitimate children, he was trying to locate her whereabouts. Nearly a month had passed since he had asked the bookseller Hookham to make inquiries around London. On December 15, at Bath, he heard from Hookham at last:

"While I was yet endeavoring to discover Mrs Shelley's address, information was brought me that she was dead—that she had destroyed herself. . . . I was informed that she was taken from the Serpentine river on Tuesday last . . . Little or no information was laid before the jury . . . She was called Harriet Smith, and the verdict was—*found drowned.*"

Even now, mystery surrounds this second death, of the lovely, despondent Harriet at twenty-one. Her farewell note to her sister, in a markedly agitated hand, contains words for "My dear Bysshe . . . if you had never left me I might have lived but as it is, I freely forgive you & may you enjoy that happiness which you have deprived me of. . . ."

Thine eyes glowed in the glare
    Of the departing light
As a starry beam
On a deep dark stream
Shines dimly—so the moon shone there
And it shone thru the strings of thy tangled hair
    Which shook in the blast of night

To the surface of the pond in Hyde Park, in London, the woman's pregnant body had floated, to be discovered by an outpatient from a nearby hospital and taken to the Royal Humane Society station at the Fox and Bull:

The moon made thy lips pale beloved
    The wind made they bosom chill
      The air did shed
      On thy dear head
Its frozen dew, and thou didst lie
Where the bitter breath of the naked sky
    Might visit thee at will.

His wife's death filled Shelley with indignation toward her family, with outrage, in time with a deep, rarely spoken grief. But one of several consequences of the tragedy followed promptly. "A marriage," Mary noted in her journal, "takes place on the 30th of December, 1816." Partly to secure custody of his two children, Shelley that morning at year's end legalized his relationship with Mary Godwin at St. Mildred's Church, London. Her father was present. The effects of the ceremony on that libertarian philosopher were, as his new son-in-law commented dryly, "magical." All could now be forgiven. To a brother Godwin was soon, at last complacently, passing along family gossip:

". . . my daughter is between nineteen and twenty. The piece of news I have to tell, however, is that I went to church with this tall girl some little time ago to be married. Her husband is the eldest son of Sir Timothy Shelley, of Field Place, in the county of Sussex, Baronet. So that, according to the vulgar ideas of the world, she is well married, and I have great hopes the young man will make her a good husband. You will wonder, I daresay, how a girl without a penny of fortune should meet with so good a match. But such are the ups and downs of this world."

"For my part," the philosopher went on not altogether candidly in that same letter, "I care but little, comparatively, about wealth, so that it should be her destiny in life to be respectable, virtuous, and contented." In the father's eyes she was respectable now, and by Mary's own lights now as always virtuous. But contentment she could only hope for in a life so intense, so extraordinary.

"How many changes have occurred during this little year," she wrote in her journal in January, on the first anniversary of the birth of her son William. And already in this new year, from Bath, she had had occasion to write Lord Byron that Claire Clairmont "was safely delivered of a little girl yesterday morning (Sunday, January 12) at four. . . . For private news," her letter to the poet at Venice continues, "Shelley has become intimate with Leigh Hunt and his family. I have seen them & like Hunt extremely. We have also taken a house in Marlow to which we intend to remove in about two months . . ." Before the end of March they were indeed settled at Albion House, Marlow, thirty miles from London—Shelley, Mary, little William, Claire, her child, nurse-maids, a gardener—and from there were anticipating a summer visit from Hunt, editor of the *Examiner*, who had been the first to notice Shelley's poetry favorably in print, as recently as the preceding December.

We know and perhaps feel closest to Mary Shelley at moments like this: "My dear Hunt" (she is writing from Marlow at one o'clock, March 5, 1817) ". . . Have you never felt in your succession of nervous feelings one single disagreable truism gain a painful possession of your mind and keep it for some months. A year ago, I remember my private hours were all made bitter by reflections on the certainty of death—and now the flight of time has the same power over me. Every thing passes and one is hardly concious of enjoying the present before it becomes the past. I was reading the other day the letters of Gibbon. He entreats Lord Sheffield to come with all his family to visit him at Lausanne & dwells on the pleasure such a visit will occasion. There is a little gap in the date of his letters and then he complains that this solitude is made more irksome by their having been there and departed. So will it be with us in a few months when you will all have left Marlow. . . ."

The visit of Hunt and at least some of his family did come and go—itself no more than a gap on a page now—and the summer at Marlow: Shelley busy with writing a political tract, with visiting and helping the neighboring poor, with composing—afloat on the Thames, under chalk hills and beech groves—the poem that would become *The Revolt of Islam*. In early September (on the very day that Washington Irving in Scotland was ending the happiest visit of his life, at Abbotsford) Mary gave birth at Marlow to a baby girl, who would be named Clara.

Within a month the mother was up, had taken her first walk, and was now, September 28, "surrounded by babes," as she wrote Shelley, off on business in London. Claire's child Allegra "is scratching and crowing—William amusing himself with wrapping a shawl round him and Miss Clara staring at the fire. It is now only four o'clock so I shall put bye my letter for the present to finish it after dinner—Adieu—dear love—I cannot express to you how anxious I am to hear from your health —affairs & plans."

For as autumn advanced, Shelley's health had grown worse. "My feelings at intervals," so he wrote Godwin in December, "are of a deadly & torpid kind, or awakened to a state of such unnatural & keen excitement that only to instance the organ of sight, I find the very blades of grass & the boughs of distant trees present themselves to me with microscopical distinctness. Towards evening I sink into a state of lethargy & inanimation, & often remain for hours on the sofa between sleep & waking a prey to the most painful irritability of thought. . . ."

They must get out of the cold and damp of Marlow, take a place on the sea, or better still, go to Italy, to blue skies and blazing sun. Allegra, Byron's baby by Claire, should in any case be with her father so that he might provide for her. The courts had taken Shelley's children by Harriet from him, from this "Atheist" who had "blasphemously derided the truth of the Christian Revelation and denied the existence of God as the Creator of the Universe," who had made friends with "a Mr. Godwin the author of a work called Political Justice," then deserted his wife and run off with Godwin's daughter, cohabiting with her and—so the petition to the Court of Chancery reads—having "several illegitimate children by her." The Lord Chancellor had denied Shelley Harriet's and his two children. The poet's health was alarming once more. *The Revolt of Islam*, in print now, had been either belittled or ignored.

To be sure, *Frankenstein* had also been published, and at the beginning of 1818 (while Irving at Liverpool was enduring the final, grim stages of bankruptcy) Shelley had sent a copy to Walter Scott "as a slight tribute of high admiration & respect" on the part of the anonymous author. Scott would express his appreciation of the book with typical generosity, but that was about all the good news of those days. Shelley had determined to leave England—would deliver Byron his daughter—for there was little to keep him and his family here. In early March, accordingly, a message was delivered to Scott's and Byron's publisher: "Mr. Shelleys Compts. to Mr. Murray & begs to inform him that if he has any books or letters to convey to Lord Byron, Mr. S. will be happy to take charge of them; as he leaves England for Italy on Monday or Tuesday . . ."

Finally money had been raised on post-obits, boxes were corded, farewells to the Hunts and other friends had been spoken. On the morning of March 10, 1818, Shelley and Mary and Claire, with the three children and two servants, set out for Dover. This time, although he did not know it, Shelley was leaving England for good.

From Calais, on the other side of the Channel, Mary wrote back to friends in London that they were heading southward "with fine weather & good hopes." The adventure for Shelley would extend over four years until it ended abruptly at the Gulf of Spezia, July 1822. During those years his genius triumphed—the genius of this "fair, freckled, blue-eyed, light-haired, delicate-looking person," as he was described precisely by one who saw him before he left England, "whose countenance was serious and thoughtful; whose stature would have been rather tall had he carried himself upright; whose earnest voice, though never loud, was somewhat unmusical." From this form, little more than twenty-nine years on earth, came the triumph. Hardly past his mid-twenties when he left England, he was already reading extensively in six languages, ancient and modern, and would soon learn a seventh; moreover, he brought a penetrating understanding of what he had read to all that he wrote. Counting the work that lay before him, those writings include political, philosophical, and aesthetic essays, travel letters, drama in both classical and Elizabethan modes, lyrics, satires, translations—writing of so astonishing a variety, in fact, as to be seldom if ever equaled by one person in the range of English literature. The works, largely ignored at the time, came forth during the Italian years: *Julian and Maddalo*, *Prometheus Unbound*, *The Cenci*, *Swellfoot the Tyrant*, *Epipsychidion*, *Adonais*, and the marvelous shorter lyrics—"Ode to the West Wind," "To a Skylark," "One word is too often profaned," . . .

Titles could be extended five times that length without including any but significant poetry. Genius is inexplicable, of course—little but the external life (and often not that) can be confidently recounted—but the exaltedness of Shelley's genius is there to read and marvel at, despite the poet's own self-denigration. For near the end he exclaimed disconsolately, "I wish I had something better to do than furnish this jingling food for the hunger of oblivion, called verse . . ."

On the contrary, the food is for the most part ambrosial: little of what he wrote was destined for oblivion, whatever might have been his own doubts; and the achievement is all the more impressive considering the neglect it met with at the time and the adversities among which it was brought into being during those years of wandering, from Milan to Leghorn, to Este and Venice and Rome and Naples, back to Leghorn, to Florence and Pisa, to Lerici at last, beside the Gulf of Spezia. He had begun by delivering Byron's child Allegra to the temperamental father at Venice, taking care to keep the equally temperamental mother, Claire Clairmont, at some remove, so that delicate negotiations might be conducted that would allow Claire on occasion to see her beloved daughter.

With the babies Clara and William, Mary awaited the outcome near
Leghorn. Byron would have nothing to do with his former mistress, but
he did in a mellow mood agree to let mother and daughter at least visit
together at Este, nearby. To facilitate other such reunions, Shelley proposed to establish his household in that town, and toward that end sent
for Mary to join him. She set out, crossing Italy over a four-day journey
with her two children, the younger of whom (unknown to Shelley) had
been ailing. During the journey the child Clara's condition grew graver.
It was serious indeed when she reached Este. From there, as soon as it
seemed safe to travel, Shelley accompanied his family to Venice, leaving
Mary and the ailing baby at an inn across the lagoon about five one
afternoon, while he hurried off in search of a doctor. "When I returned,"
so he wrote Claire the following day, September 25, 1818, "I found
Mary in the hall of the Inn in the most dreadful distress. Worse symptoms had appeared. Another Physician had arrived. He told me there
was no hope. In about an hour—how shall I tell you—she died—silently, without pain. And she is now buried."

Suddenly, all but unaccountably, a second child had been taken
from them, and the following summer, June 7, 1819, Mary would lose a
third, the last to survive of the three she had borne: William, three years
old, her adored Willmouse: "The Italian women used to bring each
other to look at him when he was asleep." He had been a healthy,
delightful boy, cheerful, blue-eyed like his father. That May, in Rome,
sickness had touched him, but he had seemed to recover completely.
Then in early June the child was again afflicted with what was diagnosed vaguely as Roman fever, and was dead within twenty-four hours.
A fragment by the father bespeaks the parents' grief:

> Thy little footsteps on the sands
> Of a remote and lonely shore;
> The twinkling of thine infant hands
> Where now the worm will feed no more;
> Thy mingled look of love and glee
> When we returned to gaze on thee—

Geneva, three years earlier: "We saw Jura and the Lake like old friends.
I longed to see my pretty babe. . . . We converse with Lord Byron till
12, and then go down to Chapuis, kiss our babe, and go to bed." He was
dead now, and Mary was once again childless. Two such devastating
losses, of the tiny Clara and William, threw her into a lethargy, made
her cold and withdrawn:

> My dearest Mary, wherefore hast thou gone,
> And left me in this dreary world alone!
> Thy form is here indeed—a lovely one—
> But thou art fled, gone down the dreary road,
> That leads to Sorrow's most obscure abode;

Thou sittest on the hearth of pale despair,
                                        where
For thine own sake I cannot follow thee.

Godwin, back at Skinner Street, added to the anguish of that dark time. During September 1819, the philosopher would pause in the midst of everlasting financial crises to pass favorable judgment on some sketches of English life published in America shortly before: "You desire me to write to you my sentiments on reading the Sketch Book, No. II., and I most willingly comply with your request. Everywhere I find in it the marks of a mind of the utmost elegance and refinement, a thing as you know that I was not exactly prepared to look for in an American." So he would opine to the Scotsman James Ogilvie about Washington Irving's essays, but he had been writing recently in a different vein to his daughter, Shelley's wife, abroad in Italy. A month earlier, in mid-August, her husband had been moved to express himself to his friend Leigh Hunt: "Poor Mary's spirits continue dreadfully depressed. And I cannot expose her to Godwin in this state. I wrote to this hard-hearted person, (the first letter I had written for a year), on account of the terrible state of her mind, and to entreat him to try to soothe her in his next letter. The *very* next letter, received yesterday, and addressed to her, called her husband (me) 'a disgraceful and flagrant person' tried to persuade her that I was under great engagements to give him *more* money (after having given him £4,700), and urged her if she ever wished a connection to continue between him and her to force me to get money for him. . . . he heaps on her misery, stiff misery.—I have not yet shewn her the letter—but I must. . . . I have bought bitter knowledge with £4,700."

Thus stains of earthliness, to use a Shelleyan phrase, continued to spread over the ideal world that the poet's life was given to realize. "One looks back," Mary wrote years later of those months of her withdrawal, "with unspeakable regret and gnawing remorse to such periods; fancying that had one been more alive to the nature of his feelings and more attentive to sooth them . . ." Yet she did not know, could only presume that his bouts with melancholy were occasioned by the almost constant physical discomfort he endured—boils, the ache in his side—and meanwhile, his most heartfelt verses he hid for fear of wounding her, who saw him still "enjoying, as he appeared to do, every sight or influence of earth or sky": peasants singing on hot summer afternoons in the fields beyond their window, the waterwheel creaking at evening, fireflies among the myrtle hedges.

Gradually, hardly aware of the scope of Shelley's anguish, Mary took on the tasks of living once more. After five childless months, hateful

months, she gave birth, in November 1819, at Florence, to a child who
would survive into maturity and respectable old age, so that we may look
upon an elderly Victorian's gentle, bewhiskered features photographed
toward the end of a long life that extended seventy years from that
beginning, in an autumn season in Italy, as the newborn Percy's father
was finishing *Prometheus Unbound*, was writing "Ode to the West
Wind."

For the most part the Shelleys in exile had lived until then a
strange, restless existence, with few friends. "But for our fears, on account of our child," wrote Mrs. Shelley in retrospect, "I believe we
should have wandered over the world, both being passionately fond of
travelling. But human life, besides its great unalterable necessities, is
ruled by a thousand liliputian ties, that shackle at the time, although it is
difficult to account afterwards for their influence over our destiny."

Thus, their days became more fixed now, became finally rooted at
Pisa, and "we were not, as our wont had been, alone—friends had
gathered round us." Byron occupied a palace across the street, on the
other side of the Arno from where the Shelleys were living. Thomas
Medwin—Shelley's cousin and early schoolmate who four years later
would be often in Irving's company in Paris—had arrived, and he attracted friends of his own who soon became friends of Shelley and
Mary: Trelawny and the Williamses—Jane and Edward Williams,
common-law husband and wife. Jane was very pretty, and on her Shelley
affixed his last of many such idealized loves, as earlier he had idealized to
adoration Harriet Grove and Elizabeth Hitchener and Mary herself, and
more recently Sophia Stacey and the Italian beauty Emilia Viviani. "I
think one is always in love with something or other," he who could speak
of love so feelingly wrote near the end; "the error, and I confess it is not
easy for spirits cased in flesh and blood to avoid it, consists in seeking in
a mortal image the likeness of what is perhaps eternal. . . ."

The group of new friends determined to forsake Pisa before the
heat of the summer arrived. They would find a place by the sea, but even
as the Williamses and Claire Clairmont were off looking for a house to
let, Shelley received word of yet another calamity: Claire's child Allegra,
five years old, whom Byron had placed in a convent some ten miles from
Ravenna to be educated, had died in a typhus epidemic, April 19, 1822.

Possessed of that new grief the party moved in May to Villa Magni,
on the very edge of the Gulf of Spezia, a fortresslike dwelling hardly
large enough—terrace, dining room, and four small bedrooms at the
upper end of a ladder over an earthen ground floor—to accommodate so
much crowding of life together: Edward and the fastidious Jane Williams and their children, the grief-stricken Claire, Shelley with feelings
overwrought, servants of the two families quarreling "like cats and
dogs," the child Percy, Mary, pregnant again and desperately ill with a
miscarriage after their arrival. She might have died: "as she was totally

destitute of medical assistance, I," Shelley wrote, "took the most decisive resolutions, by dint of making her sit in ice, I succeeded in checking the hemorrhage and the fainting fits, so that when the physician arrived all danger was over . . ."

From the first Mary loathed the place they had rented. "I was not well in body or mind. My nerves were wound up to the utmost irritation, and the sense of misfortune hung over my spirits. No words can tell you how I hated our house & the country about it." Everyone's nerves seemed on edge, in fact. Shelley had been walking with Williams one evening on the terrace facing the gulf when over the moonlit bay he thought he saw—"There it is again!—there!"—the dead child Allegra rise from the water naked, smiling and clapping her hands joyfully at sight of him. The beholder seemed in a trance, from which he was awakened with difficulty. Later, on a June night not long after her miscarriage, his wife was terrified by Shelley's continuous screams as he rushed, apparently asleep, into her room. She tried to wake him and could not. Although ill, she leapt from the bed and hurried across the hall to Jane Williams' room, "where I fell through weakness, though I was so frightened that I got up again immediately." Williams went to Shelley and calmed him, and in time they learned the dreadful occasion of his behavior. Shelley had "dreamt that lying as he did in bed Edward & Jane came in to him, they were in the most horrible condition, their bodies lacerated—their bones starting through their skin, the faces pale yet stained with blood, they could hardly walk, but Edward was the weakest & Jane was supporting him— Edward said—'Get up, Shelley, the sea is flooding the house & it is all coming down.' S got up, he thought, & went to his window that looked on the terrace & the sea & thought he saw the sea rushing in. Suddenly his vision changed & he saw," Mary records, "the figure of himself strangling me . . . All this was frightful enough, & talking it over the next morning he told me that he had had many visions lately—he had seen the figure of himself which met him as he walked on the terrace & said to him—'How long do you mean to be content?' . . ."

What contentment he felt—and Mary herself later remembered Shelley, despite the stressful interludes, as never happier than during those two months—his contentment would have arisen in part from the wild scenery of the place (so distasteful to his wife), in part from the presence of friends, above all from his boat, a twenty-four-foot schooner that had been built for him at Genoa and was delivered to the bay of Lerici May 12. Shelley was ecstatic with this plaything for the summer. To be sure, he knew little enough about sailing, but his friend Williams could manage that; indeed, "Williams declares her to be perfect, & I participate in his enthusiasm inasmuch as would be decent in a landsman." Meanwhile, Shelley did have now both "a study & a carriage" much to his liking. His health improving, he and Williams were out in the boat evening after evening through that late spring and early summer of 1822—season in which the talk of literary London, incidentally, was Washington Irving's second English work, *Bracebridge Hall*, published by Murray during that same late May.

And from London had come news earlier to add to Shelley's summer pleasure: his friend Leigh Hunt was planning a visit to Italy with his family. "My dear Lord Byron, I have just heard from Hunt . . . We may therefore expect him every day at Leghorn . . . I shall sail over to pay both him & you a visit as soon as I hear of his arrival . . ."

On Monday, July 1, Shelley and Williams and an eighteen-year-old crewman named Charles Vivian did set sail for Leghorn, some forty-five miles south, to greet the visitors from England. "A thousand welcomes my best friend to this divine country," Shelley had written excitedly. "Your arrival gives me spirits enough to laugh at almost anything." But reaching Leghorn, he and Williams found all in confusion. Byron was preparing abruptly to leave Tuscany. Hunt's six young children were about—"dirtier and more mischievous than Yahoos," Byron thought—and like their father innocent of Italian, while Hunt himself was in despair, his wife having just been informed that she was terminally ill. (In fact, she lived thirty-five years longer, much longer than did the celebrated Italian physician at Pisa who had decided that her case was hopeless.) From Pisa, Shelley wrote back to Mary, "You have no idea how I am hurried & occupied—I have not a moments leisure—but will write by next post—" On the same day, July 4, he wrote to Jane Williams: "You will probably see Williams before I can disentangle myself from the affairs with which I am now surrounded—I return to Leghorn"—fourteen miles from Pisa—"tonight & shall urge him to sail with the first fair wind without expecting me . . . I fear you are solitary & melancholy at Villa Magni—"

Still weak from her miscarriage of mid-June, Mary had not kept her journal since June 11. Now, on the eighth of July, while waiting forlornly at the villa, she attempted to catch up: "I am ill most of this time. Ill and then convalescent . . . July 1 . . . the Hunts being arrived, Shelley goes in the boat with . . . Edward to Leghorn. They are still there. Read 'Jacopo Ortis,' second volume of 'Geographica Fisica,' &c., &c."

On that same morning, Monday, July 8—having finally settled Hunt and his family at Pisa—Shelley and Williams and Trelawny were at Leghorn together, at the bank, at stores, stocking up on provisions to take back to their remote dwelling—the "white house with arches"—at Lerici. With their crewman Vivian, Shelley and Williams at last got under way about three that afternoon to make the seven- or eight-hour run northward along the coast. That same day Jane had received a letter from Edward written the previous Saturday: "How I long to see you, I had written *when*, but I will make no promises for I too well know how distressing it is to both of us to break them—Tuesday Evening at furthest unless kept by the weather I *will* say."

A thunderstorm raged over Lerici Monday night, the eighth, and all day Tuesday it rained. Wednesday was fair, and Thursday: "when twelve at night came," Mary wrote later, "& we did not see the tall sails of the little boat double the promontory before us we began to fear not the truth, but some illness—some disagreable news for their detention." The women waited anxiously for the mail on Friday. It brought no word from either husband, but rather a letter from Hunt to Shelley: "pray write to tell us how you got home, for they say that you had bad weather after you sailed monday & we are anxious."

Mary started to tremble as she read those words: the paper fell from her hands. The two women, Mrs. Shelley and Mrs. Williams, took a boat at once to Lerici, frantically posted to Pisa, knocked in dread at the door of Byron's palazzo. A servant ushered them into the gloomy building. The poet's mistress, the Countess Guiccioli, came forth smiling to welcome them. "Where is he—" Mary was just able to gasp. "Sapete alcuna cosa di Shelley"—

But she was a widow already. Sometime Monday the boat had gone down in a squall off Viareggio, and already a punt, a water keg, some bottles had been washed ashore. In time three bodies were washed ashore as well, at different points along the sandy coast. One, on July 18, was found near Viareggio, and Trelawny, hearing news of it, hurried to the spot. "The face," he wrote years afterward—ineradicable image!— "and hands, and parts of the body not protected by the dress, were fleshless. The tall, slight figure, the jacket, the volume of Sophocles in one pocket, and Keats's poems in the other, doubled back, as if the reader, in the act of reading, had hastily thrust it away, were all too familiar to me to leave a doubt on my mind that this mutilated corpse was any other than Shelley's."

When he first had seen the poet half a year earlier, Trelawny had wondered, "Was it possible this mild-looking, beardless boy, could be the veritable monster at war with all the world?—excommunicated by the Fathers of the Church, deprived of his civil rights by the fiat of a grim Lord Chancellor, discarded by every member of his family, and denounced by the rival sages of our literature as the founder of a Satanic school?" Now he lay dead on the sand near Viareggio, and soon, in conformity with an Italian statute to prevent plague, Trelawny and Lord Byron and Leigh Hunt would cremate the corpse at that wild spot, in sight of the island of Elba, along a battlemented coast with the stony Apennines behind them glistening in the sun. "I presume," wrote Byron to his publisher Murray from Pisa soon after, "you have heard that

Mr. Shelley and Capt. Williams were lost on the 7ᵗʰ Ulᵗᵒ in their passage from Leghorn to Spezia in their own open boat. You may imagine the state of their families: I never saw such a scene, nor wish to see such another." And he ended with a judgment: "You were all brutally mistaken about Shelley, who was, without exception, the *best* and least selfish man I ever knew. I never knew one who was not a beast in comparison."

At about the time that the three drowned bodies were being burnt ("Today—this day—the sun shining in the sky—they are gone to the desolate sea coast to perform the last offices to their earthly remains") the dead poet's wife had been writing to a friend in England a long account of miserable hours surrounding her loss, concluding: "Well here is my story—the last story I shall have to tell—all that might have been bright in my life is now despoiled—" What would the widow, still only twenty-four at her husband's death, do with the rest of her days? In September Jane Williams left sadly to return to London, bearing her husband's ashes in a small box, as well as letters of introduction from Mary to Hogg and others. Claire Clairmont set out to join her brother at Vienna. For a while Mary and the Hunts lingered at Pisa—"I continue to exist—to see one day succeed the other; to dread night, but more to dread morning & hail another cheerless day"—then they moved to Albaro, a village on the outskirts of Genoa. There, in October, a piece of furniture that Mary had long wanted finally arrived from England. "I have received my desk to-day, and have been reading my letters to mine own Shelley during his absences at Marlow. What a scene to recur to! My William, Clara, Allegra, are all talked of. They lived then, they breathed this air, and their voices struck my sense; their feet trod the earth beside me, and their hands were warm with blood and life when they clasped in mine. Where are they all? This is too great an agony to be written about. I may express my despair, but my thoughts can find no words."

Even so, she had not wished to leave the scene of her bereavements—this loved and lovely Italy. "My poor girl!" Godwin had written when he learned of her loss. "What do you mean to do with yourself? You surely do not mean to stay in Italy? How glad I should be to be near you . . ." But her father's quarters in Skinner Street, rent-free so long, had finally cost him more than he could pay; a technicality concerning ownership had spared him rent through all these years, but now, at the end of long legal wranglings, the court had ordered him to pay a sum in arrears far larger than he could muster. In May, in the very weeks before Shelley's death, the Godwins had been evicted, had moved to rooms on the Strand, now were maneuvering desperately to avoid the bankruptcy that did overtake the family at last three years later.

Mary meanwhile dreaded a tedious journey to England that would bring her no pleasure and only add to her father's burdens. Autumn yielded to winter at Albaro, to the new year 1823, to another spring. Only as summer approached—the perilous Italian summer—could concern for her child's health induce the widow to prepare to leave. Perhaps once in England she might negotiate with agents of Shelley's father, the wealthy Sir Timothy, to provide for little Percy's livelihood.

For the lone woman traveling with her three-year-old child, the journey northward from Albaro, put off as long as possible, finally did commence July 25, 1823. The same date would find Washington Irving in the midst of his journey toward Rotterdam with the Fosters, as that English family made its way homeward across Germany after a three years' absence in Dresden. Proceeding overland, Mary Shelley was in Paris August 12 through 20 at the Hotel Nelson in Faubourg St.-Germain, visiting friends who included, for three days, the Kenneys, near Versailles. Surely they would have mentioned—among gossip about Lamb and Hazlitt and Wordsworth—a very recent afternoon with the most famous of American writers, for Irving, who had arrived at Paris nine days before Mrs. Shelley, had on the day she reached the city awakened at the Hotel de Yorck "between 3 & 4 with . . . horror of mind," then arisen, shaved, and restlessly gone calling during the morning on the Storrows, before dining by invitation with those same Kenneys who would entertain the poet's widow. Thus both Irving and Mary, in Paris simultaneously, saw mutual friends, although neither mentions meeting the other. Their own meeting presumably would wait upon the following summer.

Mary was back in England. A friend of Godwin's had encountered her soon after her return: "She is unaltered, yet I did not know her at first. She looks elegant and sickly and young. One would not suppose she was the author of 'Frankenstein.' " So she appeared in the fall of her arrival at London. By the following spring, living near Jane Williams, her fellow sufferer, in Kentish Town on a modest allowance from Sir Timothy Shelley, she was working on assembling a posthumous collection of Shelley's poetry. Her preface to that collection is dated June 1, 1824. Four evenings before that date, Irving—just arrived from Paris to see *Tales of a Traveller* through the press—had attended a performance at Covent Garden of *Charles II*. On that occasion the playwright John Howard Payne and Payne's new friend Mary Shelley may have been with him.

During summer days that followed, when Irving was not out of town on those visits to his sister's family at Birmingham or to his friends the Fosters in the hallowed atmosphere of Brickhill, he and Mrs. Shelley were (as already noted) together in London among mutual friends on various occasions. They were, for example, in a small group attending the theater on a Tuesday evening near the end of Irving's eleven weeks' stay in England: "Private Box with Miss Holcroft—Mrs Shelley Mrs Linton." But on Friday of that same week of mid-August, 1824, Irving's visit to London was over: "Rise early. correct proof sheets till 9. . . . Murray for Tales of a Traveller Receive his drafts at 6. 9 & 12 months for 500 Guineas each. . . . Leave London at 2 oclock in coach for Brighton. Safety coach, crammed with passengers. . . . Heavy showers which drench us in spite of umbrellas—pass over downs. fine view from Ryegate Hill, arive at Brighton ½ past 8."

Even there, however, at the Ship in Distress ("a small, but civil Inn—with a comely landlady") the writer was still correcting proof sheets of his new book through the next morning, after composing last letters to Mrs. Foster, to Moore, to his Birmingham relatives while waiting for the Channel boat to leave. It would take him to Dieppe, back to France, where he would endure at Auteuil and Paris forthcoming weeks of anxious waiting. How would this third group of sketches and stories by Geoffrey Crayon be received? From Brighton, as he waited to cross the Channel, he had written to Moore, "From the time I first started pen in hand on this work, it has been nothing but hard driving with me." And had added: "Let me hear from you, if but a line; particularly if my work pleases you, but don't say a word against it. I am easily put out of humor with what I do."

In fact, whatever the verdict, as a writer he was established by then. *Salmagundi, Knickerbocker, The Sketch Book, Bracebridge Hall* had made his reputation secure on both sides of the Atlantic. Back in New York at this very time Irving was being customarily toasted in public haunts as the leading representative of American literature. In the coming month of September 1824, even as he awaited reaction to *Tales of a Traveller*, one American periodical was saluting the writer who "has certainly done more than any other to make us respectable abroad as a *literary* people." The name of so eligible a bachelor went on being linked with those of appropriate ladies; the current rumor had him engaged to the Empress Maria Louisa of Parma and Lucca. To be sure, another alarming rumor had pronounced him dead ("Washington Irving, I now hope is *not* dead," Carlyle had written Jane Welsh at the start of this year. "Do you hear anything of it?"). His actions were noted, his books widely translated, his style imitated, his likeness displayed, his worth acknowledged. Yet through trying evenings of that autumn of 1824 he would brood.

September 9: "Woke several times in the night—restless & uneasy—" The following day he received "a most kind & gratifying letter from Moore about my work. Has a great effect in reassuring me"—and so for a while Irving slept better. But by November, amid social visits and Italian lessons and a tour of the Loire, he felt his anxiety returning: "An indifferent night—awoke very early: depressed, dubious of myself

& public—" "Another night of broken sleep—" "A restless night—broken sleep & uneasy thoughts—read much in the night." Then, on November 23, at the bookseller Galignani's, "met my evil genius . . . who told me the critics were attackg me like the d———l in Engd —Retd home for a short time but could not remain—downhearted— . . . A rainy day tho mild—a Black day to me—"

The anonymous informant at Galignani's had told the truth, and not only about the British critics, though those were cruel enough. The reviewer in *Blackwood's Edinburgh Magazine*, for one, had professed to be "miserably disappointed" in *Tales of a Traveller*. After so much time, so much of an author's wandering through Germany and elsewhere, so much advance notice, Crayon "has produced a book, which, for aught I see, might have been written, not in three years, but in three months, without stirring out of a garret in London, and this not by Mr. Irving alone, but by any one of several dozens of ready penmen about town." Annoyed with Tory ways, *The Westminster Review* had exploded with pent-up rage, charging that "Geoffrey is indisputably feeble, unoriginal and timorous; a mere adjective of a man, who has neither the vigour nor courage to stand alone, though it were but for a moment . . ." In the pages of his latest work, this Whig periodical warned, the reader would find "nothing that can excite controversy, nothing that can occasion dissatisfaction; all, pensive, *gentlemanly*, and subdued; all, trifling and acquiescent as a drawing-room conversation; prevailing errors in morals and legislation carefully upheld, or, at best, left unnoticed, prevailing follies alone, in dress or address, lightly reprehended: a little pathos, a little sentiment, to excite tears as a pleasurable emotion for those who see them on no other occasion: a little point and a little antithesis to tickle the ear and divert the attention from the lamentable deficiency of solid matter."

A world away from Shelley! It was bad enough that the English reviewers were attacking Irving's descriptions of London life as "decidedly unfortunate; for the double reason that as the picture of the past they are not original, and, as of the present, they are not true." Bad enough that he was being accused of having "no inventive faculties at all," and of lacing his tales with "a vein of equivocating ribaldry," with "two or three droll indecencies," with "obscenities . . . most carefully veiled." But even worse was it that similar judgments were being voiced by his countrymen across the sea.

December 14, 1824: "recd. letter from N York signed 'a friend' containing a scurrilous newspaper tirade against me." Which review had the officious "friend" forwarded? Never mind that Irving by then and thereafter felt *Tales of a Traveller* (his only work purely of fiction) contained "some of the best things I have ever written," that Poe would in later years express his admiration of these "graceful and impressive narratives," that Longfellow and Stevenson both would single the work out for special praise, that at the very least the section called "The Money-Diggers," containing "The Devil and Tom Walker," remains fresh and delightful—vintage Irving. At the time of its publication many American reviewers, as if awaiting their chance at the expatriate, spoke of *Tales of a Traveller* only to damn it. Thus the *New-York Mirror:* "It is suggested that Mr. Washington Irving's new work would sell more rapidly if the Booksellers would alter the Title, and call it 'STORIES FOR CHILDREN' by *a Baby Six Feet High. . . .*" Thus *The Philadelphia Columbian Observer:* "With very moderate powers of *description*, he has been *puffed* to an artificial magnitude, which he cannot realize by his productions . . ." Thus the reviewer for the *United States Literary Gazette*, who, like some of his English cousins, was especially troubled by the obscenity in the book: "If the truth of the charge be denied, we refer for proof of it to the description of the comic shape of the Strolling Manager's Clown; to the indecency drowned in the crack! crack! of the postillion's whip at Terracina; the innuendoes in the 'Bold Dragoon'; . . . and finally, the shocking story of the 'Young Robber,' where a scene the most revolting to humanity"—a gang rape— "is twice unnecessarily forced on the reader's imagination . . . why is it that this fault has grown so much upon Mr. Irving since the publication of the 'Sketch Book,' which contains, as far as we remember, no traces of it?"

Obscene? In a world of Italian banditti: " 'Are they cruel to travellers?' said a beautiful young Venetian lady, who had been hanging on the gentleman's arm. 'Cruel, Signora!' echoed the estafette, giving a glance at the lady as he put spurs to his horse. 'Corpo di Bacco! They stiletto all the men; and, as to the women—, Crack! crack! crack! crack! crack!—The last words were drowned in the smacking of the whip, and away galloped the estafette along the road to the Pontine marshes."

Obscene? Assuredly in the past his writings had been warmly praised, too warmly perhaps, so that he had expected a reaction with *Bracebridge Hall*. That had not come, but now, in the fall of 1824, earlier praise was paid for, the bill rendered fiercely, and on account of a book that Irving felt with justice was better than its predecessor. To Brevoort in New York, near the end of the year, he wrote from Paris, with a try at philosophy, about his latest work, which "has met with some handling from the press. . . . However, as I do not read criticisms good or bad, I am out of the reach of attack." Nonsense. Yet he does go on to express, clearly and persuasively, what he has all along been striving for:

"I fancy much of what I value myself upon in writing, escapes the observation of the great mass of my readers: who are intent more upon the story than the way in which it is told. For my part I consider a story merely as a frame on which to stretch my materials. It is the play of thought, and sentiment and language; the weaving in of characters, lightly yet expressively delineated; the familiar and faithful exhibition of scenes in common life; and the half concealed vein of humour that is often playing through the whole—these are among what I aim at. . . ."

If his writings achieve those ends "they will out live temporary criticism; if not they are not worth caring about." Fine words; yet Irving was downcast, so much so that many years would pass before he would dare to publish any further sketches and stories of the sort found in *Tales of a Traveller*. Meanwhile, disconsolately, he would watch another year end:

December 31, 1824: ". . . retire to bed at 11. This has been a dismal day of depression &c and closes a year part of which has been full of sanguine hope; of social enjoyment; peace of mind, and health of body—and the latter part saddened by disappointments & distrust of the world & of myself; by sleepless nights & joyless days—May the coming year prove more thoroughly propitious—"

"Do you ever see Washington Irving?" Mary Shelley was asking, soon after the new year 1825 began, in a letter to her friend Louisa Holcroft, daughter in the Kenney household near Paris. "He talks of visiting England this Autumn—but he has not unfortunately fulfilled his purpose— Remember me to him & tell him I claim his promised visit when he does come—"

She was writing, she said, "in my little room beside my fire—with no change or hope—" at 5 Bartholomew Place, Kentish Town, London. Jane Williams lived nearby, and they were "much together," as she would tell Trelawny about this time, "talking of the past—or future (for the present is nought) . . ." Some months earlier Mary's posthumous collection of Shelley's poems had been printed and then withdrawn from circulation at the insistence of old Sir Timothy Shelley of Field Place, father who did not want his drowned son's name memorialized, and who threatened to cut off the allowance to Shelley's widow if it was—if any further publication by or about the radical poet should appear through her efforts. Sir Timothy's yearly allowance to her (£200, presented grudgingly as a loan) was about all the money that she and her six-year-old Percy had. Her novel *Valperga* had appeared two years earlier, but what it had earned had been devoted to helping Godwin in his struggles with bankruptcy. Now she was working on another novel, *The Last Man*, caring for her son, and visiting often with Jane Williams, whom she professed in the privacy of her journal to love "better than any other human being, but I am pressed upon by the knowledge that she but slightly returns this affection."

Jane, content enough with the present, had felt that Mrs. Shelley should get about more, and during the preceding summer—that summer with Irving and Payne and the Kenneys and Holcrofts in London—

Mary had done so, to good effect, as an entry for June 8, 1824, suggests: "I feel my powers again, and this is, of itself, happiness; the eclipse of winter is passing from my mind." But summer, and its mood, had passed as well, and such acquaintances as Irving and the Kenneys were back in Paris over the fall and through the coming winter. Moreover, the society of John Howard Payne had been denied her for reasons she could not then have known. It must have been pleasant, therefore, to have Payne reenter her life as spring came on once more. Mrs. Kenney, friend of her father, had returned to London for another visit.

Thursday evening, April 14, 1825. "My dear Sir," Mary is writing Payne from Kentish Town, "You failed in bringing me Mrs. Kenney— Why doubly fail in not calling yourself? It was not until today that I heard that our friend was gone to Brighton and I should have despaired of the possibility of inducing you to make this North Passage"—clear out to Kentish Town—"had not the kind Gods' sent me a substitute in her place—Mrs. Harwood called on me today & expressing a great desire to find some opportunity of conversing with you concerning your American friend, I thought that I might venture to say that I would ask you to meet her here—& fixed with her Sunday Evening (i.e. at 6 P.M.) Will you come . . . ?"

The American referred to was Washington Irving; Payne would be happy to drink a cup of hyson with the ladies and chat about his friend. Having received the invitation (addressed to J. Hayward, Esq., alias still in use to befuddle creditors), he set out the following Monday to walk the three miles north from the Strand to 5 Bartholomew Place. Mrs. Shelley, however, was not home when he got there. He had blundered—had misread her Sunday for Monday—"No other days *could* have done me this ill turn"—and back in his lodgings went so far as to snip the offending, nearly illegible word from her note and send it to her in extenuation.

The lady was gracious: "It was ill done indeed after causing me to form a thousand conjectures concerning your absence on Sunday, to lead you to the empty nest the day after—Will you tempt fortune again? . . . Will you walk over Saturday or Sunday or any other that may be most convenient to you . . ."

He would, eagerly. She had penned that invitation Wednesday evening, and Thursday Payne was on his way once more. Alas. "My dear Sir," Mrs. Shelley is forced to write Friday morning, "I was excessively annoyed to find that you had called fruitlessly yesterday— I had calculated that you would not receive my note in time for a visit & so did not include Thursday 'in the bond.'— Will you drink tea with me tomorrow . . . If you are in the Strand you will find stages in James St. Covent Garden every hour . . ."

After so frustrating a beginning, they got it straightened out at last, and soon had resumed their friendship more heartily than before the winter interruption. Some months earlier, as Payne notes, Mrs. Shelley "had written to me frequently for orders"—for passes to the theater— and now he was pleased to have her resume the practice. She, who enjoyed seeing plays, was poor. He, who had been for so many years involved in the world of Haymarket and Drury Lane and Covent Garden, could obtain the passes easily for her and Jane, or for her and the Godwins—for whatever party she might get together. Besides, in Mary's presence that spring he was rapidly falling in love.

Unmarried, still only thirty-four (a year older than Shelley would have been had he lived), the former boy actor with the handsome features and beautiful voice who had become a well-known playwright might have had reason to hope. Well-known he was; Shelley himself, a year before his death, had backhandedly acknowledged the American's existence, lamenting in the preface to *Adonais* the contempt that reviewers had directed toward Keats's work while celebrating, "with various degrees of complacency and panegyric, 'Paris,' and 'Woman,' and a 'Syrian Tale,' and Mrs. Lefanu, and Mr. Barret, and Mr. Howard Payne, and a long list of the illustrious obscure." Well, Payne was no Shelley, to be sure—no genius—but he was at least a man of talent. Charles Lamb would imply as much two years from now, trying his hand at putting together a play and confessing to Mary: "I want some Howard Paine to sketch a skeleton of artfully succeeding scenes . . . to say where a joke should come in or a pun be left out: to bring my *personae* on and off . . ."

Payne could do that sort of business well enough, as proved by his successes of several kinds on the London stage: tragedy, comedy, melodrama, operetta. He might understandably begin to hope, reading the notes that came from Mary that spring, hearing her share with him confidences about her life: about "Mrs. Williams, whose history she explained. They were united by a common calamity; their husbands were drowned together, and Mrs. Williams's attentions had kept Mrs. Shelley alive. . . . She also explained herself about her father"—his money problems—"and her own devotion to the memory of her husband." Such confidences were fascinating. Payne wrote her "that your yesterday's conversations filled my mind so full of yourself, that my poor pillow had but a small portion of its due. A heroine in love and friendship and duty to a parent,— . . . To any ordinary woman I should not dare to say this. It would certainly be interpreted to my disadvantage. But I think you would never have entered upon what related to yourself, with me, had you been utterly indifferent to my opinion . . . May I not, then, praise you, and like you, and more, much more than like you, without a box on the ear, or frowns, or wonder that I should presume to do so, or be so impertinent as to tell you I do? . . ."

"Do not talk of frowns," Mrs. Shelley answered ingenuously in a note written Saturday morning, April 30. "You are good & kind & deserve therefore nothing but kindness— But we must step lightly on the mosaic of circumstance for if we press too hard the beauty & charm is defaced— The world is a hard taskmaster & talk as we will of independence we are slaves. Adieu." And she closed with the conventional "I am truly yours, Mary Shelley."

To one in love, how did that sound? She had thanked him for books lent her and indicated current attractions that sounded appealing: ". . . if Virginius should be acted & the thing practicable I should like to see it." Payne's response came promptly. "My dear Mrs. S.,—Enclosed you will receive orders for the opera on Saturday . . . Macready is announced for *Virginius* on Friday, but Elliston says he does not think it will be performed. Whenever it is, four places will await you, or a private box." And he would accompany her party or not, as she chose; "if more convenient to make up your party without me, do so. . . . I am thus particular, because perhaps we may not meet in the week. I am bound to the oar, as you will infer when I mention a contract to manufacture five hundred octavo pages between this and the twenty-fifth." That is, in less than a month. "Besides, I am reluctant to wear out my welcome . . ."

Still—and the lover warms to his subject—"I am very fortunate in one respect. I can have your company without oppressing you with mine. You are perpetually in my presence, and if I close my eyes you are still there, and if I cross my arms over them and try to wave you away, still you will not be gone. This madness of my own imagination flatters itself with the forlorn hope of a delightful vagueness in part of your note. . . . I would not have you check my delusion. If in looking above my path at the sweet paradise of vapour, I am doomed to fall into a pit, I must scramble out again, as well as I can and say, 'it will all be the same a hundred years hence.'" He is emboldened to go on: "You are perfectly estimable in every way—certainly more universally so than anyone I have ever seen . . . Yet, for all your smiling, I know very well what that part of your letter means which I pretended just now not to understand. If you tread lightly on the *mosaic* of my day dreams, still *you* do tread on it, and only leave me liberty to be grateful for the grace and gentleness of the pressure—and I am grateful—and care nothing about myself, so I may care for you, and tell you so without your being angry . . ."

If not angry, Mary nevertheless had reason to check such effusions. For one thing, Payne was impecunious, even now hiding from creditors despite the octavo pages he could fill and sell. How would an alliance between the two of them benefit either one? "The engagement of Saturday," she responded—the one to the opera—"I consider fixed as fate—if you will permit it so to be; for we depend upon you as our escort." With one caution, she went on to thank him for all his kindness to her, "& I include kind thoughts as well as kind actions—although I truly know how entirely your imagination creates the admired as well as the admiration— But do not I entreat you frighten me by any more interpretations"—about treading on mosaics or whatever—"although be sure I am & always shall be Your sincere friend, Mary Shelley."

Through May their correspondence continued along its uneven path—and their times together at opera, play, diorama. Then came an invitation from Mary to dinner with the Godwins: "Will you come?— We shall all be happy to see you— . . . We dine at four."

After that occasion, or one like it at Gower Place (to which her father had recently moved), Payne at last learned the truth. "There was a long conversation in walking home with Mrs. S. from Mr. Godwin's, in which she attempted fully but delicately to explain herself upon her sentiments with regard to our correspondence." Picture the two of them near dusk, the gentleman, the widow still in her twenties, conversing intently on their walk along Camden High Street and out among the lawny uplands—swallows, odor of hay—alongside Kentish Town Road. "She said she felt herself so placed with the world that she never could expect its distinctions; and that the high feeling she entertained for the memory of her husband forbade the hope of any future connection . . ." She confessed—what letters and journal repeatedly confirm—that "she was desirous of getting to Italy, and there passing the rest of her life. . . .

"The conversation"—these words are Payne's own, reporting later in Paris to Washington Irving—"then turned upon you. She said you had interested her more than any one she had seen since she left Italy; that you were gentle and cordial, and that she longed for friendship with you." Hearing that, Payne had "rallied her a little upon the declaration, and at first she fired at my mentioning that she talked as if she were in love. Upon her reply"—denying such feelings—"I answered: 'What! would you make a plaything of Mr. I?' And then the chat sank into mere commonplace. . . ."

But Mrs. Shelley's meaning could not be misunderstood. "The scope of her remarks was that whenever she formed any alliance it must be with some one whose high character and mind should be worthy of him who had drawn her from obscurity, and that her selection must not dishonor his choice. She apologized for the remarks, and I told her I thought the better of her for all she had said, and that I understood its bearing thoroughly." A veritable Dobbin in this version of *Vanity Fair*. "She seemed considerably moved at the necessity she felt of giving pain by disclosing the truth."

That was not quite all that transpired on the walk. The playwright in passing mentioned having recently received a letter from Irving, "which Mrs. S expressed a strong wish to see, and I promised she should see it." She did, and later asked to see more. "You made me expect that *another letter* would have accompanied the book on Sunday—is it indelicate in me to ask for this? I should not of course unless you had first said that you would be good enough to shew it me. . . ."

Irving's friend was led to explain: "I did not send the letter, because I thought I might find others which would answer your wishes quite as well, and which contained less about my petty affairs . . . I will find others for you, but I send this, lest circumstances should give a false colouring to its being withheld." Does he not mean that he might be suspected of trying to divert Mary's interest from Irving? For her to understand the letter that he does send, "it is necessary you should know that Irving's advice has been of great service to me in all literary points upon which I have had opportunities of consulting him. Since chance threw me among pens, ink and paper, he and his elder brother"—Peter—"are the only persons who have ever boldly and unhesitatingly encouraged me with the hopes of ultimate success and prosperity . . . it is a very agreeable thing to be impelled by the enthusiasm of such a mind, and to hear its praises, and know they are sincere. Now you can understand the letters. . . . I am not sure you may not have expected something more chivalric and dazzling. . . . But here it is."

And might Payne not, before setting down his pen, write briefly a final time concerning his "present disease"—his infatuation with Mary? "With you, once for all, I may be explicit and bury the subject forever. A flash, as it were, and that at a time and place of which you can form no idea, gave me a thorough impression of all which I have since found confirmed of the beauty of your heart and intellect. I then knew nothing of you but what I had heard about you as a child, excepting what had been misrepresented . . . I afterwards read all you have written, and heard much in your praise. I met you afterwards, and left you with a thorough determination not to trust myself to the danger of your acquaintance . . . This is the explanation of my long neighborship without a call, and of my wish to oblige you in every way possible without again meeting you. I *did* meet you again, and presumed too much on my courage . . . I told you I knew my danger and could laugh at it. I am afraid now the laugh is not on my side. . . .

"But all this is dangerous ground and better avoided. . . . I have given way to an absurdity, and have only myself to blame. . . . It is therefore better I should not meet you till this strange fever is over. . . . I am aware how ridiculous explanations of this nature appear to cool heads and hearts, and, in this instance, rendered remarkably so by real and conventional disparities. Hence, I can the better appreciate your Saturday's conversation. I must frankly add that you may imagine I have not lived upwards of thirty years without having had some opportunity of comparing your conduct with that of others, and I must say that I have never yet met an instance of so much frankness and honest determination, the moment the truth became obvious, not to commit the feelings of the one party or the integrity of the other. . . . I am sure you will still allow me to be your friend in a corner, and to let me see your handwriting, whenever you can find any commission for me to execute, and that you will spare me anything beyond the mere matter of fact; as you are too kind not to speak kindly, and in this sort of delirium one cannot help perverting mere politeness" into cause for hope.

"To return," Payne concludes, "to the point at which our conversations began and have ended—Washington Irving—be assured I will act the hero in this business; and shall feel quite reconciled to the penalty to which my folly has condemned me, and which, I hope, I have firmness enough to make a light one, if my friendship should prove the stepping-stone to one in every way so much more gratifying and desirable."

Dobbin indeed, and to the life. Mrs. Shelley read all that, and Irving's letter to Payne as well, the latter "with great pleasure"; she was, she said, "too much of an authoress after all" not to find the concerns of such a letter interesting. In short, "W I's letter pleases me greatly as I said," but the long letter forwarding it "gives me pain because you feel it & because it seems to place a barrier to any future meeting— Thus it is ever one's hard fate either to be deserted & neglected—or, which turns out the same thing, to be liked too well, & so avoided." She will, of course, do as he bids her, "& after these last words be laconic, till you greet me with the welcome news that I may shew you all the kindness and friendship I have for you, without doing you an injury."

Regarding Irving, she will be glad to see additional letters of his, "& the handwriting, crabbed after reading your distinct syllables, will become as clear to me as Lord Byron's letterless scrawl— As to friendship with him— It cannot be—though every thing I hear & know renders it more desirable." How can such a man, "surrounded by fashion rank & splendid friendships pilot his pleasure bark from the gay press into this sober, sad, enshadowed nook?"

Thus in June. By the end of July she was jesting with Payne concerning her "favourite," Irving: "methinks our acquaintance proceeds at the rate of the Antediluvians who I have somewhere read thought nothing of an interval of a year or two between a visit— Alack I fear that at this rate if ever the Church should make us one it would be announced in the consolotary phrase that the Bride & Bridegrooms joint ages amounted to the discreet number of 145 & 3 months."

To that Payne replied the following day, July 29, 1825: "The enclosed letter from your 'favourite Irving' will tell you why I leave England. I have promised to be off on Monday, and sudden and perplexing arrangements keep me in a perpetual fret . . . I scarcely know what I have written, for my room is full of talkers. But I cannot write half so kindly as I feel, and ever shall—. I will remember your impatience, and if antediluvian modes are to be revived, I will not be an accessory but do my best to promote customs more compatible with the term to which you have limited your stay in this only world where wedlock is tolerated. Unalterably yours, J. H. P."

Earlier she had told him she meant to live but "ten years longer & to have 37 engraved upon my tomb." At the moment she was writing hastily, so as not to keep Payne's messenger, writing even before reading Irving's letter that he had forwarded: "Now, my dear Payne, tho' I am a little fool, do not make me appear so in Rue Richelieu by repeating tales out of school—nor mention the Antediluvians— But I am not afraid; I am sure you love me well enough not to be accessory in making me appear ridiculous to one whom I like & esteem, though I am sure that the time & space between us will never be shortened—perhaps it is that very certainty that makes me, female Quixote as I am, pay such homage to the unattainable Dulcinea in the Cueva de Montesinos—i.e. Rue Richelieu.

"But again be not a tell tale   so God bless you— Give my love, of course Platonic, to I."

Payne had promised, however, to act the hero in this business. He was off to Paris to meet a theatrical manager who Irving thought might ensure his "*present support*, and . . . *much future advantage*." Meanwhile: "I need not tell you how deep is my regret at leaving . . . and then to know at the same time that I must quite be forgotten in your 'favorite' . . . Who will go with you to see plays and keep your patience from rusting for want of use? Who will love you with all his heart, and not quarrel with you or with himself when you tempt him to encourage a great disposition in you to love somebody else?"

To that somebody else, in Paris on a Tuesday in August 1825, John Howard Payne delivered his and Mary Shelley's notes and letters to each other, arranged in order, from earliest to most recent. "My dear Irving," he wrote, "I have reflected a long time before I determined to show you this correspondence, because from its nature it might appear indelicate to expose the letters, especially to you, as you are more involved in it than you even appear to be. It was some time before I discovered that I was only sought as a source of an introduction to you—and I think you will, on reading the papers, feel that I might have mistaken the nature of my acquaintance with the writer, without any gratuitous vanity. But at the same time you will admit that she is a woman of the highest and most amiable qualities"—indeed, at the time surely one of the best read, most intellectual women in Europe—"and one whose wish for friendship it would be doing yourself injustice not to meet. Of course, it must be a perfect secret between ourselves that I have shown the letters. They are at present not known to any one. You must not look upon the affair in a ridiculous light, as, if you should, I shall never forgive myself for having exposed so fine a mind to so injurious a construction.

"I really wish you would see and know Mrs. S whenever you go to London. . . . No doubt it will cost you some reflection fully to appreciate the trouble I am taking to make you well acquainted with one whom I have known so well—to transfer an intimacy of which any one ought to be proud. I do not ask you to fall in love—but I should even feel a little proud of myself if you thought the lady worthy of that distinction, and very possibly you would have fallen in love with her, had you met her casually—but she is too much out of society to enable you to do so— . . .

"The letters were generally scribbled off on scraps of paper, as soon as those which prompted them came. These scraps I kept by me—accidently—or rather, most of them; when the communications grew a little serious, I kept them on purpose. . . . After I found which way the current ran, I copied all I could make out, fairly—that you might understand the matter thoroughly. . . ."

Probably the sheaf of papers was turned over to Irving August 16, which was a Tuesday, with Payne reestablished at rue Richelieu. That day—one day in a life—Irving had written letters in the morning, and later, "Walking down the Rue de la Paix I met the Duke of Wellington just coming from Plâce Vendome—column of Napoleon—He was strolling along in blue frock & white trousers—Umbrella under his arm— English—& french—& soldiers passing him, unconscious that it was the great Wellington they were elbowing.—He saunterd along with air of nonchalance—gazing at print shops &c—looks pale—face thin—cheeks fallen in—hair very grey."

Later still, in the evening, Irving entertained a couple of visitors, the painters Foy and Newton. Then, after they had left, "read Mrs Shelleys correspondence before going to bed."

What he thought of the correspondence he never committed to writing. He wrote no more than that, did nothing about the letters, returned them (with what words he may have uttered mere sounds briefly in the air of a high room in Paris, gone at once, unrecorded) to Payne, who would have the letters with him still a quarter of a century later, in Tunis, at the end of far wanderings. Nor would the "favourite" again see London until three years had passed, before that time would have moved from Paris, not westward toward Mary Shelley's enshadowed nook, but southward, into a different world entirely, sunlit, to embrace an entirely new life and undertake work of a kind unlike any he had done before.

But how, in the midst of this present barren stretch of his existence, could Irving entertain thoughts of marriage, to Mary Shelley, the Empress Maria Louisa, or anyone else? Although he might see himself as "formed for an honest, domestic, uxorious man," circumstances more than habit had condemned him to be a wanderer, as his precarious finances had "doomed" him—so he felt—"to remain single." Those finances even now, in the summer of 1825, were about to be further sapped of the substance that *Tales of a Traveller* had provided: a certain Jones in early June "promised me 50 Shares of Copper Mines at 23£ a share"—first signal of future investments in a Bolivian enterprise, made with high hopes of financial ease thereafter, that would prove in the end as imprudent as had investments in those French steamboat schemes that earlier had consumed the profits of *The Sketch Book.*

Irving would once more lose most of what his compositions had earned him. Little, in fact, among those lingering days in Paris seemed rewarding, as his low spirits continued. February 17, "awoke very much depressed"; March 21, "felt sad & heavy"; March 31, "Slept but indifferently—wanted to write this morning but could not summon my thoughts —"; April 2, "No disposition to write." Still he would go out calling, noticing new faces among the Anglo-Americans in Paris. Two in particular are of interest. On a Saturday of the preceding November: "Called on Lynch & sat some time with him—Mrs Jumel called to see Bremner —told a long story of Stephen Jumels being deranged— . . ." The middle-aged lady, married to one of the wealthiest of American merchants, would within nine years of that date be his widow and the wife, briefly, of Aaron Burr in Manhattan. Again, January 8, 1825: ". . . read Spanish till 4. Called at Mr de"—and Irving neglects to fill in the blank—"French family from America—fine family of children Mr Imlay of Carolina with them. Retd home. . . ." Doubtless the father of poor Fanny Godwin, Mr. Imlay, seventy at the time, in this same city some twenty-nine years earlier had been the lover of Mary Wollstonecraft.

Was there anyone, we finally begin to wonder, besides Byron, Shelley, and George IV, whom Irving did not meet? Through the spring and summer of 1825 he would continue to make calls—and diligently study Spanish. That latter effort had been undertaken shortly before the current year began; he had given up on Italian, had given away his German dictionary. "At present," he wrote Payne in February, "I am doing nothing but devouring my means, and studying hard." The publisher Murray would come to wonder when he might look for word from his major American author "on the subject of an original work," which he was "happy to say the public would be much delighted to receive." Murray's impatience of July had been heightened no doubt by Irving's statement six months earlier, in January: "I have nothing of my own in any state of forwardness; though my brain is teeming." But from that teeming brain had come so far only a single proposal, to translate the novels of Cervantes. To such a pedestrian suggestion Murray had not even bothered to respond: an original piece of writing was what he sought. Accordingly, he would have been pleased with a current entry in

Irving's journal, on February 5: "Good night. Mind excited. Thinking over project of an Am: Work." And off and on through 1825 the writer did labor at essays on the Manners of Americans, on Literary Reputation, on American Character—only to destroy the partial manuscript in the end. The reception of *Tales of a Traveller* was continuing to depress him. January 15, 1825: "Call at Mills's . . . Greville there—annoys me by his blunt opinion of T. T." April 29: "Walked . . . to Lynches—Otis there. Read illnatured fling at me in Am: papers. *It is hard to be stabbd in the back by ones own kin when attacked in front by strangers.*" So hard, in fact, that the essayist and storyteller could not for now go on, and had to write Murray finally, in August, "In consequence of receiving no reply from you on the subject of Cervantes' life and writings I concluded that the proposition was not sufficiently interesting and I abandoned all idea of the subject. I have nothing ready for the press, nor do I know at present when I shall have, my mind having been rather diverted from composition of late, and occupied by a course of study."

"It gives me some little dissatisfaction to perceive that you suffer yourself to be influenced in the pursuit of a great object by the squibs and crackers of criticism," his lifelong friend Paulding, back home in America, would write to reassure Irving the following month. "Whatever little rubs of this kind you may receive, place them to the account of the spleen and envy of unsuccessful rivals, who not being able to raise themselves to you, seek to bring you down to them. As to the voice of your own country, it is entirely in your favor. She is proud of you, and the most obscure recesses of the land, even old Sleepy Hollow, are becoming almost classical, in consequence of the notice you have taken of them. . . ."

Paulding might write so, and Irving in his heart might know it was true, but now—forty-two years old and listless, visiting the wine regions around Bordeaux with his brother as autumn yellowed the landscape—he seemed spent. October 17: "Awoke early—very much depressed in Spirits—My appetite has failed me of late . . ." November 2: "much depressed—& filled with anxiety . . ." Like a refrain throughout these days. November 18: "Awoke at 4. laid awake with my mind full of anxious thoughts—" November 25: "Last night dreamt of being in a large old house—found it giving way above, escaped and saw it falling to ruins— It took fire—" How vividly the dream must have imprinted itself on his anxious mind: "thot all my property & especially my Mss: were in it—rushed toward the house exclaiming I am now not worth a six pence—Found one room of the house uninjured—my brother E. I."—Ebenezer, calm in the midst of calamity—"in it. arranging papers, wiping books &c, told me that he had just managed to save every thing that belonged to us . . ."

So. A mood far different, a troubled inner man far different from the genial participant in the gay press that Mary Shelley in her byway had imagined.

Then suddenly, providentially, on the gloom of such feelings a door opened that let sunlight stream in. Irving stepped through the door to seize an opportunity that would renew his life. In a letter to Payne in early February 1826, he was exulting: "I am on the wing for Madrid!" aware now that his recent, intense studies of Spanish language and literature had all the while been preparing him for what chance had brought his way. From a forthcoming, rewarding stay of three and a half years beyond the Pyrenees, the American would emerge a different man, possessed of new achievements and with new honors won.

When he did travel north once more, in 1829, at the end of his first Spanish adventure, it was to London at last, though no record survives from that later stay of a renewal of acquaintance with Mary Shelley. Irving heard from her father: "My Dear Sir," Godwin was writing to the traveler back in England, in October 1829, "It is seven years—I am afraid I might say nine—since I had the pleasure to see you." (Seven years before that date would suggest the spring of 1822, while *Bracebridge Hall* was appearing in London—and Godwin's daughter was with Shelley at Lerici. Nine years before would place the meeting referred to in 1820, with *The Sketch Book* the current subject of London literary talk.) "In that period," the philosopher proceeds, "I have gone through many vicissitudes. In the spring of 1825 I was a bankrupt. That event was three years in concoction before it came to maturity, and I passed through considerable wretchedness. In the interval I heard of your being in London and wished much for the pleasure of seeing you." He refers to Irving's eleven weeks' stay in 1825, in Mary Shelley's company on occasion, with *Tales of a Traveller* to see through the press. "Your visit to the capital of England was, I believe, remarkably short." But what Godwin, now seventy-three, was principally writing to inquire was whether Irving would help him place his new novel with a publisher overseas.

From Cavendish Square the American, who knew of bankruptcy first hand, answered promptly and graciously, promising to do all that he could: "I would have called immediately on you to talk over this matter, but at this moment I am not as formerly my own master . . . The moment I can command a little leisure I will call on you . . . With kind remembrances to Mrs. Godwin, I am, dear sir, very faithfully yours . . ."

Thus Irving had at some point met Godwin's wife as well. During that same year, 1829, that formidable woman's stepdaughter Mary Shelley was (like the aged Godwin himself) writing her own novel, her fourth, *Perkin Warbeck*, a romance set in medieval times. In May she

had solicited the aid of Sir Walter Scott, "encouraged by the kind politeness you have afforded to others, and by the indulgence with which I
have been informed you have regarded some of my poor productions."
Mary's letter to the Wizard of the North, now near the end of his career,
seeks guidance in historical background. "I hope you will forgive my
troubling you," she concludes gracefully. "It is almost impertinent to say
how foolish it appears to me that I should intrude on your ground, or to
compliment one all the world so highly appretiates—but as every traveller when they visit the Alps, endeavours however imperfectly, to express
their admiration in the Inn's Album, so it is impossible to address the
Author of Waverly without thanking him for the delight and instruction
derived from the inexhaustible source of his genius, and trying to express a part of the enthusiastic admiration his works inspire."

Her novel appeared the following year, and two more—*Ladore* and
Falkner—in that decade of the 1830s. "I love I own to face danger
. . ." she had written Shelley years earlier, in Italy, but now in England her life had grown quiet, devoted to her son Percy, who was
making his reassuringly conventional way forward through Harrow and
Trinity College, Cambridge. In 1826, at the death from tuberculosis of
Shelley's then eleven-year-old son by his first wife, Harriet, Percy had
become heir to the baronetcy, and finally, finally, at ninety-one years of
age, old Sir Timothy Shelley breathed his ultimate unforgiving breath,
in 1844, so that the young man—then in his mid-twenties—and his
mother could move at last to Field Place, where Percy Bysshe Shelley
had been born over fifty years before.

Having declined more than one opportunity to remarry since her
return to England, Mary was often occupied during these latter years
with writing. Besides the six published novels, her work includes two
books of travel, two mythological dramas, five volumes of lives of
Italian, Spanish, Portuguese, and French writers, a couple of dozen tales
and stories, and a number of reviews. Early in 1830 she offered to write
for the *Westminster Review* an article on the latest book by Washington
Irving to come out of Spain—"for the next number *che dice?* I admire it
excessively." (About the same work, *The Conquest of Granada*, she had
earlier written Murray, "No book has delighted me so much for a very
long time—.") And she read; as always she read and read. "Routine
occupation is the medicine of my mind," she recorded in 1834. "I write
. . . in the morning. I read novels and memoirs of an evening—such
is the variety of my days and time flies so swift, that days form weeks
and weeks form months, before I am aware. . . . My heart and soul is
bound up in Percy. My race is run. . . ."

Jane Williams by then had united her life with another. That
pretty girl, who had married unwisely in India when young and had
then lived as common-law wife with Edward Williams until he was
drowned beside Shelley off the Italian coast, had set out for England,

where within a year (Mary was spared knowledge of the promptness with which the attachment had been formed) she had in turn fallen in love with the perennial suitor Thomas Jefferson Hogg. After a decent interval hers and Hogg's relationship was acknowledged publicly, and Jane began living out the long remainder of her days—she whom Shelley's latest verse had celebrated: "Dearest, best and brightest, Come away!"—before the world contentedly enough as Mrs. Hogg. She died as late as 1884.

Mary Shelley's father had died (in London, only months before Aaron Burr on Staten Island) in 1836; he had survived into his ninth decade. Some years earlier, when his daughter had returned from Italy and after his own bankruptcy, the now placid philosopher had written to her, "How differently are you and I organized! In my seventy-second year I am all cheerfulness, and never anticipate the evil day with distressing feelings till to do so is absolutely unavoidable. Would to God you were my daughter in all but my poverty! But I am afraid you are a Wollstonecraft"—with the Wollstonecraft tendency to melancholy.

Such a tendency was well developed in Mary as she grew older. She passed much of her time nourishing her lost husband's reputation, maintaining contact as best she could with those still alive who had known him. She lived among memories—"the particular shape of a room," as she wrote, "the progress of shadows on a wall—the peculiar flickering of trees—the exact succession of objects on a journey"—memories that reached back to her Skinner Street childhood, as far back as the visits of her father's friend Burr ("That family does really love me. Fanny, Mary, and Jane, also little William . . ."). Into her fleeting childhood had come Shelley, and the memories of the widow in her forties—"every impression . . . as clear as if stamped yesterday"—could treasure the intense young aristocrat close beside a sixteen-year-old girl by her mother's shaded tomb in St. Pancras Churchyard. "He never mentioned Love," she recollected, "but he shed a grace, borrowed, from his own nature . . . When he spoke of it as the law of life, which inasmuch as we rebel against, we err and injure ourselves and others, he promulgated that which he considered an irrefragable truth." She had gone with him where love took them—happily on foot down dusty French roads, from lodging to lodging in London—might now sometimes hear his voice again, with Byron's at the Villa Diodati alongside Lake Geneva—"the terraces, the vineyards, the upward path threading them, the little port where our boat lay moored"—in precious weeks while scenes of *Frankenstein* had been forming in her mind. Her memories held, indelibly, the appearance of the landscape in northern Italy, printed first as her infant child was dying, seen again on a return there in 1840: "the banks of the Brenta . . . not a palace, not a tree of which I did not recognize, as marked and recorded, at a moment when life and death hung upon our speedy arrival at Venice." And among such keen memories, and hundreds of others called back painfully while she was assembling, editing, annotating her husband's verse and prose, while she held in her hand papers his hands had touched, she might sometimes see again words scribbled in another hand on another paper—"pray write to tell us how you got home, for . . . we are anxious"—and recall the appalling emptiness before two women as they stared seaward, the ride against hope to Pisa—"Sapete alcuna cosa di Shelley"—the forming conviction.

There were, to be sure, pleasures in Mary Shelley's after days. Her son, a young man now, invited her on trips through Germany and to treasured sights in Switzerland and Italy in 1840 and again in 1843. In 1848 he married—as his mother would wish—the young widow Jane St. John, adorer in turn of the poet Shelley and protectress of his grow-ing fame. Mother, son, and daughter-in-law would thenceforth be to-gether until the end.

Claire Clairmont, governess, spinster, continued to weave her fate through Mary's; in her late forties Byron's former lover—possibly Shel-ley's too—was bustling around London teaching Italian: "this is now my life—I go by nine to Mrs. Kitchener's house where I give lessons till one—then I rush to the top of Wilton Place and get a Richmond omnibus and go to Richmond to give a lesson to the Cohens— . . ." That daughter of the second Mrs. Godwin proved tough, surviving years of loneliness in Russia, in Dresden, in France, in England. "From personal experience," she would advise the middle-aged Mary heartily, "I should say you would lose the numb feeling in your limbs if you left off *stays* entirely. I know you do not tight lace no more did I—yet I am so strong since I have worn no stays . . . leave off your stays—eat no potatoes—take ginger and you will be well." Claire spent her final days, sadly impoverished, back in Italy, in Florence—a relic still living into the 'seventies, long enough to stir the wonder and fire the imagination of the young Henry James. She died—eighty years old—in 1879.

Mary, by then, had been dead twenty-eight years, having lived somewhat beyond the thirty-seven that she had told Payne she wished to have carved on her tomb. She succumbed to the effects of a stroke, quietly in her house at Chester Square, London—her son and daughter-in-law in attendance—at the age of fifty-three, February 1, 1851.

Her friend of former days, John Howard Payne, was to die the following year, but far away from London. After Irving had left Paris in 1825 for Bordeaux and Spain, his playwright collaborator had lingered in the apartment at rue Richelieu through the following summer, and from there had insisted on acknowledging his literary indebtedness publicly, in the form of a dedication (to which Irving responded with characteristic humor: "Perhaps you might have mentioned among the many important obligations I have conferred upon you, the vast trea-sures of *excellent advice*, given freely and gratuitously, and which is by you as a solid capital, untouched. . . ."). From France Payne returned to London. There he resumed his work in the theaters and his friendship with Mary Shelley—as well as his earlier custom of furnishing her with orders for plays and operas. But her easy letters to him at that later time reveal that they were friends now and nothing more, as they would continue to be while he remained in her native land.

In 1832, after an absence of twenty years, Payne came home to America. Here he did some editing, considerable traveling in the West and South, and occasional writing on behalf of the Cherokee Indians that shows the clarity of his eye and the goodness of his heart. In 1843, he received a political appointment as consul at Tunis, and late in life the former Boy Wonder was observed there, alone among strangers, "sitting in his arm-chair, by a red-hot stove, drinking brandy and water, and looking very sad." In Tunis he died—bachelor still—April 9, 1852, and there he was buried.

But a few among the playwright's fellow countrymen were in time troubled that the author of "Home, Sweet Home" should sleep neglected in a foreign field. Friends of his memory got together funds, and in 1883, some thirty years after his death, his grave was opened, allowing one last, sobering glimpse of the once beautiful actor before his remains were transported across the ocean for reburial: "The coffin was badly decayed"; inside it, "there was little else than the blackened skeleton left. Traces of the colonel's uniform, in which Payne was buried, were distinguishable,—some gold lace and a few buttons. . . ."

Of what Irving had felt when news reached him of Mary Shelley's death in 1851, of Payne's the following year, no surviving record instructs us. The elderly author—by that time most loved and most famous of all his literary contemporaries in America—was at Sunnyside, home finally and settled for good on the banks of the Hudson. And there, within four or five years, when he was seventy-three, he would receive a letter unexpectedly from another friend whom he had known and visited in London:

"May 25, 1856. My dear Mr. Irving: I think I ought to begin by telling you who is writing to you—Emily Foster, now Emily Fuller; and I address you, after so long a time, because I hope that my eldest boy Henry may have the happiness and advantage of meeting you, and making your acquaintance personally, as he has long ago by hearsay. I have been renewing former days. I have lately been reading over my old Dresden journal, where you are a part of our daily life, and feel it all over again so completely, I cannot believe all the time since has really passed."

Since summer afternoons in Dresden's gardens, the balls, the amateur theatricals, sleds on the ice, the picnics in the surrounding countryside, their box at the opera, the boar hunts, the birthday verses, the talks by moonlight—how many sunny days and happy months . . .

"How I should like to hear from you, dear Mr. Irving! I married soon after we met in London. Do you remember you used to come, and often spend the evening with us in Seymour street? And now I have four boys and one little girl." The beautiful teenage Emily time had transformed into a fifty-one-year-old mother of five. "They are all so good and promising as to add much to our happiness." Henry, the eldest, was eager to settle in the States, "as far West as would be convenient." Hence, Emily's letter; but "I must not exceed my space. It will be such a real happiness to hear from you. Do tell me about yourself, dear Mr. Irving. You do not know how much and often I think of you."

The reply occasioned by those greetings from the wife of the vicar of Willington, Bedfordshire, was all that their writer could have wished for. "You can scarcely imagine my surprise and delight," Irving answered, "on opening your letter and finding that it came from Emily Foster. A thousand recollections broke at once upon my mind, of Emily Foster as I had known her at Dresden, young, and fair, and bright, and beautiful." Her letter had been put into his hands as he was getting into the carriage for a ride with some nieces—Ebenezer's children—who were cheering his later days. "I read it to them in the course of the drive, letting them know that it was from Emily Foster, the young lady of whom they had often heard me speak; who had painted the head of Herodias, which hangs over the piano in the drawing room, and who, I had always told them, was more beautiful than the head which she had painted; which they could hardly believe, though it was true." He went on to describe for his old friend his present, agreeable life, and to beseech her to furnish him with "more particulars about yourself, and those immediately connected with you, whom I have known. After so long an interval, one fears to ask questions, lest they should awaken painful recollections." And he ended: "Farewell, my dear Mrs. Fuller. If any of those of your family whom I ever knew and valued are at hand"—her mother, her sister Flora, her brothers—"assure them that I ever retain them in cordial remembrance; and believe me, ever, my dear Emily Foster, your affectionate friend, Washington Irving."

But though he had often talked with his nieces of his beautiful English friend of Dresden days, about that other, earlier love—about Matilda Hoffman in the village of New York when all of life was young—Irving never spoke. In this year, 1856, the girl to whom he once had been betrothed had been dead nearly half a century. "Mr. Irving," wrote his nephew and biographer, who knew him well in these later days, "never alluded to this event of his life"—his earliest love and loss—"nor did any of his relatives ever venture, in his presence, to introduce the name of Matilda." Her Bible and prayer book, however, which had been given the grief-stricken fiancé after her death in the dimity-curtained room on Greenwich Street, became—so the same source tells us—his inseparable companions "ever afterwards, in all changes of climate and country." Some thirty years after Matilda's brief life had ended—that is, in the late 1830s, after Irving, in his mid-fifties and world-renowned, had long been back in New York—he was visiting Judge Hoffman at the latter's home. A granddaughter had been asked to play the piano; in bringing forth her music from a drawer, the judge by chance extracted a piece of embroidery.

" 'Washington,' said Mr. Hoffman, picking up the faded relic, 'this is a piece of poor Matilda's workmanship.'

"The effect"—according to Irving's nephew—"was electric. He had been conversing in the sprightliest mood before, and he sunk at once into utter silence, and in a few moments got up and left the house."

Faintly over the years drift echoes of a lively adolescent voice, full of mimicry and teasing: "There Matilda come here and let me feel your arm Why Matilda you are not the same girl. You came here a puny thing and now you are a right down Country girl. It is a pleasure to feel such good solid flesh and blood. . . . *Washington* says he saw a beautiful girl at Coldenham whose name was Ellen. Tell her that. . . . Burn this letter as soon as you have read it, I beg of you I cannot bear that such nonsense should be seen by any one. . . ."

All her playfulness stilled. "She died in the beauty of her youth," he who had loved her wrote privately, more than a decade after the awful, final event he had witnessed, "and in my memory she will ever be young and beautiful."

She, too. She and Emily. Both of them—the one who died when not yet eighteen, the other who died at eighty-one—both in a manner equally doomed are alive still, as they were loveliest, through Irving's memory to ours.

DON WASHINGTON IRVING IN SPAIN

It was a dreamy sojourn, during which I lived, as it were, in the midst of an Arabian tale, and shut my eyes as much as possible to every thing that should call me back to every day life. If there is any country in Europe where one can do so, it is among these magnificent but semi-barbaric ruins of poor, wild, legendary, romantic Spain. . . .

IRVING AT SUNNYSIDE

F ROM EARLY CHILDHOOD Washington Irving had wan-
dered in imagination over the landscapes of Spain. In the domicile of
somber Deacon Irving, on William Street in the village of New York
well before the eighteenth century had ended, a boy not yet in his teens
was already finding means of freeing his fancy by poring over pages of
an old Spanish story about the conquest of Granada, a city that "has ever
been a subject of my waking dreams; and"—the adult whom the boy became would go on to reveal—"often have I trod in fancy the romantic
halls of the Alhambra." In his twenties, Irving had woven into *Knickerbocker's History of New York* numerous allusions that show an altogether comfortable familiarity with the greatest of Spanish fictions; old
Peter Stuyvesant, for example, is represented as having (like Irving
himself) "studied for years in the chivalrous library of Don Quixote."
Again, in his thirties, among the sketches and stories he wrote in France
and England for *Bracebridge Hall*, Irving included "The Student of
Salamanca," with its evocations of Inquisitorial gloom and ruined Moorish splendors in Andalucía. At Dresden in 1823, among his good and
communicative friends he could number the Chevalier de Campuzano,
"life of the Party" and Spanish diplomatic representative to that gossipy
Saxon court; such a friendship would have helped nourish an already
sturdy interest. Still later, after the disappointing reception of his *Tales
of a Traveller*, the celebrated author, now in his early forties, was pon-
dering writing a biography of Cervantes and translating his works—for
by now, in 1825, Irving had abandoned earlier efforts to master Italian,

French, or German, and was deep in a serious study of the Spanish language, the one foreign language he would learn thoroughly.

Yet as of the beginning of the year 1826 the wanderer, forty-two years old and at home in much of Europe, had not yet set solid foot on solid Spanish soil. When that year commenced he was, to be sure, near Spain, visiting friends in southern France. Toward the end of the preceding summer Irving's sometime collaborator John Howard Payne had shown him in confidence Mary Shelley's letters, at their Paris apartment on rue Richelieu. Those letters Irving had read and returned. A season had passed; autumn had separated the friends, Payne remaining in Paris with his play writing while Irving with his elder brother Peter traveled southward "to see the vintage at Bordeaux." And there, in the course of a four months' stay, the essayist and storyteller would watch another milestone pass, 1825, with "Military Music in the Street serenading the Commandant who lives opposite. So closes the year—tranquil in mind though doubtful of fortune & full of uncertainties—a year very little of which I would willingly live over again . . ."

Play writing he had tried and was done with; leave that to Payne. During these weeks he continued scribbling at essays about far-off America, but all of those he later destroyed; no doubt the savage response of critics to *Tales of a Traveller* had shaken his confidence in that kind of writing. What he needed, on the threshold of middle age, was something entirely new, some rejuvenating task to undertake. Meanwhile, and predictably: "I have been much out of order the greater part of the time since my arrival at Bordeaux—a loss of appetite, languor & great depression of spirits." For the sake of his health—and of his purse—he was trying "to get my pen into exercise," but "I find after so long an interval the effort is difficult & discouraging." To add to his worries, this was the calamitous winter in which many, including Sir Walter Scott, were ruined ("my extremity is come. . . . Came through cold roads to as cold news"), in which banking and publishing houses in Edinburgh, London, Paris, New York went under. Irving's own investments of proceeds from his most recent book were to yield him little enough in such a depressing period—or, for that matter, at any time thereafter—so that this amateur speculator in steamboats and tin mines was once more making the hard discovery that "there is nothing to be gained in looking beyond the pen. The mines are by no means so productive as I expected, and I believe I must content myself with driving my quill in a garret instead of coining the treasures of Mexico & Peru . . ."

With such cares he lingered in his brother Peter's company, the two of them suffering through their own "three or four days of cruel suspense & anxiety" caused by news of failures from the north and overseas; "It was quite a touch of old times & old horrors." Irving lingered at Bordeaux nervously awaiting what chance might put before him, as he sent back for trunks to be forwarded on, in particular for a

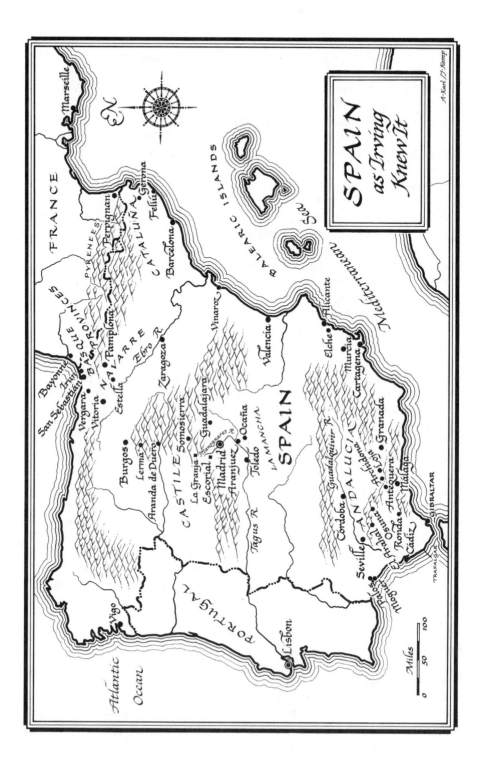

black portmanteau "with my name on it and marked *Clothes.* I find the small stock I brought with me from Paris begin to be the worse for wear and I cannot afford to buy new." He asked, moreover, that some sheets and a packet of silver spoons and forks, "for which I have no occasion," be removed from the portmanteau "and the eight or nine first volumes of Calderon marked *Comedias* put in their place . . . The exchange is easily made as the volumes of Calderon are on the top of a white wooden box marked *Italian & Spanish books* of which Mrs Storrow has the key . . ."

Delightedly he would read on in the comedies of the greatest of Spanish playwrights, determinedly would continue studying the Spanish language, while he was waiting would also dispatch one more letter on an off chance, to Alexander Everett, whom he had met three years before in Holland and had seen more recently in Paris. Older brother of the orator destined to speak alongside Lincoln at Gettysburg, the thirty-five-year-old Everett was at present head of the American Legation at Madrid. If Irving were to undertake a tour through Spain, could the minister, as a formality, to ease a countryman's progress past customs and over the countryside, attach him nominally to the embassy? The suggestion had been Everett's in the first place, as "an advantage and protection . . . in the present state of the country." But Irving had felt a scruple in pursuing the offer. "So . . . if there is the least shadow of objection, do not hesitate to say so, and there let the matter end."

The minister raised no objection at all. On the contrary, he answered Irving's request not only with a passport, but with a proposal for literary employment while in Spain that seemed providentially made to order: something well within the writer's capabilities, of certain appeal to his countrymen, easily and swiftly dealt with, and worth perhaps as much—so Everett thought—as £1,500.

The proposal was this. One of the greatest of Hispanic scholars, Don Martín Fernández de Navarrete, sailor, navigator, esteemed biographer of Cervantes, had for years been searching diligently in all the archives of Spain for every scrap relating to Christopher Columbus. The results of his searches were now beginning to appear—the monumental *Colección de los viages* that remains crucial a century and a half later to any serious study of the discoverer of America. Even then the work was understood to contain much that was previously unknown, material that should be made available as early as possible to English and American readers—the more so because, astonishingly, no full English-language account of Columbus' accomplishment existed at that time. For obvious reasons the translation would most appropriately come from the pen of an American, and what other American could do the task as well as he whose style was everywhere most highly admired? Everett accordingly proposed the assignment to Irving; and the author of *The Sketch Book*, needing money, fearing idleness, wanting a new kind of challenge, eager to ingratiate himself by means of an American subject with those of his countrymen carping about his long exile and his abandonment of native themes, accepted the assignment with alacrity.

January 31, 1826, from Bordeaux: "I must return you my thanks also for the literary undertaking you have suggested to me. The very idea of it animates me; it is just the kind of employment I would wish at present for my spare hours." His brother would help him, he said; the two of them would be working together as in the old days, a score and more years earlier in New York, over the *Morning Chronicle* and *Knickerbocker*.

All at once, then, Irving was again in motion, packing, booking seats, visiting local friends to say farewell, writing hastily to inform friends at a distance of the new direction his life was taking: "a job has suddenly presented itself which seems like a godsend . . . shall set off immediately with my Brother for Madrid, to attack it tooth & nail . . ." That to the Storrows in Paris on February 3, and four days later, exultantly, to John Howard Payne, also in Paris: "I am on the wing for Madrid! A letter from our Minister Mr. Everett has determined me to go on without delay . . ."

Accordingly, in mild and starlit darkness at six o'clock two mornings later, a diligence left Bordeaux bearing the newly appointed attaché and his brother southward. After thirty-one hours on the road "travelling day and night," they were delivered as far as Bayonne, where they changed to a Spanish diligence to cross over the Pyrenees into a land unlike any that Washington Irving had ever seen.

From the start he was enchanted: two A.M. darkness at the border, but with daybreak south of Irun, "find us among mountains—strong featurd country." For safety's sake three guards were escorting them, riding ahead. All day the diligence lumbered more deeply into Spain, past "large—desolate" dwellings, over "wild mountainous country with a stream running thro' it," into "villages of rugged looking houses" wherein might be glimpsed "Women in Mantillas—hair plaited—." Onward the brothers made their way, into the peninsula that in its isolation is more island than peninsula, that in its topography is more continent than either, most mountainous of all European countries, as African as it is European but different from both, this nation that is several nations of several languages, including Basque, incomprehensible speech of that region nearest France through which the travelers even then were passing: "Basque women handsome. Men with a kind of striped stockings & sandals. Wear jackets slung over the shoulders & turn them towards wind and weather. . . ."

Now glimpses of muleteers winding through mountain passes, of "Mules with bells—mule with velvet side saddles. priest walking before it—," and "the Scenery becomes still more wild & picturesque . . ." For a few hours each evening their diligence would stop at an inn,

"Huge rambling inns—with bed rooms within bed room. no fire-places—Braziers under the table. mats on the floor." A fitful sleep until a little after midnight, then the summons to set out again (contemporary travelers through Spain help us imagine it): voices of stable-men beyond the window, harness bells jingling as mules are led forth to be attached to the diligence, and within, the *mayoral*, lamp in hand and red cap on head, calling at the door: "*Arriba! arriba! señores! ya vamos*"—Time to get up, gentlemen; we're leaving. The groggy drawing on of outer garments, the inevitable cup of warm chocolate from the maid in the front room, the resumption of familiar places in the diligence, once more the coach door closing with a slam, the iron steps turning up with a grating sound, the *mayoral* calling out his guttural "*Arre!*" that the *zagal* out there in the night repeats, and with that command to the mules, "our diligence ceased to be stationary."

Still farther southward, accompanied by noises of hoofs, of mule bells, of clattering of wheels, past Vergara, past Vitoria, across the river Ebro and, under heavy rain, into Old Castile. Snow lay on the mountains. Sheep browsed the plains. Villages the travelers passed were poor: "shabby houses with arms on them—Castilian pride—" By early afternoon, during the hours of siesta, they had arrived at Burgos, "streets spacious idle . . . Men lounging about in great brown mantles—woman in scarlet at grate of window—." The tourists delayed—as who would not?—to see the glory of that city, and within heard "Sacristan whose cough resounds thro the Cathedral." The same night found them at Lerma, where they "Supped on kid, also old fowl well blackened in cooking—wine in a pitcher violet coloured . . . Slept 4 in a room—were awakened at 12 to resume our journey—chocolate served of course." Soon after daybreak of this fifth day out, beyond Aranda del Duero, the diligence left the snowy plains and commenced another slow winding upward into the mountains, "Bleak & barren—foggy." At the mountain village of Somosierra, "peasant girls come round us with little reliques begging charity—pour le bon dieu—one a very pretty brunette." And beyond that village, from the diligence window a solitary image against the sky: "Castilian seated on his mule with his great wrap and mantle flowing round him—his *montero* cap and his swarthy face looks with vast hauteur on all the world."

That night the weary travelers "Go to bed between 8 and 9," but "start at 4 in the morning of

"*Wednesday, 15th.*—" of February, 1826, the sixth day of hard traveling after leaving Bordeaux—and "Arrive at Madrid at 10."

Now at the end of their journey it took them a while to find accommodations, but having put up at last at the Fonda del Angel in calle Montera, Irving set out eagerly to call on his sponsor at his quarters a few blocks east off Puerta del Sol. Everett, however, was not at home. Thus the newcomer had to return and, unpropitiously, spend what was left of "a cold shivering day at my lodgings over the brazier of coals . . ."

Nevertheless, he was in Madrid finally, he and his brother Peter, with rewarding work to anticipate. The work would prove, in fact, to be different from what Irving had expected—not to be dispensed with in spare hours in a matter of weeks, but rather a task that would keep him two years and longer in this city, engaged in the hardest labor he had ever performed.

Two years of meals, of walks, of work, of hearing street cries and church bells and parlor talk in surroundings that he had not yet come to know. Those familiar with Madrid at present must adjust their vision, though keeping Puerta del Sol at the center, with the vast *Palacio Real* —the Royal Palace—down calle del Arenal to the west, the Plaza Mayor just to the southwest, and eastward along Alcalá the fountain of Cibeles and the great gate honoring Carlos III. Then as now the gardens of Retiro spread beyond an iron railing near that gate, and the Paseo del Prado stretched southward before the colonnaded museum and the Botanical Gardens beyond Neptune's Fountain, which tossed its spray high. Irving lived among those sights, but the city of his time was constructed of buildings of no more than three or four stories, bars over ground-floor windows, balconies above. The skyline was low then, dominated by palaces, churches, and convents. The streets were not of asphalt but of great paving stones, the narrow sidewalks at street level. The city itself was walled, and at its eastern edge the Puerta de Alcalá, now simply a monument within a rotary of traffic, was one of the fifteen functioning granite gates, as to the south was the then-new Gate of Toledo, being constructed in honor of Fernando VII, *el Deseado*—current, dissolute king of Spain. Beyond the walls were scarcely any suburbs: "Immediately after passing through most of the gates, the traveller enters on a desert, and looks in vain, except toward the Manzanares, for woods, or even trees, for pleasant villages or farmhouses." Only the parched, open plateau extended to the far horizon, or northward to the Guadarramas, snowcapped under the bluest of skies. The Manzanares itself, stream along the western edge of the city, was not then banked and channeled, but flowed listlessly in a narrow bed of shingle in the middle of its ravine. Sheep grazed in dry parts of the riverbed where grass grew, and near the base of grandiose bridges women would move about washing clothes, spreading them on stones to dry, returning—bundles on their heads—toward the city with their laundry done.

Within the walls was a community of some 150,000 people (three and a half million live in Madrid now). The center of activity was the Puerta del Sol, where eight major streets come together. All roads seemed to pass through this principal square. One of Madrid's thirty public fountains was then at its center, and about the fountain gathered the *aguadores*—bare-legged water carriers with their earthen jars: "*Quién quiere agua? Agua fresca ahora mismo de la fuente?*"—Who wants water; cold water just out of the fountain? Their cries would mingle with other calls: *Paja! paja! carbón! cabrito!*, chanted by vendors among the mules and asses that were laden with straw or panniers of charcoal and were ambling along the pavement oblivious of the swine, the sheep, the drove of gobbling turkeys one visitor at the time saw being prodded forward from calle de Alcalá: "*Vea usted qué pavo, Señor! Para su queridita!*"—Turkey for your sweetheart! Cinnamon smells were in the air before the chocolate shops, and melons and fruit were piled for sale on the sidewalks. Kids were for sale, hung up by their bound hind legs. Stores sold combs of gold or tortoiseshell, and silver embroidery and silk and stockings and wine. Gigs rattled by, studded with brass tacks and decorated with identifying paintings of the Virgin or of the Church of the Buen Suceso; the horses that pulled them were belled, with tassels and red woolen plumes, and their drivers wore round-brimmed hats, tasseled as well. Old women in black bearing oranges and pomegranates elbowed their way through the crowds, scolding whoever bumped against their baskets. And people everywhere: politicians, porters, friars, ladies in the inevitable black silk gowns with violet shawls and white lace mantillas, cabmen alongside the *tabernas* cracking their whips while waiting for customers, and the blind beggars whining out lottery numbers or demanding alms. "*Me da usted una limosna! Dios se lo pagará*"—God will repay you. The barefoot child begging in February. The deaf-mute with a bell in his hand.

Streets of Madrid, Irving was reporting within days of his arrival, "swarm with groups, lounging about in the sunshine." He heard their banter, those *piropos*—verbal bouquets tossed at the passing girls—saw their gesticulations. In one exchange scarcely a month after his arrival he himself became briefly and unpleasantly involved. Around noon of a Monday in mid-March he had been walking through a side street with Peter when they happened upon a group of muleteers teasing two girls, "chasing them—throwing stones at them—one overtook one of the girls & was pulling her about rather rudely." A soldier, who knew her perhaps, approached, drew his saber, and abruptly "struck the muleteer on the head. The latter . . . putting his hand to his head, found by the blood on it that he was wounded—The moment he saw the blood he began to howl—His companions came up furious—" At that same moment another soldier, on duty, arrived with a friend, and while "the soldier who had wounded the muleteer scampered," the friend covered his retreat. "A muleteer in revenge attacked the other girl—I," Irving writes in his journal, "pushed him back—He was about to attack me when the young soldier's companion stepped in in my defence—The soldier on duty finally interfered & ordered back the muleteers—& we continued our walk"—after that tense interruption—out by the Gate of Atocha, along the canal to the Bridge of Segovia, then home again through the city.

More frequently, however, the American would repair in weeks ahead to restful surroundings: "I wish you could all be here and take a sociable walk about sundown in the gardens of the Retiro, which is the pleasantest spot about Madrid, commanding a fine prospect and enjoying the most pure and delicate air. . . ." To some foreigners of the time the Retiro seemed only "a vast and ill-laid out garden and shrubbery, three or four miles in circumference," possessing "no particular attraction, excepting its fresh air, and freedom from dust." Yet from the high, exposed situation it occupied, almost treeless then, you could gaze over scarcely obstructed views in every direction: the empty Castilian plain stretching all around, here and there a melancholy hamlet, mountains far off, and nearby Madrid like a miracle in the midst of such barrenness, the setting sun turning its spires and domes to gold.

Later, in company with the rest of the city, Irving would partake of the pleasures of the *paseo*, the late-afternoon or evening walk of a mile, or two, or three, down the shaded Prado, between marble benches, around the splashing fountains. From Cibeles to San Jerónimo the railing of Retiro formed one border of the walk; gardens and palaces of grandees enclosed the other. The lanes themselves were marked by two avenues of great elms and chestnuts. Promenaders walked in the broad lane between the trees; carriages and horsemen rode on either side. One visitor to Madrid in the year of Irving's arrival, 1826, took note of the priests he saw waddling complacently along in wide hats and black capes, of a little boy wearing a soldier's cap and riding a stick horse that he beat into a gallop with his wooden sword, of a little girl supporting her doll against a railing, of new proud parents with their baby carried in the arms of its wet nurse, its *ama de leche*. Rank strutted past displaying stars, crosses, ribbons; and ladies, conscious of being observed while they strolled and chatted, would fan themselves rapidly if unattached, more slowly otherwise.

Then suddenly a drum and trumpet might sound—*el Rey!*—and an avant-courier be seen riding disdainfully along the route that His Majesty intended that day to follow. A squadron of young nobles of the bodyguard would clatter forth, mounted beautifully on horses from the royal stable, and immediately behind them would come "a gilded carriage drawn by six milk white steeds, covered with plumes, and with manes and tails that are full and flowing." Postillions in blue and gold buckskin are driving the horses. Within the coach, "the Catholic king is discovered seated on the right, conspicuous by his stars, his blue scarf, and the golden fleece which dangles from his neck." Fernando VII, this later Ferdinand, *el rey absoluto*, "glances round on the multitude with a look of mingled apathy and good humor, and salutes them mechanically by putting his hand up towards his nose and taking it down again, as though he were brushing the flies away. At his left is the queen, looking too good for this wicked world": his sickly third wife, the fanatically devout María Amelia of Saxony, twenty-three years old, whose royal father Irving had known well at Dresden—she who was "eaten up," as Longfellow observed, "by a most gloomy religious frenzy," anxious to expiate her husband's dissipations and her family's Protestant heresy. "Next comes Don Carlos, the heir apparent, drawn by six cream-colored horses, more beautiful than those of his brother. He grins horribly through his red mustaches, and frightens those whom he intended to flatter. Beside him is his wife, a large coarse woman, with heavy beetling eyebrows . . ."

Among those four people lies the destiny of Spain. Thursday, March 30, 1826: "Walked after dinner in the Retiro—with Peter— . . . Saw the King. queen & princes driving up & down the Prado— . . ." Motion among the multitude near the sovereigns has ceased. Heads have been uncovered; subjects have made their obeisance. The coaches rattle on down the boulevard, and as they pass, the crowd behind them (now quiet forever—priest, proud parents, little girl, little boy on the stick horse) resumes its movement and chatter, in that recurrent pleasure walk to see and be seen.

But the Spain of interest to Washington Irving on this first of his two sojourns was less that of the present than the glorious Spain of the past. On his second day in the city he had returned to Everett's and found him home; that same afternoon the minister had introduced Irving to Mr. Obadiah Rich, consul at Valencia living at the capital, on calle San Fernando, "an American a book collector," who "showed me Ms play of Lope de Vega never published—in his own handwriting—Letter of Cortez—& lent me Ms of Las Casas journal of Columbus."

Thus at the very start of his stay of two years in Madrid, Irving had had the good fortune to meet a fellow countryman whose resources would prove invaluable. The following morning, "After breakfast called with Peter on Mr. Rich—Hired an apartment in his house at the rate of 5 dollars a week. Looked over his collection of Spanish works—"And the day after that: "Change lodgings for Mr Richs." The brothers now found themselves in rooms "on the ground floor of a great Spanish house. We are remote from the street, with our windows opening onto a small garden; surrounded on three sides by the house. It is as still as a cloister, excepting that we have now and then the bell of a neighboring convent ringing for prayers."

Here, ideally situated, the writer could promptly get down to business. Thus, on Tuesday, February 21, within a week of arriving at

Madrid, "Called this morng on Sigr Navarette, Secretary to the academy
of history—Shewed me the work concerning Columbus voyage &c.—"
Now Irving would have his first look at what he had blithely agreed to
translate. Already he had been in touch with intermediaries in London to
approach Murray and other English publishers about the project, confident of a favorable reception despite the dismal economic times. For
dismal they were. Constable of Edinburgh had just gone spectacularly
bankrupt, carrying Ballantyne and Sir Walter Scott to ruin. One might
have guessed that Murray would not now be looking for any new ventures on which to risk capital. And sure enough; by mid-March the
verdict of the English book market had reached Madrid, where Irving
by then had examined Navarrete's tomes more closely. What he learned
on both counts was distressing.

"The Booksellers will not offer for the voyage of Columbus, they
fear it may be *dry*, and as unluckily"—to say the least—"it is so in a
superlative degree, I fear there is nothing to be done with it." So much
for agreeable and well-paid labor translating in his spare hours, before
setting out on a leisurely tour of Spain. "I have the five volumes at
present in my possession . . . almost entirely made up of Documents"
—postille, capitulations, pleitos, letters of credence, decrees, passports,
wills, conditional grants—"which none but an historiographer would
have appetite to devour or stomach to digest. I must," he concluded
grimly, "turn my attention therefore to something else."

But what, in this foreign city? Wednesday, March 8, 1826: "Read
a little, but felt unfit for any occupation—walked in the Retiro—warm
weather—reposed on grass in shade of an almond tree full of blossoms &
swarming with bees—." What might he do with his time? Saturday,
March 18: "Commenced lessons in Spanish ½ past 10. Went to Court
with Mr Everett—there was a Besamanos"—a ceremonial kissing of the
royal hands—"in honour of Queens Saints day—St Joseph. was presented to the king, Queen—Don Carlos & Don Francisco. . . ." But
could anything of his original purpose in coming to Madrid be salvaged?
Friday, March 24: "Good Friday—& as bad a day as could well be.
Cloudy. cold—harsh & windy. Every body depressed. . . . The Streets
silent—no Bell rings no carriages to be seen—only here and there a
Muleteer—the Centinels on duty with reversed arms—the churches
shut— . . . —went to bed at ½ past 8 & extinguished the day as
soon as possible." For all that, he could not yet abandon his idea "of
doing something with the work concerning Columbus; though it is very
voluminous and husky . . . I am turning and turning it over and considering it. . . ." Then, in his journal entry the following day occurs
the first mention of a new course to pursue: Saturday, March 25,
"Wrote a little at life of Columbus—Great ringing of bells in commemoration of resurrection—."

Thereafter, through all of April, all of May, well into June, Irving's journal contains one refrain. April 1: "Busy all the morng at Columbus." April 12: "Write all day at Columbus—." April 28: "Write all day & till 8 o'clock in Evg at Columbus." April 30: "Write all day at Columbus—." May 19: "20 pages." May 20: "Rise at ½ past 4—write at Columb all day. . . . —29 p." May 29: "All day at Columb. from 5 in morng until 8 at night. Evg at Mrs Everetts. . . . return home and write a little."

At last here was something, as the author chose to phrase it, that he could take his coat off to: not a translation of dry documents but a narrative account, the first adequate account in English, that would draw upon Navarrete's sources as well as Rich's invaluable collection of manuscripts—here in the very building where Irving was living—in order to tell the discoverer's wonderful story. "It will require great attention hard study & hard work, but I feel stimulated to it, and encouraged by the singular facilities which are thrown in my way."

Concerning facts and dates, Irving meant "to be scrupulously attentive & accurate, as I know I shall be expected to be careless in such particulars & to be apt to indulge in the imagination." This was to be solid history, "a minute and circumstantial narrative," no burlesquing as in *Knickerbocker*, no hasty sketching or picturesque romanticizing. How long would such a trial of skill in an entirely new line take him to complete? By mid-June, within three months, he had achieved his immediate ends. "I never worked so hard, nor so constantly for such a length of time; but I was determined not to stop until I had made a rough draft of the whole work. I have succeeded in so doing."

He could slow down then, spending some time revising and enlarging what he had put together. In late June a nephew—William's son—then twenty-four years old and fated to become the author's executor and earliest biographer, passed through Madrid on a European tour and encountered Irving "in the midst of books and manuscripts, full of the subject on which he was engaged, and in excellent spirits, though once" —Pierre Munro Irving did recall of that brief visit—"in a long walk which we took together on the Prado, he adverted with deep feeling to the cloud which had been thrown over him by the persevering malignity with which all sort of disagreeable things had been forwarded to him from America by some secret enemy." Well, the expatriate might hope that his anonymous ill-wisher—and however many he spoke for—would be appeased by this present national subject, assuming so ambitious an undertaking could ever be finished. And if it could be, the author would have achieved, so he was beginning to feel, something more lasting than anything he had ever written before.

Time would disprove that assumption, but it had sustained him during these past weeks, keeping him at his desk among old Spanish parchment-covered books and manuscripts day after day and into the evenings through spring and early summer. Now Irving did relax a little, attended the theater, saw the Armory, in Plazuela de la Cebada witnessed an execution of "a man for Robbing & murder—hanged— took place at about 1." (That same year, in the same spot, a spectator on a cold, sunless morning took note of balconies crowded with gentlemen and ladies, of boys hanging from *rejas*, of muleteers and tradesmen crowding the square below, of blind men singing ballads about the condemned, of cowled monks chanting a death dirge, of grenadiers in bearskin caps, of the criminal shrouded, his legs tied under the belly of the ass that bore him, his hands bound around a copper crucifix as he was led to the gallows.) And Irving, relaxing, journeyed with Peter to nearby La Granja, dined more often with his new friends in the city— the Everetts, the D'Oubrils, the Riches—went to bullfights. Indeed, two days after his nephew's arrival, he accompanied friends to see the bulls: "Little round bellied Spanish Marquis with us a battered rake of 60. as round as a pumpkin yet pale & withered in the face—His plan of amusement for the day To the Bull fight in the morning—then to dine at a Fonda to the bull fight in the evening then to the theatre—then to have a girl for the night— . . ."

Irving's own days were being spent differently. In mid-August he fancied, mistakenly, that though he had much work on Columbus still before him, "all the heavy & anxious toil is over." Another, related subject had attracted his interest in the meantime, so that by early fall he had turned to that: to Ferdinand and Isabella's campaigns, culminating in the fateful year 1492, to wrest from the Moors their last Spanish stronghold, at Granada. Thus in the autumn he had two books partially written but neither close to completion. And the weeks continued to pass.

In mid-November the Riches moved from calle San Fernando to a house in the highest part of Madrid, to the north near the Puerta de Santa Barbara, now deep within the business district but then commanding "a view over a great part of the city and the adjacent country." The brothers Irving moved with them. The Riches "occupy the first floor of the house, we have rooms on the second. The house is one of those great habitations peculiar to Spain. Great entrances and staircases about which you might drive a French Diligence. . . . Our household concerns are attended to by a Spanish family that lives half a mile off in a remote corner of the mansion on the same floor with us." In such surroundings, among barking pug dogs and caterwauling cats, the author would see the year end and the work that began as a task of a few weeks still unfinished. Sunday, December 31: "return home and write a little—but sleepy & go to bed—and so ends the year 1826 which has been a year of the hardest application & toil of the pen I have ever passed. I feel more satisfied however with the manner in which I have passed it than I have been with that of many gayer years. & close this year of my life in better humour with myself than I have often done."

Just before Christmas—times having improved—he had written optimistically to Murray in London, "informing him of Columbus being nearly ready for the press," and in mid-January of the new year 1826 "get letter from Murrays agreeing to publish Columbus." Thus the toil-worn author had fresh incentive to finish. But "it is a kind of work," so he was protesting a month later, "that will not bear hurrying; many questions have been started connected with it which have been perplexed by tedious controversies, and which must all be looked into. I had no idea of what a complete labyrinth I had entangled myself in when I took hold of the work. . . ."

He was still slaving over his task in March, when "Mr Longfellow arrives." Twenty years old at the time, two years out of college, Henry Wadsworth Longfellow was a young friend of Irving's nephew—the one who had passed through Madrid nine months before—and holder of an appointment to teach languages at Bowdoin; hence the travels through Europe, as preparation. From the Spanish capital the future poet was soon writing his father: "The society of the Americans here is very limited; Mr. Everett and family, Mr. Smith his secretary, Mr. Rich the consul, Washington Irving and his brother Peter, Lieutenant Slidell of the navy, and myself compose the whole." To this fervent admirer of *The Sketch Book* ("I was a school-boy when it was published," he testi-fied years later, "and read each succeeding number with ever-increasing wonder . . . spell-bound . . .") the famous author's presence was de-lightful: Irving "has a most beautiful countenance," Longfellow wrote home, "and at the same time a very intellectual one, but he has some halting and hesitating in his conversation, and says very pleasant, agree-able things, in a husky, weak, peculiar voice. He has a dark complexion, dark hair, whiskers already a little gray. This is a very off-hand portrait of so illustrious a man." And further: "he is one of those men who put you at ease with them in a moment. He makes no ceremony whatever with one, and, of course, is a very fine man in society, all mirth and good humor."

In society yes; Irving would not spoil social occasions by revealing his private cares. Yet during those weeks he was often disheartened, as his journal discloses. Money worries vexed him. He was having bad dreams, couldn't find copyists, feared that his book was not well enough written, was weary with it, weary with Madrid, and eager to be on tour in Andalucía. About that proposed trip he had written in late February, "Six weeks since I thought I should certainly have been off by this time, and yet here I find myself toiling & fretting, and my work still requiring the finishing hand." There was no leaving Rich's library, however, until the job was done; in fact, exactly twelve months more would pass before Irving was free to resume his roaming.

Another birthday came upon him in April: forty-four. Already in the preceding month he had noted almond trees in the Retiro in bloom again. By May, with the author still much of the day at his desk, the blossoms had fallen; bees no longer hummed in those branches. "Literary men are said to be generally bad calculators of their time & trouble, but I never was more completely out, than in my idea of the toil this work would have cost me, or I doubt whether under present circumstances I should have undertaken it." Moreover, Irving's brother Peter, ever in feeble health (and helpless to aid him with his researches after all), was now being bothered by an "old enemy the head ache . . . I feel sorry on his account to linger so long in Madrid which can no longer possess any interest for him . . ."

June, July. A second summer, and ices were being served again at tables in shade along the Prado. Irving had "nearly got the work ready for launching," but was continuing to feel "doubts and anxieties. It is an important affair for me . . ." He had "now been nearly eighteen months in Spain, during which time I have laboured harder than ever I did in my life; with what success remains to be seen." The first chapters of his effort he would dispatch to London that month, and by mid-August was about to send more: "I am waiting with great anxiety to hear of the fate of my manuscript, and until I hear I shall be good for nothing."

In September: sheepishly writing friends in Paris with his superscription still Madrid, hurrying because "Peter is waiting for me with his hat on to go to dinner, when I must put this letter in the Post office. . . ." Brief excursions in the autumn to Escorial, to Toledo. And still no word from Murray. Not until almost the end of October did Irving finally learn from his agent in London that the publisher had accepted the hefty manuscript on its author's terms: three thousand guineas, payable in installments over two years.

What relief that news must have brought him! All at once money worries were in the past; at least financially those hours of tedium among Rich's papers had been vindicated, and the trip so often deferred could now go forward. Thus, as soon as the worst of winter was over, on March 1, 1828, near the start of a third Spanish spring, Irving at long last did set out by diligence past the surrounding wheat fields toward Córdoba—although without Peter. The delays had cost him the company of that special traveling companion, whose headaches had grown worse in recent months, and whose present health forbade his taking part in the rugged journey that lay ahead.

Spires and domes and rooftops of the capital, its walls and familiar gates, treeless Retiro and the shaded Prado were slowly receding behind the lumbering diligence; fourteen years would pass before Washington Irving—by that time transformed into a portly, official ambassador nearing sixty—would see Madrid again. Now he was on his way south to Andalucía, rolling through barren La Mancha past "scenes of some of the exploits of Don Quixote," then ascending under a full moon into the Sierra Morena, bandit-infested, "wonderfully wild and romantic," the road winding along precipices "overhung with cragged and fantastic rocks." The traveler was exhilarated to find himself one dawn among "the stern and savage defiles of the Despeña Perros." And down from those heights the awkward carriage rumbled into balmy regions of orange trees, aloes, and myrtle. Through weather suddenly delicious to the senses it continued along its way to Córdoba—greatest of European cities nine centuries earlier, now shrunk to a squalid settlement of some twenty thousand souls, with little more than the wondrous mosque to detain a stranger. At Córdoba the diligence abandoned its passengers. From there (as frail Peter was making his way northward in slow stages back to the comforts of France) the trip to Granada awaiting his younger brother would have to be managed by horse and mule.

"I would reccommend no one to take the route we did, from Cordova to Granada," Irving concluded at the far end of that next leg of his journey. "It is through monotonous dreary country, where the traveller passes many long tedious miles without meeting a habitation, and where he is obliged to put up with all kinds of privations at the wretched dens called posadas." The American had been charged with informing friends in Madrid of the advisability of traveling with a family in southern Spain. Eight days it had taken to get this far. "As few strangers . . . pass through these parts, there are no accommodations to be met with at the posadas. You must forage through the village to collect materials for a repast"—one imagines a dusty uneven street, low earth-colored houses, ragged children gaping among garbage, the flies, the rancid smells, a dog stretched in shade, an old woman in black retreating around a corner—and you will be lucky at night "if you can have a private room to sleep in and a mattress spread on the earthen floor. The Spanish travellers generally, who pass through these mountains, are of hardy and simple habits. They wrap themselves in their cloaks, and lie on the mantas of their mules and horses, with a saddle or a pair of alforjas for a pillow."

Yet Irving's first glimpse of the city that had formed the subject of his childhood's waking dreams now made the trip all worth it: at twilight, from the plain where Columbus had petitioned his Catholic sovereigns as they encamped some three centuries earlier before this Moorish capital and its crowning citadel of the Alhambra: "The evening sun shone gloriously upon its red towers as we approached it, and gave a mellow tone to the rich scenery of the vega. It was like the magic glow which poetry and romance have shed over this enchanting place." At Granada the traveler was to linger ten days on this first visit, seeking imprints of the Moors, wandering among redolent gardens where fig trees were beginning to bud, writing one gossiping letter near sunset in the Alhambra itself, diluting his ink in the fountain of the Court of the

Lions: "Good heavens! after passing two years amidst the sunburnt wastes of Castile, to be let loose to rove at large over this fragrant and lovely land!"

By March 19, he had resumed his journey—rugged once more—across the Alpujarras on his way toward the southern coast of Spain. Travel through such desolate heights continued to be wearing—nine days from Granada circuitously to Málaga, a distance that the modern driver might cover in scarcely more than a morning. "Every day is passed in incessant action and fatigue; on horseback or on foot, scrambling among rocks and precipices . . ." The country Irving described as "destitute of comforts," but sternly beautiful: the very weeds underfoot—thyme, rosemary—were aromatic, the very mountains were of finest marble. Along dry riverbeds the travelers advanced through ravines with gigantic red boulders "absolutely impending over us." Finally in sight of the blue Mediterranean, "our road at times wound along the face of vast promontories . . . from whence we looked down upon the surf beating upon the rocks, at an immense distance below us." Fishermen could be seen drawing their nets on the sandy beaches, their voices just audible as they shouted at their labor.

Exhausting was such travel, in file on muleback—and dangerous as well. Here, as all over the Spanish countryside, crosses had been stuck in fissures of rocks at bends in the road to mark where previous hapless wayfarers had been ambushed and murdered by brigands who roamed the hills unchecked. Irving might joke about it: "our greatest risk," he had insisted on an earlier leg of his journey, "has, I am convinced, been from our own escort, which for part of the way has been composed of half-reformed robbers, retired from business, but who seemed to have a great hankering after their old trade." Yet the danger was real. Contemporary travelers witnessed and vividly recorded details of such encounters: the jogging carriage suddenly, unaccountably stopped, the lantern at the top lighting up olive trees a little way into surrounding darkness, in place of the easy clop of mule hoofs the abrupt and violent sound of unfamiliar voices: "*La bolsa!*" Forms out there, muskets leveled, mounting panic and pleadings from within: "*No me quita usted la vida!*"—Don't kill me!—cries for mercy, *piedad, Jesucristo, ay Santiago apóstol y mártir*, as one at a time each passenger is made to descend from the coach, deliver up watch, jewels, money, and lie flat on his face among the dirt of the road. "In these unsettled times"—within clear memory of years when roving mountain bands survived by plundering the French invader—"the police has become so negligent and the robbers so daring that the roads are infested in every direction and the first question you ask of a friend, on arriving from a journey, is whether he has been robbed?" So Irving himself had reported a short time earlier, and conditions since then had not improved. His friend Lieutenant Slidell had had to watch helplessly, a few months before on his way south from Barcelona, while *bandoleros* took a rock and beat out the brains of the postillion, face down with the others, so that he would not identify them. The boy had moaned in the darkness of the roadside for an hour or longer, but nothing could be done to save him.

Irving, for his part, met some rough types along the way—one "singular character," for instance, on muleback miles from anywhere, in Andalucían hat and jacket, "a cartridge belt of crimson velvet slung over one shoulder and passing under the other arm; two carabines slung behind his saddle, pistols in front, a cutlass by his side, a long Spanish knife in the pocket of his vest . . ." But despite such encounters at posadas and on the lonely road, the American did reach moonlit Málaga finally and in safety, in time for his forty-fifth birthday.

From Málaga his route wound through the mountains of Ronda—the only bad weather of the trip: "for three days . . . we were drenched by frequent and heavy rains"—then on to Gibraltar, where he made a four-day visit. From Gibraltar along a road bordered by cork forests, with herdsmen's voices in the perfumed darkness amid the sound of nightingales: "In the course of the morning ride very drowsy, & could hardly keep to the saddle" on the way to Cádiz. That city of liberal hopes had maintained its independence throughout the Napoleonic invasion near the start of the century. From its streets the proclamation of the Constitution of 1812 had provided a battle cry for progressives thereafter; from within its walls the devious Ferdinand had less than five years ago been delivered by means of another foreign intervention, French vessels offshore bombarding the port into submission. To Irving Cádiz seemed "a beautiful city—one of the most beautiful I have ever seen, but one is continually reminded that all the outward gayety and splendor of its snow-white and spacious mansions cover internal poverty, ruin, and wretchedness." On the signal tower, Sunday, April 13, 1828, the sightseer was gazing over a panoramic view of the white port and its blue harbor, while "Veteran soldier who attends it—gives acc^t of the distressing scenes he has witnessed—says when he considers the state of the world he thanks God for his Gray hairs that his time will soon be over. . . ."

On several occasions in months ahead Irving would return to the city, but this first visit was brief. "I heard nothing while there but repinings at past prosperity and present distress." The following morning at seven he set out "in the Steam boat Betis—bound to Seville . . . arrive at Seville ½ past 5. Put up at Fonda de la Reyna." And there he did stop. In Seville and its vicinity he would remain more than a year, writing and studying, with only occasional brief forays into surrounding regions to vary his new routine.

One such trip we might anticipate, although he did not make it until that summer, in August: to Moguer and Palos, near the coast beyond fertile plains, westward some sixty miles away. "Palos—Church of St. George where Columb read the royal order—Stands on crown of hill . . . At Moguer Visit Church of St Clara—21 Franciscan Nuns—rich—In church Columbus watched all night—Church lighted by parafin lamps. . . . La Rabida—two internal cloisters—convent silent—cells of monks closed—solitary cat—a scattered fig tree or two—olives &c shew where had been an orchard—The French destroyed it . . ." At the time of Irving's visit Palos was "a wretched hamlet," a "Small town in hollow of hills—two streets.—houses one story high—white washd . . . on the river a Mystick or two with latine sails—gliding—." The couple of boats he saw were coming to shore for fruit and wine, and as he gazed down upon them in the water, the biographer of Columbus noted that they were about the size of the caravels in the little fleet that, three hundred and thirty-six years earlier, had sailed from this same river out into the Atlantic to discover a world.

"If my work does not please," he had written from Madrid with it only just blocked out and the bulk of the task before him, "I must say it will not be the fault of the subject." By now Irving knew that his *Life and Voyages of Christopher Columbus* had indeed pleased the vast majority of readers in both England and America. Because of it he would soon win unanimous election to the Real Academia de Historia—signal honor—and largely because of it would receive the prestigious Medal of the Royal Society of Literature: ". . . to WASHINGTON IRVING, ESQ., Author of the 'Life of Columbus,' . . . &c. &c. . . ." The American historian George Bancroft would find in Irving's account of the discoverer "all kinds of merit—research, critical judgment, interest in the narrative, picturesque description and golden style." And Navarrete himself would conclude that Irving "*ha logrado dar á su historia aquella extensión, imparcialidad y exactitud que la hacen muy superior á las de los escritores que le precedieron*"—that the author has succeeded in giving his history a breadth, an impartiality, an accuracy that make it very much superior to the works of writers who preceded him. Even now, as he stood overlooking the boats on the Tinto River at Palos, the American would know that the four volumes of Columbus, which had cost him "more toil and trouble than all my other productions," had not only repaired his fortunes but had enlarged his already sizable international reputation. Its success in the United States was particularly gratifying, for all the while that he had been laboring to finish it, he had (as he would later admit in print) "been chiefly animated by the hope, that the interest of the subject would cause the work to remain among my countrymen, and with it, a remembrance of the author, when all the frail productions of his fancy might have perished and been forgotten."

Irving's fanciful creations—Rip, Ichabod, Knickerbocker—live on. *The Life and Voyages of Christopher Columbus*, although still consulted and respected by serious modern historians, stands most of the time neglected on library shelves. Yet it is a fine achievement. The idiom, of course, is nineteenth century, but even now the sweep of the story that Irving tells exerts—as one of its earliest admirers justly said—"all the fascination of a novel, with the additional interest of real history." The author's facts remain for the most part unsuperseded; in the background his impressive scholarship (all that voluminous mass of old Spanish documents) is reassuringly evident without ever being allowed to clog the narrative. Through a series of brief, unified chapters, and in that easy, golden style that Bancroft and so many others have admired, Irving tells—for "those who learn the history of Columbus . . . for the first time"—the marvelous adventure from beginning to end. The magic of his prose leads us to imagine afresh the world through which the Genoese moved with his obsession, a world of oceans that had no farther shores, wherein roamed mighty fishes, across which blew haughty winds. Monsters might be out there, and the lost Atlantis, and St. Brandan's inaccessible isle, and if the world were round, people at the antipodes walked upside down over distant stars. Perhaps the earth's middle was belted by an impassable "region of fire, where the very waves, which beat upon the shores, boiled under the intolerable fervor of the heavens." On mainlands in longitudes beyond where Europeans yet had gone, beyond jungle and mountain, lay the legendary kingdom of the Christian potentate Prester John. And eastward at the other ends of the earth were Mangi and Cipango, provinces with cities of ivory and alabaster—one hundred miles in circuit—their palaces roofed with gold, their lords and ladies, in silks and gorgeous brocades, benignly awaiting on arched marble bridges the coming of the Christian.

Through this world of superstition and fierce bigotry and idealism Columbus—sojourner *par excellence*—had made his restless way. On the docks of Lisbon he would have beheld the wealth of vast Africa—elephant tusks, gold dust, pepper, coffles of black slaves—from the coastline that was even then lengthening, promontory by promontory, headland by headland, southward slowly into the fearful unknown. From the Portuguese court, to the Canaries, to Spain, Irving's account follows its persistent subject as he carries his wild scheme at last to the thrones of the Catholic sovereigns:

"Because, most Christian and very exalted excellent and mighty Princes, King and Queen of the Spains and of the islands in the Sea, our Lord and Lady, in this present year 1492, after Your Highnesses had made an end to the war with the Moors who ruled in Europe, and had concluded the war in the very great city of Granada, where in the present year, on the second day of the month of January, by force of arms I saw the royal standards of Your Highnesses placed on the towers of Alhambra . . . and I saw the Moorish King come forth to the gates of the city and kiss the royal hands . . ."

For seven years Columbus had followed the court about Spain, vainly applying for royal favor. "During all this time," as Irving tells us, "he was exposed to continual scoffs and indignities, being ridiculed by the light and ignorant as a mere dreamer, and stigmatized by the illiberal as an adventurer. The very children, it is said, pointed to their foreheads as he passed, being taught to regard him as a kind of madman." Yet the madman finally had his way; *La empresa de las Indias* could at last go forward:

"I departed from the city of Granada on the 12th day of the month of May of the same year 1492, on a Saturday, and came to the town of Palos, which is a seaport, where I fitted for sea three ships well suited for such an undertaking, and I departed from the said harbor well furnished with much provision and many seamen, on the third day of the month of August of the said year, on a Friday, at half an hour before sunrise . . ."

Irving's text bestirs images of that fateful morning, of the little caravels—none of them more than seventy feet long, shorter than a tennis court—among the three vessels fewer than a hundred men, singing their chanteys as the creaking windlasses raised the anchors, the day gray about them, the sea calm, sails limp. An outgoing tide was carrying the vessels across the bar and downriver. From the shore friars at the convent of La Rábida could be heard chanting their liturgy in the still dawn:

> *Deo Patri sit gloria,*
> *eiusque soli Filio . . .*

Through Irving's pages we follow the tiny fleet seaward on its southwesterly course to the Canaries, where the ships were detained for three weeks before striking out westward "into the region of discovery." Early on, sailing through darkness, "they saw a singular jet of flame fall from the sky into the sea some 4 or 5 leagues distant from them"—a meteor no doubt, but an alarming occurrence to the superstitious crew. Westward they made their way: a mast floated by, dolphins were sighted, dark clouds appeared to the north. For thirty-three days, through fair weather, through rain, the three little caravels sailed, alone and pressing forward where European had never sailed before. The sailors' beards lengthened. Bilges began to stink. Food grew weevily. Water dwindled. Cockroaches multiplied. But " 'Thanks be to God,' says the Admiral, 'the breezes were softer than in April at Seville, and it is a pleasure to be in them: they smell so sweetly.' They saw some fresh green seaweed, and many land birds, of which they caught one—they were flying south-west—terns and ducks and a booby."

That was on the thirtieth day out. Two days later, the distance widening and widening from Spain and home, "the men could now endure it no longer; they complained of the long voyage. But the Admiral reassured them as best he could, holding out to them bright hopes of the gains which they could make . . ." And the following night at two A.M., October 12, with the moon past full, *Pinta* in the lead, sails of the three vessels silver in all that empty darkness, suddenly a cry from the forecastle mast: "*Tierra! Tierra!*"

A low sand cliff was gleaming some six miles ahead. There, quite unintentionally, Columbus had encountered not Cipango, not Japan at all, but a world he never suspected existed, found himself not among spices and pearls and gold, but on white beaches confronting coarse-haired natives with red paint over their faces. "They are a people very guileless and unwarlike, all naked, men and women, as their mothers bore them. It is true that the women wear merely a piece of cotton big enough to cover their genitals but no more, and they are very handsome . . ." After more than a month out of sight of land, the Admiral finally was standing on firm ground, trading hawks' bells and amber beads and bottles of orange water among thatched huts with strange-tongued savages who, when asked about *oro*, about gold, would point just over the horizon or farther inland beyond the mangroves. But the land was beautiful, so lushly green to the weary sailors, and the native women were well shaped and without shame, and as the caravels sailed from island to island brightly colored fishes swam through the clear, green, sunlit water alongside.

From these paradisaic regions of the Caribbean Irving's account lets us follow Columbus eastward again, bearing (in addition to small gold souvenirs, yams, and a sampling of perplexed Indians) the most stupendous secret in geographical history, as he guided the little *Niña*, alone now, along the perilous voyage through midwinter storms, against head winds and human treachery, to arrive at last, battered but intact, March 15, 1493, in "the harbor of Palos; whence he had sailed on the 3d of August in the preceding year, having taken not quite seven months and a half to accomplish this most momentous of all maritime enterprises."

The remaining pages in Irving's highly readable and comprehensive account tell of the Admiral's reception in Spain and of his three later voyages, specifically (in the author's words to his publisher) of "the troubles of himself and his brothers in the island of Hispaniola with the natives and the rebels. His being sent to Spain in chains. His fourth voyage, in the course of which I have brought forward many particulars of his singular and disastrous voyage along the coast of Veraguas or Isthmus of Panama. The transactions in the island of Jamaica, where he lived for a year in the wrecks of his stranded ships &c. &c. so that the latter part of the work is full of incident and interest."

So it is. But the first voyage holds our wonder longest—that bold expedition from this now insignificant port of Palos and back again. And from Palos, from a past of frustration and daring and triumph in which Irving among Rich's documents had been living so long, the newly acclaimed historian was making his way now back into the present, returning by calesa through Moguer, through Villaalba, on the road to nineteenth-century Seville. At Villaalba, August 14, 1828: "Meet with a young spaniard at the Inn—good countenance though full of care—talks freely—Speaks of lamentable state of Spain.—wishes to go to america—Sup together of a gaspacho a ragout made of the leveret & a rabbit he had purchased. Conversation about Bull fights—robbers—contrabandistas—all the people on this side of Seville incline to smuggling—all on the other side toward Cordoba &c incline to Robbery. . . ."

Back thus into the present. Next day, Friday: "arrive at Seville at ½ past 2."

During his stay in Seville, before the excursion to Palos, Irving had been working to finish that second book begun while at Madrid—the book to which his studies of Columbus had led him, wherein he was recounting the conquest (the final scene of which the great discoverer himself had witnessed) of the Moslem kingdom of Granada by the Catholic Monarchs late in the fifteenth century. Seville was a city altogether appropriate for pursuing such an undertaking. From his rooms in Barrio de Santa Cruz (made agreeably cool by Moorish walls of prodigious thickness), the American would sally forth to study at the Biblioteca Columbina nearby, or at the Archives of the Indies a few blocks farther away. Both held much of value. In the former, for example, he had recently, in late June, come excitedly upon "work of Pedro Aliaco Imagine del mundo with marginal notes by Columbus and his brother Bartholomew." That medieval volume—*Tractatus de Imagine Mundi*—remains a prize of the library, and acknowledgment is made to this day that Washington Irving was the first to appreciate the significance of the writings inserted along its margins in the 1480s by a previously unidentified hand.

Columbus still held his interest; at this very time the biographer was preparing a second edition of the Admiral's life and voyages. But he was also deep in a study of the final years of Moslem sovereignty in Spain. "It is impossible," he wrote, "to travel about Andalusia and not imbibe a kind of feeling for those Moors. They deserved this beautiful country. They won it bravely; they enjoyed it generously and kindly." For seven hundred years and more, through generation after generation, they had lived in the peninsula, and "no lover ever delighted more to cherish and adorn a mistress," this latest witness was concluding, "to heighten and illustrate her charms, and to vindicate and defend her against all the world than did the Moors to embellish, enrich, elevate, and defend their beautiful Spain."

The city in which Irving now resided, though much diminished from its former greatness, displayed the Moslem achievement in every quarter. "The whole character of the place is peculiar, retaining a strong infusion of the old Moresco," like an oriental city—so he felt—out of *A Thousand and One Nights*. Women were veiled. Clothing that people wore on the streets of Seville—unlike the dark garb of Castile—was brilliant and varied. "As you pass by the houses you look into beautiful courts, with marble pillars and arcades . . ." On warm evenings lanterns would allow the passerby glimpses within of groups seated in patios, in air fragrant with orange trees and honeysuckle, amid sounds of a guitar and of a fountain gently splashing on tile. Flowerpots of geraniums hung from walls and porticoes.

And even when he journeyed beyond the limits of the city into surrounding plains, past olive groves and bright green barley fields that Moorish irrigation had made to flourish, Irving would encounter additional recollections of Moslem life. In April, for instance, he had set out with friends at five in the morning to attend the cattle fair of Mairena, four leagues and two hours away. "Fine view sunburnt hills from one part of the Fair over a broad rich plain. with the ruins of Moorish castle in the near ground . . . The fair like an arab or Moorish encampment after a foray." Goya (dying this same month, April 1828, in Bordeaux) might have painted the scene for a tapestry design: "Cattle sheep horses scattered about. rude tents—men scouring about on horseback on fine horses in Andaluzian dresses—Some in groups—some sleeping in shade. some drinking, singing—Landscape trembling with heat of sun. . . . clouds of dust from various parts of landscape telling the arrival of other parties . . . tinkling of bells—oxen standing patient & immovable—horses prancing & neighing with the generous impatience of their nature—groups of gipsies." The description preserves one morning fashioned from Spain's African heritage, against which the American was led immediately to set a note from the utilitarian present: "Fat landlady of the Posada for the use of the room for 5 hours, with a few glasses of orangeade—& the use of plates &c charges 9 $. We give her 4 $."

And let her scold. Back in Seville on succeeding days he would frequently mount after breakfast "to the top of the Giralda for exercise & prospect"—up the ramp the three hundred and fifty feet to the summit of what remains a landmark of the city, what in Moslem Seville had been the minaret, rising over mosque, alcázar, and crowds in burnooses astir in the bazaars below. Toward the end of May, on the feast day of San Fernando—deliverer of Seville from the Moslems in 1248—Irving had entered the great echoing cathedral to find "the body of the Sainted King . . . exposed in a coffin of gold and silver with a glass side—Body envelloped in rich gold brocade see feet & dimly the face which appeared to be very dark—like mummy had on a crown." That same evening the city was alight with festivities: "Fine appearance of the Giralda illuminated—studded with flames which sent off volumes of smoke—it seemed as if the tower were on fire." And a little later, in early June, had occurred the feast of Corpus Christi: "after breakfast walk thro the streets—covered with awnings"—shaded as are the narrow streets of the city on present summer days—"fronts of houses—balconies &c hung with red damask &c. Ceremonies in cathedral. Boys in old Spanish dress with hats on, dance before the altar"—exactly as other boys had danced on that same feast day in sight of the Catholic sovereigns themselves more than three centuries before. "Procession with Crosses, Images of saints—immense silver shrine with the host."

Evidences of the two Spains—Moorish and Catholic—thus were everywhere about him as Irving worked to tell the story of the concluding achievement of the Reconquest that had taken nearly eight hundred years to accomplish. Occasionally he was away from the city: in August to Palos, as already described, later back to Cádiz. Sunday, August 24, 1828: "all last night on board steam boat—Sleep on deck wrapped in my cloak—but harrassed by Mosquitoes arrive at Cadiz at 11 . . ." There, he called on "Miss Shaw & family—all go to Circus & see experts on Slack rope &c." A few days later he was visiting the wine vaults: "brother of Mr Domecq there   taste wine of vintage of 1764 . . ." And near Cádiz, in October 1828, in the village of El Puerto de Santa María, Irving finished his *Chronicle of the Conquest of Granada.* By the following month he was back in Seville.

"I am lingering here in Andalusia," he wrote his American friend Brevoort in December, "waiting until the publication in England of the work on the Conquest of Granada, and occupying myself with researches in the old Cathedral library and the archives of the Indias. All the summer months have been passed by me in the country, first in a cottage about two miles from Seville and afterwards at a small country house near Port S'Mary." Now he was resettled in Seville itself, at Mrs. Stalker's English boardinghouse, taking his daily walks along the palm-lined Alameda or out to Delicias, in the shade of acacias and willows on the banks of the Guadalquivir. Wednesday, December 31, 1828: "Thus ends the year: tranquilly—It has been one of much literary application. and generally speaking one of the most tranquil in spirit of my whole life. The literary success of the Hist of Columb has been greater than I anticipated and gives me hopes that I have executed something which may have greater duration than I anticipate for my works of mere imagination. . . ."

Mere we might quarrel with. Yet after two works of Spanish history, the author had been applying himself lately to yet another book— this one not historical but imaginative after all, a sort of Spanish Sketch

Book that was to become for many of his readers the most appealing of all his writings. For some time he had been setting down legends of Moorish enchantment. "For my part I do not believe above one half of all these stories," so he insisted the following spring, April 1829, to a young female correspondent in Madrid; "yet one half is enough to make a reasonable person stare." At Alcalá de la Guadaira, for example, "just a pleasant drive from here . . . there is an old Moorish castle on a hill, in one of the ruined towers of which a most beautiful princess was confined in old times; and there she is to be seen on Moonlight nights, with a turban all sparkling with diamonds and rubies, waving a white veil from the top of the tower . . ." Elsewhere hereabouts had been encountered a strange little monk, three feet high, reading by the road-side in a great book that he would slam shut if spoken to. Moreover, Irving himself had often passed a certain fountain on the outskirts of Seville; and "Not very far from the fountain there are the ruins of an old Spanish Country seat, that was very grand and gay in former times; and used to be a great resort of all the fine people of the country round; but now the walls are all broken, the chambers roofless, and nothing inhabits it but bats and owls and lizards. But Some times it will appear all lighted up at night, and there will be such a rattling of carriages as if all the gay people of Seville had come forth and were driving up to its gates. Some of the Country people say they have seen great old fashioned carriages drawn by Six Mules; with coachmen and footmen with cocked hats and old fashioned liveries; and gentlemen and ladies seated inside in ancient Spanish court dresses; but if they venture to speak to these gay people, of a sudden the whole vanishes. All night too there will be heard from the old country seat the Strumming of guitars and the rattling of castanets, and Singing and dancing, and talking and laughing; but in the morning all is again a ruin, with the owls and bats and lizards swarming about it."

Assuredly, over this romantic region, so full of strange stories, his imagination that April of 1829 was roving once more. His spirits felt restless with another spring. Perhaps a visit to Moslem Africa, "merely Tangiers and Tetuan, for a few days to get a peep at the turbaned Infidels in their own towns." But the Austrians happened to be blockading the North African coast at the time, so Irving had to look in other directions for a destination toward which he might journey. Soon he had made up his mind. On the first day of the following month, he set out on horseback with one traveling companion and a guard to return to Granada—and the Alhambra.

This time he went directly overland, a distance of some hundred and forty miles, eastward across the plains from Seville and up once more into the sierras. It took his little party five days, much of it over roads no better than mule paths, to complete the journey that takes four hours now. The valuable part of their luggage had been sent ahead; the travelers would keep "merely clothing and necessaries for the journey and money for the expenses of the road; with a little surplus of hard dollars by way of *robber purse* . . ." Irving was on one horse; his Russian friend from Madrid, Prince Dolgorouki, then in his early thirties, was on a second; and a third horse was "for our scanty luggage and the conveyance of a sturdy Biscayan lad, about twenty years of age, who was to be our guide, our groom, or valet, and at all times our guard. . . . He was, in truth, a faithful, cheery, kind-hearted creature, as full of saws and proverbs as that miracle of squires, the renowned Sancho himself . . ."

Their preparations made—and having laid in besides, above all, "an ample stock of good humor, and a genuine disposition to be pleased" —they set off that bright May day a hundred and fifty some years ago at six-thirty in the morning. The route took them through Alcalá de Guadaira, where the ghost of the turbaned princess was still confined. As one does at the start of journeys, they noticed everything: the Guadaira winding about the base of the hill on which stood the castle ruins, waters of the river "whimpering among reeds, rushes, and pond-lilies, and overhung with rhododendron, eglantine, yellow myrtle . . ." A fisherman's net they saw hung against a tower wall to dry; "a group of peasant women in bright-colored dresses, crossing the arched bridge, were reflected in the placid stream."

On eastward they proceeded, across open plains empty of house, tree, or any kind of shelter. Through that afternoon the three riders were doused repeatedly with heavy rain showers: "Our only protection was our Spanish cloaks, which nearly covered man and horse, but grew heavier every mile. By the time we had lived through one shower we would see another slowly but inevitably approaching; fortunately in the interval there would be an outbreak of bright, warm, Andalusian sunshine, which would make our cloaks send up wreaths of steam, but which partially dried them before the next drenching."

That first night out was spent at a posada at El Arahal, where Irving and the prince distributed cigars to win over the local populace; and at seven of the balmy next morning they were on their way again, "with all the posada at the door to cheer us off." Over verdant, fertile country they traveled, alighting "beside a brook in a rich meadow" for the midday meal—ham brought along from Seville, Valdepeñas wine from their leather *bota*—and afterward, with cloaks spread out under a tree, all took a siesta. Farther on, at Osuna, they passed their second night, in a cheerless posada outside the walls of the town, with the sierras directly before them.

Now the road they would follow ascended through picturesque but lonely mountain landscape. Vultures might sometimes be seen wheeling above the travelers, or groups of shy bustards might stalk over the heaths below. But no songbirds would break the silence of places so barren of tree or shrub. What might startle the ear would be the sudden hoarse cries of a herd of wild bulls on some green fold of upland; their low bellowing and black, menacing aspect as they looked down from their rocky height added to the wildness of the scenery. Or the wayfarers might hear a sound of bells of lead mules in a train still out of sight, or hear the muleteer's voice, chanting a ballad or admonishing an animal from straying. "At length you see the mules slowly winding along the cragged defile, sometimes descending precipitous cliffs, so as to present themselves in full relief against the sky, sometimes toiling up the deep arid chasms below you." Always the muleteer in passing would call out his solemn salutation—"*Va usted con Dios, Caballero!*" or "*Dios guarde á usted*"—before riding on, seated sideways on his mount, which would seem to be listening gravely and keeping pace with the chant that his rider had resumed. The bend of the mountain hides him; voice and bells fade; and the silence, the awesome loneliness return.

In the wild passes of these same mountains that Irving now was entering, "the sight of walled towns and villages, built like eagles' nests among the cliffs, and surrounded by Moorish battlements, or of ruined watchtowers perched on lofty peaks, carries the mind back to the chivalric days of Christian and Moslem warfare, and to the romantic struggle for the conquest of Granada." Indeed, these same remote regions, east of Osuna, were "often ravaged during the reign of Ferdinand and Isabella by Ali Atar, the old Moorish alcayde of Loxa, father-in-law of Boabdil . . ." Boabdil the Unfortunate: through what had once been the kingdom of this last Moorish ruler Irving, companion, and guide were slowly passing, beyond Fuente de Piedra, on to Antequera—"in the very heart of the country famous for the chivalrous contests between Moor and Christian"—next day on to Archidona (where the threesome dined under olive trees on cold roasted kid, partridge, salted codfish, half a pullet, bread, oranges, figs, raisins, walnuts: "I assure you I never made more savoury meals in my life" than on this trip)—on over the Puerta del Rey, through which Ferdinand had invaded the Moorish kingdom, and on still farther, until finally, toward sunset of the fourth day out, they were in sight of Loja itself, ancient frontier town and key militarily to *bellísima Granada*. Of course every village and every feature of the landscape one of their number was observing with the keenest interest, he whose most recent work had been a chronicle of the campaigns waged in the fifteenth century between Crescent and Cross through these same regions.

Chronicle of the Conquest of Granada had been for Irving a labor of love. Moreover—as often with this author, who had already written

mock letters, journalistic satire, burlesque, tales, essays, plays, a fragment of novel, serious history—it was an effort to try something different from what he had done before. But initially the book did not please
as had much of his earlier writing, so he abandoned the experiment for
many years thereafter. To be sure, some of his readers were impressed
from the start. "No book has delighted me so much for a very long time,"
the widely read Mary Shelley was informing Murray in London soon
after publication, and she sought to interest the *Westminster Review* in
letting her prepare an article about it: "I admire it excessively." Coleridge was prompt in referring to Irving's new book as a masterpiece of
romantic narrative. Bryant later judged it "one of the most delightful
of his works." And Prescott, whose own classic account of the reign of
Ferdinand and Isabella is warrant for the value of his judgment, felt that
the chronicle superseded "all further necessity" for a history of the conquest. Moreover, modern studies of Moorish Spain continue to notice
Irving's account; one published as recently as 1975 includes *The Conquest of Granada* in its bibliography as "a colourful narrative still
surprisingly close to the facts."

Those facts concern the final years in western Europe of Moorish
sovereignty, which had been imposed on al-Andalus as long ago as the
early eighth century, after some seven thousand Berbers had crossed the
fifteen miles of water from North Africa in the spring of 711 and occupied the flanks of Mount Calpe, thenceforth to be known by the Arab
name *Jabal Tariq*, Gibraltar. From that base the Moslems had swept
over the face of Iberia with astonishing rapidity, in two years driving the
Christian Visigoths before them across plains and plateaus and as far as
the cold, fogbound peaks at the very northern edge of the peninsula,
against the sea. Into such inclement regions the invader, a people of
desert and sun, did not choose to press, but proceeded to establish kingdoms over the remainder of what we know as Spain and Portugal. Three
hundred years later—consider the sense of stability in maintaining possession so long—Islam still dominated two-thirds of Iberian soil. But the
long effort at Reconquest had begun from those northern peaks, and
would continue with increasing success through the thirteenth century.
Toledo fell to the Christians in 1085; Córdoba fell in 1236, Seville
(after more than five hundred years in Moorish hands) in 1248.

Yet the kingdom of Granada in the south of Spain—some forty-five
miles deep, a hundred and fifty miles wide, possessed of fourteen cities
including the Mediterranean ports of Almería and Málaga—the
Moorish kingdom of Granada survived, ever more crowded with refugees from Catholic triumphs to the north. Too devout to endure life
under Christian rule, those refugees strengthened the will of the little
kingdom to preserve itself. Its situation, however, came to be as perilous
as has been that of modern Israel: "Granada," Irving observes early in
his book, "had risen to splendor on the ruin of other Moslem kingdoms;

but in so doing had become the sole object of Christian hostility, and had to maintain its very existence by the sword. The Moorish capital accordingly presented a singular scene of Asiatic luxury and refinement, mingled with the glitter and the din of arms."

The din grew clamorous through the decade preceding the capitulation of Granada to investing forces of Castile and Aragón early in January 1492. During those ten or twelve culminating years, the Moslems under al-Zaghal and Boabdil, the Christians under Ferdinand, had disputed al-Andalus, as Irving tells us, piece by piece, inch by bloody inch. To evoke their fierce campaigns his account draws on old chronicles from Rich's library in Madrid, with no facts intentionally misrepresented, although in the process the author does try to enhance scenes by using "a little freedom of pencil in the coloring, grouping, &c, &c." in order to create something "between a history and a romance." This, indeed, is the novelty about his literary experiment, his attempt, not at historical romance, but at romantic history.

Romance imposes itself on Irving's chronicle in several ways. With his fondness for assuming personae—Oldstyle, Knickerbocker, Geoffrey Crayon—the author has chosen to represent what he has written here as the work of one Fray Antonio Agapida, a zealous monk of the period being described. Thus, liberties taken to color and vivify the narrative may be accounted for as those found in Agapida's manuscripts. Yet the cleric never existed—a truth not long kept secret—and the moment the narrator is known to be fictional, readers are bound to wonder how much of what this imaginary monk records must be discounted.

The device may seem to have allowed its creator "freer scope in touching up and coloring the subject," but it had the unfortunate consequence of casting doubts on what in fact is reliable history. Lockhart in England, reading the manuscript for Murray before publication, raised another objection. The son-in-law of the Great Unknown complained in confidence that Irving with his elegant style was "not the man to paint tumultuous war, in the lifetime of Scott, when Byron is fresh." One does feel the influence of Scott while reading these descriptions of forays, ambushes, skirmishes, surprisals of castles, sieges, plunderings. But if Scott's superior example encouraged Irving to enliven dry medieval accounts, the American's achievement in turn exerted its own influence on later historians, helping to explain the vividness with which Prescott—to mention one great practitioner—recreates the past of this same Spain, of Mexico and Peru. For Irving, through his Agapida, has let us witness much that is sharply focused and memorable: plumed cavaliers before the battle, trumpets signaling and pennons snapping over tents on the plains, engineers with their lombards and foot soldiers with their arquebuses and crossbows, alarm fires blazing atop the mountains, hamlets put to the torch and the smoke rising as villagers keen and wail, soldiers battered from horses and left sinking in their armor to the

bottom of mountain rivers, the besieged dying of thirst on their battlements, "raving mad, fancying themselves swimming in boundless seas
. . . parched and panting . . . no longer able to draw a bowstring
or hurl a stone," scaling ladders overturned, Moors transpierced, Christians in triumph throwing turbaned heads of the conquered from the
ramparts, *Te Deum*s chanted while beyond the walls wild dogs in the
fields feed on corpses of warriors stripped and plundered.

We are even allowed to glimpse the requisite Moorish female,
beautiful, beheld "by the light of a silver lamp" in "an apartment of
superior richness to the rest." The fortress has fallen. She is "the wife of
the alcayde of the castle, whose husband was absent, attending a wedding feast at Velez Malaga. She would have fled at the sight of a Christian warrior in her apartment, but, entangled in the covering of the bed,
she fell at the feet of the marques, imploring mercy. . . ."

Here is more romance, and in a more dubious form. Although
Irving deplores earlier accounts of the Conquest, "woven over with love-
tales and scenes of sentimental gallantry, totally opposite to its real character," his own chronicle proceeds to assure us at this point that the
"Christian cavalier, who had a soul full of honor and courtesy towards
the sex, raised her from the floor, and endeavored to allay her fears; but
they were increased at the sight of her female attendants, pursued into
the room by the Spanish soldiery. The marques reproached his soldiers
with unmanly conduct, and reminded them that they made war upon
men, not on defenceless women. . . ."

And so on, at some little length. Yet the spirit of what Irving
acknowledges to have been "one of the sternest of those iron conflicts,
sanctified by the title of *Holy Wars*" seems here and elsewhere to partake more of the decorous nineteenth century during the decade before
Victoria's ascension than it does of the rugged fifteenth. As for readers
of our own war-ridden day, readers perhaps grown chary of crusades in
any case, we may feel remote indeed from the attitude, even allowing it
to be the worthy monk Agapida's, that watches "two valiant alcaydes,
Nicholas de Roja and Sancho de Avila," Christians both, fall in combat
against the enemy in the court of the castle at Alhama, then merely
remarks "but they fell honorably, upon a heap of slain," before turning
its unafflicted glance elsewhere. We may, indeed, finally tire altogether
of these "valiant cavaliers" rampaging through Irving's chapters—of the
gallant, fearless flower of Spanish chivalry, of the Moors that are hardy,
brave, vigilant, true. Assuredly we will grow impatient with those
windy, sanctimonious speeches printed verbatim and represented as having been delivered to inspirit troops in the heat of battle by commanders
who never could have spoken them for the general ear. We may view
with a cynicism hardly felt in Irving's prose the manner in which the
Boabdil for whom he feels sympathy has secretly attended to his own
future welfare, by accepting a bribe of fertile lands and "thirty thousand

castellanos of gold," before delivering his kingdom into the hands of the conquering Christian.

All that said, Irving's romantic history nevertheless does at times convey grandeur and genuine emotion, as in the closing scenes that describe the capitulation of Granada itself. Boabdil descends through a gate of the Alhambra that henceforth will be walled up forever. He makes his way down past the Hill of Martyrs to the banks of the Genil and the assembled Catholic host: Cardinal Mendoza, the king with his splendid, proud escort of cavalry. To Ferdinand are delivered the keys of the city, last relics of the Arabian empire in Spain. On that momentous occasion, witnessed by Columbus, the Moslem throne was lost forever. Now firearms are thundering in triumph from within the city, as the defeated Moor, before passing into exile, pauses on the heights at the edge of the stern Alpujarras for one last glimpse of the terrestrial paradise, of all that beauty no longer his. "You do well," his mother beside him chides, "to weep like a woman, for what you failed to defend like a man!" The Catholic Monarchs take possession that afternoon. And four days later, January 6, 1492, courtiers of Castile and Aragón set foot for the first time in the citadel of the Alhambra, wandering "with eager curiosity over this far-famed palace, admiring its verdant courts and gushing fountains . . ."

"I have been trying to conjure up images of Boabdil passing in regal splendor through these courts; of his beautiful queen; of the Abencerrages, the Gomares, and the other Moorish cavaliers who once filled these halls with the glitter of arms and the splendor of oriental luxury; but I am continually awakened from my reveries by the jargon of an Andalusian peasant who is setting out rose bushes, and the song of a pretty Andalusian girl who shows the Alhambra . . ." Thus from the Court of the Lions within the Moorish citadel, Washington Irving had written a friend in Madrid on his first visit to Granada more than a year earlier. But during that brief visit, in mid-March 1828, "the Spring was not sufficiently advanced, and the trees were not in full leaf. I wish," he explained later from Seville, "to see Granada in all its glory; with its gardens and groves covered with flowers and foliage, and the Alhambra fragrant with orange & citron blossoms, and resounding with the song of the nightingale. . . ."

So by mid-May 1829 he had returned, after his trip on horseback through the mountains of the Conquest. "I thought Granada one of the loveliest spots I had ever seen when I visited it last year, but now it seems a vast deal more beautiful." Through the Alhambra, at the time largely uncared for and falling into ruins, he might wander at will, through "Great halls, and courts, with gardens and fountains, and all silent and deserted; not a living being to be seen." His friend Dolgorouki, with whom he had made the overland trip, after four days in the city resumed his travels across Andalucía; with a spyglass "I looked out for you from the tower of the Gomares, and . . . descried you making your way up the arid hills beyond the Vega." But Irving remained behind. The governor of the city had offered the American the use of modern apartments alongside the Alhambra itself; furnished and maintained for that administrator's convenience, they were seldom occupied. Gratefully Irving accepted the offer, and thus found himself for almost eleven weeks a solitary guest in the strangest of all his many habitations.

"Here then I am, nestled in one of the most remarkable, romantic and delicious spots in the world. I have the complete range and I may say control of the whole palace, for the only residents beside myself are a worthy old woman, her niece and nephew, who have charge of the building, and who make my bed, cook my meals, and are all kindness and devotion to me." Breakfast in days ahead he would frequently take in the Hall of the Ambassadors, high over the shimmering *vega*, among cool morning breezes from the Sierra Nevada, under a ceiling of wonderfully intricate fretwork, surrounded by elaborate stucco decorations of airiness and grace. The meal finished, "I lounge with my book about these oriental apartments or stroll about the courts and gardens and arcades, by day or night with no one to interrupt me. It absolutely appears to me like a dream; or as if I am spell bound in some fairy palace." At night he would swim, under bright stars, in the sun-warmed waters of the pool of the Court of Myrtles.

Though empty of furnishings, and though sadly abused by neglect and the ravages of French invaders and tatterdemalion families living in decaying towers and under staircases about the grounds, the Alhambra even in 1829 was a magic place. Other travelers who saw it bemoaned its ragged condition and prophesied its total ruin within a generation. But Irving came upon it just in time, to gaze beyond the depredations— graffiti scratched into stucco, rags hung to dry from windows and loopholes or between marble pillars of the courtyards. His writings did their part to help preserve this historic pile, as earlier to Stratford-on-Avon, to the Catskills, he had directed attention that has been unflagging since. What he was responding to here were vestiges of a high civilization that had cultivated the arts and sciences, had promoted agriculture and manufacturing and commerce, had written wise and equitable laws: a civilization of philosophy, of poetry, of music that seemed to linger in tile and cedarwood chambers, around refreshing fountains, under ceilings penciled with lapis lazuli, over white marble pavements; a civilization where divans and worked ivory and glass lamps and gorgeously patterned carpets had once heightened luxury, at a time when the rest of Europe was spreading rush mats on earthen floors.

He was enraptured by it. "You remember," he wrote Dolgorouki in mid-June, "the little suite of rooms locked up, where the Italian artist worked who had been repairing the Alhambra. It is an apartment built either by Charles V. or Philip, and terminates in the open gallery where Chateaubriand wrote his name on the wall. I have taken possession of that apartment, and one room is very comfortably fitted up as my bedroom and study." His attendants—little Dolores, old Tía Antonia—had tried to dissuade the American from moving into quarters so remote, where only owls or an occasional fox or wildcat would be his company. If he stubbornly insisted, then Mateo Jiménez, son of the Alhambra, would have to secure doors and windows as a precaution against burglars. Legends of treasure were always rife, treasure buried hastily in the fifteenth century by wealthy Moors expecting to return; indeed, such legends formed much of the conversation between the American visitor in his mid-forties and the teenage Mateo—historian, valet de chambre, descendant of humble folk whose lives had been scraped out among these vine-covered ruins.

Yet even with Mateo's bolts in place, Irving had a rough first night of it, ushered to his distant quarters in the very heart of the deserted palace by his apprehensive attendants. Dolores gravely crossed herself as they forsook him there.

Now all alone, the New Yorker in remote darkness had felt "a vague and indescribable awe" creeping over him. "Every thing began to be affected by the working of my mind. The whispering of the wind, among the citron-trees beneath my window, had something sinister. I cast my eyes into the garden of Lindaraxa; the groves presented a gulf of shadows; the thickets, indistinct and ghastly shapes. I was glad to close the window, but my chamber itself became infected. There was a slight rustling noise overhead; a bat suddenly emerged from a broken panel of the ceiling, flitting about the room and athwart my solitary lamp . . ."

Seizing the lamp, Irving issued out into the passageway that initiatory night: "I walked, as it were, in a mere halo of light, walled in by impenetrable darkness. The vaulted corridors were as caverns; the ceilings of the halls were lost in gloom. I recalled all that had been said of the danger from interlopers in these remote and ruined apartments. Might not some vagrant foe be lurking before or behind me, in the outer darkness? My own shadow, cast upon the wall, began to disturb me."

Then suddenly, in the Hall of the Ambassadors, he heard sounds more ominous than any echoes of his footsteps. "I paused and listened." They appeared to be coming from beneath the floor, or outside the tower—low moans, something resembling the howling of an animal, stifled shrieks mingled with inarticulate ravings. That was enough. The adventurer turned and scampered back along arcades through which he had just passed, breathing more easily only when in his chambers once more, "and the door bolted behind me."

Not until morning were the dismal howlings accounted for. Dolores explained that they were "the ravings of a poor maniac, a brother of her aunt"—of Tía Antonia—"who was subject to violent paroxysms, during which he was confined in a vaulted room beneath the Hall of Ambassadors."

But sunshine beaming throughout the palace had restored Irving's equilibrium in any case. His apartments—four high rooms—offered beauty from every viewpoint. "One of my windows looks into the little garden of Lindaraxa; the citron trees are full of blossoms and perfume the air, and the fountain throws a beautiful jet of water; on the opposite side of the garden is a window opening into the saloon of Las dos Hermanas, through which I have a view of the fountain of Lions, and a distant peep into the gloomy halls of the Abencerrages. Another window of my room looks out upon the deep valley of the Darro, and commands a fine view of the Generalife"—and of the Torre de las Damas nearer at hand, and the Silla del Moro high above.

The fortunate visitor today looks on the same superb vistas. So much did Irving come to love these quarters that he professed to find it hard to leave them even to take walks for exercise. Happy now, genuinely so, for once he set down no private notations that would disclose a troubled mind. Seldom did he even descend from his enchanting hilltop to visit Granada, although he would pass hours at the railing of his mirador gazing upon the alameda far below, where the life of the city unfolded each day: morning hum and murmur, streets "thronged with man, and steed, and beast of burden," then midday and siesta, with windows closed, curtains drawn, locusts chirping in the sultry air, as "the full-fed monk snores in his dormitory; the brawny porter lies stretched on the pavement beside his burden . . ." With the declining sun the scene would gradually revive, bells ringing vespers, the evening promenade of *majos* and *majas* under way, and later still, up from the city sounds of "guitars, and the clinking of castañets; blending, at this lofty height, in faint but general concert." Darkness, and the starlike lights of ice gatherers among the snows of the Sierra Nevada, while Granada sleeps in moonshine. "I sit by my window until late at night, enjoying the moonlight and listening to the sound of the fountains . . ."

And he was writing. "Nothing could be more favorable for study and literary occupation than my present abode." He was writing—or had in readiness from productive days at Madrid and Seville—so his nephew and biographer later determined, legends of the conquest of Spain, a history of the Visigothic king Roderick, voyages of the companions of Columbus, a sketch of the life of Mahomet, chronicles of Don Pelayo, more chronicles of the successors of Don Pelayo, still more chronicles, of the Ommiades, and of Don Fernando Gonzalez, Count of Castile, and of his successor Don García Fernandez, and something put together about the Seven Sons of Lara, and about Fernando el Santo, conqueror of Seville, whose mummified face he had gazed upon.

One hardly can blame him for this diligent mining of what seemed to be literary gold; hadn't Murray just agreed to pay £2,000 for *The Conquest of Granada?* Yet the bulk of what he was scratching away at didn't amount to much. It would lie in manuscript for years—might have remained unpublished altogether without altering the author's reputation.

One other work, however, did claim some of his time, a book begun at Madrid a couple of years earlier, continued in romantic mood at Seville, and now brought almost to completion during these weeks of isolation in the very atmosphere it described.

WASHINGTON IRVING

ESCRIBIO EN ESTAS HABITACIONES SUS

CUENTOS DE LA ALHAMBRA

EN EL ANO DE 1829

So reads the plaque outside the room where the bat got in: In these quarters Washington Irving wrote his tales of the Alhambra in 1829. Some of them he did write there, even though the finishing touches were applied in London, and the book itself was not published for another three years, not until 1832, at the time of the return of America's foremost man of letters to his homeland, where fame was to engulf him utterly.

So the long-deferred, triumphant return was to be accompanied by the publication of this work now being composed—one of the three best books he ever wrote. This was not history, not even romantic history, but pure romance—one of those products of "mere imagination" that may have seemed ephemeral to its author, but that (like the delicate arabesques of the Alhambra itself, "apparently as unsubstantial as the crystal fabrics of a morning's frost") have proven more durable than structures of gray granite fact weightier and far more solid. No other book of his—not even *Knickerbocker*, not even *The Sketch Book*—is so consistently engaging. In its pages distant past blends with present, and both become exotic, both magical. From the past Irving has captured and preserved in his silken prose those legends that Mateo and others had guided him to—the "Legend of the Arabian Astrologer," the "Legend of the Three Beautiful Princesses," the "Legend of the Moor's Legacy"—and through such evocations has saved for us a gorgeous world, a world of ladies on white palfreys "with velvet caparisons, embroidered with gold, and sweeping the ground," of steeds with bits and stirrups of gold, with silken bridles adorned with pearls and precious stones. Before generations of captivated readers his legends have displayed love notes perfumed with musk and roses, scimitars flaming with damascene, boxes of sandalwood containing silken carpets from the throne of Solomon the Wise. Through wickets among towering cyprus trees his words guide us into small gardens, where the waters of fountains run cold as ice and clear as crystal. Robes of those about us are of tissue or brocade; shawls are of cashmere. In bazaars we behold dervishes and faquirs, and on the battlefield warriors with glittering poignards and cuirasses gold-embossed . . .

The brilliant past of the legendary Saracen ended with the completion of the Reconquest, here in the Alhambra, in the Hall of Justice, where "the very cross is still to be seen upon the wall" before which knelt Ferdinand and Isabella. "I picture to myself," writes Irving in the course of *The Alhambra*, "the scene when this place was filled with the conquering host, that mixture of mitred prelate and shaven monk, and steel-clad knight and silken courtier; when crosses and crosiers and religious standards were mingled with proud armorial ensigns and the banners of the haughty chiefs of Spain, and flaunted in triumph through these Moslem halls. I picture to myself Columbus, the future discoverer of a world, taking his modest stand in a remote corner, the humble and neglected spectator of the pageant. I see in imagination the Catholic sovereigns prostrating themselves before the altar, and pouring forth thanks for their victory . . ."

Yet an instant later "the transient illusion is over—the pageant melts from the fancy"—and Irving is back in his present world, where smoke from modern fireplaces has discolored the fretted walls, where no white arm beckons, no dark eyes flash behind the latticed jalousies, where patterns of the once dazzling tiles are shattered, and swallows circle through the empty rooms.

But even the sixteen chapters of *The Alhambra* that, scattered among Moorish legends and history, describe the present—Irving's attendants and occasional visitors, his wanderings to surrounding towers or over the hills nearby or down to the cool grottoes of the baths, his frugal suppers of fruit and milk, the coming of summer that stills the nightingale and withers the scarlet blossom of the pomegranate—these chapters, too, have their charm. "Behold for once a day-dream realized." He had not, he insisted, embroidered on the details of his sojourn in the Alhambra in any way: "the account of my midnight rambles about the old palace is literally true. . . . Every thing in the work relating to myself and to the actual inhabitants of the Alhambra is unexaggerated fact: it was only in the legends that I indulged in *romancing*." So an old man in his mid-seventies would declare as he remembered that marvelous spring and summer already almost thirty years behind him. The marvel was that fact and fancy at least for a little while had melded in his life, in a castle on a hilltop, and become indistinguishable.

It couldn't last, no more than could those visions of Boabdil in regal splendor, of Ferdinand victoriously at prayer within these walls. In May Irving had listened from his mirador to the church bells of Granada pealing the death of that later Ferdinand's gloomily pious queen. For Amelia of Saxony, the present king's frail third wife, was dead at twenty-six, and the times in Spain beyond the citadel of the Alhambra clamored to be heard. "If you can put me up a parcel of French and English newspapers"—this appeal to Dolgorouki in mid-June—"and forward them to me by any *Corsario*, you will do me a vast kindness, for I am totally behindhand in the news of the day, and do not know which way the world is rolling. I do not care how old the papers are, for it is two or three months since I have seen any . . ."

In the contemporary Spain that Irving had lost touch with, the king possessed of three wives and a thousand concubines was a widower again, without ever having produced an heir. Moreover, his dissipations made it unlikely that he ever would; gouty, apoplectic, he was—though a year younger than Irving—not expected to live much longer. Meanwhile his brother, the dwarfish dogmatist Don Carlos, grinned at the populace from his carriage and waited his turn on the throne.

Irving would learn more of all that, and more very soon of the way the world elsewhere was turning. For suddenly, July 13, 1829, the author "received letters informing me of my appointment as Secretary of Legation to London." To London? Leave the Alhambra, leave Spain: should he not refuse so unexpected an offer? "I have," he wrote his brother, "a thorough indifference to all official honors, and a disinclination for the turmoil of the world: yet having no reasons of stronger purport for declining, I am disposed"—after some agony of thought, and surely without much enthusiasm—"to accord with what appears to be the wishes of my friends."

But how could he bring himself to leave this place? "Never shall I meet on earth with an abode so much to my taste, or so suited to my habits and pursuits." And when he did leave, where he most wanted to go was not to England, but home. During recent months in Seville and Cádiz, that longing had found expression again and again. The final entry, for example, in Irving's private journal of the preceding year, December 31, 1828, reads: "The only future event from which I promise myself any extraordinary gratification is the return to my native country, which I trust will now soon take place." From Seville again, writing to Peter in March 1829: "I have a craving desire to return to America, which has been increasing on me for the two years past, until now it incessantly haunts my mind and occupies all my dreams." And from the Alhambra itself, in late May of this same year, to his American friend Brevoort at New York: "the happiest day of my life will be when I once more find myself among you all."

Yet such happiness was to be postponed still longer. As July drew to a close Irving was preparing to set out not westward, but east and north toward London. A young Englishman of good family named Sneyd chanced to be passing through Granada on his way home and presented letters of introduction to the famous American. Amiable, an

Oxford graduate in his late twenties, Sneyd was engaged to the daughter of the British consul at Cádiz, and accordingly was eager to return to Spain to be married. But first he had to travel back to that Jane Austen world he seemed to have derived from, meaning to get there by the end of August in order to be presented with a living he had come into worth £1,000 a year. His route to England had been laid out; his conveyance was ready. Irving could hardly expect timing or company more agreeable on a journey that might be perilous and should not be undertaken alone. He wrenched himself away.

Tuesday, July 28, 1829. ". . . Evg, at five oclock leave Granada in company with Mr Raphael Sneyd in Tartana for Murcia escorted by Antonio a long legged tall swarthy portuguese—armed with escopeta—Wind up among wild mountain scenery—Get a last look at the Alhambra Mountains arid & stern." The sun was low in the sky as Irving paused. "The hill on which I stood commanded a glorious view of the city, the Vega, and the surrounding mountains." All this his eyes would never see again: "The setting sun as usual shed a melancholy effulgence on the ruddy towers of the Alhambra. I could faintly discern the balconied window of the tower of Comares, where I had indulged in so many delightful reveries. The bosky groves and gardens about the city were richly gilded with the sunshine, the purple haze of a summer evening was gathering over the Vega; every thing was lovely, but tenderly and sadly so, to my parting gaze." Before the sun did set he must hurry on, in order to carry with him precisely this recollection of the Moorish citadel at its most beautiful. The rumble-tumble mule-drawn *tartana* was staggering forward; Irving, on foot, joined the others—Sneyd and the musket-bearing Antonio—and they proceeded together.

"To our right is the Sierra Nevada—at three leagues distance"—twelve miles—"come to Huetor, a pretty village among trees—put up at posada kept by a Frenchman—."

So he was on his way, was once more to resort, as he noted, to "the expedients of a Spanish posada," whether kept by Frenchmen or otherwise: "break sugar with knife & the back of a chair—Heat water in a chocolate pot, make tea in a jug—spread our mattress on the floor." And up and on the road again at three in the morning.

Inside the *tartana*—a clumsy, gloomy carriage, so Irving described it when the trip was done—"we had two mattresses on which we lolled and which broke the jolting of the machine, these Served us likewise as beds at night; for the matresses of the Spanish Inns are apt to be too dirty and *populous* to be Slept upon with comfort." At least the covering of the cart provided some relief from heat; in early mornings and late afternoons the vehicle would trundle along at something under thirty miles a day. The pace allowed for observation of the countryside: eagles soaring, flocks of white goats, the Moorish look of flat-roofed villages, great firs near Murcia "with grape vines clambering about them &

clusters of grapes hanging among their branches." On past the date groves and glazed-tile domes of Elche they trudged, and through and beyond Alicante, where the hills looked like cast iron and fields were bare and dry that in springtime would be green. The mule plodding ahead of them with its worsted tufts and profusion of bells brought them to the level *vega* of Valencia, beyond those innumerable crosses set along the roadway, beside rice plantations and fields of Indian corn, past "a kind of rude obolisk, with the scull of a robber & murderer hanging in an iron cage: some of the hair remained on the scull . . ."

Nearly two weeks it had taken the travelers to get that far—maybe three hundred and fifty miles—with stops both midday and evening at various primitive inns, where they supped on musk melon or sent Antonio foraging in the village for eggs and tomatoes. In the inns Irving observes that windows in these parts have no glass, notes the muleteers wrapped in their *mantas* asleep on the floor, sees the begging friars and "a little tempest of a chamber maid; in a great fury because she had to prepare rooms for us—Antonio," he adds, is "very authoritative at the Inns with a voice as if from a barrel." And at one squalid *venta* beyond Alicante, "Our mattresses were spread on the floor and, as usual, we lay down in our clothes—much incommoded by fleas and by hungry cats that came prowling after ham that we had brought with us." In fact, "we have been about twelve days in reaching this place," he calculated wearily from Valencia, "in all which time I have not taken off my clothes to go to bed . . ."

But finally they had got to the coast, and lay over a couple of days, resting, awaiting the luggage sent separately. Before breakfast one morning Irving was walking in the crowded market place of Valencia: "Soldiers & housemaids. friar talking & laughing with buxom wife of grocer—a young woman observing them from behind the curtain of an opposite shop." Ever alert to the passing moment, the note taker did what he could to arrest it. "After breakfast walk out with Mr. Sneyd. Ascend the tower of the Cathedral . . ."

But just here, among passing moments at Valencia in the late summer of 1829, Irving's long youth was ending. Pampered youngest son, recipient of his older brothers' benefactions on Grand Tour and later, seeker after secure domestic nests in New York, Birmingham, Dresden, padder about marble courtyards of fairy-tale Granada and loller on mattresses over romantic Spanish mountainsides—ever youthful adventurer gives way at last to a portly middle-aged man of affairs. Irving has yet to journey beyond the frontiers of the New World, hunting buffalo and sleeping beneath prairie stars, but it is a middle-aged man who will travel there, and a noble old man who will return to Spain.

Meanwhile, here at Valencia, having arranged for his trunks to be sent on, Irving was leaving the *tartana*, leaving his seemingly endless youth behind and, with Sneyd, was boarding the regular diligence for Barcelona. Now the dark blue Mediterranean is on their right, and a pleasant breeze blows over them. The countryside abounds with vineyards, figs, corn. At Vinaroz, "a good dinner—fish, flesh, fowl, & game. fine melons, tomatoes, sweet peppers &c black wine. A Catalan at table (merchant of Barcelona) . . . & his companion amuse themselves with bantering a young Frenchman who had been boasting of his good fortunes among the Spanish women." On past the *barranca* separating Valencia from Cataluña, past more crosses, past "an arm of a Robber elevated on a pole & blackening in the Sun." Then, approaching Barcelona from the surrounding mountains, "the huge jingling diligence" is being pulled by seven wild mules that are plunging down the road "without parapets & winding & passing Zig Zag down vast declivities among awful cliffs & ravines—grand sight," with "two or three wild looking fellows scampering beside them, banging them with sticks & lashes, & whooping & hallowing like indians." Thus noisily down toward the city, until at last they were lumbering at more measured pace along its wide streets. "Put up at the Posada de los quatres Naciones Took a warm bath—Excellent baths, wall tiled."

Sneyd had got too much sun and was ill with a fever, so the travelers delayed again to let him rest and to await the arrival of their trunks. A few days passed with Irving reading newspapers to come abreast of the times, sightseeing, making calls: "Dined," on the sixteenth of August, "at the Village of Gracia, in the country house of Mr Ryan— present Mr ———" (the name was retrieved soon after: Dobel, Captain Dobel) "a captain of a Scotch ship—a crusty dry Scotchman. has two young wild boars on board of his ship which at my suggestion he promises to make a present to Sir Walter Scott." For feasting on, or for hunting through the plantations of Abbotsford? Unknown to Irving, who was out of touch with matters at Edinburgh, the enfeebled Scott was past hunting now. But another visit at Barcelona while young Sneyd was recovering put the American firmly in touch with the unsavory present in Spain. Monday, August 17. ". . . We dine" in the Royal Palace "at the Count D'Espagne's—Capt Genl of the province . . . in a very large and handsome salon Dinner a mixture of Spanish, French & English Cooking. and among the dishes were Roast beef & plum pudding. The Count speaks English and is partial to the English."

What precisely did Irving know of this horrifying specimen of humanity, King Ferdinand's iron-fisted administrator of the refractory province of Cataluña? "I had heard much," he later conceded, "of the cruelty of his disposition, and the rigor of his military rule." The Conde de España was a cultivated madman, moved to dance gleefully before the spectacle of his enemies suffering, to exult in mass hangings and mutilations, capable of leveling a troublesome town and leaving only one stone standing, inscribed "*Aquí estuvo Ripoll*"—Here stood Ripoll—

to mark the site. Ruthless, secretive, hated by his own men, half insanely tyrannical in his own family, within a decade he would be beaten mercilessly and drowned by rebellious subordinates. But now at dinner with Irving and other foreign diplomats, the uniformed general was strutting at the summit of his power.

"Capt Gen*l* very affable, talkative, merry—in one of his gay moods. Has the argument & jokes all his own way—He is a Lion," wrote Irving at the time, "joking in his own den." And fifteen years later, from the same city, having returned to the same palace, the American would remember the way the count after this present dinner, among cigars and wine, had amused himself with an underling, come "bustling into the apartment with an air of hurried zeal and momentous import, as if about to make some great revelation." What the functionary brought, however, was news that the captain general had already been told, and had discussed with his English cronies over the roast beef: that the lovely Neapolitan princess María Cristina, then in her early twenties, would be visiting Barcelona on her way to her nuptials; for the princess' gouty uncle, that dissolute king of Spain Ferdinand VII, had decided to be wed again after all, a fourth time, and to his blooming niece, who even then was en route to the ceremony. As Irving watched, the polished governor, possessed in advance of all that the functionary was breathlessly communicating, nevertheless feigned interest, affecting "to receive the information with great surprise," having it repeated over and over, "each time deepening the profundity of his attention; finally he bowed the city oracle quite out of the saloon, and almost to the head of the staircase, and sent him home swelling with the idea that he had communicated a state secret, and fixed himself in the favor of the Count. The latter returned to us laughing immoderately at the manner in which he had played off the little dignitary, and mimicking the voice and manner with which the latter had imparted his important nothings. . . ."

The wit of it may escape us: "his jokes were coarse," as Irving did note, "and his humor inclined to buffoonery." And we may be ready to leave that company. Sneyd is better now, and the travelers have been "overjoyed by the sight of our Trunks which came in the Diligence this morning," Friday, August 21. The following day the American and his eager young companion are on their way north once more, past Gerona, with a stop briefly at the cathedral: "Fine windows of painted glass—women confessing—whispers in twilight . . ."

Scarcely ten days earlier, before reaching Barcelona, Irving had written, "I assure you . . . I shall leave Spain with feelings of great regret. A residence of between three and four years in it has reconciled me to many of its inconveniences and defects, and I have learned more and more to like both the country and the people." But on Sunday, August 23, 1829, after breakfast, he must finally bring this long, productive stay to an end, along the road "leading up the Junquera to the Spanish custom house. a peseta saves the examination of our luggage. At Puente Puerto we come to the frontier line. . . . our baggage slightly examined and sealed—proceed—pass over Zig zag road leading round precipices—our horses going furiously—."

In truth the Spanish years had been productive, redirecting and vigorously stimulating Irving's literary zeal. Some three thousand pages, a million words—a third of what he wrote in a lifetime—are calculated to be about Spain. Even as he left the country in 1829 on his way to Perpignan and Paris, he had in his trunks materials all but completed that would eventually be printed in the form of four separate books as well as numerous shorter sketches, these in addition to his accounts of Columbus and the conquest of Granada already successfully published.

So if the travelers were hurrying now, the speed was more for Sneyd's sake, to get him home to lay claim to his living. Nor for that object could they go fast enough. Nine days and nights through France they traveled incessantly. "The consequence" to the Englishman, Irving records, "was a return of his fever, which confined him to his bed for several days at Paris." Poor Sneyd and his prospects!—that living of £1,000 sterling awaiting him the first of September, and "another living of about the same income would fall to him in the course of a few years, and he was to have about fifteen thousand pounds from his mother." But the amiable Oxonian would never collect, or return to Spain, or marry the following spring the beautiful daughter of the British consul at Cádiz. "All these prospects which had animated him throughout our journey, and had been the themes of our frequent conversation, had made him more and more impatient to get on the nearer he arrived to his journey's end." Thus from his bed in Paris the young man had risen with his first return of strength and hurried ahead. Irving would follow soon after.

To a journey's end, and not in Jane Austen country after all. "Poor fellow! on my arrival in London I was shocked at receiving intelligence of his death!" He had succumbed at the age of twenty-eight. So Irving's early days back in England perforce included scenes, "too painful to be repeated," with the afflicted parents of the deceased, his companion over long Spanish roads through many languorous mornings and evenings.

The present days in London would have been crowded in any case. The new member of the legation was soon established at 9 Chandos Street, Cavendish Square, far from the dreamy Alhambra, and ready to assume his diplomatic duties; but friends were everywhere: Jeffrey and Moore and Campbell and Newton and Leslie and Rogers and Kemble. And the Russian envoy Dolgorouki had been transferred from Madrid to London, and John Howard Payne was on hand, "fresh and fair as a rose . . . as usual up to the ears with negotiations for some half dozen pieces of various kinds." People Irving knew well and those he knew hardly at all applied for help. Could he interest some London bookseller in the poems of the American poet Bryant, in the paintings of Audubon? Could he intercede with an American publisher on behalf of Tom Moore, whose *Life of Byron* was almost finished, or on behalf of old William Godwin, Mary Shelley's father, who had ventured to start another novel this late in life? Irving could and did perform those services, and others like them, to the best of his considerable abilities during these months. And at Lockhart's home he had his heartrending reunion with the ruin of Sir Walter Scott—"Ah, the times are changed, my good fellow, since we went over the Eildon hills together"—and at their London town house found time for frequent visits to the Fosters, dear Dresden friends: "Do you remember you used to come, and often spend the evening with us in Seymour street?"

Indeed, the whole of a varied, eventful past seemed coalescing in these two and a half years Irving spent in England as member of the American Legation. The very appointment of secretary, he had been led to understand, resulted from the recommendation to the State Department of a friend of his youth, Commodore Jack Nicholson—"Little Jack has had a kind of dogged, determined kindness for me now for about twenty-five years, ever since he took a liking for me on our getting tipsy together at Richmond, in Virginia, at the time of Burr's trial." But however it had come about, Irving meant to do his best with the assignment, with petty chores of filing claims and signing passports and attending to destitute seamen, as well as with more delicate matters of negotiating national treaties over West Indian trade. As seldom before—as only during Burr's trial and the War of 1812—he plunged now into the midst of public affairs. "What a stirring moment it is to live in," this in the spring of 1831, from *Middlemarch* England on the eve of the Reform Bill. "I never took such intense interest in newspapers. It seems to me as if life were breaking out anew with me, or that I were entering upon quite a new and almost unknown career of existence . . ." And when his superior became ill, the writer-functionary found himself installed, from June 1831 to April 1832, as acting chargé d'affaires, virtually head of the most crucial of American diplomatic posts. Martin Van Buren, Jackson's newly appointed ambassador to the Court of St. James's, when he arrived in London in the midst of that term, in September, was impressed to discover Irving's vast popularity despite much anti-American feeling—and wrote the President about his fellow officer's competence, about his "untiring disposition for the prompt and successful discharge of business": penning all those official letters on behalf of his country to the likes of Wellington and Earl Aberdeen.

The man of affairs was busy all right, and actively in the center of public life. In other ways he seemed different. "I have a villainous propensity to grow round and robustious, and I fear the beef and pudding of England will complete the ruin of my figure." Thus it was a stouter Irving who accepted the medal of the Royal Society of Literature in London, who journeyed to Oxford in June 1831 to be presented with the degree of Doctor of Civil Law, amid the acclaim of affectionate students calling out the well-loved names: "Knickerbocker!" "Ichabod Crane!" "Rip Van Winkle!"

Yet what the transplanted New Yorker wanted most of all at this time of his life was not awards or service or money or companionship, however agreeable those might be. Most of all he wanted to go home. As far back as five years ago he had written from Madrid, "The fact is that the longer I remain from home the greater charm it has in my eyes and all the colouring that the imagination once gave to distant Europe now gathers about the scenes of my native country. I look forward to my return as to the only event of any desirable kind that may yet be in store for me." The event had been delayed, but the feeling persisted. In London early in 1830 he was still expressing "a most craving desire to visit old friends and old scenes." Now he did have money from royalties— more money perhaps than he had ever had—and had accomplished something during these years abroad, and could return with his head high, as he had longed to be able to do when still in his early thirties and struggling with bankruptcy at Liverpool. Finally he was freed from his duties at the legation, was packing at last, had actually set out for Southampton April 2, 1832, was boarding ship.

Thus, after a brief visit with his brother Peter in Le Havre, Irving began the journey to America. His protracted exile was ending. After forty boisterous days on the ocean the ship dropped anchor; and soon, near sunset of May 21, in his fiftieth year, from the deck of a newsboat and "with a heart swelling with old recollections," Washington Irving was viewing, like Rip himself, a familiar scene that time had transformed. Beyond a thousand crowding masts in the harbor, late sunshine was lighting up steeples and windows of New York, no longer a town but a city, "extending itself over heights I had left covered with green forests."

On one of the city wharves he stepped ashore.

"The packet ship *Havre* arrived last evening," Philip Hone, New York's sometime mayor, gossipy man-about-town, and next-door neighbor of the Irvings in childhood, noted in his diary the following day. "Among the passengers is our distinguished countryman and my old friend Washington Irving, who visits his native country after an absence of seventeen years. I called to see him this morning at his brother's,

Ebenezer Irving. He has grown very fat since I saw him in England in 1821, looks exceedingly well, and is delighted in being once more in his native city. I passed half an hour with him very pleasantly. He talks a great deal, and is in high spirits, a thing not usual with him except when under excitement, as he is at this moment. . . ."

And would continue to be for many days following. Much there was to excite the homecomer—most obviously, all the changes. "The city," the absent John Howard Payne had learned from his sister three years earlier, "has enlarged well on toward Bloomingdale. The Village of Greenwich is in the city—more than a mile beyond is city also . . ." And Hone's own diary is a record of change, as, for example, in an entry the previous fall, mid-November 1831: "A new theater was opened a few evenings since called the Richmond Hill Theater. The house, formerly Col. Aaron Burr's, which was removed some years ago to the corner of Varick and Charlton Streets, has been fitted up, and is, I am told, a very handsome theater." Changes everywhere. For Irving, the sight of so many friends gathering on Bridge Street at Ebenezer's, friends who "absolutely overwhelmed" him with their welcomes and felicitations, together "with the increased beauty, and multiplied conveniences and delights of the city, has rendered my return home wonderfully exciting. I have been in a tumult of enjoyment ever since my arrival; am pleased with everything and everybody, and as happy as mortal being can be."

Those sentiments he transmitted to Peter, on the other side of the Atlantic, ten days after the return, on a Wednesday that he had designated in response to a petition from those varied friends. "Sir," they had written hard upon his heralded reappearance, "A number of your townsmen, many of them the associates of your youth, impatient to evince to you their feelings of gratification at your return among them, to express the interest they have felt in your career in every period of its increasing brilliancy, to pay a just tribute to private worth, and to give you a warm and cordial welcome to your native city, beg that you will appoint some day when you will honor them with your company at"— (it was not to be avoided, the ceremony that the diffident Irving dreaded above all others)—"a public dinner." The petition had been signed by forty-three of New York's most illustrious citizens: Renwick and Ogden and Hoffman and King and Livingston and Kent and Gracie and Colden and Stuyvesant and Hone and too many others to gainsay. "I will, if suitable to your convenience, appoint Wednesday next for that purpose," their townsman had dutifully responded amid appropriate phrases of gratitude, and thus at the City Hotel on the afternoon specified found himself surrounded by three hundred convivial gentlemen, in whose presence he was made to bear with twelve regular toasts, numerous volunteer toasts, speeches of five vice-presidents of the occasion, and at least one speech "in a strain of surprising eloquence" that lasted an hour and a quarter. "A regular Knickerbocker affair," the well-satisfied Hone pronounced it: excellent dinner, enormously successful, even to the utterance of Irving's own remarks. He who had unwittingly bent and cracked a silver fork in his anxiety as he groped to address a small dinner group at Gibraltar had here risen once more, shakily, doubting his self-control, and begun to speak in a voice at first hard to make out. "I trembled for him," one friend admitted later, "until I saw him seize the handle of a knife and commence gesticulating with that; then I knew he would get on."

Although it was the last such speech but one that the writer would ever give—he made sure of that—Irving did manage to articulate thoughts that brought forth applause, huzzas, cheers: about this proudest, happiest moment of his life, about the auspiciousness of his return, about the contrasts between despotic Europe and a free land. "I am asked, how long I mean to remain here?" he intoned. "They know but little of my heart or my feelings who can ask me this question. I answer, as long as I live." And the room exploded with shouts and prolonged clapping, so that the speaker, who had meant to go on, seized his chance and sat down.

His friend Brevoort, whom he had seen in Europe before setting sail, read of the performance and from Fontainebleau in the course of his travels wrote a month later, "I doubted whether your nerves would carry you through a public speech, upon an occasion so trying—but go to, you are an orator." Be that as it may, Irving had soon grown restless with the adulation pouring out of the City Hotel and into the following weeks. It showed no signs of diminishing. *The Alhambra*, just published, swelled the interest in his person and the plaudits for what he had achieved; *The New-York Mirror*, for example, was exulting at length in late June about "delightful grace of language . . . impressed in every page, every line, every word, with the reality of truth and the glow of nature . . . scenes stretch away before you; his people move, look, and walk with an individuality and a force only to be produced by the hand of a master . . ."

The only sure course for avoiding further embarrassment was for the master to stay out of New York till the clamor died down, to see for himself this vast and bustling country so long forsaken. Already, soon after the banquet, he had journeyed to Washington, and as the season progressed visited the White Mountains and Saratoga Springs. By late summer the chronicler of byways was on the move again, but over more distant terrain, having reached as far as the river town of Cincinnati, after "a very interesting tour through Ohio." His traveling party had landed "at Ashtabula, a small place on the shore of Lake Erie. From thence we proceeded along the ridge road parallel to the lake to Cleveland, and thence through the centre of the State to this city, where we arrived last evening," the first of September, 1832. "I have been greatly delighted with the magnificent woodland scenery of Ohio, and with the exuberant fertility of the soil . . ."

That fertile soil, Irving presumed, would eventually make Ohio "a perfect garden spot. When the forests are cleared away, however, the country will be a vast plain, diversified here and there by a tract of rolling hills; and nothing will compensate for the loss of those glorious trees, which now present the sublime of vegetation."

John Brown, Ohio settler, had done his share to clear trees in these parts—had, in fact, a few years earlier removed from the white house in Hudson, near Cleveland, that he had built for his family along the Underground Railroad, in order to clear trees from more wilderness, eighty miles away, in northwestern Pennsylvania. Land was cheap out there, and the woods were oak and hemlock, good bark for tanning. So in May 1826, with Irving at Madrid buried in Rich's library ("all day at Columbus"; "at Columb all day"), John Brown had sold his house and led his growing family eastward to Randolph Township, ten miles into the forest beyond the village of Meadville.

That summer the tanner cleared twenty-five acres and built a two-room log house and a barn and a tannery large enough for eighteen vats. The few other settlers in the area viewed him with awe: a doer. By October he had ten or a dozen hands working for him. He was surveying roads, introducing blooded stock into the region, starting a school, distributing "good moral books and papers," soon had set up a post office and applied for the position of postmaster. As others followed him into the area, he would inquire of the head of the household "whether he was an observer of the Sabbath, opposed to Slavery and a Supporter of the Gospel and common Schools, if So all was right with him, if not he was looked upon by Brown with Suspicion. . . ."

And Brown's wife, the *"remarkably plain"* Dianthe, was having more children. She had ten in all. Her husband reared strictly the eight who survived. There would be no foolish noise in that household, no idleness, no disobedience, no lies, no fantasies. When he was three Jason was thrashed severely for insisting that a dream he had dreamed was real. John, Jr., kept an account book:

For disobeying mother . . . . .8 lashes
  " unfaithfulness at work 3   "
  " telling a lie 8   "

Food at Brown's table "was always plain and Simple all luxuries being despensed with and not allowed in the family and in the year 1830 he rigidly adopted the tetotal temperance principles." Breakfast would be followed by a Bible reading, and on Sundays Brown would herd his family and employees and what neighbors he could cajole into the second floor of his tannery and preach to them: "Our stupidity ingratitude & disobedience we have great reason to mourn & repent of." "Is not the reflection that full, & complete justice will at last be done enough to make the very Heavens & Earth to tremble?"

But the tanner's new life in Pennsylvania was not prospering as well as it had begun. Brown's wife had grown distracted, was ill, some said was out of her mind. Through 1831 Brown himself was suffering with ague. The four-year-old Frederick died that year, and in the following year Dianthe, pregnant once more, grew even worse, so that in the very month when Washington Irving, triumphantly restored to his homeland, was making his way through Ohio, this obscure woman gave birth to her tenth child, stillborn, and herself expired. "Randolph, Pa., August 11, 1832. Dear Father: We are again smarting under the rod of our Heavenly Father. Last night about eleven o'clock my affectionate, dutiful and faithful Dianthe (to use her own words) bade 'farewell to Earth.' My own health is so poor that I have barely strength to give you a short history of what passed . . ."

Brown would marry again, ten months later, this time a girl half his age, a blacksmith's daughter, sixteen years old, engaged to come spin for the widower's household. His second wife, Mary Day, bore him thirteen children ("Be fruitful, and multiply"), but their offspring would enter a world increasingly grim. The tannery business was failing. Now the father was short of money, was falling ever more deeply in debt. He had hardly enough funds for a down payment on an ox team. Cash was scarce everywhere; credit became scarcer.

Beset with such adversities, John Brown nevertheless continued throughout his thirties to ponder and react to the outrage of slavery. During the decade when such names as William Lloyd Garrison and Nat Turner and Elijah Lovejoy became prominent, the tanner in his clearing in northwestern Pennsylvania was forming a plan. To his brother in Hudson he wrote in the fall of 1834: "Since you left me I have been trying to devise some means whereby I might do something in a practical way for my poor fellow-men who are in bondage, and having fully consulted the feelings of my wife and my three boys, we have agreed to get at least one negro boy or youth, and bring him up as we do our own,—viz., give him a good English education, learn him what we can about the history of the world, about business, about general subjects, and, above all, try to teach him the fear of God." The family had "all agreed to submit to considerable privation in order to buy" a slave, if no other way to acquire the youth were possible.

But times got worse; no amount of privation could make Brown's plan feasible. By the following spring, 1835, the tanner had resigned his postmastership, abandoned his luckless holdings in Pennsylvania, and, on borrowed money, was leading his family back to the village of Franklin Mills—now Kent—not far from where he had set out nearly a decade earlier to make his way to prosperity.

The period that followed Brown's return to Ohio, from 1835 forward, was even bleaker than before, a period filled with what seemed apparently endless and unrelieved failures and losses. The Panic of 1837 all but destroyed him. He tried his hand at land speculating, disastrously. He tried surveying, sheepherding, cattle droving. "The cattle business has succeeded about as I expected, but I am now some what in fear that I shall fail of getting the money I expected on the loan. Should that be the will of Providence I know of no other way but we must consider ourselves verry poor for our debts must be paid . . ."

He did fail, and the debts could not be paid. Creditors harried him, hauled him into court. He borrowed more, shuffled loans, could not redeem them. His affairs became hopelessly entangled, and finally, in September 1842, John Brown was declared bankrupt.

Of those very times, however—grim as they seem—a son of his grown into old age in our century would recall affectionately "a large living-room" with "a fireplace ten feet long, with huge andirons and a crane and hooks to hang kettles upon. We boys would cut logs two and three feet through for the fireplace, and at night, in winter, two great back-logs were covered with ashes to hold fire. Father would sit in front of a lively fire and take up us children one, two, or three at a time, and sing until bedtime." The house was a whitewashed log house in Richfield, Ohio, with a creek dam and millpond, and mud turtles to fatten and feed on. Another "favorite dish with us children was corn-meal mush cooked the whole afternoon long in a huge iron caldron, and served with rich milk or cream." Scripture and prayer would start and end each day's work. And the image of the stern Calvinist, readier than most fathers to thrash in an age when few spared the switch, seems softened in recollection: "During prayers all stood, father leaning against the back of a chair upreared on its forward legs, dead to the world and to the pranks of his unregenerate boys, who slyly prodded each other with pins and trampled upon each other's toes to relieve the tension. . . ."

Like Job, John Brown had need to pray for strength to bear his lot. These same years, he later admitted, he had felt "a steady, strong, desire; *to die*." He had been declared bankrupt in 1842, but that was not the end of his troubles. The following year, he wrote an absent member of the family concerning four of his children, ages nine to one: "On the 4th Sept Charles was taken with the Dysentery and died on the 11th, about the time that Charles died Sarah, Peter, & Austin were taken with the same complaint. Austin died on the 21st, Peter on the 22d & Sarah on the 23d and were all buried together in one grave. This has been to us all a bitter cup indeed, and we have drunk deeply, but still the Lord reigneth and blessed be his great and holy name forever." Then simply, poignantly the dazed father adds: "They were all children towards whom perhaps we might have felt a little partial but they all now lie in a little row together. . . ."

His fellow countryman Washington Irving had fared far better than had Brown during this decade, although Irving's life, too, had been visited with cares. From Cincinnati in the fall of 1832 the author restored to his homeland had proceeded to roam the American frontier, where he had experiences that furnished him with the basis for a different kind of writing, as well as with renewed interests and new and renewed friendships to be considered in later pages. In brief, during the 1830s Irving was engaged in reestablishing himself permanently in his native country after a long absence: publicly by publishing books on American subjects, privately—after returning from his western travels —by purchasing and lavishing improvements on a fixed abode at last, near Tarrytown along the east bank of the Hudson north of Manhattan. A farmhouse purchased in 1835 was remodeled, enlarged, and eventually rechristened Sunnyside, and at this altogether comfortable residence of turrets and terrace with views of the Tappan Zee, the famous author gathered his family around him: his brother Ebenezer and Ebenezer's five daughters, his sister Catharine and her daughter—as well, finally, as his cherished brother Peter, who had left America as long ago as 1808 with a letter from Theodosia Burr to her father in exile in England. Now, twenty-eight years later, in 1836 (the year of Burr's death, on Staten Island), the aged and ailing Peter had been induced to brave the transatlantic crossing a last time, enduring the dreaded month and more of continuous seasickness in order that he might live out his days among family on native ground.

But the days that remained to him were not many. Peter died unexpectedly, in his sixty-sixth year, in the summer of 1838, some twenty-five months after having returned to New York to take his place, "cozily quartered," among the family at what would become Sunnyside. His death was a severe blow to his younger brother, who had been for so long his companion—in early New York, in England, France, Spain: "Every day, every hour I feel how completely Peter and myself were intertwined together in the whole course of our existence"—this to their sister nearly three months after the death. All the other members of the immediate family had long since married, "and had families of their own to engross or divide their sympathies, and to weaken the fraternal tie." But Peter, like Washington, had remained a bachelor. Now, although "surrounded by affectionate relatives," the survivor felt after the loss of his favorite brother "that none can be what he was to me; none can take so thorough an interest in my concerns; to none can I so confidingly lay open my every thought and feeling, and expose every fault and foible, certain of such perfect toleration and indulgence."

In this dejected state of mind Irving tried to write, but even that activity—especially that—reminded him of Peter: "My literary pursuits have been so often carried on by his side, and under his eye." The *Morning Chronicle* and *The History of New York. The Sketch Book.* The plays in Paris. *Columbus* in Madrid. "I have been so accustomed to talk over every plan with him, and, as it were, to think aloud when in his presence, that I cannot open a book, or take up a paper, or recall a past vein of thought, without having him instantly before me, and finding myself completely overcome . . ."

Yet he struggled on to cope with his loss, and before the end of that year, 1838, had begun to write himself out of his despondency. "Happily, within the last month," Irving could report at the beginning of December, "I have been once more enabled to get my pen into motion; and the effect has been most salutary on my spirits." All the more so because his investments, as usual, were unproductive, the number of his dependents had increased through these years of panic and depression, and he had been unable for a long time past to drive himself to write for publication.

What he had now turned to with renewed interest had emerged from his Spanish experiences. Already, in 1835, he had published additional prose on early Spain, developed, as he said, from "venerable, parchment-bound tomes, picked up here and there about the peninsula": the "Legend of Don Roderick," the "Legend of the Subjugation of Spain," the "Legend of Count Julian and His Family." But in the aftermath of Peter's death he recalled a task begun more than a decade ago in Madrid and noted in his journal as having occupied a week or so of labor at the end of 1827: "wrote all day at Friar Sahaguns conquest of Mexico." Again, in Seville a year and a half later, Irving was writing through eighty-six leaves of manuscript translating further from Sahagún's *Historia de la conquista de México.* Near Cádiz, at Puerta de Santa María, October 21, 1828: "Read in Solis Hist. Mexico." Next day: "Write at Mexican Story. . . ." And in 1832, not long after his return to America, he had confided to a friend, who had recorded the confidence that Irving "had formed his plan to write some standard works, which should long be read—He selected the history of Columbus for one—and let me tell you he has the conquest of Mexicco, and the life of Washington for two others—"

To that stirring subject, then—Cortés and the Aztec Moctezuma— Irving had now returned with mounting excitement: "I had intended to write Marianne a letter the week before last, but I got into a vein of literary occupation—the first I had had for a long time—and it was too important an event to be trifled with; so I nursed the mood along, to get it completely under way, and had to give up all letter writing."

Now, late in 1838, having served as Irving's "daily occupation for about three months," the rough draft that would form the first volume was done, and the author was deep in the contemplation of this other astounding adventure, in describing which he meant to carry along "the reader with the discoverers and conquerors, letting the newly explored countries break upon him as it did upon them . . ." We were to accompany Cortés on his march across Mexico, growing familiar with "objects, places, customs, as they awakened curiosity and interest, and required to be explained for the conduct of the story." Along the way, from people on the seaboard, from messengers of Moctezuma, we would have overheard vague accounts of a great and powerful city ahead of us, farther inland. Every step, as we advanced westward with Cortés and his band of four hundred, "would"—so Irving intended—"have been a step developing some striking fact, yet the distance would still have been full of magnificent mystery." With the conquistadores we would behold Mexico at last from surrounding heights, the incredible city spread out far below us, "shining with its vast edifices, its glassy lakes, its far-stretching causeways . . ." And over those causeways—the snow-capped volcanoes silent against the blue sky—we would at length pass with Cortés and enter, "full of curiosity and wonder, on every side beholding objects of novelty, indicating a mighty people, distinct in manners, arts, and civilization from all the races of the Old World. . . ."

Thus at a later date did Irving reflect wistfully on the book he never got to write, this "pendant to my Columbus," full of narrative and action and character in strong relief, as well as fascinating, accurate information that he would have allowed to emerge naturally in the course of the story. But with his materials assembled and the writing three months along, the author was at work one winter day in the New York Society Library on Chambers Street when he was accosted by an acquaintance, a friend of the historian William Hickling Prescott, whose *History of the Reign of Ferdinand and Isabella* had recently been published in Boston. Irving's present interlocutor was sounding him, on behalf of Prescott, to discover what subject America's most famous author was then occupied with, as the younger historian in Boston "did not wish to come again across the same ground with him"—Irving's *Columbus* and *Conquest of Granada* having treated two of the most interesting aspects of Prescott's own subsequent book. "Mr. Irving asked: 'Is Mr. Prescott engaged upon an American subject?' 'He is,' was the reply. 'What is it? Is it the Conquest of Mexico?' Mr. Irving rapidly asked. 'It is,' answered Cogswell. 'Well, then,' said Mr. Irving, 'I *am* engaged upon that subject, but tell Mr. Prescott I abandon it to him . . .' "

The gesture arose "from a warm and sudden impulse," and Irving professed never to have regretted making it. But "I doubt," he did allow himself to mention privately some five years later, when the other historian's work was done, "whether Mr. Prescott was aware of the extent of the sacrifice I made." For a long time the subject had been a favorite one, and "when I gave it up to him, I in a manner gave him up my bread, for I depended upon the profit of it to recruit my waning finances . . ."

Those profits would unquestionably have been substantial. But now Prescott (who admitted frankly that he would otherwise have forsaken the field in despair) had his subject to himself, while Irving turned listlessly to contributing trivialities to the recently founded *Knicker-bocker* magazine in order to help pay bills at Sunnyside. But he was harassed by worries—Ebenezer's declining health, for one, that made it increasingly difficult for the older brother to support himself. Moreover, "How I"—Irving, here in the early 1840s—"shall be able to keep all afloat with my cramped and diminished means, and with debts incurred on behalf of others hanging over and threatening me is an equally harrassing question. These things break my rest and disturb my waking thoughts . . . However, as poor Scott said, 'I have a good deal of work in me yet' . . ."

Relief did come, but not from his writing. It came from an entirely unexpected source. Daniel Webster, Secretary of State, recommended to President Tyler that Washington Irving be appointed America's ambassador to Spain. In Manhattan, February 10, 1842, the nominee heard the news, and in the capital Webster remarked that "Washington Irving is now the most astonished man in the city of New York." For the honor had been unsolicited and unsought. During the decade since his return home Irving had been urged to run for Congress and had declined. He had been urged to run for Mayor of New York and had declined. President Van Buren had offered him the Secretaryship of the Navy, and that office, too, he had declined. But Spain was different, so that hardly more than a week later the veteran of the London legation was formally addressing Secretary Webster: "Sir, I accept, with no common feelings of pride and gratitude, the honorable post offered me by the Government, of Envoy Extraordinary and Minister Plenipotentiary to Spain. . . ."

He would come to regard this as the crowning honor of his life, this appointment that the Senate had warmly, bipartisanly approved. "Ah," Henry Clay had exclaimed, "this is a nomination everybody will concur in! If the President would send us such names as this, we should never have any difficulty." And soon after, to Irving personally, Clay had written: "Take with you, my dear sir, the fervent wishes of one whose sentiments of regard have remained unabated during twenty-eight years, for your success in your public mission, and for increased fame in your literary pursuits." The senator from Kentucky was expressing the feelings of many about what Webster called the most distinguished appointment of Tyler's administration.

But before he could set out, Irving had much to do—assigning his nephew power of attorney, putting his brother Ebenezer in charge of Sunnyside ("Try if you cannot beat me at farming and gardening"), shopping, packing, making his will, journeying to Washington to receive instructions. And in late March the author-diplomat was again being proffered a public dinner, this one of farewell, by his persistent townsmen. But stoutly, if courteously, he begged off this time: "I cannot but remember with deep sensibility a similar testimonial of their good will with which I was surprised and overpowered ten years since, on my return home from so long an absence . . . it is a proud gratification to me to find that, after ten years of familiar intercourse, the same good will still appears to be exhibited. . . . Thus have I continually been paid, and overpaid, and paid again for all the little good I may have effected in my somewhat negligent and fortuitous career, until, at times, I feel as if, in acquiescing in such over-measured rewards, I am tacitly pocketing what is not due me.

"In the present instance," however, "that shall not be the case." The business of preparing to assume a post "of important and untried responsibility," so the ambassador-designate deftly explained, left him neither the leisure nor the frame of mind to join in such a festivity. But no doubt equally in Irving's thoughts to urge a refusal were memories of the discomfort he had experienced a few weeks earlier at a dinner that he had not been able to escape, in honor of someone else, to be sure, but over which America's favorite author had been obliged to preside.

Many years before, in 1823, Irving in Dresden had sent Lord Byron, whom he had never met, an inscribed copy of *The Sketch Book*. The action is notable because of its rarity; the American had almost never presumed to initiate correspondence with other writers to whom he was personally a stranger. But recently he had done just that again, this time sending a note of appreciation to "that glorious fellow" Charles Dickens. And the author of *The Old Curiosity Shop* had responded at length and most earnestly. "My dear Sir: There is no man in the world who could have given me the heartfelt pleasure you have, by your kind note of the 13th of last month. There is no living writer, and there are very few among the dead, whose approbation I should feel so proud to earn. And with everything you have written upon my shelves, and in my thoughts, and in my heart of hearts, I may honestly and truly say so. . . . My dear Washington Irving, I cannot thank you enough for your cordial and generous praise, or tell you what deep and lasting gratification it has given me. . . ."

Not long afterward, the popular young novelist and social reformer in London was all alive to cross the Atlantic: "Washington Irving writes me that if I went, it would be a triumph for me from one end of the States to the other, as was never known in any nation." Thus, early in 1842, with Irving in the midst of preparations to depart for Spain,

Dickens, just turned thirty, was arriving for his first visit to America. Along the East River to the Bay, among "localities, attractive to all readers of famous Diedrich Knickerbocker's History," the Englishman was observing villas and heaps of buildings and ships' mast and flapping sails and crowded ferries, and up Broadway was noting all the ladies in rainbow silks and satins with their blue parasols and fluttering ribbons, and the beaux in tasseled cloaks thronging the sidewalks under the Lombardy poplars. He took note of vagabond pigs rooting in the gutters, of huge blocks of ice being lugged into shops and bars, of pineapples and watermelons piled up for sale, of "the city's hum and buzz, . . . the ringing of bells, the barking of dogs, the clattering of wheels . . ." And while he was here Dickens, too, the beloved Boz, must be given a public dinner, over which only one American could be allowed to officiate.

Accordingly, at seven on Friday evening, February 18, 1842, two hundred and thirty gentlemen were sitting down together at the Carlton House, and an abashed Washington Irving was on hand, dreading the moment when he must rise before them all. "I shall certainly break down!" he had predicted glumly and repeatedly beforehand, and now with the manuscript of his speech—maybe a dozen pages—under his plate, the moment had come. The president of the assembly, Irving himself, was arising amid long-continued and deafening applause that only made matters worse. Forgetting his notes in his terror, he opened his mouth, got through two or three sentences, hesitated, made a couple of attempts to proceed, gave up, and ended lamely with the toast, "Charles Dickens, the guest of the nation."

" 'There!' said he, as he resumed his seat under a repetition of the applause which had saluted his rising; 'there! I told you I should break down, and I've done it.' "

It mattered to no one but Irving. The crowd loved him and loved Dickens, too, that master public performer who even then had stood to respond felicitously with a speech of his own: "Washington Irving! Why, gentlemen, I don't go upstairs to bed two nights out of the seven . . . without taking Washington Irving under my arm; . . . Washington Irving—Diedrich Knickerbocker—Geoffrey Crayon—why, where can you go that they have not been there before? Is there an English farm—is there an English stream, an English city, or an English country-seat, where they have not been?" Who, Dickens asked, could travel among Italian peasants or the bandits of the Pyrenees without remembering Irving? "Go farther still—go to the Moorish fountains, sparkling full in the moonlight," and had not Irving "peopled the Alhambra, and made eloquent its shadows?" Had he not crossed the dark Atlantic with Columbus, and made Rip Van Winkle at his game of ninepins an inseparable part of the Catskills? America well knew, the visitor was gracefully concluding, "how to do honour to her own literature, and that of other lands," by choosing "Washington Irving for her representative in the country of Cervantes."

Applause, and more applause. The dinner was a huge success, and equally successful were meetings in weeks ahead between Boz and Geoffrey Crayon in Washington (where in a crowd at the White House a lady grabbed the hat of the dismayed Irving and put it on her head so that she might have that to boast about for the rest of her life), and in Baltimore (where the two authors were observed sipping through separate straws at one mighty mint julep, Irving moved often to utter "that captivating laugh of his," which Dickens described as "the brightest and best that I have ever heard").

When the meetings ended, the English visitor would write this to Irving: "Wherever you go, God bless you! What pleasure I have had in seeing and talking with you, I will not attempt to say. I shall never forget it as long as I live. What *would* I give, if we could have but a quiet week together! Spain is a lazy place, and its climate an indolent one. But if you have ever leisure under its sunny skies, to think of a man who loves you, and holds communion with your spirit oftener, perhaps, than any other person alive—leisure from listlessness, I mean—and will write to me in London, you will give me an inexpressible amount of pleasure." He signed the letter, "Your affectionate friend, Charles Dickens."

As for Irving, however mellow were his own recollections, he had at any rate been cured of public dinners, and declined the one proposed to bid him farewell shortly before his departure for Madrid, as he avoided—when the time came to leave—saying goodbye even to his beloved relatives at Sunnyside. Instead, he wrote them a letter aboard the *Independence* as the ship made ready to set sail from New York, April 10, 1842, to bear its reluctant passenger a third time—and this the last—eastward to Europe.

Now he was landing in Bristol. No longer by horse-drawn coach, now on a lovely spring day he was being hurried across England by railroad, twenty-five miles an hour and in amazing comfort, as though the rider were still in his Voltaire chair at Sunnyside. And now he was quartered in London, in the Little Cloisters of Westminster Abbey, within hearing of chimes and an organ pealing. "Our windows look out upon a green lawn, shaven like velvet, shaded by lofty trees, with rooks sailing and cawing about them, and partly surrounded by Gothic edifices." From within this unlikely dwelling an older Irving—fifty-nine now, almost twice young Dickens' age—could remember earlier visits to the same building, which had inspired one of the best essays in *The Sketch Book*. Living within the Abbey walls was "like my sojourn in the halls of the Alhambra. Am I always to have my dreams turned into realities?"

But the England of postchaises was all but gone, and the people had changed. Irving visited Murray's drawing room with heart in throat, saw Tom Moore looking thinner, more careworn (and the Irish poet and friend of Byron rushed to Irving with delight: "the man of all others I wanted to shake hands with once more"). Leslie was on hand, but white-haired, and old Rogers hung on, almost eighty now, and Irving met the twenty-three-year-old Queen Victoria: "quite low in stature, but well formed and well rounded. Her countenance, though not decidedly hand-some, is agreeable and intelligent." And he managed emotional visits to his sister's family at Birmingham.

Then across the Channel, up the Seine to Rouen. But everything seemed different; he was older, and alone. Peter, who had so often ac-companied him among these scenes, was no longer with him. One quiet garden, "with shady walks, and shrubberies, and seats, behind the old Gothic church of St. Ouen, at Rouen," had been Peter's "favorite resort during his solitary residence in that city, and where he used to pass his mornings with his book, amusing himself with the groups of loungers and of nursery maids and children. I felt my heart completely give way when I found myself in that garden. I was for a time a complete child. My dear, dear brother! As I write, the tears are gushing from my eyes."

Thus, from Paris, an older traveler set words down as another spring advanced. "My visit to Europe has by no means the charm of former visits. Scenes and objects have no longer the effect of novelty with me. I am no longer curious to see great sights or great people . . ." Irving's favorite niece was here in Paris, married to a son of his old friend Storrow, so he might rest agreeably through six weeks, until he was joined by his attaché, young Carson Brevoort, son of another old friend, and by his secretary of legation, the twenty-nine-year-old Alex-ander Hamilton, grandson of the patriot who had fallen at Weehawken. At last the diplomatic party had assembled and was moving southward together, through Bordeaux, Bayonne, over the Pyrenees. By mid-summer, July 25, 1842 (shortly before a federal court in distant Ohio declared the tanner John Brown bankrupt), they arrived in Madrid.

Irving was here, so far from Sunnyside, in part out of a sense of duty, in part for the salary that he felt his household needed: "I shall be able to bestow a little more money on the place now, to put it in good heart and good order." But while he was here he also meant to make progress on a literary undertaking already begun, more ambitious than anything attempted before, nothing less than a complete and long-delib-erated life of his namesake, George Washington. "I shall," he had in-formed Ebenezer overconfidently, recalling the different Spanish capital he had known fifteen years before, "apply myself steadily and vigorously to my pen, which I shall be able to do at Madrid, where there are few things to distract one's attention . . ."

*　*　*

The coming weeks and months would reveal much in Madrid to distract the ambassador, so that through the four and a half years of this second stay he would advance his work on Washington no more than a few brief chapters. "Spanish history has at all times born the air of romance," he would be writing not long after this second arrival, "and does so especially at this moment." On his earlier sojourn the author had immersed himself in Spain's past: the Moorish subjugation of the penin-sula, the Christian reconquest, the unification under Ferdinand and Isabella, the voyages of Columbus that offered the newly unified state the basis of a global empire. Now Irving came to know intimately the country that, from such grand beginnings, Spain had become in his own day.

When the ambassador reached Madrid this second time, a coach-maker's son and soldier of fortune was firmly in command of the Spanish nation. That blooming Italian princess, arriving to marry her uncle King Ferdinand in 1829, just as Irving was leaving Spain at the end of his earlier sojourn, had done her duty by presenting the dissolute monarch with heirs: two daughters. The elder of the two was now, on Irving's return, still only eleven. On the child's behalf her mother, María Cristina, had reigned for a while after the king's death in the 1830s; but she had quarreled with ministers and generals and retired into exile in France. The most prominent of those generals had succeeded the queen mother at the center of power. Accordingly, to Baldomero Espartero as regent was His Excellency Washington Irving, in gold-braided uniform and dress sword, presenting his credentials August 1, 1842.

For his audience Irving was "introduced into an anteroom of spacious dimensions, with busts of Espartero in two of the corners, and a picture of him in one of his most celebrated battles"—standard totali-tarian décor. "Some of his officers and aides-de-camp were in this room . . . After a little while, we (Mr. Vail, Hamilton, and myself) were ushered into an inner saloon, at one end of which Espartero stationed himself, with Count Almodovar, Minister of State, on his right hand. I advanced, and read in Spanish a short address": To the illustrious Regent the American envoy is honored to deliver a message from the President of the United States for Her Majesty the Queen of Spain, and to express sentiments of good will and abiding respect of the peoples of America for the peoples of Spain, with hopes of still closer bonds of comity between the two nations, and the ardent wish of the one for the prosperity and glory of Spain under its present constitutional form of government. Etc., etc. The Regent answered with comparable flourishes, finding somehow a basis for comparing Presidents Tyler and Washing-ton, before the brief ceremony at Buena Vista was concluded.

But more was to come. "It being signified to us that the Queen would receive us at the royal palace, we drove thither"—the mile or so across town along Alcalá, through Puerta del Sol, to the palace gates.

At his destination the American emissary was kept waiting some little time in the apartment of the Minister of State, before word arrived that the Queen was ready. "We accordingly passed through the spacious court, up the noble staircase, and through the long suites of apartments of this splendid edifice, most of them . . . vacant, the casements closed to keep out the heat, so that twilight reigned throughout the mighty pile."

Sixteen years earlier Irving had walked through these chambers that were "now silent and somber," in attendance at "grand court occasions in the time of Ferdinand VII, when they were glittering with all the splendor of a court . . ." Now, in a dim salon hung with tapestries, under a high vaulted ceiling, the party of the American ambassador was being directed to wait for the arrival of that deceased king's reigning daughter. A door at the far end was opened "to an almost interminable range of other chambers, through which, at a distance, we had a glimpse of some indistinct figures in black. They glided into the saloon slowly, and with noiseless steps": three figures—an elderly tutor, a middle-aged governess, and the child who was queen.

Isabella—namesake of the most excellent of Spanish monarchs— "received me with a grave and quiet welcome, expressed in a very low voice." I hear, she told him, with the greatest satisfaction the expressions of true friendship which you have conveyed in the name of the President of the United States, in delivering to me the letter which accredits you near my Person. . . . "She is nearly twelve years of age, and is sufficiently well grown for her years. She has a somewhat fair complexion, quite pale, with bluish or light gray eyes; a grave demeanor, but a graceful deportment." The agreeable recollection, the eleven-year-old was continuing, which you mention to me of the illustrious queen whose name I bear and whose throne I occupy doubly strengthens my affection toward this part of the New World which she discovered, and whose prosperity is for the same reason dear to my heart. . . .

"I could not but regard her with deep interest," writes Irving of that interview, "knowing what important concerns depended upon the life of this fragile little being, and to what a stormy and precarious career she might be destined." The destiny of the child was being shaped even as she and the elderly gentleman from America stood exchanging compliments in a dim palatial hall. Even now, her mother in exile in Paris—together with "certain reverend crowned heads and grey diplomatists, in neighbouring countries"—was plotting a dynastic marriage from among several possibilities, intent on choosing not the bridegroom suited to Isabella, but the one who would further the interests of those plotters best. And beyond the palace, debates were swirling among politicians concerning when the girl should be declared of age. Fourteen was the expected time—two years hence—but one party wanted her to assume the throne earlier, to forestall any effort by her uncle Don Carlos to seize power; the other wanted to delay the ascension—to eighteen perhaps—to allow her liberal tutor more time to instruct her in constitutional ways. Now the object of such attentions was finishing her reply to the American ambassador: The proper appointment which your country has made of the worthy interpreter of its feelings will be a new proof of the friendliness which happily exists between the United States and the Spanish nation. And Irving, listening, was moved again by her vulnerability: "her solitary position, also, separated from all her kindred except her little sister, a mere effigy of royalty in the hands of statesmen, and surrounded by the formalities and ceremonials of state . . ."

Of those ceremonials he would see more a few weeks later, in the fall, when the queen again received the American ambassador at the Royal Palace in company with other envoys—"a row of dignified diplomatic personages, some of them well stricken in years, and all of them sage representatives of Governments, bowing with profound reverence, and conjuring up nothings to say to a couple of little girls." Light was flooding through the windows, and Isabella was dressed in white: "my whole impression," wrote the ambassador, "is of a more cheerful kind than at my first audience." With some apprehension the children were approaching the diplomatic line, but after the first couple of exchanges, they seemed more at ease. At his turn before the queen, Irving expressed regret that his limited command of Spanish made it difficult for him to address her as he would wish. ("I do not know," he later teased when writing his sister at Sunnyside, "whether I ought to impart these diplomatic conversations with royalty, as these are the verbal links that connect the destinies of nations. However, for once, I'll venture confiding in your secrecy.") But you speak it very well, the queen had answered, "with a smile, and a little flirt of her fan. I shook my head negatively. 'Do you like Spain?' said she. 'Very much,' replied I, and I spoke sincerely. She smiled again, gave another little clack of her fan, bowed, and passed on."

Her skin, by the way, is not good, but rather "rough and somewhat mealy"; so Irving confides further to his rapt relatives back home. She bathes often, however, and (he feels sure) will outgrow the defect. Meanwhile, her younger sister, although still very much a child, is as pretty as any princess should be. At the end of the line the two girls have crossed the hall to return to their places, and "on being prompted, bowed to us; upon which we made respectful reverences, and retired, taking care, as we withdrew, not to turn our backs upon royalty."

Already the emissary from overseas had felt his heart go out to the little monarch, as it would for the rest of his life—no matter how she grew and changed, no matter what he heard about her in the sensational years that lay ahead. For Isabella was destined to become the scandalous laughingstock of Europe, in her twenties and thirties would conduct the most dissolute and at the same time rigidly pious court on the Continent, praying for hours on cold church stones, then rising to indulge herself with lovers beyond number—Serrano and Mirall and the Marquis de Bedmar and Colonel Gandara and Don José de Arana and Tirso Obregón and Emilio Arrieto and Puig Moltó and an American dental assistant named McKeon and the swaggering Carlos Marfori and a certain Haltman—until efforts had finally to be made to explain her "terrible constitutional malady" in physiological terms, as the result of a vaginal eczema. Some explanation would seem called for; yet all the while, in beginning her later days at three in the afternoon and ending them at five in the morning, this little girl grown to porcine womanhood was to dance and play through much of her reign "without a thought for business, careless of the world's talk, and no more anxiety upon her brow than if her life had been one of perpetual sunshine."

Even now, however, in the fall of 1842, during Irving's second audience with the twelve-year-old, clouds were hovering. An insurrection would soon emphasize the instability of her position. Barcelona, on the east coast, was in revolt again, and Espartero as regent was assembling his troops to march the three hundred and fifty miles from Madrid overland to deal personally with the troublesome Catalans. "The present insurrection," according to Irving, "seems to have broken out suddenly and accidentally, some trifling affray with custom house officers having been the spark which has set the combustible community in a flame." And on the grand esplanade of the Prado, near the Regent's palace (in modern Madrid, headquarters of the Ministry of War, cater-cornered from the great post office at Cibeles), several thousand government troops were on parade:

"It was a bright, sunshiny day. About two o'clock, the Regent sallied forth from Buena Vista, at the head of his staff. He is a fine martial figure, and was arrayed in full uniform, with towering feathers, and mounted on a noble gray charger with a flowing mane, and a long silken tail that almost swept the ground. He rode along the heads of the columns, saluting them with his gauntleted hand, and receiving cheers wherever he went."

Before his soldiery the general pauses from time to time, greeting troops of horsemen. When he returns to the center of the esplanade, he draws his sword as if to speak to the entire assembly. At once all is silent: "I do not know," writes the witness Irving, "that ever I was more struck by anything, than by this sudden quiet of an immense multitude." Pacing his horse slowly back and forth over a space of some thirty yards, Espartero brandishes his sword and addresses his troops in a voice so loud and clear that every word can be heard distinctly. He is determined, he cries, to protect the constitution, to preserve the liberties of Spain, to defend the nation against both despotism and anarchy. During his absence suppressing insurrection, he relies—as he has in the past—on the loyalty of the National Guard to maintain peace in the capital and safeguard the young and innocent queen. The ruler's avowals have been met with acclamations. Sheathing his sword, he wheels on his mount, and at the head of his disciplined and well-armed forces marches through the Gate of Alcalá eastward out of the city.

"Spain," Irving had written to the American Secretary of State three months earlier, "is a Country accustomed to violent remedies . . ." One such remedy was now being prepared for the Catalans. The troops of the regency reached the coast and, on December 3, 1842, bombarded Barcelona. Four hundred dwellings were destroyed. Next day the stunned city capitulated.

General Espartero "has before him a grand career, if he follows it out as he has begun, and is permitted to carry it to a successful termination." So the American ambassador had surmised during the autumn. "If he can conduct the affairs of Spain through the storms and quicksands that beset his regency; if he can establish the present constitutional form of government on a firm basis, and, when the Queen arrives at the age to mount the throne, resign the power into her hands, and give up Spain to her, reviving in its industry and its resources, peaceful at home and respected abroad, he will leave a name in history to be enrolled among the most illustrious of patriots."

Worthy goals for the most part, but the name Baldomero Espartero has hardly rung down the corridors of time through these hundred and forty years. The erratic, dilatory, chocolate-drinking general (first of many such soldiers of fortune, culminating in Franco, who have ruled modern Spain) did by no means all that Irving hoped he could, and indeed would last as regent scarcely seven months after the bombardment of the Catalan capital. That very act—impulsive, excessive, brutal—would contribute to his downfall, playing as it did into the hands of his enemies. And the queen—generous of heart but wondrously inept at every age, from inattentive schoolgirl to barely literate adult—would not have been the one to give Spain up to in any case, if the multitude of problems that beset the divided nation were to be solved.

Assuredly Irving understood only a part of what was happening, being "new to the ground and surrounded by mystery and legerdemain." His own duties he could meanwhile perform well enough. To officialdom, as occasions arose, he was explaining American policy concerning Cuba. He lobbied for Spanish recognition of the independent state of Texas. He strove to lessen tensions over trade between America and Spain. Through tactful and patient correspondence he sought to obtain the release of an American held in a Havana jail and to ease the punishment levied by authorities on another unlucky American citizen in Spain. He supervised the consular offices at Barcelona and Málaga. And he reported regularly and at length to his own government.

Such matters occupied his routine calls and deskwork. One typical day in these early months of his incumbency the ambassador obliges us by describing, in a letter home in mid-August 1842, during the torpid season of late summer. To get "a good start of the sun, which rules like a tyrant throughout the day," he rises about five in the morning. In early breezes that flow through open doors and windows he reads and writes until eight, when "the distant sound of military music gives notice of the troops on their way to relieve guard at the royal palace." Soon the horse guards are passing beneath his window, with a band on horseback playing some waltz or military air: "I watch and listen as they prance down the street, between spacious dwellings of the nobility, and turn into the passage leading to the palace . . ." The foot guards follow, and by the time those have marched by, the ambassador is customarily summoned to breakfast.

Over the breakfast table will soon be heard further strains of military music from the street below, as the relieved guard reverses direction to return to its barracks. "This pageant, which invariably takes place at the same hour every morning, is a regale of which we never get tired." *We* includes Irving's fellow New Yorkers, young Alexander Hamilton and Brevoort—his good friend's son—and Hector Ames, all attached to the embassy. On the table before them have been placed the Madrid papers, but in this censored society those "seldom contain anything of peculiar interest." After breakfast, however, papers from London and Paris arrive, along with the mail. "Should the mail bring, as it sometimes does, a packet of letters for the different members of the household, giving us the news and gossip of home, there is a complete scene of excitement"—a scene as agreeably encountered as it is readily imagined —"each hurrying on his letters, and calling out, every moment, some piece of intelligence, or some amusing anecdote."

That interlude ended, during the summer weather Irving will generally pass his day in the spacious bedroom that serves as well for his study, about thirty feet by twenty-two, with front windows looking down on a busy thoroughfare of the city, and other windows overlooking a little square—Plazuela de la Villa—with a public fountain, "thronged all day, and until a late hour of the night, by water carriers, male and female servants, and the populace of the neighborhood"—endlessly noisy, endlessly picturesque in their various costumes and groupings.

"At five o'clock we dine, after which some take a siesta, or lounge about until the evening is sufficiently advanced to take a promenade either on the Prado, or on the esplanade in front of the royal palace." Often, however, during these warmer weeks, the ambassador prefers to seat himself "in the balcony of my room, where I can catch any night breeze that is stirring, and can overlook the street. Between nine and ten a running footman gives notice, by the sound of a bugle, of the approach of the Queen, on her return from her evening's drive in the Retiro and in the Prado." Mounted soldiers follow the runner. Then comes the royal carriage—an open barouche drawn by six horses, passing directly under the balcony to allow a full view of "the little Queen and her sister, and their *aya*, or governess, Madame Mina." Attendants on horseback ride alongside, and another carriage-and-six follows, bearing those "whose duties bring them in immediate attendance upon the persons of the Queen and Princess." All that sudden clatter moves on down the street until it rounds the corner toward the palace, as have the guards of morning. Then, amid the resumption of sounds of ordinary street life— another Madrid evening, of which some fifty thousand have passed near the Casa de Villa since then—Irving lingers at his balcony "until a late hour, enjoying the gradually cooling night air, which grows more and more temperate until toward midnight, when I go to bed."

He got out more often in cooler weather. By mid-September he had changed his residence, from the noisy quarters near the Royal Palace to ones farther east, on calle de las Infantas, in a nobleman's mansion with a fine view of Buena Vista and the distant groves of the Retiro. Like so many Spanish dwellings these were commodious: "I have such a range of *salons*, that it gives me quite an appetite to walk from my study to the dining room." Now he slept in an octagonal chamber—once the chapel of the building—with a gilded cupola and little windows, fifteen feet above the floor, that caught the first rays of dawn: "You have no idea what a splendid waking up I have sometimes in the morning. . . ."

He would keep these apartments for most of the rest of his stay in the capital, and within them in time would set about "to play the Ambassador on a cautious scale," entertaining small parties—no more than twenty-four people—from among the resident diplomatic corps, with torches held by servants at the street entrance and along corridors to light guests the way. Modest he insists these occasions were—nothing like those of the British minister Aston, whose immense fortune put social competition out of the question. Even so, surviving documents of the customhouse let us form an idea of Irving's domestic effects and ambitions—as well as of what modest diplomatic living involved back then: equipment for horses and carriages, clothing, furniture (brass lamps, candelabra), dinnerware (fingerbowls, eighteen decanters, eight dozen wineglasses), in addition to a small case of wine, three barrels of wine, twelve hundred bottles of wine, a hundred bottles of liqueurs, six dozen packs of playing cards, five thousand cigars—all of it on the way from the frontier, then delivered, then set into use by housekeeper, cook, butler, footman, coachman, each "bowing to me with profound respect," and all presumably kept busy unpacking, serving, cleaning, as they moved around those sprawling halls and chambers.

What a contrast to the ways of that earlier frugal and all but solitary denizen of the Alhambra! Yet the unaccustomed master of such

Mary Wollstonecraft. The likeness was made within the last year of the subject's life, when she may already have been pregnant with the child who would become Mary Shelley. Portrait by John Opie.

Shelley. This is presumably the watercolor, long thought to be lost, by Edward Ellerker Williams, done near the end of Shelley's life.

Claire Clairmont. Copy of an oil painting by Amelia Curran.

Villa Magni, Lerici. From here Shelley departed to his doom; here Mary Shelley awaited her husband's return. The photograph was taken in the 1880s.

John Howard Payne as Hamlet. The portrait is by Irving's friend Charles R. Leslie.

Mary Shelley in later life. The subject was approaching her mid-forties when this painting was done, by Richard Rothwell, in 1841.

Irving during his first sojourn in Spain. The drawing, by David Wilkie, was made in Seville in 1828, when Irving was forty-five.

Interior of the Alhambra. A nineteenth-century view.

New York in the 1830s. The view is along Broadway, looking south from Liberty Street. The four-storey building to the right of Trinity Church is the City Hotel, where Irving was welcomed at a public dinner on his return to America in 1832.

Sunnyside in Irving's lifetime. Purchased in the mid-1830s, the house was gradually transformed, through Irving's efforts, into the form here pictured.

Madrid in the time of Isabella II. The view is from the Prado along calle de Alcalá in the direction of Puerta del Sol. Modern views of Madrid are often taken from the same vantage point, although now the fountain of Cibeles, at the right in the photograph, has been relocated in the center of the boulevard, with traffic circling around it.

bella as Irving knew her. The portrait, by
nte López, was made in 1842, during
ng's first year as ambassador, and when
subject was twelve.

Isabella in maturity.

Irving a few years after his return to
America from the Spanish court. The
photograph is from a daguerreotype
made in 1849.

John Jacob Astor in 1794. The subject was thirty-one years old at the time, a rising merchant in New York City. Copy by Jacob H. Lazarus after the original by Gilbert Stuart.

Astoria in 1813. Engraving in Gabriel Franchere's *Narrative of a Voyage to the Northwest Coast of America*. Franchere was among the original colonizers.

Astor in old age. So he would have
appeared when Irving knew him best.
Portrait by E. D. Marchant, painted
about 1838, when the subject would
have been seventy-five.

Hell Gate. Astor's country home was located
near what is now the eastern end of
Eighty-sixth Street, New York City.

Irving seated at the entrance to Sunnyside. A
stereoscopic slide, made about 1856 by
Frederick Langenheim.

John Brown in May, 1859. Two
months later the abolitionist
would arrive at the Kennedy farm
in Maryland, intent on launching
his attack on Harpers Ferry.

Skirmish at Harpers Ferry. Colonel Lee has ordered Lieutenant J. E. B. Stuart to
attack the engine house, inside which Brown and his men have retreated. From a
contemporary print.

a scale of living was lonely—much lonelier than on his previous visit to Spain, homesick for his cottage on the Hudson and constantly reminded of absent friends here at Madrid whom he had known fifteen years before: Everett, Rich, the D'Oubrils, Navarrete, Dolgorouki. "I miss all my former intimates," he writes the last named, now Russian minister at Naples, in October. "Navarrete, grown old and infirm, has been absent from Madrid ever since my arrival. I look with an eye of wistful recollection at the house once inhabited by the D'Oubrils, which was my familiar and favorite resort. It is undergoing great repairs and alterations, to become the residence of some millionaire who has made a fortune by speculation. . . . I am," he goes on, "continually retracing the scenes of past pleasures and friendships, and finding them vacant and desolate. I seem to come upon the very footprints of those with whom I have associated so pleasantly and kindly, but they only serve to remind me that those who made those footprints have passed away."

Moreover, inconveniences of Spanish life—noise, dirt, primitiveness—annoyed the older diplomat more than they had the younger author. Worse still, Irving felt some responsibility for the widespread enthusiasms toward the peninsula that his writings had helped create. "A stranger from the gayer, more polished and luxurious countries of Europe has much to tolerate in coming to Spain," he was conceding to his niece at Paris that same month, October 1842. For the elderly resident at Madrid could (perhaps like some of his readers) feel discomfort more readily than he had "sixteen or seventeen years since, when my imagination still tinted and wrought up every scene. I am at times affraid that these involuntary tintings of my imagination may have awakened expectations in others with respect to this country which the reality will disappoint; and that they will concur with an English traveller in the south of Spain in pronouncing me 'the easily pleased Washington Irving.' "

Easily pleased: Richard Ford's condescending sneer had rankled. But nearing sixty now, he who had led a long life, author of legends and romance whose prose had brought and would bring so many through Spanish customs and across a rugged landscape to the Alhambra, was uncharacteristically moved to share with his favorite niece revealing thoughts about himself. "Would to god," he wrote, "I could continue to be 'easily pleased' to the end of my carreer. How much of a life checquered by vicissitudes and clouded at times by sordid cares, has been lighted up and embellished by this unbought trickery of the mind. 'Surely' says the bible 'man walketh in a vain shadow and disquieteth himself in vain'—but this has not been the case with me—Shadows have proved my substance; and from them I have derived many of my most exquisite enjoyments; while the substantial realities of life have turned to shadows in my grasp." The export business dissolved in bankruptcy at Liverpool, investments evaporated, esteem become scorn and caviling, friends gone, loved ones dead. But "when I think what revelry of the mind I have enjoyed; what fairy air castles I have built—*and inhabited*—when I was poor in purse; and destitute of all the worldly gear on which others build their happiness; when I reccollect how cheap have been my most highly relished pleasures; how independent of fortune and of the world; how easily conjured up under the most adverse and sterile circumstances; I feel as if, were I once more on the threshold of existence, and the choice were given me I would say, give me the gilding of the imagination and let others have the solid gold—let me be the 'easily pleased Washington Irving' and heap positive blessings on others, until they groan under them."

So he expressed his feelings that fall, late in life and far from home, in the midst of a substantial world of diplomatic paperwork, of attendance at court functions and *besamanos*, of study and report and spectacle.

As the weeks passed Irving continued to prepare his long dispatches on peninsular affairs for the State Department in Washington. The reaction of Spaniards to Espartero's bombardment of Barcelona in early December surprised the American ambassador; he had felt that a show of force would strengthen the regency and let the general proceed with his program of creating a truly constitutional monarchy. "Beside, the Spanish Public," he was repeating to Secretary Webster, "is exceedingly tolerant of strong measures and accustomed to those severe remedies, incident to what may be called a national state of intermittent revolution."

But Irving was wrong about public tolerance this time. So hostile had been the Catalans that the regent had not dared enter Barcelona after it surrendered, and throughout the winter and into the spring of 1843 revolts against the central government continued to erupt all over Spain. "It is lamentable," our envoy reported, "to see . . . how all patriotic feeling is lost in the violence of parties"—*carlistas, cristinos, isabelitas, moderados, progresistas, exaltados*—"and how opposite factions coalesce in their efforts to fan a partial flame into a general conflagration."

Anarchy seemed at hand. By late June, "in the midst of plots, conspiracies, and insurrections," Espartero was once more marching at the head of troops, southward this time, toward fractious Seville, and once more was leaving the capital—and the queen—to the protection of the National Guard. But too many people stood to gain by the regent's fall. In his absence armies loyal to rival parties moved against the city, so that on the afternoon of July 12, 1843, Irving, attracted by "an uncommon bustle and confusion of voices in the street," looked out his window to discover as far as he could see men, women, and children scurrying noisily for cover. All the city gates were shut and heavily guarded, and Madrid was under siege.

Periodically during the preceding winter and spring the ambassador had suffered from an old affliction, the inflammation of hands and ankles, brought on by overwork, that had crippled him twenty years earlier and that now had led his doctor to prescribe days during which he must not read or write at all. But in the martial excitement of that summer evening the invalid was not long getting off his sofa and about again, hurrying from his rooms "with as much eagerness as, when a boy, I used to break bounds and sally forth at midnight to see a fire." For feebly old as he might occasionally feel, the author of the battle-crowded *Conquest of Granada* was unable to "resist the desire to see something of a city in a state of siege."

What he beheld, riding about in his carriage that first night, was the whole of Madrid "illuminated, as is generally the case when any popular movement is apprehended"—in those times before aircraft—"so that an enemy may not have darkness to favor his designs." Torchlight revealed armed troops in public squares and ready at windows and balconies, cannon in place at mouths of thoroughfares, trenches being dug, breastworks thrown up, shops all fastened shut, and at the Prado only "two carriages besides my own on the drive, usually so crowded. I drove from gate to gate of this end of the city, all closed and guarded. As the night advanced, I drove through most of the principal streets. The houses were illuminated from top to bottom. Few people were walking in the streets; but groups were gathered about every door. Troops were patrolling in every direction, and in the main squares, which formed military posts, both officers and men were bivouacking on the pavements. The appearance of a solitary carriage rumbling through the streets attracted universal attention . . ."

But no one halted him. Thus, by eleven o'clock, this aging lover of spectacle had got home again safely. From then through a number of days and nights the issue of Espartero's regency awaited events. Newspapers stopped publishing, but rumors came fast, from all directions. Espiroz with an insurgent army was at the Puerta de Hierro, half a league away. Narváez, coming to join him, had reached Guadalajara. The militia had resolved to defend the city street by street, balcony by balcony. "One of my windows," Irving wrote of the siege, "commands a view of one of the city gates and its vicinity, and I could hear every discharge, and, at night, could see the flash of guns." He lay in bed not far from Puerta de Alcalá, listening to the occasional sound of a drum in the street, "the report of two or three distant shots." And by day, mindful of an earlier attempt before his arrival to kidnap the child queen, the

American ambassador persuaded all the resident foreign diplomats to offer in writing "to repair in person to the palace and be near the Queen at any moment their presence might be deemed useful." For the militia, rumor insisted, meant to make a last stand if need be at the Royal Palace itself.

Irving's offer of a diplomatic cordon was declined, "the ministry thinking the safety of the Queen and her sister sufficiently secured by the devotion of the inhabitants of Madrid, &c." Yet the peril seemed real: opposing forces had gathered, and the regent's troops under General Zurbano had finally marched through the city gates to engage the enemy.

The conflict would resolve itself to everyone's astonishment. "July 23d. The question is decided. The armies met yesterday morning; a few shots were exchanged when a general embracing took place between the soldiery, and the troops of the regency joined the insurgents": Narváez and his fellow generals entered Madrid unopposed. *Madrileños* could now behold "bands of rough soldiery, and Catalan guerrillas, who look like demi savages, roaming about their streets with triumphant air . . . " The existing cabinet had resigned. Informed at Seville of the loss of the capital, Espartero was fleeing south to board a British warship off Cádiz, accepting a twenty-one-gun salute before departing into pampered exile at Belgrave Square, London. And in Spain, "Clause one and only," the victors proclaimed, "Don Baldomero Espartero . . . deprived of all . . . titles, ranks, offices, honours, and orders. August 13."

A new government would be formed. Early in August Irving was writing home to Washington that "there are already three rival generals in the Capital each watching with jealousy the honors accorded to the others. There are opposite factions each claiming the merit of the recent victory and grasping at the lions share of the spoils." The story was familiar—"It would be difficult and indeed unprofitable to unravel the complicated web of intrigues and cross purposes, woven over the whole surface of public affairs in this country and impeding every effort for the general good"—a story that would continue to unfold around the center of power in bewildering ways and without much public benefit well beyond the end of Isabella's reign.

Long after Irving's departure from Spain that end would come, as late as September 30, 1868, a troubled quarter of a century into the future, when the monarch, by then obese at thirty-seven, huge in her crinolines, eyes red from sleeplessness and weeping, with her ineffectual husband and the latest of a long succession of lovers beside her, would board a special train at San Sebastián and cross the border into France and exile; behind her, banners would be exulting that "the accursed race of the Bourbons is banished for evermore." For by that time royal outrages had reached the limit of a people's tolerance, so that insurgent generals at last could easily topple the Spanish monarchy.

Earlier, before mid-century, soon after Irving's arrival at the embassy, the new ambassador had voiced his own frustrations over trying to operate in the midst of such instability: "It appears that, within the last eight years, there have been *forty two* changes in the department of war; *twenty five* in that of the Marine, and so on with the rest. This consumption of ministers is appalling. It is true the lowest number of changes occurs in the department of State, with which we would have to negotiate, but even here it is *nineteen;* which is at the rate of nearly two ministers and a half per annum. To carry on a negotiation with such transient functionaries is like bargaining at the window of a railroad car, before you can get a reply to a proposition the other party is out of sight."

Out of sight now was the Regent Espartero, fled to England, and another train was pulling in, bearing this time the short, alert figure of General Ramón María Narváez, intent on ruling with an iron hand and without the vacillations of his predecessor. To celebrate the outcome of these recent events the child queen and her new set of counselors was attending a two-hour High Mass in late August. Irving positioned himself where he could see her distinctly, accompanied by "the crowd of veteran courtiers, in court dresses that had weathered many a political storm in this revolutionary country, and which, like their owners, were much the worse for wear. In fact," the envoy reflected, departing from description in writing his family at Sunnyside, "men are so often turned in and turned out of office by the frequent and sudden changes in this government, that they and their coats are worn threadbare and limber as rags. Scarce a man about court, I might almost say about the streets, but has been, or is, or expects to be a cabinet minister or other high functionary; and I am careful now to pull off my hat to every dabbler in politics, however shabby his looks or low his condition, as I do not know but by a sudden turn of the wheel, I may have to treat with him about affairs of State. . . ."

But the queen, the young nieces at home would be wondering—the little queen, how did she look when their uncle saw her on that occasion? She was wearing lace over a skirt of white satin, with a train of velvet, scarlet embroidered with gold. Around her forehead was a circlet of diamonds, from which a lace veil fell over her face. A broad ribbon of some aristocratic order crossed from her shoulder to her rather too ample waist. Almost thirteen now, and plump; still, "it was a beautiful sight to see her at various parts of the service, rise from her chair, advance to the Prie Dieu and kneel down at it, with her prayer book; her long train extending behind her across the throne."

That little girl at prayer was fated, after a protracted life, to die in exile in Paris as late as 1904, past seventy by then, and an enigma still—charming, ludicrous, generous, on occasion regal, despite the girth and the giggle, on other occasions like some dilapidated charwoman. And yet the "poor old wrinkled face" that time would foist upon her was to the last (so an observer insisted at the end of the century) one that "no number of *toreros*' kisses had been able to reduce to baseness." Now she was thirteen with all those questionable adventures before her, as Irving witnessed her devotions—"a beautiful sight"—young girl at her praying desk, wearing bejeweled circlet, lace, and velvet gold-embroidered.

But should a responsible American be transmitting such luxurious images to his republican relatives back in New York? "I fear, to be sure, that I may turn the heads of my nieces with these descriptions of the little Queen and her royal state; her diamonds, and brocades and regal robes; and that they may be sighing now and then to go to Tarrytown church in long velvet trains and diamond coronets; and have Doctor Creighton"—their Episcopal minister—"officiate to them in pontifical state and ceremony, like the Patriarch of the Indias—but," he concluded playfully, "let them recollect that they have a safer seat on the sofa than the little Queen on her throne; that the cottage, if it has not the pomp, is at least free from the perils of the palace, and that they reign without dispute over the whole empire of Sunnyside. . . ."

Despite such evidences of an abiding gift for drollery, Irving during these weeks was still struggling with his illness, which added to his longing to be with the family back at his cottage above the Hudson. But the book trade at home was depressed, his royalties from that source sadly shrunken, so much so that had he returned to America, "without income to meet current expenses, and all the sources of future profit suddenly dried up" by this tormenting swelling of hands and ankles, "I should have been driven to despair." He must stay at his post, deferring the biography of Washington (another precious year gone by, and nothing done on it!), while dictating his long, entertaining, and often astute dispatches to the successive Secretaries of State—Webster, Calhoun, Buchanan. Daily business went forward, as Irving considered with appropriate Spanish ministers such matters as the offensive treatment of an American vessel by the *intendente* of Málaga, or the rumored conspiracy among slaves and Creoles in the ever sensitive island of Cuba. Then, in early autumn, the still ailing envoy received permission from overseas to take a brief leave, in order to rest in Paris at his niece's home.

While he was gone young Hamilton managed the embassy—that small domain still without enough shelves, so that boxes of books remained stacked in a corner while the secretary went on pleading with the State Department for funds to purchase at least a desk and a walnut bookcase. During this eventful fall and winter Barcelona was again in revolt, as were at various times Vigo and Zaragoza and Cartagena and Alicante. Narváez moved fiercely to discipline dissent, declaring martial law, rounding up his enemies in midnight searches, shooting hostages.

The foe fought back; the brusque general narrowly, miraculously escaped being assassinated on his way to join the queen at her royal box at the theater. Those shocks to the state occurred while Irving was away, but he felt their repercussions when he returned to Spain in early December 1843, not long after Isabella II had been formally declared of age, competent to rule without a regent, and had sworn at a picturesque and elaborate ceremony to abide by the most recent constitution.

She was just two months past her thirteenth birthday. That she was now ruler in her own right was owing to the unwillingness of Narváez to delay declaring her majority, however premature; his action would help frustrate other political generals eager to seize power. For its part, the citizenry was jubilant, so that houses, as Irving saw on his arrival at the capital, "were decked out with tapestry; there were illuminations by night; games, dances, spectacles and parades by day; fountains were running with wine and milk, and the streets thronged by the populace in their holiday garbs . . ."

Hindsight may lead us to wonder why. The course before the young monarch would be ill marked and hazardous at best, and of little profit to that festive populace. Moreover, the child who, powerless, had been "the only rallying point of national feeling" had now become something different, as Irving had foreseen: "the moment her minority ends," he had noted months before, "and, as queen, she favors either party, that moment she will become an object of hostility, and her very throne may be shaken in the violent convulsions which are likely to arise."

Her earliest test at statecraft came promptly. A former tutor, Salustiano de Olózaga, now first minister of the queen as Narváez hovered behind the throne, was charged with having forced—physically forced—the young girl to sign an unpopular measure. "I rose," she deposed to the Cortes, "and turned to the door which is on the left of my desk. Olózaga placed himself in front of me and bolted that door. I turned to the opposite door; and Olózaga again came before me and bolted that door also. He caught hold of my dress, and obliged me to sit down. He seized my hand, and forced me to sign. After that he left, and I withdrew to my apartments."

At such an outrage the nation was understandably incensed, yet the minister denied guilt as well as he could without calling his queen a liar outright; she had, after all, been seen at the door cordially offering him candy for his daughters as he was leaving, and the several witnesses of that departure had at no time heard noises inside the room—of locks being thrown, or scuffling, or voices raised. While Irving was taking up his Spanish life again, the crisis simmered, in a city that gleamed with bayonets as in time of war, along streets where "dark knots of politicians muffled in their cloaks" were holding mysterious conversations at every corner. Soon the minister had fled into exile, even as he was polling an ominously larger vote than formerly for his seat in the Cortes. Had the little queen made it all up, to get rid of an opponent? Was the thirteen-year-old already a tool of Narváez and his intriguing *moderados?*

For most Spaniards she did retain her popularity a few years longer, and some would find other matters to think and talk about, whatever happened. Occasionally Irving had access at this period to Madrid high life, occupied with its own timeless vanities no matter which ministers came and went; and once or twice he lets us hear them in their self-absorptions, as, for instance, when he attends two aristocratic ladies gossiping behind their fans about his lovely acquaintance the Princess of Carini, wife of the ambassador of the Two Sicilies. One lady is developing a critique of her person at length, as the other turns to the American to insist that, although she herself has only the highest regard for the princess, she is "obliged in candor to admit, one by one, all the censures of the marchioness." Both ladies "(being handsome women) agreed that the princess had no pretensions to beauty." That was too much. No beauty? Did not the princess, a diffident Irving dared ask, have fine eyes? "Fine eyes!" the marchioness snorted; "pooh! what are fine eyes in Spain, where they go begging about the streets?" No, the princess was not beautiful, and worse yet, she was, so her critic disclosed, *"positively fond of her husband."* Irving glosses that fondness as "a crime almost unheard of in high life in Madrid"—a charge, however, that the marchioness proceeded to substantiate by quoting "some over tender speeches made by the Princess to her husband in society . . . which were given with a provoking humor and mimicking that compelled me to laugh in spite of my secret predilection for the Princess. It was ungenerous however," this veteran of drawing rooms slyly concludes, "in the marchioness to attack the poor princess on a point on which she herself was so secure: since no one can accuse her of devotion to her own husband, though she is said to be full of loving kindness to all mankind beside!"

That in February 1844, as certain lives, amid plots and public doubts, went on with their town talk undeterred. The same month the little queen, exercising her new power, issued a command to Irving and other diplomats through her minister: "As the day approaches on which Her Majesty the Queen, DOÑA MARÍA CRISTINA"—absent in opulent exile in Paris the last three years and more—"will set foot on Spanish soil on her return to this Court, the Queen, My Royal Mistress, has decided to proceed to the Royal Residence of Aranjuez, to await there the arrival of her august Mother. In a moment so solemn, the happiness which her Majesty will experience would be greater, if those persons who through their exalted character, have the honour to be present often about the throne, would repair there to be witnesses of the disclosure of her filial love."

So María Cristina was making the journey back from France to be reunited with her two daughters by Ferdinand. "She returns," Irving noted, "by the very way by which she left the kingdom in 1840, when the whole world seemed to be roused against her, and she was followed by clamor and execrations. What is the case at present? The cities that were then almost in arms against her, now receive her with fêtes and rejoicings. Arches of triumph are erected in the streets; *Te Deums* are chaunted in the cathedrals; processions issue forth to escort her . . ." And at six in the morning of March 21, 1844, His Excellency Washington Irving issued forth as well, from Madrid in the carriage of the Mexican ambassador, to traverse the thirty miles to the reunion.

It was to take place about five in the afternoon, at a royal tent erected in a field three miles southeast of Aranjuez. "The road was full of carriages and horsemen, hastening to the rendezvous, and was lined with spectators, seated by the roadside in gaping expectation." Over the tent itself waved flags and streamers, and in the vicinity were three or four smaller tents, as well as "an immense assemblage of carriages, with squadrons of cavalry, and crowds of people of all ranks, from the grandee to the beggar." Two hours beyond the expected time the queen and her younger sister were kept waiting among a throng of courtiers. During that anxious interval Isabella would hurry to a nearby height that allowed her a view far down the road toward Ocaña, then return impatiently to the tent. "At length the royal cortege was seen descending the distant slope of the road, escorted by squadrons of lancers, whose yellow uniforms, with the red flag of the lance fluttering aloft, made them look at a distance like a moving mass of fire and flame." At the news, the excited daughter and queen of Spain, defying etiquette, forsook her designated position near the entrance of her tent and rushed forward pell-mell "through the avenue of guards, quite to the road"— filial love disclosed—to receive her mother's homage and embrace.

María Cristina was back, but only as a mother, with (it was emphasized) no role to play in the political affairs of the nation. And she returned as she had left, "gorged with riches." During the queen mother's exile, General Espartero as regent had discontinued her pension, but a royal decree restored it now, with arrears for the whole of the past three years as well. Those reached £120,000—an amount that would allow her to pay back the £80,000 with which an earlier government commission had found her guilty of absconding at the time of her departure into France—pay it all back and still show a handsome profit. Moreover, another royal decree was soon concerning itself with the domestic arrangements of Ferdinand's widow: "Having regard to the considerations submitted to me by my august mother, Doña Maria Cristina de Bourbon, I have authorized her to contract a marriage with Don Fernando Muñoz, Duke of Rianzares; and I further declare that in contracting this alliance with a person of inferior station, she has in no way forfeited my favour and affection, and shall suffer no prejudice in her style and title, or in any of her honours, prerogatives, and distinction . . ." Signed, "I the Queen."

And thirteen-year-old daughter. Corporal Muñoz, father of half a dozen of the queen mother's other children, was thus publicly acknowledged, a duke and grandee, and his wife might well beam complacently upon her daughter's subjects. "Long live Spain's Guardian Angel!" they called to her, as she proceeded in triumph alongside the queen from Aranjuez to Madrid. And through the spring and longer after her return, the capital was relatively tranquil, even as the ministry of the parvenu González Bravo fell in May and the aristocracy entered upon a new era of splendor—glittering balls and garden parties as in earlier times—those noble families assured that with the queen mother back, and with Narváez vigilant as president of council and minister of war, life would again be well.

Irving, meanwhile, continued to recuperate during the warming months, bathing his ankles daily until he was able at last to anticipate full mobility: "I am afraid, when I once more sally forth and walk about the streets, I shall feel like a boy with a new coat, who thinks everybody will turn round to look at him. 'Bless my soul, how that gentleman has the use of his legs!' " By late April he had "taken a walk in the green alleys of the Retiro"—more leafy now than a score of years before—"for the first time in upward of fifteen months, and performed the feat to admiration." And when the court removed to Barcelona in late May, the American ambassador was recovered enough to be able to make arrangements to follow along with the rest of the diplomatic corps.

Consequently, during a month of that summer of 1844, Irving found himself returned to a Spanish city he had visited earlier—at times to the very palace, in fact, in which he had dined with the Conde de España before leaving Spain those many years ago. The fierce old count had subsequently joined the cause of Don Carlos—Isabella's uncle and claimant to the throne—had committed more of his "sanguinary acts," to put the matter as gently as Irving does, and finally had been "murdered . . . with savage cruelty, while being conducted a prisoner among the mountains." In ascending toward the queen's apartments, his American dinner guest of 1829 was led to remember: "Fifteen years had elapsed since I took leave of the Count at the top of this staircase, and it seemed as if his hard-hearted, derisive laugh still sounded in my ears. . . ." The ambassador had been summoned to Isabella's presence, and he found her "standing in the centre of the room . . . dressed to take her evening drive. She had a pinkish bonnet, with pinkish flowers, and, altogether, her whole dress has left a kind of pinkish idea in my mind. She had even a slight pinkish bloom in her face, which is usually pale.

Indeed, her whole appearance is improved; it is more healthful. She is growing more and more womanly . . ."

The envoy delivered her his President's messages, just lately arrived, congratulating her on her ascension and condoling with her on the death of an aunt during the winter. He responded appropriately when she expressed, "in a low voice, the hope that I had made a pleasant journey, &c." Then he withdrew, to give place to each of the other diplomats in turn.

After the interview Irving remained near the court in Barcelona through four weeks, amid drives, dinners, balls, and other entertainments, before he was able in late July to take a steamer for France. He meant to avoid the worst of the Spanish summer and to rest again at his niece's while consulting his doctor in Paris.

For more and more often he was feeling his age, and acting it: "I am now at that time of life when the mind has a stock of recollections on which to employ itself; and though these may sometimes be of a melancholy nature, yet it is a 'sweet-souled melancholy,' mellowed and softened by the operation of time, and has no bitterness in it. My life has been a chequered one, crowded with incidents and personages, and full of shifting scenes and sudden transitions. All these I can summon up and cause to pass before me, and in this way can pass hours together in a kind of reverie. When I was young, my imagination was always in the advance, picturing out the future, and building castles in the air; now, memory comes in the place of imagination, and I look back over the region I have travelled. . . ."

Perhaps he was doing just that on the steamer to Marseille; for a long time, at any rate, he lingered outside the cabin, enjoying "a beautiful sail by moonlight, which kept me a great part of the night on the deck." And while on board, to friends and relatives far away he had earlier been writing discursively "at a table in the cabin," sensible at one point as he did so "of the power of a pair of splendid Spanish eyes which are occasionally flashing upon me, and which almost seem to throw a light upon the paper." In these moments the present did become insistent again, and beautifully so. Since he could not break the spell, he would describe the owner of those eyes. "She is a young married lady, about four or five and twenty, middle sized, finely modelled, a Grecian outline of face, a complexion sallow yet healthful, raven black hair, eyes dark, large, and beaming, softened by long eyelashes, lips full and rosy red, yet finely chiselled, and teeth of dazzling whiteness. She is dressed in black, as if in mourning; on one hand is a black glove; the other hand, ungloved, is small, exquisitely formed, with taper fingers and blue veins. She has just"—that very instant. That gesture—"put it up to adjust her clustering black locks. . . . Really, if I were a young man, I should not be able to draw the portrait of this beautiful creature so calmly."

But now he was interrupted. The lady had noticed his glances in her direction. " 'Really Señor,' said she, at length, with a smile, 'one would think you were a painter, taking my likeness.' " And the distinguished elderly gentleman had to confess that he had been doing just that—was "writing to a friend the other side of the world, discussing things that are passing before me, and I could not help noting down one of the best specimens of the country that I had met with." Soon he was rendering his description into Spanish for her and her husband. "It occasioned a world of merriment, and was taken in excellent part. The lady's cheek, for once, mantled with the rose. She laughed, shook her head, and said I was a very fanciful portrait painter; and the husband declared that, if I would stop at St. Filian, all the ladies in the place would crowd to me to have their portraits taken—my pictures were so flattering."

Before long the steamer had pulled alongside the tiny port of San Feliú, and it was time for the Spanish couple to leave. The courtly Irving "helped the beautiful original of the portrait into the boat, and promised her and her husband, if ever I should come to St. Filian, I would pay them a visit. The last I noticed of her, was a Spanish farewell wave of her beautiful white hand, and the gleam of her dazzling teeth as she smiled adieu. So there's a very tolerable touch of romance for a gentleman of my years." And the *Villa de Madrid* steamed on to Marseille, where around eight in the morning of July 31, 1844, this romancer in his early sixties was able to recognize, just outside the fort in the harbor, "a little cove where I used to bathe when I was here, just forty years since," as a young New Yorker on the Grand Tour in the fall of 1804. Soon he was landing "on the quay where I had often walked in old times."

A rest in Paris, a hasty visit—slipping unremarked through London—to his sister's family at Birmingham, then in mid-November Irving was back in Madrid, delighting his servants by his return: "Juana threw her arms round my neck. Old Pedro, the coachman, cut a most uncouth caper, and I had much ado to avoid the embraces of the cook's aide-de-camp and the footboy." It was good to get home. "I found everything prepared to make me comfortable for the winter: my bedroom fresh papered, curtained, and carpeted"—all so inviting, in fact, that the ambassador felt about ready to nestle in and "give up the world until spring time."

But social life around the courts had grown ever more active with the queen mother's presence. "The nobility and the wealthy are vieing with each other in display, during this interval of political sunshine; and as many fortunes have been made by men in office and political speculators, all Madrid rattles and glitters with new equipages." For such changes had the street mobs been made jubilant at Isabella's ascension, at María Cristina's return. "One would hardly suspect," notes Irving, "from the luxury of the capital, that the country was so wretchedly impoverished." The returned traveler had arrived "just in time for a *Besa manos* at the palace, and a ball at General Narvaez', on the young Queen's saint's day."

That latter had cost the general plenty. People wondered where his money was coming from; for Narváez, who had not been rich before acquiring power, had recently been indulging a taste for prodigality. In an elegant section of the city, on calle de la Luna (drab enough street at the present day), this bewigged gallant, "ambitious of the smiles of the ladies," had purchased a mansion "built around an open court, with great saloons." But even though huge, on that particular November night the resplendent palace "was exceedingly crowded, there being about fifteen hundred persons present." The royal family was among them—"a compliment rarely paid to a subject at this punctilious Court"—and Irving was permitted to see a side of Isabella that he had not seen before. "She was in high glee. Indeed, I never saw a schoolgirl at a school ball enjoy herself more completely. . . . There were blunders in the quadrille, which set the little Queen laughing; and queer, old-fashioned dancing on the part of the Portuguese Minister, which increased her risibility. She was at times absolutely convulsed with laughter, and throughout the whole evening showed a merriment that was quite contagious. I have never seen her in such a joyous mood, having chiefly seen her on ceremonious occasions, and had no idea that she had so much real *fun* in her disposition."

At four that morning Isabella was still dancing, and protested that she would willingly go on through eight more dances. "The Queen Mother, however, got her away between four and five." Irving, pleading lameness—age might not have sufficed as an excuse for royalty—had managed to avoid the quadrille and leave the ball about three. But soon he was in attendance at another command performance, at a banquet in the Royal Palace, seated immediately at Maria Cristina's left before a vast circular table in the Hall of the Pillars. In the midst of those festivities the fourteen-year-old queen, elsewhere at the table and a full eighty feet away, suddenly rose and left. Was she ill? Messengers periodically approached the queen mother to report. Isabella, Irving was informed, had been "too tightly laced: They had endeavored to make a *fine figure* of her . . . 'Well,' said the Queen Mother smiling 'tell her to leave her dress loose, to put on a shawl and to come back.' In a little while the young queen returned to the banquetting hall, not envelloped in a shawl, but free from the misery of a fine figure. . . ." And free, presumably, to eat on, for Irving had already revealed to his interested nieces some months before that "by the by," the little monarch "will soon cease to deserve the adjective *little*," looking as she does on occasion "rather full and puffy . . . being perhaps rather too straitly caparisoned . . ."

But despite the scenes of court splendor he went on describing, that world held less and less for the aging diplomat. What might have been thought an infatuation with royalty arose from his desire in letters to gratify the tastes of his domestic circle at Sunnyside. For his own part, at court functions he frequently felt himself "the very dullest of the dull," having grown too old or too wise—he hoped the latter—to take much pleasure in such spectacles. As a servant of his government he continued carrying out official duties, at the time directed primarily toward renegotiating the restrictive tariff on flour imported by Cuba, and toward frustrating British designs to purchase that tempting relic of Spain's lost empire. And during these months his health improved. He was accordingly able to greet the arrival of another birthday, April 3, 1845, with complacence, recalling "the time when I did not wish to live to such an age, thinking it must be attended with infirmity, apathy of feeling, peevishness of temper, and all the other ills which conspire to 'render age unlovely;' yet here my sixty-second birthday finds me in fine health, in the full enjoyment of all my faculties, with my sensibilities still fresh, and in such buxom activity that, on my return home yesterday from the Prado, I caught myself bounding up stairs three steps at a time . . ."

Hardly the proper demeanor for an ambassador; he had checked himself in order to avoid offending the astonished porter. But if such good spirits continued, His Excellency was ready to live to the age of Methuselah. Meanwhile, he was spending more of his days agreeably alone now: morning hours in his study, afternoon drives, the opera, summer evenings along the Prado, where, seated, he would gaze with pleasure upon groups of children in moonlight, "who gather about the fountains, take hands, and dance in rings to their own nursery songs. . . ."

His life in Spain he saw drawing to a close. By then, by the summer of 1845, the Tyler administration in Washington had been replaced by that of Governor Polk, and envoys such as Irving might anticipate an end to their service. "I am kept," he wrote that June, "in a state of irksome suspense as to the intentions of government towards me." Later: "I long to throw off diplomacy, and to return to my independent literary pursuits. My health is now excellent." But weeks had passed, and months, and still no word arrived concerning the appointment of a successor. He watched the mails, scanned the newspapers. And finally, from Paris once more, in December, he submitted his resignation: ". . . The unexpected manner in which I was called to this high trust from the retirement of private life, without reference to any political considerations; and the cordial manner in which I was welcomed to it by my countrymen of all political creeds, have ever made me regard it as the crowning honor of my life. . . . In now offering my resignation I am actuated by no party feeling . . . but solely by an earnest desire to return to my country and my friends."

The brief recuperative visit to France that late autumn lengthened. Early in 1846 Irving was in London, "where my friends think I may be of more service, during the present crisis"—concerning the settlement of the Oregon question—"than in Spain." Those friends included Louis McLane, Polk's emissary to the Court of St. James's and Irving's former superior there. Not until late March, after a delicate and fruitful contribution of his diplomacy to negotiations that helped settle our northwestern border with Canada, was Irving (this friend of both America and England, this ambassador, as Thackeray called him, from the New World of Letters to the Old) finally able to return a last time to Madrid.

He took stock of events when he arrived. "There have been several changes in the Cabinet here, which have caused great agitation in the political circles. Narvaez, who had been in eclipse for a short time, is restored to power, and is again at the head of the Government . . ." But the Cortes had been suspended, the press gagged, the country under stern autocratic rule. Those measures were increasing the premier's unpopularity, and gossip had grown interested in his debts and speculations. Although he might later boast on his deathbed that he had no enemies to forgive—had had them all shot—at present the foes of Narváez (now styled Duke of Valencia) seemed active enough, and among them was María Cristina—another speculator—in Spain at the start solely as a mother, but of course increasingly a political force to deal with. The queen mother's apostolic tastes had found Narváez not zealous enough in serving the secular interests of the clergy. Thus, in the tempestuous spring of 1846 his ministry fell, and the duke, like Espartero before him, passed into exile. From beyond the border not long before, Don Carlos, Ferdinand's aging brother and claimant to Isabella's throne, had abdicated his pretensions in favor of his squint-eyed son, who meant to pursue them more aggressively. At home a new constitution had been promulgated, dissatisfying all parties. And through the turmoil, business circles at the capital were spinning erratically, fortunes being won and demoralizingly lost by speculations in vast, corrupt projects to modernize the backward nation.

One other problem was perhaps the most urgent of all. "The question of the marriage of the young Queen," Irving had noted in March, "becomes more and more embarrassing. Until it is settled, the affairs of Spain will always be in a precarious state, and the kingdom liable to convulsions." But the envoy—well past a year into the new American administration, seven months beyond the date he had submitted his resignation—was "getting tired of courts," as he admitted privately, "and shall be right glad to throw off my diplomatic coat for the last time." In midsummer, with his successor, former Congressman Saunders of North Carolina, finally on hand (and Isabella's bridegroom still not chosen), the outgoing American ambassador was having a last royal audience, at ten o'clock of an evening in late July 1846.

"*Con mucho sentimiento mío,*" the queen addressed him on that occasion, "*recibo el anuncio . . .*"—It is with much regret that I receive the announcement of your recall from the post of Envoy Extraordinary and Minister Plenipotentiary of the United States near my person. . . . You may take with you into private life the intimate conviction that your frank and loyal conduct has contributed to draw closer the amicable relations which exist between North America and the Spanish nation, and that your distinguished personal merits have gained in my heart the appreciation which you merit by more than one title.

The personal allusion, departing from form, was unusual and highly complimentary. At his turn, Irving had ended his own more formal remarks with a sincere hope, carefully rendered into Spanish (elderly American gentleman in diplomatic uniform reading before the young monarch for the last time): "I now take leave of your Majesty, wishing you, from the bottom of my heart, a long and happy life, and a reign which may form a glorious epoch in the history of this country."

"Thus closes my public career," the ambassador wrote home soon afterward. "At six o'clock this evening I set off from Madrid, in company with Mr. Weismuller, a connection of the Rothschilds, stationed at this capital, to post for France in a private carriage." By mid-August Irving had reached England. In early September he was aboard the steamer *Cambria* bound for Boston, and on September 19, 1846, he was restored to the happiness of Sunnyside—and the evening of life among his friends and devoted family.

But now he possessed new matter for reflection as he dreamed with a book on the terrace above the Tappan Zee: not only memories of the Alhambra at sunset high over Granada, and of the rush-shaded streets of Seville on summer days, and of the rocks of Ronda echoing thunder; not only the date groves of Elche and the flat-roofed villages and the muleteers chanting their songs as they ambled along bleak mountain paths; and not only memories of long-ago Christians and Moors, about whom he still had sketches to publish. Now Irving's recollections could embrace as well present-day court life and diplomacy: a fête champêtre in springtime, for instance, among nightingales singing and lilacs in bloom at the queen mother's villa outside Madrid, where the envoy had seen gondolas bearing court ladies on canals, with swings and roundabouts at the shore, and crossbow games, and bands playing and fireworks, and laughter in the evening reaching him from beneath the Chinese lanterns over the lawns. Or he might abruptly remember the sight of a young queen reviewing her troops—twelve or thirteen thousand soldiers and she for the first time as their commander in chief, on a beautiful dun-colored horse and wearing a blue cloth riding habit and a black beaver hat and a captain-general's badges. So much he might muse over: the author-diplomat had witnessed enough pageantry of Spain's past and present to furnish his mind, in the decade and more remaining, with a broadly extended "stock of recollections on which to employ itself."

Moreover, he was entitled to feel satisfied. As ambassador, Irving had served his country perhaps better than any other American could have done in that post at that particular time. Through "the tortuous course of Spanish politics where every thing is perplexed with mystery and intrigue," he had made his way adroitly, without encountering one personal enemy. Espartero, Narváez, María Cristina, Isabella, Spaniards of every party knew and respected him. "Why does not your government send out Washington Irving to this court?" a high official from Madrid was asking the editor and poet Bryant some years later. "Why do you not take as your agent the man whom all Spain admires, venerates, loves? I assure you, it would be difficult for our government to refuse anything which Irving should ask . . ."

But that was in 1857, when the subject of the appeal was past venturing far. Scarcely two years remained by then of a long life that had urged this traveler, old now, to roam from earliest childhood—often in fancy and sometimes in fact—with love and wonder over the landscapes of Spain.

OLD MR. ASTOR &
"VASHINGTON IRVING"

---

*He was altogether one of the most remarkable men I
have ever known: of penetrating sagacity, massive intellect, and possessing elements of greatness of which
the busy world around him was little aware . . .*

IRVING AT SUNNYSIDE IN 1851,
OF JOHN JACOB ASTOR

A FTER CONCLUDING his second sojourn in Spain, Washington Irving returned to America—this time for good—and proceeded to reestablish his life at Sunnyside. Once more a private citizen, the former ambassador would decline further opportunities for public service, content in his mid-sixties to enjoy the company of friends and family. His brother Ebenezer and Ebenezer's daughters—Kate, Sarah, Julia, Mary—would help enrich those final years at the cottage overlooking the Hudson. Manhattan lay a brief train ride to the south; and friends—some of whom, like Paulding and Gouverneur Kemble, he had known since boyhood—had estates nearby. Irving had cause to be satisfied, so that a visitor who saw him in the years after 1846 might well remark an old man's merry countenance, "still handsome, in which youthful little dimples and smiles bear witness to a youthfully fresh and humorous disposition and soul."

That same witness would record as well appealing impressions of Irving's domestic surroundings now—cows in the meadow, ivy-covered walls, breezy warmth within—over which the celebrated author had been laboring since his return. "I want to get my study in order, and my books arranged," he had written soon after taking up residence once more among his relatives. "But the fact is, I am growing a confounded old fellow; I begin to be so studious of my convenience, and to have such a craving desire to be comfortable." Nevertheless, within weeks of landing at New York, he had entered vigorously into home-improvement schemes, having outhouses built, chimneys plastered, a kitchen yard and stable enclosed, "making a new ice pond in a colder and deeper place, in the glen just opposite our entrance gate," adding a laundry, storerooms, pantries, servants' quarters, coal cellar, hennery, until (as he could end by boasting) he had converted "what was once rather a make-shift little mansion into one of the most complete snuggeries in the country."

Nor is it disagreeable to find that restive nature thus occupied, settled at last and henceforth, he who had been often adrift (though a welcome member of familial groups before so many other hearths: at the Hoffmans' in early New York, the Van Warts' in Birmingham, the Fosters' in Dresden, the Storrows' in Paris, the D'Oubrils' in Madrid). Now in the seventh decade of his life he was cozy in his own home—and might have been excused had he done no more than putter thus, taking his honorable ease surrounded by loved ones, among the plaudits of his adoring countrymen.

We might pause over one specimen reaching him in those years that will serve for many such testimonials to the worth of his long life. On a summer day in 1852, after he had complimented the work of a younger writer, Irving would receive a letter from Concord, Massachusetts. "I beg you to believe, my dear Sir, that your friendly and approving word was one of the highest gratifications that I could possibly have received, from any literary source. Ever since I began to write," Nathaniel Hawthorne was therein confessing, "I have kept it among my cherished hopes to obtain such a word; nor did I ever publish a book without debating within myself whether to offer it to your notice. Nevertheless, the idea of introducing myself to you as an author, while unrecognized by the public, was not quite agreeable, and I saw too many faults in each of my books to be altogether willing to obtrude it beneath your eye." Those books would have included *The Scarlet Letter* and *The House of the Seven Gables*. Incapable of flattery, the reserved Hawthorne went on: "Pray do not think it necessary to praise my 'Blithedale Romance'—or even to acknowledge the receipt of it. From my own little experience, I can partly judge how dearly purchased are books that come to you on such terms. It affords me—and I ask no more—an opportunity of expressing the affectionate admiration which I have felt so long; a feeling, by the way, common to all our countrymen, in reference to Washington Irving, and which, I think, you can hardly appreciate, because there is no writer with the qualities to awaken in yourself precisely the same intellectual and heart-felt recognition."

So despite what he judged to have been a precarious and desultory career, the denizen of Sunnyside had become a unique national possession, and—according to Hawthorne—was affectionately regarded as such by all his countrymen, founding their Irving Societies and building their Irving banks and naming their ships and streets and towns for him. The object of such adulation might understandably have been content to rest on what he had achieved. Yet in those thirteen years after his

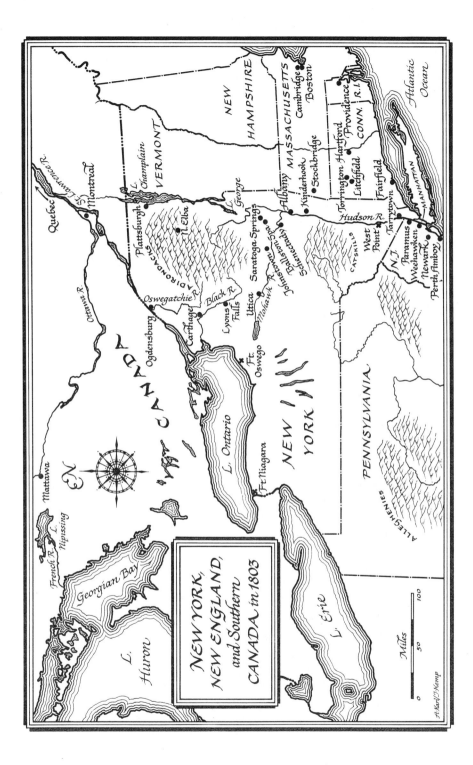

NEW YORK,
NEW ENGLAND,
and Southern
CANADA in 1803

final return to America, Irving would go on writing almost to the very end, preparing a revised edition of his complete works, composing his engaging study of Goldsmith, publishing various Spanish sketches that had lain a long time unfinished, and heroically committing his diminished strength to what would prove by far his longest piece of prose: the five-volume biography of Washington, not finally completed until the last, tormented months of his life.

Those efforts did meanwhile urge Irving from time to time to bestir himself from the comforts of Sunnyside, so that his closing years were not entirely sedentary. Several trips he took by train to Washington, to visit Mt. Vernon and talk with descendants of his namesake. More than once he journeyed north to Saratoga Springs, mingling for rest and health among fashionable guests on the porches of the United States Hotel. And in 1853, in the late summer, he traveled in company from that resort, fleeing the heat, "down Lake Champlain in a steamer to Plattsburg, whence we made a night journey by railroad to Ogdensburg. Here we passed part of a day—a very interesting one to me."

The seventy-year-old gentleman had been at Ogdensburg before, along the St. Lawrence in upper New York State, when it was only the empty lots of a future town. Exactly fifty years earlier, as a young man of twenty, Irving had been at this very spot, "quartered in some rude buildings belonging to a ruined French fort at the mouth of the Oswegatchie." And now in 1853, somehow he was seventy. Seventy years old! And then he had been twenty, and in that earlier summer of 1803 exploring the Black River country and lingering a week or longer with the Hoffmans and the Ogdens here where all had been romance. What happy days they had been: "rambling about the woods with the young ladies; or paddling with them in Indian canoes on the limpid waters of the St. Lawrence; or fishing about the rapids and visiting the Indians, who still lived on islands in the river. Every thing was so grand and so silent and solitary. I don't think any scene in life made a more delightful impression upon me."

So he adjudged when that same life, full of impressions, was finally nearing its end. Chance had brought the old gentleman back, moving with the dignity of his years through a tour that would take him on up the river and across Lake Ontario to Niagara. But first he must search out the French fort that had sheltered that other party of which his young self, with most of life before him, had been a member.

Alas, not a trace of the fort remained. With some difficulty he did, however, find where it had stood, and there under a tree sat down "and looked round upon what I had known as a wilderness—now teeming with life—crowded with habitations—the Oswegatchie River dammed up and encumbered by vast stone-mills—the broad St. Lawrence ploughed by immense steamers."

After a while he rose and walked to the point of land where, half a century earlier, with two young ladies he had sometimes launched a canoe onto the water, "while the rest of the party would wave handkerchiefs, and cheer us from shore." That spot had become a busy landing place for steamers. "There were still some rocks where I used to sit of an evening and accompany with my flute one of the ladies who sang." Once more, and for a long time, the old gentleman sat on those rocks, "summoning recollections of bygone days, and of the happy beings by whom I was then surrounded."

All of them—Mr. and Mrs. Hoffman, and Anne Hoffman, and Mr. and Mrs. Ludlow Ogden, and Miss Eliza Ogden—"all were dead and gone; of that young and joyous party I was the sole survivor; they had all lived quietly at home out of the reach of mischance, yet had gone down to their graves; while I, who had been wandering about the world, exposed to all hazards by sea and land, was yet alive. It seemed almost marvellous. I have often, in my shifting about the world, come upon the traces of former existence; but," the old gentleman, back home at Sunnyside that autumn, would conclude about this recent encounter, "I do not think any thing has made a stronger impression on me than this second visit to the banks of the Oswegatchie."

Reverse the flow of time. Restore (as we can) the bewigged septuagenarian to youth, to childhood. A child is poised at the outset of experiences destined to figure so prominently in his many-sided life as to lead some readers to value, most highly of all Irving's work, the writings they ultimately inspired. We have yet to consider this final aspect of Washington Irving's life and achievement.

Back in time, and he is only five or six, the family—Deacon Irving, his wife, their five sons and three daughters—all together for a brief while yet, living in the high wooden house among the greengages on William Street at the tip of Manhattan. The year is 1788. The eldest daughter, Anne, already at seventeen has determined to marry and move far away to the frontier, up the Hudson to Albany and forty miles west along the Mohawk River, where her bridegroom means to trade with Indians for furs. Washington's oldest brother, William, has been coaxed into accompanying the newlyweds, and in fact will remain in the wilderness four years, until 1791, before tiring of the trader's life and returning home. Irving's sister, however, and another recently married sister, Kitty, will eventually establish homes in Johnstown, north of the Mohawk; and at the start of the new century, in 1800, their youngest brother, seventeen himself by that time, will prevail on his family to let him ascend the river to visit them.

"A voyage to Albany then, was equal to a voyage to Europe at present, and took almost as much time," so the elderly Irving recalled at mid-century. Along the wide river the sloop, with boom creaking, would tack its leisurely way, anchoring each night at the foot of mountains or alongside forests, where "every thing grew dark and mysterious; and I heard the plaintive note of the whip-poor-will from the mountain-side, or was startled now and then by the sudden leap and heavy splash of the sturgeon." With daylight the vessel glided farther northward until in sight of the Catskills: "Never," wrote Irving later, "shall I forget the effect upon me of the first view of them predominating over a wide extent of country, part wild, woody, and rugged; part softened away into all the graces of cultivation. As we slowly floated along, I lay on the deck and watched them through a long summer's day . . ."

In three years the youth would again behold such views (haunts that his pen would make famous in "Rip Van Winkle") and much else besides, on the trip that would lead him to Ogdensburg along the St. Lawrence and beyond in 1803. He was twenty by then, the anonymous author of some mildly satirical letters by Jonathan Oldstyle published in his brother Peter's Burrite newspaper. But *Salmagundi* and *Knickerbocker* and all the rest of his literary achievement lay in the future of this young clerk in the New York law office of Josiah Hoffman. Hoffman, thirty-seven, was responsible for the present trip—he and his thirty-year-old cousin Ludlow Ogden. Both had interests in land bought on speculation in upstate New York, and the overland voyage would allow them to examine what they had purchased.

In Hoffman's family were two daughters. The younger, Matilda, was only eleven or so, too young yet to awaken the intense love that Irving was to feel for her in time, in the months before her early death in the Greenwich Street bedroom six years later. But the other daughter, Ann, was thirteen, and old enough already to accompany her father and stepmother, Hoffman's second wife, only twenty-three herself in that adventurous summer. These, then, with Ogden's wife and Miss Eliza Ogden, twenty-one, chiefly comprised the party that launched forth by sail from Manhattan for Albany about three on Saturday afternoon, July 30, 1803.

Irving's journal of that trip—the first long trip of his well-traveled life—survives, a booklet of fifty-nine pages of notes in brown ink that let us ascend the Hudson in pleasant company, going ashore for milk and cheese when the breezes die, or on deck underway trying the echoes with fowling pieces and pistols at every mountain. From Albany overland the group rode to Ballston Springs, then in a hired stage to Utica, from which the punishing part of their journey commenced.

For this was veritable frontier then. They were setting out into the backwoods beyond Utica by wagon, "having sent the chief of our baggage in a waggon the preceding afternoon. The roads were very bad and the countery around afforded but little variety of prospect." So the young journalist recorded at the end of that day's progress. "We however found sufficient entertainment in the waggon to make the time pass pleasantly along & the jolting of the rugged roads seemed rather to heighten our amusement." He had been reading passages of Shakespeare to the ladies as they jogged forward, "& was much entertained with Ann Hoffmans reading several scenes in Romeo & Juliet," wilderness all about them. That night they spent at "a very decent log house tavern," where "in the course of the evening Mrs Hoffman sung & I accompanied her on the flute."

Such good spirits near the start would be well taxed before the journey ended. At daybreak next morning they were up and soon proceeding along roads that grew worse, obliging all of them more than once to get out of the wagon and walk alongside. Near what is now Lyons Falls they discharged the wagons and prepared to descend the Black River in a scow, some forty miles to the falls at present-day Carthage. Even now the area is hardly dense with people, tucked off on the other side of the Adirondacks, but then it had been opened to settlers only a decade; a day might elapse without these travelers' seeing another human face. Now descending the winding river, Irving and his friends were passing between banks "covered with lofty trees which entirely confine the prospect except now and then in the course of several miles you may pass by a log house round which the land is partially cleared exhibiting a dreary scene of burnt stumps and fallen trunks of trees." And before they could reach their landing place, rain had started pouring down. "We had just stopped by a brook that ran into the river to get some cold water and eat crackers when it began." By the time they got ashore and to another log house, about dark, it had soaked them through. Inside before a fire they dried their clothes, then "retired to a back room (the house consisting only of two rooms) where we had beds spread on the floor and made out to pass the night as comfortably as a numerous regiment of fleas would permit us."

Even so, that lodging was far better than the following night's, at what is now Carthage, in a structure that the travelers dubbed the Temple of Dirt: "a dirtier house was never seen . . . it was impossible to relish any thing in a house so completely filthy. The Landlady herself was perfectly in character with the house. A little squab french woman with a red face, a black wool hat stuck upon her head her hair greasy & uncombed hanging about her ears and the rest of her dress and person in similar stile We were heartily glad to make an escape from a house so extremely disgusting."

From there they ventured overland again, "60 miles thro the woods" to Ogdensburg. But those sixty miles would take them five days to negotiate, on a road "dreadfully rugged and miry. The horses could not go off of a walk in any part." At times the path could hardly be distinguished from the rest of the forest. It rained some more, and the wagon "stuck fast in the mire and one of the horses laid down refusing to budge an inch further." The ladies and gentlemen transferred to the second wagon, leaving their drivers to try levering out the forsaken vehicle. But the second wagon had not gone far down the road, "full of deep mud holes," before it, too, was "fairly stuck fast in one where the mud & water almost covered the Horses back." The only recourse was for all to walk. "The rain by this time descended in Torrents. In several parts of the road I had been up to my middle in mud and water and it was equally bad if not worse to attempt to walk in the woods on either side. We helped the ladies to a little shed of bark laid on crotches about large enough to hold three when they set down; It had been a nights shelter to some hunter but in this case it afforded no protection, one half of it fell down as we were creeping under it and though we spread great coats on the other, they might as well have been in the open air. The rain now fell in the greatest quantity I had ever seen. The wind blew a perfect hurricane."

Over the huddled travelers trees were creaking and bending alarmingly. A house, they had been told, was half a mile away; and the women, now thoroughly frightened, wanted to look for it. "We therefore dragged along—wet to the skin wading through mud holes—it seemed as if the whole forest was under water"—dragged along until they reached what turned out to be no more than a hut. A man named Hazelton lived there alone. Accommodations were primitive: "the fire place (which was nothing but a large part of the floor left bare and an aperture in the roof over head) took up a fourth part of the room, the spaces between the logs were not filled up and admitted the light and air in every direction." A berth in one corner served for a bed, "and on it a peice of old carpet by way of mattrass—An old chest of drawers laid on their back & shoved under the birth. two or three crazy chairs a rough table & 4 or 5 kegs of rum made up the furniture of this dwelling."

Irving and his friends had arrived to find a couple of brothers, who had been driving an ox team to Ogdensburg, already sheltering there. Their name was Sharp, and they promptly revealed themselves to be "extremely noisy and boisterous. One of them in particular was the most impudent chattering forward scoundrel I ever knew." Soon Hoffman's wagon drivers caught up and came in to get dry, making "15 people in this small room" (it measured eighteen feet by sixteen) "the men began to drink immediately and were very noizy in their greetings and welcomings to each other. The Ladies appeared almost ready to give up We had now been two days travelling and had got but 21 miles into the wilderness."

Worse was to follow. One of the drivers went out to chop firewood, but "wounded his foot very badly with the axe he entered the hut with his foot bleeding." Catching sight of the blood, Mrs. Hoffman fainted, and Irving, in this dreariest night of his young life, felt despairing, "here in a wilderness, no medical aid near, among a set of men rough and some of them insolent (the Sharps) with ladies of delicate minds and constitutions sinking under fatigue and apprehension."

Yet for all that, the city folk held up surprisingly well. Mrs. Hoffman came to, and the party got tea made and had boiled corn and potatoes, then arranged beds—Hoffman and Ogden on the floor, Mrs. Hoffman and Mrs. Ogden on the carpet-covered berth, Ann and Miss Eliza on a mattress laid over the chest of drawers. In the opposite corner, at full voice, the drivers went on playing cards for liquor with the Sharps, "very boisterous." Ann was in tears. Beside the girls' bed Irving had stationed himself across two chairs, over the backs of which greatcoats were spread to shield the women from the gamblers' leers. The rain poured down. Drunk, the cardplayers at last slid to the floor to sleep, leaving a wakeful Irving to sit through the rest of the night holding an umbrella over the ladies, listening to the crash of trees outside, and from time to time distinguishing in the darkness some wolf's long dreary howl.

Worse still: to those same brothers Sharp the traveling party from New York was obliged to become indebted next day, a long Sunday night having finally turned into Monday morning, the fourteenth having turned at last into the fifteenth of August, 1803. "We found it impossible to travel the roads with horses and therefore engaged the Sharps to take our baggage through on their ox cart." After the storm the skies had cleared, but the woods were marsh, the oxen sinking deep in mud, Irving and the others forced among sun patches "to jump from trunk to trunk of dead trees that laid along side of the road." They pressed on, annoyed by "musquitoes and *punkies* or gnats an insect so minute that you cannot see it till it is on your skin where it bites very severely." Hornets—"(a poisonous kind of insect which had frequently annoyed us on the road)"—assailed them anew. They endured the scoundrelly Sharps, apportioned out their dwindled rations of potatoes and bread until forced for a day to go without food entirely, and slept the night in an open hovel with their "trunks &c on the roof (which was flat) to keep the dew from falling on us."

But at last, to their joy, they came within sight of Ogdensburg. "The prospect that opened upon us was delightful after riding through thick woods for several days where the eye is confined to a narrow space and fatigued with a continual repetition of similar objects, the sight of a beautiful & extensive tract of country is inconceivably enlivening." Alongside, some twenty feet below the path, flowed the Oswegatchie River, entering the broad St. Lawrence ahead. The juncture formed a point of land "on which stood a few houses called the Garrison which had formerly been a fortified place built by the french to keep the indians in awe they were now tumbling in ruins excepting two or three which were still kept in tolerable order by Judge ford, who resided in one of them and used the others as stores and out houses. We recrossed the Oswegatchie river to the Garrison as we intended to reside with Judge ford for some time. . . ."

This was the fort, then, and these the happy summer days, stretching forward into two weeks and more, that Irving himself, exactly a half-century older and nearing the end of his lifelong journey, would seek to recreate, recalling the fishing, the shooting, the visits with Indians and laying out of town lots, recalling a young law clerk's helping with bonds and deeds, and his launching a canoe bearing two girls just at this spot on the limpid river, while friends were waving merrily from the shore.

Not many—and those often traders with Indians—had penetrated into upper New York when young Irving made his first visit there. But one in particular who had preceded him through these regions would, during their friendship of future years, have been an understanding listener to the author's reminiscences about backwoods adventures—all the more so considering the direction that the Hoffman party had followed after leaving Ogdensburg. Irving's earliest journal ends while he and his friends are still in the vicinity of the old French fort along the St. Lawrence, but elsewhere we learn from an older Irving that he had, on this as on one or two later occasions, crossed into Canada and made his way to Montreal. There the young New Yorker had entered a colorful world that his predecessor in these remote parts, the immigrant John Jacob Astor, had already come to know.

"In the course of visits in early life to Canada," a world-famous Irving would write from Sunnyside, "I had seen much of the magnates of the Northwest Company, and of the hardy trappers and fur-traders in their employ, and had been excited by their stories of adventurous expeditions into the 'Indian country.' " And elsewhere, at the beginning of a book composed in Astor's home, Irving remembered again those late summer days in Canada in 1803, among "the principal partners of the great North West Fur Company, who at that time lived in genial style at Montreal, and kept almost open house for the stranger. At their hospitable boards I occasionally met with partners, and clerks, and hardy fur traders from the interior posts; men who had passed years remote from civilized society, among distant and savage tribes, and who had wonders to recount of their wide and wild peregrinations, their hunting exploits, and their perilous adventures and hairbreadth escapes among the Indians. I was at an age when the imagination lends its coloring to every thing, and the stories of these Sinbads of the wilderness made the life of a trapper and fur trader perfect romance to me."

To be sure, by 1803, with young Irving and the Hoffmans on their way to Ogdensburg and Montreal, Astor's own years as a trader in the backwoods were behind him. But for a number of seasons he, too, had trudged through the forests north and west of Albany, had negotiated mud holes, slapping at mosquitoes, and built his camp fires at dusk before lying down in a makeshift lean-to to listen to the cry of the wolf late at night under the summer moon. In 1788, in fact, when Irving's eldest brother and brother-in-law were first setting out from Manhattan to trade for furs along the Mohawk River, Astor in his mid-twenties had already passed through regions not far from those wilds to engage in the same enterprise.

This immigrant had sailed from Europe for America in 1783, the very year of Washington Irving's birth, the year when independence from England was finally won. Astor's own birth had occurred twenty years before that date, at the end of the war between England and France that delivered French forts along the St. Lawrence—and all that vast fur country—to the British once and for all. The fort that Irving would see falling in ruins in 1803, the fort that had disappeared without a trace by his return in 1853, had been functioning as a French bastion, out there beyond the edges of civilization, during the struggle for the control of Canada and up to the year when Astor was born: in 1763, on July 17, in the village of Walldorf some ten miles from Heidelberg, state of Baden, Germany.

But the Astor family would hardly have been concerned with distant political upheavals across an ocean. They were humble people. Astor's father was a butcher—remained a butcher in that same German village for forty years, then retired and lived there thirty years longer until his death past ninety, well into the nineteenth century. The son John Jacob, one of several children, had been set to the task of learning the butcher's trade as soon as he reached fourteen. But an older brother had emigrated to England by then, and another, after serving in the English navy in those years before the American Revolution, was already settling into a new life in colonial New York. Their example beckoned an adventurous youth condemned to a present of delivering slabs of meat to village customers, to a future of hacking at carcasses until he was old and feeble. For a couple of years young Astor did serve his cheerless apprenticeship at his father's shop; but in 1779, he set out on foot from Walldorf to try his hand elsewhere. Walking the few miles to the Rhine, he got a job on a timber raft that furnished him passage down to the sea, then traveled by Dutch smack across the Channel to England.

When he arrived in London he was sixteen, and spoke no English. But his brother George had established a music shop in that city, so that for the next four years, while the American Revolution was in progress on the other side of the Atlantic, the younger brother worked among fifes and organs and hautbois, gaining competence in the business, putting aside some money, and more or less learning the English language —though he would speak it all his life with a thick German accent. How he would write it we shall have occasion to see.

The treaty of peace between England and America, signed September 3, 1783, opened the way for the twenty-year-old Astor to set out from Bristol two months later, aboard the *North Carolina*, bound for America, for that land that his other brother's letters from New York had long been extolling. The years of working at the music shop in England had provided him with a savings of fifteen guineas. Five of these paid Astor's steerage passage, including salt beef and biscuit for as long as the voyage might last. Five more the young man invested in a few flutes from his brother's factory to sell at a profit on the other side of the Atlantic. What was left of the last five guineas when he got there he would use to establish himself in the New World.

His arrival was badly timed. A day's sail from Baltimore the ship lay locked in ice in the midst of a severe winter at Chesapeake Bay—and remained locked for two months after its January landfall in American waters. Most passengers soon grew weary with waiting and crossed the ice on foot to shore, but for a long time the frugal Astor stayed with the vessel, eating his rations of biscuit and salt beef, maybe learning from shipboard talk about opportunities in this free new country. Finally, however, even his patience was exhausted: "having then been more than four months on board"—and more than half that time icebound in sight of land—"I was desirous to get on shore as soon as I could. which I did . . . I think it was on the 24ᵗʰ or 25ᵗʰ of March 1784 that I arrived in Baltimore. Some days previous to the arrival of the ship N. Carolina in which I came passenger."

He is writing to his friend Washington Irving, half a century later. "I remember," he goes on, "the day on which I first arrived at Baltimore I took a walk to see the town. getting up Market Sᵗ. while standing and looking about, a little fat man came out of his shop. This was Nicholas Tuschdy he addressed me saying—young man I believe you are a stranger, to which I replied yes.—Where did you come from.—from London—but you are not an Englishman no a German. Then says he we are near country men I am a Swiss—we are glad to see people coming to this conitry from Europe. On this he asked me into his house and offered me a glass of wine and introduced me to his wife as a countryman. He offered his services and advice while in Baltimore and requested me to call again to see him. I did call again to see him when I stated that I had some articles of merchandise to dispose of chiefly music and musical—instruments, he observed that if I would put some in his store that he would sell them free of any commission or expense, and I gave him some to sell. He was a very worthy & kind man and for many years one of my correspondents." From the beginning good fortune was attending the young immigrant. "I remained about three weeks in Baltimore and recᵈ. much kindness & civility for which I could not myself account in any way but the kindness of the people all which I recollect with much pleasure."

Such a welcoming atmosphere may have tempted him to tarry: "we are glad to see people coming to this conitry." But Astor was bound for New York, where his brother Henry lived. That town of just over twenty thousand people he reached in the late spring of 1784, and was promptly hired as a baker's delivery boy in the shop of a fellow country-man. Before long the new arrival had other wares than bread and cakes for sale; for a Mrs. Noble later assured her daughter that she could remember having "bought pins, needles, tape, beads, from John Jacob Astor when he peddled them in a basket around the streets."

Within this heterogeneous little city such a peddler would have encountered many backwoodsmen: traders, Indians, riverboatmen, farm-boys bearing furs down from surrounding forests to exchange for goods in the port at the mouth of the Hudson. That summer Astor traded trinkets—those beads and pins perhaps—for his first pelts. And before the summer ended, he was working for an old Quaker named Bowne, who dealt in furs—was beating the pelts to keep out moths, at the same time learning much about the business.

Which furs are valuable? Who pays most for them? How are they trapped, cured, stored, packed, transported? He had come to America to sell musical instruments, but perhaps on the ship over, perhaps in these early weeks in the New York of Irving's infancy, Astor began to take an interest in furs. He traded for them where he could—along the water-front, aboard sloops in the harbor—stored them away as he got them, then went out and traded for more. For his labor in Bowne's shop he received two dollars a week and board; most of the pay went for trinkets to trade for still more furs. And so successful was he in amassing those random pelts that before the autumn of that same year, his first in America, he was on his way back across the ocean to England to sell what furs he had in the London market.

Few in America yet wore garments made from such elegant pelts, but in Europe they had been highly valued for centuries; we think of Chaucer's opulent merchant with the "Flaundryssh bevere hat" on his head, in company with the plump monk, sleeves trimmed with costly gray fur, on their fourteenth-century pilgrimage to Canterbury. Europe was where furs had always commanded high prices, Europe and China, so that on this first of several return trips to the Old World, Astor could make a substantial enough profit to pay for the voyage and leave him money to pick up English-made merchandise—knives, awls, kettles, tin mirrors—valued more highly than furs in a New World still abundantly primitive.

It seems so easy in retrospect: be diligent, apply yourself, squander nothing. Astor, like many tradesmen then, trafficked in several wares: in musical instruments, in toys. Get more than one iron in the fire. But furs absorbed his talents more and more; and after he had returned to New York, his employer Bowne, impressed, agreed to meet expenses for a risky expedition into upstate Indian fur country if Astor would go. Obviously the young man already knew which pelts to look for among bark lodges near the hunting grounds of the Oneidas and Cayugas, and how much to give for what he found.

Know your business, and keep at it. See Astor, then, in the late spring of 1785, dressed in his woodsman's cap and rough cotton shirt and thick boots and mackinaw, on his back the sack of finger rings and ribbons and pans to barter, in his pocket maybe some coins, clay pipe in hand, flintlock under his arm as he boards the sloop for Albany. Others later remembered having encountered him thus in the backwoods. "John Jacob Astor, with a pack of Indian goods upon his back, wandered from the Indian trail, got lost in the low grounds at the foot of Seneca Lake in an inclement night, wandered amid the howl and the rustling of wild beasts, until almost morning, when he was attracted by the light of an Indian cabin, near the old castle, and following it, obtained shelter and warmth." That was around where Canandaigua is now. Another contemporary deposed: "Many times I have seen John Jacob Astor with his coat off, unpacking in a vacant yard near my residence a lot of furs he had bought dog-cheap off the Indians and beating them out, cleaning them and repacking them in more elegant and salable form to be transported to England and Germany, where they would yield him 1,000 per cent on the original cost." On foot, by canoe, by pack horse, by wagon he was seeking out tribes in order to barter with them, on two expeditions for Bowne, thereafter for himself alone. His face was browned by the sun, swollen by insect bites. "His wagon had broken down in the midst of a swamp. In the *mêlée* all his gold had rolled away through the bottom of the vehicle, and was irrecoverably lost; and Astor was seen emerging from the swamp covered with mud and carrying on his shoulder an axe—the sole relic of his property. . . ."

Keep at it, though. Not for Bowne, but for himself alone he was soon laboring—and for his family. So it would be for the rest of Astor's long life. He had married by now, in the autumn of 1785, a local girl a year older than he was. She brought him a dowry of $300, connections with some of the better families in town, and a base—in his mother-in-law's boardinghouse on Queen Street—from which to operate. By May 1786 he had opened a shop there, "two doors from the Friends Meetinghouse," as the advertisement under the name of Jacob Astor specified in the New York *Packet*. At the shop could be purchased clarinets, German flutes, violins, violin strings. But the rank smell of furs was elsewhere in the establishment, from two back rooms and the stable, where his wife would often help him with beating, grading, packing the beaver pelts for shipment overseas. Eventually, on April 29, 1788, to the usual newspaper notice by J. Jacob Astor, reporting the arrival of an assortment of pianofortes "per the ship Ann from London," was added for the first time the information: "He gives cash for all kinds of Furs; and has for sale a quantity of Canada Furs, such as beaver, beaver coating; raccoon skins, raccoon blankets, and spring musk rat skins; which he sells by large or small quantities—a considerable allowance will be made to every person who buys a quantity."

For only a while longer would Astor venture out to the woods himself to trade for pelts with white trappers and Indians. Now he had a partner, Peter Smith—and "I have," he could still write Smith years after the partnership ended, "the Highest oppinion of your judgement & prudanese." In the Mohawk Valley, in a room in his house at what is now Utica, Smith had set up a trading post, acquiring furs that found their way to Astor's shop on Queen Street, there to be sold locally or to be transported abroad. For his part, the German did continue to journey from home, leaving his competent wife to manage affairs at the store; but now he would make his way to Montreal, departing in summertime and negotiating the two-week trip by sloop, wagon, and canoe, up to Albany, thence to Lake Champlain and over to Plattsburgh, from there to the St. Lawrence and on into Canada. Once arrived at Montreal, he would generally remain a couple of months purchasing furs, extending his personal contacts, and deepening his knowledge of the business before returning home in the middle of autumn.

This journey Astor was to make year after year, from as early as 1788 to as late as 1809. For as the recollections of Irving have suggested, Montreal was at the time the center of the fur trade for as much of North America as had yet been explored; and the magnates of that trade—Scotsmen almost to a man—were living there in high style on the proceeds of the barter. Whoever wanted furs in quantity must come to them. Long before the French (in the year of Astor's birth) lost Canada, furs had already become the principal resource of that immense region. As spices had stirred Columbus to search for Cipango, furs had brought the French to the St. Lawrence, the Dutch to Manhattan, the Swedes to Delaware. Dutchmen and Swedes were gone now, and the furs of the Connecticut Valley and New England all but exhausted. Around the Great Lakes, however, both north and south, beaver and other fur-bearing animals remained plentiful. And beaver above all was needed, for hats in Europe—tricorns of soldiers and high hats of gentlemen. So people overseas would pay well for the beaver that Indians had valued hardly at all. Accordingly, the magnates at Montreal were living through these years in fur-lined splendor.

All the more so because they had a monopoly. For a while after the French left, the fur trade in the forests back from the clear waters of Ontario and Erie and Huron had been in chaos—ruthless competition among trappers who were murdering rivals, pillaging each other's pelts, routinely debauching Indians with cheap rum for more furs. To restore order a group of prominent traders at Montreal had come together (this was in 1783, the year that Irving was born, the year that Astor left England for America) and formed the North West Fur Company. Trappers and traders must deal with them henceforth. From England those partners would regularly import blankets and scarlet cloth and buttons and whatever glittering ornaments of English make the Indians currently coveted. Then once a year, in forty-foot-long, resin-daubed, birch-bark canoes, with all the pomp of Highland chieftains, they would set out from Montreal in lordly caravans to deliver goods to the backwoods posts, to which the solitary traders might come to get them. Astor went along at least once, ascending the Ottawa River, making the portage near what is now Mattawa (all the four thousand pounds of cargo having been packed in hundred-pound lots for the purpose) to Lake Nipissing, then by water again down to Georgian Bay. At that juncture the canoes would emerge under the wide skies of the Great Lakes, with access to all the forts and posts, and to the backwater rivers and creeks from which pelts were being delivered. Astor went on that glorious inland voyage, which Washington Irving repined throughout his life that he never got to make. For as a young man Irving, too, had "meditated at one time a visit to the remote posts of the company in the boats which annually ascended the lakes and rivers, being thereto invited by one of the partners; and I have ever since regretted that I was prevented by circumstances from carrying my intention into effect."

The regret is altogether understandable. What a trip it would have been to a sensibility like his! The boatmen—ten paddlers per canoe, most of them French and carefree—singing responsively to the steersmen as they moved the huge canoes smoothly forward, foreman at the bow calling back notice of snags, steersman barking commands from the stern, the cleaving of water, the good cheer and clear air, the deep green of spruce and hemlock forests, blue summer sky overhead, camps along the shore—accompanying cooks and bakers busy now—with all the lavish food and fine wines spread out that this annual ceremony commanded. Then the arrival at the posts—Detroit, Michilimackinac, Fort William—to be welcomed before the palisades and led to the bourgeois' quarters to feast again, among antlers and furs and thick beams and a huge stone fireplace, on venison and beaver tail, with the bustle in the stockade of unpacking, the accounting among the clerks, and the repacking, this time of furs that would return with the canoes full of song to Montreal:

> Tous du lông de la rivière,
> Legérément ma bergère,
> Legèrement, ye ment . . .

Not that the aesthetics of the enterprise would have mattered much to Astor. He was along to learn the fur trade thoroughly, but nothing about his later life suggests that the magic of the frontier ever touched him. As soon as he could he left to agents all treks into the wilderness. Indeed, though his commercial empire in time spread westward far beyond these Great Lakes, he never evidenced a longing to see the places with names that would become familiar in his New York count-inghouse: the Mississippi, the Missouri, the Rockies, the Columbia, Canton. So on this trip up the Ottawa he traveled not for the scenery, but for what more his shrewd mind and observant eye could learn of the economics of furs.

Winter pelts are best, of course, when the fur grows longest. Indian and white trappers, almost indistinguishable in appearance, were scattered thinly about pursuing their forest lives, along riverbanks near beaver dams, pursuing their lonely callings. You trapped a beaver with a metal trap, carefully dug down or raised up to be hidden four inches below the surface of the stream. Over the spot a twig would be set, one end in the river bottom. On the other end, maybe four inches above the water, bait would have been rubbed, an odor imperceptible to humans, extracted from glandular pouches in the beaver itself. Other beavers assuredly could smell the odor, and would be drawn to it, until one creature lifted itself toward the twig over the hidden trap and stepped a paw down onto its destruction. Caught, the beaver would make for mid-stream, but the trap was chained to a stake that had been driven deep into the river bottom. Returning later in the day to his set, the trapper would draw in the chain and find the drowned beaver. Maybe four or five such he could catch with traps enough on a lucky day.

About eighty beavers made up a pack weighing a hundred pounds, worth maybe three hundred dollars. That might be a whole year's labor to get together, and the proceeds for those who successfully protected their annual haul and delivered it downriver to Montreal would be squandered in a few days of wild living before the trappers headed back to the woods again. Indians would sew beaver skins together and wear them as garments, fur side in, for several months; such pelts, softened and made downy by skin grease, were most valuable of all. White men, mostly loners in the backwoods for years at a time, might trade for skins instead of trap them, using those coveted tin pots and jew's harps for which they had been overcharged on credit at the fort. Or Indians from the Mississippi might come to the forts themselves, setting up their wigwams or birch-bark camps on the beach nearby so the bargaining could begin. But one way or another beaver furs were moved down the streams and rivers to the lakes, from the lakes to Montreal, from Mont-real overseas to stylish London.

In that mercantile age English law forbade the transporting of Canadian furs anywhere except to London. But some—more and more—were finding their way to Astor's shop in Manhattan. The still modest demand for beaver in America was being satisfied legally in a roundabout way: not overland across the Canadian border and down the Hudson, but by ship from Montreal clear across the ocean to England, then back across the ocean to New York. Even so, profits were such that it paid "Astor, John J. furr trader, 40, Little-Dock street" to deal in Canada furs, supposing (doubtful supposition) no smuggling occurred across the St. Lawrence. And his partner, Peter Smith, meanwhile went on providing him with some American furs from the Mohawk Valley.

So Astor was prospering. He moved in 1790 from his mother-in-law's boardinghouse at 81 Queen Street to larger quarters, as listed in the registry for that year, on Little Dock Street. Four years later he had moved again to a still larger establishment at 149 Broadway, where his residence was located on the second floor, over the shop. By then he was a merchant of some consequence, and the father of a growing family. A daughter, Magdalen, had been born in 1788. His first son, John Jacob, Jr., was born in 1791, and a second son, William, the following year. In the spring of 1795 Astor was back in Europe, extending his connections with London merchants, assessing the European fur market, allowing himself the pleasure of revisiting relatives in the village of Walldorf from which he had set out on foot all but penniless sixteen years earlier. Already the emigrant had so heartily thrived in the New World that he could afford to sit for two portraits by Gilbert Stuart, subsequently the painter of Washington; they show the German in his early thirties, slender still, handsome enough, with thin mouth and strong chin and penetrating eyes. This was the well-dressed and successful John Jacob Astor whom his aging father and stepmother—the butcher and egg seller—were to welcome on that springtime return to Baden in 1795. By late summer the voyager had completed his visit to "Gearmaney & francs," as he wrote, and was home in New York ready to set out once more for the fur capital at Montreal.

Judging by his letters, however, success was not so easily wrought as here appears. To Smith he confides that he has returned from Europe to find business "very mush Derangd So that I Shall am afraid fall short of Cash Even to Comply with my Engagements." A characteristic of Astor's prose, now and later, is that note of cautious pessimism, but events had occurred recently that must have buoyed his spirits nevertheless. When America had won its independence from England, one triumph of the diplomacy of Franklin and his fellow negotiators at Paris had been the drawing of a boundary between Canada and its new neighbor that bisected the Great Lakes and gave all of Lake Michigan to the latter. But a decade had passed, and the English garrisons in the New World had simply refused to vacate those crucial forts along the right banks of the Lakes and rivers, at Michilimackinac, Detroit, Niagara, Oswego, Oswegatchie. Too much was at stake to give them up "with all possible speed"—whatever faraway diplomats had ordained; and fur merchants of Montreal and fur traders in the wilderness both north and south of the Lakes (almost all at the time Canadian) were naturally content to have the forts remain in English hands. Now, late in 1794, John Jay had shaped a new treaty with the English in London. In the months ahead the forts would be evacuated after all. The time was near—as Astor saw more clearly than most—when an entirely American fur enterprise could be developed, independent of Montreal and the Scots magnates to the north.

Meanwhile, the range of his commercial interests continued to grow. Smith, out there in the wilderness where Utica stands now, was acquiring land, and Astor was also coming into possession of certain sprawling expanses in the back country, most of them received as payment for debts owed him. He sounded doubtful sometimes about such holdings as investments. "I Dont think I Can buy as I have nothing to get Cash with un Less it be Bank Shares which Cost me 40 p Ct & now Sell but at 15 p Cent advance which you knaw would be making a very grate sacrificig . . ." That to Smith in 1793. And five years later, litigation connected with upstate lands would cause him to erupt to the same correspondent: "I am very Sick of the Busniess all the mony I Can muster gos for this Damd businiss it is too much for me to Lay aut of . . . if we have no prospect of Success Lets be Done with it at ances and thraugh no more mony away for if no Stop is put to it I shall yet be ruind with it."

But Astor was not ruined, in 1798 or at any time thereafter. Not only did he possess wealth in backcountry real estate, like Hoffman and Ogden and others of the period. He was also enlarging his interests in much else besides: in real estate nearer Manhattan, in musical instruments and toys still, in firearms for sale locally, in imported English goods, in various American goods for export in increasing quantities to Europe. But above all he was interested in furs. In 1800, as he was moving his store yet again, to 71 Liberty Street (keeping his residence at the Broadway address), the German was learning from a dealer in distant St. Louis that he already was "beyond question the greatest of the fur merchants. Your relations at home and abroad give you facilities which no other house in the United States possesses." And as the new century began, the once humble butcher's boy, sixteen years after his arrival in America, was already worth $250,000, a stupendous fortune in an age when a good house rented for $350 a year, when a gentleman and his family might live very well, in fact, on no more than $800 a year.

A quarter of a million: Astor was thirty-seven. Three years later he moved his family—now increased to two sons and three daughters—to 223 Broadway, into a house built by the wealthy and impeccable Federalist statesman Rufus King, confidant of Hamilton. Thus far had the fur beater come by 1803.

That same year, in the summer, young Washington Irving— twenty years old—was making his first long trip, with the Hoffmans and Ogdens through Black River country in upstate New York to Ogdensburg and on to Montreal. By then Irving's family undoubtedly knew Astor and was known by him; and during this same visit to Montreal in 1803 Irving was to meet Astor's agent and nephew by marriage Henry Brevoort, the young man who would introduce Walter Scott to *Knickerbocker* on a trip to Europe a decade later, who would share bachelor quarters with Irving in New York before the latter's long absence overseas, who would become himself one of the rich men in the New York of the 1830s, whose son would become attaché with Ambassador Irving at Madrid in the early 'forties, and whose correspondence from and to the writer and diplomat reveals him to be perhaps Irving's closest lifelong friend.

So 1803 was a significant year in Irving's life, as in Astor's. It was, as well, a significant year in the life of the nation; for during this same summer, in mid-July, a courier had arrived from Europe bringing news of momentous import to the government in Washington: the preoccupied Bonaparte had just agreed to sell the remaining French territory in North America to the United States for $15,000,000. How much land was involved was unclear: assuredly the port of New Orleans and the valley of the Mississippi River, with, presumably, most of the Missouri River Valley as well, westward to the Rockies. But not enough was known about the farther reaches of the purchase to be certain. Was the source of the Missouri, for instance, in Canada or within the newly acquired territory? The President had long been curious about the West in any case. Accordingly, well before the Senate in October had ratified the treaty that made official the transfer of some eight hundred and thirty thousand square miles of wilderness, Jefferson had been responsible for the exchange between two soldiers of letters concerning a bold project: "If therefore there is anything . . . in this enterprise, which would induce you to participate with me in it's fatiegues, it's dangers and it's honors, believe me there is no man on earth with whom I should feel equal pleasure in sharing them as with yourself . . ." That, on June 19, 1803, from Jefferson's private secretary, Meriwether Lewis, and the answer, dated July 17, the day after its receipt, came from William Clark: "This is an imense undertaking fraited with numerous dificulties, but my freind I can assure you that no man lives with whom I would prefer to undertake and share the Dificulties of such a trip than yourself."

Irving (as we shall see) would come to know William Clark in future years. Now, in the fall of 1803 and the winter of 1804, that lieutenant and Captain Lewis were assembling the party and supplies to set out on a voyage of exploration to the headwaters of the Missouri River wherever they might rise, then across the Rockies beyond American territory and to the Pacific. The journey, which would be made (in Jefferson's words) "to explore the Missouri river . . . across this continent, for the purposes of commerce," would prove of intense interest to such citizens of the republic as John Jacob Astor.

Not, in Astor's case, so much for the hardships endured and surmounted, although later readers of the adventures of Lewis and Clark may understandably find that aspect of their achievement most thrilling. The two officers had got together their measuring instruments and blunderbusses and ammunition and swivel gun, the kegs of pork and barrels of flour and bushels of meal, their presents for the Indians—twenty-one bales of tobacco and small bells and rings and beads and brooches—and had recruited their hunters and blacksmiths and house joiners and soldiers and half-breed interpreters to the total number of forty-five; and on Monday, May 14, 1804, were setting out westward at last in three boats—two pirogues and a keelboat—sails raised, where the Missouri empties its muddy waters, just above St. Louis, into the Mississippi. Clark's journal notes their departure matter-of-factly, "at 4 oClock P. M, in the presence of many of the neighbouring inhabitents," after which they proceeded "under a jentle brease up the Missourie to the upper Point of the 1st Island 4 Miles and camped on the Island." Thus this freshwater voyage of discovery began, with a configuration that may remind us of three sailing vessels elsewhere, at another time. "This little fleet," Lewis would write nearly a year later, after their first wintering some thirteen hundred miles along their way, "altho' not quite so rispectable as those of Columbus or Capt. Cook, were still viewed by us with as much pleasure as those deservedly famed adventurers ever beheld theirs; and I dare say with quite as much anxiety for their safety and preservation. we were now about to penetrate a country at least two thousand miles in width, on which the foot of civilized man had never trodden; the good or evil it had in store for us was for experiment yet to determine, and these little vessells contained every article by which we were to expect to subsist or defend ourselves. . . ."

Astor would have been interested in other aspects of the journey than this, but we may imagine briefly "the men in the water from morning untill night hauling the cord & boats walking on sharp rocks and round sliperery stones which alternately cut their feet & throw them down," their wary encounters with Sioux along the riverbank, the abundance of rattlesnakes and grizzlies ("I find that the curiossity of our party is pretty well satisfyed with rispect to this anamal"), the prickly pears underfoot, the toothaches, the "toumers," the icy waters of the rapids and the portages on paths hacked through forests, the agony of the winter crossing of the Bitterroots, the hunger in the mountains and withal the "danceing and Singing Songes in the most social manner" at every opportunity, square dancing among themselves at the campsites and before delighted Indians at their villages. That endurance stretched through two and a half years without a single argument between the leaders, who brought their men over eight thousand miles of exploration and—with one exception (a soldier had died of a ruptured appendix when they were three months out)—safely home to St. Louis, September 23, 1806.

It stands, so the greatest authority on the fur trade adjudged at the beginning of our century, "as incomparably the most perfect achievement of its kind in the history of the world." But Astor in New York would have spent little time admiring the wonder of so complex and perilous an undertaking managed so successfully, nor would most of the abundant specimens sent back have held much interest for him: the bows and arrows, the pressed flowers and earthen pots and living prairie dogs, the ram's horns. What would have captured his interest, had he been granted the opportunity of reading the journals, would have been, say, a notation (one of several such) by Clark on August 7, 1805, near the Three Forks of the Missouri: "all those Streams Contain emence number of Beaver orter Musk-rats &c." His eye might have lingered over Captain Lewis' entry a year later, on August 12, 1806, recording an encounter with two hunters from the Illinois: "I gave them a short discription of the Missouri, a list of distances to the most conspicuous streams and remarkable places on the river above and pointed out to them the places where the beaver most abounded." He would have noted Clark's entry of August 22 in the same year, after an Indian parley with the Cheyennes: "as I was about to leave the cheifs lodge he requested me to Send Some traders to them, that their country was full of beaver and they would then be encouraged to kill beaver, but now they had no use for them as they could get nothing for their skins and did not know well, how to catch beaver. if the white people would come amongst them"— and this surely would have interested Astor—"they would become acquainted and they would learn them how to take the beaver. . . ."

If white people would come among them. Yet it was not necessary to read the journals of the expedition to find out what the whole country soon knew and what Astor had already suspected: at a stroke the fur-bearing regions of the United States had been trebled, and the furs in those regions abounded as plentifully as did the fabled buffalo. To be sure, the Napoleonic wars had temporarily limited markets for furs in Europe. But here in America, along the East Coast, fashions were steadily increasing sales of the more elegant pelts—marten and mink and fox and always beaver—as New Yorkers and Bostonians and Philadelphians acquired the wealth to ape the dress of the Continent.

One other aspect of Lewis and Clark's achievement would have impressed Astor, this most of all. The explorers had made it overland to the Pacific and back again: to the Pacific, where swam in the coastal waters furs more precious even than beaver—to the Pacific, on the farther shores of which lay a market more lucrative than Europe and America combined.

China and the United States had been trading since the year, coincidentally, of the immigrant Astor's arrival in America. A young German peddler of beads and bread would have had nothing to do with that beginning, of course; but in February 1784, the *Empress of China*, sponsored by a group of East Coast merchants, had sailed on an initial voyage from New York to Canton. Profits from the venture had encouraged others to invest in similar undertakings in succeeding years. Astor meanwhile had married into a New York family; his wife, as it happened, had a brother and nephew who were both ship captains, as well as a niece who had married a captain engaged in the China trade. So there were ample means through the 'eighties and 'nineties for the rising fur trader in his Little Dock Street shop to become familiar with the attractions of commerce between America and the Far East. Moreover, as Chinese merchandise began to find its way into American homes, a general merchant (such as Astor had become) of musical instruments, pelts, English cutlery, and the like would readily add to his inventory silks and teas for sale.

In 1800, as noted, Astor's fortune stood at a quarter of a million dollars. That year he used some of his wealth from furs to enter the China trade directly. He joined others (though he was principal owner) in outfitting the ship *Severn* to make the long journey south, around Cape Horn into the Pacific, and northwestward across more than fourteen thousand miles of ocean to Canton. The vessel set out in late April, bearing in its hold a thousand beaver skins and more, in addition to other furs from American waters and ginseng gathered by backwoods traders from fields in New York State. For the Chinese, with goods that Americans coveted, coveted in turn ginseng—an herb from which they made medicines of doubtful efficacy; and they coveted furs, for which they would pay better than would any other nation in the world. The principal obstacle confronting an American dealer was encountered in trying to get pelts over the great distances that lay between their source and that most profitable market: distances that separated creeks and rivers in the backwoods of the Old Northwest from warehouses at Whampoa on the South China Sea. Money—a lot of it—was needed to have furs delivered overland and downriver to New York, then to outfit a ship and hire the captain and crew, then to abide the year and more of absence that the uncertain voyage around the Horn and across the Pacific and back consumed before that same ship might be safely anchored off the Battery with valuable Oriental merchandise in its hold. Astor, however, had the money. Accordingly, by 1804, the year after he moved into Rufus King's porticoed mansion and four years after he had entered the trade, he was sole owner of a vessel departing for China. Sole owner: he alone would take the risks; he alone would make the profits now.

What a wonderful web was drawn by traders' tracks and vessels' wakes in years ahead! At the center, within his countinghouse, sat Astor, alert to the Indian market in the interior of America, alert to the retail market in American cities along the East Coast, alert to the markets of London and Hamburg and Marseille, alert as well to the insatiable market in far-off China. All of it interconnected. From England and Europe, in exchange for furs and in ships of his own now, came wire and milk-glass lamps and looking-glass plates and lead pencils and toys and gold paper and pocketbooks and much else of European manufacture besides. Some of those items he sold in his store or auctioned off for sale or distributed for a price to agents up and down the East Coast. Some—blankets and firearms and cutlery, for instance—he had transported over American rivers to the interior, marking the goods up, of course, before trading them for furs of trappers and Indians. Marking them way up: a fat profit would be shown already. But the furs for which they were traded, obtained at the lowest rates in exchange for goods inflated in value, he would next put into a ship of his own in New York Bay that was bound for China. In China Astor's agents would receive a thousand times the value of what other agents had given for the furs in the American backwoods. Furthermore, payment from the Chinese would be taken in goods of theirs—in souchong teas and silk handkerchiefs and Nankin fans and chinaware and vermilion and nutmegs and cloves and camphor and sweetmeats and "black India lutestrings and taffeties," all loaded in the hold of Astor's ships to be brought back to America, to yield yet another huge profit—in New York and among correspondents in Europe—over the value of the same merchandise in Canton.

The pattern came full circle. As early as 1802 Astor was already sending some of the Chinese tea to Europe, from which he had acquired barter initially to trade with the Indians. Nor was that all: the pattern was to develop intricacies even more rewarding. A few years later, when Astor the fur merchant was also one of the largest shipowners in America, he would encourage his vessels to increase the number of their trading stops in order eventually to take on board sandalwood from Hawaii, quicksilver from Spain, opium from Turkey, brandy from Leghorn, rum from St. Croix. And within his countinghouse the German continued to spell out his singular letters and shuffle his invoices and prosper, by means of those piculs of cochineal in transit, those covids of camlets, those bales of cotton and barrels of high wine and poods of whalebone and puncheons and hogsheads of peltries changing hands all over the world. Methodically he prospered, rising early, applying his shrewd and retentive mind to business every day until two, then putting it all aside to go home and eat his dinner, have his glass of beer, and play his three games of checkers before taking a horseback ride and attending the theater in the evening. Stolid and steady, avoiding risks, thoroughly familiar with all aspects of his widespread enterprises, looking over all their details, Astor prospered and continued to prosper.

He was ensconced in success by the fall of 1806, as the explorers Lewis and Clark, bearing reports that would interest him, were descending the Missouri River at last, on their way back to the United States near the end of their own far-flung enterprise. September 3: The returning party of explorers meets boats headed upriver with a license to trade with the Sioux; and in the midst of a thundershower Lieutenant Clark for the first time, in the shelter of a tent on shore, hears from the outbound traders of the "maney changes & misfortunes" that have occurred in the nearly two and a half years of his absence: "that Gen! Wilkinson was the governor of the Louisiana and at S! Louis . . . 2 Indians had been hung in S! Louis for murder and several others in jale. and that M! Burr & Gen! Hambleton fought a Duel, the latter was killed &ᶜ. &ᶜ. . . ."

The duel between the Vice President and the Federalist leader was already more than two years in the past before Lieutenant Clark learned of it in the tent along the Missouri. Young Washington Irving had read the shocking news in a letter received in Genoa some four or five months after its occurrence and during his first trip to Europe, on which he had set out after his return from Ogdensburg and Montreal. The effects of the duel, fought on the morning of July 11, 1804, had touched Astor's life as well, for the merchant had known and worked with Burr. Indeed, to Astor, among others, Burr had turned for help in the weeks that followed that fateful interview at Weehawken.

The two men—the German merchant and the New York lawyer and politician—had had dealings together in the late 'nineties, when the prodigal Burr had found occasion to borrow (as many others would borrow) from Astor. In addition, Astor, considering yet another kind of investment, had been able on several occasions to make use of Burr's outstanding professional talents. Profits from furs had already allowed the merchant to enter the China trade. Profits from the China trade were now allowing him, in the decade after 1800, to extend his wealth in another direction, toward more holdings in land, in acres of earth that would provide appealingly tangible acquisitions to an Old World son of humble origins. Acres and acres of earth. And in making such acquisitions Aaron Burr's knowledge and circumstances had several times of late proven helpful.

The lands, however, that had come to interest Astor were no longer tracts that extended over wilderness in back-state New York. By now he had realized that profits from that source would be slow to accrue, with acreage so abundant out there and the numbers of settlers sparse. But he did see, more clearly than anyone else, the implications of what was happening closer to home. Harman Blennerhassett, arriving in the New World from Ireland in 1796, had noticed activity around him, but from that notice was no more able than others to draw Astor's profitable conclusions or to act on them. What the Irishman did observe in passing through Manhattan—and wrote of in a letter home—was a citizenry busily making new docks, filling in swamps, digging cellars for new buildings. Blennerhassett continued westward to construct his own fine house on an island in the Ohio River and await there the unfolding of a fate that would entwine his life lamentably with Aaron Burr's. But meanwhile, Astor the fur merchant was being led to calculate from what he, too, saw happening among the lanes and alleys and lots and wharves near his countinghouse, now on Liberty Street—and from what he had observed of the growth of New York since his own arrival. Just over twenty thousand people had been located on the southern tip of the island when the immigrant had come up from Baltimore and begun to peddle his bakery goods in the spring of 1784. Thirty-three thousand were there only six years later, in 1790. Sixty thousand people lived on the island only a decade after that, almost doubling the population in ten years. Here, then, not in backwoods New York, was the land that Astor should buy. Accordingly, during the first decade of the nineteenth century he proceeded to invest an immense sum in Manhattan real estate— over half a million dollars, most of it from the China trade.

Profits from furs beyond the frontier had brought him profits from teas and silks in distant Canton. Now wealth from China would bring Astor more profits from land near at hand. But for the most part he purchased only a certain kind of land—orchards and ponds and undeveloped fields that lay on the island above Canal Street, to the north of the city's upper boundary. All those people he had observed were huddled on the southern tip; more were coming and would have to live somewhere. Thus in the summer of 1803, the canny Astor invested $25,000 in the Eden farm, seventy acres that extended over bucolic hill and dale from Broadway west to the Hudson in the area of what is now Times Square. Two years later he paid $75,000 for half of the Clinton farm, comprising much of what is now Greenwich Village. Later still he came into possession of the Cosine farm, from the present Fifty-third Street to the present Fifty-seventh Street and westward as far as the river. He bought those sizable tracts, and waited. Occasionally he might sell lots of an acre or so at a profit of up to two hundred percent, but far more often Astor simply held on to the land until the city grew up to it. He could afford to: his ships kept anchoring in the harbor laden with wealth (he could make as much as $70,000 from a single voyage to China and back). As for real estate, when the right time did come, he would lease, not sell, the land he owned nearby. That way others would do the improving—building their shops and brownstones and outbuildings as the city spread northward—but rent would be paid to Astor, who continued to possess what would sooner or later revert to him or his descendants, with all improvements intact.

And Aaron Burr had played his part in adding to Astor's holdings. Many years earlier, while New York was still an English colony, a colonial governor had beneficently granted extensive lands to Trinity Church, though a law subsequently had been passed—while the lands were increasing in value—limiting how much income the church could realize from all that property. The figure had been set at $12,000. In 1767 (with Astor a butcher's child of four in tiny Walldorf) the church on Broadway had leased, for ninety-nine years, at the absurdly low annual rental of $269, four hundred and sixty-five lots that it owned to one Abraham Mortier. Thirty years had gone by, with the fortunate Mortier using that spaciousness (in our day bounded by Hudson, Spring, and Greenwich streets) for a country place. Then, in 1797, a New York legislator became interested in how Trinity Church was managing its wealth: Was its income from holdings really limited to the $12,000 specified by law? A committee was appointed to conduct an investigation; and the legislator himself, Aaron Burr, became its chairman.

For whatever reason, the investigation of Trinity Church, which might have proved awkward, was never completed. Burr, however, emerged from the episode in possession of the Mortier lease, using which as collateral he proceeded to borrow $38,000 from a bank with which he was associated. The attorney lived well, we remember, entertaining opulently with his teenage daughter as hostess in his mansion at Richmond Hill near the century's end. And we recall the widower's labyrinthine financial dealings that made such living possible during those years in New York before Theodosia married and Burr went off to Washington to become Vice President of the United States.

But the Vice President had returned from Washington and run for governor of New York. And he had lost in the spring of 1804, and had called out General Hamilton, and been rowed to Weehawken; and his world was shattered in the noisy public outrage awakened by that calamity. Even before then, to be sure, Burr had turned to Astor for money. That ninety-nine-year Mortier lease, as one asset, still had had more than sixty years to run before reverting to Trinity Church when he sold it to Astor for $62,500. Other lots and lease remainders Burr sold the merchant at various times. But now, within weeks after the duel, with the Vice President's stealthy, benighted departure by boat southward from New York City pending, yet another transaction with Astor brought him an additional $8,000. Not that the politician would ever grow rich through those maneuvers. Almost all the money would go to satisfy his creditors; indeed, for years during and after his forthcoming western adventure the former Vice President would have to avoid New York or finally pass through it in disguise, in part because of creditors still unappeased. Meanwhile, the house and grounds of his beloved Richmond Hill were falling into Astor's hands: a hundred and sixty acres of land to add to the merchant's other holdings.

In contrast to Burr, Astor never had a creditor. None of Astor's land was ever mortgaged.

A story is told that illustrates the merchant's methods as property owner. About this time in his life he did, uncharacteristically, sell rather than lease a lot, and that lot was, also uncharacteristically, downtown, on Wall Street. The new owner was exultant. He had got the property from the fur dealer for $8,000 and, considering how land was increasing in value in the city, could be sure it would be worth $12,000 within a few short years. He enlightened Astor accordingly. The German is supposed to have answered to this effect: True, your lot will be worth $12,000 in a few years. Meanwhile, let me tell you what will become of the money you've just paid me for it. I mean to invest that money in eighty lots north of Canal Street, each costing a hundred dollars. In the same few years that the value of your land will be increasing to $12,000, the value of mine will have increased to $80,000. Your profit: $4,000. My profit: $72,000.

The phrasing is assuredly not Astor's, and doubtless so shrewd a dealer would never have revealed his intentions so openly, but such a lot downtown is on record as having been sold for that amount at about that time by Astor, who through the early nineteenth century was involved in thousands of conveyances, acquisitions of water rights, grants, leases, transfers of titles, and similar transactions, until he had come to own enormous acreage of real estate on Manhattan. And it was those possessions, even more than the furs and the Chinese merchandise, that finally would make this ill-lettered German by far the wealthiest person in America—would make him wealthy by his merely waiting for the city to grow and imbue the land he owned with a sterling value.

His store was at 71 Liberty Street now, his home the King mansion on Broadway, with its pillars and arches and open piazza. Among those more gracious surroundings he continued his orderly life of simple habits, rising early and spending the morning at business, which included still, in addition to land purchases, the scrutinizing of four widely different markets: the American market in East Coast cities, the Oriental market, the European market, and the backwoods market of trader and Indian. And every fall Astor continued to make the journey to Montreal, where as late as 1806 he was as usual being entertained by the fur magnates with whom he mingled, this time in company with his eldest daughter, Magdalen. That September a Manchester merchant noted her presence among others at a party at the Frobishers: ". . . Miss

Magilvray, Miss Caldwell Miss Henry, a Miss Astor from New York (her father who is at present here is said to be worth 200,000£—report says he will give this daughter 25,000£) Mr. Cartwright & 2 Daughters . . ." And a couple of days later, September 17, "Went to the Library at 11 & staid till 3. At 4 to Mr. Frobisher to dinner, where I met Judge Ogden, Lady & 2 Daughters, Mr. Astor & daughter, a Miss Ergene . . ." And other young ladies. But the girl whose father would endow her so generously did make a stir. Within a week at Alexander Henry's was assembled "a very large Party . . . we consisted of abt 40. Lady Johnston amused herself at Whist whilst the sprightly dance was kept up till past twelve—chiefly country dancing but some few Reels & one Cotillion in complement to Miss Astor, as they scarcely dance anything else at New York."

Obviously Magdalen would not stay single long. The following year she was married, at nineteen, to Adrian Bentzon, former governor of Santa Cruz in the Danish West Indies: a "very ugly" gentleman who "wears a shoe with the heel two inches thick," so a schoolgirl in New York alive to gossip was informing her sister by letter after the event, "and to crown all he is a modern philosopher." Thus Matilda Hoffman at sixteen was already wryly observing society, as she grew toward that womanhood she would never experience, in those years when she was attracting the notice and love of Washington Irving. For young Irving had returned from Europe and was now engaged with friends in composing *Salmagundi*, a little magazine appearing at intervals through these same months in 1807 to satirize the foibles of the New York that Astor and his family were part of—town of cotillions and concerts, of "the moss-crowned roof of the Bear-market" and the Powles Hook ferryboats, of parades on the Battery and performances of *Macbeth* or *The Fair Penitent* at the Park, which the theater-loving Astor incidentally had by then acquired, refashioned, and leased out to plump up his profits a bit more. A pleasant acquaintance with surfaces of Astor's world develops through the pages of the popular *Salmagundi*, for the magazine may still amuse us with its whim-whams and high spirits, with its incidental revelations of salt marshes and haystacks on the far side of Hackensack bridge, or of the vanity of Will Wizard, just returned from Canton with gifts of tea for the ladies, and wearing his waistcoat of China silk, the roses and tulips upon it "the work of *Nang-Fou* . . . who had fallen in love with the graces of his person, and sent it to him as a parting present." We may smile, as well, in coming to know this world better, over Cousin Christopher Cockloft, in a dither because he "had got his silk stockings bespattered with mud by a coach, which it seems belonged to a dashing gentleman who had formerly supplied the family with hot rolls and muffins": the leading fur merchant, to be sure, was hardly dashing at any time, but a bakery boy he had been in truth, who now owned a fine enough coach. *Salmagundi*, this earliest of Irving's literary successes, does show us a fluid society in that increasingly fashionable if muddy little city, where more than one person was observed to have risen from paltry beginnings.

Irving's periodical lets us see surfaces of the world through which Astor was making his astonishingly successful way. But depths of that world are to be sought elsewhere. Some may be able to discern them among dry titles and invoices of the countinghouse: "To disct. on £242.9.6 @ 2½ pCt. . . . Brokerage on £236.8.3 1 pCt . . . Duty p money & Water charges . . . Housing Cartage & warehouse rent . . . Unpack^g. sorting lotting & . . . Sale charges of 4 lots . . . Excise on £236.8.3 @ 1 pCt Errors £9.9.2 . . . Interest on duties advanc'd 73 days . . ." Or here perhaps: "That the above named John Jacob Astor, his Heirs or Assigns, shall be intitled to, and have aright to possess one other Fourth part or share of all such Tracts as may be acquired under the agreement or arrangement made by the said David Alexander Grant . . . one Third proportion of all such Sums so advanced by the said John Jacob Astor, which Receipts or Notes shall be made payable to him or assigns in two equal payments: That is to say . . ."

Some will find Astor's substance there, within the countinghouse on the walls of which the merchant hung furs that his trained eye could admire more than any picture. Others will assemble his real self from scanty details of private life that have survived those years: the often apocryphal anecdotes, or his fondness for flute playing, or remembered images of his son William beating furs in the back of the shop as his father had, or the occasional personal references in letters, or the genuineness of the father's devotion to his wife and the mother of his children, or the lifelong heartache that the condition of one of those children brought him. For Astor's eldest son, John Jacob, Jr., was mentally defective. Whether he was born so or whether an early accident rendered him so is not clear; the father did not speak of the cause, nor did anyone else. But even in old age, with the son by then nearing sixty, Astor still had not given up hope of improvement: "I direct my executors to provide for my unfortunate son John Jacob Astor," the old man willed. "And in case he should be restored then I direct them . . ." Everything that the merchant had achieved, as he wrote his former partner Peter Smith, now and later was for his children: "I workd for tham & I wish tham to have all the Good of it the more they enjoy it the more happy am I—" However, one (and he the eldest, bearing his father's name) would understand little enough of what a butcher's son from a village in Baden was accomplishing here in the New World. One would not know, and he the eldest son for whom the amassing fortune had been intended.

Some of what Astor was may be sensed, perhaps, in the way he bore misfortune—his son's tragedy and other griefs to follow: "the best is to travel about & to attend to bussiess—to keep body and mind engaged &

not reflect too much on our Afflections which we all must have at Some Period or other these will came . . ." So he attended to business even when griefs did come, and always he formed his visions.

Those were extraordinary. The "elements of greatness" that Irving came to admire, the "penetrating sagacity" and "massive intellect"— what was grand about Astor seems most clearly evident through his skill at forming reality out of vast dreams. No more able than his business contemporaries to enter imaginatively into the often miserable lives and feelings of distant trappers or Indians or sailors or Sandwich Islanders, he nevertheless did have an awesome grasp of possibilities extending forward in time and outward across the globe. We have noted his vision, clearer than anyone else's, of a future New York covering all the hills and fields of Manhattan, and have commented already on his vision of trading lanes connecting the farthest points of earth, all to his profit. But that mind of his could fashion still bolder conceptions, and the merchant by now possessed means to act upon the very boldest of them.

He determined to monopolize the fur trade in America. Furs were his first love; and we who have learned to wince in imagining the muffled sound of metal snapping underwater, in considering a terrified, dumb, drowning creature's desperate, futile gnawing on a chain—struggles that sometimes will tear pitiful furred body from trapped leg—we remind ourselves that not until our own day has the acquisition of furs been regarded in any light other than as blameless and sensible. In Astor's young manhood the textile industry hardly existed in America. Furs and skins clothed people who could not afford imported cloth from Europe. Moreover, as already implied, furs from Chaucer's day and earlier provided not only warmth and beauty but a mark of status. Laws in medieval England, for instance, had legislated that no one with an income under forty pounds a year could wear martens; the poor must wear lambskins; no one but officers in the king's household could wear ermine and sable.

Of course from European rivers furs had long since been depleted, and supplies from the hinterlands of Russia had grown scarcer. But in the New World lived creatures enough to satisfy all but inexhaustible cravings. Thus, Sir Humphrey Gilbert, exploring in Canada in 1579, gratified his sponsors with reports of "hares, dogges, wilde ounce, and a kynde of Beaste like a Connye, Bevers, Martins, Badgers, Otters, Weeselles, Wolves . . ." Henry Hudson aboard the *Half Moon*, passing a forested island to starboard and ascending a New World river in 1609, encountered natives who "brought us Bevers skinnes and otter skinnes which we bought for Beades, Knives, and Hatchets." Captain John Smith five years later was exploring New England, pleased to calculate that "of Bevers, Otters, and Martins, blacke Foxes, and Furres of price, may yeerly be had six or seven thousand, and if the trade of the French were prevented, many more." Champlain on the St. Lawrence and Ottawa rivers about the same time was noting for his French sovereign's satisfaction the presence of deer, moose, buffaloes, beavers, martens, wolves, foxes, weasels. And shortly thereafter, in 1620, the Pilgrims at Plymouth were not long in commencing trade with the willing Wampanoags, loading on board a couple of hogsheads of peltries before the *Fortune* returned to England.

For many years the bulk of furs that the white man took from the New World was acquired in traffic with Indians. That is, he did not so much trap the animals as trade for them; through that traffic Dutch and Swedes and French and English first became acquainted with the tribal life of Algonquins and Hurons and Iroquois. By the eighteenth century the center of the fur trade was at Montreal, and the chain of lakes and far-stretching rivers and plausible portages gave assurance that Montreal would remain the emporium of the trade for years to come.

Astor in the closing decade of the eighteenth century accepted and utilized that situation, continuing to make his annual pilgrimage to Canada, in fact, as late as 1809. In 1805, for instance, it was noted in Montreal that "Mr. Astor has been here & purchased largely I believe for £16,000 of Otter, Beaver & Martins . . ." But why should the New York merchant be required to make so arduous a journey to buy pelts that in most cases had been trapped south of the Great Lakes, in America's own territory? By treaty the Old Northwest was open to traders from both nations; Canadians could exploit those largely uninhabited regions of the United States, in what are now Illinois and Michigan and Wisconsin—just as Americans could, by law at least, trade in Canadian woods. The vast majority of traders and trappers, however, were of Canadian nationality (the total number of such hermit types was never large in any case), and the North West Company and the Hudson's Bay Company and the Michilimackinac Company held their monopolies so jealously that the occasional American adventurer would find the solitary life of trapper or trader risky, should he meet with Canadians anywhere through those broad regions in which law was hardly enforceable.

Still, the situation rankled. Jay's Treaty in 1794 had cleared the English from forts along the southern shores of the Lakes. During that same decade troubles with Indians south of the Lakes had been ruthlessly laid to rest at Fallen Timbers. Moreover, the Canadian market for furs—a Europe closing behind the dike of Napoleonic militarism—was growing stagnant at the very time that the American trade was discovering a domestic market and a vast new outlet for furs in China. Why should wealth from American rivers go to the magnates at Montreal? As Astor was writing the governor of New York early in 1808: "It is a fact known to yaurself that we are obligd to Drow ¾ of aur furrs for ham consumption frum Canada." Why?

The time had come to change all that. The field was open. Astor, devising schemes in his New York countinghouse, would seek the prestige of governmental sanction to found a company as strong as the Canadian fur companies, with sufficient resources to compete against them effectively. He who heretofore had been a merchant, buying and shipping other people's furs, would now extend his interests to producing pelts directly, by means of his own trappers scouring the backwoods. But the North West Company of Canada—to name only one potential rival—possessed, in addition to the friendship of the Indians, a capital of over a million dollars. Some comparable amount must be amassed down here in Manhattan even to enter the field. Toward that end, perhaps a group of American businessmen might be persuaded to involve themselves in capitalizing an organization based in New York to compete with such fiscal strength to the north? Astor did his figuring, then petitioned his state government for support.

"WHEREAS John Jacob Astor, has presented his petition to the legislature, representing among other things, that he is desirous of forming a trading company, for the purpose of carrying on an extensive trade with the native Indian inhabitants of America; but that an undertaking of such magnitude would require a greater capital than any individual or unincorporated association could well furnish, and who would be less able to support a fair competition with foreigners who are at present almost in the exclusive possession of the fur trade; and has prayed that he and such other persons as may be associated with him, may be incorporated, the better to enable them to carry into effect this design . . ."

The preamble to an act of April 6, 1808, opens with that stately jargon, then proceeds to indicate public benefits that will arise from such an enterprise as Astor and his associates are seeking to initiate: "AND WHEREAS, such an establishment may be of great public utility, by serving to conciliate and secure the good will and affections of the Indian tribes toward the government and people of the United States, and may conduce to the peace and safety of our citizens inhabiting the territories bordering on the native Indian tribes: Therefore

"*Be it enacted by the people of the state of New-York, represented in senate and assembly,* That the said John Jacob Astor, and such persons as shall hereafter be associated with him for that purpose . . . hereby are erected, a body corporate and politic, by the name of 'The American Fur Company' . . ."

The name would come to be known throughout the West and all over the world. Astor had his charter in the spring of 1808, with every advantage that governmental recognition gave him over unchartered local competition. He and his "associates"—but that last was a joke known only to the German. Although the preamble acknowledged that the undertaking was of a size that "would require a greater capital than any individual or unincorporated association could well furnish," in fact a single fur merchant did hold the corporation in his hands. Despite the respectable assurances of stock to be offered for public subscription at $500 a share, of nine directors to be elected by stockholders, and so on, the company was in fact one man's entirely. No stock would be offered. The directors Astor would appoint, to serve at his pleasure. Astor was president, for life if he chose. The million dollars of capital stock projected would all come from Astor. As with his ships to China, Astor alone would take the risks, but only he would make the profit.

Washington Irving, in the merchant's confidence in later years, would verify authoritatively, when the secret no longer mattered, that "the capital was furnished by himself; he, in fact, constituted the Company; for though he had a board of directors, they were merely nominal; the whole business was conducted on his plans, and with his resources, but he preferred to do so under the imposing and formidable aspect of a corporation, rather than in his individual name; and his policy was sagacious and effective."

Sagacious in part because Astor's liability was limited, in part because favors could be extended less objectionably to a petitioner on behalf of what was presumably a corporate group of worthy capitalists than they could to one individual New York fur trader of boundless ambition. But the merchant went a step farther. In addition to the sanction of his state, Astor besought federal support as well, appealing to President Jefferson's conviction that the wealth of furs south of the Great Lakes should benefit American citizens rather than Canadians. Indeed. One citizen in particular stood to benefit, although the President could hardly have discerned, behind the well-wrought corporate facade of the American Fur Company, how focused Astor intended those benefits to be. "Gov. Clinton speaks well of Astor, as a man of large property & fair charactor, and well acquainted with the fur & peltry business." So Jefferson was informed by his Secretary of War. Accordingly, July 17, 1808, the President felt secure in writing Meriwether Lewis, now governor of the Missouri Territory, that a company was forming to carry on trade with the Indians on a sizable scale, in order to give the United States "exclusive possession" of profits by wrenching the commerce from Canada. Profits to the United States? The new company, the President went on to explain to Lewis, was "under the direction of a most excellent man, a Mr. Astor, merch't of New York, long engaged in the business, & perfectly master of it."

During the next quarter century the most excellent Astor would fashion his company into an all but unchallenged monopoly, forcing the Canadians out of United States territory and crushing or absorbing all competition nearer at home. But bringing about that state of affairs was not always easy. Hardly were his efforts well started, for

instance, before war between England and America erupted, a catastrophe that by itself would have ended a lesser man's dreams. Of course
the German had not wanted war to come, and had joined other merchants on the East Coast to do what he could to prevent it. "We are
happey in the hope of Peace & have not the Smalest Idia of a war with
england," he had been writing as recently as four months before the
outbreak of hostilities, in the summer of 1812, that were to lead at once
to the disruption of the China trade, to the derangement of trade with
Europe, to the blockade of New York and New Orleans, to the closing of
the Great Lakes. Moreover, no sooner had the conflict started than Indians friendly to the British forsook the trading posts and took to the
warpath. And during succeeding months, as English ships patrolled
offshore, the New York trader in furs, European hardware, and luxurious Chinese merchandise was reduced to dealing in goods from the
American South that were ordinarily, as he wrote, "not in my line": pig
lead, goat skins, cornmeal.

Yet so lucky and so wealthy was Astor that the calamity of war
itself could be made to work to his benefit. Some of his ships had got
away just before the blockade clamped down; two others laden with
merchandise from China—cassia, nankeens, teas, nutmeg, silks—that
the war would make all the more rare and valuable had slipped into New
York Harbor before the blockade had entirely closed: the *Enterprise*
three days after war was declared, the fortunate *Hannibal* four months
later. With foreign trade all but extinguished now, the price of tea soon
doubled; as one consequence, Astor found himself during the war with
enough money to spare to lend large sums to the government at favorable terms. By the time peace was restored, matters looked promising
indeed. "My losses by Sea are made up in the peace by the rise on my
Stocks of which I have something more than 800m$." Close to a million
there—and the war, that "most unfortunate period," was over, and "I am
glad of peace, because it puts every thing on safe ground & I can always
make money if I will be prudent at all events I have enough, since it can
make all my children independent, this I however mention only to you."

Good family man still in his prime, the merchant in his early fifties
was thus ready and well equipped to carry other schemes forward. Furs
remained his passion: "Minck & Martin Skins as also fisher & Silver fox
and Musrat Skins if any   all these take Little Room and will Sell here
. . . furrs the Skins Should be thin & the furr thick—Racown Skins if
well furrd & Large are worth 4/- Muss Skins if thick 16/- Musrat Skins
3/ if very good   you may find Still Same ather Skins & if So bring
Some . . ." He knew the trade thoroughly, had trudged through the
backwoods himself to barter for pelts and beat them and grade them and
pack them. Moreover, he owned the American Fur Company still, and in
the years following the war with England would proceed to use that
corporate tool to transform all the vast, uninhabited area from the Mis-

sissippi to the Rockies, wherever furred creatures abided, into something approximating his own private reserve. But he was able to do so only after waging a series of conflicts with others, sometimes cannily, sometimes ruthlessly.

The government at Washington, one potential obstacle, had already been persuaded of the advantages that a series of privately owned trading posts would bring to the territory of the Louisiana Purchase: "the Enthusiasm of Intercourse & good will with the Natives," Astor had argued, "would itself be a great object to the country and without it the company could not succeed for it would be the best & True Policy to trade honourably with them & to treat them well, with Independent traders its not so, they go one year to trade with the Indians perhaps never to see them again, why then they care little how much they Cheat them." That is, it would be in Astor's interests (and thereby the nation's) to treat the Indians fairly, inasmuch as his posts were to be permanent. But the Canadians, still plundering furs from American streams, must at the same time be prohibited from trading south of the Great Lakes; and toward that end, Astor used all his formidable influence with Madison and Monroe and any legislators at the capital who might help change the present law. By the spring of 1816, his efforts had yielded success; that April Congress passed an act decreeing that "licenses to trade with the Indians within the territorial limits of the United States shall not be granted to any but citizens of the United States." Foreigners were thus removed from the field, and henceforth Astor and his company had only to concern themselves with competition from domestic sources. All three such sources were closed off in the coming decade.

One the government itself had opened. As far back as the administration of President Washington, in 1796, two government posts, or factories, had been set up to trade with Indians, and in Jefferson's administration the number of factories had increased. Their purpose was simple: to secure goodwill by sparing Indians the more ruinous exploitations that private traders were routinely practicing. For Indian furs, agents at government posts would exchange manufactured goods (tin pots, knives, blankets) at cost, not marked up ten or a hundred times their value. But Jefferson, eager by every means to lure Indians from trading with Canadians, did permit private American traders to continue dealing for furs as well, and the private traders were left with a number of advantages over their hampered rivals in the factories. Private traders had liquor. Most Indians wanted and expected firewater to figure in any business dealings with the white man, but government factories were prohibited for humanitarian reasons from including that inducement in their bargains. Moreover, the more powerful private traders—Astor, for instance—could offer superior English hardware, whereas government posts were required to deal only in American-made goods for furs. In addition, Indians would have to bring their pelts to the factories, and be denied credit when they got there. The private trader, by contrast, could journey through forest and over plain to Indian encampments and spread out his wares in the lodges themselves, in a whiskey-soaked atmosphere with credit abounding.

However well intentioned, goverenment factories that were still in business after the War of 1812—at Detroit and Michilimackinac and Prairie du Chien and elsewhere—were for all those reasons doing poorly. Astor wanted to be rid of them just the same, and through that second decade of the century worked with others to bring the system down. Lewis Cass, governor of Michigan Territory, proved obliging; and when Thomas Hart Benton was elected first senator from Missouri in 1820, that gentleman joined Cass on Astor's payroll—and remained on it as he became chairman of a powerful Senate Committee on Indian Affairs, remained on it even as he steered through Congress "An Act to abolish the United States Trading Establishments with the Indian Tribes." The act became law May 6, 1822, and through one of Astor's lieutenants Senator Benton was promptly receiving "the unqualified thanks of the Community for destroying the pious monster."

So much for the teetotal factories. The Canadians had been driven out, and now the naive American government. Another competitor proved tougher. That took the form of rival American companies or partnerships, most with headquarters in St. Louis, some founded by early French and Spanish settlers trading with Indians along the Mississippi and Missouri while Astor's interests had still been centered at Montreal. The range of those interests had broadened, however, and had come to trespass on territories of these more westerly companies—the Missouri Fur Company, the Rocky Mountain Fur Company, as well as others less formidable but no less determined to hold their own against intruders. Undeterred, Astor established at St. Louis a Western Department of his American Fur Company in the same year, 1822, that the government's factory system expired. Henceforth, he would be in open competition with all comers, intent on driving them all out of business and keeping the bulk of the profits from American furs for himself.

He practically succeeded. Some of his opposition he bought out; some found it attractive to merge with his company; some he outbid by having posts built beside theirs and offering Indians more for their furs—as much as four times as much—until the competition crumbled. For behind the American Fur Company, uniquely, lay Astor's enormous wealth, which allowed that company—his company—to give more credit, to furnish better goods from Europe, and to absorb temporary losses that would have destroyed any other trading organization.

His company it remained in truth, for Astor himself continued entirely and solely in charge, determining what products would be bought in Europe for trade in the interior, which furs from the interior would be sent to what markets at home and abroad. Accordingly, profits came to him from every direction, every transaction: from the difference between what he paid overseas for goods and what he traded them for upriver, from the difference between what he paid for furs upriver and what he sold them for overseas, from freight charges in his ships carrying goods both ways across the Atlantic, from interest (more than a million dollars in all) paid him on capital that he lent to his company, from markups on subsistence articles that he provided his agents at the trading posts, from the value of land holdings that Indians would surrender to pay off debts they had let swell on credit, from dividends that his company paid shareholders during these same lucrative years—the majority shareholder being, of course, John Jacob Astor.

Once he had all but disposed of rival companies, the third source of domestic competition was easy enough for Astor to deal with. Indeed, those lone, independent traders who might have offered a last alternative for Indians to barter with had for the most part already been either ruined or absorbed into the company along the way. By 1828, then, the term "The Company" had come to mean only Astor's company, the American Fur Company, not merely to disgruntled survivors but to everyone else in the West. And for the remaining thirty years of its existence, until long after its founder had withdrawn to concentrate on making money elsewhere, the Company would continue supreme in the fur trade. Moreover, during those years it would be generally and thoroughly hated. Zachary Taylor, who served as an infantry officer along the Upper Mississippi in the 1820s, put the feeling succinctly: "Take the American Fur Company in the aggregate, and they are the greatest scoundrels the world ever knew." Or, as another qualified observer wrote from St. Louis in 1831, the agents of the company "entertain, as I know to be the fact, no sort of respect for our citizens, agents, officers or the Government, or its laws or general policy."

Why did they have to respect citizens or laws, in desolate regions where the trading post (presage of a civilization still to the eastward) could shape matters the way it wanted them? Concerning intoxicants, for instance, Astor might have preferred that liquor be excluded from the Indian trade, but British competitors to the north had for years used it regularly and abundantly as a means of floating advantageous bargains. Likewise, the independent American trader had no other means than liquor—whiskey, shrub, brandy, high wines—to compete against the advantages that Astor's wealth gave his company. "The trader with the whisky, it must be admitted, is certain of getting most furs." Accordingly, the Company was not long in supplying its own liquor illegally to Indians, in greater quantities than did anyone else. The consequences were inhuman. About whiskey we hear repeated that, as of 1819, "so violent is the attachment of the Indian for it that he who gives most is sure to obtain the furs, while should any one attempt to trade without it he is sure of losing ground with his antagonist." Thus, we learn further, "the neighborhood of the trading houses where whisky is sold"—and none sold more than Astor's—"presents a disgusting scene of drunkenness, debauchery and misery; it is the fruitful source of all our difficulties, and of nearly all the murders committed in the Indian country. . . . For the accommodation of my family," this second witness, an army officer near Detroit in 1825, goes on, "I have taken a house three miles from town, and in passing to and from it, I have daily opportunities of seeing the road strewed with the bodies of men, women and children, in the last stages of brutal intoxication. It is true there are laws in this territory to restrain the sale of whisky, but they are not regarded. . . ."

Astor's men knew how to get around laws, as they knew how to add to a couple of gallons of unrectified spirits thirty gallons of water and red pepper and tobacco and sell that concoction, which cost them five cents a gallon to make, for fifty cents a bottle. For such a bottle an addict (and many Indians became addicted) could be persuaded to trade whatever furs he had. So it had been for years. At the French fort on the Oswegatchie in upper New York that young Irving saw in ruins, one who knew it before Irving's birth and when it was flourishing as Fort La Galette had written of the nearby Indians and their craving for rum: "they have not now the resolution to refrain from the use of it;—on the contrary, it is become so familiar, and even necessary to them, that a drunken frolic is looked upon as an indispensible requisite in a barter, and anticipated with extreme delight." So it had been, and so it was continuing; within such a durably hazy setting the Company might easily sell a pound of gunpowder, worth twenty cents in England, for four dollars—four dollars' worth of pelts, which themselves were worth much more than that in East Coast and European marketplaces. Tobacco that was bought at ten cents a pound sold to the Indians five twists for six dollars—or the whole pound for eighteen dollars. Astor, to be sure, did not create so deplorable a situation, but no one exceeded him in profiting from it.

Certainly the backwoodsmen themselves profited little enough. These—the white trappers and traders with Indians—worked under conditions so bleakly unrewarding as to leave us wondering why they kept at it. Their pitiful wages, one employer reported, "almost all the men take up as fast as they earn—and would faster, if I would let them—in goods at about five hundred per cent on original cost." Prudence was not a trait of those mountaineers. Most of the time they lived dourly alone; and when they got paid—maybe once a year, maybe to the value of $130 for eleven perilous months of lonely trapping, skinning, curing, dressing, packing, and transporting of furs in all weathers—convention urged that they squander any cash they got as fast as they could, on squaws and drink and gewgaws at the post, then move on back with their traps to willow and cottonwood streams in the uplands. Why did they not forsake such a life? It got in their blood, and most of them could do nothing else. Meanwhile, these white Indians—as exploited as were the red—had of course to purchase the few supplies that their meager backwoods life required—rifle and knife and traps, tobacco and sugar and salt and coffee—at Astor's store in the wilderness, and at Astor's prices.

So one way or another the money flowed back to the Manhattan countinghouse of John Jacob Astor & Son. Nor does the German himself seem ever to have doubted the justice of the arrangement. Devoid of what we have learned to call a social conscience, he, like the great majority of his merchant contemporaries, used the system to the exclusive benefit of his family and—though far less often—of those few employees he personally knew. The hundreds, even thousands, beyond his acquaintance but in his employ or affected by his actions—the sailors and clerks and voyageurs and auctioneers and Indians and trappers and storekeepers and agents scattered about the world—must take care of themselves, as Astor had done. From him they could hope for no more than the least possible pay for the most possible labor. That was simply good business, and his imagination not then or ever could see the matter otherwise.

He knew, after all, what he was working for, and it was not to improve social conditions. This butcher's son from the village in Baden was working for his family, that his wife might have ease and all his children be independent. For this family, as noted, he had amassed a fortune, "& I wish tham to have all the Good of it the more they enjoy it the more happy am I." Primogeniture, European principle of ancient standing, thus governed his actions in this brash new democracy, so that, from his earliest trust funds for the children to the final codicils of his will, he revealed his intention of using the money he made almost solely to benefit his relatives and establish an Astor dynasty.

Of the two sons on whom that establishment depended, the older, being deranged, could not participate in Astor's designs. The younger, after studying and traveling in Europe, did become the junior member of his father's firm in 1818—John Jacob Astor & Son—and in that capacity William Backhouse Astor soon developed into all that his father could have desired. Stolidly he devoted the rest of his long life to augmenting the family fortune. Moreover, the young man married sensibly and fathered seven children, who brought their grandparents pleasure both in present fact and in future hope: the Astor name would endure.

As for the senior Astor's daughters, they could be troublesome, as when, in 1812, Dorothea (not yet eighteen) eloped on a visit to Washington with a Colonel Langdon, one of a large family and without resources of his own. The Langdon relatives themselves disapproved of an involvement with what one of them referred to as that "fat German, Dolly Astor," even as the bride's father was refusing in his bitterness to admit the newlyweds to his home or have any relations with them whatsoever. The unpleasantness continued through a number of years, until in time Astor mellowed to the extent of providing his daughter and son-in-law with a New York mansion—and lavishing his affection on their expanding family. But in the wake of the elopement he had clear-headedly written his old friend and former partner Peter Smith, in 1813, and offered that devout melancholiac a dearly bought insight: "know that every one has trouble & those who have tham by Imagination as you have have the worst & the most of tham—."

The pragmatist would not brood over imaginary cares or inevitable losses. One preventable loss, however, that all but prostrated him derived from the marriage of his eldest daughter, Magdalen—former belle at Montreal parties—with the ugly "philosopher" and minor diplomat Adrian Bentzon. The marriage had produced a son, John Jacob Bentzon, whom the proud grandfather took with him to Washington when the child was seven years old, in the late winter of 1818. Somehow, while in Astor's charge, the boy drowned there, in a shallow stream (long since drained) that ran at the time along the base of Capitol Hill. More than a year after the accident, writing again to Smith, ever morose in central New York: "I was Sorry," the still devastated Astor reported, "to See you ware in bade or Low Spirits, this indeed has been my case for these 13 Months past . . ." The best he could do now—and all he could recommend to others—was "to travel about & to attend to bussiess —to keep body and mind engaged." Afflictions come to everyone, poor and rich alike, and when they do, "we must Suport aurselfs as well as we can—"

That spare philosophy, learned in a hard school, may have helped the merchant during the same year endure a different kind of family misfortune, a divorce instituted by Magdalen against the absent Bentzon, returned to his original haunts in the Virgin Islands and charged now with desertion and adultery, both of which lapses the errant husband readily admitted. Single again, Magdalen was not long in marrying an English gentleman named Bristed, but that marriage proved even shorter lived than her first, lasting scarcely more than a year. "Mr. Jnọ Bristed goes in this Packet for England," Henry Brevoort (Astor's nephew by marriage) was writing his friend Washington Irving in Europe, October 9, 1821. "He finds it impossible to bear the matrimonial yoke any longer with that Lamb of Beelzebub, my well beloved Couzen the late Mrs Bentzon.—He is literally wasted to the bone by the severity of her discipline. Their fracas have furnished the Town with scandal these six months. She is certainly a maniac. . . ."

Magdalen and Dolly both made difficulties. The third of Astor's daughters was, happily, more tractable. Eliza was with her father in

Paris in 1821, and there was seen by her expatriate townsman Washington Irving. The writer, then nearing forty, found her on that occasion to be "quite a clever, agreeable girl."

Stanley Williams, best and generally exemplary twentieth-century biographer of Irving, locates the first encounter between the German merchant and the American writer in Paris, in that year: 1821. But that the meeting of the two New Yorkers would have been delayed so long seems unlikely. Irving's beloved eldest brother, William, a prominent member of the small New York community of the late eighteenth century where the German likewise had thrived, was only three years younger than Astor. Moreover, we have seen that in his early manhood William had briefly tried his hand at trading for furs in the Mohawk valley; could his interests have failed to bring him together with that other fur dealer whose shop was only blocks from the Irving home? To William's grown son, Washington Irving would later write of Astor as "an early friend of your father, for whose memory he entertains great regard; and he has always been on terms of intimacy with your uncle Peter and myself, besides knowing more or less of others of our family." That clarification was set down in 1834; many years later Irving referred to his "long intimacy with Mr. Astor, commencing when I was a young man." Neither utterance would seem to support a first meeting between them as late as 1821, when the writer was already approaching forty. Indeed, a decade before that date, in 1811, Astor's relative Brevoort, serving at the time as an agent for the merchant at Mackinac in the Old Northwest, had forwarded his friend Irving in New York copies of Indian speeches for hand delivery to his employer: "Shew old Astor the speeches if he wishes to see them"—nor does that sound like a charge to be entrusted to one who had not yet met the fur trader. Incidentally, during that same year, 1811, Irving himself had been briefly flirting with a mercantile career in his brothers' New York hardware store: "By all the martyrs of Grubstreet," he had exclaimed then, "I'd sooner live in a garret . . . than follow so sordid, dusty, soul killing way of life; though certain it would make me as rich as . . . John Jacob Astor himself."

Probably the beginning of Irving's friendship with Astor—though unrecorded—dates from around the start of the century. Thus, when the German was in Paris in 1821, he was looking up an old acquaintance rather than meeting a new one. By then his son William Backhouse had shown himself capable of managing business affairs back home, so that Astor (past his middle fifties and ailing) had sailed not westward toward the exotic sources of his wealth—never did he see those places— but eastward again, alone, toward the land of his childhood, on June 2, 1819, aboard the "elegant new ship Stephania, Captain Burke . . . for

Havre." Once in Europe, he had traveled to Paris, Geneva, Rome, Naples (where he spent the first winter of this extended stay), Frankfort, and back to Paris for the second winter, 1820–21. There his youngest daughter had joined him, as well as his eldest son, accompanied by a nurse. One purpose of Astor's current European travels was to seek medical advice for the unfortunate John Jacob Astor, Jr., now thirty, whom Irving, successful author of *The Sketch Book*, found on this occasion in Paris to be "in very bad health, and seems in a state of mental Stupor—His Situation causes great anxiety & distress to his father & sister; and there appears but little prospect of his recovery." The son's present journey did prove futile; that same summer Astor booked passage for his return home.

But the father and daughter stayed on. "The Astors passed a few Days in London lately but have gone off on a tour," Irving would write in August from England, where he had removed himself to oversee the publication of *Bracebridge Hall*. In fact, the merchant spent the greater part of these seven or eight years from 1819 to 1826 in Europe. He bought a villa on Lake Geneva, and from there continued to write his remarkable letters and issue directives through the agency of his younger son William in New York. Although approaching sixty and on the other side of the Atlantic, Astor showed little diminution of attention to his various businesses, and his influence was as potent as ever. From Rome, for example, he had written in 1820 to a long-term debtor strategically placed: "under standing that Landed property in the US. is at present not verry Saleble I presume you have not Sold any of your estates & there for it may not bee convenient to repay me the Sume Lend to you nor am I particularly in want of it it will however bee agreable to have the Intrest paid & have taking the Liberty to Drow an you for 2100$ fav^r. of my son at 90 Days"—that to the then President of the United States, James Monroe. As evidence of a continuing and detailed knowledge of his business affairs, one communication after his return to New York will serve to typify many such to his subordinates—this one dispatched from Albany in 1828: "I think you best have at least 10,000 of the very poor Racoon put up and sent to Hamburgh, those that have little *or no* fur on them, those that were baled of better kind, I kept will go to London, and you will be so good as to tell Custer to have his martin and mink skins, as also about 150 to 200 of his best Red Fox, and some Cross Fox put up to be sent, and next packet to London. . . . If application for deer skin, you will of course sell. . . . Muskrat you will of course sell, also Beaver."

Wherever he went, Astor kept close touch on anything affecting his profits. His youngest daughter was married now, to a Swiss count, so that the father had sailed for home alone in 1826. He would return a last time, in 1832, to his villa at Geneva, and in fact would have spent in all a third of his long life in Europe. In this present American interval, meanwhile, from 1826 to 1832, he finally began at New York to disengage himself from some of his many enterprises. The China trade, which his ships had dominated through the decade after the second war with England, now interested him less, not because the imported teas and silks were failing to make him money, but because the intricacies of the trade were distracting him from attending to new and nearer sources of wealth. He sold the last of his ships, and at about the same time, around 1826, began extending his American investments in canals, in railroads, in hotels, in banking, in insurance, in state and city stocks. Furs he did continue to send to Canton for a while, but in other people's ships, and even his career as a furrier was coming to an end. Dull pains over his body would force him back to consult specialists in Europe in June 1832, the season in which the expatriated Washington Irving was experiencing the triumph attendant upon his long deferred restoration among family and friends in Manhattan. When Astor departed, his wife Sarah (then as always) remained at home, through no lack of affection—the marriage was a close and happy one—but because of a lifelong aversion to travel.

The merchant turned seventy in Geneva. His illnesses persisted; his planned trip home was postponed. Required to linger in Europe, he would need whatever solace his simple philosophy could marshal. His daughter Magdalen, Lamb of Beelzebub, had died in 1832, in her midforties. His brother Henry, the butcher whose residence in New York before the Revolution had inspired an illiterate German immigrant with the desire to seek his fortune abroad, died the following year. Astor's life, that well-oiled machine of interconnecting triumphs, appeared to be winding down. He was ill. Moreover, his son William had shown himself to be less interested in furs than in other aspects of his father's commercial empire. The very supply of furs was being depleted at an awesome rate; the slaughter would continue, but future profits would inevitably decline, even as fashions in hats (so Astor had noted) were changing from beaver to silk. He noted all the signs, and from Geneva began the complicated process of disengaging himself from the intricacies comprising the American Fur Company: "Gentlemen   Wishing to retire from the Concern in which I am engaged . . . you will please to take this as notice thereof . . . I am Gentlemen your humble Servt. John. Jacob.Astor For Self & AmfurCo."

That was getting out in good order, after having collected, over the years, his share in abundance of the ravages of the West, about which a disillusioned John Quincy Adams would later lament: "Ages and ages of continual progressive improvement, physical, moral, political in the condition of the whole People of this Union, were stored up in the possession and disposal of those lands." As it turned out, not the whole People of this Union but only a few had benefited from the slaughter; skins and furs had been possessed to the benefit of one man in particular, one old man landing in New York now for the last time, on the *Utica*, April 4, 1834, past seventy and still ailing as he hobbled down the gangplank to learn sad tidings from his ever faithful son William. Mrs. Astor, beloved wife of nearly fifty years, had died seven days before.

"As to me," the nerve-shattered widower would soon write a friend, Wilson Price Hunt, then postmaster of St. Louis, "while absent, I lost Wife Brother Daughter Sister, Grandchildren & many friends & I expect to follow very soon. I often wish you were *near me*, I should find much in your society which I am in need of. being no longer disposed to business, or rather not able to attend to it, you know that I gave up a good part, & am about to dispose of the rest. . . ."

Although expecting to follow his wife to the grave "very soon," Astor in fact survived her sixteen years. Nor did he (as we shall see) quite forsake business after all. Moreover, during those years of continued activity that remained to him, he would have occasion to assuage loneliness partly by deepening his friendship with a man unlike himself in most respects, with the writer and longtime acquaintance restored to his homeland, "Vashington Irving."

In contrast to the dogged and purposeful Astor, Irving had, as he told a friend not long after his return to America in 1832, "staggered *through the world like a drunken man.*" The staggering had drawn out a pattern of its own, to be sure, and apparently one not without merit; for New York was roundly cheering the writer in the spring and early summer weeks immediately after his arrival from Europe, and talking about their pride in him, and about their memories of him. "The return of Geoffrey Crayon," his friend the diarist Philip Hone noted May 26, 1832, during those happy days of spring, "has made old times and the associations of early life the leading topics of conversation amongst his friends." And the friends were multitudinous. To escape their attentions, the genuinely modest Irving had, we remember, ventured forth in June of that year to reacquaint himself with the rest of America: with Washington, with New England, and with the Old Northwest—that last by steamboat over the Great Lakes as far as the village of Ashtabula, then by road to Cleveland and south through forested Ohio to the river town of Cincinnati.

Thus far we followed him in previous pages. He was traveling with friends met on the ship that had brought him earlier that year from Europe. One friend was Charles Joseph Latrobe, an Englishman in his thirties, amateur botanist, mountain climber, nephew of the architect Latrobe whom Irving had known in Washington twenty years before. Count Albert-Alexandre de Pourtalès, nineteen years old and wild to see Indians and live in Indian style, was also along, as the ward, presumably, of Latrobe, who seems to have been charged by the count's wealthy Swiss parents with keeping the young man out of trouble. On the Lake Erie steamboat these three traveling friends had joined forces with a fourth, a gentleman of forty named Ellsworth, on a government commission. Henry Leavitt Ellsworth was bound for Indian territory in what is now Oklahoma, to explore the region and adjudicate tribal disputes between Creeks and Cherokees. The opportunity seemed made to order for the new arrivals in America, including Irving, home after seventeen years abroad. They were invited to accompany Ellsworth on his explorations. The four would set out from Fort Gibson, on the Arkansas River, and spend several weeks roaming together as pioneers where white men had not ventured before.

All of them wrote of this excursion, the commissioner in a long letter to his wife, the worthy Latrobe in a rather flat and verbose book, the high-spirited count in a journal, and Irving in both journal and published essay. Together the five accounts provide a vivid experience of life on and beyond the frontier in the first half of the nineteenth century, beginning with the departure of the party down the Ohio on Monday, September 3, 1832, as recorded by Irving: "Left Cincinnati at 5 oclock in the steam boat Messenger, for Louisville—thunder showers—after which a remarkably clear tract in the west—moonlight night—mist on riv—passenger on board wounded with slash in the face."

Thus early was encountered an emblem of this land of brawls and gouging that they were to enter, a long way from Switzerland, England, or even New York. Through ten days and seven hundred miles the oddly formed group descended the Ohio and ascended the Mississippi to St. Louis, recording glimpses of people and riverscapes along the way: black steward aboard with gold earrings and checkered apron to his armpits, gamblers ("a young river dandy—green merino short coat—domestic cloth trousers—low crowned broad brimmed white hat—plays cards with a kindred genius"), on the banks occasional clearings that might reveal a "solitary log hut with corn fields among the forests—canoe by the shore." The very voices striking their ear were recorded, of two Kentuckians quarreling, for instance: "Put down that rock & I'll fight you," or a black man overheard driving his team of six oxen in Louisville: "Get along, you fat money making rascals." And nights on the river: "Beautiful moonrise on Illinois—fire of woodman at front of island—red-yellow moon—silver star—calm, cobalt-green sky reflected in river—here & there at distances a solitary light twinkles down from some big house among the trees." Nights new to Irving as to his friends: "moonlight—light of fires—chant & chorus of negro boat men—men strolling about docks with cigars—negroes dancing before furnaces—glassy surface of river.—undulations made by boat—wavering light of moon & stars—silent, primeval forest sleeping . . . on each side still forest—forest—forest."

How vastly green it must have looked to the homecomer, after his

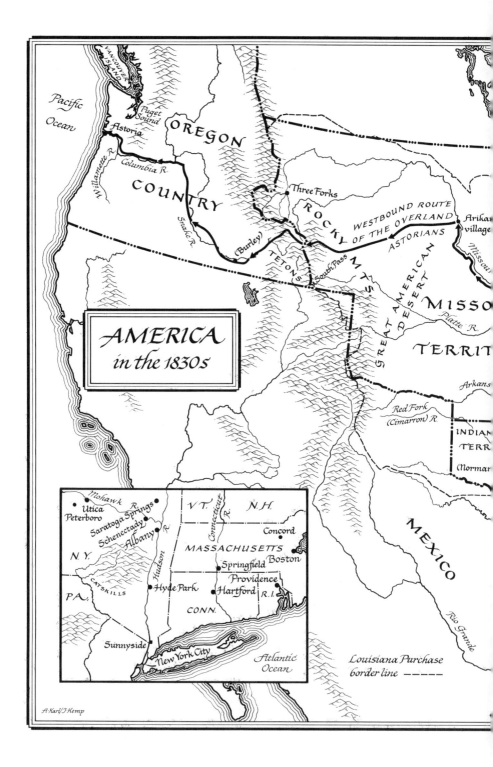

Pacific
Ocean

VANCOUVER
ISLAND

Puget
Sound

Astoria

Willamette R.

Columbia R.

Snake R.

(Burley)

OREGON

COUNTRY

ROCKY MTS.

Three Forks

TETONS

South Pass

WESTBOUND ROUTE
OF THE OVERLAND

ASTORIANS

Arikara
village

Missouri

GREAT AMERICAN DESERT

Platte R.

MISSO

TERRIT

AMERICA
in the 1830s

Arkans

Red Fork
(Cimarron) R.

INDIAN
TERR

(Mormar

MEXICO

Rio Grande

Mohawk

Utica
Peterboro

Saratoga Springs

Schenectady

Albany

N.Y.

CATSKILLS

PA.

Hudson R.

VT.

Connecticut R.

N.H.

Concord

MASSACHUSETTS

Springfield

Boston

Providence

Hyde Park

Hartford

R.I.

CONN.

Sunnyside

New York City

Atlantic
Ocean

Louisiana Purchase
border line -----

A·Karl/J·Kemp

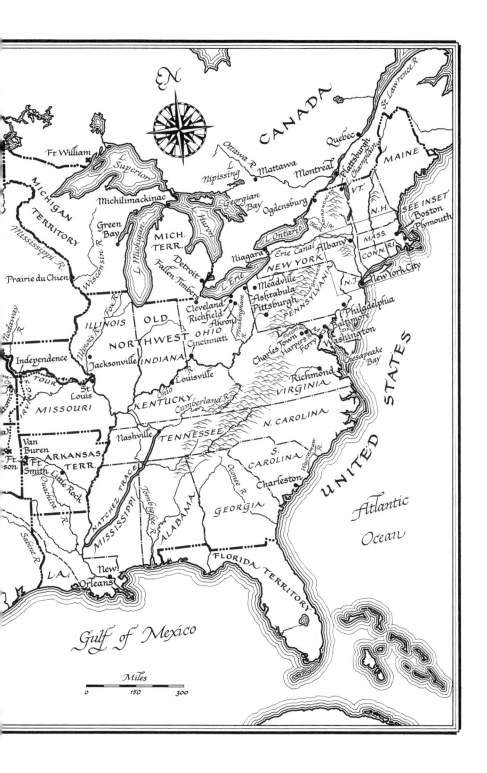

years in brown, bare Spain. Along the way he and his friends would attend stories of settlers in this different world. "Man & his wife from Philadelphia County—good looking man, & woman & children decently clad—been here 15 years—if it were to be done over would not come here—no means of educating his children—wants neighbours—people in neighbourhood rough & rude—some live by hunting, poaching, &c. —says he finds a great difference in himself since he has been here—his sons prefer hunting to learning—." Or, soon after meeting that family, "Stop at log house on the shore—pretty, delicate woman from near Nashville Tennessee—wishes herself back—no church in neighbour-hood—people rude. If there comes a Quaker the rude fellows pelt him, & cut his horse loose, & play all kinds of tricks. . . . Has lease for 4 years, after which will return to Tennessee."

Not everyone journeying westward would find what he longed for. On the morning of September 13, Irving and his three friends reached St. Louis, headquarters of the Western fur trade and outfit station for all parties into the interior—trappers, traders, army units, explorers, missionaries, settlers. Irving's party briefly formed one such group, laying over two days to purchase supplies: "We had not brought any with us from New York, since we had not anticipated this adventurous expedition." A quarter of a century earlier, Aaron Burr had visited this same river port: "St. Louis is on the banks of the Mississippi," he had instructed Theodosia in 1805, "about twenty miles below the mouth of the Missouri. It contains about two hundred houses, and some very wealthy people. The inhabitants are French; retain the French manners of the last century; are said to be hospitable; gay to dissipation; the society polished and fashionable." Irving's two days in 1832 scarcely gave him time to verify Burr's impressions, though he did take note, in a town now swollen to 7,000 inhabitants, of the "old rackety gambling house—noise of the cue and the billiard ball from morning till night—old French women accosting each other in the street." The new arrivals had put up at the Union Hotel; and after a morning of getting together their various purchases, many from the store of the American Fur Company (horses, a covered wagon for baggage, tents, provisions, glass beads, "some scissors for the young ladies and harmonicas for the Indian youngsters") —after those purchases, they had taken advantage of one opportunity to sample the hospitality of the place, in an outing to visit Governor Clark.

By that time Meriwether Lewis had been dead twenty years and more, either murdered or a suicide at thirty-five, in the back room of a tavern on the Natchez Trace near Nashville. But his old friend William Clark at sixty-two was still vigorous; indeed, Clark's appearance led his visitor Irving to think he was much younger: "fine healthy robust man—tall—about 50—perhaps more—his hair, originally light, now grey—falling on his shoulders—frank—intelligent—." The celebrated writer had driven out from St. Louis the few miles to the governor's ranch, set among nut trees and grapevines. The level prairies, alive with the chirp of insects, spread away green nearby, shading to blue at the horizon. In an open-air sitting room ("rifle & game bag &c. in corners— Indian calumet over fireplace—") Irving had awaited his host's arrival, and the veteran of the great expedition to the Pacific had approached from the distance "on horseback with dogs—guns. His grandson on a calico poney hallowing & laughing—." In an orchard that was "bending & breaking with loads of fruit," all had sat down to a plentiful dinner of fried chicken and bacon and grouse and roast beef and roasted potatoes and tomatoes and tasty cakes and bread and butter. "Gov. C. gives much excellent information concerning Indians. . . ."

What information we are not told in detail, but his advice would have been more enlightened than most that Irving would hear. After that helpful and agreeable visit, the party set out from St. Louis across Missouri, toward Independence and beyond, three hundred miles along a road that was "merely a track over the natural sod of the prairie." Now they were starting to rough it in truth, traveling on horseback ("Bringing up the rear, wrapped in the coats was Washington Irving," young Pourtalès bore witness, "ruefully inhaling gigantic clouds of dust kicked up by the horses. This is the description of our expedition for the next few days") maybe fifteen miles each morning, another ten or twelve miles after the midday dinner stop, finishing the day's push an hour before sundown in order to make camp. Or generally so. Monday, October 1, 1832: "Camp after sunset in a beautiful grove at the foot of immense trees—by a brook opposite a prarie—moonlight—owl hoots— prarie wolf howls—barking of dogs—bells of our horses among the trees—supper—beef, roast ducks & prarie hens . . . Fine effect of half moon among lofty trees—fire of camp with guides Indians & others round it—dogs lying on grass—waggons—tents by fire light—groups of attendants lying at foot of trees & round fires." Thus such days might end, and other days begin as did Wednesday, October 3: "Beautiful morng—breakfast scene—men round pans and kettles—groups of little hounds looking on— . . ."

That same morning they met in their travels parties of Osages— "lads with bows & rifles walking—fine, erect port of Osage warriors . . . Squaws riding with umbrellas—warm day—wide, treeless prarie—trembling with heat—columns of smoke hanging lazily in various directions of horizon—." And on the following morning they beheld "flights of Perroquets," cackling, chattering, flashing gemlike green and gold overhead. By the eighth, among such marvels, they had reached their present destination: "Arrive on banks of Arkansas—tolerably clear stream—neat look of white fortifications—blockhouses. &c. of Fort Gibson opposite. Cross in scow and arrive at gate of garrison—."

This was Irving again being "easily pleased." If no dinner to suit his taste, then a taste to suit his dinner: trait of a born traveler. Commissioner Ellsworth, as new to the country as was his author friend, viewed the fort differently: "numerous little log buildings . . . on the opposite side of the river—Although I had formed no definite idea of the Fortress, yet it did not equal my expectation." Irving was passing the guards at the gate, a sergeant (he notes) "with Irish brogue—culprits in pillory & riding the wooden horse—arrive at Col. Arbuckle's quarters—log house."

Shortly before, this Arbuckle, the fort's commander, had been assigned a company of rangers, which he had dispatched under a Captain Bean westward into Indian country. "The principal object of your command," Bean had been instructed, "is to preserve peace between the different Tribes on this Frontier with which the United States have Treaties: and between these and our Citizens: and you will, as far as may be in your power, protect our Citizens and the Indian Tribes refered to, from injury from the Pawnee and Commanchee Indians." So Bean's rangers were out there in the woods somewhere, and in Arbuckle's whitewashed log headquarters (no closets or presses, the easterner Ellsworth remarked; just nails on the walls for coats) it was determined that the newly arrived commissioner and his friends would set out promptly to join and travel in safety with them. A couple of Creeks would carry a message ahead to tell the rangers to await their arrival.

All this frontier bustle arose from a policy pursued by that warhorse Andrew Jackson, never a friend of the Indians. President Jackson, however, had not initiated the cruel program of Indian removal to these western regions. Years earlier, in 1803, Thomas Jefferson as President had undertaken "to encourage agriculture, domestic manufactures, stock raising and to abandon hunting" among Indians in the southeastern United States—that is, to "civilize" them on their tribal lands. But after the War of 1812, Jefferson's more moderate ambition was abandoned in favor of a brutal treatment of the Indian problem, pursued under President Monroe. His Secretary of War, the southerner Calhoun, had inspired and guided it, supported by governors of the interested southern states and by Indian agents—political appointees for the most part, unconcerned about tribal welfare. Calhoun meant simply to drive all Indians from the United States by removing them westward to Indian territory that was inhabited at the time by Osages, Comanches, Apaches, and other nomadic tribes of the plains. Wrenching the sedentary, agricultural Cherokees and Creeks from their ancestral lands in Georgia and Tennessee would inevitably create conflicts—but at a distance, out West; and meanwhile, white settlers in the Southeast would take possession of the appropriated lands. The policy was finally sanctioned by law under Jackson; through the Indian Removal Act of June 30, 1830, all remaining Indians living east of the Mississippi would be forcibly driven west of the river.

Some Cherokees had been moved already, by a treaty of 1828 that granted them land in present-day Oklahoma formerly occupied by a few hundred Creeks. White squatters had intruded into the territory as well, and the Creeks had besought the government at Washington to adjust boundaries within the region to end quarrels that had arisen. Ellsworth had been charged with accomplishing this mission, part exploratory, part adjudicatory, part informative—all of it, of course, created by that crass and inhuman policy of greed that troubled the great majority of white Americans of the early nineteenth century hardly at all.

We in the late twentieth century have our own national injustices to ponder. Irving, to his credit, was more bothered than were many of his contemporaries by the white man's callous behavior in such instances. *The Sketch Book*, with its worldwide circulation, contains two essays about Indians written as early as 1814; the tone of both is responsive to the dignity and sympathetic to the plight of native Americans. In "Traits of Indian Character," for instance, an Irving twenty years younger had already noted that the coming of the white man among Indians "has enervated their strength, multiplied their diseases, and superinduced upon their original barbarity the low vices of artificial life. It has given them a thousand superfluous wants, whilst it has diminished their means of mere existence." Elsewhere in the same essay, the author acknowledges Indian cruelty to whites, but suggests good reasons for it: "They cannot but be sensible that the white men are the usurpers of their ancient dominion, the cause of their degradation, and the gradual destroyers of their race." Nor was such sympathetic understanding merely impulsive. His admiration for Indians was informed and consistent. Writing from Madrid in 1827, the far-traveled Irving remarked that there were "more natural gentlemen among the common people of Spain than among any people I have ever known, excepting our Indians." And his books on the American West that this present tour would inaugurate, books that remained immensely popular throughout his lifetime and long afterward, would furnish Irving's contemporaries with their most accurate, thorough, and panoramic view of Indian life, whether as led by the abstemious Chinooks or the honest Flatheads, the shy Shoshones or the gaily dressed Creeks, the unrelentingly hostile Blackfeet or the peaceful Nez Percés. In his Western writings the popular author would recount legends of the Osages, rituals of the Arikaras, orations of the Crows—and thus make all that colorful heritage a part of our Saxon awareness. Nor would such writing have been possible from the pen of bigotry, apathy, or indifference.

Thus Irving was on the point of enlarging a long-held interest, riding out with "Col Arbuckle, Genl Houston" (like a character in implausible romantic fiction, our protagonist, who had recently dined with William Clark, now rode alongside Sam Houston) "to Col. Choteau's," at the Creek Agency a few miles northwest of the fort. From there the group, reduced to Irving, Ellsworth, Latrobe, Pourtalès, a few rangers, and a couple of Creole hands to guide and hunt for them, would push westward into the interior on the trail of Captain Bean's company. "You may desire to know what Provisions we took from Fort Gibson," Ellsworth wrote home to Hartford; "nothing but pork—flour coffee & sugar & a little salt . . . as we depended on game after that period" of the opening days. In addition, they did pack weapons and camping gear. Irving tells us that "Mr. E." was wearing "half Osage, half chasseur dress—embroidered leather Indian pouch—powder horn with red worsted band." Latrobe and Pourtalès had brought along six horses: a racehorse apiece for the prairie hunts they anticipated, plus riding horses and two pack horses. "Mr Pourteles loaded one," according to the disapproving Ellsworth, "with shawls blanketts & & & presents to the squaws—"

For Pourtalès at nineteen meant to live with the Indians, despite his guardian Latrobe's protests, despite the dangers that the guides were warning of if he pursued that resolution. Wearing his beads and moccasins, possessed of his ingratiatory presents, he now detached himself from the group to search out an Osage village that he had learned was somewhere nearby. Latrobe felt constrained to follow along; the others doubtfully watched them disappear into the woods. Ellsworth was feeling depressed anyway. This was the time to travel all right, trees begilt with autumn, "for the flies & musquitoes abound in summer—in the spring the streams are high & the mud deep." But he confessed in writing to his wife that he was starting the expedition "with a heavy heart— . . . the danger from wild Indians, and some of them cannabals too—the exposure to so much inclement weather far from medical treatment & good nursing—the conflagration of the praries—the reptiles that must every night be my companions & the wild beast on all sides!"

Moreover, they had forgotten plates and silverware; "in our hurry to get away it is not strange that we should forget some things very necessary for our comfort." But the mood of the Connecticut insurance man would soon improve, as the guides fashioned bowls for him out of tree knots, while their evening campfires spread warmth and a light that revealed in time the wanderers Pourtalès and Latrobe, moved by wiser second thoughts, reappearing at the edge of the clearing, drawn by the cheerful firelight and ready to stay with the others the rest of the way. Another day's trek, and the little group had encountered ashes of the rangers' fires still warm; so that the following morning, Saturday, October 13, as Irving records, they "set off about 7—after riding some distance . . . we come to a bottom of woodland—see horses among the trees, recognized by the men as horses belonging to their troop." From a ridge they discovered the camp below, "in beautiful open wood by a stream of water—undergrowth of low shrubs—blanket tents—venison hanging on stick to smoke over fire—buckskins spread—cooking at fires—horses—stacks of saddles & rifles—congratulation of men with their companions."

Henceforth all would travel together. We might picture them briefly, these rangers when rangers were a novelty, young recruits without discipline, mostly having a lark for the short duration of their service, no uniforms yet, their hats of "many colors & shapes—every one, wore that, which he supposed would not return—the only arms, were a rifle for each—." Irving first glimpsed them now, here in camp: "men of all kinds of dress—some lying under trees—rifles leaning agst trees." Always the high jinks, the target practice, the pot-stirring and snoozing and storytelling, the "Shooting—leaping—wrestling—in the camp—."

During their progress together they would soon have to ford the Arkansas River at the mouth of the Red Fork. "Some of the rangers who could not swim, and whose horses could not carry them over, threw in a dry log, and clung to that stemming the current as well as they could." Irving was persuaded to cross the river another way. The guides were using a buffalo skin for a boat, piling it high with saddlebags and shot pouches and bridles and greatcoats: "Mr Irving said it would certainly sink." Nevertheless, the amiable author of *The Alhambra* was presently "taken in the arms of Billet & Tonish and placed with great care in the centre of the tottering craft, and requested to sit *perfectly still*—The swimmers plunged in with their hideous yells"—exuberant Indian yells—"and Mr Irving sat *motionless*, proud enough to be borne across the deep in a Buffaloe skin!!—when the swimmers had passed more than half the distance, and become able to touch the bottom, Mr Irving was more careless as to his perpendicular stillness, and seizing one of the guns which lay beside him, he fired a salute to those who were behind— He soon reached the shore, and strided the sand along the beach on the opposite side as one who had just discovered and was taking possession of a new country!!—" When the exclamatory Ellsworth reached the southern bank on a subsequent crossing, he found "my friend Mr Irving . . . busily filling his little sketch book, with the interesting events of the day—" There among the forest of oaks and mimosas, the meandering Arkansas visible for miles from rocks above, and far off the yellowish line of the prairies, what Irving was writing just there and at those moments we can read, his journal having survived from which would be fashioned the appealing essay of "A Tour on the Prairies."

He was having a splendid time. "Mr. Irving," that frequent insomniac, "declares for all to hear that he has never slept or eaten so well as he does now that he is a nomad." All of them were eating enormously. Pourtalès spoke of their roasting the ribs of a fat female bear and cooking fritters in the grease—indeed, of consuming "moose, deer, bear, and turkey; we drank coffee and prairie tea, and we made grilled corncakes. There was such an abundance of everything that I ate every half-hour from seven in the morning to six in the evening." Ellsworth, too, discovered that "the appetite is voracious—the stomach is constantly braced by the cool air, and the system is not enervated by warm rooms or by dissappation." And in his little sketch book, the nearly fifty-year-old Irving, who admitted to being positively ashamed of his new gluttony, was sounding half his age, lyrical over this novel existence, all aspects of it: "Delightful mode of life—exercise on horseback all the fore part of the day—diversified by hunting incidents—then about 3 oclock encamping in some beautiful place with full appetite for repose, lying on the grass under green trees—in genial weather with a blue, cloudless sky—then so sweet sleeping at night in the open air, & when awake seeing the moon and stars through the tree tops—such zest for the hardy, simple, but savory meats, the product of the chase . . . turkeys just from the thicket—honey from the tree—coffee—or delightful prarie tea. The weather is in its perfection—golden sunshine . . . skies without a cloud—or if there be clouds, of feathery texture and lovely tints . . . How exciting to think that we are breaking thro a country hitherto untrodden by white man, except perchance the solitary trapper—a glorious world spread around us without an inhabitant."

Virtually uninhabited, to be precise. They did occasionally come upon encampments of Indians, and Commissioner Ellsworth would proceed dutifully to introduce himself "as a big man come from their father the President—I told them I came to establish peace among all the Indian tribes, and wished that the Osages and Pawnees, might bury the hatchet, and smoke the calumet of peace—they replied all very good—" But the commissioner was privately having trouble adjusting to Indian ways, to the "*very indecent* manner," for instance, that the Creeks had "of making pictures on the trees . . . warrior in such attitudes of amorous feeling . . . I forbear giving details—" Or to the pot-bellied Indian children: "They were many of them, naked—several little boys 13 years old came out before us, and when I was addressing them and urging them to peace & not to fight the Pawnees, or steal horses, and provoke revenge; these little boys made water before all the women, and even *upon* some of them, laughing, heartily to show us how they could, wet the folks around by their jet . . ."

After such encounters before the noisome wigwams it was doubtless good to have your duty behind you, pushing forward toward evening camp through forests of cottonwood and pecan and elm and sycamore, or coming on prairies sometimes with grass to the horses' shoulders, or fording mud-red waters of the streams: "We are about eighty or more in number, and our group looks absolutely warlike," so young Pourtalès thought. "If you just imagine a long line of individuals on good mounts, armed with carbines, dressed in moccasins, leggings, leather shirts, coats, trousers, hats of all possible descriptions, part American, part Indian, living in the wilderness on what we can hunt . . ." and having a wonderful time so far, none more so than Pourtalès himself. While

Mr. Latrobe was content to collect his botanical specimens, storing them in the little bag tied to his coat button, Pourtalès "must follow the Osage trail—he must sleep in Osage huts amidst lice and brawling brats & dirty squaws—." The proper Ellsworth remained offended. "From a hint dropped one day, I infer the parents wish to have the child absent from Switzerland to change some previous attachments, and to sow his wild oats in a foreign country—Whether the first object named will be accomplished I know not—The last I am sure will be done, unless his wild store is beyond measurement—" Ah, but "the deep mortification," as the commissioner feared, "which may be inflicted upon his future domestic felicity . . . by the appearance of red progeny, who will rise up to call him father! I forbear to add more—"

Actually, he seems to have understood the count hardly at all, could not know of the goals forming in the idealistic mind of the young Swiss, who was determining to give himself to the task of imparting civilized skills to these Osages and becoming their advocate before the American government: "It would be a beautiful life!" so Pourtalès resolved exultantly in his journal. "This is a new career, an untried career, a never-ending career in its implementation and its results. Alas, will it be mine, or is the future still enveloped in its impenetrable veil?" The veil we might lift a moment to disclose the young count returning to Europe after all, joining the Prussian diplomatic corps, most respectably marrying in his mid-thirties the eldest daughter of the curator of Bonn University, by her fathering two daughters of his own before dying in his late forties, in 1861, while Prussian ambassador to Paris. Ellsworth's fears, and the count's own dreams on the prairies, proved equally wide of the mark.

If he knew little of Pourtalès, the commissioner was coming to understand Irving better. They were almost constantly together during these five weeks: "Mr Irving Latrobe & myself, used generally to shave ourselves before sunrise—you would laugh to see us, drawing our razors over our faces apparently at random; for we all shaved without a glass"; or, "Mr. Irving & myself went to the Creek and washed our linnen & wollens—it was a *new employment to both*—"; or, "One night I dreamed a bear had caught me, and I called out lustily as you know I do at home in such dreams—Mr Irving reached over my head, and in trying to awake me scratched my neck—I awaked at this moment, and thought my dream reality, and that the bears paws were upon me—."

Through such intimacies Ellsworth was able to perceive and record not only obvious traits—the author's sweet tooth, his touchiness about disrespect from social inferiors, his skin problems, his penchant for physical cleanliness—but more subtle attributes as well. "Mr Irving is quick in his feelings . . . ridicules the idea of taking thought for tomorrow . . . will live & die a batchelor and yet make more conquests among the females than other dry fellows can ever do . . ." And on those long

nights by the campfires ("Our nights were very long—for we had no
candles, and *could* only amuse ourselves, by conversation") the sociable
author confided much to his new friend, of a childhood in early New
York, for instance: "He was a poor scholar—fond of roguery, with no
disposition to bone down to study—he had a great thirst for reading
voyages . . . a book of travels was like a coach at the door—he must
jump in & take a ride . . ." Or about the surprising success of *Knickerbocker*, followed by the business partnership with his brothers, who
thought it better that he "join them, and become rich; than to live in an
authors chamber—a poor garret—." Irving told of Ebenezer among
friends in New York hearing read, after long silence, the first manuscript pages of *The Sketch Book*: the joy of those listeners "*could not be
repressed* and *loud applause echoed from every side*—The brother was
so affected *at the reception that he burst into tears* and *was obliged to
leave the room*—." And the author described for his friend the episode at
Oxford, then scarcely a year into the past: "he said he was never so
much embarrassed . . . appearing on the stage dressed for the occasion, before a vast audience" to receive his honorary degree. The solid
Latin phrases were rolling about him. Did the undergraduates know
who this man was? From the multitudes before him "some one would cry
out, yes 'sketch book'—and that would resound with deafning applause;
another cried out *Knickerbocker* with like satisfacction— . . ." And so
on, Irving recalled by the campfire, of a memorable half hour.

Something about those western nights—fire warmth and bright
sparks leaping into darkness and the company at ease with the black
forests all around and bells of the grazing horses tinkling—had encouraged the usually self-effacing author to survey his achievements
with honesty and pleasure. A hunter, meanwhile, might be seen entering
the clearing with a slain deer on his back; or one would bring in the ribs
of an elk, and "he is hoisted on the shoulders of his companions—groups
round fire examining the sport." Long shadows move against the tree
trunks; men carve meat, skim pots, sprawl fashioning skins into moccasins; voices drone, lazy in story. At last the bugle sounds tattoo. Fires
crackle more softly and seldom, burning down. Stories end; the last
straggling voices finally cease. From the surrounding forest comes the
sound of an owl's hoot. A horse neighs. Then silence. Sleep, and before
dawn to awaken deliciously: "fine night—moon shining feebly down
into the camp—fires nearly extinguished—men lying about their fires—
light clouds drifting across the moon . . . Yellow leaves showering
around us . . ."

Reveille. The rangers stir, arise to morning sounds: "imitations of
cocks crowing, hens cackling, among the youngsters of the camp—
horses driven in—breakfast—whistling—singing—dancing—hallooing
after horses—joking, laughing . . . Have you seen my horse? cries one.
What horse is that broke loose over the brook? . . . Whose wallet is

this? Why, I guess its mine." The bugle calls to mount and march, and behind the company are left the shambles of a camp: fourteen dead fires and the ground appearing like "a slaughter house—a camp is a most offensive place after 24 hours—."

Now the terrain changes, grows more rugged farther westward: "ride through tangled bottoms and up and down rough, broken, rocky hills—picturesque look of troop winding thro thickets and up heights." They have passed by honey trees, by a deer's moss-covered skull, by beaver dams, by an Indian's burial place, bones blanching in tree limbs. Overhead, wild geese squawk past in a line. And finally all about the party are signs of buffalo: short grass, then tracks, recent dung, low bare limbs of trees where the creatures have been scratching, and their wallowing holes in the earth, maybe ten feet across and up to two feet deep. "We soon saw 3 large Buffaloe walking slowly along, their humpy backs & little horns just projecting above the bushes on the opposite side of the marsh—Buffaloe! Buffaloe! Buffaloe look at them—there they go—." And more of them lumbered into sight, and still more. "Before long we saw the huge piles coming down the hill—" Irving, who had bagged one hare while hunting a decade earlier with the royal party in the snow-filled forests near Dresden, now joined his mates in the wild pursuit to kill. "The animal," Ellsworth had noted, "when he first sees you looks with *astonishing firceness*, with his *full round eye fixed intently upon* YOU—His great size, (often 2000 lbs) his shaggy head, his hump back, and short sharp horns, are terriffic, not only to horses but their riders—" Here came one, bellowing most horribly in distress, dust rising, with the Creole Billet yelling and firing at his flank, "untill he came very near us . . . blood was streaming from his mouth & nose— an awful picture indeed—." Irving was galloping with the rest of them, and with Pourtalès was shooting at one bull "again & again, while Tonish kept him at bay for their sport Mr Irving found his pistols too small to be effectual, as he could not get near enough to the animal, with his horse He took Pourteles gun (double barrell) and shot two balls with that, which took effect— . . ."

Thus: Western sport in the early nineteenth century. The squeamish will look elsewhere while Billet skillfully opens the flesh under the jaw of the creature, removes the tongue, and ties that trophy to the saddle. The chase has ended. Slabs of hump are brought to camp to feed the weary, satisfied party. Meanwhile, the image of stout Irving as hunter lingers, matched for vividness by only one other glimpse, in camp a couple of days earlier, when Captain Bean, reconnoitering on a nearby hill, had suddenly screamed down the alarm: Pawnees! We read of it, presumably, in safety, but the terror the word awakened was genuine: "*Pawnees. Pawnees—get the horses—to arms!* to arms!—"

Ellsworth was in the thick of the camp when its calm was disrupted. "Shots were heard over the hill!—2 of our men killed? next 7

killed!—500 Pawnees coming with bows and guns—'every man get his
horse and mount'— What *consternation!* I cannot describe it—my horse
had gone down the Creek . . . charity began at home—every one took
care of himself—Some horses were soon ready, and Rangers seen riding
with a *quick* gallop to the brow of the hill, where the Pawnees might be
seen—Oh! the confusion! the cooking dishes were upset as matters of no
moment, for many a poor soul, thought he should need no more nourishment—Some actually shed *tears*—Mʳ Irving could find only one *Leggin*, and he was calling through the camp loud, and louder still, for his
odd leggin, of mighty little consequence in a battle—He was as *pale* as
he could be, and much terrified—"

Their plight was no joke, of course; nor was Irving the only one
frightened. "Latrobe seized his saddle, and put it on wrong side before
and girted it in this manner—Pourteles wanted to know, whether it was
best to take saddle bags or not? One young chap went running around,
wringing his hands, crying 'Lord jesus help me find my bridle'!" And the
horseless Ellsworth, gun primed and dirk at his side, hastened to join
others in piling up a brushwood breastwork "to guard us from the
arrows of the Pawnees—"

Fortunately those arrows never came. The captain on his hilltop
had mistaken a distant sight of two rangers scouting; they, in turn, had
seen Bean's own stealthy figure as that of an Indian, "so that the Capt
and two of his men were frightened at each other—." Nevertheless,
Pawnee tracks had been sighted; thus the horses that night were staked
and the guard doubled, while around the campfires "a long evening was
filled, by comparing notes of bravery on the occasion—all denied being
frightened, and most boasted what *he* meant to do to the damned
Pawnees!"

By now the high spirits of the camp had more than once been
dampened. The rangers' zestful imitations of animals were less often
heard around reveille. During the day, terrain before the party was more
hostile, "excessively fatiguing to men and horses—a broken, hilly country
covered with Scrub oaks, with interlacing limbs as hard as iron, & intersected by deep ravines of red clay, down which the horses fairly slide,
& then scramble up the other side like cats." The weather was growing
cloudier as autumn wore on. "Oh how glad shall I be, to get bread again,
and sugar & milk and coffee": the plaint is Ellsworth's. They had been
from Fort Gibson more than two full weeks, the rangers longer. Friday,
October 26: "Last night wild horses came neighing about our camp and
took off some of our gallant steeds—they cannot be found this morning . . ." By the end of the month Irving was noting "discontent in the
camp as among the children of Israel in the wilderness—want of
bread—for a week past the troops have been out of flour. A corporal last
night was put under arrest for mutinous talk on the subject. . . ." Rain
had begun to fall, making campsites dismal. "The mud around our tent

was over shoe," according to Ellsworth. "I got some grape vines, & bushes to lay down before our door . . . The day was very uncomfortable—the storm was cold—our horses stood shivering and the wet hobbles wounded their feet or legs—very badly." The company had to push on in rain: "The violence of the storm was only resisted by stopping & turning our backs to the storm, after the manner of cattle." Or it would start raining in the middle of the night; Irving on November 4 "had prepared my bed in the open air . . . when it began to rain, crept into the tent—sound of the axe in all quarters—men cutting poles to make booths of blankets &c."

All of them longed to see the fort again. It was very cold. On the seventh, "I have never," Ellsworth testified, "known so cold a day in November in Hartford as today—my hands & face suffered severely as did my feet—." By that time his and Irving's flour was gone, like the troops' before them; "pepper also—salt nearly gone—we live on soup & stewed game." That same night was clear and frosty; a cup of water by where Irving slept froze half an inch. But the next day, dragging themselves eastward alongside their skinny, exhausted horses, the adventurers at last reached log houses among trees, Creek houses—frontier promise of civilization not far beyond—presenting their "delightful sight of hogs—poultry, crowing of cocks &c.—horse pricks his ears—."

So the month's tour of the prairies was to be safely concluded. In fact, three days later Irving would be aboard a steamboat on his way down the Arkansas toward New Orleans, pigeons in clouds overhead, cows on the banks staring in wonder at the passing craft before galloping into the woods. Fort Smith would appear alongside and drop astern ("on rocky Bluff—ruinous old wooden buildings & block house"), then Van Buren ("at present 4 or 5 straggling log huts"); next the boat would dock at Little Rock, with a population at the time of five hundred and twenty-seven, for the benefit of whom so notable an arrival was to be recorded in the local *Arkansas Gazette*: "among the passengers on board . . . our distinguished countryman WASHINGTON IRVING, Esq. the accomplished author . . . on his return to New-York, from a tour among the Indian tribes west of Arkansas." Along with Irving (besides John James Audubon, coincidentally on the same steamboat) was the little "sketch book" that Ellsworth had seen the author scribble in so often. Notes would awaken memories that would be used when Irving finally reached Manhattan; even now, about to leave the West, he was still observant: "In general," one undated entry concludes dryly about this time, "the frontiersmen seem to think themselves imposed upon by the Indians, because the latter, having lost nearly all their property, seek to hold on to what is left.

"They have got the Indians' coat & now begrudge them the fringe."

At the fort Irving had been forced to say his good-byes hastily, to the now devoted Ellsworth, to Latrobe and Pourtalès, because the sudden appearance of the steamboat had provided an unexpected opportunity to set off at once for home. The departure, a mile below the Osage Agency, had occurred near dawn—"beautiful dawn—while yet twilight pass a fire on the shore—Indians around it—canoe fastened close by." Down the Arkansas River to Little Rock, on down to the Mississippi, on down to New Orleans, then by mail stage through the pine forests of Alabama and Georgia, on through the Carolinas and Virginia, to Washington for an extended visit with friends through that winter and until March of the new year, 1833. Irving was in excellent spirits, "cheerful, gay, talkative," according to one who saw him then, "no longer subject to those moody fits which formerly obscured his fine intellect at times." Materials for work on a wholly American theme lay to hand at last; and in succeeding months, back in New York, the author would develop jottings from his memorandum book into the long, appealing essay published in the spring of 1835 as Volume I of the three volumes of *The Crayon Miscellany*. (The essay describing his visit two decades earlier with Scott at Abbotsford made up much of the second volume; legends of Moorish Spain filled the third.)

As for the narrative on the West, though self-professedly containing no "moving accidents by flood or field," it was particularly warmly received both in America and in Europe. "I have passed a few hours delightfully in reading Washington Irving's 'Tour on the Prairies,'" Philip Hone wrote in his diary that May. "It is the very best kind of light reading . . . Killing buffaloes, hunting wild horses, sleeping every night on the ground for a whole month . . . —all events of ordinary occurrence to the settlers of the great West, but matters of thrilling interest to comfortable citizens who read of them in their green slippers, seated before a shining grate, the neatly printed page illuminated by a bronze astral lamp . . ."

Enough for an account to aspire to, surely; the author's own introduction alludes to this "simple narrative of every day occurrences; such as happen to every one who travels the prairies." But no one (Latrobe's turgid book on the same events makes an instructive comparison) has described more deftly than Irving such occurrences, which, to be sure, are past anyone's experiencing around Norman or Tulsa in our own time.

Moreover, finishing his book and with firsthand knowledge of the frontier to draw on, Irving back in New York was in a position to consider a literary task that his old friend Mr. Astor proposed to him during the summer of 1834. That same spring Astor had returned from Europe for good, to be met with the grievous news of his wife's recent death. In the weeks that followed, life must have seemed about over for the widower, now past seventy and retired from the fur trade. Meanwhile, years that had accumulated so quickly continued to bury earlier events of his life in oblivion; in fact, the most magnificent of Astor's many undertakings—one that he had conceived and launched more than a quarter of a century ago—seemed destined to be forgotten. It had proved to be the only commercial failure of his life—but a glorious failure for all that. Perhaps Irving, home and with no work pending, could be prevailed upon to tell the adventurous story: another book on an American theme, but this one far grander than was any tour of the prairies. To his friend, Astor urged the subject: "John Jacob Astor is extremely desirous of having a work written on the subject of his settlement of Astoria, at the mouth of Columbia River; something that might take with the reading world, and secure to him the reputation of having originated the enterprise . . . The old gentleman has applied to me repeatedly in the matter . . ."

And in this, as in so many other matters, the old gentleman had his way. "For upward of a month past," Irving was accordingly reporting in September 1835, "I have been quartered at Hellgate, with Mr. Astor, and I have not had so quiet and delightful a nest since I have been in America. He has a spacious and well-built house, with a lawn in front of it, and a garden in rear. The lawn sweeps down to the water edge, and full in front of the house is the little strait of Hellgate, which forms a constantly moving picture. Here the old gentleman keeps a kind of bachelor hall. . . ."

And here, in compatible surroundings, Irving set about to recreate the greatest of all the projects that Astor's bold mind had conceived and brought into being. At the beginning of the century, with France still in possession of the immense Louisiana territory beyond the Mississippi, the New York merchant (as one measure of the dimensions of his schemes) had hit upon a plan for forming a syndicate to purchase the entire Mississippi and Missouri river valleys from Napoleon, in order to resell them to the American government at a commission that might yield a profit up to $30,000,000. That fantastic proposal he had actually made to Gouverneur Morris and De Witt Clinton, but before steps could be taken to organize an approach to the French ruler (who, Astor correctly surmised, had seen as indefensible a region that he was nevertheless eager to keep from the English), Louisiana had been negotiated for and acquired by the federal government at Washington.

That was in 1803. For forty years after that date, what Jefferson had bought for $15,000,000 was put to hardly any use at all. Lands east of the Mississippi sufficed to accommodate however many citizens in those less populous times might desire to clear woods and farm on the frontier. As for the nearly million square miles of acreage from the Mississippi to the Rockies, much of it was reported to be mountain or desert, fit for Indians, traders, trappers, and not much else. The sod of treeless prairies seemed to defy farming; the mineral wealth of the region went mostly undetected.

The region did possess furs of course, and in abundance. Astor, acting on that realization as early as 1807, envisaged a future shaped to his own advantage: a series of forts and trading posts to exploit those furs, set out along the route westward to the Pacific that the explorers Clark and Lewis had recently followed. Through the width of the territory over which that same Lewis was then serving as governor, Astor meant to establish posts, following the course of the Missouri to the Rockies and even beyond, into an area beyond what Jefferson had purchased, into Oregon country that the English in Canada could claim as legitimately as could Americans, like them, on the other side of the continent.

Indeed, we recall from Burr's escapade along the Mississippi about that time, in 1807, that far from coveting what are now the states of Washington and Oregon, most Americans cared little about such far-off regions, and the few who did care supposed that an autonomous sister republic might be formed eventually on the other side of the Divide. Jefferson, for instance, confided to Astor himself in May 1812 that the President—the former President by then—had hoped for the establishment of an independent nation on the Pacific Coast, "unconnected with us but by the ties of blood and interest . . ." That is, almost no one so early in our history foresaw a single country stretching from the Atlantic seaboard westward across forest and prairie and desert and snowcapped mountain to the Pacific, at a distance at the time of no less than four months away.

Astor saw his line of forts, however, crossing that distance, and may even have dreamed of forming an independent republic himself, in the valley of the Columbia River, about which newspaper readers had learned from returning members of the Lewis and Clark expedition: "One of the hands, an intelligent man, tells me," a correspondent to a Kentucky newspaper had written in 1806—and his letter was reprinted in newspapers farther east—"that Indians are as numerous on Columbia as the whites are in any part of the U States— . . . They have brought several curiosities with them from the ocean. The Indians are represented as being very peaceable. The winter was very mild on the Pacific . . ."

Oregon could be reached overland, and was desirable country. The thought was intriguing. From modest origins Napoleon had recently become emperor of the French; and Aaron Burr, whom Astor had dealt with in New York, was being charged at Richmond in the summer of 1807 with having aspired at least to become emperor of Mexico. The butcher's son from Walldorf was nourishing his own ambitions, in a mind spacious enough to contain thoughts of a western republic, founded by him and spreading back from the wide mouth of the Columbia River into the rich interior. Such a dream on his part is at least conceivable. What is certain is that he did undertake to plant a settlement on the other side of the continent, where the Columbia flows into the Pacific. Partly by sea, partly overland, he meant to supply that settlement until it had grown self-sufficient and was on its way to becoming a city. He would call the settlement Astoria; and from Astoria, from the very beginning, furs from the west-flowing rivers would be shipped directly to China.

Why shouldn't such a port, so advantageously located, grow with all the vigor of New York itself? A metropolis founded by John Jacob Astor. Undeterred by the risks, by the expense, by the enormous logistical problems, he set about realizing his dream. How he did so, and what came of it, make an absorbing story of dedication, hardship, bad luck, and heroism played out against scenes of perilous grandeur. And this was the story that Astor, grown old, succeeded in persuading Washington Irving to tell.

In these pages we shall briefly follow the adventure; but before doing so, some attention must be directed to how confidently we may accept the account that Irving has given us. Is he reliable, or does he indulge his fondness for romance in the pages of *Astoria*? In the spring of 1835, by the time the middle-aged author had settled to work at Astor's country home, he could bring to his literary task proven skills of the historian, for Irving owed his present fame in part to his accurately rendered accounts of Columbus and the conquest of Granada. Moreover, he brought with him recent memories of frontier existence. Memories of youthful adventures on another frontier with the Hoffmans and Ogdens, and of the world of the fur magnates of Montreal, added to the equipment he possessed: "From those early impressions," as he wrote, "the grand enterprizes of the great fur companies, and the hazardous errantry of their associates in the wild parts of our vast continent, have always been themes of charmed interest to me; and I have felt anxious to get at the details of their adventurous expeditions among the savage tribes that peopled the depths of the wilderness."

To do so, he had the advantage of access to hundreds of documents at Hell Gate concerning that colonizing effort on the Pacific Coast that had occurred a quarter of a century earlier. All those letters, accounts, journals, invoices of merchandise Astor made available to Irving, although most have since been destroyed. In the 1870s, some twenty-five years after the merchant's death, fifteen large packing cases containing "the miscellaneous records & papers left behind by John Jacob Astor," were systematically burned. Some ten years after that, "to save a few dollars' truck hire" when offices of the Astor estate were being moved a few blocks in Manhattan, nearly all that remained of the papers and manuscripts were likewise put to the flame. So at Astor's home in 1835

Irving had before him what no longer exists. The reliability of his handling of that material becomes, therefore, a matter of considerable
interest.

He hired his nephew to help with research, to sort through and
digest the multitude of documents and published material that had come
into Astor's possession over the years. For a recompense, as Irving explained, the nephew would be responsible for looking over "the various
papers, letters, and journals in the possession of Mr. Astor, written by
various persons who have been in his employ." Moreover, he was "to
draw anecdotes and descriptions" from Astor himself, "and from Northwest traders who occasionally visit him; to forage among various works
in French and English that have been published relative to these regions,
and thus to draw together and arrange into some kind of form a great
body of facts." All this the nephew willingly agreed to do.

Here, then, is one brief sample of what Pierre Irving proceeded to
summarize for his uncle's use, a description of days along the Missouri
in 1811: "On leaving the village of Charete, about 50 miles above St
Charles, saw Daniel Boone—see Bradbury, p 16. Boone died in 1818—
The next day saw Colter. See Lewis & Clark Vol II p. 407, & Bradbury,
p 17. A very interesting note in relation to him . . ."

And so on. John Bradbury, an English naturalist who had accompanied an expedition part way up the Missouri and written an account of
his experience, was one of several published sources that Washington
Irving was able to consult in fashioning his history of Astor's colonizing
enterprise. Of that encounter above St. Charles, Bradbury writes: "On
leaving Charette, Mr. Hunt pointed out to me an old man standing on
the bank, who, he informed me, was Daniel Boone, the discoverer of
Kentucky. As I had a letter of introduction to him . . . I went ashore
to speak to him . . . He informed me, that he was eighty-four years of
age; that he had spent a considerable portion of his time alone in the
backwoods, and had lately returned from his spring hunt, with nearly
sixty beaver skins."

That and no more. Irving follows his nephew's suggestions and
Bradbury's facts, but he relates those facts in his characteristic style,
transmuting a record into the stuff of literature: "On the afternoon of the
third day, March 17th," we learn from *Astoria*, "the boats touched at
Charette, one of the old villages founded by the original French colonists. Here they met with Daniel Boon, the renowned patriarch of Kentucky, who had kept in the advance of civilization, and on the borders of
the wilderness, still leading a hunter's life, though now in his eighty fifth
year. He had but recently returned from a hunting and trapping expedition and had brought nearly sixty beaver skins as trophies of his skill.
The old man was still erect in form, strong in limb and unflinching in
spirit, and as he stood on the river bank, watching the departure of an
expedition destined to traverse the wilderness to the very shores of the

Pacific, very probably felt a throb of his old pioneer spirit, impelling him to shoulder his rifle and join the adventurous band. . . ."

In such a passage, altogether typical, conjectures are indicated clearly, while what is factual in the record is scrupulously followed. *Astoria* appeared in 1836, to wide and unanimous praise. "The modesty of the title," Edgar Allan Poe wrote in the *Southern Literary Messenger*, affords "no indication of the fulness, comprehensiveness, and beauty, with which a long and entangled series of detail, collected, necessarily, from a mass of vague and imperfect data, has been wrought into completeness and unity." Others in America and Europe were similarly impressed at the time. For example: "With all his power of humor and pathos," the author of *Astoria* "is conscientious, and does not permit his imagination to *make* facts, to be passed off as real occurrences." And an English reviewer remarked on "materials not very favorable to his purpose" out of which the author had "succeeded in weaving a connected and exciting narrative. Great art has been employed, though none appears."

But somehow, in the second half of the nineteenth century, after Irving's death, *Astoria* came gradually to acquire a reputation for being overly tinted with colorful fictions, in general delightful entertainment but unreliable in specifics. Indeed, not until very late in the century did the careful researches of Hiram Chittenden, most thorough and respected scholar of the American fur trade, at last furnish a definitive judgment on the matter of Irving's accuracy. Initially Chittenden had shared the prejudice prevailing by then: *Astoria* would be discovered to have taken casual liberties with its subject in the interest of romance. But the more the scholar considered Irving's book, the more his respect for it grew. Verifiable dates proved trustworthy; locations were identifiable by Irving's descriptions; journeys recounted in the text could be followed precisely along riverbeds and through mountain passes of the western landscape. The book, Chittenden concluded, preserves "the most real and graphic picture now in existence of a phase of life which has entirely passed away. . . . Not in allurements of style alone, but in the essential respects of accuracy and comprehensive treatment, Irving's work stands immeasurably above all others upon the subject." In a word, it was a classic, "unapproached and unapproachable" in its particular field, and incapable of ever being surpassed.

Modern scholars have confirmed Chittenden's judgment of 1902. For example, Bernard De Voto has set down his conclusion that *Astoria* should be regarded as an original source, in some contexts as the only source for the events it relates; its accuracy, according to De Voto, is "remarkable," its literary quality "superb." As for the occasional, quite minor discrepancies between what Irving includes and what journals subsequently discovered and published may omit (a particular Indian's stature, the intention of trappers to bring a noble horse back to Astor), might we readers not be justified if, instead of charging Irving with inventing whole cloth, we assume that he is making use of conversations at Astor's home with people who had taken part in the settlement of Astoria? Such conversations occurred. Directly from the actors in the drama, so the nephew assures us, the author obtained "many personal anecdotes for the enriching of his work."

Those anecdotes concerned events that had begun to unfold in 1808. In the spring of that year Astor, then in his mid-forties, had secured his charter for the American Fur Company, which in the coming years he would fashion into a world-famous monopoly. That autumn he had returned to Montreal as usual. But on this visit Astor had proceeded to recruit various traders to join him in a venture that promised almost limitless profits on the other side of the continent. He had to recruit Canadians, because few Americans at the time yet knew the fur trade intimately, and the best of those few were already employed by the established companies north of the Great Lakes. A group of knowledgeable Scotsmen with such fine names as McKenzie and McDougall and McKay did agree to join the American enterprise, and the following June they arrive at New York to arrange a partnership with Astor. Managing matters from his Greenwich Street office, the German would put up all the money and run all the financial risks for the first five years. His partners' risks would be physical, as they made their way westward by sea and land to establish their colony on the Columbia River. Of this new subsidiary of his recently formed fur company—this new Pacific Fur Company—Astor retained exactly half the shares, allowing the various partners (a few Americans were included as well) to divide a number of the remaining shares among themselves.

So matters were progressing altogether to his liking by the new year 1810, and during that year two expeditions would indeed set out to fulfill Astor's dream. A key to the success of what he was trying to accomplish lay in the ships he owned in whole or part. He had shares in several by now—the *Beaver*, the *Magdalen*, the *Severn*, the *Fox*, the *Sylph*—and thus was uniquely able to furnish supplies to a colony established at his sole expense thousands of miles from New York, on the Pacific coast somewhere north of the Spaniards in California and south of the Russians in Alaska. Once set up in that mild though rainy climate, such a colony could presumably sustain itself with ease through intervening months on the wealth of the region that Lewis and Clark had visited—salmon in the rivers and game in the woods—if the new settlers could look forward once a year to the arrival of a ship bearing tools and arms and produce from the States to ease the rigors of their primitive days. The ship delivering those desirables could then pick up the year's catch of furs and sail directly and economically for China.

Or another option was open to it—an even more profitable one—and Astor, of course, had considered that too. Swimming off the coast of the Pacific were the most valuable fur-bearing creatures in the Western Hemisphere—more valuable than beaver, more valuable than marten or mink or ermine. The smooth, jet-black fur of the sea otter made it, of all animals, the most coveted in world markets, including markets at Canton, where its existence in small quantities had been known and valued for centuries. In small quantities—but Captain Cook had abruptly discovered enormous herds of the creatures during his Pacific explorations in 1778. Indians along the coast of Vancouver Island, for instance, had that year traded the captain six exquisite sea otter pelts for twelve glass beads; and those six pelts, taken to China, had proved to the astonishment of the English to be worth over a hundred dollars apiece—a dozen cheap beads thus effortlessly transformed into $720, enough for a Westerner to live on very well for a year. About details of the good fortune they had chanced upon Cook's entire crew were sworn to secrecy, but so exciting a secret could not keep. Soon it had found its way into print on the East Coast of America, where merchants trading with China were not long in routinely including a stop along the wild Pacific coast in their itineraries.

Thus vessels were already occasionally entering coastal waters off Oregon during the first decade of the century. Astor, who knew what sea otters were worth, meant to take his share of profit from their sudden abundance. Moreover, he would trade with the Russians farther north, too—at New Archangel, near where Sitka is now—and, toward the end of removing competition, had his son-in-law Bentzon work out an arrangement with proper authorities in Washington and at St. Petersburg, whereby the ill-furnished outpost at New Archangel could count on the regular arrival of an American vessel each spring with needed supplies from the States—the same efficient vessel that would relieve the Astorians farther south. The merchandise (vinegar and duffel cloth and casks of lead and superfine flour and shoes and candles and what not) would be bartered for sealskins and sea otter pelts, to the satisfaction of the Russians, who had been prohibited from trading directly with China since 1785. Further, with all their wants now secured through Astor's vessels, those same Russians at their Alaskan outpost would agree henceforth to refrain from any dealings with Indians farther south, along the Columbia, or with Canadian traders or American vessels (if not Astor's) nearer at hand.

A monopoly was thus being negotiated by the dutiful Bentzon, whose wife, by the way, in that same promising year of 1810 was presenting her merchant father with a first grandchild, the boy named John Jacob Bentzon. All was propitious. Late that summer Astor was overseeing the loading of his newly acquired ship *Tonquin*, three hundred tons, as it lay tied up not far from the Greenwich Street countinghouse: doubtless muskets, grindstones, tobacco, springs, resin, molasses, felt hats, fowling pieces, axes, chisels, scissors, razors, awls, adzes included among the multitude of goods being stored in the hold. Meanwhile, Astor's new partners from Canada, those picturesque Scotsmen, had returned to New York once more, this time in one of their great canoes from Montreal, sweeping down the Hudson with their entourage as though on their way to yet another rendezvous at some post far back in the interior. The ship's crew of twenty-one seamen was hired, the captain put in charge, the partners aboard, the loading completed (coat buttons, blue bunting, pitchers and white bowls and chamber pots and rum and gin and a pewter inkstand); and on September 8, 1810, the *Tonquin* cast off moorings at last and set a course seaward that would eventually raise Cape Horn.

The vessel was to sail around the southern tip of South America and northward again to the Columbia River, where she would deliver those passengers who were aboard for the purpose of setting up the new colony at the river mouth. She was to supply the colonists with what was needed from the cargo (from the tablespoons and padlocks and seeds and jack planes and men's worsted hose and needles and nun's thread and camp kettles in her hold), then proceed along the coast to trade with Indians for fur. Eventually the furs were to find their way to China. From Canton, Chinese goods—valued silks and hyson teas and the rest —would afterward be brought back home to America, to this same New York Bay at the outer verge of which the departing *Tonquin* was even now diminishing.

The captain of the vessel was named Thorn. Young Washington Irving, that idling Lad of Kilkenny, had known him among the chophouses in those early days when New York was of manageable size: "we remember him well in early life," writes the author in *Astoria*, "as a companion in pleasant scenes and joyous hours. When on shore, among his friends, he was a frank, manly, soundhearted sailor." Not so on board ship, however. Before assuming command of the *Tonquin*, Jonathan Thorn had served as naval officer under Decatur off the coast of piratical Tripoli. He was on leave from the navy now, and no doubt his military experience had seemed an asset when Astor was seeking a captain for the vessel that was plotted to sail through seas over which the English were becoming increasingly troublesome (as they pursued policies that led, in fact, to war between the two countries within a couple of years). Astor's ship was mounting twelve guns just in case. But in addition, she carried, besides the crew and her rigid captain, those partners of Astor's from Montreal with their sprawling retinue of landsmen and freshwater sailors—eleven clerks and five artisans and thirteen Canadian backwoodsmen—all of whom were in anything but a disciplinable mood. The backwoodsmen, promptly and predictably seasick, would stagger to the gunwales and (in Irving's phrase) offer up their tributes to windward, to the disgust of the contemptuous Thorn, frowning from the quarterdeck. The clerks, young men of good families all, were for their part prepared to serve apprenticeships through ordeals awaiting them ashore, but now meant to enjoy a cruise over tropical seas. The partners —McKay and McDougall and the two Stuarts—were sufficiently apprised of their own importance as to be ready to take issue with any order from the captain that might prove inconvenient. So the motley bunch sailed forth with their different purposes to pursue.

Thorn, it turned out, was a disastrous choice as captain to lead them. Riding the high seas now, he was not long in ordering all lights extinguished at eight each evening. Darken ship at twenty hundred. But the partners would have none of that militant imposition upon their civilian ease; they and Astor owned the vessel, after all. The captain commanded her, however, and meant to throw in irons whoever on board disobeyed. At that, the irascible McDougall drew his pistol, and bloodshed this near the start of the venture was only narrowly averted. Tensions mounting, the *Tonquin* proceeded along its course southward, as the regular sailor at the helm viewed with ever increasing distaste the set of fellows riding aboard.

"His letters to Mr. Astor," writes Irving, "wherein he pours forth the bitterness of his soul, and his seamanlike impatience of, what he considers, the *'lubberly'* character and conduct of those around him, are before us, and are amusingly characteristic. The honest Captain is full of vexation on his own account, and solicitude on account of Mr. Astor, whose property he considers at the mercy of a most heterogeneous and wasteful crew." Alas, those same letters, that moment on the author's desk, were subsequently reduced to ashes by Astor's careless descendants; but in some of the best writing he ever did, Irving uses them to put us aboard the troubled ship on its outward passage, among those suffering backwoodsmen, for example, "lurking below in their berths in squalid state, or emerging now and then like spectres from the hatch ways, in capotes and blankets; with dirty night cap, grizly beard, lanthorn visage and unhappy eye, shivering about the deck . . ." The clerks, by contrast, were soon scribbling in their journals and chattering merrily together in holiday mood, "having got into fine latitudes, upon smooth seas, with a well stored ship under them and a fair wind in the shoulder of the sail." They meant to see the world, even to urging the fuming captain to detour eastward and touch the Cape Verde Islands, that they might say they had been to Africa. As for the partners, who ashore with Astor had bragged of their backwoods hardihood, McDougall and the others were now complaining loudly about shipboard fare, despite the fresh porks and tongues and pudding. "When thwarted in their cravings for delicacies," Irving quotes from a letter of Thorn's, "they would exclaim that it was d——d hard they could not live as they pleased upon their own property, being on board of their own ship, freighted with their own merchandize.—And these," adds the captain sourly, "are the fine fellows who made such boast that they could 'eat dogs.' "

No, he would never again take such effeminate types to sea "without having Fly Market on the fore castle, Covent Garden on the poop and a cool spring from Canada in the main top." The words are Thorn's, not Irving's, and make us regret the loss of his letters the more. They had crossed the Equator now, were sailing southward in the tropics, past a turtle sleeping on the waves, past porpoises and sea bladders. Flying fish glided through their rigging. And now they had reached the bleak Falkland Islands, deep in the South Atlantic four hundred miles east of the southern tip of present Argentina. There, with the ship anchored to take aboard water, the partners were stretching their legs on shore, chasing sea wolves and wild geese and forgetting their promise not to delay the departure. Once before it had happened; now it happened again. The wind hauled fair, and signals were made for the boat on shore to return to the ship. No response. A half hour passed, and still no boat put off. "The Captain reconnoitered the shore with his glass and, to his infinite vexation, saw the loiterers in the full enjoyment of their 'wild goose chase.' " In a fury, he made sail at once. "When those on shore saw the ship actually under way they embarked with all speed, but had a hard pull of eight miles before they got on board, and then experienced but a grim reception, notwithstanding that they came well laden with the spoils of the chase."

Eight miles of salt-water rowing, with sore palms, stiff backs, and vile tempers at the end of it. Two days later, the *Tonquin* put in for repairs elsewhere in these same remote, unpeopled islands. And when— it was December 11—the time came to hoist sail once more, once more two of the partners, McDougall and David Stuart, were out of earshot, away to the south of the island chasing penguins. Six others ashore with the boat must await their return. But the captain had had enough. "This was the third time his orders had been treated with contempt, and the ship wantonly detained, and it should be the last." Spreading all sail, he put to sea—and they might rot there among the bats and sea lions, the lot of them. "It was in vain that those on board made remonstrances and entreaties and represented the horrors of abandoning men upon a sterile and uninhabited island: the sturdy Captain was inflexible."

Eight men, then, were about to be marooned, as they now realized, hurling themselves into the boat and starting to row for their lives. Through three and a half hours the desperate clerks and partners pulled at the oars, "swashed occasionally by the surging waves of the open sea, while the ship inexorably kept on her course and seemed determined to leave them behind." On board, a nephew of Stuart's—the boat still far astern—finally seized a pistol and threatened to blow out the captain's brains if he didn't put about. But even that was not enough to deter him.

Writing to Astor later, Thorn insisted he had meant to carry out his resolve. "Had the wind," he wrote, "(unfortunately) not hauled ahead soon after leaving the harbour's mouth, I should positively have left them." But the wind did shift and come ahead, and the boat was able at last to row alongside the stalled ship, and the weary, drenched laggards clambered aboard.

Thereafter, doubling Cape Horn on Christmas Day and edging into the Pacific, the tiny craft confronting ever more distant seas held men crowded aboard whose tempers were continuously smoldering. The backwoodsmen would grumble together in their French patois; the partners spoke only in Gaelic now; the clerks recorded privacies in those everlasting journals of theirs; and the captain came to see conspiracies wherever he looked, hear them in every unintelligible speech that struck his ear. On they sailed, to Hawaii by mid-February, to a village of a couple of hundred thatched houses on poles facing the bay at Waikiki, in which the *Tonquin* briefly cast anchor. Some desertions in those benign latitudes; some harsh floggings ordered by the relentless Thorn; some strutting ashore by the partners in their Highland kilts to impress the natives. And then the ship, still laden with ill humor, began the last leg of the voyage, arriving after a stormy passage at the mist-beshrouded mouth of the Columbia River, March 22, 1811.

The landscape now before them loomed wild and threatening: the mouth of the river, four miles in width, blocked by a sandbar and fearsome breakers, dark forests to north and south, the snowclad mountains beyond them to eastward, and all that rumbling solitude. But despite the perils of boisterous weather, Thorn would enter the river at once, and toward that end ordered the whaleboat to sound the bar for the channel, while the ship stood off shore. The chief mate, a man named Fox, with an old seaman named Martin and three Canadians, reluctantly obeyed, setting forth about one in the afternoon, all hands on shipboard watching apprehensively as the little boat pulled away, "rising and sinking with the huge rolling waves, until it entered, a mere speck, among the foaming breakers and was soon lost to view." Afternoon gave way to evening, evening to morning, while the ship waited.

The boat never came back.

That second long day stretched into night, and on the morning of the third day—the wind having abated and the weather grown serene at last—the captain determined to follow his pinnace into the river mouth. Aboard this other boat would be an able mariner named Aiken, the sailmaker Coles, the armorer Weekes, and two Sandwich Islanders, recruited during the layover at Waikiki. The pinnace would lead, sounding for four fathoms, while the ship followed under easy sail. "In this way they proceeded until Aiken had ascertained the channel, when signal was given from the ship for him to return on board."

The rudderless pinnace was near at hand. Suddenly it was caught in the breakers, was hurled away from the vicinity of the ship, became unmanageable, its crew "crying out piteously for assistance" as the distance between the two crafts rapidly widened. From the *Tonquin*'s mizzen top the little boat could be seen still struggling, but broaching broadside to the waves now. The ship itself, drifting into shoal water, was meanwhile in danger of foundering, waves breaking over her, her hull repeatedly striking. Finally she did manage to find seven fathoms and cast anchor, as night came on.

Then darkness. "The wind whistled, the sea roared, the gloom was only broken by the ghastly glare of the foaming breakers, the minds of the seamen were full of dreary apprehensions, and some of them fancied they heard the cries of their lost comrades mingling with the uproar of the elements. . . ."

Dawn finally. Next day those on board got ashore at last. But of the ten men who had preceded them off the ship, only the armorer Weekes and one of the Sandwich Islanders, both severely battered, had managed to make it to land. Obeying orders of their obstinate captain, eight of the crew had perished, eight men out of a total complement of just over fifty.

An ominous commencement to the enterprise. In ensuing days the new colonists, grumbling over their needless losses, made contact with the Indians, chose a site on the southern shore, and felled trees to establish in a cleared thicket the storehouse and powder magazine and lodgings and stockade that were to be the fortress and trading post of Astoria. A garden was prepared and seeds planted, while the *Tonquin*, eager to proceed on her voyage now that partners and clerks and artisans were ashore, impatiently awaited the completion of the storehouse in order to unload her cargo—that rice and tar, those faggots of Crowley steel and darners and gunlocks and sole leather. Finally, in early June, with seeds in the earth and flag waving over the fortified clearing, the ship at last made sail and dropped down to Baker's Bay, where early on the morning of June 5, she stood out to sea once more, a fine breeze swelling her canvas.

She was to trade for peltries along the coast to the north, then return to Astoria in the autumn. Aboard, in addition to the captain and crew, were one of the partners, McKay, with Mr. Lewis as ship's clerk, and an Indian named Lamazee induced to come along to act as interpreter. Against the interpreter's advice the *Tonquin* was at Vancouver Island now, putting in to the harbor of Neweetie to trade with the natives. The captain had been cautioned that this tribe could behave treacherously, but he nevertheless proceeded to spread on deck "a tempting display of blankets, cloths, knives, beads and fish hooks, expecting a prompt and profitable sale." And from shore the local Indians put out in their canoes and came alongside and climbed aboard.

Among them was an old chief named Nookamis, experienced in

trading with earlier Yankee vessels in these parts. To Thorn's first offer of barter—a couple of blankets for a sea otter pelt—the wily old fellow answered with scorn, demanding more than double the amount that the captain proposed. "Thorn," says Irving, "was a plain, straight forward sailor, who never had two minds nor two prices in his dealings, was deficient in patience and pliancy and totally wanting in the chicanery of traffic." Indignant now, the captain thrust his hands in his pockets, turned, and began sullenly pacing up and down the deck, the cunning old chief following close beside him, "holding out a sea otter skin to him at every turn, and pestering him to trade." The native's scorn had given way to cajoling, but soon the chief "began to jeer and banter him upon the mean prices he offered." Abruptly the frustrated Thorn seized the otter skin, rubbed it in the chief's face, and ordered him off the vessel—him and all the Indians, all of them take their pelts, get off his ship. He scattered furs left and right beneath his feet, breaking up the market, then strode about the quarterdeck to cool his fury while the disgruntled natives were reclaiming their pelts, descending to their canoes, paddling to shore.

McKay, the partner along from Astoria, had been at the Indian village during the encounter. Now he returned to the ship and learned what had happened from the interpreter, who pleaded with him to convince the captain to weigh anchor and stand out to sea. But Thorn among his cannon dismissed all fears of mere savages, the more confidently as the day passed with no sign of hostile groupings on the island. Night fell, and only customary precautions were taken among the *Tonquin*'s watch.

The evening went undisturbed, and the depth of night. Early next morning, however, with McKay and the captain still asleep, a canoe bearing twenty Indians paddled alongside the ship. Carrying otter skins but no arms, the men in the canoe seemed friendly enough, signaling their wish to come aboard and resume trading. In "any River, Bay or Port among the Natives," Astor had two years earlier instructed one of his captains bound for the Northwest, "be carefull of them"; don't permit them "to come on board, nor even near the Ship, as I understand several Ships have been taken and with their Crews destroy'd by them." The captain of the *Tonquin* had been similarly warned before leaving New York; yet the officer on watch this morning, having received no orders to the contrary, was allowing the twenty Indians to mount the sides of the vessel, while another canoe was approaching, and another.

Unarmed or not, so many about to board alarmed the officer. He summoned McKay and the captain, who arrived on deck to find it already thronged with natives. Most were wearing mantles of skins, causing Lamazee, the interpreter, to suspect that those might have weapons hidden on their persons after all. His suspicions he passed on to McKay, who told Thorn. More canoes were alongside, and more were putting off from shore. Finally, tardily the captain did order the crew to weigh anchor. Deckhands were sent aloft to set sail.

But the Indians were ready now to trade on Thorn's terms of yesterday. Hurriedly a barter was commenced while the sails were loosening and the anchor rising. Knives seemed what interested the natives most—gorgeous sea otters in exchange for knives. One would trade and move off to make room for another. The anchor was up now. "The Captain, in a loud and peremptory tone, ordered the ship to be cleared."

Out there in one of earth's lonely places, the friend of Irving's youth had uttered his last command. Ashore among agreeable companions he had seemed "frank, manly, soundhearted." At sea, however, through this voyage he was harsh and stern and hated. Now the last cry of his dictatorial voice was answered almost simultaneously by signal yells from the Indians, all of them armed with those newly purchased knives or with hidden war clubs, as they leapt forward vengefully to assault the weaponless white men around them. Lewis, the ship's clerk, "was leaning with folded arms over a bale of blankets, engaged in bargaining, when he received a deadly stab in the back and fell down the companionway." On the taffrail, McKay was bludgeoned with a war club and flung backward into the sea, to be dispatched by women in the canoes. Thorn was cut down near the tiller, unable to fight his way to the cabin and firearms. The crew on deck strove to protect themselves with handspikes and whatever makeshift weapons happened to be in reach, but the numberless Indians overpowered them and slaughtered them every one.

As for the seven seamen aloft in the shrouds, they had watched the start of the massacre in horror and helplessness. They were to be butchered, too, of course; so while the struggle was raging below them, those seven slid down the running rigging to get between decks. One fell from the rigging and was killed. Another was murdered in the descent, a third as he stepped through a hatchway. But four seamen did make it to the cabin, where they barricaded themselves inside with the mortally wounded Lewis. Armed with muskets now, they fired through holes and were soon able to clear the ship of Indians—even to emerge and train the cannon on departing canoes with telling effect.

But it was almost over, there among sprawled corpses of shipmates on a blood-washed deck—gone to naught all the high plans that had accompanied the long, contentious voyage from the wharves of Manhattan. Lewis was doomed in any case. Later that evening the four surviving seamen sneaked away from the *Tonquin* by small boat and left her there in the darkness.

The following morning the ship still lay off shore, apparently deserted. Cautiously a canoe pushed off from the beach, and another. The Indians were circling the vessel at a distance, when a figure was seen at the gunwales signaling them to come aboard. The interpreter Lamazee, whose life had been spared and who was accompanying the returning Indians, recognized the man, before he disappeared from sight, as Lewis, the clerk.

The empty ship tossed at anchor. The sails flapped free. Time passed, as the Indians circled and pondered. Finally the bolder among them came alongside and climbed to the deck. Nothing seemed to oppose their plunder. Others soon followed. More and more of them clambered aboard, their footsteps pattering on the decks beneath which, in the hold among kegs of powder, a dying white man bided his time, with fire in his hand.

One June day in 1811. Aaron Burr, in the third year of his impoverished exile after the Richmond treason trial, was wandering over Holland, about to return to Paris and longing only to be home once more with Theodosia and her child. In Edinburgh, the poet Walter Scott, encouraged by the success of *The Lady of the Lake*, was that month making his first purchase along Tweedside of land that he would convert into the grounds of Abbotsford. Mary Shelley was still Mary Godwin, virginal child of thirteen, living with her stepmother and philosopher father in London, among the books at Skinner Street. Shelley himself, recently expelled from Oxford and as yet unaware of Mary's existence, was at nineteen on the point of eloping with Harriet Westbrook. Emily Foster was a seven-year-old in Bedfordshire—all of Dresden, all of a long life before her. Matilda Hoffman was dead two years. Her lover Washington Irving had by that month set up bachelors' quarters with Henry Brevoort at Mrs. Ryckman's, on Broadway near the Bowling Green, aimless of purpose, alternately morose and flippant with his unspoken grief and the earlier success of *Knickerbocker*. A June day in 1811. And off an island along the northwest coast of America an explosion that would have looked from on high like a puff of gray smoke, drifting and soon dispersing. Briefly the waters had been roiled with the mutilations of arms and torsos and legs, with what was left of that cargo (the bullet molds and striped shirting and "bandanoes" and tin pails, stored so carefully in the hold, so conscientiously guarded by the vigilant Thorn) tossed high and then sinking, sinking, and flotsam on the water briefly, until wind and current washed away the last traces of the *Tonquin*, and the sea was as it had been before.

Weeks passed before the hopeful colonists at Astoria heard even rumors of the calamity off Vancouver Island. The four white survivors who had fled the doomed ship in darkness had soon been driven ashore in those fierce currents and captured. Before the natives tortured them and put them to death, the interpreter Lamazee was allowed to question them; he in turn managed to make his escape later and find his way back to his own tribe at the mouth of the Columbia. From him, then, came details of the *Tonquin*'s fate, but those details would not reach the settlers at Astoria for weeks, and a full year would pass before the news finally arrived at Astor's countinghouse on the other side of the continent.

The merchant was too shrewd to underestimate the effects on his schemes of a loss so appalling. Yet the evening of the summer day in 1812 that he learned of the disaster, he appeared "with his usual serenity of countenance" at the theater. "What would you have me do?" Irving quotes Astor as answering a friend who, knowing of the calamity, expressed surprise that he could attend frivolous entertainment at such a time. Vat vould you hef me do? "Would you have me stay at home and weep for what I cannot help?"

He had done all he could—which was a great deal—and, to be sure, the colony might still have a chance of success. During each of the last three autumns Astor had undertaken the formidable expense of fitting out a ship and hiring a crew and sending her over the long course southward, to round Cape Horn at Christmas, in the height of the southern summer, and make her way across the Pacific to the Northwest coast. In 1809 he had sent out the *Enterprise*, in 1810 the doomed *Tonquin*, in 1811 the *Beaver*—as he said he would—and the third costly vessel set sail when the fate (lucrative or otherwise) of the first two ships was still unknown. A faint heart would not do; faith was needed to reap those distant rewards, and faith of a sort the visionary merchant had in abundance.

For a moment we might follow the chronology, made confusing because each China voyage took longer than a year—sometimes two years and more—to complete. Nevertheless: the *Enterprise* departed New York in the fall of 1809. In the spring of 1810 she was on the Pacific coast, preparing the compliant natives of the Columbia for the impending arrival of white colonists eager to trade. From the Columbia she sailed north to New Archangel and concluded trading arrangements with the Russians. Then to China that summer. That same fall, of 1810, the *Tonquin* sailed from New York, reaching the Pacific coast (as we have seen) in the following spring, to be destroyed that second summer, of 1811. During the fall—with the *Enterprise* unaware of the *Tonquin*'s fate and still trading between Canton and New Archangel—the *Beaver* set sail from New York. She did reach the Astorians on schedule in the spring of 1812. In June 1812, the *Enterprise* returned to New York, after a voyage of two and a half years, with a valuable cargo of Chinese merchandise. She had not yet revisited the Columbia in the interval, but did presumably bring home with her the confirmation of the *Tonquin*'s fate that Astor took with him to the theater that summer evening.

But the *Beaver* would have arrived with supplies at Astoria by that time, and the overland expedition would have long since reached the fort at the mouth of the Columbia. All might yet be well.

In Astor's own words: a short while earlier, in March of this present year 1812, he had caused a letter to be written to Thomas Jefferson, bringing that western enthusiast up to date. "In June 1810"—the summer in which the *Tonquin* had been loading at New York—"I sent a party of men," so he explained to the former President, "say about seventy in number to ascend the Missouri, with a view to make Columbia River and meet the people who had gone by water, as well as to ascertain the points at which it might be most proper to establish posts for trade, &c." (The correctness of the style betrays the intervening hand of an amanuensis.) He wrote also about the sailing of the *Tonquin* in September 1810, "with sixty men and all the means which were thought necessary to establish a post at or near the mouth of that river," and about the sailing of the *Beaver* in October 1811, "with above sixty men and all necessaries, to fix a post and to remain at or near Columbia River, and to cooperate with those who had gone before." While the letter to Jefferson was being drafted, Astor still did not know the fate of the *Tonquin*, gone from New York a year and a half. "The last account which I had of the party which ascended the Missouri was by letter of 17 July last, about 180 miles below the Mandan Village, where they left the Missouri, and took the Big River in a southern course, this being recommended as nearer and easier to the south branch of the Columbia than the route taken by M^r. Lewis: they were well provided, and had procured near a hundred horses to transport their baggage.—The accounts as to ultimate success were fair and encouraging, and they had no doubt of meeting their friends who went by sea; which I think they must have done in October last."

That is, in October 1811, before winter set in. Thus, if by some time warp into the twentieth century, Astor in his countinghouse had been able to learn within hours of the destruction of the *Tonquin* in the summer of 1811, he might have found comfort in this thought, that the forsaken survivors of the seagoing expedition, ashore within their palisades at Astoria, would be joined in three or four months by the overland party. Yet any such comfort would have been delusive. Actually, that latter group was nowhere near Astoria in the October when the merchant presumed it would be arriving. In October 1811, the weary overland adventurers—first flurries of snow falling about them—were on foot and still a thousand miles to the east of the Pacific, destined to spend the worst of winter struggling for survival in the mountains.

Their story, too, is of interest. The overland expedition was commanded by one of the partners of the enterprise, a gentleman from New Jersey named Hunt; and as Jonathan Thorn had been the wrong choice to command the *Tonquin*, Wilson Price Hunt, for different reasons, was not the man to lead a party across the unmapped wastelands of America. His experience as an outfitter of traders out of St. Louis had not supplied him with that firsthand knowledge of woodcraft and Indian lore acquired by any number of wilderness traders, some of whom were along in the party but resentful of this shopkeeper's elevation over them—and thus inclined to withhold the help they might have provided to make the going easier. They might, for instance, have told him right at the start about how to deal with Canadian backwoodsmen.

Hunt had arrived at Montreal in July 1810 to recruit the back-woodsmen and boatmen he would need—French Canadians having developed (far beyond their American rivals) not only the necessary skills but the insouciance to ply them under trying conditions. But delays beset him each step of the way. Canadian fur companies kept the best men from joining. The few who did agree to join would insist on being paid a part of their wages in advance, promptly squander the sum on drink and whoring in those obliging environs, then disappear. Days mounted up as the recruitment lagged. Finally some knowing soul along the way advised the innocent Hunt to furnish recruits not with cash but rather with feathers and ostrich plumes as inducements, thereby making an appeal to their boundless vanity. The good-natured Canadians succumbed to those lures; at last Hunt and his party of boatmen were able to get under way in their forty-foot birch-bark canoe, following the familiar passage up the Ottawa River, by portage to Lake Nipissing, then on to Georgian Bay.

But even embarked, "their progress was slow and tedious. Mr. Hunt," as Irving explains in *Astoria*, "was not accustomed to the management of 'voyageurs' and he had a crew admirably disposed to play the old soldier, and balk their work, and ever ready to come to a halt; land, make a fire, put on the great pot and smoke, and gossip and sing by the hour." So they advanced intermittently, across the wide waters of Lake Huron, down Lake Michigan to Green Bay, up the Fox River, and after a final portage down the Wisconsin to the Mississippi. Around the first of September they reached St. Louis.

But that was late. With its mountain sources in high latitudes, the Missouri, which they meant to ascend, freezes early. By November, in any event, they must be wintering, and here in this frontier village on the Mississippi much still needed attention before they could set out, as Hunt gathered together supplies and sought to persuade hunters to join his party. (Canadian boatmen were the best to be had—and American hunters.) A more efficient leader might have expeditiously brought the group between July at Montreal and early November to a wintering, say, as far along as the Three Forks of the Missouri in present-day Montana, awaiting spring and an agreeable passage over the Rockies to the Columbia. But Hunt's party, which had misspent its time, now found itself establishing a winter encampment November 16 (two days before ice formed), no farther than four hundred miles or so up the Missouri, at the mouth of the Nodaway River, still within the boundaries of modern Missouri state. Only thus far, near the end of 1810, had they proceeded, while the *Tonquin* was sailing southward from New York to Cape Horn. And just after the New Year (the *Tonquin* in the Pacific by then) Hunt left his men dug in beside the shelter of their bluff along the frozen Missouri and returned on foot and horseback to St. Louis, to recruit an interpreter and any more hunters who might be willing to lend a hand in helping the expedition pass well-fed and unmolested that spring through Sioux and Blackfoot country.

So with the coming of the thaw in 1811 (and the *Tonquin*'s arrival at the Columbia), Hunt was still at St. Louis, about to set out a second time to ascend the Missouri to rejoin his party at the Nodaway wintering site. On this second ascent, in April, he had aboard the naturalist Bradbury, whose entertaining account of the upriver voyage allows us to experience day by day events now a hundred and seventy years in the past: the encounter with Daniel Boone along the riverbank, the rain that fell to augment spring floods, the pleasing progress by sail when the wind was southeasterly, but far more often a tedious, toilsome advance by poling against the current, by grappling overhanging limbs with hooks, by dragging the boat forward laboriously with towlines, men tugging in frigid shallows or along the shore. The boat zigzagged its slow way upward past snags and sandbars. Alongside, bulky drowned buffaloes were drifting downstream, their carcasses at one stretch attracting "an immense number of turkey buzzards," beautiful in flight but up close revolting with their stench; "as the preceding night had been rainy, multitudes of them were sitting on the trees, with their backs toward the sun, and their wings spread out to dry . . ."

In surrounding woods were passenger pigeons in such numbers that the gentle Bradbury was able within a few hours ashore to shoot two hundred and seventy-one of them with his fowling piece—birds in such numbers and of such beauty that Irving (who saw them himself on other occasions) is moved to describe what such wanton slaughter has by now erased forever: "They appear," he writes in *Astoria*, calling on his own recollections, "absolutely in clouds, and move with astonishing velocity, their wings making a whistling sound as they fly. The rapid evolutions of these flocks, wheeling and shifting suddenly as if with one mind and one impulse; the flashing changes of colour they present, as their backs, their breasts, or the under part of their wings are turned to the spectator, are singularly pleasing. When they alight, if on the ground, they cover whole acres at a time; if upon trees, the branches often break beneath their weight. If suddenly startled while feeding in the midst of a forest, the noise they make in getting on the wing is like the roar of a cataract or the sound of distant thunder." All are gone now—the last passenger pigeon died in 1914 in the Cincinnati Zoo—and never again will such a sight astound the eye, such sounds delight the ear. "We might have obtained a great many more," writes Bradbury elsewhere after helping kill three buffaloes from the deck, "but for once we did not kill *because* it was in our power to do so." And on still another occasion, "Mr. Crooks joined me"—who had killed his two hundred and seventy-one pigeons—"in remonstrating against this waste; but it is impossible to restrain the hunters, as they scarcely ever lose an opportunity of killing, if it offers, even although not in want of food."

But why not, with sport apparently limitless among all that fecundity? Clumps of roses and currant bushes bloomed along the banks, "mixed with grape vines, all in flower, and extremely fragrant." Quantities of water snakes were sunning themselves on lily pads, and ashore under flat stones on a bluff lay snakes in a torpid state: "The number of snakes . . . was astonishing." And elks and antelopes and bears and deer and wolves and wild turkeys and geese and prairie hens and prairie dogs, and plains "literally covered with buffaloes as far as we could see . . ." bellowing in springtime. And lowly mosquitoes "in numbers inconceivably great. In walking it was necessary to have one hand constantly employed to keep them out of the eyes; and although a person killed hundreds, thousands were ready to take their place."

Why not lay waste, and enjoy? Squaws hung around forts where the boat would stop, "for the same purpose as females of a certain class in the maritime towns of Europe crowd round vessels lately arrived from a long voyage, and it must be admitted with the same success." The Canadians, Bradbury reports, "were very good customers, and Mr. Hunt was kept in full employ during the evening, in delivering out to them blue beads and vermillion, the articles in use for this kind of traffic." In dusky lodges the white travelers would squat on buffalo robes smoking the calumet before somber Indians under scalps and raccoon tails that hung from the rafters.

They reached the wintering encampment in good time, and by late April, when the rains finally subsided, the reassembled party broke camp under the familiar bluff by the Nodaway's mouth and pushed off in four boats—some sixty adventurers—bound up the long Missouri. Simultaneously, at a spot on the western coast of America, others in Astor's employ had begun clearing thickets and felling trees to build the fort at Astoria, the *Tonquin* impatiently at anchor nearby in that far-off bay. The overland party passed the mouth of the Platte, reached the Omaha village, by mid-May had left that Indian town and were making their way northward along what are now the eastern borders of Nebraska and South Dakota. Signs of war parties were on the banks. Smoke from prairie fires stained the skies. And in late May three white hunters, heading south, appeared in two canoes around a bend in the river above them. These Kentuckians had passed through lands toward which the outbound settlers were heading; and following their veteran advice, Hunt now made a change in plans. He would not after all pursue the more northerly route of Lewis and Clark, along the river into Blackfoot country, through present North Dakota and Montana. Rather, he would strike out overland on horseback to the south of that hostile region, across terrain that these three hunters knew, where game was plentiful. Horses could be bartered for at the Arikara village upriver; and there at ten in the morning of June 12, 1811, the four boats were putting to shore while curious old squaws and giggling children and barking curs clustered about them. The conical huts these Indians lived in were "like so many small hillocks," covered with earth in this treeless landscape. The smells of the place were villainous, but the Arikaras were friendly, and their horses a welcome sight, grazing in numbers over the surrounding plains.

Here, in these early days at the village, or just before, came the one indifferent morning when, westward across two thousand miles, the white man Lewis among the stench of bilge water in a ship's dark hold touched fire to powder and blew to bits the *Tonquin* and all those Indians swarming over it. And from this Arikara village Hunt wrote to New York with predictions of ultimate success; "the last account which I had of the party which ascended the Missouri," Astor next spring would inform Thomas Jefferson, "was by letter of 17 July last." On the following morning, the eighteenth, the expedition, now possessed of eighty-two horses laden with traps and corn and ammunition, had left the river, the boats, the friendly Arikaras and filed westward into the Dakota wastelands, into that region that a later generation would come to know as the Great American Desert.

"It is a land," wrote Irving in 1835, "where no man permanently abides; for, in certain seasons of the year there is no food either for the hunter or his steed. The herbage is parched and withered; the brooks and streams are dried up; the buffalo, the elk and the deer have wandered to distant parts, keeping within the verge of expiring verdure . . ." So bleak seemed that immense wilderness that a quarter of a century after Hunt and his men were entering there, Irving could still express the view "that a great part of it will form a lawless interval between the abodes of civilized man, like the wastes of the ocean or the deserts of Arabia." Hence the long-entertained presumption of one nation east of the Mississippi, a sister nation west of the Rockies—with this no-man's land between.

The valley of the Missouri lay behind them now. They pushed at first through "prairies where grass was knee-deep and the horses could graze to their satisfaction. The country was bare. Only a few cottonwoods grew along the rivers." In early August, "we crossed many ridges . . . composed of a red earth having the consistency of brick"—the terse notes are Hunt's own. "This rough country has scanty grass." They were discoverers now, seeing what no other white man had yet recorded. Mountains spread before them, and water was scarce. A dog with them died of thirst. "The road was irksome because of steepness and the great number of stones." Bighorns and black-tailed deer were sighted among the peaks. "The evening was very cold. At the north were mountains covered with pines. They were crossed on the 15th. The country was extremely rugged; it became more so on the 17th, and a way out of these mountains could not be found." On the nineteenth they unwittingly set up camp near tracks of the black bear, "so that, with the slightest breeze moving in the bushes, one felt in spite of oneself a shiver of dread."

Fifteen, sometimes twenty miles a day: past the bald country of the Cheyennes, the Crows, the Snakes, guiding for a hundred miles and more in that crystalline atmosphere on "three immensely high and snow-covered peaks" far ahead of them, the Tetons. Lingering by a river near buffalo herds through precious days to dry and pack meat before ascending from watered plains to where buffalo would not follow. Days slipping by, as the party searched for defiles through the mountains, sometimes retracing their steps: "the country for some distance down appears to be very favorable for hunting beaver. Geese and ducks are very common." They were half way through September. "On the 16th, snow was frequently encountered." The northern faces of mountains were already deep in snow. "We had snow on all the heights to each side of us and in front of us." Mountain rivers flowed with fierce currents, hard to ford. "One of our horses fell with his pack into the river from a height of nearly two hundred feet, but was uninjured. . . ."

They had made their way across what is now northwestern South Dakota, across the southeastern corner of modern Montana, across the width of present Wyoming—but how the mere names of the states tame what was then strange and wild! By late September they were close upon those Pilot Knobs, the three great Teton peaks toward which their course had been so long directed. All seemed well. They stood beside a tributary of the great Columbia itself, current flowing westward under the delighted gaze of the travelers.

But here Hunt made the most grievous of his several wrong decisions. He determined to forsake the horses and take to the water again. All were in favor of it—the Canadian boatmen, the weary pedestrians, the saddle-sore partners. But western rivers, rising in altitudes comparable to those flowing east, have much shorter runs to the sea; their drop is thus more precipitous, their currents far stronger. Now while the group set about building canoes, one of their number was sent to explore farther downstream. "The 1st of October, it rained in the valley and snowed in the mountains." A couple of forlorn Snake Indians came among them and warned that the fast-flowing river was unnavigable. Reed returned from his downstream reconnoitering and confirmed that the current was too rapid for canoes. "All day long on the 3rd, rain and sleet fell." And crucial time slipped by as the party removed in search of a more serviceable waterway farther north. At last, on October 19, "the cargoes being placed in our canoes, we embarked in them"—down what is now the Snake River in eastern Idaho: "The force of the current made us travel rapidly."

For a couple of blissful days "the river grew lovelier and wider; a space of 1200 to 1800 feet separated the two banks. On the 20th, we travelled 40 miles," still with light hearts through half that distance, "but, during the last twenty of them, the bed of the river was intersected by rapids."

From there on, progress became an unintermitted trial—rapids ever more tumultuous, falls of thirty feet and more, portages, towings of the canoes from among brambles and prickly pears ashore. The width of the river soon narrowed to sixty feet—all that pouring water confined between canyon walls. "One of the small canoes filled and capsized, some goods were lost." The current poured forward, raging, relentless: "we let down the canoes by a tow-line. Several filled with water in crossing a series of rapids. We lost some more goods. The river was winding, the country uneven and rocky. The mountains crowded to the water's edge on the left or south bank. . . ."

And at a spot probably near present Burley, Idaho, they arrived at their day of disaster, the twenty-eighth of October, 1811, that month and year when Astor assumed they would have reached Astoria for sure. Swirling in rapids still a thousand miles from the mouth of the Columbia, a canoe bearing five men was hurled against a rock, split, and overturned. "Mr. Crooks and one of his companions were thrown amidst roaring breakers and a whirling current, but succeeded, by strong swimming, to reach the shore. Clappine"—a Canadian veteran, the cheerful steersman—"and two others clung to the shattered bark and drifted with it to a rock. The wreck struck the rock with one end and swinging round flung poor Clappine off into the raging stream, which swept him away" —drenched body tumbling from sight—"and he perished."

After that last glimpse, the mangled form was not seen again. As for the others, they did survive their encounter with death, but the party could go no farther by water. Falls forty feet high awaited them, canyon walls rising three hundred feet straight up. Much farther than they suspected from the Pacific, they were lost in wilderness, with supplies drastically reduced by the destruction of canoes in recent days. Less than a week separated them from famine. They had no horses, no guides, no paths to follow. Winter was coming on.

It seemed best to detach three parties, in hopes that one might get through or find Indians. Hunt stayed with the main body. Nine days were wasted by the river, trying to fish, to trap food. Finally the group —some forty of them—buried what goods they couldn't carry, divided the corn, the grease, the bits of dried meat, then proceeded on foot to follow the river, soon far below them. "For supper we had only some fruits of the rose bushes, and then we lay down near the fire . . . very tired and very hungry." Rain fell almost continuously. "On the 9th"—in

November now—"I set out on the north of the river with nineteen men . . . Mr. Crooks, with nineteen others, marched on the south. It rained in the afternoon." Thereafter the worst of their ordeal began. Dead salmon stank from the river. The group ill-advisedly abandoned the Snake and struck out northward across a prairie, "where we found no water. Everything seemed to indicate that we would be no more fortunate on the following day. What vexation for men whose food consisted principally of dried fish!" Their thirst became acute in days that ensued. Several Canadians had begun to drink urine before rain fell at last. But the fish gave out. They lived on haws and chokeberries. The snow was to mid-leg. All of one day they toiled forward and made four miles. Some were frostbitten. Some ate the soles of old moccasins. On the fifth of December "the abundant snow which was falling did not allow us to see three hundred feet ahead of us." On the sixth, to their surprise, they encountered Crooks and his wandering party, dreadfully wasted by their deprivations. On the seventh, "we were reduced to marching slowly, because Mr. Crooks was so feeble that he had great difficulty in keeping up with us. Most of my men had gone on ahead." On the eighth, those still with Hunt began grumbling over the delay, "saying we all would die of hunger; and importuned me in every way to go on. To add to my troubles, Mr. Crooks was quite ill in the night . . . I left three men with him; and departed on the 9th with two others to rejoin my party. I had three beaver skins, two of which I left with them. We supped off the third. The weather was extremely cold." By the tenth, some of the men had not eaten for four days. They chanced upon a few scraggy Indian horses, killed one, ate that, and hoarded the others gratefully. Ice was running in the rivers now. The days were stormy, snow piling up. "On the 16th, we emerged from the mountains, and camped on the banks of the river that we had crossed on the 26th of last month. Thus, for twenty days, we had uselessly tired ourselves in seeking a route along the lower part of the river." They ate dried cherries and roots. A bedraggled band of Indians they encountered told them that to get to the western side of the mountains would take maybe twenty more nights; "we would have snow up to our waists."

But Hunt pressed on, he and about thirty-five others, with "only five wretched horses for our food during the passage of the mountains." New Year's Day they rested. "My men urged me that . . . we should not travel on January 1st, 1812. I willingly consented because most of them were very fatigued from having, each day, only a scanty meal of horseflesh and from carrying their packs on their shoulders . . ." On the sixth the pitiful, emaciated band saw the sun for the first time since entering the mountains. But not until the eighth of January was the worst of their trial at last behind them, as they came joyfully in sight of an Indian camp to the west on plains below. There succor was found, and guidance to the Columbia.

By then one man had gone insane from hunger and killed himself by drowning. One had lost his way and was never found. Three had given up and chosen to stay with a wandering Indian tribe. A sixth had been too weak to continue, and was left with other Indians. But Hunt himself and most of his party did finally straggle into Astoria, February 15, 1812. McKenzie and McLellan, detached from the group at the Snake, had arrived there nearly a month before. Much later Crooks and John Day were discovered still miraculously alive upriver, though robbed by Indians and stripped, half dead from exposure. They reached Astoria May 11, the day after the *Beaver*, filled with supplies from New York, dropped anchor in the bay.

The *Beaver*—beautiful sight—had arrived at last. All might yet be well. With the American Hunt now commanding the post and a full ship anchored offshore, the struggling enterprise might still be somehow salvaged. Perhaps what had so long been an ill-fated venture could flourish at last, and the tiny settlement be allowed to grow into Astor's dream: a "great emporium of the American fur trade in the Pacific and the nucleus of a powerful American state."

Yet never was a feasible undertaking more dogged by misfortune. The *Beaver* reached Astoria in mid-May, 1812. In mid-June, on the other side of the continent, President Madison declared war against England. Six months and more would pass before the news of the hostilities reached the mouth of the Columbia; and even so, these possessions might have been defended against Indians and English alike, if leaders of the colony had been judicious and loyal. But during that same summer Hunt was innocently making another of his several injudicious decisions, this time determining to journey northward in August when the *Beaver* sailed on her mission to replenish the Russian outpost at New Archangel. Unaware of the outbreak of war, the American, restored to health, meant to familiarize himself with the coastal trade, then return to Astoria in the fall. The fort would meanwhile be left in charge of Duncan McDougall, penguin chaser of earlier times who had quarreled so often with Thorn on the *Tonquin*'s long voyage out. McDougall, we remember, was a Canadian, a Scotsman, a British citizen—and ultimately disloyal to Astor's interests.

So Hunt was gone aboard the *Beaver*, nor did he reappear at Astoria when he said he would. Delays beset his visit to New Archangel. To take peltries that would pay for supplies delivered, the *Beaver* had to sail to an even more distant Russian outpost. A storm battered the ship in those northern waters, so that her cautious captain with his valuable cargo of furs feared to attempt the grueling entrance at the mouth of the Columbia. It was late autumn now. Better to sail, he thought, straight to the Sandwich Islands—to Hawaii—repair the ship, leave Hunt there to catch the annual supply vessel that Astor would have dispatched from New York, and head the *Beaver* on toward Canton to continue her trading mission.

The new year opened: 1813. Still no news of war had reached the Northwest coast, where the Astorians could only surmise gloomily what might have delayed Hunt's return. Had the *Beaver* suffered the fate of the *Tonquin*? Hunt meanwhile was three thousand miles away in tropic climes, waiting in vain for the arrival of a supply ship from the East Coast that should have reached Hawaii (as had the *Tonquin* two years before) in February.

As for the *Beaver*, she had long since sailed for China, dropping anchor at Whampoa early in that year. There Sowle, her captain, did at last learn of war between England and America. Astor's orders, received at Canton, instructed the ship to proceed directly to Astoria in order to support the endangered colony. Yet the timid skipper elected to wait out the war where he was, snugly anchored, so as not to risk a valuable cargo of merchandise on the high seas.

What could one man do from the other side of the world? All that he could, Astor did. He had warned the stubborn Thorn about letting Indians in numbers aboard his ship. He had ordered Sowle to return to the Columbia River. He had placed Hunt in command of Astoria with the expectation that an American loyal to his interests would be directing the colony. And even with a war in progress and no profits to count yet, Astor persisted in outfitting another annual ship—after the costly *Enterprise*, the *Tonquin*, the *Beaver*. Like the others, this present vessel, the *Lark*, intended to get under way in the fall, though dislocations of war would delay her leaving New York through several months, until early March 1813, the very time that Hunt was anxiously watching for her sails to appear in the bay at Waikiki. The *Lark* did finally reach the Sandwich Islands, but the vessel that arrived in August was a mockery of the ship that had sailed from Manhattan the previous March. Nearing the islands, the luckless craft had been savagely raked by a typhoon; four men had drowned in the storm, and the rest of the crew almost starved before the hulk drifted at last to shore: "a varey little of the Cargo nor aney part of the Ship was Saved," her captain would write Astor later; "that which was, was Taken by the king"—of that Polynesian realm— "and plundred by the natives, we was here treated with greate inhumanity, Stripte to ashirte & trowes unable to make aney resistance against so maney natives, with a crew almost helpless worn down with Starvation & thirste . . ."

What more could Astor do? Four sumptuous ships had already set sail, and meanwhile he had been appealing urgently to his government to detach a "Smal Garison" of troops westward over Hunt's route to defend the fort—or a sloop of war by sea: "Good god what an objit is to be securd by Smale means—" For by now reports had reached him at his countinghouse that the country through which the Columbia flowed "abound with fish & game and the quantity of valuable furrs fare exceeding our most Sangguine exspectations." Yet the distracted government failed to act to protect the territory. Whereupon Astor outfitted yet another ship, his fifth. This one, however, that was scheduled to sail in the fall of 1813 was halted by the British blockade off Manhattan and sent back to port to be unloaded.

What more could he do? In truth it was too late to save Astoria anyway. As far back as the beginning of 1813, with Hunt languishing in the Sandwich Islands and the *Beaver* driving for Canton, Duncan McDougall had finally learned at the fort that war between England and America was in progress. "Having maturely weighed our situation," one of his associates later wrote, "after having seriously considered that being almost to a man British subjects, we were trading, notwithstanding, under the American flag: and foreseeing the improbability or rather, to cut the matter short, the impossibility that Mr. Astor could send us further supplies or reinforcements while the war lasted, as most of the ports of the United States would inevitably be blockaded by the British; we concluded to abandon the establishment in the ensuing spring, or at latest, in the beginning of the summer."

In fact, the wily McDougall and his Scottish cohorts yielded the post without an effort to defend it. In July 1813 a manifesto was signed by the four partners present (three of whom were British subjects), whereby furs on hand were to be sold to English traders for what amounted to a third of their value, after which McDougall and most of the other agents and clerks would obligingly join the North West Company, Astor's Canadian rivals along the Pacific. From his outlandish wanderings Hunt finally returned in August, too late to save what had already been forfeited. Astoria became Fort George before the year was out, and over its stockade fluttered the Union Jack.

"We have been sold," the furious Astor wrote one partner when he learned what had happened. But did it have to end that way? Ill-equipped English traders were never really a threat, farther from their sources of supplies across Canada than were the Americans. And the British frigate that was said to be on its way north from Rio might have arrived at the mouth of the river in vain, for agents loyal to Astor could easily have retreated with their furs to outposts upstream, beyond pursuit. Let the warship batter down an empty stockade. After that futile bombardment and the ship's departure, the Astorians could have paddled back down to Point George and leisurely rebuilt their post under the Stars and Stripes.

Simply put, Astor's partners had betrayed "my once Darling objict the Settlement at Columbia," Hunt by ineptitude, McDougall by disloyalty. The merchant, to be sure, had chosen both men as his agents, and had signed on the bullheaded Thorn. But that much conceded, he could hardly have done more to prevent the final catastrophe. Nevertheless, through the remainder of the war the fort that he had striven to establish was held by the British; and on November 12, 1814—so much for a dream—appeared in New York newspapers the announcement, signed by Astor and two partners, that "the firm of the Pacific Fur Company is dissolved."

The war ended the following year. Shortly thereafter, the American flag again flew over the distant outpost beyond the Rocky Mountains; for in 1818, an agreement between England and the United States restored the settlement, technically at least, to its earlier claimants. Not to Astor, but to his adopted country. By then the merchant had forsaken his Far Western ambitions forever; and indeed, the trading post itself, though under the American flag for a while, remained in the hands of the North West Company of Canada. Theirs were the traders who had remained on the spot, to take full advantage of treaty stipulations that "all territories and their waters, claimed by either power, west of the Rocky Mountains, should be free and open to the vessels, citizens, and subjects, of both for the space of ten years." The few white people at the mouth of the Columbia now were English.

When that first decade of joint claim ended in 1828, the compromise was extended another ten years, so that as Washington Irving in 1835 was writing his account of Astor's great enterprise (his glorious failure, the only mercantile failure of his life, and yet the spacious project that he chose to have memorialized through Irving's prose), dominion over the Pacific Coast remained unsettled: "the second period of ten years is fast elapsing," *Astoria* takes note in conclusion. "In 1838, the question of title will again come up . . ."

And again the arrangement of joint ownership would be extended. Long before then, of course, it had become clear that despite his best efforts, despite all the money poured into the venture, Astor had lost. In another sense, however, he had won—if not for himself, for his country. Very likely had a colony not been hacked into existence at Astoria, the northwestern limits of the contiguous United States would now follow the northern boundary of California and Nevada, just as surely as would our western boundaries now extend northward along the entire Pacific Coast to merge with Alaska if Astor's dream had been realized. That we possess the states of Washington, Oregon, and Idaho, on the far side of the Great American Desert, is owing to Astor's efforts to achieve his vision. For Hunt's long, arduous overland trek in 1811 on the German's behalf had in fact located the path that others would follow. His party, together with the eastbound party of Robert Stuart, bringing messages to Astor from the Columbia in 1812 (Irving tells that incredible story too), had hit upon the best route for future settlers to follow to the Northwest—and had published the news. Wagons could make it all the way. Where Hunt had gone wrong, Stuart went right, and together the two explorers provided landmarks that thousands after them would watch for as they headed westward, past Court House Rock and Chimney Rock and Scotts Bluff and Independence Rock through South Pass and on to Fort Bridger and Salmon Falls and to Fort Vancouver at the end of the trail. By the mid-1840s this route, this Oregon Trail, would become a great highway, two thousand miles long, often a hundred feet wide or more, "smooth as a barn floor swept by the winds, and not a blade of grass can shoot up on it on account of the continual passing." The deep furrows that the wagon wheels cut can be seen in places still; the names of those hopeful settlers can still be read carved into the stone of bluffs along the way. They would come in astonishing numbers, and their presence in the Willamette Valley, northward to Puget Sound, and back along the Columbia River would lead diplomats to agree at last, in 1846, to a border settlement that Washington Irving, ambassador to Spain in London at the time, had a hand in fashioning: neither the California boundary nor the "fifty-four forty" that some were ready to fight for, but rather the forty-ninth parallel that is the boundary still. Thus, not until 1850 (California taken from the Mexicans in the meantime), while revising his account of foiled empire-building in the Pacific Northwest for the Complete Edition of his works, could Irving properly end the compelling story: "Since the above was written, the question of dominion over the vast territory beyond the Rocky Mountains, which for a time threatened to disturb the peaceful relations with our transatlantic kindred, has been finally settled in a spirit of mutual concession, and the venerable projector whose early enterprise forms the subject of this work had the satisfaction of knowing, ere his eyes closed upon the world, that the flag of his country again waved over 'ASTORIA.' "

The War of 1812 had occasioned the doom of Astor's settlement on the Columbia. Most of his agents and clerks had been Canadians; at the time Canadians were the best (and often the only) people in the business of trapping and trading for furs. But a war with England had meant almost certainly that such a distant venture, however magnificently conceived and supported, would be untenable if manned by British subjects, no matter which partner was put in charge—McDougall, McKay, McKenzie, Stuart—just as peace through those same years would have assuredly resulted in success beyond the founder's hopes, regardless of who his agents might have been.

Astor had survived the surrender of his fort at the mouth of the Columbia, as he had survived the war itself. Indeed, from the latter he profited, recovering the million and more dollars misspent in pursuit of his "favorite plan," the Astoria enterprise. And he had gone forward in the years after 1815 to make the American Fur Company supreme over all its rivals. But no subsequent commercial success entirely compensated him for the sense of loss that memories of Astoria bestirred; so that even when he was seventy, a widower keeping bachelor hall at Hell Gate, he prevailed on his friend Irving to tell the world of that one failure that was the most wonderful of all his undertakings.

Hell Gate, Astor's country home, was a thirteen-acre farm centering on what is now Eighty-sixth Street. There, with his deceased daughter Magdalen's son, and with the poet Fitz-Greene Halleck to act as secretary, the old gentleman played host to Washington Irving and to Irving's nephew, who in the summer of 1835 had been pleased, after accepting the tasks of researcher, to find himself "a devourer of oysters and regaler upon Champagne at other people's expense—an eater with silver forks, a user of napkins and washer of the hands in blue bowls . . ."

During those same months Irving's newly acquired stone cottage on the banks of the Hudson was undergoing the earliest of the alterations that would finally shape it into Sunnyside, while in the opposite direction, southward across fields and above Canal Street downtown, another residence was being built, but this one for Astor, because the merchant's old Broadway mansion bought from Rufus King had been destroyed to make way for a new hotel. The year before, the ailing millionaire had returned for the final time from Europe, in part presumably to watch over the construction of those two edifices—hotel and home. Philip Hone, the indispensable diarist, had noted his arrival April 4, 1834, aboard the *Utica*—a homecoming that Astor's illness in Europe had delayed a year, and at which he had been confronted with the melancholy news of his wife's death one week before. "He comes," wrote Hone, "in time to witness the pulling down of the block of houses next to that on which I live—the whole front Barclay to Vesey Street on Broadway—where he is going to erect a New York *palais royal*, which will cost him five or six hundred thousand dollars." But within a month of that entry, from among the dust and noise and rubbish that the changes were creating around City Hall Park, the diarist felt "sorry to observe since Mr. Astor's return from Europe that his health is declining. He appears sickly and feeble, and I have some doubt if he will live to witness the completion of his splendid edifice."

We remember that Astor himself had expected to follow his wife to the grave "very soon," and had withdrawn that same year, 1834, from the American Fur Company entirely. But shortly before, in wistful mood, he had written his old friend Wilson Price Hunt, postmaster of St. Louis, that "had we succeeded in keeping Astoria, ere now we should all have made great fortunes there, and even more and much more than the Hudson's Bay Company now do."

Doubtless the postmaster regretted the loss of a fortune as much as the millionaire who was reminding him of it. In any case, Astor's health, benefiting from his horseback rides over Manhattan, did improve in coming months, and the merchant's spirits rose as he set about to supply "abundance of materials in letters, journals, and verbal narratives" to Irving and his nephew at Hell Gate, hopeful that their literary efforts would prevent his magnificent venture in the Pacific Northwest twenty-five years earlier from passing entirely out of the world's notice.

Meanwhile, the hotel he was having erected on Broadway—the Park Hotel, soon to be known as the Astor House—had progressed to the amazement and delight of fellow New Yorkers. Earlier its owner had acquired the other leading hostelry, the City Hotel, at auction in 1828; within the dining salon of that building, on Broadway above Trinity Church, Irving had been welcomed back to America at a celebrated public dinner in the spring of 1832. But the City Hotel was to be eclipsed in splendor by this block-long Astor House, which would contain on its ground floor eighteen shops that offered wigs and clocks and jewelry and trusses and fancy drygoods and gold leaf, as well as numerous other items of quality for sale. More than three hundred guest rooms and parlor suites would each be furnished in costly black walnut, with the innovation of water closets above ground level, and ten bathing rooms, and all the floors to be "regularly overlaid with superior oilcloth of various tasteful patterns," Brussels carpets to be put over those, and marble-topped tables, and "mosaik work" in the vestibule, and frescoes on the ceiling over the hundred-foot-long dining room; throughout would shine the novelty of gaslight—and the silver and china alone would cost $20,000. All such wonders came to pass, so that for some years into the future the Astor House was the leading hotel of New York City, suggestive of the dominance of its namesake, the Waldorf-Astoria, through at least a part of the twentieth century.

But hotels were only one of the interests to which the septuagenarian Astor's restless mind turned during these years after his retirement from the fur trade and from the trade with China. He retained ownership of the Park Theater (remodeled this year of 1834), as well as of thousands of acres of land on Manhattan, where others were building both public and private edifices. The new Erie Canal, the swift steamboats, those first shiploads of immigrants, all were urging the city to expand even more rapidly now. Remarking in his diary that "the whole of New York is rebuilt about once in ten years," Philip Hone comments in entry after entry on this continuing tendency that Astor had predicted and of which Astor was principal beneficiary: "There is a great deal of moving in the streets out of Broadway, in the upper part of the city"— that is, just below Washington Square. "But the pulling down of houses and stores in the lower parts is awful. Brickbats, rafters and slates are showering down in every direction. There is no safety on the sidewalks, and the head must be saved at the expense of soiling the boots." In the year that Irving at Hell Gate was writing *Astoria*, land across the East River on Long Island, so Hone tells us, was making fortunes overnight: "Men in moderate circumstances have become immensely rich, merely by the good fortune of owning farms of a few acres of this chosen land." If, for example, Abraham Schermerhorn four years ago would have taken $18,000 for his farm three miles from Brooklyn, "today he pockets $102,000, and regrets that he sold it so cheap!" Again, "Francis B. Cutting and Robert Bayard bought two or three years ago the country-place, as it then was, of the late William Bayard, for a sum between $50,000 and $60,000 (a great price at that time), and sold it at auction in lots the day before yesterday"—April 21, 1835—"for $225,000." On Manhattan, in every downtown street, dwellings were being cleared away or converted into stores, their owners "tempted with prices so exorbitantly high that none can resist, and the old downtown burgo-masters . . . will be seen, during the next summer, in flocks, marching reluctantly north to pitch their tents in places which, in their time, were orchards, corn-fields, or morasses . . ." When they got there, however, those flocks were to find that Astor already owned many of the orchards and cornfields, land more valuable than even the golden fields beyond Brooklyn. The new arrivals could lease his vacant lots, but they would have to improve them at their own expense, pay rent and taxes on the buildings they erected, keep them in repair, and surrender them to the owner of the land when the lease expired. Nor was Astor done buying. From this year, 1835, until his death, he would invest an additional $832,000 (a quarter then would buy a pound of beef) in Manhattan real estate—wealth making wealth—and would find in his son William the perfect temperament for profitably managing those enormous and increasing holdings.

Thus, accumulating more money than ever before, the old man moved through the 1830s, hardly the indifferent superannuate that his letters early in the decade had suggested he meant to become. On the contrary, his health was much better than a few years back, even though he was well into his seventies now. A famous lady of a later age, Julia Ward Howe, near the end of the century recalled one New Year's Day of her childhood, at about this time, when "a yellow chariot stopped before our door. A stout, elderly gentleman descended from it, and came in to pay his compliments to my father. This gentleman was John Jacob Astor . . ." During the same decade, the then Miss Ward's brother would marry one of Astor's granddaughters, so Julia Ward was often invited to the new town house that the merchant had built on Broadway between Prince and Spring Streets. "He was very fond of music, and sometimes engaged the services of a professional pianist. I remember that he was much pleased at recognizing, one evening, the strains of a brilliant waltz, of which he said: 'I heard it at a fair in Switzerland years

ago. The Swiss women were whirling round in their red petticoats.' "
The talented Julia would sometimes join William's daughter—her sister-
in-law—in song at "old Mr. Astor's musical parties, and at one of these
he said to us, as we stood together: 'You are my singing birds.' . . ."

Trivial moments, but not unappealing. The old man continued to
delight in the lives of his family—was building mansions for his various
grandchildren as he felt such benefactions appropriate. They knew little,
of course, of the ruthlessness in backwoods and on high seas that had
gathered their grandfather's fortune together—and as for that, would
perhaps have found nothing remarkable in the details of his dealings.
Whether as merchant or fur trader or moneylender or landlord, Astor—
good friend of three presidents—had himself never acted illegally, nor
were his methods different from those of other businessmen of the time,
except that the results they rendered were so much more successful.
Understandably his family was devoted to the aged, affectionate gentleman with the long white hair and silver-buckle shoes and courtly Old
World manners and generosities. Some years earlier, to morose Peter
Smith, Astor had written illuminating advice concerning that former
partner's family in back-state New York: "all your wealth," he had reminded Smith, "will Do you no good in your Grave Devid Som of it with
tham   See tham happy & Comfordable & you will bee So your Self
Donte tell me that it is easey to give advise—I Say to you that I Do
Devid with my Children . . ."

He did divide, and in addition, occasionally, shared his wealth with
a few rare, close friends—or might try to. *Astoria* had been finished by
now and published, in the fall of 1836, to the acclaim from Poe and
others that was remarked on earlier. "Old Mr. Astor appears to be
greatly gratified, which is very satisfactory to me," Irving reported at the
time. The merchant had reason for gratification: that book would fix his
name in the popular mind thereafter as a model for the rugged individ-
ualist, self-made, enormously resourceful, enormously rich, a Titan
among men. And so he was. Is the book, then, an apologia? Admittedly a
social critic will not be detained long among the pages of *Astoria*,
colorful as they are, for nothing in the account qualifies Irving to claims
as an early muckraker—no exposures of robber barons, no jeremiads
against malefactors of great wealth. Which is to say that Irving was
writing, in 1835 and not seventy years later, for different purposes, as a
romantic responding to heroic enterprises. The inspirer of the narrative
was of course delighted with this thrilling and accurate recapitulation of
what had been a colossal enterprise indeed. Accordingly, the friendship
between the two men thrived even more stoutly after the literary task
was completed. "Old Mr. Astor most unexpectedly paid me a visit at the
cottage about a month since," the author was writing from his new home
in December of that year, 1836, when the book appeared. "He landed at

Tarrytown, and hired a vehicle, which brought him to the cottage door. He spent two days here, and promised to repeat his visit as soon as there shall be good sleighing . . ."

Moreover, the millionaire had tried to pay Irving for the service rendered. In later years, after Astor's death, a report circulated to the effect that he had paid the author $5,000 to write *Astoria*. As soon as the charge reached his ears, Irving set about publicly to deny it. Astor "was too proverbially rich a man," the historian wrote for publication in the New York *Literary World*, "for me to permit the shadow of a pecuniary favor to rest on our intercourse." The merchant had not been allowed even to subsidize an elegant binding for the book; "it must be produced," Irving had insisted, "in the style of my other works, and at my expense and risk," and whatever profits the book made must come solely "from its sale and my bargain with the publishers."

Gratitude for financial favors need not be adduced to explain that friendship. Astor was a man of parts. Jefferson knew and liked him; Madison liked him; Monroe did; Gallatin did; Henry Clay did (though Clay, to be sure, was busy in 1835 borrowing $20,000 from him on easy terms). The poet Fitz-Greene Halleck admired Astor, and when Joseph Cogswell met him in 1837, that distinguished bibliographer was surprised to discover him to be "not the mere accumulator of dollars, as I had supposed him; he talks well on many subjects and shows a great interest in the arts and literature."

Talks better than writes, no doubt. Old Peter Smith, by the way, had taken his former partner's advice and divided his wealth with his children. Peter's heir Gerrit, in his thirties now, had become a reformer out there at Peterboro, a man as unlike Astor as could be imagined, campaigning tirelessly then and through much of his long life for rational religion, for peace, for women's rights, for land reform, for reforms in education, for vegetarianism, for prohibition. Indeed, the younger Smith had written his father's old friend while the Astor House was under construction early in 1835 to urge that liquor be banned from its premises. "I admire much your ideas on the subject of temperance," the German had answered, with perhaps a touch of humor; "but I fear our folk here are not good enough to admit of the introduction at the Hotel I am building of the temperance principles." Nevertheless, these two men, with some thirty-five years' difference in their ages and a world of difference in their temperaments, also became friends, visiting cordially together on a number of occasions and corresponding on matters of railroad business in which both had an interest. When the old man died, Gerrit Smith paid him tribute: "I have lost a fast friend—a friend, too —who had the ability, as well as the disposition to render me very important Services—"

Indeed, the reformer had held tangible evidence of the old gentleman's regard in 1837, after an economic panic had rendered Smith—inheritor of nearly a million acres of New York State—land-poor, in need of cash. Willingly and promptly the landlord of New York City had lent him $200,000, for uses ultimately (had Astor known what they were) that would have seemed to him incomprehensible.

Gerrit Smith meant to pay off his debts in preparation for giving away the bulk of whatever else he owned. August 10, 1837: "I this week receive a letter from my friend, and my father's friend, John Jacob Astor, in which he consents to loan me for a long period the large sum of money which I had applied for to him. This money will enable me to rid myself of pecuniary embarrassments, and to extend important assistance to others . . . This is a great mercy of God to me." Simplify, simplify. Five years earlier Smith had given up using tea and coffee, as even before then he had stopped using all spices and condiments. Two years before Astor's loan the reformer had commenced abstaining from "fish, flesh and gravies," as well as from all products of slave labor destined for the table. For in addition to the other causes he espoused, Peter Smith's son was an abolitionist. In 1836, while writing to his wife to eschew "the accursed spirit of aristocracy," he referred to their daughter: "I hope our dear Lilly, if she has one particle of that wicked thing in her heart called prejudice against people of color, will make haste to get rid of it. This prejudice is a quarrel with God." But he meant to do more than simply exhort. Smith would use his wealth to purchase slaves their freedom, then provide them with land from the holdings over New York State that were his father's bequest; for the right to the soil, Gerrit Smith would later insist, is "as absolute, universal and equal as the right to the light and the air."

A remarkable attitude toward property on the part of a property owner, and in marked contrast to the attitude of his friend John Jacob Astor. In the coming decade Smith set about realizing his intentions. During the summer of 1846 he wrote to three local ministers: "For years I have indulged the thought, that, when I had sold enough land to pay my debts, I would give away the remainder to the poor." Would the Reverend Mr. Wright and Dr. Smith and the Reverend Mr. Ray furnish him with a list of 1,985 colored men between ages twenty-one and sixty, temperate, decent, and at present without property? "Could I receive the list by the first day of next month (and I most earnestly hope that I can), I should be able to put a considerable share of the deeds into your hands by the first day of the following month; and, in that case, the grantees might be put in possession of them by the middle of October. . . ."

To this unusual man's white-pillared home at Peterboro, Madison County, in central New York, on April 8, 1848, came the like-minded John Brown. Brown, another eschewer of luxuries, teetotaler, reformer, idealist, had been driven to bankruptcy in Ohio six years earlier, in

1842. Soon afterward, at Richfield, the unfortunate father had watched four of his children die of dysentery, then buried them in a common grave. "*I expect nothing* but to 'endure *hardness.*' " Since then Brown's career had led him from Richfield to Akron, from Akron to Springfield, Massachusetts, as he tried to glean a living for the surviving members of his family. "Sometimes the prospect seems quite disheartening, & at other times it brightens." But the bright periods were brief. In 1846, he lost another child, Amelia, a year old, when one of her sisters accidentally scalded her to death. And at Springfield, in April 1848, still another child, Brown's most recent, died of consumption, held in her father's arms as he was pacing the bedroom trying to give her comfort. A daughter remembered watching him calmly close the dead girl's eyes and fold her little hands and lay her back in the cradle. But after the infant Ellen was buried, "father broke down completely, and sobbed like a child."

So far his life had been, in his words, one of "poverty, trials, discredit, & sore afflictions." That same month, however, undeterred by this latest grief, John Brown traveled to central New York to pay his visit to Gerrit Smith. The tanner was considering moving his family to the community that he had learned Smith was establishing in the Adirondacks, on 120,000 acres of Essex County, across from Burlington, Vermont, where blacks were being given means to become farmers and useful citizens. "I can think of no place where I think I would sooner go; *all things considered* than to live with those poor despised Africans to try, & encourage them; & show them a little so far as I am capable how to manage."

Smith was agreeable. To this decent, nearly impoverished, teetotaling enemy of slavery at his door the philanthropist agreed to sell what land was required at a dollar an acre; so that in the late spring of the following year Brown's family was established in a rented house among the mountains of northern New York, not far from regions through which young Washington Irving had made his tortuous way toward Canada nearly fifty years earlier.

The land was rugged for farming. Only a few blacks had taken advantage of Smith's generosity, but to those few the newly arrived white family brought barrels of flour and a willingness to share skills and time and energy. Among these mountains, then, Brown built yet another of the several homes that his gnarled hands raised, but this time in surroundings "where every thing you see reminds one of Omnipotence"—let others bemoan the taskings of long winters and lean crops in rocky soil—"and where if you do get your crops cut off once in a while, you will feel your dependence."

Each affliction served God's purposes; Thy will be done. Of course neither ease nor worldly success would follow Brown's latest move. As summer was ending, he left his family at North Elba and traveled to

Europe on a business venture to offer wool for sale in continental markets. Thus, we may form the unlikely picture of this somber and godly Ohio frontiersman, in the fall of 1848, craning his long neck in the Paris that Irving had known or pacing out tactics on the field of Waterloo. He was at Hamburg, at Leeds, at London, but the foray proved disastrous, as had so many of his temporal undertakings. From London he reported in October, "I find that with all the prejudices that exist against American wools that have come to this country for the most part, that a good sale is out of the question." This was not sea otter he was offering, and times had changed in any case. Brown had to sell at ruinous prices. The venture cost the partnership of Perkins & Brown an estimated $40,000—a partnership, incidentally, for which the near-saintly Simon Perkins had put up the capital.

After he returned home, business importunities would continue to force Brown to travel from place to place. Yet he loved North Elba: "*Nothing* but the strong sence of duty, obligation, & propriety, would keep me from laying my bones to rest there; but I shall cheerfully endeavour to make that sense my guide; God always helping." Often in coming years he was away from his family, in Pennsylvania, in Massachusetts, trying to redeem losses and scrape together a little profit for the partnership. But times remained meager, so that in March 1851 Brown was forced to abandon the farm in Essex County, New York, and once more lead most of his family back to Ohio.

A daughter and son-in-law stayed behind. Four years later, in June 1855, the father moved his family, for the last time, again to North Elba, where his wife would be living during the years of Bleeding Kansas that lay ahead, where she would await the outcome of events at Harpers Ferry. Indeed, Brown's bones would finally be laid to rest in the Adirondacks after all. For now, however, he had begun to involve himself more militantly in the cause of the blacks, who were oppressed afresh by the recent passage of stricter fugitive slave laws as part of the federal Compromise of 1850. From Springfield early in 1851, the tanner was writing his wife: "Since the sending off to slavery of Long from New York, I have improved my leisure hours quite busily with colored people here, in advising them how to act, and in giving them all the encouragement in my power. . . . I can only say I think I have been enabled to do something to revive their broken spirits. I want all my family to imagine themselves in the same dreadful condition. . . ."

What he had done was form the League of Gileadites, to protect fugitive slaves in Springfield from being recaptured. And he had been providing the League with words of advice, writing them down at the Massasoit Inn, often until late in the night, thereby staving off "gloomy homesick feelings which had before so much oppressed me: not that I forget my family at all." He was advising blacks that they would find strength only in union: "Should one of your number be arrested, you must collect together as quickly as possible, so as to outnumber your adversaries who are taking an active part against you." Keep weapons hidden, but come armed. " 'Whosoever is fearful or afraid, let him return and part early from Mount Gilead' (Judges, vii. 3; Deut. xx. 8). . . . Be firm, determined, and cool; but let it be understood that you are not to be driven to desperation without making it an awful dear job to others as well as to you."

The law that Brown's League was resisting had been enacted to appease the South, at a time when concessions were being made to the North as well. In 1850, with the question of slavery ever more broadly dividing the nation, California had been admitted to the Union as a free state, and the slave trade abolished at last in the nation's capital. That much for the North. But slaves from southern states who managed to escape to freedom would now be relentlessly pursued by federal marshals and returned to their owners. The outcry against Senator Clay's compromise was instantaneous in northern cities. "It now seems," Brown could write as early as November 1850, "that the fugitive slave law was to be the means of making more abolitionists than all the lectures we have had for years."

One question that the carefully wrought compromise had purposely evaded concerned those sparsely settled spaces torn from Mexico two years earlier at the end of the Mexican War. California, filling with new immigrants come to pan for gold, must be granted statehood at once. But what of the empty regions that the Forty-niners had crossed? Would those territories between the Mississippi and the Far West finally enter the nation as slave states or free? As a solution to a problem that could no longer be postponed, Congress in 1854 passed the Kansas-Nebraska Act. Slaveowners and free-soil advocates alike might move into territories beyond the Mississippi until the various regions had amassed a large enough population to qualify for statehood. Then citizens of each territory would decide, by popular vote, the attitude that their new state would take toward slavery.

Nebraska was far enough north that it would become a free state, but Kansas lay directly across the river from the slave-holding state of Missouri. Soon proslavery supporters were moving westward from Independence and other frontier towns to stake out claims on those prairies that Irving had traversed a score of years earlier; through "Annoyance Associations," many meant to make sure that Kansas would not be voted a haven for escaping slaves in the future. At the same time, abolitionists were forming Emigrant Aid Societies in the North to encourage free-soil farmers to remove to the new territory on the prairies. And among the farmers who caught the Kansas fever first were three of John Brown's sons, setting out from Ohio on horseback in November 1854, to drive eleven head of cattle before them across Illinois. After a wintering, the boys reached eastern Kansas in the spring, in time to lay claim to farmland a few miles northwest of Osawatomie.

And John Brown—he who had lost nine children by then and suffered through fifteen business failures in an arduous lifetime—set off westward himself in August 1855, traveling through Ohio and on by one-horse wagon to join his sons and help settle Kansas for freedom. In his wagon the old man was carrying specimens of "Kansas furniture"— guns, revolvers, powder, caps, artillery broadswords. He reached the territory in October. The terrible prairie winter closed down upon him and his family. But spring came at last; and on the night of May 24, 1856, the broadswords from Ohio were in the hands of a party under Brown's command as he knocked at the door of a proslavery settler's cabin near Pottawatomie Creek.

The door was forced open. The Northern Army had come. Old Doyle, the settler inside, and two of his boys must surrender. "I told you what you were going to get," Doyle's wife, in tears, began railing at her husband there in the log-chinked darkness. "Hush, mother, hush." Out of the cabin into the night the men were shoved, and a hundred yards down the windswept road two of Brown's sons lifted their broadswords and began hacking at the struggling victims. The three mutilated bodies were left by the roadside, and the avenging party rode on, to the Wilkinsons' cabin. Rode on to Dutch Sherman's cabin.

Better that a score of bad men should die than that one man who came here to make Kansas a free state should be driven away. So Brown explained his actions later. "I believe," he said, "that I did God service in having them killed." Now he was resolved to go to whatever lengths to remove the curse of slavery from this land: better indeed that a whole generation perish than that slavery survive.

In the three years remaining to him Brown would return east and speak often and effectively about conditions in Kansas, soliciting funds from whoever would join him in his eternal war. On one occasion he journeyed back to Kansas, swooped with a party across the river into Missouri, gathered a number of slaves together, and guided them boldly northward to freedom in Canada. Describing that strike to a group assembled in central New York in April 1859, the old fighter would speak with a simple eloquence that moved Gerrit Smith to tears. Smith rose and proclaimed, "If I were asked to point out—I will say it in his presence—to point out the man in all this world I think most truly a Christian, I would point out John Brown. . . ."

Three months later, on the Fourth of July, Brown arrived at the Kennedy farm in Maryland, five miles from the federal arsenal at Harpers Ferry. There a contingent of young volunteers would stand ready to follow his orders: John Kagi and Will Leeman and Oliver Brown and Dangerfield Newby and others, some of them veterans of Kansas, some down from North Elba, some white, some black. As soon as the time was right, Brown meant to lead them forth to take possession of the arsenal— meant to descend with his band of twenty or so on Harpers Ferry, grab and distribute arms, then withdraw into the surrounding hills with armed slaves augmenting their numbers. Thus, a free state would be created in the very midst of thralldom; and as soon as that happened, the North would rise in support, and throughout the South slavery would crumble and vanish.

Later Gerrit Smith wrote that "my gifts to Brown show only a small part of my relations with him. For many years, and down to the last year of his life, he had business transactions with me. He borrowed money from me. He deposited money with me. He bought farms from me. The title to eighty acres of land, which he bought from me in 1858 and then paid for, he left in my name, when he bade me 'Farewell!' on the 14th of April 1859 . . ." And when Brown—his little band of men formed in twos behind his wagon—rode forth from the Kennedy farm toward Harpers Ferry in that same year, on the Sabbath evening of October 16, he was carrying a check from Smith to the amount of a hundred dollars, nourishment for the seed of freedom he intended that night to plant.

By then, by 1859, old Mr. Astor had been dead for more than a decade. Even so, the fur merchant who years earlier had lent Gerrit Smith $200,000 had managed, despite middling health, to extend his days on earth through eighty-five years, longer indeed than he himself would have chosen to. "I am broken up," Astor had told the abolitionist near the end, in 1847. "It is time for me to be out of the way." Yet one who knew him well at the last found much that was admirable in how the old gentleman accepted physical decline: "Although he lived many years beyond the age when 'the grasshopper is a burden,' and was the victim of much suffering, he did not murmur, nor did he become unreasonable and peevish. . . ."

Astor's daughter Eliza, she who had married the Swiss count, had died childless near Geneva in 1838. "There are, therefore," the diarist Hone recorded, "but three children to inherit the largest fortune in the State—William B. Astor, Mrs. Langdon, and a son who is not likely to interfere with the claims of the others." As for that deficient son— Astor's eldest—one of the merchant's final projects had been to provide a home for him in New York City, where John Jacob Astor, Jr., lived until his death in his mid-seventies, in 1867, "the sole occupant of a large and commodious mansion. He was here under the care of Dr. O'Donnel, now of Brooklyn, who devoted his attention exclusively to him . . ."

The Langdons (the "fat German, Dolly Astor," and the husband with whom she had eloped at seventeen) passed their days in their own Manhattan mansion and at their home up the Hudson that Astor had purchased in 1840 from the estate of Dr. David Hosack, the same who early in the century had tended Alexander Hamilton in the barge from Weehawken, rubbing spirits of hartshorn on the moribund patriot's neck and hands. Hosack's home that the Langdons acquired was at Hyde Park: "This is the finest place on the North river"—on land adjoining the estate of the Roosevelts, another old New York family, though of Dutch rather than German extraction.

The third of old Mr. Astor's surviving children, the wondrously efficient William, was to become his principal beneficiary, to the dismay of some democrats. "No man born under the influence of our free institutions," one editorialist pronounced after the death of the immigrant from Walldorf, "could be so unmindful of his own fame and so recreant to the Republican Spirit as to dedicate his whole life to the sole object of endowing his eldest son with a more than imperial fortune."

Not his eldest—but the point is a quibble. The fortune was imperial, to be sure, by far the largest fortune ever amassed in the United States up to that time. At Astor's death in 1848 it stood at between twenty and thirty million dollars, ten to twenty times as large as that of the next wealthiest Americans: the Goelets, Cornelius Vanderbilt, the Lorillards, Peter Cooper. Indeed, Astor was by then one of the five richest men in the world. Only the wealth of Baron Rothschild, Louis-Philippe, the Duke of Devonshire, and Sir Robert Peel exceeded his, and none of those had been born the son of a village butcher. Moreover, the bulk of Astor's estate did go to his son William, and only a relatively small portion (about a half-million dollars) was set aside for public uses, mostly for the founding of what would become the New York Public Library, which his friend Washington Irving had long urged him to endow.

The attenuated decline and death of such a man as Astor calls forth reflection. "We remember seeing Mr. Astor two winters since, when going down Broadway," the reporter Walt Whitman, hardly yet a poet, wrote in a New Orleans newspaper within a fortnight of the old man's passing. "A couple of servants were assisting him across the pavement . . . The old gentleman's head seemed completely bent down with age and sickness; he was muffled in furs and entirely unable to help himself. The very groom, a hearty young Irishman, with perhaps not two dollars in his pocket, looked with pity upon the great millionaire! Certainly no man, of the crowds that hurried along that busy promenade, would have accepted the rich capitalist's wealth tied to the condition of being in his shoes." To be sure, youth (Irish or otherwise) regularly regards great age that way, and money has little to do with it; but who can resist uttering commonplaces when kings or plutocrats die? "So a rich man has the advantage of rotting in *velvet*, *gold*, and *silver* trappings; *silver* headed screws, exquisite needlework, and *bullion* fringe . . ." Hone tells of the gawking crowds at Astor's funeral, "from the house of Mr. William B. Astor, in Lafayette Place. . . . There were six Episcopal clergymen and a long train of followers. The occasion caused great excitement, and the curiosity of the people was intense; the street was filled, the walks obstructed all the distance from the house to St. Thomas's Church, where the funeral ceremonies were performed, and in the cemetery of which the wornout remains were deposited. Mr. Astor's house was filled with curious persons, principally females, who were admitted to see the pale features of the deceased, and, walking round the coffin, had each a brief view of the lineaments. . . ."

At that interesting ceremony Washington Irving served as a pall-bearer, and he was named in the will as an executor of Astor's enormous estate. Thus his friendship with the merchant continued to the very last. Irving had finished *Astoria* and seen it published in 1836. Later in that decade he had written *The Adventures of Captain Bonneville* (another western history) and begun his work on the conquest of Mexico, forsaking the latter subject when he learned that Prescott was similarly employed. July 11, 1841, from Hell Gate: "I am just now on a brief visit to Mr. Astor. I came here yesterday (Saturday) and think I shall return home tomorrow." During that particular stay Irving "accompanied Mr Astor in an excursion on the water," by sloop from Hell Gate down the East River to Corlears Hook, past beautiful green shores, "and I saw the old Jones country seat peering through the trees, with its half ruined out houses and weedy garden"—not far from where the United Nations Building rises now. October 3, 1841: "I have been passing a few days partly in town on business and partly at Mr Astor's . . . " December 1: "I am passing a few days in town at Mr Astor's . . ." And even after Irving had departed early the following year to assume his post as ambassador at Madrid, he could rely on Brevoort to forward news of the merchant, as on December 28, 1842: "Our old friend Mr Astor has been confined to his room, & mostly to his bed these three months past. I saw him yesterday. He was lying in his bed, in his parlor, looking feeble & emaciated, but much recovered. His appetite remains healthy & his mind as clear & as much occupied with old cares, as usual. His years are bearing him downward, & probably his next, the eightieth, will be his last. He asked, as he always does, about you"—about Irving—"with the liveliest interest & in the kindest manner."

Time passed beyond that eightieth birthday, and Astor abided. In October of the following year, Brevoort wrote the ambassador at Madrid that "Old Mr Astor still holds out, & is better, body & mind, than he was before you left us." The following fall, in 1844, Philip Hone saw the merchant socially. "He sat at the dinner table with his head down upon his breast, saying very little, and in a voice almost unintelligible; the saliva dropping from his mouth, and a servant behind him to guide the victuals which he was eating, and to watch him as an infant is watched." But even thus reduced, according to Hone, Astor loved money as fervently as ever. Indeed, this late in life he could bestir himself to resent a bill for eighty-seven cents wrongly charged to him. "His mind is good, his observation acute, and he seems to know everything that is going on. But the machinery is all broken up, and there are some people, no doubt, who think he has lived long enough."

Yet he lingered. A full year later, in the fall of 1845, his health was "such as to permit him to take a drive occasionally on the 3ᵈ Avenue and almost daily to be rolled over the garden walks at Hell Gate in his Bath Chair, and he is stronger, I think than he was a few weeks ago." When Ambassador Irving, after four years in Spain, returned home in the autumn of 1846, he found his old friend alive to greet him, still "able to move about in his Carriage & Bath Chair." These twilights Astor would sit before his summer house at the river's edge below his country home, waiting to "watch the Boston night boat go through Hell Gate to the Sound . . . he would refuse to go in to his dinner until it passed, no matter how cold and dark it was. . . ."

And still he lingered, although in early November 1847 he left Hell Gate for the last time, moving to his town house on Broadway. So fragile had he become by then that he was existing, we are told, "on the milk of a wet nurse," was each day gently being "tossed in a blanket for exercise." Even this late, however, in February 1848, he could enjoy a visit of several days with his literary friend Irving, at the time eager to resume work on his biography of Washington. Indeed, Irving was among the last of the old man's visitors; for late the following month John Jacob Astor took to his bed and stayed there. No disease doomed him—simply old age. In his parlor within the brick mansion on Broadway he died, without pain or struggle, at nine in the morning of March 29, 1848.

DREGS

I have got to the dregs, and must take them.

IRVING AT SUNNYSIDE, 1859

Irving as Astor's executor—Tasks of old age—You should write one more book—Irving's death—His funeral—Harpers Ferry—The wagon comes to a halt.

T<small>ODAY</small>, J. J. Astor goes to the tomb," the novelist Fenimore Cooper wrote his wife on the first day of April, 1848. "Irving is an executor, and report says with a legacy of $50,000. What an instinct that man has for gold! He is to be Astor's biographer!" Columbus and Astor, the novelist snorted: no doubt Irving would make of Astor the greater figure. But Cooper, ever cool toward the only American writer who rivaled (and far exceeded) him in popularity, was in error—not only about the legacy paid for performing a trying task, but also about Irving's literary endeavors in the years when the task was ended. As for the legacy—and helping to execute the will of the richest man in America was wearisome work at best—Irving received about $10,000: what the other five executors received and the fee that was legally set. In any case, was it his fault that Astor admired and loved him? As for the literary endeavors, we have seen what those would be—a biography not of the German fur trader but of one far greater, and a hero from childhood, George Washington. We have seen, too, what the effort of finishing that monumental work cost the old man who was courageous enough to undertake it.

He had few illusions: every writer thinks his last work is his best, as Irving was aware, whereas history thinks otherwise. So he needed incentive other than what could be fashioned from self-deception to prod his labors forward. Not that poverty forced him to his desk in his old age, although whatever wealth did soften his late years—and the amount never approached dimensions that gossips assumed—arose less from Astor's munificence than from the reissue, by an imaginative young publisher named George Putnam, of the Works of Irving in a uniform edition. Indeed, by the very year 1848, when the author was sixty-five, his collected works were selling so well that he could have afforded, as his nephew reminded him, "to take his ease." Yet he fagged on. "I know my nature," he explained. "I must get through with the work I have cut out for myself. I must weave my web, and then die."

We have seen him in his study and at his leisure during the eighteen fifties, at Sunnyside. To a friend of his youth, James Kirke Paulding —now, miraculously, grown old as well—he offered this additional glimpse when he was seventy-two: "You hope I am 'sliding smoothly down the hill.' I thank you for the hope. I am better off than most old bachelors are, or deserve to be. I have a happy home; the happier for being always well stocked with womankind, without whom an old bachelor is a forlorn, dreary animal. My brother, the 'General,' is wearing out the serene evening of life with me; almost entirely deaf, but in good health and good spirits, more and more immersed in the study of newspapers (with which I keep him copiously supplied), and, through them, better acquainted with what is going on in the world than I am, who mingle with it occasionally, and have ears as well as eyes open. . . ."

The brother—the "General," Ebenezer, father of those "four blessed nieces" whose presence at Sunnyside so enlivened their uncle's later years—would have been reading in his newspapers about the furor created by a new novel of 1852, *Uncle Tom's Cabin*, about the opening of Kansas to settlement and the formation, in 1854, of the New England Emigrant Aid Society to colonize free-soil settlers there, about the troubles between those newcomers and proslavery settlers that followed, about the brutal caning on the floor of Congress, in May 1856, sustained by the abolitionist Senator Charles Sumner of Massachusetts at the hands of a hotheaded young southern congressman, about the massacre that same month of five settlers near a place called Pottawatomie Creek, about the Dred Scott decision and the emergence of a new lanky figure from the prairies as a politician of consequence, debating Senator Douglas in towns and villages of Illinois. But Washington Irving himself—though his nephew tells us he was "not without foreboding at the signs of the times"—says little of all these happenings in his ample prose that has survived that tempestuous decade. True, as he remarked, he was living "only in the Revolution. I have no other existence now—can think of nothing else." He had friends, moreover, on both sides of the developing quarrel, in the North obviously, but doughfaces like Pierce and Buchanan as well, and southern senators like Preston and Henry Clay. Then too, his field was ever European diplomacy; and of politics overseas, in England, France, Spain, and elsewhere in Europe, his letters of these years are both knowledgeable and full. But most of all, through changing decades Irving's aims as a writer had remained consistent: "If," he had concluded as long ago as 1820, while writing *The Sketch Book*, "I can by any lucky chance, in these days of evil, rub out one wrinkle from the brow of care, or beguile the heavy heart of one moment of sorrow; if I can now and then penetrate through the gathering film of misanthropy, prompt a benevolent view of human nature, and make my reader more in good humour with his fellow beings and himself, surely, surely, I shall not then have written entirely in vain." That modest and—despite the rhetoric—humane ambition would now be best fulfilled, as Irving must have thought, by his devoting what remained of his talent to depicting the life of America's founding father, recreating a crucial era in the past as an example for the present. It was a typically Irvingesque response to crisis—a conciliatory response that was, however, hardly more indicative of a man's weaknesses than of his strengths.

And despite self-doubts he saw the work through. "You have done with Washington just as I thought you would," one reader wrote him in 1856, after the second volume had appeared, "and, instead of a cold, marble statue of a demigod, you have made him a being of flesh and blood, like ourselves—one with whom we can have sympathy. The general sentiment of the country has been too decidedly expressed for you to doubt for a moment that this is the portrait of him which is to hold a permanent place in the national gallery." Nor was that a naive opinion. The reader was no less responsible a critic than the mature historian Prescott, brilliant author of *Ferdinand and Isabella*, of *The Conquest of Mexico* and *The Conquest of Peru*.

The effort, then—the taxing, fearful effort of researching and composing those five volumes—had been worth it. Bancroft, equally eminent in the field of history, in a letter to Irving in 1855, responded to the portrait of Washington this way: "I was up late and early, and could not rest until I had finished the last page. Candor, good judgment that knows no bias, the felicity of selection, these are yours in common with the best historians. But, in addition, you have the peculiarity of writing from the heart, enchaining sympathy as well as commanding confidence; the happy magic that makes scenes, events, and personal anecdotes present themselves to you at your bidding, and fall into their natural places, and take color and warmth from your own nature."

No doubt such testimonials were gratifying, but the effort that earned them had cost an old man repose. In the midst of his labors Irving had worried whether he could ever finish so lengthy and complex a project. "I am constantly afraid," he had told his nephew one morning, in clear allusion to his mind, "that something will happen to me." The final, pitiful months of Scott's life, the equally pathetic closing months— a mind eclipsed—in the life of his once witty friend Tom Moore, haunted him: senility, a failed intelligence, had always seemed, so the nephew tells us, "the saddest possible fate." On one occasion Irving

confided forcefully to the same listener, who had been helping to edit the
Life: "All I fear is to fail in health, and fail in completing this work at
the same time. If I can only live to finish it, I would be willing to die the
next moment."

He was granted his wish to finish the final volume. Perhaps the
next moment of that mid-March day in 1859 should have claimed his
last breath, for we have seen the agony of mind that followed:

> Not poppy, nor mandragora,
> Nor all the drowsy syrups of the world,
> Shall ever medicine thee to that sweet sleep
> Which thou ow'dst yesterday.

Was not death preferable to an old man's asthmatic cough that racked
his heart and the hearts of those who heard him, preferable to the Can-
nisis and the Balm of Gilead, lately prescribed by Dr. Peters, and the
Protoxyd of Iron and the Dulcamara and the olive tar and the medicated
papers to be burned in vain, preferable to his dread of long, long
nights—the sleeplessness, the fears and evil dreams? Of death itself he
had no fear, wanted only to go down "with all sail set." At last, indeed,
he came to long for it: "Misery—misery—misery—Will this never
come to an end?" But more characteristically he would murmur as
calmly as he could, "I am getting ready to go. I am shutting up my doors
and windows." His will was written, his gravesite chosen.

Visitors kept calling; even to the end, a few were allowed to see
him. One made bold to suggest: "You should write one more book."

"What is that?"

"Your reminiscences of those literary friends."

"Ah"—Irving sighed—"it is too late now! I shall never take the
pen again. I have so entirely given up writing, that even my best friends'
letters lie unanswered. I must have rest. No more books now!"

The visitor, in what was to be the last month of Washington Irving's life, departed Sunnyside soon after, having been granted a final
image that clings to our minds as well: "As I came away, the old gentleman bundled his shawl about him, and stood a few moments on the
steps. . . ." Of what was this sojourner through the wilds of New York,
through the hills of Scotland and the forests beyond Dresden and the
mountains of Spain and the Oklahoma prairies—of what was he thinking? How far might his musings have rambled still?

Sunset over the Hudson Monday, November 28, 1859, was of
notable splendor. "The whole western sky was hung with clouds of the
richest crimson, while the scene had all the softness of our lingering
Indian summer." The party at Sunnyside were in the dining room,
where windows look westward past the piazza to the river and the hills
beyond. Watching the changing hues, "Mr. Irving exclaimed again and
again at the beauty of the prospect." He had spent a part of that day

walking about his grounds, and now, when the spectacle of sunset was ended, would try to sleep until teatime.

That late afternoon he did have luck dozing, but woke finally from his nap "heavy, and a good deal depressed, as he had been more than usual during the day." Yet he was spared his dreaded nervous attacks, so that from ten to ten-thirty he was able to join in the family's evening conversation. In the parlor was a game of whist, and as frequently happened now, Irving was read to, on this occasion from Page's history of the Paraguay expedition. His mind was still roaming, as it had from childhood, over the world displayed. When ten-thirty came, he kissed his loved ones goodnight and started up the steep, narrow stairs to bed.

It was the last time he would mount them. Soon his niece Sarah, Ebenezer's eighth child, then in her forties (she would live past eighty and never forget), entered his bedroom to place the medicines nearby, as she did each evening at bedtime. Her uncle's pillows would have to be arranged for yet another weary night. "*When will this end?*" the old man said softly by the foot of the bed, as though to himself, so softly indeed that his niece, standing near, was not even certain what she had heard. "If this could only end!" he might have murmured, but there was no time to question, for at that same instant he uttered a brief cry, pressed a hand to his left side, clutched at the footboard, then fell backward to the floor.

Elsewhere in the house they heard Sarah's scream and heard the fall. All rushed into the room, and the nephew, who had been of help so often before, bent down and lifted and cradled his uncle's head. A few slight gasps, then nothing. Desperately the family worked over the body, trying to restore a life that had left them—administering brandy, bathing the feet—through long minutes that passed before Dr. Caruthers arrived from two miles away and confirmed that their efforts were useless. Washington Irving was dead at last, of what was diagnosed later— one wants to say fittingly—as an enlargement of the heart.

News of the death of America's first great imaginative writer inspired tributes unprecedented for a private citizen of the republic. Flags on ships and public buildings were flown next day at halfmast; church bells tolled; shops and schools closed; courts adjourned. The funeral itself, on December 1, crowded the village of Tarrytown with mourners. Lines of carriages spread away from the gate to Sunnyside and from Christ Church, where services had been scheduled for half past one in the afternoon. Nearly a thousand people viewed the remains—the attenuated frame, the now thin features—when the sexton opened the lid of the rosewood coffin, after the anthem, the lesson from Corinthians, the chorale within the Tudor brick church. Then the carriages—a hundred and fifty of them—followed by five hundred pedestrians, filed slowly toward the cemetery a mile away, on a hill overlooking on one side the Hudson River, on the other the very Sleepy Hollow that Irving's pen had made legendary: "If ever I should wish for a retreat, whither I might steal from the world and its distractions . . . I know of none more promising than this little valley." The procession wound past local landmarks: the monument commemorating the captors of Major André, the bridge, now hung in black, over the resounding planks of which Ichabod Crane was represented as having thundered in terror, half on and half off Gunpowder long ago. The weather had remained unseasonably beautiful for so late in the year, another Indian summer day, balmy and clear, "one of his own days," as many of the mourners noted. Yet even as the coffin was being lowered into the oak-shaded southern slope of ground he had chosen, that first day of December was already nearing its end. Soon above the hillside by Sleepy Hollow would spread once more a glorious sunset, as glorious as the one three afternoons earlier that had soothed the living Irving, radiant like that earlier one across the Hudson, declining in turn beyond this land that the vagabond New Yorker had loved more than anywhere else on earth.

The sun that sets in the evening rises the following day on a different world. Washington Irving, born in the year of the birth of our nation, was buried December 1, 1859. The next morning, shortly after eleven, in a field on the outskirts of Charles Town in what was then Virginia, they hanged John Brown.

Old Brown and his band of liberators had descended on Harpers Ferry that drizzly Sunday evening a month and a half before, and by noon Monday, October 17, over the lovely village in the mountains at the juncture of the Potomac and the Shenandoah, all the church bells were ringing in alarm, and the entire populace beneath those tolling bells knew that a slave insurrection had begun. By then the first blood had been spilled, ironically that of a free black, Hayward Shepherd, innocent and unarmed, mistakenly shot by one of Brown's raiders. But much more blood would flow before the streets of Harpers Ferry were quiet again. Mobs of whites had formed quickly, and through the afternoon they grew in size and fury and drunkenness, as the Gault House saloon did a fine business. The first of Brown's men to fall, the black man Dangerfield Newby, was dragged to a gutter where his ears were cut off for souvenirs. Another raider was shot and thrown off the railroad trestle into shallow water to lie "at the bottom of the river, with his ghastly face still exhibiting his fearful death agony," while sharpshooters on the bridge used him all afternoon for target practice. Three of Brown's men, including his son Watson, were cut down under a flag of truce. The day continued dark and foggy, and there was rain later, and through the rain-drenched streets white mobs raced screaming, "*Kill them, Kill them.*" Later still, in the engine house, where the bewildered old man and the last of his supporters had retreated, cries of the wounded could be heard the whole night long. It was an all but endless night they suffered through, pitch-black in there and cold. The old man was wearing a presentation sword he had confiscated, Frederick the Great's gift to George Washington, and he paced among hostages and the surviving raiders, explaining his purposes, while yet another son, Oliver, wounded, in agony, was heard begging to be shot and released from his pain.

The boy, just twenty, died before the daybreak that would disclose, outside the engine house, a company of marines in position under Colonel Robert E. Lee. The steel trap had sprung without any slaves having willingly answered Brown's summons to freedom. The old man was taken from the engine house wounded, and in the days ahead, lying on a cot, was tried hastily for treason at the nearby courthouse in Charles Town. On November 2, he was sentenced to hang.

When the morning of his execution came, one month later, Brown sat serenely, in a broad-brimmed hat, atop his coffin in the wagon that took him to the gallows. During the brief journey out of town he gazed about him: "This *is* a beautiful country," he was heard to say. "I never had the pleasure of seeing it before."

Then he was standing alone. Names destined for fame or notoriety were attached to some among the spectators that morning. Stonewall Jackson, still merely Professor Thomas J. Jackson of the Virginia Military Institute, was there; John Wilkes Booth was there, member of a Richmond rifle company. In all, fifteen hundred troops were on hand to see that this old man was dealt with. His elbows had been bound together. He stood in old clothes and carpet slippers; over his head the jailer was fitting a linen hood. After an agonizing delay, the sheriff at last raised his hatchet and cut the rope that let the trap door fall; and as John Brown's body swung in space, one age ended and another began.

CHRONOLOGY,
NOTES, INDEX &
ACKNOWLEDGMENTS

	WASHINGTON IRVING	AARON BURR	SIR WALTER SCOTT
1760		60. AB 4 yrs old. (Born Newark, NJ, Feb. 6, '56. Father dies '57; mother '58.) Now living with uncle, Timothy Edwards.	
1765			
1770		68. AB enters Princeton.	
			71. Aug. 15. WS born Edinburgh.
		72. AB graduates from Princeton.	
		73. AB studying theology.	73. Paralysis discovered; WS to Sandyknowe.
		74. AB studying law, Connecticut.	
1775		75. Lexington-Concord. AB with Arnold to Quebec.	
		76. AB at battle of Manhattan.	
		77. Valley Forge.	
		78. Monmouth.	78. WS rejoins family at Edinburgh.
		79. AB resigns from army.	79. Enters Edinburgh High School.
1780			
		82. Marriage of AB and Theodosia Prevost.	
	83. Apr. 3. WI born NYC.	83. Daughter Theo born. Dec. AB to NYC.	83. WS at Kelso; discovers Scottish ballads.
1785			

MARY SHELLEY	IRVING AND SPAIN	JOHN JACOB ASTOR	JOHN BROWN
(William Godwin born 1756; Mary Wollstonecraft, 1759.)			
	63. Louisiana to Spain at end of French and Indian War.	63. July 17. JJA born Walldorf, Baden (Germany).	
	67. Jesuits expelled from Spain.		
		77. JJA in butcher's trade, with father.	
	79. Spain joins France against Britain during American Revolution.	79. Leaves Walldorf for London.	
	83. Spanish Empire reaches its greatest extent.	83. Treaty of Paris. JJA leaves London for America.	
		84. Jan. Arrives Chesapeake Bay. Apr. JJA in NYC.	
		85. JJA marries Sarah Todd.	
		86. JJA opens music store. On furbuying expeditions in NY State, Canada.	
	88. Death of Carlos III. Ascension of Carlos IV.	88. JJA in Montreal. First child (daughter) born.	

WASHINGTON IRVING	AARON BURR	SIR WALTER SCOTT
89. Washington inaugurated first president, NYC.		
	91. AB elected to US Senate.	92. WS becomes advocate. On first visit to Liddesdale.
1790		
94. WI's friendship with John Anderson.	94. AB's wife dies.	
1795		95. In love with Williamina.
	97-99. AB practicing law; speculations in NYC.	97. Williamina marries. WS meets, marries Charlotte.
99. WI in law office, NYC.		99. Scotts established at Castle St. Sophia born.
1800 00. WI's first trip up Hudson.		
	01. AB VP of US. Theodosia marries Joseph Alston.	01. Walter (son) born.
02. WI in Hoffman's law office. "Jonathan Oldstyle."		02. *Minstrelsy of Scottish Border. Edinburgh Review* founded.
03. Summer. WI to upper New York, Montreal.		
04-06. WI in Europe: Bordeaux, Marseille, Genoa, Palermo, Paris, London.	04. AB defeated for NY Gov. July 11: Duel with Hamilton.	
1805	05. AB leaves Senate. Spring. Down Ohio, Mississippi.	05. *Lay of the Last Minstrel.*
06. WI in NY, passes bar exam.		06. WS Clerk of Sessions.
07. *Salmagundi* WI at Burr's trial, Richmond.	07. AB arrested in Ala. Spring, summer. Trial at Richmond.	
	08. AB to England, Edinburgh.	08. *Life of Dryden. Marmion.*

MARY SHELLEY	IRVING AND SPAIN	JOHN JACOB ASTOR	JOHN BROWN
89. Opening scenes of French Revolution.	89. French Revolution begins.	89. JJA purchases first lots in NYC.	
91. Mary Wollstonecraft meets William Godwin.			
92. *Vindication of the Rights of Woman.* MW to Paris.		92. Son William born.	
93. *Political Justice.* MW with Gilbert Imlay.	93. Louis XVI beheaded. Spain and France at war.	93. Gray enters Columbia River.	93. Whitney's cotton gin.
94. May. Fanny Imlay born.		94. JJA to England on business.	
95. MW in London, attempts suicide.	95. Peace between Spain and France.		
96. MW calls on Godwin.	96. Spain declares war on England.	96. Jay's Treaty in effect. JJA in following years becomes leading fur trader.	
97. Godwin, MW marry. Aug. 30: Mary Godwin born. Sept. 10: Mary Wollstonecraft dies.			99. NY begins emancipation of slaves.
	99. Napoleon as First Consul.	00. JJA enters China trade.	00. May 9. JB born Torrington, Connecticut.
	00. Spain returns Louisiana to France.		
01. Godwin marries Mrs. Clairmont.			
		03. Louisiana Purchase.	
		04-06. Lewis and Clark Expedition.	
			05. Brown family moves to Ohio.
07. Godwins at Skinner St.		07-09. Embargo.	
	08. Bourbons deposed. French enter Spain. Joseph Bonaparte proclaimed king. Beginning of War of Independence.	08. Am. Fur Co. chartered.	08. Prohibition of African slave trade.

WASHINGTON IRVING	AARON BURR	SIR WALTER SCOTT
09. Apr. 26. Matilda Hoffman dies. Dec. *Knickerbocker*.	09. To Sweden, Denmark.	
1810 10. WI in silent business partnership with his brothers.	10. In Paris.	10. *The Lady of the Lake*.
	11. AB obliged to return London.	11. WS makes first purchase of land for Abbotsford.
12-14. WI edits *Analectic*.	12. AB returns to America. To NYC in June. Grandson dies.	12. Byron's *Childe Harold*.
	13. Theodosia dies at sea. Burr practicing law in NY through following years.	13. WS rediscovers abandoned manuscript of novel.
14. Col. WI, aide-de-camp.		14. *Waverley*.
1815 15. May 25. WI embarks for England. In Liverpool.		15. *Guy Mannering*. WS to London, Waterloo, Paris.
	16. Alston dies.	16. *The Antiquary. Old Mortality*.
17. Late summer. WI to Scotland, Abbotsford.		17. WS ill, recovers. Irving visits Abbotsford, Sept.
18. Bankruptcy of P & E Irving. WI to London to write.		18. *Rob Roy. Heart of Midlothian*.
19-20. *The Sketch Book* published serially.		19. *Ivanhoe*.
1820		
21. Paris. WI meets Tom Moore, sees Payne, Astor.		21. *Kenilworth*.
22. *Bracebridge Hall*. WI in Dresden. Dec. Meets Fosters.		22. George IV visits Scotland.
23. WI with Fosters. Aug. In Paris, writing plays.		23. *Quentin Durward*.

MARY SHELLEY	IRVING AND SPAIN	JOHN JACOB ASTOR	JOHN BROWN
		09. Partnership to establish colony at mouth of Columbia.	09. Abraham Lincoln born.
		10. Overland expedition sets out. *Tonquin* sails from NY.	
		11. May. Astoria established. June. *Tonquin* destroyed.	
12. Mary to Scotland.	12. Constitution proclaimed at Cádiz.	12. Overland party reaches Astoria. War with England. JJA's daughter elopes.	
	13. French driven from Spain.		
14. Mary meets Shelley. July. Elopement. Six-weeks' tour.	14. Ferdinand restored to power.	14. Astoria abandoned to North West Co.	
15. Mary loses child.			
16. William born. To Geneva. Fall: suicides Fanny, Harriet. Shelley marries Mary.			
17. Marlow. Clara born.			
18. *Frankenstein.* Shelleys go into exile. Clara dies.		18. Astoria formally restored to US, but NW Co. retains control. JJA's grandson drowns.	
19. William dies. Percy born.	19. US acquires Florida from Spain.	19. JJA to Europe for health.	19. JB working as tanner at Hudson, Ohio.
20. Shelleys at Pisa.	20. Liberals in ascendancy.		20. Missouri Compromise.
	21. Mexico, Venezuela, Peru declare independence.	21. JJA sees Irving in Paris. Fall.	21. JB marries Dianthe Lusk.
22. Claire's child by Byron dies. July. Shelley drowns.			
23. Mary returns to England, by way of Paris.	23. French intervention. Ferdinand restores repression. Monroe Doctrine.	23-26. JJA in Europe. Begins withdrawing from China trade.	

	WASHINGTON IRVING	AARON BURR	SIR WALTER SCOTT
	24. WI meets Mary Shelley in London. *Tales of a Traveller*.		24. *Redgauntlet*. Abbotsford completed.
1825	25. WI in Paris, Bordeaux.	25. Completion of Erie Canal.	25. WS begins *Journal*. Dec. Financial crisis.
	26. Feb. WI to Madrid.		26. Ruin. WS leaves Castle St. Wife dies.
			27. WS publicly acknowledges writing Waverley novels. Working to erase debt.
	28. *Columbus*. WI tours Andalucia. At Seville.		
	29. *Granada*. WI at Alhambra. Leaves Spain for London.		
1830	30-32. WI in England at Legation.		
			31. Last visit with Irving, in London.
	32. WI returns to NY. *Alhambra*. Fall. Tour on prairies.		32. Sept. 21. WS dies at Abbotsford.
		33. AB marries Mrs. Jumel.	
	34. WI purchases Sunnyside.		
1835	35. "Tour on Prairies," "Abbotsford."		
	36. *Astoria*.	36. Sept. 14. AB dies on Staten Island.	
	37. *Bonneville*.		
	38. Peter dies. WI abandons subject of Cortés, Mexico.		

MARY SHELLEY	IRVING AND SPAIN	JOHN JACOB ASTOR	JOHN BROWN
24. Death of Byron. Mary's friendship with Irving.			
25. Aug. Payne shows Mary's letters to Irving, Paris.			25. JB postmaster, Randolph, Pa.
26. *The Last Man.*	26. WI to Spain.		
27. Jane Williams marries Hogg.			
	28. WI in Andalucia. Seville.		
	29. WI at Alhambra. Leaves Spain in late fall. Ferdinand marries Cristina of Naples.		
30. *Perkin Warbeck.*	30. Oct. 10. Birth of Isabella.		
			31. Nat Turner's insurrection. Garrison founds *Liberator.*
	32. Birth of Infanta Luisa.		32. JB's wife Dianthe dies.
	33. Death of Fernando VII. María Cristina as Regent. First Carlist War begins.		33. JB marries Mary Day.
		34. Wife dies. JJA withdraws from Am. Fur Co. Devotes himself to real estate, lending.	
35. *Ladore.*		35. WI with JJA at Hell Gate.	35. JB returns to Ohio.
36. Death of Godwin.	36. Republic of Texas.	36. Astor House opens on B'way.	
37. *Falkner.*			37. Panic. JB loses heavily. Abolitionist Lovejoy murdered.
		38. First steps in plans to found Astor Library.	
39. Annotated edition of Shelley's poems.	39. End of First Carlist War.		

WASHINGTON IRVING	AARON BURR	SIR WALTER SCOTT

1840

42. Dickens dinner. WI
to Madrid as envoy.

43. Madrid under siege.

44. Cristina returns. WI
to Barcelona, Paris.

1845   45. Dec. WI resigns as
envoy.
46. WI to England.
Summer. Farewells
in Madrid. Fall.
Returns to NY.
48. Putnam's Complete
Revised Edition of
WI's works begun.
49. *Life of Goldsmith.*

1850

53. Revisits Ogdensburg,
N.Y.

1855   55. *Wolfert's Roost.*
Washington, I.
56. *Washington*, II, III.

57. *Washington*, IV.

59. *Washington*, V. Nov.
28. WI dies at
Sunnyside.

MARY SHELLEY	IRVING AND SPAIN	JOHN JACOB ASTOR	JOHN BROWN
40. Mary with Percy on tour of Continent.	40. Cristina abdicates.		
	41. Espartero as Regent. Oct. Plot to kidnap queen.		
	42. WI arrives Madrid as Am. envoy. Barcelona bombarded.		42. JB declares bankruptcy.
	43. Siege of Madrid. Narváez in power. Queen of age.		43. Four of JB's children die.
44. Death of Shelley's father. Percy becomes baronet.	44. Reunion at Aranjuez.		
	45. Texas annexed to US.		
	46. WI leaves Spain. Marriage of Isabella II. Second Carlist War.	46. England recognizes US claim to Oregon country.	46-8. Mexican War.
48. Percy marries.		48. March 29. JJA dies in his town house, NYC.	48. Gold discovered in Calif.
	49. End of Second Carlist War.		49. JB in Europe on business.
			50. Compromise of 1850.
51. Feb. 1. Mary dies at Chester Sq., London.			
52. Payne dies in Tunis, age 60.	52. Attempt on Isabella's life.		
	54. Abortive revolution. Return of Espartero.		54. Five sons of JB to Kansas.
			56. Pottawatomie massacres.
	57. Birth of Isabella's son, to become Alfonso XII.		57. Dred Scott Decision.
			58. Lincoln-Douglas Debates.
			59. Oct. Raid on Harpers Ferry. Dec. 2. JB executed.
	('68. Isabella retires to France. '70. Abdicates. 1904, Apr. 9. Dies in Paris, age 73.)		

Notes and Sources of Citations

PMI refers to Irving, Pierre M., *The Life and Letters of Washington Irving*, 4 vols. (New York, 1863–64).

STW refers to Williams, Stanley T., *The Life of Washington Irving*, 2 vols. (New York, 1935).

A list of full titles of sources referred to in the notes appears on pages 565–72.

DEPARTED YEARS

1   Epigraph. Irving to R. C. Winthrop, 4-4-1853. PMI, IV 142.

2   Contemporary descriptions of John Brown. Oates, 186, 183, 237.

2   Laughter making "not the slightest sound." Recollection of Mrs. T. B. Russell, with whose family Brown was staying in April 1857. Ruchames, 236.

2   Mrs. Wilkinson about Brown. Sanborn, 267–68.

3   Watchdogs raging and barking. Same, 267.

3   Brown's "flock of sheep." Villard, 328; Hinton, 177.

3   "Worse plague than the fleas." Annie Brown Adams' recollections. Villard, 417. See also Nelson, 15.

4   Gideon, and host in flight. Judges 7:19–22. One of Brown's favorite biblical passages.

4   "God has seen fit to visit us." Brown, from Richfield, Ohio, to John, Jr., 9-25-1843. Ruchames, 50.

4   *Eternal war* with slavery." Brown, from Red Rock, Iowa, to Henry L. Stearns, 7-15-1857. Same, 38.

5   "Queer figure . . . coattails floating." Recollection of George Grant. Oates, 170.

5   "Brains" and "piece of skin." Affidavit of 6-6-1856 by James Harris, who discovered the body. Villard, 164.

5   "Blood, as with sweet wine." Isaiah 49:26. Another favorite passage.

5   "Beat up a slave quarter." Hugh Forbes to New York *Herald*, 10-27-1859.

5   "Mechanical arts" and "business of life." Oates, 245.

5   "Impressive beyond expression." Anderson, 28.

6   "Men, get on your arms." Same, 31.

6   Brown's "one unconquerable weakness." Webb, 297.

6   "Honest Rich, . . . good-hearted man." PMI, II 316; Leslie, 271.

7   Dolley "portly, buxom dame." Irving, from Washington, to Brevoort, 1-13-1811. Irving, *Letters 1802–23*, 297.

7   "Any man, in any country." W. C. Preston, from Charlottesville, Va., to Irving, 5-11-1859. PMI, IV 286.

7   "Less honored than loved." Same, 309.

7   Irving most loved American. See Hellman, *Esquire*, 341.

7   "No living writer . . . few among the dead." PMI, III 164.

7   Irving "*a great* fellow." Johnson, *Dickens*, 391.

7   "Communion with your spirit." Dickens, from Washington, to Irving, 3-21-1842. PMI, III 187.

7   Irving's "writings are my delight." Byron, from Ravenna, to Thomas Moore, 7-5-1821. Marchand, *Byron*, 912.

7   "Such a man, and such a friend." David Wilkie, from Madrid, to Thomas Lawrence, 2-11-1828. Cunningham, II 502.

7   Scott's opinion of Irving. Leslie, 217.

7   Longfellow on Irving. Address before Mass. Hist. Soc., 12-15-1859. *Irvingiana*, xxxvi.

8   Bryant on Irving's contribution. See Canby, 93.

8   Gotham. Irving, *Oldstyle, Salmagundi*, II (83), III (96), etc. Reference is to the English town where wise men could be counted on to speak nonsense.

8   The almighty dollar. "The Creole Village," *Wolfert's Roost*. Irving, *Works*, XVI 40.

8   "No irreverence was intended." Wagenknecht, 81.

8   Christmas customs. *Pickwick* appeared in 1836–37, *The Sketch Book* in 1819–20. See in the latter "Christmas," etc. Citations from "The Christmas Dinner." Irving, *The Sketch Book*, 184, 191.

8   "American authors . . . school-books excepted." Statement of H. C. Carey. STW, II 395, n. 129.

9–10   Irving and Irvington. PMI, IV 173. The five citations that follow are from the same source: II 431 ("saturnalian applause"); IV 196 ("Revolution"); IV 219 ("Since my return": Irving to Mrs. Emily Fuller [Emily Foster], 7-2-1856); IV 106 ("Rusty or fusty": 7-15-1852); III 129 ("Twice the market price": 5-18-1838).

10   "Little old-fashioned stone mansion." "A Chronicle of Wolfert's Roost," *Wolfert's Roost*. Irving, *Works*, XVI 9.

10   "Funny little in-and-out cottage." Thackeray, from New York City, to his daughter, 12-3-1852. Wilson, *Thackeray*, I 45.

10   Pig "of peerless beauty." Wagenknecht, 43.

10   "Musing" in Voltaire chair. 8-27-1847. PMI, IV 25.

10   "Horrific alarum." Pochmann, liii, n. 113.

11   Changing trains at Harpers Ferry. PMI, IV 150.

11   Account of homecoming. Irving, from Sunnyside, to Mrs. J. P. Kennedy, 3-11-1853. Same, 135–36.

11   "May be five feet six or seven." The visitor was Benjamin Silliman of Yale, 8-20-1856. Fisher, G. P., II 250.

12   "Conversation was likely to be recorded." Irving, from Sunnyside, to Charles Lanman, 5-9-1857. PMI, IV 228–29.

12   "Erratic and precarious career." Hellman, *Esquire*, 338.

12   "Now half-past twelve at night." Irving to Sarah Storrow, 1-13-1852. PMI, IV 102.

12   "My fifth volume is launched." Irving, from Sunnyside, to J. P. Kennedy, 5-11-1859. Same, 283.

12–14　"Sadly out of spirits." PMI, IV 275. Subsequent citations are from the same source; specifically, 265, 264, 296, 273, 278, 244 (Irving's earlier birthday), 290, 275 ("haunted chamber"), 272, 291, 270, 265, 300 ("looked very feeble"), 312, 280, 260, 306 ("long wind").

14　"Good God! what shall I do—" P. Irving, MS Journal, 3-3-1859.

14–15　"Played whist." PMI, IV 310. Citations to the end of the chapter are from the same source: 313, 285, 268.

YOUNG WASHINGTON IRVING & AARON BURR

17　Epigraph. 6-29-1859. PMI, IV 301.

18–19　"Our sweet infant . . . taken ill." Mrs. Burr, from Albany, to Burr, 8-14-1783. Davis, *Memoirs*, I 246.

19　"For whom else do I live?" Burr, from Albany, to Theodosia, 1-4-1799. Same, 396.

19　"I had rather not live." Theodosia, from Rocky River Springs, S.C., to Burr, 8-1-1809. Davis, *Journal*, I 285.

19　"Bastard Bratt." Adams, from Quincy, Mass., to Jefferson, 7-12-1813. Cappon, II 354.

19　Woman of "very good Sense." Joseph Shippen, Jr., to his father, 8-1-1752. Parmet and Hecht, 2.

19–22　Burr's mother's diary. Entries for 4-13-1756, 9-2-1757; Fisher, J., 300, 314–15.

22　Edwards on his future wife. Dwight, 115.

23　Burr's "handsome estate." Davis, *Memoirs*, I 25.

23–24　"Them rogues eyes of your." Mrs. Theodore Sedgwick to Burr, 8-3-1779. Parmet and Hecht, 52.

24　Intrigues "without number." Davis, *Memoirs*, I 91–92.

24　"Climeing on all fours." Journal of Matthias Ogden. Wandell and Minnigerode, I 48–49.

24　Arnold's testimony. In letter of introduction to General Richard Montgomery, 11-30-1775. Same, 52.

25　"Now is your time." Davis, *Memoirs*, I 120.

25　"Country enjoyed security." Samuel Young, from Mount Pleasant, N.Y., to Commodore Valentine Morris, 1-25-1814. Same, 165–66.

26　The Hermitage. As observed in 1974. Restorations are under way; see *New York Times*, 9-1-1977.

27　"Stroke my head with your little hand." Burr, from Albany, to Theodosia Prevost, 12-5-1781. Davis, *Memoirs*, I 233.

27　"Our being the subject of much inquiry." Mrs. Prevost, from Litchfield, Conn., to Burr, 5-1781. Same, 226.

28　"The old family nest." PMI, I 22. The description of New York in 1783 is developed primarily from Booth, Hellman's *Esquire*, Hemstreet, Lamb, and Smith.

29　Irving's mother "of elegant shape." "Recollections," 690.

29　"Every thing that was pleasant was wicked." PMI, I 25.

29　"A bairn that's called after ye." STW, I 10.

30　"I wander about the pier heads." "The Author's Account of Himself." Irving, *The Sketch Book*, 8.

31　The barber and Louis XVI. PMI, I 30–31.

31　"Ourang Outang." Smith, 183.

32 "My guardian angel." Mrs. Burr, from New York City, to Burr, 11-1787. Davis, *Memoirs*, I 279.

33 Furnishings at Richmond Hill. From bill of sale prepared in 1797. Wandell and Minnigerode, I 125–26.

33 "Most delicious spot." Abigail Adams, from New York City, to Thomas Brand-Hollis, 9-6-1790. Adams, C. F., *Letters of Mrs. Adams*, 402.

33 "The grand and sublime." Abigail Adams, from Philadelphia, to her daughter, 11-21-1790. Same, 405.

33 "Two thousand five hundred and fifty Dollars." Wandell and Minnigerode, I 123–24.

34 "A Miss Woolstonecraft." Davis, *Memoirs*, I 363. The two citations that follow are from the same source: 362 ("Your mind": 2-15-1793); 361–62 ("souls!": 2-8-1793).

34–35 Burr's letters to his daughter. Davis, *Memoirs*, I 382, 317, 388, 395, 394 (two citations), 384–85, 371, 370. [The misspelling and solecism in the next-to-last citation are Burr's.]

35 "Come . . . to your wretched." Parmet and Hecht, 67.

36 Death of Mrs. Burr. See Wandell and Minnigerode, I 113.

36 Brant "a man of education." Parmet and Hecht, 116.

36 "Nation of newspaper readers." *Port Folio*. Mott, I 160.

36 "Too small a share . . . to politics." 3-20-1802. Same, 161.

36 "The daemon of party spirit." Washington, from New York City to Gov. Arthur Fenner, 6-4-1790. Fitzpatrick, XXXI 48.

37 "Mankind . . . are vicious." Hamilton before the Constitutional Convention, 6-18, 6-22-1787. Lodge, I 382, 388.

37 "Wonderfully perfect instrument." "Answers to Questions . . ." propounded 1-24-1786. Lipscomb and Bergh, XVII 112.

37 "The most restless . . . intriguer." Adams, from Quincy, Mass., to James Lloyd, 2-17-1815. Adams, C. F., *John Adams*, X 124.

37 Jefferson's distrust of Burr. *Anas*, 1-26-1804. Padover, 1285.

38–40 Irving's Oldstyle letters. Citations are from Letters I, IV, III, and IX. Irving, *Oldstyle, Salmagundi*, 3, 4, 14, 10, 32–35.

40 Irving's first pseudonym. See Hedges, 17.

40 Burr on Oldstyle. Burr, from Washington, to Theodosia, 1-29-1804. Davis, *Memoirs*, II 274.

40 "Mewed up, during the livelong day." "The Birds of Spring," *Wolfert's Roost*. Irving, *Works*, XVI 34–35.

40 "A mile of terra incognita." "The Author's Account of Himself." Irving, *The Sketch Book*, 8.

41 "Literary carreer." So Irving was spelling the word as late as 1845, when he was past sixty. STW, II 190.

41 John Anderson's journal. Hellman, *Esquire*, 17–18.

41–42 "The ponderous fathers of the law." Irving, from New York City, to Gouverneur Kemble, 5-24-1806. PMI, I 169. The four citations that follow are from the same source: 62 ("share the world"); 63 ("overboard"); ("severest moments"); 65 ("main topsail yard": Irving, from Bordeaux, to William Irving, 7-1-1804).

42 "Scribble this nonsense." Undated entry, sometime between late January and late March, 1806. Irving, *Journals 1803–06*, 580. [Two dashes inserted for clarity, after "flute" and "scolds."]

43 "A *young man* and in *Paris*." Irving, from Paris, to Peter Irving, 7-15-1805. PMI, I 150. The four citations that follow are from the same source: 153 ("vice": to Peter Irving, 10-20-1805); 155

("small-clothes": from London, to William Irving, 10-1805); 78 ("insolence"); 87 ("convent bell").

43   "A taste to suit my dinner." 8-10-1804. Irving, *Journals 1803–06*, 86.

43–44   "I recognized the house." Irving, from Paris, to Mrs. Catharine Paris, 11-1-1845. PMI, I 72.

44   Bordeaux girls and New York girls. 7-13-1804. Irving, *Journals 1803–06*, 43. The five citations that follow are from the same source: 140 ("freedom": 12-1804); 194 ("shut up" and "Sicily": 2-10-1805); 206 ("handsome nuns": 2-14-1805); 524 ("lascavious gestures"; Sunday, 2-10-1805; see Wagenknecht, 128).

44–46   Irving and the pirates. 12-30-1804. The letter to William Irving describing the encounter is in Irving, *Letters 1802–23*, 145–48. Citations are from that source. Compare Irving, *Journals 1803–06*, 148–52.

46   "*Gallop through Italy.*" William Irving to Irving, 7-8-1805. PMI, I 139–40.

46   "Never meddle any more in politicks." 10-27-1804. Irving, *Letters 1802–23*, 106.

46–47   "*Pet* or *Peet.*" Burr to Theodosia, 2-23-1802. Davis, *Memoirs*, II 178.

47   "*Ere this have been president.*" Federalist Congressman William Cooper to Thomas Morris, 2-13-1801. Same, 113.

47   "Opinion . . . of serious . . . men." 12-2-1800. Morris, A. C., II 396–97.

47–48   "The wishes . . . of the United States." Burr, from New York City, to Representative Smith of Maryland, 12-16-1800. Davis, *Memoirs*, II 75.

48   "The fictions of slander." Burr, from New York City, to unidentified correspondent, 10-6-1799. Same, I 423.

48   "A religious duty." Hamilton to unknown correspondent, 9-21-1792. Syrett and Cooke, 17. Lamb (II 387) identifies the correspondent as Rufus King.

49   Philanderers. Mitchell, B. (II 399), is authority for the assertion concerning Hamilton's faithfulness to his wife.

49   "18 to ask 45." Lamb, II 386–87.

49   Hamilton "vain, and opinionated." 7-13-1804. Morris, A. C., II 456.

49   Hamilton's opinions of Adams. Morris, R. B., 532.

49   His opinions of Jefferson. Hamilton to James A. Bayard, 1-16-1801. Same, 540.

49   And of Burr. Same, 537, 536. Wandell and Minnigerode, I 207.

50   Jefferson "a contemptible hypocrite." Hamilton to James A. Bayard, 1-16-1801. Morris, R. B., 540.

50   Adams on the Vice Presidency. Syrett and Cooke, 32.

50   Hamilton "intriguing . . . against A. B." Burr, from New York City, to Theodosia, 2-16-1804. Davis, *Memoirs*, II 277.

50   Campaign attacks against Burr. Wandell and Minnigerode, I 265–72.

50–51   "Election is lost . . . *tant mieux.*" Burr, from New York City, to Theodosia, 5-1-1804. Davis, *Memoirs*, II 285.

51   Effect "present and palpable." Burr, from New York City, to Hamilton, 6-21-1804 (a phrase in the correspondence preceding the duel). Syrett and Cooke, 58.

51   "First man of any respectability." Biddle, C., 305.

51–53   Burr-Hamilton correspondence. The entire correspondence is conveniently available in the well-edited volume of Syrett and Cooke.

51   "My animadversions." Hamilton's remarks on the impending duel, New York, 6-27 to 7-4-1804. Syrett and Cooke, 100.

51-52 "A still more despicable opinion." Dr. Charles Cooper, from Albany, to Philip Schuyler, 4-23-1804. Same, 48.

52   "A variety of engagements." Same, 50.

53   "A disappointed and mortified man." "Veritas," in New York *American-Citizen*, 8-8-1804, p. 2, col. 3.

54   Letters on the eve of the duel. Burr later expressed disgust for Hamilton's letter, which, he said, "read like the confession of a penitent monk." Todd, 31. Correspondence in Syrett and Cooke.

54   "I have called out General Hamilton." Davis, *Memoirs*, II 325–26.

56   "Take care of that pistol." Account of Dr. David Hosack to William Coleman, 8-17-1804. Coleman, 20–21.

56   *"Remember, my Eliza."* Same, 23.

56   "Adieu best of wives." Hamilton, from New York City, to Elizabeth Hamilton, 7-4-1804. Syrett and Cooke, 111.

57   "These things must have an end." Burr, at Richmond Hill, to Van Ness, a verbal communication for Hamilton, 6-22-1804. Syrett and Cooke, 69.

57   "I must go and speak to him." Van Ness's recollection. Same, 155.

57   "Burr has killed General Hamilton!" Parton, *Burr*, II 13.

57   "Present state of Gen¹. H." Burr, from New York City, to Dr. David Hosack, 7-12-1804. Syrett and Cooke, 143.

57   "Voltaire less." The remark was provoked by hearing a reading from *Tristram Shandy* concerning the gentleness of my Uncle Toby, who could not kill a fly. Hague, 78.

57   "Odium on . . . Burr." Hamilton's remarks on the impending duel, New York, 6-27 to 7-4-1804. Syrett and Cooke, 101.

58   "Hamilton died yesterday." Burr, from Richmond Hill, to Joseph Alston, 7-13-1804. Davis, *Memoirs*, II 327.

58   "Insulted majesty of the law." Coleman, 47.

58   An "unexampled measure." Burr to Joseph Alston, 7-18-1804. Davis, *Memoirs*, II 327.

58   "I propose leaving town." Burr to Alston, 7-13-1804. Same, 327.

59   "A dish of good coffee." Parton, *Burr*, II 16.

59   "A hearty welcome." Same, 17.

59   "Drinking the nasty puddle-water." Burr, from Lexington, Ky., to Theodosia, 5-23-1805. Davis, *Memoirs*, II 373.

60   "One of the best presiding officers." Wandell and Minnigerode, I 219.

60   "Angel, but . . . devil." Burr, from Washington, quoting to Theodosia, 3-13-1805. Davis, *Memoirs*, II 360.

60   This house a "sanctuary." Parmet and Hecht, 230–31.

60   "Sympathy of the Senators." Senator Samuel Mitchill of New York, as quoted in Wandell and Minnigerode, I 323.

61   "Take a Bed with you." Wilkinson to Burr, 5-23-1804. Ford, W. C., 122.

61   "Booted to the middle." *Knickerbocker.* Irving, *Works*, I 313.

62   Wilkinson's prose. McCaleb, 205. Adams, H., III 315–16. Wilkinson, II, Appendix XCIX, C.

62   Burr's elegant flatboat. Burr, from Pittsburgh, to Theodosia, 4-30-1805. Davis, *Memoirs*, II 368.

62-63 Blennerhassett's island. The description is based on Schneider, 7–8.

63   Blennerhassett's reason for fleeing Ireland. Blennerhassett-Adams, 353.

63   "Honored in being associated with you." Blennerhassett to Burr, 12-21-1805. Safford, 118.

63   "Frank, ardent souls." Burr, from Lexington, Ky., to Theodosia, 5-23-1805. Davis, *Memoirs*, II 372.

64   "A corps of volunteers." Burr to John Smith; Smith to Jefferson, 3-27-1807, as quoted in McCaleb, 183.

64–65   "A host of choice spirits." The text of the letter, dated 7-29-1806, is printed entire as Appendix D of Beveridge, III 614–15. Compare Parmet and Hecht, 251–52.

65   "No enterprise too hazardous." Hamilton to John Rutledge, 1-4-1801. Parmet and Hecht, 124.

65   "Separate them, if it be better." Jefferson, from Monticello, to John Breckenridge, 8-12-1803. Lipscomb and Bergh, X 410.

65   "All will be settled." Burr to Wilkinson, in cipher, 7-29-1806. Beveridge, III 615.

66   "I pledge you my honour." Burr, from Louisville, to Gov. Harrison. Clark, Appendix 17.

66   "More . . . from the *manner*." Presley Neville and Samuel Roberts, from Cannonsburg, Pa., to Madison, 10-7-1806. Schachner, 326.

66   Wilkinson *v.* the Spanish. Beveridge, III 314–15.

66–67   Wilkinson writes Jefferson. Natchitoches, 10-21-1806. Wilkinson, II, Appendix XCV.

67   "Dark and wicked conspiracy." Wilkinson, from near Natchez, to Jefferson, 11-12-1806. Wilkinson, II, Appendix C.

67   Jefferson's proclamation. Ford, P. L., VIII 481 ["knolege" as in source].

67   Flotilla "bound to market." Quoted in Beveridge, III 361. My description of the flotilla derives from Todd, 38.

67   "Dirks & Pistolls." Schachner, 380.

67–68   "For five thousand dollars." Wilkinson to Silas Dinsmore, 12-4-1806. McCaleb, 275.

68   "A miracle of beauty." Same, 278.

68   "My great offense." Lieutenant Edmund Pendleton Gaines to Wilkinson, 3-4-1807. Same, 279.

69   "I am Aaron Burr." Parton, *Burr*, II 101.

69   "Tried and concluded." Burr, from Richmond, to Theodosia, 3-27-1807. Davis, *Memoirs*, II 405. See Parmet and Hecht, 284.

69–70   Brown's family moves West. All citations in the section are from the mature Brown's description of his childhood, written from Red Rock, Iowa, to young Henry L. Stearns, 7-15-1857. Ruchames, 35–41.

70   A "*travelled man*." STW, II 256.

70   Mumford the favorite. PMI, I 163.
      "Paris by the Tail." 5-28-1805. Irving, *Journals 1803–06*, 422. The six citations that follow (through "the engineer's *lady*") are from the same source: 285 (4-5-1805); 80 (Marseille, 8-27-1804); 131 (11-14-1804); 135 (12-1804); 221 (3-1-1805); 88–89 (9-

70–71   11-1804).

71–72   Irving's youthful letters. PMI, I 187, 172, 181. The three citations that follow (through "*D——d* little") are from the same source: 168, 166, 173.

72   "Technical rubbish." "Captain James Lawrence." Irving, *Spanish Papers*, II 38.

72   "What a Salmagundi is." No. I, 1-24-1807. Irving, *Oldstyle, Salmagundi*, 67.

73   "The man I most loved on earth." PMI, I 63.

73   "Nonsense and 'Salmagund.'" Thomas Green Fessenden, in the *Weekly Spectator*. Leary, 14.

73   "Mr. Jefferson's * * * * *." Irving, *Oldstyle, Salmagundi*, 75.

74   Fungus on *Salmagundi*. No. II, 2-4-1807. Same, 81.

74   "Tending Burrs trial." Irving to Mary Fairlie. Irving, *Letters 1802–23*, 234.

74   "Enchanted with Richmond." PMI, I 196.

75   "I set off for Richmond." Irving to Mary Fairlie. Irving, *Letters 1802–23*, 236. The description of Richmond in 1807 is based principally on Beveridge and Beirne.

75   "A veto on that." 6-29-1859. PMI, IV 301.

75   Burr "retains his serenity." Irving, from Richmond, to Mrs. Hoffman, 6-4-1807. Irving, *Letters 1802–23*, 238.

76   "Culpable to evince . . . sympathy." Irving, from Washington, to Mary Fairlie [?], 7-7-1807. Irving, *Letters 1802–23*, 244.

76   "Where his history will end." Jefferson to George Morgan, 3-26-1807. McCaleb, 315.

76   "Guilt is placed beyond question." Ford, P. L., IX 15.

76   Adams on Burr's guilt. Adams to Benjamin Rush, 2-2-1807. Biddle, A., 129.

76   Halter should "get its due." Jefferson to Gov. Langdon, 12-22-1806. McCaleb, 288.

77   "Judiciary as a stronghold." Beirne, 51.

77   "Aid and Comfort." Constitution, Article III, Section 3.

78   Toasting Aaron Burr. Parton, *Burr*, II 127.

78   "Canova's living marbles." Scott, Winfield, *Memoirs*, 13. "It was there [at Richmond] that I first made the acquaintance of this charming man and distinguished author [Irving]—an agreeable acquaintance continued through England, France, and America, down to his death." Same, 15.

78   "Dangerous . . . to acquit." Safford, 465.

78   Jackson on Burr. Parton, *Burr*, II 107. Parton, *Jackson*, I 334–35.

79   "Col Burr at liberty." Irving, from Washington, to Mary Fairlie[?], 7-7-1807. Irving, *Letters 1802–23*, 244–45.

79   "Most unpleasant case." Beirne, 277.

79   Marshall on the subpoena. Coombs, 52.

80   "Day after day." Irving, from Richmond, to Mrs. Hoffman, 6-4-1807. Irving, *Letters 1802–23*, 238.

80   Irving on Maison Carrée. Irving, *Journals 1803–06*, 71, 72.

80   "Finest & richest girls." Irving, from Fredericksburg, Va., to Mary Fairlie, 5-13-1807. Irving, *Letters 1802–23*, 236.

80–81   Irving and Cabell. Irving, *Journals 1803–06*, 405, 417.

81   "An old fellow traveller." "The Stage Coach." Irving, *The Sketch Book*, 157.

81   "An *interesting young man*." Irving, from Washington, to Mary Fairlie[?], 7-7-1807. Irving, *Letters 1802–23*, 244.

81   "W is a pensioner." John Randolph to Judge Joseph H. Nicholson, 5-31-1807. Beirne, 120.

81–82   Irving on Wilkinson's entrance. Irving to James Kirke Paulding, 6-22-1807. Irving, *Letters 1802–23*, 239–40.

82   Wilkinson's version. To Jefferson, 6-17-1807. Beveridge, III 457.

82   "What a spectacle." Beirne, 124.

      "Busy, busy, busy." Burr, from Richmond, to Theodosia, 6-3-1807.

82   Davis, *Memoirs*, II 406.

82   "Really were an Emperor." 8-13-1807. Safford, 324.

82   "The wondrous cargo." Irving, from Richmond, to Paulding, 6-22-1807. Irving, *Letters 1802–23*, 239.

82–83   "The most finished scoundrel." Randolph, from Richmond, to Joseph Nicholson, 6-28-1807. Schachner, 422.

83   "The mammoth of iniquity." Randolph, from Richmond, to Nicholson, 6-25-1807. Adams, H., III 458.

83   Indictment against Burr. Coombs, 140–41.

83   "Treasonable *intent*." Luther Martin, 8-17-1807. Robertson, I 461.

84   Truxtun's testimony. Coombs, 167.

84   "Federal bull-dog." Jefferson, from Washington, to Hay, 6-19-1807. Ford, P. L., IX 58.

84   Speeches in court. See Robertson, I 128 ("hell-hounds": Luther Martin, 6-10-1807); II 96–97 ("Who is Blennerhassett?": William Wirt, 8-25-1807).

84   "Every kind of sense." Dudley Woodbridge's testimony. Beirne, 187.

84–85   Burr invites Theodosia to Richmond. Burr to Theodosia, 7-24-1807. Davis, *Memoirs*, II 410.

85   "A scene of uninterrupted gayety." Todd, 67–68.

85   Irving's visit to Burr in prison. Irving, from Washington, to Mary Fairlie[?], 7-7-1807. Irving, *Letters 1802–23*, 245.

86   "I visited Burr this morning." Safford, 402.

86   "About fifteen hundred." 11-3-1807. Same, 481.

86   "I firmly believe." Mrs. Blennerhassett to her husband, concerning their son Dominick. Schneider, 31.

87   "The trip to the other world." Abernethy, 273.

87   Self-judgments of Wilkinson. Beirne, 257; McCaleb, 337.

88–91   "Left in a skiff." Bixby, I 1. Sources of passages derived from Burr's Journal are sequentially as follows: 12-5-1808, I 29 ("Lamb"); 1-3-10, I 350; 7-11-09, I 165 ("memorandum"); 12-3-08, I 27; 4-4-09, I 93; 12-12-08, I 36 ("pipe"); 5-1-09, I 101; 11-29-09, I 282 ("tooth"); 2-2-10, I 398 ("rooms"); 9-1-11, II 239 (fleas); 12-4-09, I 290–91 ("bite"); 6-13-09, I 138 (three women); 12-8-10, II 73; 10-23-09, I 250 (chambermaid); 10-25-09, I 253; 5-17-11, II 146–48 (nobleman's wife).

91   "It was his theory." Davis, *Journal*, I vi.

91   "X is abandoned!" Theodosia, from New York, to Burr, 10-31-1808. Davis, *Journal*, I 72.

91–92   *"Pensant a T."* Bixby, I 12 (11-17-1808). The four citations that follow are from the same source: 11-21-08, I 14 ("about you"); 11-28-08, I 21 ("non-existence"); 1-17-09, I 58 ("Erskine"); 11-30-08, I 23 ("jubilee").

92   "Your presence threw a lustre." Davis, *Journal*, I 75.

92   "Dr. P. Irving." Theodosia, from New York, to Burr, 1-3-1809. Davis, *Journal*, I 130.

92   "I had rather not live." Theodosia, from Rocky River Springs, S.C., to Burr, 8-1-1809. Same, 285.

92   "I can only thank you." Burr, from Göteborg, Sweden, to Theodosia, 10-13-1809. Same, 315–16.

92   "Burying you *alive*." Bixby, I 267 (11-18-1809). The thirteen citations that follow are from the same source: 11-8-09, I 263

93–95 ("picture"); same ("Gampy"); 11-24-09, I 274 ("A. B."); 9-6-10, I 477–78 ("heart kick"); 4-25-10, I 438 ("rascal's"); 6-14-11, II 175; 9-12-11, II 244 ("heighho" and "we shall go"); 9-14-11, II 245 ("windows"); 4-23-12, II 422–23 (iceberg); 4-25-12, II 425 ("moon"); 5-7-12, II 436 ("wig"); 5-30-12, II 459; 6-8-12, II 477.

95 Aaron Burr had returned. Parton, *Burr*, II 245.

95 Theodosia's letter. Davis, *Journal*, II 439.

95 "Gamp. is well." Same, 398.

95–96 "Alas! my dear father." Theodosia, from Seashore, S.C., to Burr, 8-12-1812. Same, 439–40.

96 "Anxiety into dread." "The Voyage." Irving, *The Sketch Book*, 13.

96–97 "I am miserable." Alston, from Columbia, S.C., to Burr, 1-19-1813. Davis, *Memoirs*, II 429. The four citations that follow are from the same source: 431 (2-25-1813); 437 (2-16-1816); 441 (8-6-1805); 433 (10-16-1815).

97 "That queer little old man." Duncan, 262.

97 "Some terrible old man." The child was James Parton, who became Burr's biographer. Parton, *Burr*, I xii.

97 "*Je n'aime pas.*" Bixby, II 146.

98 "One good turn." Nevins, *Hone*, I 98.

98 "I don't see him any more." 6-19-1834. Dunlap, III 796.

98 "I once knew Aaron Burr." Todd, 61–62.

98 "Little dirty Noisy Boy." Fisher, J., 315.

98 "Unprincipled and dangerous." Hamilton to James A. Bayard, 8-6-1800. Morris, R. B., 536.

99 Jackson on Burr. Orally to John Overton, 5-29-1806. Beirne, 80.

99 Adams on Burr. 11-16-1837. Nevins, *Adams*, 487.

99 Mme. Jumel on Burr. Duncan, 246.

99 Theodosia on Burr. Davis, *Journal*, I 75.

99 Irving on Burr. PMI, I 191.

99 "I am not a libertine." Wandell and Minnigerode, II 340.

99 "What manner of man." Todd, 62.

THE GREAT UNKNOWN
& GEOFFREY CRAYON, GENT.

101 Epigraph. 10-31-1858. PMI, IV 261.

102 "Snug gentleman's cottage." "Abbotsford," *The Crayon Miscellany*. Irving, *Works*, IX 202.

103 "Scott's family well remember." Lockhart, IV 88. Lockhart's wife Sophia was Scott's daughter—and present at the breakfast table, nearly eighteen at the time and as yet unmarried.

103–6 "I knew him at once." "Abbotsford," *The Crayon Miscellany*. Irving, *Works*, IX 202–3. The five citations that follow (through "auld world trumpery") are from the same source: 203–4.

106 "Burr was acquitted." Pochmann, xix, n. 16.

107 "Parody a small hand-book." "The Author's Apology," *Knickerbocker*. Irving, *Works*, I 11. This and the two citations that follow (through "I altered the plan") are from the explanation that Irving wrote in 1848 to accompany the revised edition.

107 "It took with the public." Manuscript Fragment. STW, II 258.

107–8   Scott's response to *Knickerbocker*. Scott, from Abbotsford, to Brevoort, 4-23-1813. PMI, I 240.

108   "Too honest and too sincere." Brevoort, from London, to Irving, 6-24-1813. Same, 300.

108   Modern judgments of *Knickerbocker*. Robert E. Spiller and others, *Literary History of the United States* (New York, 1953), 244; Walter Fuller Taylor, *A History of American Letters* (Boston, 1936), 96; George Haven Putnam in *The Cambridge History of American Literature* (New York, 1917), I 254; Saxe Commins, *Selected Writings of Washington Irving* (New York, 1945), xviii, xi.

108–9   "Divers ingenious theories." *Knickerbocker*. Irving, *Works*, I 35. The twelve citations that follow are from the same source: 86 ("trumpet"), 215, 211 (inventions), 220, 434 ("economy"), 521, 313, 312 ("windy"), 354, 399, 177, 246–47 ("Minuits").

109   "The style of Dean Swift." Scott, from Abbotsford, to Brevoort, 4-23-1813. PMI, I 240.

110–11   "Bull hides of the invincible Ajax." *Knickerbocker*. Irving, *Works*, I 177. The six citations that follow are from the same source: 295 ("trumpet"), 247, 95 ("poop"), 100, 381, 385 ("ox-fly").

111   "The traditions of our city." "The Author's Apology," *Knickerbocker*. Irving, *Works*, I 13. The two citations that follow are from the same source: 12, 14.

111–12   "A wretched state of doubt." Manuscript Fragment. STW, II 257. The seven citations that follow (through "any romantic story") are from the same source: 256–58.

112   "Engaged every day to dine." STW, I 91.

112   "A withered little apple-John." Irving, from Washington, 1-13-1811. Irving, *Letters 1802–23*, 297.

112   "His travels . . . go a great way." Mary E. Fenno, from New York, to G. C. Verplanck, 12-29-[1810?]. STW, I 91.

113   "D——d stringy." Irving, from New York, to Brevoort, 7-8-1812. Irving, *Letters 1802–23*, 340.

113   "Honestly rodgers." Irving, from New York, to Brevoort, 6-8-1811. Same, 322.

113   "To Hamilton's monument." Irving, from New York, to Mrs. Hoffman, 6-23-1810. Same, 287.

113   "Reading Lady of the Lake." Notebook, 1810. PMI, I 254.

113   Dealers in "whitehead . . . &c." *New York Gazette*, 3-1-1811: "P. & E. Irving & Co., 162 Front Street." STW, I 126.

113   "Your other habits and pursuits." Peter Irving, from London, to Irving, 5-31-1810. PMI, I 257.

113   "A musselmans paradise." Irving, from Philadelphia, to Brevoort, 4-11-1811. Irving, *Letters 1802–23*, 314.

113   "No prospect ahead." Irving, from Albany, to Mrs. Hoffman, 2-26-1810. Same, 284.

113   "Among hardware and cutlery." 5-15-1811. *Irvingiana*, ix.

113   "Up hill work." PMI, I 253.

114   "Not ambitious of being either wise or facetious." *Analectic Magazine*, 3-1814. STW, I 416.

114   "Never again undertake the editorship." Irving, from Philadelphia, to G. C. Verplanck, 1-21-1815. Irving, *Letters 1802–23*, 387.

114   "Nothing so irksome as having nothing to do." Irving, from New York, to Peter Irving, 12-30-1812. Same, 351.

114   "Break off . . . from idle habits." Manuscript Fragment. STW, II 259.

115–16   John Brown's youth. Citations in the section, with the one exception below, are from John Brown's letter, from Red Rock, Iowa, to Henry L. Stearns, 7-15-1857. Ruchames, 37–38.

115   "Fashionable dissipation." Irving, Manuscript Fragment. STW, II 259.

116   "I am like another being." Irving, from Birmingham, to Brevoort, 7-5-1815. Irving, *Letters 1802–23*, 399. The two citations that follow are from the same source: 397–99.

116   "Do not be unhappy about me." Theodosia Burr Alston, from New York City, to Burr, 1-3-1809. Davis, *Journal*, I 130.

116   "He lives like a man of sense." PMI, I 333.

116   "Your part in our little partnership." Peter Irving, from England, to Irving, early 1810. Same, 256.

117   Irving at Chepstow. Same, 336–37.

117   "I . . . made them teach me." "Autobiographical Notes of Washington Irving," 5-16-1857. STW, I 150.

118   "The whole tenor of my life." Quoted by Edward Everett, undated. Same, 150.

118   "I have no intention." Irving, to Ebenezer Irving, late 1815. PMI, I 346.

118   "Anxious days and sleepless nights." Irving, from Liverpool. Same, 347.

118   "Dry rubbish of accounts." Irving, from Liverpool, to Mrs. Jane Renwick, 4-5-1816. Irving, *Letters 1802–23*, 440. ["Leisure" and "liesure" as in source.]

118   "Mud of Liverpool." Irving, from Liverpool, to Brevoort, 10-17-1815. Irving, *Letters 1802–23*, 426. The three citations that follow are from the same source; all were written from Birmingham: 12-28-1815, 430; 7-16-1816, 449; 11-6-1816, 457.

118   "Own individual interests." Irving to William Irving. PMI, I 357.

118–19   "Disliked the very name." Manuscript Fragment. STW, II 259. The seven citations that follow (through "affection of a son") are from the same source, same page.

119   "Nothing . . . would induce me to remain." Irving, from Liverpool, to Brevoort, 3-24-1817. Irving, *Letters 1802–23*, 474.

119   "Your letter urging my return." Irving, from Birmingham, to Brevoort, 5-26-1817. Same, 481.

119–20   "I took my resolution." Manuscript Fragment. STW, II 260.

120   Edinburgh "remarkably picturesque." 8-26-1817. Irving, *Tour*, 28.

120   "At the gate of Abbots Ford." Same, 39–40.

120   "Golden hearted old worthy." Irving, from Abbotsford, to Peter Irving, 9-1-1817. Irving, *Letters 1802–23*, 501.

120–21   Scream "like a bullcalf." Scott, from Edinburgh, to John Morritt, 3-18-1817. Grierson, IV 414. The two citations that follow are from the same source: 414–15.

121   Scott on a Highland pony. [Gillies], 237.

121   Avoiding what "tends to acidity." Scott, from Abbotsford, to John Morritt, 8-11-1817. Grierson, IV 493.

121   "Household affairs to attend to." "Abbotsford," *The Crayon Miscellany*. Irving, *Works*, IX 204.

122   "I am *not* the Author of *Waverley*." Pope-Hennessy, 149.

122–23   "Gray waving hills." "Abbotsford," *The Crayon Miscellany*. Irving,

Works, IX 216. The four citations that follow (through "native dialects") are from the same source: 213, 204, 226, 227.

123   "Sunshine that plays round his heart." Irving, from Abbotsford, to Peter Irving, 9-1-1817. Irving, *Letters 1802–23*, 501.

123   Scott "in his ordinary dress." STW, I 422, n. 105.

123–24   "Under the roof of Scott." "Abbotsford," *The Crayon Miscellany.* Irving, *Works*, IX 229. The five citations that follow (through "future glory") are from the same source: 229–30, 243, 246, 248.

125   "Grim features / glared." Scott, *Works.* Introduction to Canto Third, *Marmion*, 105.

125–26   "Uncommonly healthy." Autobiographical Notes, 1808. Lockhart, I 14. The three citations that follow are from the same source: 14–17.

126   "In a *clean clean* parlor." Lockhart, I 83–84.

126   "To stand, to walk, and to run." Autobiographical Notes, 1808. Lockhart, I 20. The two citations that follow are from the same source: 17, 3.

126   "And still I thought . . ." Scott, *Works.* Introduction to Canto Third, *Marmion*, 104–5.

127   Trusting "my juvenile reminiscences." Autobiographical Notes, 1808. Lockhart, I 21.

127   "The bursts of applause." Lockhart, I 85.

127   "Indulged brat." Autobiographical Notes, 1808. Lockhart, I 25. The citation that follows is from the same source: 26.

127   *"Suppressed bitterness."* Lockhart, I 98.

127   "What a godsend." Pope-Hennessy, 23.

128   Reading Shakespeare in his mother's bedroom. Autobiographical Notes, 1808. Lockhart, I 36.

128   Young Scott at Kelso. Same, 34, 38–39.

128   "The huge Platanus had died." Scott, "Essay on Landscape Gardening" (1828); quoted in Lockhart, I 116.

129   "Unhappy years . . . ?" 4-4-1826. Scott, *Journal*, 124–25.

129   "A roaring boy in my youth." 3-21-1827. Same, 290.

129   "Wilderness of forms and conveyances." Lockhart, I 44.

129   Law's "musty arts." Fyfe, 53. The phrase "law's dry, musty arts" appears in Burns' verse epistle "To William Simpson of Ochiltree" (1785).

130   "German language and the Lowland Scottish." Quoted in Lockhart, I 204.

130   "Love and Ambition awaking." 3-28-1826. Scott, *Journal*, 121.

130   Laboring "hard and well." Lockhart, I 44.

130   "Laughing or roaring and singing." Sheriff Robert Shortreed's testimony. Same, 198, 195–96.

131   A *"gangrel scrape-gut."* Lockhart, I 152.

131   "You my closet are." Johnson, *Scott*, 70.

131   *"Chère adorable."* Scott, from Rosebank, to William Clerk, 9-30-1792. Grierson, I 25. Compare 6-16-1827: Scott, *Journal*, 315.

131   "Kind honest friend." 1-20-1826. Scott, *Journal*, 62.

131–32   "What a life mine has been." 12-18-1825. Same, 42–43.

132   Charlotte's suitors. Pope-Hennessy, 53.

132   Irving about Scott's wife. "Abbotsford," *The Crayon Miscellany.* Irving, *Works*, IX 234–35.

132   Scott's "nonsense." Pope-Hennessy, 237.

132 "Wrap you in *my Tartan plaid*." Scott, from Edinburgh, to Charlotte Carpenter, 11-28-1797. Grierson, XII 78.

133 "All might be safely confided." 5-11-1826. Scott, *Journal*, 142.

133 "Bad dreams about poor Charlotte." 6-11-1826. Same, 157.

134 "Resembling the style of Dean Swift." Scott, from Abbotsford, to Brevoort, 4-23-1813. PMI, I 240.

134 "The last of all the Bards." Scott, *Works. The Lay of the Last Minstrel*, 1.

134 "Scott's vivacity and force." Cockburn, 211.

134 "My staff, but not my crutch." Scott, *Works*. Introduction to *The Lay of the Last Minstrel*, xxvii.

135 "Advances were like . . . Napoleon." Cockburn, 212.

135 "Called on Walter Scott." Bixby, I 46–47: 1-1-1809. Burr, from London, to Theodosia, 2-15-1809. Davis, *Journal*, I 172.

135 "A *Scotch novel* on the stocks." Lockhart, II 201.

135 "Enough to tear me to pieces." Same, 173.

135 "The post-horse duty in Scotland." Testimony of Robert Cadell. Quoted in Lockhart, II 292.

136 "Monarch of Parnassus." Byron's journal, 11-24-1813. Quennell, I 220. "To the Monarch of Parnassus from one of his subjects": inscription by Byron to Scott in a presentation copy of *The Giaour* (published June 1813). Pope-Hennessy, 157–58.

136 "The reign of Scott." Fyfe, 217.

136 "I like the man." Byron's journal, 11-17-1813. Quennell, I 210.

136 "The sons of song." Byron, *Works. Poetry*, I 311–12.

136 "The noble imp of fame." Scott, to Robert Southey, 8-7-1809. Grierson, II 214.

137 "A poem of most extraordinary power." Scott, from Abbotsford, to John Morritt, 5-4-1812. Grierson, III 114–15.

137 Scott's first letter to Byron. Scott, from Edinburgh, to Byron, 4-3-1812. Grierson, III 137–38.

137 And Byron's reply. Byron, from London, to Scott, 7-6-1812. Marchand, *Letters*, II 182.

137–38 Joanna Baillie's letter. Joanna Baillie, from London, to Scott, 2-21-1817. *Familiar Letters*, I 415.

138 "A thorough good man." Byron, from Genoa, to Henri Beyle, 5-29-1823. Quennell, II 733.

138 "Pseudo-romance of pseudo-chivalry." Buchan, 104.

138 "Byron hits the mark." Quayle, 81.

139 Lockhart's anecdote. Lockhart, III 128–29. But compare Johnson, *Scott*, I lxiv, n. 82.

140 "Motive for publishing . . . anonymously." Scott, *Works*. Introduction to *Waverley*, xxv, xxvi.

140 "Instant and universal" impression. Cockburn, 281. The citation that follows is from the same source, same page.

140 "Mr. Wright, the author of *Waverley*." Pope-Hennessy, 149.

141 "With such a work, Doctor." Lockhart, VI 57.

142 A "snug little dinner." Lockhart, III 341.

142 "A cottage & a few fields." Scott, from Ashestiel, to James Ballantyne, 5-12-1811. Grierson, II 492–93.

143 "I assure your ladyship." Scott, from Ashestiel, to Lady Alvanley, 5-25-1812. Grierson, III 122.

143 "Armour, advertised." Scott, to Daniel Terry, 6-20-1813. Lockhart, III 64.

143–44   "Social, Joyous, full of anecdote." 8-27-1817. Irving, *Tour*, 31.

144   "Laidlaw, to-morrow morning." "Abbotsford," *The Crayon Miscellany*. Irving, *Works*, IX 266.

144   "I felt happiness then." Irving to Duyckinck. *Irvingiana*, viii.

144–45   "Jeffrey was delightful." 10-31-1858. PMI, IV 260–61.

145   Scott's pronunciation. Scott, *Journal:* Preface [by W. E. K. Anderson], viii.

145   "Half a hundred scribblers." Irving, from Paris, to Richard Rush, 10-28-1820. Irving, *Letters 1802–23*, 600.

146   "An imitation of Washington Irving." 5-28-1826. Scott, *Journal*, 151.

146   "Guter Wein gute Milch." Notebook, 1818. STW, I 166.

147   "I left abbots ford." Irving, from Edinburgh, to Peter Irving, 9-6-1817. Irving, *Letters 1802–23*, 502–3.

147   "Scott is the author." 8-27-1817. Irving, *Tour*, 31.

147   "By chaize, by coach, by gig." Irving, from Edinburgh, to Peter Irving, 9-20-1817. Irving, *Letters 1802–23*, 504.

147   "My tour in the Highlands." Irving, from Hawick, to Scott, 9-23-1817. Same, 507.

147–48   Notes on the tour. Irving, *Tour*, 45–46; 48 (Sterling, 9-9-1817).

148   "Devouring melancholy." Irving, *Notes* 79 [original indents after both dashes]. The three citations that follow are from the same source: 64, 70 ("lovd"), 55.

148   "Why . . . go home." Irving, *Tour*, 104–5.

148–49   "Excessively disappointed." Irving, from Hawick, to Scott, 9-23-1817. Irving, *Letters 1802–23*, 507–8.

149   "Best & pleasantest acquaintances." Scott, from Abbotsford, to John Richardson, 9-22-1817. Grierson, IV 532.

149   "Gentleman dressed in black." Yarborough, 425–26.

149   "Your letter of Aug. 20th." Irving, from Liverpool, to Brevoort, 10-10-1817. Irving, *Letters 1802–23*, 508.

149   "You may get married." "Abbotsford," *The Crayon Miscellany*. Irving, *Works*, IX 264.

150   "I long to see you all." Irving, from Liverpool, to Mrs. Hoffman, 11-23-1817. Irving, *Letters 1802–23*, 513–14.

150   "Thump, thump, thump." "Autobiographical Notes of Washington Irving," 5-16-1857. STW, I 151–52. The citation that follows continues the passage from that source.

150   "This loathsome entanglement." Irving, from Liverpool, to Brevoort, 1-28-1818. Irving, *Letters 1802–23*, 516–17.

150–51   Ogilvie's letter to Irving. Ogilvie, from London, to Irving, 7-22-1817. PMI, I 369–70. [Original indents after "awakened" and "mockery."]

151   "New life & health." Notebook, 1818. STW, I 165.

152   "Building up a fortune. Irving, from Leamington, to Brevoort, 7-7-1818. Irving, *Letters 1802–23*, 528.

152–53   "Whoever has made a voyage." "Rip Van Winkle." Irving, *The Sketch Book*, 29. The three citations that follow are from the same source: 38.

153   Who is it that can tell me who I am? *Lear*, I iv.

153   "It had all come back to him." E. Burritt, "The Birthplace of Rip Van Winkle," *Packard's Monthly* (11-1869), 333–34. STW, I 169.

153–54   "Roof fallen in." "Rip Van Winkle." Irving, *The Sketch Book*, 36. The six citations that follow are from the same story: 32, 34, 31.

155 "Commodore Decatur informed me." William Irving, from New York, to Irving, 10-24-1818. STW, I 170.

155 "Proud mind and an empty purse." "The Wife." Irving, *The Sketch Book*, 25.

155 "Attending to literary pursuits." Irving, to Ebenezer Irving, 11-1818. Irving, *Letters 1802–23*, 536.

155 "Days in the best of society." William Irving, from New York, to Irving, 10-24-1818. STW, I 171.

156 "Fancy, humor—all." Mitchell, D. G., *American Lands and Letters. Works*, XIV 226–27.

156 "Left for a little while." Irving, from London, to Ebenezer Irving, 3-3-1819. Irving, *Letters 1802–23*, 541.

156 "My pride was up." Manuscript Fragment. STW, II 260.

156 "Severity . . . by the British press." "Preface to the Revised Edition." Irving, *The Sketch Book*, 3.

157 "I feel great diffidence." Irving, from London, to Brevoort, 3-3-1819. Irving, *Letters 1802–23*, 543.

157 "Anxious to hear from you." Irving, from London, to Brevoort, 5-13-1819. Same 548.

157 "*Far* beyond my most sanguine expectations." Irving, from London, to Brevoort, 9-9-1819. Same, 559.

157–58 Early judgments on *Sketch Book*. PMI, I 418–19.

158 "Appalled by such success." Irving, from London, to Brevoort, 9-9-1819. Irving, *Letters 1802–23*, 559–60.

158 "Generous and happy feelings." "Christmas Day." Irving, *The Sketch Book*, 176.

158 "It is a random thing." Irving, to Ebenezer Irving, 12-29-1819. Irving, *Letters 1802–23*, 573.

159 Godwin to Ogilvie. 9-15-1819. PMI, I 422. [Original indents after "request."]

159 "The 'prince of Booksellers.' " Irving, from London, to Brevoort, 9-9-1819. Irving, *Letters 1802–23*, 559.

160 "Materials enough on hand." "Preface to the Revised Edition." Irving, *The Sketch Book*, 3. The two citations that follow are from the same source: 3–4.

160–61 "Nothing will give me more pleasure." PMI, I 439–40.

161 "At the end of my *fortune*." Irving, from London, 5-13-1819. Irving, *Letters 1802–23*, 548.

161 "Wooden bowl . . . Silver tankard." Irving, from London, to Walter Scott, 11-20-1819. Same, 570.

161 "Let it sink or swim." "Preface to the Revised Edition." Irving, *The Sketch Book*, 6.

162 "Sticking in the mire." Same, 7.

162 "You doubted the success." Irving, from Granada, to John Murray, 5-9-1829. McClary, 124.

162 "I began my literary career." "Preface to the Revised Edition." Irving, *The Sketch Book*, 7.

162–63 "Blank page in existence." "The Voyage." Irving, *The Sketch Book*, 11. Citations that follow from that source appear on 9–10.

163 Byron on Crayon. Byron, from Ravenna, to John Murray, 10-12-1820. Byron, *Works. Letters and Journals*, V 94.

164 "Very monument a ruin." "Westminster Abbey." Irving, *The Sketch Book*, 142.

164   "No lofty theme." Irving, from London, to Brevoort, 3-3-1819. Irving, *Letters 1802–23*, 543.

164   "A most fortunate fellow." Peter Powell to Irving, 12-3-1820. PMI, II 32.

164   "This will never do!" Jeffrey, opening his review of *The Excursion*, 11-1814. Jeffrey, 457.

164–65   Reactions to *The Sketch Book*. McClary, 36: *Quarterly*, 4-1821; STW, I 190: *Monthly*, 11-1820, *Ed. Mag. and Lit. Misc.*, 9-1819.

165   Lockhart's critical judgments. These were written in 1818, two years before the review of *The Sketch Book*. Lochhead, 40–42.

165   "Best English writings of our day." *Blackwood's*, 2-1820. STW, I 190.

165   "I have dedicated my second volume to Scott." Irving, from London, to Ebenezer Irving, 8-15-1820. Irving, *Letters 1802–23*, 589.

165   "Its success . . . is unparalleled." Murray, quoted by G. S. Newton, summer, 1821. PMI, II 48.

165   "As readily believed a fairy tale." Irving, from Paris, to John Murray, 10-31-1820. Irving, *Letters 1802–23*, 601.

165   "A small, shrivelled, deformed man." Irving, from London, to James Kirke Paulding, 5-27-1820. Same, 584.

166   Hallam, Belzoni, Mitchell, Cohen. Irving, from London, to Brevoort, 8-15-1820. Same, 592.

166   Irving's "circle of acquaintance." Irving, from London, 5-13-1820. Same, 581.

166   Glimpse of Coleridge. STW, I 156.

166   "Most fashionable fellow of the day." Reported by Charles Leslie, from London, to Irving, 12-24-1820. Leslie, 230.

166–67   "Walter Scott . . . is in London." Leslie, from London, to his sister, 4-9-1820. Same, 217.

167   "Old D'Israeli is a staunch friend." Irving, from London, to Brevoort, 5-13-1820. Irving, *Letters 1802–23*, 581.

167   "I have led . . . such a lonely life." Irving, from Liverpool, to William Irving, 12-23-1817. Same, 515.

167   "I must take my leave." Irving, from London, to Brevoort, 8-15-1820. Same, 593.

167   "This bloated sensualist." Irving, from Liverpool, to Brevoort, 8-23-1815. Same, 418.

167   "Let loose his belly." Lord Folkestone to Creevey, early in 1818. Priestley, 213.

168   "The first creation of my reign." Fyfe, 280.

168   "Full enjoyment of his . . . reputation." Leslie, 42.

168   "A description of his personal appearance." Leslie, from London, to his sister, 6-28-1820. Same, 218–19.

169   "A most ungrateful wretch to complain." Scott, from Abbotsford, to Robert Southey, 4-4-1819. Grierson, V 338.

169   "The very image of Death." Scott, to Captain Ferguson, 4-16-1819. Same, 355.

169   "Strange to hear anything." Paris, 10-31-1826. Scott, *Journal*, 226.

169   "Did not recollect one single incident." Lockhart, IV 274.

170   "No sigher in shades." 6-16-1826. Scott, *Journal*, 159.

170   "J. G. L. kindly points out." 4-22-1826. Same, 134.

170–71   "I . . . do it more natural." 10-18-1826. Same, 214.

171   "Mere cairngorms." Scott to Irving. PMI, I 335. Compare Scott, from Edinburgh, to Irving, 12-4-1819: "In my hurry I have not

thanked you in Sophia's name for the kind attention which furnished her with the American volumes [of Scott's own poems]. I am not quite sure I can add my own, since you have made her acquainted with much more of papa's folly than she would ever otherwise have learned, for I had taken special care they should never see any of these things during their earlier years." PMI, I 444.

171   Scott on *Pride and Prejudice*. Scott, *Journal*, 114.

171   "Churls over their evening ale." Scott, *Works*. *Ivanhoe*, II 96. Cited in Keith, 71.

172   "Sir Walter Scott is probably responsible." Mark Twain, *Life on the Mississippi*, XL ("Castles and Culture"). *Works* [Hillcrest Edition, 9 vols., New York, 1906], IX, 308-9.

172   "Literature seems his sport." Irving, from London, to Paulding, 5-27-1820. Irving, *Letters 1802–23*, 584–85.

173   "Let him come up." Lockhart, V 194.

174   "The Irish harper." Scott, from Edgeworthstown (Ireland), to John Morritt, 7-31-1825. Grierson, IX 195 ["very" expanded to "verily"].

174   "No real comfort sacrificed to fantasy." 11-26-1826. Scott, *Journal*, 246.

174   "Oaks will outlast my laurels." Scott, from Abbotsford, to Countess Pürgstall, 1821. Grierson, VI 507.

175   "The most wealthy . . . nobility." Ballantyne, 96.

175   "Years I was in his service." Dalgleish, LXXI 225.

175   "Overwhelming pecuniary ruin." John Richardson's testimony. Pope-Hennessy, 261–62.

176   "Shall we receive good?" Job 2:10.

176–78   "Gurnal . . . A hard word." Title page. Scott, *Journal*, opposite 1. The indicated citations that follow are from the same source: 11-21-1825 ("enamourd"), 3; 11–20 ("Lady's Album"), 1; 12-2 ("correcting proofs"; original indents after "smoothly"), 23–24; 12-9, 30; 12–14 ("Affairs very bad"), 37; 12–18, 38–42 (eight citations, through "When I die" ["s" supplied on "these day"]); 1-5-1826, 55.

178   He had felt "mortal fear." Scott, *Journal*, 55, n. 2.

178   "Came through cold roads." 1-16-1826. Scott, *Journal*, 60. 1-17: Same.

178   Dalgleish's recollections of ruin. Dalgleish, LXXI 228.

178–79   "The opening of the year 1826." Cockburn, 430.

179   "Scott ruined!" Quayle, 213–14.

179   "The pillow of a debtor." 1-18-1826. Scott, *Journal*, 61.

179   "Not your ordinary way." Dalgleish, LXXI 228–29.

179   "We dined of course at home." 1-19-1826. Scott, *Journal*, 62.

180–81   "Chucking about of our old furniture." 3-13-1826. Scott, *Journal*, 112. The nine citations that follow are from the same source: 2-14-1826, 89–90; 3–19 ("melancholy letter"), 117; 3-23 ("better than I expected"), 119; 4-1 ("12 or one"), 122; 5-11 ("take leave"), 142; 5-15, 144; 5-16 ("I have seen her—"), 145; 5-18 ("coffin"), 146; 12-30,31-1826, 258.

181   "It is easy no doubt." Scott, to Lockhart, 1-20-1826. Grierson, IX 370–71. [Dashes inserted before "a" and after "end."]

182   "Such a plan, judiciously adopted." Scott, from Edinburgh, to James Ballantyne, 4-22-1800. Grierson, I 97.

182   "Dabble in trade." Cockburn, 430.

183   "He was worth £80,000." 1-29-1826. Scott, *Journal*, 71.

183   "Let us dig on . . . at that extraordinary quarry." Cadell to Constable, spring, 1822. Quayle, 157.

183   *"Are these men never to get easy?"* Cadell to Constable, 1-1823. Same, 175.

184   "Save my library." Scott, *Journal*, 68 ["imagina" expanded to "imagination"].

184   "Large nose." Same, 67.

184   "Well do I remember." Cockburn, 431.

185   "I the said Sir Walter Scott." Quoted in Scott, *Journal*, Introduction [by W. E. K. Anderson], xxvi.

185   "It is worth £300 more." 6-29-1826. Scott, *Journal*, 165.

185   "Selling my horse." London, 10-24-1826. Moore, V 125.

185   "I wrote a good task." Scott, *Journal*, 153. The citation that follows is from the same source: 294.

185   "It grieves me." Irving to David Wilkie, quoted in Wagenknecht, 81.

185   "Too tranquil for repining." Scott, *Journal*, 207.

186   "The old salve to the old sore." 8-25-1826. Same, 189.

186–87   The Theatrical Fund Dinner. Scott, from Edinburgh, to Lady Louisa Stuart, 3-8-1827. Grierson, X 173. Lockhart, VII 18–19. Scott, *Journal* [2-24-1827], 282.

187   "A gift little worth having." 4-24-1831. Scott, *Journal*, 650.

187   "Blisterd bled and criticized." 5-8-1831. Same, 653.

188   "Sir Walter had had his head shaved." 5-10-1831. Lockhart, VII 281.

188   "The stern sullen unwashed artificers." 11-24-1826. Scott, *Journal*, 245.

188   "They have much to answer for." 5-13-1831. Same, 655.

188   "The geese on the green." 3-21-1831. Lockhart, VII 267.

189   "He be damned." Scott, to Robert Cadell, 4-1831. Grierson, XII 14.

189   "What the subject is." Quayle, 247.

189   "At sea in the dark and the vessell leaky." 5-6,7-1831. Scott, *Journal*, 653.

189   "I must not complain now." Scott to J. L. Adolphus, at Abbotsford, 8-1827. Lockhart, VII 53.

189   "Red-sandy complexion." Testimony of Sir Frederic Madden, autumn, 1831. Scott, *Journal*, 667, n. 2.

190   Irving's last meeting with Scott. PMI, II 459.

190   "It shall be one of the best." Scott, from Portsmouth, to Cadell, 10-24-1831. Scott, *Journal*, 685, n. 1.

190   "We slept reasonbly." Same, 713.

191   "He sprang up with a cry of delight." Lockhart, VII 385.

191   "A moment sooner than I can help it." Scott, from Edinburgh, to his son Walter, 6-2-1829. Grierson, XI 196.

191   "This is sad idleness." Lockhart, VII 389.

191   "An infant of six months old." Laidlaw to Skene, 8-15-1832. Skene, 208.

192   "As wild and violent as before." Sophia to Walter (Scott's son). Johnson, *Scott*, 1276. The citation that follows is from the same source, same page [source prints "landanum"].

THREE WOMEN, FRIENDS OF IRVING'S

193   Epigraph. Irving, from Sunnyside, to Mrs. Emily Fuller, 7-2-1856. PMI, IV 218.

194   "Haphazard, schemeless life." Irving, from London. Irving, *Letters 1802–23*, 585–86.

195   "Entering into a New World." Irving, from London, to Brevoort, 8-15-1820. Same, 593.

195   "A *young man* and in *Paris*." Irving, from Paris, to Peter Irving, 7-15-1805. Same, 196.

195–98   "Paris or myself has changed." Irving, from Paris, to William Irving, 9-22-1820. Same, 597. The three citations that follow are from the same source: 596–97.

198   "I did not half know you." PMI, II 26.

198–99   "One of my greatest gratifications." Irving, from Paris, to Richard Rush, 10-28-1820. Irving, *Letters 1802–23*, 600.

199   "Urge me to return to New York." Irving, from Paris, to Brevoort, 3-10-1821. Same, 614–15.

199   "Dined with M'Kay." Moore, III 182.

199–200   "Irving called near dinner time." 3-19-1821. Same, 211.

200   "The man I most loved." PMI, I 63.

200   "One of the dismallest blows." Irving, to Ebenezer Irving. PMI, II 66.

200   "I am still preyed upon." Irving, from Edgbaston (England), to Charles Leslie. Irving, *Letters 1802–23*, 654.

200   "I have fagged hard." Irving, from London, to Peter Irving, 9-6-1821. Same, 647.

201   "Demi-savage, with a feather." "The Author." Irving, *Bracebridge Hall*, 3. The citation that follows is from the same source, same page.

201   "The fault of the book." Quoted in the *Port Folio*, 1823. STW, I 208.

201   "Singular sweetness of the composition." *Edinburgh Review*, 11-1822. Same, 210.

201–2   "I have not a moment to myself." Irving, from London, to Brevoort, 6-11-1822. Irving, *Letters 1802–23*, 677. The citation that follows is from the same source, same page.

202   "Absolutely rude and churlish." Irving, from the Deep Dene, Surrey, to Catharine Paris, 6-21-1822. Same, 682.

202   "One grand obstacle removed." Irving, from London, to Brevoort, 6-11-1822. Same, 678.

202   "Streets so lively with people." 8-6-1822. Irving, *Journals 1819–27*, 8.

202   "It would amuse you to see me." Irving, from Wiesbaden, to Sarah Van Wart, 8-20-1822. Irving, *Letters 1802–23*, 697.

203–7   "The rocks, the mossy stones." Foster, 53 [4-1822]. The twenty-two citations that follow (through "I prefer reading travels") are likewise from Emily Foster's journal: 151 ("sunny days"), 33 (black clouds), 36–37, 124–25 ("*lilacced*"), 83 (two citations), 88 ("irretrievably eternally lost"), 59 ("like mad" [4-22-1822]), 73, 63 ("honey words"), 62 ("sour cherries"), 72 ("extasies"), 62 ("candle light"), 100 ("Lammermoor"), 63 ("Rob Roy"), 48, 70 (the exchange on friendship and love, which is recorded entirely in French: "L'amitié voit les defauts . . ." etc.), 84 ("*going*"), 85 ("bête"), 85–86 ("Pumperlin"), 92 ("*les amours*"), 96.

207 "No praise . . . so sweet, so genuine." Flora (Foster) Dawson's reminiscences. Appendix, PMI, IV 340.

208 "Dresden . . . a place of taste." Irving, from Vienna, to Mrs. Sarah Van Wart, 11-10-1822. Irving, *Letters 1802–23*, 719.

208 Entering Dresden. 11-28-1822. Irving, *Journals 1819–27*, 88.

208 "Intoxication of the heart." Irving, from Heidelberg, to Mrs. Sarah Van Wart, 9-18-1822. Irving, *Letters 1802–23*, 706.

208 "The leaves of past pleasures." Irving, *Journals 1819–27*, 22.

208 "Attempt to please the world." Same, 18.

209 "Herr Washington Irving . . ." 1-22-1823. STW, I 230.

209 "A prettily furnished appartment." Irving, from Dresden, to Charles Leslie, 12-2-1822. Irving, *Letters 1802–23*, 725.

209 "To the Kings appartments." 12-22-1822. Irving, *Journals 1819–27*, 99.

209 "Your old-fashioned, high bred gentleman." Contemporary description (1822), quoted in STW, I 213.

209-10 "There's the mystery!" Flora Dawson's reminiscences and journal extracts record details of the meeting between Irving and the Fosters. Appendix, PMI, IV 340–41.

210 "Mʳ Irving . . . was introduced to us." Foster, 108–9.

210 "Miseries of an indulgent mistress." 12-19-1822. Irving, *Journals 1819–27*, 97.

210 "Mʳ Irving is always with us." Foster, 116.

210 "Hair of a man of genius." Same, 110–11.

210-12 "Walked out with Col Livius." 12-23-1822. Irving, *Journals 1819–27*, 99 ["interted" expanded]. The ten citations that follow are from the same source: *100*, *101*, 102, *104* (New Year's Eve), *104* (New Year's Day), 108 (1-8-1823), 108 ("spangles"), 109 ("hares"), 110, 126. [Italicized page numbers indicate citations where I have disregarded Irving's paragraphing, printing the extract without his indentations.]

212 "Practically wiped out the city." Parkinson, 451. The paragraphs on the bombing of Dresden derive from accounts in that source and in David Irving's *The Destruction of Dresden* (New York, 1963), H. Essame's *The Battle for Germany* (New York, 1969), and Charles B. MacDonald's *The Mighty Endeavor* (New York, 1969).

213 "Our house now *his home*." Flora Dawson's reminiscences and journal extracts. Appendix, PMI, IV 344–46.

213 "Evening after evening in happy converse." Same, 357.

213 "A sweet little poem on spring." Foster, 126.

213 "He would write in the morning." Flora Dawson's reminiscences and journal extracts. Appendix, PMI, IV 357–58.

213 "The springs of mental energy." Irving, *Notes*, 79.

214 "Never beat a more kindly heart." Flora Dawson's reminiscences. PMI, IV 353.

214 Bancroft on Irving. 7-5-1821. Howe, M. A. DeW., I 110.

214 "Absolutely nothing!" Irving, from Dresden, to Leslie, 3-15-1823. Irving, *Letters 1802–23*, 736.

215 "When I was very young." Manuscript Fragment. STW, II 255. The two citations that follow (through "Matilda . . . timid") are from the same source: 256.

216 "Perfect liberty of private conduct." Irving, from Paris, to Peter Irving, 7-15-1805. Irving, *Letters 1802–23*, 196.

216   Irving from Genoa, about the Hoffmans. Irving to William Irving, 12-20-1804. Same, 125.

216   "I resumed my legal studies." Manuscript Fragment. STW, II 256.

216   "Good solid flesh and blood." Matilda Hoffman to Ann Hoffman, 9-20-1805. Introduction by Stanley T. Williams to Irving, *Notes*, 37. The citation that follows is from the same source: 37–38.

217   "Matalinda dinda dinda." Matilda Hoffman, from Philadelphia, to Ann Hoffman, 11-12-1804. Same, 37.

217   "She went with us to the theatre." Rebecca Gratz, from Philadelphia, to Maria Fenno Hoffman, 3-1805. Osterweis, 99.

217   Matilda's frocks. Rebecca Gratz, from Philadelphia, to Maria Fenno Hoffman. Same, 101–2.

217   "A modern philosopher." Irving, *Notes*, 40.

217   "*Washington* says . . ." Matilda Hoffman, from New York, to Ann Hoffman, 8-29-1807. Irving, *Notes*, 39–40.

217   "No body knew her so well as I." Manuscript Fragment. STW, II 256.

217–18   Hair playing "carelessly in the wind." "Recollections," 694.

218–19   "Intuitive rectitude of mind." Manuscript Fragment. STW, II 256. The nine citations that follow (through "last one she looked upon") are from the same source: 256–57 [*s* supplied on "three day & nights"].

219   "Died on the 24th instant." *New-York Commercial Advertiser*, 4-29-1809. STW, I 405, n. 176. Compare "Recollections," 696.

219–20   "The frightful gloom of my own thoughts." Manuscript Fragment. STW, II 257–58. The seven citations that follow (through "worlds thoughts") are from the same source: 258–60.

220   "Mat died in April." Notebook, 1810. STW, I 119.

220   "M Hff died April 26, 1809." Same, 106.

220   "The recollection of Matilda." Irving, *Notes*, 63. The citation that follows is from the same source, same page.

220–21   "Your memory is as tenacious as mine." PMI, I 431.

221   "The bed of death." "Rural Funerals." Irving, *The Sketch Book*, 116.

221   "Departed beings that I have loved." "St. Mark's Eve." Irving, *Bracebridge Hall*, 85.

221   "You wonder why I am not married." Manuscript Fragment. STW, II 261.

221   "Some of the *real* causes." Same, 261–62.

221–22   "He has written." Flora Dawson's reminiscences and journal extracts. Appendix, PMI, IV 358. The two citations that follow are from the same source: 361.

222–23   "They occupy part of a palace." Irving, from Dresden, to Peter Irving, 3-10-1823. Irving, *Letters 1802–23*, 732. The eight citations that follow (through "matters of the kind") are from the same source: 732–33.

223   "A small party at Mrs Fosters." 4-3-1823. Irving, *Journals 1819–27*, 134. The citation includes "Conclude the evening by waltzing," in the paragraph that follows in the text.

223   Emily on the "vivid painting." Foster, 122–23. The three citations that follow after Irving's in the next paragraph (through "want of excitement") are from the same source: 126, 128–29, 118.

224   "An intercourse become so dear to him." Flora Dawson's reminiscences and journal extracts. Appendix, PMI, IV 358.

224 Citations from Irving's journal. Irving, *Journals 1819–27*, 137–41.

224 "That good dear nice Mr Irving." Foster, 130.

224 "My mother encourages him." Flora Dawson's journal extracts. Appendix, PMI, IV 358.

224–25 "Our last evening with Irving." Foster, 138–39.

225 "Talk of stars &c." Irving, *Journals 1819–27*, 154.

225 "Delightful letters from Irving." Foster, 141.

225 "They were the sweetest moments." Irving, from Hirschberg, to Mrs. Foster, 5-23-1823. Irving, *Letters 1802–23*, 751.

225 "Fifty plans of what I ought to do." Same, 754.

225–26 "Your letter of Wednesday." Irving, from Prague, to Mrs. Foster, 6-1-1823. Same, 757.

226 "An unlucky journey for us both." 6-2-1823. Same, 758–59.

226 "A great Humbug." 6-4-1823. Irving, *Journals 1819–27*, 171.

226 "We determine to push for Dresden." Same, 176.

226 "A pair of handsome moustachios." Foster, 147.

227 "Love cooled down into friendshp." Irving, *Journals 1819–27*, 184.

227 "Fidgetty." Flora Dawson's reminiscences. Appendix, PMI, IV 365.

227 "A sprinkling of rain." 7-12-1823. Irving, *Journals 1819–27*, 188.

227 "The three philosophers." Flora Dawson's reminiscences. Appendix, PMI, IV 366. The citation that follows is from the same source, same page.

227 "Oh, Dresden, Dresden!" Same, 364.

227 "I am annoyed at myself." Foster, 158.

227–28 Glens "very still & lonely." 7-16-1823. Irving, *Journals 1819–27*, 192. The four citations that follow are from the same source: 190, 191 (7–14), 196 (7–20; dash inserted after "to be had"), 197 ("Konig von Preuss").

228 "We arrived at Cassel." Foster, 161. The citation that follows is from the same source: 163.

228 "Readg Ms: to ladies." 7-23-1823. Irving, *Journals 1819–27*, 198.

228 "Irving has given up the Rhine." Foster, 163.

228 "We are now in Holland." Irving, *Journals 1819–27*, 199.

228 "Walked about Rotterdam." Same, 200 ["retu" expanded to "return"].

228 Flora's account of Rotterdam. Flora Dawson's reminiscences. Appendix, PMI, IV 376.

229 "Poor Mr I. is out of spirits." Foster, 167.

229 "Feelings too quick to analyse." 7-30-1823. Same, 167–68.

229 "Steamboat goes off finely." Irving, *Journals 1819–27*, 200. The citation that follows is from the same source, same page.

229 Voyaging briefly with the Fosters. Citations from Foster, 168–69 (to "pirates hung").

229 "Ships gliding along fields." Irving, *Journals 1819–27*, 201.

229–30 "More like relatives than friends." Irving, from Paris, to Peter Irving, 8-5-1823. PMI, II 162–63.

230 Emily on August 3, 1823. Foster, 169–70. Citations to the end of her journal are from 170–71.

230 "For life, as it were." Conclusion to *Washington Square*, by Henry James.

231 "Wretchedly out of spirits." Irving, from Paris, to Peter Irving, 8-20-1823. PMI, II 165.

231 "A strange horror on my mind." 8-11-1823. Irving, *Journals 1819–27*, 209.

231   "That little spot of earth." Irving, from Paris, 12-11-1824. Hellman, *Letters to Brevoort*, II 183.

231–32   John Brown's marriage. The citations, with the exceptions noted, come from Brown's letter from Red Rock, Iowa, to Henry L. Stearns, 7-15-1857. Ruchames, 37–40.

232   "The seport of religion." Villard, 13.

232   "A meal of Potatoes & Salt." James Foreman, from Youngsville, Pa., to James Redpath, 12-28-1859. Ruchames, 163.

232   "Brown was an austere feller." Sanborn, 34.

232   A firebell in the night. The warning about slavery is contained in a letter from Monticello to John Holmes, 4-22-1820. Ford, P. L., X 157.

232–33   John Brown, Jr.'s reminiscence. Boyer, 216.

233   "Dismal feeling still hanging about me." 8-11-1823. Irving, *Journals 1819–27*, 210. The two citations that follow are from the same source: 210, 208.

233   "Her budget of wonderful stories." Irving, from Haerlem, to T. W. Storrow, 7-11-1822. Irving, *Letters 1802–23*, 692.

233–34   "Scott's manner must . . . be . . . avoided." Irving, from Paris, to Peter Irving, 9-4-1823. PMI, II 166.

234   "Call on Bradish." 8-8-1823. Irving, *Journals 1819–27*, 207. The two citations that follow (through "met with Payne") are from the same source: 208, 209.

234   A "secret history of the times." Payne, from Schenectady, to Brevoort, 10-14-1806. STW, I 78.

234–35   Promoting "the interests of American drama." First number of *The Thespian Mirror*. Overmyer, 47. The six citations that follow are also from Overmyer: 57 ("delicacy"), 49 (Brevoort's letter), 45 ("tedious"), 46, 50 (*Port Folio*), 54–55.

235–36   "If you, sir, can reclaim this youth." John E. Seaman to Dr. Eliphalet Nott. Overmyer, 69.

236   Irving to Payne. Irving, from Philadelphia, 11-2-1809. Irving, *Letters 1802–23*, 276; STW, I 84–85.

237   "You will have friends present." Overmyer, 112.

237   "A face almost too beautiful." Harrison, 61–62.

237   "I blush to own it." Overmyer, 123.

237   "To *fatten* on trouble." PMI, II 169.

237   "A party to persuade the folks not to hiss." Irving, *Letters 1802–23*, 536–37 [source indents after "please"].

237–38   Creditors "quiet before." Overmyer, 172.

238   Entries in Payne's journal. Same, 192–93.

238   "Breakfasted . . . with . . . Payne." PMI, II 41.

238   "Returning thro palais royal." 8-9-1823. Irving, *Journals 1819–27*, 209.

238   "The situation . . . is very central & desirable." Irving, from Havre, to Payne, 9-27-1823. Luquer, 470.

239   "Up several pairs of stairs." Irving, from Paris, to Catharine Paris, 10-24-1824. PMI, II 216.

239   "You would be quite charmed with them." 10-3-1823. PMI, II 168.

239   "This fund of Dramatic talent." Irving, from Dresden, to Charles Leslie, 3-15-1823. Irving, *Letters 1802–23*, 736 ["wit" (torn) is expanded to "within"].

239   "Payne is busy upon Azendai." Irving to Peter Irving. PMI, II 169.

239   "I delivered all your letters." Payne, from London, to Irving, 11-7-1823. Same, 170.

239   "Dramatic stuff within me." Luquer, 475.

239–40   Captain Copp's song. Irving, from Paris, to Payne, 11-26-1823. Same, 477.

240   "200 guineas down." Overmyer, 229.

240   "The points all told *amazingly.*" Payne to Irving, spring, 1824. PMI, II 172.

240   "Charles Lamb tells me." Same.

240   Payne's preface. Harrison, 101.

240   "I cannot afford to write." Irving, from Paris, to Payne, 1-31-1824. Luquer, 480.

240–41   "The teeming little world below me." "Sketches in Paris in 1825," *Wolfert's Roost.* Irving, *Works,* XVI 195.

241   "A rawness about every attempt." Irving's recollections to Pierre Irving. PMI, II 178.

241   "Sooner you take the field the better." Murray to Irving, 11-8-1823. Same, 177.

241   "Feel intolerably triste." Irving, *Journals 1819–27,* 288.

241   "A fit of sterility." Irving, from Paris, to Leslie, 2-8-1824. Leslie, 260.

241–42   "Again a Watchful night." 12-21-1823. Irving, *Journals 1819–27,* 260. The eight citations that follow (through "vivid dream") are from the same source: 277 (1-23; 1-24-1824), 287 (2-10), 278 (1-26), 280 (2-1), 267 (1-8), 278 (1-25; "Raphsodical letter"), 270 (1-10-1824).

242   "Bedevilled by the fumiste." Irving, from Paris, to Payne, 11-5-1823. Luquer, 471. The citation that follows is from the same source, same page.

242   "Tenacious in money matters." Irving to Payne, 6-20-1825. STW, I 285.

242   "Bills brot of Mr Paynes." 1-30-1824. *Journals 1819–27,* 280.

242   "Capt Medwin calls." 2-19-1824. Same, 292.

242   "Materials for two volumes prepared." Irving, from Paris, to John Murray, 3-26-1824. McClary, 50. See n. 78 on that page.

242–43   "Find letter from Murray." 3-22-1824. Irving, *Journals 1819–27,* 307. The three citations that follow are from the same source: 334, 335, 336.

243   Irving with Mrs. Shelley. "Beside him sat on this evening, presumably, Payne and Payne's friend Mary Wollstonecraft Shelley . . ." STW, I 259. But during these months was Payne avoiding Mrs. Shelley, having fallen in love with her earlier? See 287 of the present work.

243   Murray "behaved like a gentleman." Irving, from London, to Peter Irving, 5-31-1824. PMI, II 193–94.

243   Payne "copied part of my MS." Irving, from Lyndhurst, to Peter Irving, 6-10-1824. Same, 198.

244   "Called on Col Aspinwall." Irving, *Journals 1819–27,* 340–42 [6-2 to 6-6-1824].

244   "Go to White Lion." 6-14-1824. Same, 349. The citations that follow are from the same source: 6-17, 351 ("retreat"); 6-18, 352.

244   "Moore . . . gives me great encouragement." Irving, from Sloperton Cottage, Devizes, to John Murray, 6-18-1824. McClary, 56.

244   "Rather tremble for its fate." 6-17-1824. Moore, IV 208.

244   "One of the serenest periods of my life." Irving, from Birmingham, to Mrs. Storrow, 6-25-1824. Williams, *Storrows,* 35.

244-45   "Down the river quite into the sea." 7-30-1823. Foster, 167.

245   "Passed thro Islington—" 7-6-1824. Irving, *Journals 1819–27*, 358.

245   "Welcomed . . . in the kindest manner." Same.

245   "Seven or eight days at least." Irving, from Brickhill, to Peter Irving, 7-7-1824. PMI, II 202.

245   "Walked in the grounds & to Bedford." 7-7-1824. Irving, *Journals 1819–27*, 358. The five citations that follow (through "Mr Simeon") are from the same source: 360 (7-8), 363 (7-13), 359 (7-7), 359 (7-8), 361 (7-10).

245   "Let us pray!" Dawson, II 139.

246   "You were all wound up." Irving, from Paris, to Emily Foster, 8-23-1825. Williams, "Irving's Religion," 416, 415.

246   "Plenty of the needful." Irving, from Brickhill, to Peter Irving, 7-12-1824. PMI, II 204.

246-47   "The Revd Mr Grimshaw." Irving, *Journals 1819–27*, 364. The four citations that follow are from the same source: 364, 374 ("Book work," 7-27), 366 ("Mrs Shelley"), 378.

247   Mrs. Shelley's "favourite." Shelley, M., *Letters*, I 336.

247   "No doubt of seeing the animal." Mary Wollstonecraft to William Godwin, 8-30-1797. Wardle, 119–20.

247   "In *her* an able advocate." Burr, from Philadelphia, to Mrs. Burr, 2-16-1793. Davis, *Memoirs*, I 363.

247   Citations from *A Vindication*. Wollstonecraft, *Rights of Women*, 212, x, 107. See also 138 (exercise), 220 (women in government), 251 (coeducation). My account of Wollstonecraft's life is indebted to Tomalin and Flexner.

248   "Let them stare!" From Paris, 1-1-1794. Wollstonecraft, *Imlay*, 24. The two citations that follow are from the same source: 27 (1-1794), 178 (9-27-1795).

249   "A system of fraud." Godwin, *Justice*, II 381. The work is analyzed in Woodcock, 47–97.

249   "Legal prostitution." Wollstonecraft, *Rights of Women*, 104, 222. To be sure, she is referring to one type of marriage, although by no means rare. Compare the sentiment with this: ". . . I respect marriage, as the foundation of almost every social virtue . . ." Same, 119.

249   "Extraordinary married pair." Thomas Holcroft to William Godwin and Mary Wollstonecraft Godwin, 4-6-1797. Paul, I 240.

249   "I may be termed happy." Mary Wollstonecraft to Godwin, 6-6-1797. Wardle, 82.

250   "Dying in the evening." Paul, I 275.

250   "The poor children!" William Godwin to Mrs. Cotton, 10-24-1797. Same, 281.

250   "Widow with green spectacles." Charles Lamb to John Rickman, 9-16-1801. Lucas, I 273.

250   "That Bitch." Lamb, from London, to Thomas Manning, 9-24-1802. Same, 317.

250   "To take another wife." Southey to Coleridge, 2-1804. Southey, II 268.

250   "Infernal devil." Brown, 296.

250   "Books not worth reading." Same, 308.

251   "I have seen the two daughters." Burr, from London, to Theodosia Alston, 11-21-1808. Davis, *Journal*, I 99. The citation that follows is from the same source, same page.

251   "The girls sang and danced." Bixby, II 326.

251   "Subject to sea-sickness." Godwin, from Skinner Street, London, to William Baxter, 6-8-1812. Marshall, I 27–28.

251   "My own daughter is . . . very pretty." Godwin to unknown correspondent, 1812. Paul, II 214.

252   Shelley's first letter to Godwin. Shelley, P. B., *Letters*, I 219–21.

252   And the second letter. Shelley, from Keswick, to Godwin, 1-10-1812. Same, 227–28.

252   "Shall I be torn to pieces?" Godwin to Francis Place, 9-5-1813. Brown, 282.

253   "A wiser and a better man." Shelley, from Keswick, to Godwin, 1-10-1812. Shelley, P. B., *Letters*, I 227.

253   "All the females of my family." Godwin, from London, to Shelley, 3-14-1812. Paul, II 207.

253   "Partner of my thoughts and feelings." Shelley, from Keswick, to Godwin, 1-26-1812 [?]. Shelley, P. B., *Letters*, I 242.

253   "We have seen the Godwins." Harriet Shelley, from London, to Catherine Nugent, 10-1812. Same, 327, n. 8.

253   Christie Baxter's recollection. Brown, 271.

253   "Romantic woes or wonderful events." Shelley, M., *Frankenstein*, Introduction, 6.

253   "Harriet is a noble animal." Peacock, 92.

254   "Bysshe strode about the room." Hogg, II 538–39.

254   "To defecate life of its misery." Shelley, P. B., *Poetical Works*, Preface, I viii.

254   "Distress and misery that prevails." Irving, from Birmingham, 12-9-1816. Hellman, *Letters to Brevoort*, I 194–95.

254   "Passion for reforming the world." Preface to *Prometheus Unbound*. Shelley, P. B., *Poetical Works*, II 6.

254–55   "This book is sacred to me." White, I 338–39.

255   "One mile distant from London." Godwin, from Skinner Street, to John Taylor, 8-27-1814. Godwin, *Elopement*, 11. The four citations that follow are from the same source: 10–11.

255   "In the silent summer morning." Claire Clairmont's testimony. Brown, 287.

255   "A letter on my dressing table." Godwin, *Elopement*, 11–12.

255   "The contemplation of female excellence." Shelley, from London, to Hogg, 10-4-1814. Shelley, P. B., *Letters*, I 401.

255–56   "A fat lady had arrived." 7-29-1814. Shelley, M., *Journal*, 4. The citation that follows is from the same source, same page [7-30; original indents before "Mrs. Godwin"].

256   "Watch, chain, &c." 8-4-1814. Same, 5.

256   "Cottages roofless, rafters black." Shelley, M., "History," 15.

256   "Stinking bacon, sour bread." Same, 16.

256   "I do not forget you." Shelley, from Troyes, to Harriet Shelley, 8-3-1814. Shelley, P. B., *Letters*, I 391–92.

256   French "exceedingly inhospitable." Shelley, M., *Journal*, 8.

256   "Cold paws on her face." 8-12-1814. Holmes, 237.

256   "Ephemeral summers of joy." Bigland, 48.

256   "Too happy to sleep." 8-2-1814. Shelley, M., *Journal*, 5 [Shelley's entry].

256   "Thinking of Don Quixote." Shelley, M., "History," 13.

256–57   "Delight giving scenes." Clairmont, 25, 26 (8-17; 8-19-1814; "att" expanded to "attempt").

257   "Waving with the golden harvest." Shelley, M., "History," 13.

257   Stars wove "a wild dance." Same, 24.

257   "Thou Friend, whose presence." Dedication of *The Revolt of Islam*. Shelley, P. B., *Poetical Works*, I 158.

257   "Detestable" slow diligence. 9-6-1814. Shelley, M., *Journal*, 14.

257   "Things, past, present, and to come." 9-8-1814. Same.

257   Brother "treats us very ill." 9-13-1814. Same, 15.

257   "Why cannot I be with you." 10-25-1814. Shelley, M., *Letters*, 3.

258   "*Friday, Sept. 16.*" Shelley, M., *Journal*, 15.

258   "I return your cheque." Bigland, 70.

258   "Prostitutes and seducers." Shelley, from London, to Godwin, 3-6-1816. Shelley, P. B., *Letters*, I 459.

258–59   "Cutting squares of skin." Shelley, M., *Journal*, 18–19.

259   Jane's "horrors." 8-27-1814. Same, 12.

259   "Jane walks in her sleep." 10-14-1814. Same, 20.

259   "I sigh yet feel no pain." 10-14-1814. Clairmont, 51.

259–60   "He came to Edinburgh." Shelley, from Keswick, to Elizabeth Hitchener, 11-14-1811. Shelley, P. B., *Letters*, I 182.

260   "Dearest Hogg." The series of letters from Mary to Hogg are reprinted and discussed by F. L. Jones in "Mary Godwin to T. J. Hogg: The 1815 Letters," Cameron, 84–120. My citations are from that source: 96, 98, 99, 106.

261   "My little dead baby." 3-13-1815. Shelley, M., *Journal*, 40. The four citations that follow are from the same source: 41 (3-19), 40 (3-14; 3-12), 47.

261   "Twice as fat." Testimony of Charles Clairmont. Bigland, 72.

261   "Commencement of several literary plans." Shelley, from Bishopsgate, to Hogg, 9-22-1815. Shelley, P. B., *Letters*, I 432.

262   "The best feelings of the human heart." Shelley, from London, to Robert Southey, 3-7-1816. Same, 462.

262   "Altogether a most complex affair." Shelley, from Bishopsgate, to Godwin, 2-18-1816. Same, 452.

262   "My design of settling in Italy." Shelley, from London, to Godwin, 2-16-1816. Same, 450.

262   "Silent as the grave?" Marchand, *Byron*, 591.

262–63   "She, who is not in love." Same, 603–4.

263   "I therefore take Mary to Geneva." Shelley, from Dover, to Godwin, 5-3-1816. Shelley, P. B., *Letters*, I 472.

263   "Scent of flowers and new-mown grass." Mary Shelley, from Geneva, to unknown correspondent, 5-17-1816. Shelley, M., *Letters*, I 11.

263   "Her silken robe, and inner vest." Holmes, 329.

263   "His hand to his head." Marchand, *Byron*, 630, quoting from Polidori's diary.

263   "Threw water in his face." Holmes, 329.

263–64   "Nature of the principle of life." Shelley, M., *Frankenstein*, Introduction, 8–10. [Source indents before "I opened mine."]

264   "A dreary night of November." Same, 57.

264   "As to all these 'mistresses.' " Byron, from Diodati, to Augusta Leigh, 9-8-1816. Same, from Venice, to same, 12-18-1816. Marchand, *Letters*, V 92, 141.

264–65   "More serious and threatening aspect." Fanny Godwin, from London, to Mary Shelley, 7-29-1816. Marshall, I 153–54.

265   "Kiss our babe, and go to bed." Shelley, M., *Journal*, 55. The three citations that follow are from the same source: 63, 65, 66.

266 "Put an end to the existence." *The Cambrian*, 10-12-1816. Paul, II 242.

266 "Go not to Swansea." Godwin to Mary Shelley, 10-13-1816. Dowden, II 58.

266 "The spot from which I hope." Fanny Imlay, from Bristol, to Godwin, 10-8-1816; quoted in a letter from Godwin to Mary Shelley. Dowden, II 58.

266 Hookham's letter of December 15. Cameron, "The Last Days of Harriet Shelley." Cameron, 234.

266 "If you had never left me." Same, 261. The letter is headed "Sat. Eve."

267 "Thine eyes glowed in the glare." Same, 258.

267 "A marriage . . . on the 30th." Shelley, M., *Journal*, 71.

267 "Magical" effects. Shelley, from London, to Claire Clairmont, 12-30-1816. Shelley, P. B., *Letters*, I 525.

267–68 "To church with this tall girl." Godwin, from London, to Hull Godwin, 2-21-1817. Paul, II 246.

268 "Changes . . . during this little year." 1-24-1817. Shelley, M., *Journal*, 75.

268 Claire "safely delivered." Mary Shelley, from Bath, to Lord Byron, 1-13-1817. Shelley, M., *Letters*, I 18.

268 Mary's letter to Leigh Hunt. Same, 21.

269 Mary "surrounded by babes." Mary Shelley, from Marlow, to Shelley, 9-28-1817. Same, 34.

269 "Feelings . . . of a deadly & torpid kind." Shelley, from Marlow, to Godwin, 12-7-1817. Shelley, P. B., *Letters*, I 572.

269 Shelley this "Atheist." Appendix III, Medwin, 463–64.

269 "A slight tribute of high admiration." Shelley, from Marlow, to Sir Walter Scott, 1-2-1818. Shelley, P. B., *Letters*, I 590.

269 "Mr. Shelleys Compts." Shelley, from London, to John Murray, 3-7-1818. Same, 598.

270 "Fine weather & good hopes." Mary Shelley's postscript to Shelley's letter to Leigh Hunt, 3-13-1818: Shelley, P. B., *Letters*, II 2.

270 "Fair, freckled, bue-eyed . . . person." Testimony of Horace Smith, remembering his first impression of Shelley in 1816. Beavan, 137.

270 "This jingling food for . . . oblivion." Bigland, 173.

271 "She is now buried." Shelley, from Venice, to Claire Clairmont. Shelley, P. B., *Letters*, II 41. [Source indents after "distress."]

271 "The Italian women used to . . . look at him." Shelley, from Livorno, to T. J. Hogg, 7-25-1819. Shelley, P. B., *Letters*, II 104.

271 "Thy little footsteps on the sands." Shelley, P. B., *Cambridge Works*, 482.

271 "I longed to see my pretty babe." 7-27-1816. Shelley, M., *Journal*, 55.

271–72 "Wherefore hast thou gone." Shelley, P. B., *Cambridge Works*, 481.

272 "My sentiments on reading the Sketch Book." Godwin, from Skinner Street, to James Ogilvie, 9-15-1819. PMI, I 422. [Source indents before "Everywhere."]

272 "I wrote to this hard-hearted person." Shelley, from Livorno, to Leigh Hunt, 8-15-1819. Shelley, P. B., *Letters*, II 109.

272 "Unspeakable regret and gnawing remorse." Mrs. Shelley's note (written in the late 1830s) on her husband's poems of 1818. Shelley, P. B., *Poetical Works*, III 162. The citation that follows is from the same source, same page.

273   "A thousand liliputian ties." Mrs. Shelley's note on her husband's poems of 1820. Same, IV 54.

273   "Friends had gathered round us." Mrs. Shelley's note on her husband's poems of 1821. Same, 149.

273   "One is always in love." Shelley, from Lerici, to John Gisborne, 6-18-1822. Shelley, P. B., *Letters*, II 434.

273   Quarreling "like cats and dogs." Mary Shelley, from Lerici, to Maria Gisborne, 6-2-1822. Shelley, M., *Letters*, I 171.

273–74   "Making her sit in ice." Shelley, from Lerici, to John Gisborne, 6-18-1822. Shelley, P. B., *Letters*, II 434.

274   "I was not well in body or mind." Mary Shelley, from Pisa, to Maria Gisborne, 8-15-1822. Shelley, M., *Letters*, I 179.

274   "There it is again!" 5-6-1822. Jones, 147. (Williams' testimony.)

274   "I fell through weakness." Mary Shelley, from Pisa, to Maria Gisborne, 8-15-1822. Shelley, M., *Letters*, I 180. [Slight alterations for clarity: quotation mark inserted before "Get"; superfluous "the" deleted before "his widow"; final period written as question mark.]

274   "I participate in his enthusiasm." Shelley, from Lerici, to Trelawny, 5-16-1822. Shelley, P. B., *Letters*, II 421.

274   "A study & a carriage." Shelley, from Lerici, to Lord Byron, 5-1822. Same, 420.

275   "I have just heard from Hunt." Shelley, from Lerici, to Byron, 5-12-1822 [?]. Same, 417–18. [Source does not punctuate after salutation.]

275   "A thousand welcomes." Shelley, from Lerici, to Leigh Hunt, 6-19-1822. Same, 438–39.

275   "More mischievous than Yahoos." Byron, of Hunt's children, to Mrs. Shelley, 10-6-1822. Quennell, 708.

275   "I have not a moments leisure." Shelley, from Pisa, to Mary Shelley, 7-4-1822. Shelley, P. B., *Letters*, II 444.

275   "I fear you are solitary & melancholy." Shelley, from Pisa, to Jane Williams, 7-4-1822. Same, 445.

275   "I am ill most of this time." Shelley, M., *Journal*, 180.

275   The "white house with arches." Shelley's description to Hunt; Shelley, from Lerici, 6-19-1822. Shelley, P. B., *Letters*, II 438.

275–76   "How I long to see you." Edward Williams, from Leghorn, to Jane Williams, 7-6-1822. Jones, 163. [Original has only the *k* of "to break."]

276   "Disagreable news for their detention." Mary Shelley, from Pisa, to Maria Gisborne, 8-15-1822. Shelley, M., *Letters*, I 182. The two citations that follow are from the same source, same page.

276   "This mutilated corpse." Trelawny, 123.

276   "This mild-looking, beardless boy." Same, 26–27.

276–77   Byron's letter to Murray. Byron, from Pisa, 8-3-1822. Howarth, 331–32.

277   "Today—this day—" Mary Shelley, from Pisa, to Maria Gisborne, 8-15-1822. Shelley, M., *Letters*, I 185.

277   "I continue to exist." Mary Shelley, from Pisa, to Maria Gisborne, 8-1822. Same, 186.

277   "I have received my desk to-day." 10-7-1822. Shelley, M., *Journal*, 182.

277   Godwin's letter to Mary. Brown, 358.

278   Awake "with . . . horror of mind." 8-12-1823. Irving, *Journals 1819–27*, 210.

278   "She is unaltered." 11-26-1823. Robinson, II 260.

279   "Private Box with Miss Holcroft." 8-10-1824. Irving, *Journals 1819–27*, 378. The two citations that follow are from the same source: 381 (8-13-1824).

279   "Nothing but hard driving with me." Irving, from Brighton, to Thomas Moore, 8-14-1824. PMI, II 207–8.

279   "Respectable abroad as a *literary* people." *United States Literary Gazette*, 9-15-1824. STW, I 281.

279   "Washington Irving . . . is *not* dead." Carlyle to Jane Baillie Welsh, 1-8-1824. Same, 459, n. 10.

279–80   "Woke several times in the night." Irving, *Journals 1819–27*, 393. The five citations that follow are from the same source: 394, 421 (11-7), 427 (11-19; 11-21), 428 (11-23-1824).

280   Criticism of *Tales of a Traveller*. Reichart, 159 (9-1824); STW, I 278, 277, 276 (*Universal Review*); Reichart, 162.

280   "Recd. letter from N York." Irving, *Journals 1819–27*, 436.

280   "Some of the best things I have written." Irving, from Paris, to Mrs. Catharine Paris, 9-20-1824. PMI, II 214.

280   "Graceful and impressive narratives." "Tale-Writing . . . ." Poe, *The Complete Works*, ed. James A. Harrison (New York, 1902), XIII 153–54.

281   American reviewers on *Tales of a Traveller*. Wagenknecht, 13; Reichart, 162; STW, I 276.

281   "Are they cruel to travellers?" "The Inn at Terracina," *Tales of a Traveller*. Irving, *Works*, VII 262.

281–82   "I am out of the reach of attack." Irving, from Paris, 12-11-1824. Hellman, *Letters to Brevoort*, II 184–86.

282   "A dismal day of depression &c." Irving, *Journals 1819–27*, 442.

282   "Do you ever see Washington Irving?" Mary Shelley, from Kentish Town, to Louisa Holcroft, 1-6-1825. Shelley, M., *Letters*, I 313. [Original reads "W Irvin."] The citation that follows is from the same source: 312. (Louisa was the daughter of Godwin's close friend Thomas Holcroft. After Holcroft's death in 1809, his widow married the dramatist James Kenney, a friend of Payne's and of Irving's.)

282   "For the present is nought." Mary Shelley, from Kentish Town, to Trelawny, 2-22-1825. Same, 315.

282   "She but slightly returns this affection." 1-18-1824. Shelley, M., *Journal*, 192.

283   "I feel my powers again." Same, 194.

283   "Sunday Evening . . . Will you come?" Shelley, M., *Letters*, I 319.

283   "This ill turn." *Romance*, 24.

283   "It was ill done indeed." Mary Shelley, from Kentish Town, to Payne, 4-20-1825. Shelley, M., *Letters*, I 320. The citation that follows (4-22) is from the same source: 321.

284   Writing "frequently for orders." *Romance*, 20.

284   "A list of the illustrious obscure." Shelley's preface to *Adonais*. Shelley, P. B., *Poetical Works*, IV 86.

284   "I want some Howard Paine." Lamb to Mary Shelley, 7-26-1827. Lucas, III 110.

284   "United by a common calamity." *Romance*, 28.

284   "A heroine in love and friendship." Same, 30–31.

284–85   "Do not talk of frowns." Shelley, M., *Letters*, I 322.

285   "Four places will await you." *Romance*, 33–36.

285–86   "Your sincere friend, Mary Shelley." 5-4-1825 [?]. Shelley, M.,

Letters, I 322–23. [Complimentary close is indented, without punctuation.]

286   "We dine at four." 5-11-1825 [?]. Same, 324.

286   "A long conversation in walking home." *Romance*, 60–62. F. L. Jones dates the walk Saturday, 6-25-1825. See Shelley, M., *Letters*, I 332, n.

286–87   "Is it indelicate to ask for this?" Mary Shelley, from Kentish Town, to Payne, 6-28-1825. Shelley, M., *Letters*, I 331.

287–88   "I did not send the letter." *Romance*, 69–74. [Source indents immediately before "I am aware" and "I am sure."]

288   "Too much of an authoress after all." Mary Shelley, from Kentish Town, to Payne, 6-29-1825. Shelley, M., *Letters*, I 332–33.

288   "At the rate of the Antediluvians." Mary Shelley, from Kentish Town, to Payne, 7-28-1825. Same, 336.

288–89   "Unalterably yours, J. H. P." *Romance*, 83–84.

289   "37 engraved upon my tomb." Mary Shelley, from Kentish Town, to Payne, 6-29-1825. Shelley, M., *Letters*, I 333.

289   "I am a little fool." Mary Shelley, from Kentish Town, to Payne, 7-29-1825. Shelley, M., *Letters*, I 337.

289   "*Much future advantage*." Irving, from Paris, to Payne, 6-21-1825. Luquer, 601.

289   "A disposition to love somebody else." *Romance*, 87–88.

289–90   "I do not ask you to fall in love." Same, 17–19.

290   "I met the Duke of Wellington." Irving, *Journals 1819–27*, 509–10.

290–91   "An honest . . . uxorious man." Irving, from London, to J. K. Paulding, 5-27-1820. Irving, *Letters 1802–23*, 585. The citation that follows is from the same source, same page.

291   "50 Shares of Copper Mines." 6-1-1825. Irving, *Journals 1819–27*, 488. The six citations that follow are from the same source: 456, 467, 471 (two citations), 430 (11-27-1824), 443–44.

291   "Devouring my means, and studying hard." Irving, from Paris, to Payne, 2-21-1825. Irving, *Journals 1819–27*, 458, n. 39.

291   "On the subject of an original work." PMI, II 238.

291   "My brain is teeming." Irving, from Paris, to John Murray, 1-26-1825. McClary, 68.

292   "Project of an Am: Work." Irving, *Journals 1819–27*, 453. The two citations that follow are from the same source: 446, 480 [source indents before "It"].

292   "Nothing ready for the press." Irving, from Paris, to John Murray, 8-19-1825. McClary, 74 ["no" expanded to "not"].

292   "The squibs and crackers of criticism." Paulding to Irving, 9-3-1825. PMI, II 239.

292   "My appetite has failed me." Irving, *Journals 1819–27*, 531. The three citations that follow are from the same source: 537, 544, 546 [dash supplied after "house"].

293   "I am on the wing for Madrid!" Irving, from Bordeaux, to Payne, 2-8-1826. Irving, *Journals 1819–27*, 564, n. 104.

293   "Seven years since I had the pleasure." Godwin to Irving, 10-1829. Paul, II 300.

293   "Kind remembrances to Mrs Godwin." Irving, from Cavendish Square, to Godwin, 10-14-1829. Same, 302.

294   "Their admiration in the Inn's Album." Mary Shelley, from London, to Sir Walter Scott, 5-25-1829. Shelley, M., *Letters*, II 15.

294 "I love I own to face danger." Mary Shelley, from Pisa, to Shelley, 8-10-1821. Same, I 147.

294 "I admire it excessively." Mary Shelley, from London, to Sir John Bowring, 1-7-1830. Same, II 27.

294 "No book has delighted me so." Mary Shelley, from London, to John Murray, 12-7-1829 [?]. Same, 21.

294 "The medicine of my mind." 12-2-1834. Shelley, M., *Journal*, 203. [Source indents before "My heart."]

295 "Dearest, best and brightest." "The Pine Forest." Shelley, P. B., *Poetical Works*, IV 174.

295 "I am all cheerfulness." Godwin to Mary Shelley, 10-9-1827. Paul, II 299.

295 "The particular shape of a room." Shelley, M., *Rambles*, II 78.

295 "That family does really love me." 3-26-1812. Bixby, II 398.

295 "Clear as if stamped yesterday." Mrs. Shelley's preface to the 1839 edition of her husband's poetry. Shelley, P. B., *Poetical Works*, I xvi.

295 "He never mentioned love." Mary Shelley's note on her husband's poems written in 1818. Same, III 159.

295 "The terraces, the vineyards." Shelley, M., *Rambles*, I 139.

295 "The banks of the Brenta." Same, II 79.

296 "Tell us how you got home." This and the citation that follows are from Mary Shelley's letter to Maria Gisborne, 8-15-1822, containing the account of Shelley's death. Shelley, M., *Letters*, I 182.

296 "This is now my life." Claire Clairmont to Mary Shelley, 10-30-1840. Grylls, 233.

296 "Leave off your stays." 4-11-1849. Same, 236.

296 Henry James. "The Aspern Papers" was inspired by Claire Clairmont's situation in the final years of her life.

296 "The many important obligations." Irving, from Bordeaux, to Payne, 1-3-1825. Luquer, 598.

297 "Drinking brandy and water." A. Chapolie, from Tunis, 4-28-1883. Harrison, 252.

297 "The coffin was badly decayed." John Worthington, from Tunis, 1-5-1883. Same, 271.

297–98 "Emily Foster, now Emily Fuller." PMI, IV 217–18.

298 "Imagine my surprise and delight." Irving, from Sunnyside, to Mrs. Emily Fuller, 7-2-1856. Same, 218–20.

298–99 Irving and Matilda. PMI, I 229–30. [I have introduced an indentation after "workmanship."]

299 Her mimicry and teasing. Irving, *Notes* [Introduction by Stanley T. Williams], 37, 40.

299 "Ever young and beautiful." Notebook, 1822. PMI, I 231. Compare Irving, *Journals 1819–27*, 281, n. 478.

DON WASHINGTON IRVING IN SPAIN

301 Epigraph. "Recollections of the Alhambra," *Wolfert's Roost*. Irving, *Works*, XVI 366.

302 "The romantic halls of the Alhambra." "Important Negotiations . . ." *The Alhambra*. Irving, *Works*, XV 69.

302 "The chivalrous library of Don Quixote." *Knickerbocker*, V v. Irving, *Works*, I 294.

302   "Life of the Party." 12-30-1822. Irving, *Journals 1819–27*, 103.

303   "The vintage at Bordeaux." Irving to Peter Irving, 8-26-1825. PMI, II 241.

303   "So closes the year." Irving, *Journals 1819–27*, 557.

303   "Great depression of spirits." Irving, from Bordeaux, to T. W. Storrow, 10-31-1825. Williams, *Storrows*, 52–53. The two citations that follow are from the same source: 53.

303   "My extremity is come." 12-18-1825; 1-16-1826. Scott, *Journal*, 38, 60.

303   "The treasures of Mexico & Peru." Irving, from Bordeaux, to T. W. Storrow, 10-31-1825. Williams, *Storrows*, 53.

303   "Cruel suspense & anxiety." Irving, from Bordeaux, to T. W. Storrow, 11-8-1825. Same, 55.

305   "Marked *Clothes*." Irving, from Bordeaux, to T. W. Storrow, 12-25-1825. Same, 62–63.

305   Irving's letter to Everett. Irving, from Bordeaux, to Alexander H. Everett, 1-12-1826. PMI, II 246.

306   "I must return you my thanks." Same, 248.

306   "Attack it tooth & nail." Irving, from Bordeaux, to T. W. Storrow, 2-3-1826. Williams, *Storrows*, 64.

306   "On the wing for Madrid!" Irving, from Bordeaux, to Payne, 2-8-1826. Irving, *Journals 1819–27*, 564, n. 104.

306   "Travelling day and night." Irving, from Madrid, to Susan Storrow. 2-26-1826. Williams, *Storrows*, 71.

306–44   My citations incorporate changes kindly furnished from the manuscripts by Professor Andrew Myers, who is editing Irving's Spanish journals for future publication; thus discrepancies exist between citations printed throughout this chapter and those found both in Trent and Hellman and in Penney.

306–7   "Strong featurd country." 2-12-1826. Trent and Hellman, III 2. Citations that follow through "Huge rambling inns" are from the same source: 2-4 (2-12 and 2-13-1826).

307   "*Arriba! arriba!*" [Mackenzie], I 85.

307–8   "Castilian pride." Trent and Hellman, III 4–6 (2-13 to 2-15-1826). Citations from these pages include all through "a cold shivering day." [Dashes inserted for clarity around "Castilian pride."]

308–9   Madrid in 1826. The description draws on [Mackenzie], I 171–75, on Inglis, I 65–111, and on Bowers, 15–18.

308   "After passing through most of the gates." *Modern Traveller*, II 108.

309   Streets "swarm with groups." Irving, from Madrid, to Susan Storrow, 2-26-1826. Williams, *Storrows*, 72.

309–10   Irving and the muleteers. 3-20-1826. Trent and Hellman, III 16–17.

310   "I wish you could all be here." Irving, from Madrid, to T. W. Storrow, 3-30-1826. Williams, *Storrows*, 77.

310   "An ill-laid out garden." Inglis, I 96–97.

310–11   "Six milk-white steeds." [Mackenzie], I 306. The two citations that follow are from the same source.

311   "Gloomy religious frenzy." Longfellow, I 120.

311   "Next comes Don Carlos." [Mackenzie], I 306.

311   "Walked . . . in the Retiro." 3-30-1826. Trent and Hellman, III 19–20.

311   "An American a book collector." 2-16-1826. Trent and Hellman, III 7. The three citations that follow are from the same source, same page (2-16, 2-17, 2-18-1826).

311   "The ground floor of a great Spanish house." Irving, from Madrid, to Susan Storrow, 2-26-1826. Williams, *Storrows*, 73.

312   "Called this morng on Sigr Navarette." Trent and Hellman, III 10.

312   "The Booksellers will not offer." Irving, from Madrid, to T. W. Storrow, 3-15-1826. Same, 74.

312   "Unfit for any occupation." Trent and Hellman, III 13. The citations that follow are from the same source: 16, 18 (3-18, 3-24-1826).

312   "Turning and turning it over." Irving, from Madrid, to T. W. Storrow, 3-30-1826. Williams, *Storrows*, 77.

312–13   "Great ringing of bells." Trent and Hellman, III 18. The citations that follow from Irving's journal appear in Trent and Hellman, III 20–27.

313   "Hard study & hard work." Irving, from Madrid, to T. W. Storrow, 4-14-1826. Williams, *Storrows*, 80. The citation that follows is from the same source, same page.

313   "A minute and circumstantial narrative." "Preface," *Life and Voyages of Columbus.* Irving, *Works*, III xv.

313   "I never worked so hard." Irving, from Madrid, to T. W. Storrow, 6-12-1826. Williams, *Storrows*, 83.

313   Irving's nephew in Madrid. PMI, II 253.

314   "Robbing & murder—hanged." 8-11-1826. Trent and Hellman, III 36.

314   The spectator at the execution. [Mackenzie], I 342–52.

314   "Round bellied Spanish Marquis." 6-26-1826. Trent and Hellman, III 30.

314   "The heavy & anxious toil is over." Irving, from Madrid, to T. W. Storrow, 8-16-1826. Williams, *Storrows*, 95.

314   "A view over . . . the city." Irving, from Madrid, to Susan Storrow, 12-28-1826. Same, 103. The description of Irving's quarters that follows is from the same source: 102–4.

314–15   "So ends 1826." Trent and Hellman, III 49. The two citations that follow are from the same source: 48, 51 (12-22-1826, 1-16-1827).

315   "It will not bear hurrying." Irving, from Madrid, to Pierre M. Irving, 2-22-1827. PMI, II 257.

315   "Mr Longfellow arrives." 3-7-1828. Trent and Hellman, III 56.

315   "Society . . . is very limited." Longfellow, from Madrid, to his father, 3-20-1827. Longfellow, I 108.

315   "A school-boy when it was published." 12-15-1859. *Irvingiana*, xxxvi.

315   Longfellow's description of Irving. Longfellow, I 108–9.

315   "Still requiring the finishing hand." Irving, from Madrid, to T. W. Storrow, 2-26-1827. Williams, *Storrows*, 109.

316   "Bad calculators of their time." Irving, from Madrid, to Mrs. Storrow, 5-5-1827. Same, 112. The citation that follows is from the same source, same page.

316   "An important affair for me." Irving, from Madrid, to T. W. Storrow, 7-9-1827. Same, 117.

316   "Waiting with great anxiety." Irving, from Madrid, to Col. Thomas Aspinwall, 8-19-1827. Aderman.

316   "Peter . . . with his hat on." Irving, from Madrid, to T. W. Storrow, 9-14-1827. Williams, *Storrows*, 121.

316–17   "Exploits of Don Quixote." Irving, from Granada, to Antoinette Bolviller, 3-15-1828. PMI, II 286. The three citations that follow (through "Despeña Perros") are from the same source: 286–87.

317   "The route . . . from Cordova to Granada." Irving, from Granada, to Alexander H. Everett, 3-15-1828. Aderman.

317   "No accommodations . . . at the posadas." Irving, from Seville, to Everett, 4-15-1828. PMI, II 305–6.

317   "The evening sun shone gloriously." Irving, from Granada, to Antoinette Bolviller, 3-15-1828. PMI, II 288.

318   "This fragrant and lovely land!" Same, 288–89.

318   "Among rocks and precipices." Irving, from Málaga, to Prince Dolgorouki, 3-29-1828. PMI, II 294. The citation that follows is from the same source, same page.

318   Boulders "impending over us." Irving, from Málaga, to Antoinette Bolviller, 4-2-1828. Same, 301.

318   "Along the face of vast promontories." Irving, from Málaga, to Prince Dolgorouki, 3-29-1828. Same, 294–95.

318   "Our greatest risk." Irving, from Granada, to Antoinette Bolviller, 3-15-1828. Same, 285.

318   *"No me quita usted la vida!"* [Mackenzie], I 90.

318   "In these unsettled times." Irving, from Madrid, to Mrs. Storrow, 5-5-1827. Williams, *Storrows,* 113–14.

319   A "singular character." Irving, from Málaga, to Antoinette Bolviller, 4-2-1828. PMI, II 299.

319   "Drenched by . . . heavy rains." Irving, from Seville, to Alexander Everett, 4-15-1828. PMI, II 306.

319   "Very drowsy" in the saddle. 4-12-1828. Penney, 7.

319   Cádiz "a beautiful city." Irving, from Seville, to Everett, 4-15-1828. PMI, II 307.

319   "Veteran soldier." 4-13-1828. Penney, 8.

319   "Repinings at past prosperity." Irving, from Seville, to Everett, 4-15-1828. PMI, II 307.

319   "In the Steam boat Betis." 4-14-1828. Penney, 8–9.

319–20   Irving at Palos. 8-13-1828. Penney, 53–54, 51, 55. [Dash omitted between "21" and "Franciscan."]

320   "Not be the fault of the subject." Irving, from Madrid, to T. W. Storrow, 8-31-1826. Williams, *Storrows,* 97.

320   "To washington irving, esq." STW, II 14.

320   "All kinds of merit." Address to New York Historical Society, 12-6-1859. *Irvingiana,* xxxi.

320   *"Ha logrado dar á su historia."* "Preface," *Life and Voyages of Columbus.* Irving, *Works,* III xviii.

320   "More toil and trouble." Irving, from Seville, 12-20-1828. Hellman, *Letters to Brevoort,* II 207.

320   "A remembrance of the author." Advertisement, dated from Seville, 12-1828, for Irving's condensation of *Columbus; New York American,* 4-4-1829. STW, I 492.

321   "All the fascination of a novel." Charles Leslie, from London, to Irving, 3-19-1828. Leslie, 280.

321   "Those who learn the history." Irving, from Seville, to Alexander Everett, 4-23-1828. PMI, II 313.

321   A "region of fire." *Life and Voyages of Columbus.* Irving, *Works,* III 38.

321–22   Citations from Columbus' letter. Morison, I 203–4. References indicating this distinguished historian's regard for Irving appear on I 36, 117, 219, 309, 426.

322   "Exposed to scoffs and indignities." *Life and Voyages of Columbus.* Irving, *Works,* III 99.

322   "Into the region of discovery." Same, 131.

322–23　"A singular jet of flame." Saturday, 9-15-1492. Columbus' journal, as retold by Las Casas. Landström, 61. The two citations that follow are from the same source: 66 (10-8 and 10-10-1492).

323　"A people very guileless." Morison, I 340–41.

323　"Most momentous of all maritime enterprises." *Life and Voyages of Columbus.* Irving, *Works*, III 258–59.

323　"The latter part of the work." Irving, from Madrid, to John Murray, 7-29-1827. McClary, 92.

324　"Meet with a young spaniard." Penney, 57 [source indents before "Conversation"]. The citation that follows is from the same source: 59.

324　"Work of Pedro Aliaco." 6-26-1828. Same, 39.

324–25　"They deserved this country." Irving, from Seville, to Antoinette Bolviller, 5-28-1828. PMI, II 322.

325　"The whole character of the place is peculiar." Irving, from Seville, to Alexander Everett, 4-15-1828. PMI, II 309.

325　"You look into beautiful courts." Irving, from Seville, to Catharine D'Oubril, 4-19-1828. Aderman.

325–26　At the cattle fair. 4-27-1828. Penney, 16–17. The seven citations that follow are from the same source: 21 (5-9, Giralda), 31–32 (5-30), 33 (6-5), 61–62 (8-24), 63 (8-28-1828, taste wine).

326　"Lingering here in Andalusia." Irving, from Seville, 12-20-1828. Hellman, *Letters to Brevoort*, II 208.

326　"Thus ends the year." Penney, 90.

327　"One half is enough." Irving, from Seville, to Catharine D'Oubril, 4-21-1829. Aderman. The citation that follows is from the same source.

327　The ruins of the country seat alight. Irving, from Seville, to Nathalie Richter, 4-22-1829. Aderman.

327　"Merely Tangiers and Tetuan." Irving to Everett. PMI, II 379.

328–29　"By way of *robber purse*." "The Journey," *The Alhambra.* Irving, *Works*, XV 19. The twelve citations that follow (through "the very heart") are from the same source: 16–30.

329　"Savoury meals." Irving, from Granada, to Sarah Van Wart, 5-12-1829. Aderman.

330　"No book has delighted me so." Mary Shelley, from London, to John Murray, 12-7-1829 [?]. Shelley, M., *Letters*, II 21. And to Sir John Bowring, 1-7-1830. Same, 27.

330　Coleridge's reaction, and Bryant's. PMI, II 376–77.

330　Prescott's judgment of *The Conquest.* Prescott, II 109. ". . . the reader, who will take the trouble to compare his [Irving's] Chronicle with the present more prosaic and literal narrative, will see how little he has been seduced from historic accuracy by the poetical aspect of his subject." Same.

330　A modern study of Moorish Spain. Jan Read, *The Moors in Spain and Portugal* (Totowa, N.J., 1975), 251.

330–31　"Granada had risen to splendor." *Conquest of Granada.* Irving, *Works*, XIV 20.

331　"A little freedom of pencil." Irving to Prince Dolgorouki, 12-13-1828. PMI, II 349.

331　"Between a history and a romance." Irving to Thomas Aspinwall, 4-4-1829. Harbert, 307.

331　"Freer scope in . . . coloring." Irving, from Seville, to Alexander Everett, 2-14-1829. PMI, II 369.

331   "Not the man to paint tumultuous war." Smiles, II 258.

332   The besieged "raving mad." *Conquest of Granada*, VI. Irving, *Works*, XIV 53.

332   The beautiful Moorish female. Same, V. *Works*, XIV 43.

332   "Love-tales and . . . gallantry." Irving, *Spanish Papers*, II 380.

332   "Sternest of those iron conflicts." "Note to the Revised Edition," *The Conquest of Granada* [Holly Edition, New York, 1892], I xxiv.

332   "Two valiant alcaydes." *Conquest of Granada.* Irving, *Works*, XIV 42.

332–33   "Thirty thousand castellanos." Same, 513. The two citations that follow are from the same source: 526, 530.

333   "Trying to conjure up images." Irving, from the Alhambra, to Antoinette Bolviller, 3-15-1828. PMI, II 289.

333   "Granada in all its glory." Irving, from Seville, to Mme D'Oubril, 4-17-1829. Aderman.

333   "The loveliest spots I had ever seen." Irving, from Granada, to Sarah Van Wart, 5-12-1829. Aderman. The citation that follows is from the same source.

334   "From the tower of the Gomares." Irving, from the Alhambra, to Dolgorouki, 5-23-1829. Aderman.

334   "Delicious spots in the world." Irving, from the Alhambra, 5-23-1829. Hellman, *Letters to Brevoort*, II 212–14. The citation that follows is from the same source.

334–35   "My bedroom and study." Irving, from the Alhambra, to Prince Dolgorouki, 6-15-1829. PMI, II 393.

335–36   "Vague and indescribable awe." "The Mysterious Chambers," *The Alhambra.* Irving, *Works*, XV 100. The four citations that follow (through "violent paroxysms") are from the same source: 100–102.

336   "The little garden of Lindaraxa." Irving, from the Alhambra, to Prince Dolgorouki, 6-15-1829. PMI, II 393.

336   "Man, and steed, and beast of burden." "The Balcony," *The Alhambra.* Irving, *Works*, XV 122. The two citations that follow are from the same source: 122–23.

336   "I sit by my window." Irving, from the Alhambra, to Prince Dolgorouki, 6-15-1829. PMI, II 393–94.

336   "Nothing . . . more favorable for study." Irving, from the Alhambra, to Peter Irving, 6-13-1829. Same, 391.

337   "Crystal fabrics of . . . frost." "The Court of Lions," *The Alhambra.* Irving, *Works*, XV 128.

337   "Velvet caparisons, embroidered with gold." "Legend of the Three Beautiful Princesses." Same, 280.

338   "The very cross . . . upon the wall." "The Court of Lions." Same, 129. The two citations that follow are from the same source: 129–30.

338   "A day-dream realized." "Important Negotiations . . ." *The Alhambra.* Irving, *Works*, XV 69.

338   "The account of my midnight rambles." Irving, from Sunnyside, to S. A. Allibone, 11-2-1857. STW, I 375.

339   "Put me up a parcel." Irving, from the Alhambra, to Prince Dolgorouki, 6-15-1829. PMI, II 395.

339   "Secretary of Legation to London." 7-18-1829. Diary entry quoted in PMI, II 396.

339   "Indifference to all official honors." Irving, from the Alhambra, to Peter Irving, 7-18-1829. Same, 398.

339 "An abode so much to my taste." Irving, from Valencia, 8-10-1829. Hellman, *Letters to Brevoort*, II 220.

339 "The return to my native country." Penney, 90.

339 "A craving desire to return." Irving, from Seville, to Peter Irving, 3-3-1829. PMI, II 372.

339 "The happiest day of my life." Irving, from the Alhambra, 5-23-1829. Hellman, *Letters to Brevoort*, II 218.

340 "Leave Granada . . . with Mr Sneyd." Trent and Hellman, III 64.

340 "A glorious view of the city." "The Author's Farewell to Granada," *The Alhambra.* Irving, *Works*, XV 424–25.

340 "To our right is the Sierra Nevada." Trent and Hellman, III 64. The citation that follows is from the same source: 65.

340 "Two mattresses on which we lolled." Irving, from Valencia, to Catharine Paris, 8-10-1829. Aderman. Irving's sister Catharine Paris, to whom he wrote many letters in later life, was the Kitty who had been courted as a young New Yorker by the luckless John Anderson (page 41 above). After her husband's death Mrs. Paris lived at Sunnyside. Her daughter Sarah, Irving's favorite niece, married the son of his good friend Thomas Wentworth Storrow and lived out her adult life in Paris.

340–41 "Grape vines clambering." 8-4-1829. Trent and Hellman, III 76. The three citations that follow are from the same source: 83 (8-8), 72 (8-2), 80 (8-6-1829).

341 "Twelve days in reaching this place." Irving, from Valencia, to Catharine Paris, 8-10-1829. Aderman.

341–42 "Soldiers & housemaids." 8-10-1829. Trent and Hellman, III 86. The six citations that follow are from the same source: 86 (8-10: "tower"), 87 (8-12), 87–88 (8-12: "arm"), 90 (8-14: "diligence"), 93 (8-16: "Gracia"), 94–95 (8-17: "Count D'Espagne's").

342 "The rigor of his military rule." Irving, from Barcelona, to Mrs. Catharine Paris, 7-5-1844. PMI, III 350.

343 "Capt Gen*l* very affable." 8-17-1829. Trent and Hellman, III 94. ["Argnt" expanded to "argument."]

343 The Count and the functionary. Irving, from Barcelona, to Mrs. Catharine Paris, 7-5-1844. PMI, III 351.

343 "His jokes were coarse." Same, 350.

343 "The sight of our Trunks." 8-21-1829. Trent and Hellman, III 95. The citation that follows is from the same source: 96 (8-22-1829).

343 "I shall leave Spain with . . . regret." Irving, from Valencia, 8-10-1829. Hellman, *Letters to Brevoort*, II 224.

343–44 "To the Spanish custom house." 8-23-1829. Trent and Hellman, III 97.

344 Irving's writings on Spain. Williams, *Background*, II 38.

344 "A return of his fever." Irving, from Paris, to Catharine Paris, 10-6-1829. PMI, II 413. The three citations that follow are from the same source, same page.

344–45 "Fresh and fair as a rose." Hellman, *Esquire*, 220.

345 "Ah, the times are changed." PMI, II 459.

345 "Spend the evening with us in Seymour street?" Emily Fuller, to Irving, 5-25-1856. PMI, IV 218.

345 "Getting tipsy together at Richmond." Irving, from the Alhambra, to Peter Irving, 7-18-1829. PMI, II 399.

345 "What a stirring moment it is to live in." Irving, from London, 3-31-1831. Hellman, *Letters to Brevoort*, II 230.

345   Irving's "untiring disposition." Van Buren, from London, to President Jackson, 11-25-1831. STW, II 11.

346   "A villainous propensity to grow round." Irving, from London, to Gouverneur Kemble, 1-18-1830. PMI, II 427.

346   "The greater charm it has." Irving, from Madrid, 4-4-1827. Hellman, *Letters to Brevoort*, II 196.

346   "Old friends and old scenes." Irving, from London, to Gouverneur Kemble, 1-18-1830. PMI, II 427.

346   "A heart swelling with old recollections." *Irvingiana*, xv. The citation that follows ("extending") is from the same source.

346–47   The *"Havre* arrived last evening." 5-22-1832. Nevins, *Hone*, I 62–63.

347   "Greenwich is in the city." Lucy Payne to John Howard Payne, 3-29-1829. Overmyer, 277.

347   "The Richmond Hill Theater." 11-15-1831. Nevins, *Hone*, I 53.

347   "Absolutely overwhelmed." Irving, from New York, to Peter Irving. PMI, II 486. The citation that follows is from the same source.

347   "A public dinner." 5-23-1832. STW, II 336, n. 41.

347   "Wednesday next for that purpose." 5-24-1832. Same. Both letters appeared in the *New-York Mirror* for 6-9-1832.

347–48   "A strain of surprising eloquence." 5-30-1832. Nevins, *Hone*, I 65. The citation that follows is from the same source.

348   "I trembled for him." The friend was the painter Gilbert Stuart Newton. PMI, II 491.

348   "As long as I live." *Irvingiana*, xvi.

348   "You are an orator." Brevoort, from Fontainebleau, to Irving, 7-28-1832. STW, II 336, n. 41; Hellman, *Letters to Irving*, II 91.

348   Opinion of *The Alhambra*. 6-23-1832. Quoted in PMI, III 20.

348–49   "A very interesting tour." Irving, from Cincinnati, to Mrs. Catharine Paris, 9-2-1832. PMI, III 34. The citation that follows, immediately after the section break, is from the same source.

349   "Good moral books and papers." Oates, 21.

349   "Looked upon . . . with Suspicion." Testimony of James Foreman, from Youngsville, Pa., 12-28-1859. Ruchames, 167.

349   *"Remarkably plain"* Dianthe. Brown, from Red Rock, Iowa, to Henry L. Stearns, 7-15-1857. Same, 40.

349   John, Jr.'s account book. Sanborn, 92.

349   "The tetotal temperance principles." Testimony of James Foreman, 12-28-1859. Ruchames, 167.

350   Brown's sermon topics. Oates, 22.

350   "The rod of our Heavenly Father." Brown to Owen Brown. Ruchames, 41.

350   "Teach him the fear of God." Brown, from Randolph, Pa., to Frederick Brown, 11-21-1834. Same, 42.

351   "Our debts must be paid." Brown, from New Hartford, to his family, 6-12-1839. Villard, 30.

351   Recollections of Brown's home. Testimony of Salmon Brown, who died in 1919. Ruchames, 183, 185–86.

351   A "strong, desire; *to die*." Brown, to Franklin B. Sanborn, 2-24-1858. Oates, 50.

351–52   "In a little row together." Brown, from Richfield, Ohio, to John Brown, Jr., 9-25-1843. Ruchames, 50.

352   "Cozily quartered." Irving, from Wolfert's Roost [Sunnyside], to Pierre M. Irving, 5-18-1838. PMI, III 129.

352–53   "Intertwined together." Irving, to Sarah Van Wart, autumn, 1838.

PMI, III 130. The five citations that follow (through "completely overcome") are from the same source: 130–31.

353 "Get my pen into motion." Irving, from Sunnyside, to Sarah Van Wart, 12-1-1838. PMI, III 132.

353 "Venerable, parchment-bound tomes." Irving, *Spanish Papers*, I 457.

353 "Wrote at . . . conquest of Mexico." 12-12-1827. Myers, A., 410.

353 "Read in Solis Hist. Mexico." 10-21-1828. Penney, 75.

353 "Plan to write some standard works." Ellsworth, 78.

353 "A vein of literary occupation." Irving, from Sunnyside, to Sarah Van Wart, 12-1-1838. PMI, III 132.

354 "Daily occupation for three months." Irving, from New York, to William H. Prescott, 1-18-1839. Same, 138.

354 Irving's projected Conquest of Mexico. Irving, from Madrid, to Pierre Irving. PMI, III 144–45.

354 The "pendant to my Columbus." Same, 143.

354 "Across the same ground." Same, 133.

354–55 "A warm and sudden impulse." Irving, from Madrid, to Pierre Irving. Same, 143. The citation that follows is from the same source.

355 "These things break my rest." Irving, from New York, to Sarah Storrow, 10-3-1841. Williams, *Sunnyside and Spain*, 38.

355 "The most astonished man in the city of New York." PMI, III 176.

355 "I accept . . . the honorable post." Irving, from New York, to Hon. Daniel Webster, 2-18-1842. Same, 180.

355 "Send us such names as this." Same, 179.

355 Clay's letter to Irving. Clay, from Washington, to Irving, 3-29-1842. Same, 188.

356 "Beat me at farming." Irving, from New York, to Ebenezer Irving, 2-17-1842. Same, 179.

356 "Pocketing what is not due me." Irving, from New York to Philip Hone, 4-4-1842. PMI, III 190–91.

356 "That glorious fellow" Dickens. Irving, from Sunnyside, to Sarah Storrow, 5-25-1841. Same, 164.

356 Dickens' letter to Irving. Same, 164–65.

356 "A triumph . . . as was never known." Dickens to William Hall, 9-14-1841. Johnson, *Dickens*, 352.

357 "All readers of famous Diedrich Knickerbocker's History." *American Notes*, Chapter V [in *Dickens's Works*, London, 1874], 90. The citation that follows is from the same source, same page.

357 "I shall certainly break down!" Recollection of C. C. Felton, quoted in PMI, III 184–85. See also Wilson, *Halleck*, 437.

357–58 Dickens' speech. Wagenknecht, 95; Johnson, *Dickens*, 389.

358 "That captivating laugh of his." Johnson, *Dickens*, 406.

358 "Your affectionate friend." Dickens, from Washington, D.C., to Irving, 3-21-1842. PMI, III 187.

358 "Our windows look upon green lawn." Irving, from Little Cloisters, Westminster Abbey, to Sarah Storrow, 5-10-1842. Aderman.

358 "Dreams turned into realities?" Irving, from London, to Catharine Paris, 5-9-1842. PMI, III 197–98.

359 "The man . . . I wanted to shake hands with." 5-10-1842. Moore, VII 319.

359 Irving describes Queen Victoria. Irving, from Birmingham, to Catharine Paris, 5-7-1842. PMI, III 196.

359 The garden at Rouen. Irving, from Paris, to Sarah Van Wart, 6-8-1842. Same, 204.

359   "The charm of former visits." Irving, from Paris, to Sarah Irving, 5-29-1842. Same, 204.

359   "In good heart and good order." Irving, from New York, to Ebenezer Irving, 2-17-1842. PMI, III 179. The citation that follows is from the same source: 180.

360   "The air of romance." Irving, from Madrid, to Sarah Storrow, 11-26-1842. STW, II 142.

360   Irving presents his credentials. Irving, from Madrid, to Mrs. Catharine Paris, 8-3-1842. PMI, III 220–23.

360–62   Isabella's reception of Irving. STW, II 141–42. Irving's description that continues is taken from his letter to Mrs. Paris cited immediately above: 223.

361   "Certain reverend crowned heads." Irving, from Madrid, to Hon. Daniel Webster, 11-5-1842. Hellman, *Esquire*, 287.

362   "A mere effigy of royalty." Irving, from Madrid, to Mrs. Catharine Paris, 8-3-1842. PMI, III 223.

362   "A couple of little girls." Irving, from Madrid, to Catharine Paris, Same, 256.

362   "My whole impression." Irving, from Madrid, to Catharine Paris, 11-20-1842. Williams, *Sunnyside and Spain*, 49.

362   "Confiding in your secrecy." Irving, from Madrid, to Catherine Paris. PMI, III 257–58. The citation that follows is from the same source: 258.

362   Her skin is "*mealy*." Irving, from Madrid, to Catharine Paris, 11-20-1842. Williams, *Sunnyside and Spain*, 49.

362   "We made respectful reverences." Irving, from Madrid, to Catharine Paris, 11-15-1842. PMI, III 258.

363   Isabella's "constitutional malady." The Countess of Cardigan's phrase. Aronson, 176.

363   "Careless of the world's talk." Testimony of a contemporary visitor to Spain. Same, 63.

363–64   "The combustible community in a flame." Irving, from Madrid, to Mrs. Catharine Paris, 11-25-1842. PMI, III 259–60. The description of the Regent reviewing his troops is from the same source: 260–61.

364   "Violent remedies." Irving, from Madrid, to Hon. Daniel Webster, 8-27-1842. Hellman, *Esquire*, 282.

364   "A grand career." Irving, from Madrid, to Catharine Paris, 8-3-1842. PMI, III 224.

364   "Mystery and legerdemain." Irving, from Madrid, to Hon. Daniel Webster, 11-5-1842. Hellman, *Esquire*, 290.

365–66   One typical day. Irving, from Madrid, to Mrs. Eliza Romeyn, 8-16-1842. PMI, III 225–27.

366   "Such a range of *salons*." Irving, from Madrid, to Miss Charlotte Irving, 9-16-1842. Same, 247–48.

366   "Ambassador on a cautious scale." Irving, from Madrid, to Mrs. Moses H. Grinnell, 9-30-1842. Same, 250.

366   Irving's customs declarations. Bowers, 148; STW, H 143.

366   Servants "bowing . . . with profound respect." Hellman, *Esquire*, 266.

367   "I miss all my former intimates." Irving, from Madrid, to Prince Dolgorouki, 10-18-1842. PMI, III 252–53.

367–68   "Much to tolerate in Spain." Irving, from Madrid, to Sarah Storrow, 10-8-1842. STW, II 147. The citation that follows ("fairy air castles") is from the same source: 147–48. Irving identifies Ford as his critic in a letter of 1850 quoted in PMI, IV 76.

368   "A state of intermittent revolution." Irving, from Madrid, to Hon. Daniel Webster, 12-10-1842. Hellman, *Esquire*, 293. The citation that follows is from the same source, same page.

368   "Conspiracies, and insurrections." Irving, from Madrid, to Sarah Storrow, 6-27-1843. PMI, III 281.

368   "Voices in the street." Irving, from Madrid, to Sarah Storrow, 7-14-1843. Same, 283.

369   "Sally forth to see a fire." Irving, to Sarah Storrow. Hellman, *Esquire*, 270.

369   "A city in a state of siege." Irving, from Madrid, to Sarah Storrow, 7-14-1843. PMI, III 284. The two citations that follow are from the same source: 284–85.

369   "The flash of guns." Irving, from Madrid, to Sarah Storrow, 7-13 [for 18?]-1843. PMI, III 288.

369   "Two or three distant shots." Same, 289.

370   "Repair in person to the palace." Irving, from Madrid, to Hon. Hugh S. Legare, 7-22-1843. Hellman, *Esquire*, 298.

370   "The safety of the Queen." Irving, from Madrid, to Sarah Storrow, 7-13-1843. PMI, III 288.

370   "The question is decided." Irving, from Madrid, to Hon. Hugh S. Legare, 7-23-1843. Hellman, *Esquire*, 299.

370   "Bands of rough soldiery." Irving, from Madrid, to American Secretary of State, 8-3-1843. Same, 304.

370   "Clause one and only." Clarke, 190.

370   "Three rival generals." Irving, from Madrid, to American Secretary of State, 8-3-1843. Hellman, *Esquire*, 303.

370   "The complicated web of intrigues." Irving, from Madrid, to Hon. Daniel Webster, 11-5-1842. Same, 285.

370   "The accursed race of the Bourbons." Gribble, 270.

371   "At the window of a railroad car." Irving, from Madrid, to Hon. Daniel Webster, 11-11-1842. STW, II 150–51.

371   The "veteran courtiers." Irving, from Madrid, to Catharine Paris, 8-25-1843. Williams, *Sunnyside and Spain*, 60. The citation that follows is from the same source: 63.

372   The "poor old wrinkled face." Testimony of an acquaintance of Isabella's in old age. Aronson, 177.

372   "Descriptions of the little Queen." Irving, from Madrid, to Catharine Paris, 8-25-1843. Williams, *Sunnyside and Spain*, 65.

372   "Sources of profit dried up." Irving, from Madrid, to Mrs. Catharine Paris, 5-6-1843. STW, II 159.

373   "The populace in their holiday garbs." Irving, from Madrid, to Hon. A. P. Upshur, 12-8-1843. Same, 164.

373   "Rallying point of national feeling." Irving, from Madrid, to the American Secretary of State, 8-19-1843. Hellman, *Esquire*, 308. The citation that follows is from the same source, same page.

373   Isabella's deposition about Olózaga. Clarke, 195.

373   "Dark knots of politicians." Irving, from Madrid, to Hon. A. P. Upshur, 12-8-1843. STW, II 164.

374   Irving defends the Princess of Carini. Irving, from Madrid, to Sarah Storrow, 2-10-1844. Same, 170–71.

374   "The disclosure of filial love." González Bravo, from Madrid, to Irving, 2-16-1844. STW, II 173. ["CHRISTINA" in source.]

375   "What is the case at present?" Irving, from Madrid, to Catharine Paris, 3-16-1844. PMI, III 325.

375   Irving witnesses María Cristina's return. Irving, from Madrid, to Catharine Paris, 3-23-1844. Same, 327–28.

375   "Gorged with riches." Testimony of the French minister Guizot. Aronson, 47.

375–76   "Marriage with Don Fernando Muñoz." Gribble, 115.

376   "Long live Spain's Guardian Angel!" Aronson, 47.

376   "Like a boy with a new coat." Irving, from Madrid, to Catharine Paris, 4-17-1844. PMI, III 338–39.

376   "The green alleys of the Retiro." Irving, from Madrid, to Pierre M. Irving, 4-28-1844. Same, 340.

376–77   The count's "sanguinary acts." Irving, from Barcelona, to Mrs. Catharine Paris, 7-5-1844. PMI, III 351. The four citations that follow (through "low voice") are from the same source: 352–53.

377   "My life has been a chequered one." Irving, from Madrid, to Sarah Storrow, 3-27-1845. PMI, III 374.

377–78   Describing the married lady. Irving, on board the *Villa de Madrid* and at Marseille, to Mrs. Catharine Paris, 7-29 and 7-31-1844. PMI, III 358–60. The two citations concerning the arrival at Marseille are from the same source: 360.

378–79   "Her arms round my neck." Irving, from Madrid, to Mrs. Catharine Paris, 11-26-1844. PMI, III 364. The three citations that follow (through "*Besa manos*") are from the same source, same page.

379   "Ambitious of the smiles of the ladies." Irving, from Madrid, to Hon. James Buchanan, 7-10-1845. Hellman, *Esquire*, 320.

379   Narváez's ball. Irving, from Madrid, to Catharine Paris, 11-26-1844. PMI, III 365–66.

379   The banquet in the Royal Palace. Irving, from Madrid, to unidentified correspondent, 1844. Williams, *Sunnyside and Spain*, 75.

379   "Rather full and puffy." Irving, from Madrid, to Catharine Paris, 4-17-1844. PMI, III 337.

380   "The dullest of the dull." Irving, from Madrid, to Sarah Storrow. PMI, III 368.

380   "Three steps at a time." Irving, from Madrid, to Sarah Storrow, 4-3-1845. Same, 374–75.

380   "Dance . . . to their own nursery songs." Irving, from Madrid, to Catharine Paris, 8-9-1845. Same, 377.

380   "A state of irksome suspense." Irving, from Madrid, to Sarah Storrow, 6-5-1845. STW, II 193.

380   "Throw off diplomacy." Irving, from London, to Pierre Irving, 2-3-1846. PMI, III 382.

380   Irving's letter of resignation. Irving, from Paris, to Hon. James Buchanan, 12-12-1845. Hellman, *Esquire*, 324.

380–81   "I may be of more service." Irving, from Paris, to Pierre Irving, 12-29-1845. PMI, III 380.

381   "Several changes in the Cabinet." Irving, from Madrid, to Catharine Paris, 3-29-1846. Same, 383. The citation that follows is from the same source, same page.

381   "Getting tired of courts." Irving, from Madrid, to Mrs. Paris, 4-25-
381   1846. Same, 384.

     "*Con mucho sentimiento mío*." STW, II 196; PMI, III 392.

382   "I now take leave." PMI, III 391–92.

382   "Thus closes my public career." Irving, to Mrs. Paris, late July, 1846. PMI, III 393.

383   "Stock of recollections." Irving, from Madrid, to Sarah Storrow, 3-27-1845. PMI, III 374.

383   "The tortuous course of Spanish politics." Irving, from Madrid, to Hon. James Buchanan, 5-25-1845. Hellman, *Esquire*, 315.

383   "Why . . . not . . . send out Washington Irving?" Bryant, 35.

OLD MR. ASTOR & "VASHNGTON IRVING"

385   Epigraph. Irving, from Sunnyside, to Henry R. Schoolcraft, 11-10-1851. *Irvingiana*, xvii.

386   "Youthful little dimples." Fredrika Bremer, from Brooklyn, to her sister, 11-5-1849. Bremer, I 59.

386   "Get my study in order." Irving, from Sunnyside, to Mrs. Pierre M. Irving, 3-12-1847. PMI, III 399.

387   "Making a new ice pond." Irving, from Sunnyside, to Mrs. Catharine Paris, 9-9-1847. PMI, IV 26.

387   "One of the most complete snuggeries." Irving, from Sunnyside, to Gouverneur Kemble. PMI, III 402.

387   Hawthorne writes to Irving. Hawthorne, from Concord, to Irving, 7-16-1852. STW, II 205–6.

389   "A very interesting one to me." Irving, from Sunnyside, to Miss Mary E. Kennedy, 9-8-1853. PMI, IV 157.

389–90 "Quartered in some rude buildings." Irving, from Sunnyside, to Sarah Storrow, 9-19-1853. PMI, I 60. The six citations that follow are from the same source: 60–61.

390–91 "A voyage to Albany then." Irving, in an unfinished article begun 6-1851. PMI, I 40. The two citations that follow are from the same source: 42.

391–92 "Little variety of prospect." Irving, *Journals 1803–06*, 11 (8-8-1803). The four citations that follow are from the same source, same date: 11–12.

392–94 "Burnt stumps and fallen trunks." 8-10-1803. Irving, *Journals 1803–06*, 13. The sixteen citations that follow are from the same source: 14 ("crackers"), 14 ("fleas"), 16-17 (Temple of Dirt), 17 ("60 miles"; 8-12), 17 ("miry"), 20 ("stuck fast"; 8-13), 20 ("mud holes"), 20–21 ("Torents"), 21 ("under water"), 21 ("fire place"), 21 ("furniture"), 22 ("scoundrel"), 22 ("15 people"), 22 ("axe"), 22 ("apprehension"), 22 ("boisterous").

394–95 "Engaged the Sharps." 8-14-1803. Irving, *Journals 1803–06*, 23. The six citations that follow are from the same source: 23 ("dead trees"), 24 (*"punkies"*), 26 (hornets; 8-16), 24 ("dew"; 8-14), 27 ("enlivening"; 8-16), 27 ("Judge ford"; 8-16-1803).

395   "Visits in early life to Canada." Irving, from Sunnyside, to Henry R. Schoolcraft, 11-10-1851. *Irvingiana*, xvi.

395   "Perfect romance to me." Irving, *Astoria*, 3.

397   "I arrived in Baltimore." Astor, from New York, to Irving, 11-25-1836. Porter, I 352, 351–52.

398–99 "In a basket around the streets." Porter, I 24. The three citations that follow are from the same source: 29, 38, 35–36 (wagon broken down).

399   "The Friends Meeting-house." Advertisement in *New York Packet*, 5-22-1786. Porter, I 26.

399–400   "Per the ship Ann." *New York Packet*, 10-28-1788. Porter, I 31.

400   "The Highest oppinion of your judgement." Astor, from New York, to Peter Smith, 4-1-1802. Porter, I 403.

401   "A visit to the remote posts." Irving, *Astoria*, 3.

401   "Tous du lông de la rivière." Bradbury, 39, n. 10.

403   "Astor, John J. furr trader." *The New-York Directory and Register for the year 1790*. Porter, I 40.

403   "Gearmaney & francs." Porter, II 1098–99.

403   "Very mush Derangd." Astor to Peter Smith, late summer, 1795. Same, I 53.

404   "I Dont think I Can buy." Astor, from New York, to Peter Smith, 3-31-1793. Porter, II 956.

404   "Sick of the Busniess." Astor, from New York, to Peter Smith, 3-17-1798. Same, I 386.

404   "Greatest of the fur merchants." Charles Gratiot, from St. Louis, to Astor, 4-29-1800. Chittenden, I 165, n.

405   "No man on earth." Meriwether Lewis, from Washington, to William Clark, 6-19-1803. Thwaites, VII 230.

405   "This is an imense undertaking." Clark, from Clarksville, Ky., to Lewis, 7-17-1803. Same, 259.

406   "Explore the Missouri river." Jefferson's instructions to Lewis. Same, 248.

406–7   Departure "at 4 oClock P. M." Thwaites, I 16–17. The four citations that follow are from the same source: I 284–85 (4-7-1805), II 161 (6-15-1805), II 4 (5-6-1805), II 139 (6-9-1805; "danceing").

407   "The most perfect achievement." Chittenden, I 81.

407   "Emence number of Beaver." Thwaites, II 320. The two citations that follow are from the same source: V 243, V 357.

409   "Black India lutestrings." Among the cargo of the *Severn*, from Canton, arriving at New York 5-11-1801. Porter, I 133.

410   "Maney changes & misfortunes." Thwaites, V 374–75.

410–13   Burr and Astor. See the account in Myers, G., I 166–68.

413–14   "A Miss Astor from New York." Journal of Samuel Bridge, 9-15, 9-17, 9-24-1806. Porter, I 412–13.

414   "A modern philosopher." Irving, *Notes*, 40.

414   "Roof of the Bear-market." Irving, *Oldstyle, Salmagundi*, 187 (No. X). The two citations that follow are from the same source: 124 (No. V), 136 (No. VI).

415   "To disct. on £242.9.6." "Sales of Furs . . . on Acc^t of J. J. Astor" (New York, 2-3-1807). Porter, I 411.

415   "The above named John Jacob Astor." "Agreement . . . for the Acquisition of Crown Lands in Lower Canada . . ." 10-17-1795. Same, 381–82.

415   "My unfortunate son." Codicil VII to Astor's will. Porter, II 1267.

415   "I workd for tham." Astor, from New York, to Peter Smith, 4-13-1819. Same, 1162.

415–16   "The best is to travel about." Astor, from New York, to Peter Smith, 3-16-1819. Porter, II 1160.

416   "Elements of greatness." Irving, from Sunnyside, to Henry R. Schoolcraft, 11-10-1851. *Irvingiana*, xvii.

416–17   "Hares, dogges, wilde ounce." Phillips, I 24, n. 39. The two citations that follow are from the same source: 147 (Hudson), 69 (Smith).

417   "Mr. Astor has been here." James McGill, from Montreal, to Isaac Todd, 10-17-1805. Porter, I 65.

417   "A fact known to yourself." Astor to De Witt Clinton, 1-25-1808. Same, 64.

418   The charter of the American Fur Company. Porter, I 413–14.

419   "He . . . constituted the Company." Irving, *Astoria*, 17.

419   "Clinton speaks well of Astor." General Henry Dearborn, Secretary of War, to Jefferson, 4-8-1808. Porter, I 167.

419   "A Mr. Astor, merch't." Jefferson, from Washington, to Meriwether Lewis, 7-17-1808. Ford, P. L., IX 200.

420   "Happey in the hope of Peace." Astor, from New York, to Charles Gratiot, 2-28-1812. Porter, I 249.

420   "Not in my line." Astor, from New York, to Thomas Wilson, 5-18-1814. Same, 294.

420   "The rise on my Stocks." Astor to John Dorr, 2-25-1815. Same, 338.

420   "I am glad of peace." Astor, from New York, to Andrew Daschkoff, 3-11-1815. Porter, I 344.

420   "Minck & Martin Skins." Astor, from New York, to Captain John Ebbets, 11-13-1809. Same, 430.

421   "Intercourse & good will with the Natives." Astor to De Witt Clinton, 1-25-1808. Phillips, II 133–34. Punctuation inserted.

421   "Licenses to trade." The law was passed 4-29-1816. Porter, II 694.

422   "An Act to abolish." Phillips, II 95.

422   "Destroying the pious monster." Ramsay Crooks, from New York, to Thomas Hart Benton, 4-1-1822. Porter, II 713.

423   "The greatest scoundrels." Same, 756.

423   "No sort of respect." Andrew S. Hughes, from St. Louis, to Lewis Cass, Secretary of War, 10-31-1831. Myers, G., I 118.

423   "The trader with the whisky." Thomas L. McKenney, Supt. of Indian Affairs, to Secretary of War, 2-14-1826. Same, 117.

423   "Sure to obtain the furs." Thomas Biddle to Henry Atkinson, 10-29-1819. Chittenden, I 23, n.

424   "A disgusting scene." Col. J. Snelling, from Detroit, to James Barbour, Secretary of War, 8-23-1825. Myers, G., I 115–16.

424   "A drunken frolic." *John Long's Journal 1768–1782.* Thwaites, Reuben Gold, *Early Western Travels 1748–1846* (Cleveland, 1904), II 47.

424   "Take up as fast as they earn." Testimony of Nathaniel J. Wyeth. Chittenden, I 59.

425   "The more happy am I." Astor, from New York, to Peter Smith, 4-13-1819. Porter, II 1162.

426   That "fat German, Dolly Astor." Same, 1040.

426   "Every one has trouble." Astor, from New York, to Peter Smith, 11-28-1813. Porter, I 546.

426   "Keep body and mind engaged." Astor, from New York, to Peter Smith, 3-16-1819. Porter, II 1160.

426   "Certainly a maniac." Brevoort, from New York City. Hellman, *Letters to Irving*, I 150.

427   "A clever, agreeable girl." Irving, from Paris, to Brevoort, 4-14-1821. Irving, *Letters 1802–23*, 626.

427   Irving's first meeting with Astor. The case for a meeting between Irving and Astor earlier than 1821 is persuasively argued by Andrew B. Myers in "Washington Irving and the Astor Library," *Bulletin of New York Public Library*, LXXII (6-1968), 380–81. Compare STW, II 74.

427   "An early friend of your father." Irving, from New York, to Pierre M. Irving, 9-15-1834. PMI, III 61.

427   "Long intimacy with Mr. Astor." 11-10-1851. *Irvingiana*, xvi–xvii.

427   "Shew old Astor the speeches." Brevoort to Irving, 6-28-1811. Hellman, *Letters to Irving*, I 35.

427   "As rich as . . . John Jacob Astor." Hedges, 12–13.

427–28   "Elegant new ship Stephania." *New-York Gazette and General Advertiser*, 6-3-1819. Porter, II 1099.

428   "Little prospect of his recovery." Irving, from Paris, to Brevoort, 4-14-1821. Irving, *Letters 1802–23*, 626.

428   "A few Days in London." Irving, from London, to Mrs. Storrow, 8-26-1821. Same, 642.

428   "Drow an you for 2100$." Astor, from Rome, to President Monroe, 4-5-1820. Porter, II 726 ["proper" expanded to "property"].

428   "You will of course sell." Astor, from Albany, to Ramsay Crooks, 5-8-1828. Porter, II 851.

429   "Wishing to retire." Astor, from Geneva, to Bernard Pratte & Co., 6-25-1833. Same, 1224.

429   "The disposal of those lands." Alexander, 225.

430   "About to dispose of the rest." Astor, from New York, to Wilson Price Hunt, 5-4-1834. Porter, II 1225.

430   "*Like a drunken man.*" Ellsworth, 74.

430   "The return of Geoffrey Crayon." Tuckerman, I 54.

430   Irving to Cincinnati. See page 349 in the present work.

431–34   "Left Cincinnati at 5 oclock." Monday, 9-3-1832. McDermott, 69. The eight citations that follow are from the same source: 72 ("river dandy"; 9-7), 70 ("corn fields"; 9-4), 86 (voices), 78 ("cobalt-green"; 9-11), 71 ("cigars"; 9-6), 74 ("Philadelphia County" and "Nashville"; 9-9-1832).

434   "Not brought any . . . from New York." Letter from St. Louis, 9-14-1832. Pourtalès, 24.

434   Burr's visit to St. Louis. Burr, from Washington, to Theodosia, 3-10-1805 [erroneously dated 1804 in Davis]. Davis, *Memoirs*, II 359.

434   "Old rackety gambling house." 9-13-1832. McDermott, 83 [superfluous ampersand omitted].

434   "Scissors for the young ladies." Letter from St. Louis, 9-14-1832. Pourtalès, 24.

434–35   "Fine healthy robust man." 9-13-1832. McDermott, 81. The four citations that follow are from the same source, same date: 81-82.

435   "A track over the natural sod." Latrobe, I 148.

435   "Bringing up the rear." Journal, 9-15-1832. Pourtalès, 25.

435   "Camp after sunset." 10-1-1832. McDermott, 95. The four citations that follow are from the same source: 98 ("breakfast"), 98 ("umbrellas"), 100 ("Perroquets"; 10-4), 111 ("Arrive"; 10-8-1832).

435   Irving "easily pleased." STW, II 147.

436   "Did not equal my expectation." Ellsworth, 2.

436   "Culprits in pillory." McDermott, 111.

436   "The principal object of your command." Col. Matthew Arbuckle, from Fort Gibson, to Capt. Jesse Bean, 10-5-1832. McDermott, 32 [editor's introduction].

436   "To encourage agriculture." Jefferson to Congress, 1803. Phillips, II 79.

437   "A thousand superfluous wants." "Traits of Indian Character." Irving,

The Sketch Book, 226. The citation that follows is from the same source: 229.

437   "Excepting our Indians." Irving, from Madrid, to Mrs. Storrow, 5-5-1827. Williams, *Storrows*, 115.

437   Irving's writings on the Indians. See Hough, Robert L., "Washington Irving, Indians, and the West." *South Dakota Quarterly*, VI [Winter, 1968].

437   "Col. Arbuckle, Genl Houston." 10-10-1832. McDermott, 111.

438   "What Provisions we took." Ellsworth, 9–10.

438   "Mr. E." wearing "Osage . . . dress." 10-10-1832. McDermott, 113.

438   "Shawls blanketts & & &." Ellsworth, 7. The three citations that follow are from the same source: 6 ("musquitoes"), 9 ("heavy heart"), 8 ("hurry").

438–39   "Set off about 7." 10-13-1832. McDermott, 118. The citation that follows is from the same source, same page.

439   "Many colors & shapes." Ellsworth, 9.

439   "All kinds of dress." McDermott, 119. The citation that follows is from the same source: 120.

439   Irving crosses the Arkansas. 10-14-1832. Ellsworth, 40–42 ["carless" expanded to "careless"].

439   "Never slept or eaten so well." Letter from Canadian Fork, 10-9-1832. Pourtalès, 40.

439   "Ate every half-hour." Journal, 10-17-1832. Same, 55.

440   "The appetite is voracious." Ellsworth, 106.

440   "Delightful mode of life." 10-16-1832. McDermott, 130–31.

440   "A big man from their father." Ellsworth, 114. The two citations that follow are from the same source: 136, 18.

440   "About eighty or more in number." Journal, 10-14-1832. Pourtalès, 50.

441   "Must follow the Osage trail." Ellsworth, 69. The two citations that follow are from the same source: 68, 67.

441   "A beautiful life!" Journal, 10-21-1832. Pourtalès, 63.

441–42   "Mr Irving Latrobe & myself." 10-25-1832. Ellsworth, 108. The eight citations that follow are from the same source: 46 (10-17), 100 ("bears paws"; "lustly" expanded), 46–47 ("ridicule" changed to "ridicules") and 133–34, 22 ("conversation"), 74–75, 76 ("garret"), 77–78, 79–80 (Oxford).

442   "Hoisted on the shoulders." 10-14-1832. McDermott, 124.

442–43   "Fine night—moon shining feebly." 10-16-1832. McDermott, 128–29. The citation that follows is from the same source: 124 (10-15) and 122 (10-14-1832).

443   "A most offensive place." Ellsworth, 52.

443   "Ride through tangled bottoms." 10-14-1832. McDermott, 123.

443   The buffalo hunt. Ellsworth, 103. The four citations that follow are from the same source: 104, 81 ("*intenly*" expanded to "*intently*"), 104, 105.

443–44   The Pawnee threat. Ellsworth, 93–94.

444   "Excessively fatiguing." 11-1-1832. McDermott, 142.

444   "Oh how glad shall I be." Ellsworth, 113. The citation that follows is from the same source, same page (10-26-1832).

444   "Discontent in the camp." 10-31-1832. McDermott, 139.

444–45   "The mud was over shoe." Ellsworth, 119. The citation that follows is from the same source: 58.

445   "Sound of the axe." 11-5-1832. McDermott, 146.

445   "Never known so cold a day." 11-7-1832. Ellsworth, 141.

445   "Salt nearly gone." 11-7-1832. McDermott, 148. The citation that follows is from the same source: 149 (11-8-1832).

445   "Wooden buildings & block house." 11-11-1832. McDermott, 156. The citation that follows is from the same source: 157.

445   "WASHINGTON IRVING, Esq." *Arkansas Gazette*, 10 [for 11?]-14-1832. McDermott, 38 [editor's introduction].

445   "Begrudge them the fringe." McDermott, 166.

446   "Beautiful dawn." 11-11-1832. Same, 155.

446   "Cheerful, gay, talkative." 3-11-1833. Nevins, *Hone*, I 89–90.

446   No "moving accidents." "Introduction," "A Tour on the Prairies." *The Crayon Miscellany.* Irving, *Works*, IX xiv.

446   "By a bronze astral lamp." 4-14-1835. Tuckerman, I 138.

446   "Narrative of every day occurrences." "Introduction," "A Tour on the Prairies." *The Crayon Miscellany.* Irving, *Works*, IX xiv.

447   "The old gentleman has applied to me." Irving, from New York, to Pierre M. Irving, 9-15-1834. PMI, III 60.

447   "For upward of a month past." Irving, from Hell Gate, to Peter Irving, 9-26-1835. PMI, III 78.

448   "The ties of blood and interest." Jefferson, from Monticello, to Astor, 5-24-1812. Ford, P. L., IX 351.

448   "Winter . . . mild on the Pacific." Letter in the Philadelphia *Register*, 10-28-1806, taken from "a Kentucky paper" of 10-4-1806. Thwaites, VII 348.

449   "Themes of charmed interest." Irving, *Astoria*, 3.

449   "The miscellaneous records & papers." Porter, II 1299. The citation that follows is from the same source, same page.

450   "Papers, letters, and journals." Irving, from New York, to Pierre M. Irving, 10-29-1834. PMI, III 63.

450   Pierre Irving's research. Irving, *Astoria*, xxiv [editor's introduction].

450   Bradbury and Daniel Boone. Bradbury, 43.

450–51   And Irving's transmutation. Irving, *Astoria*, 100–101.

451   Poe on *Astoria*. *Southern Literary Messenger* 3 (1837), 59. Irving, *Astoria*, xxxi [editor's introduction].

451   "Does not *make* facts." *Western Monthly Magazine*, 685. Same.

451   An English judgment. *The London and Westminster Review* 27 (1837), 188. Same, xxxii.

451   Chittenden's opinion of *Astoria*. See Chittenden, I xiv, 239, 240, 243.

451   And DeVoto's. DeVoto, 427. Edgeley Todd provides another informed opinion of Irving's reliability: "Working closely with *Astoria* and the hundreds of pages of its sources, the researcher comes in time to respect what Irving says and learns that he should not lightly impugn Irving's accuracy." Edgeley W. Todd (ed.), *Astoria* . . . (Norman, Okla., 1964), Editor's Introduction, xli.

452   "Many personal anecdotes." PMI, III 81.

454–61   The cargo of the *Tonquin*. The invoice of merchandise shipped on the *Tonquin* does not survive, but that for the *Beaver* in the following year does (Porter, I 484–507). Setting out from the same port, the latter ship was on a comparable mission to the same destination; I have drawn on its cargo list in the present section.

454   "We remember him well." Irving, *Astoria*, 78 (Chapter XI).

455–59   Thorn's "letters to Mr. Astor." Same, 34 (Chapter V). The seventeen citations that follow are from the same source: 34 ("lurking below"), 36 ("fine latitudes"), 35 ("d——d hard"), 35 ("Fly Market"), 38 ("'wild goose chase'"), 38 ("third time"), 39 ("inflexible"), 39 ("swashed"), 39 ("hauled ahead"), 52 ("mere speck"), 53 ("signal"), 53 ("piteously"), 53 ("apprehensions"), 73 ("tempting display"), 73 ("chicanery"), 73–74 ("pestering"), 74 ("jeer"). In addition to using portions of the account in *Astoria*, my narrative incorporates details—fish through the rigging and the like—from Ross and Franchere.

459   In "any River, Bay or Port." Astor, from Philadelphia, to Capt. John Ebbets, 11-1809. Porter, I 432.

460   "Ordered the ship to be cleared." Irving, *Astoria*, 75. The citation that follows is from the same source, same page.

462   Astor "with his usual serenity of countenance." Irving, *Astoria*, 78–79.

463   Astor's letter to Jefferson. Astor, from New York, to Jefferson, 3-14-1812. Porter, I 508–509.

464   "Their progress was . . . tedious." Irving, *Astoria*, 87.

465   "Number of turkey buzzards." 4-16-1811. Bradbury, 68.

465   "They appear . . . in clouds." Irving, *Astoria*, 107.

465–66   "We might have obtained . . . more." 6-9-1811. Bradbury, 126. The seven citations that follow (through "this kind of traffic") are from the same source: 148–49 (6-22), 100 (5-28), 69 (4-19), 189 (7-20), 155 (6-23), 61 (4-8), 140 (6-17-1811).

467   "So many small hillocks." Irving, *Astoria*, 139 (Chapter XX).

467   "The last account I had." Astor, from New York, to Jefferson, 3-14-1812. Porter, I 509.

467   "A land where no man abides." Irving, *Astoria*, 151 (Chapter XXII). The citation that follows is from the same source: 152.

467–69   "Grass was knee-deep." Hunt, 281. The sixteen citations that follow (through "left or south bank") are from the same source: 282–91.

469   "Mr. Crooks . . . amidst roaring breakers." Irving, *Astoria*, 198 (Chapter XXXII).

469–70   "For supper . . . some fruits." Hunt, 292. The nine citations that follow (through "January 1st") are from the same source: 293–301.

471   "Great emporium of the fur trade." Irving, *Astoria*, 307 (Chapter LI).

472   "A varey little of the Cargo." Samuel H. Northrop, from the Columbia River, to Astor, 3-1814. Porter, I 554 ["avarey" and "somaney" each broken into two words].

472   A "Smal Garison." Astor, from New York, to Jefferson, 10-18-1813. Same, 542.

472   "Good god what an objit." Astor, from Philadelphia, to Department of State, 4-4-1813. Porter, I 524.

473   "Most Sangguine exspectations." Astor, from New York, to Jefferson, 10-18-1813. Same, 542.

473   "Having maturely weighed our situation." Franchere, 280.

473   "We have been sold." Astor to Donald McKenzie, 9-27-1814. Porter, I 239.

473   "My once Darling objict." Astor, from Philadelphia, to Department of State, 4-4-1813. Same, 524.

474   "Pacific Fur Company is dissolved." 11-12-1814. Same, 235.

474   "All territories and their waters." Treaty of 10-20-1818. Same, 242.

474   "The second period of ten years." Irving, *Astoria*, 356.

475   "Smooth as a barn floor." Testimony of Father De Smet. Chittenden, I 462.

475   "Since the above was written." Irving, *Astoria*, 356.

475   Astor's "favorite plan." Astor, from New York, to Gabriel Shaw, 7-11-1814. Porter, I 342.

476   "A devourer of oysters." Pierre Irving, from Hell Gate, to Daniel Roberts, 1-16-1835. Kime, 40.

476   "A New York *palais royal.*" Nevins, *Hone,* I 121.

476   "His health is declining." 5-1-1834. Same, 126.

476   "Should all have made great fortunes." Astor, from New York, to Wilson Price Hunt, 1-21-1832. Porter, II 773.

477   "Abundance of materials." Irving, from New York, to Pierre M. Irving, 9-15-1834. PMI, III 60.

477   Astor's Park Hotel. Williamson, 33, 49.

477–78   "New York is rebuilt." 5-1-1839. Tuckerman, I 360. The four citations that follow are from the same source: 359 (same date), 131 (1-14-1835), 138 (4-23-1835), 203 (3-9-1836).

478–79   "A yellow chariot before our door." Howe, J. W., 32. The two citations that follow are from the same source: 74, 75.

479   "I Do Devid." Astor to Peter Smith, 4-13-1819. Porter, II 1162.

479–80   "Astor . . . greatly gratified." Irving, from Tarrytown, to Pierre M. Irving, 12-12-1836. PMI, III 92. The citation that follows is from the same source, same page.

480   "Too proverbially rich a man." 10-10-1851. *Irvingiana,* xvii.

480   "In the style of my other works." Same, xvi.

480   "Talks well on many subjects." Porter, II 1094.

480   "I admire much your ideas." Astor, per William B. Astor, from New York, to Gerrit Smith, 2-18-1835. Porter, II 904.

480   "I have lost a fast friend." Gerrit Smith, from Peterboro, N.Y., to William B. Astor, 4-6-1848. Same, 1259.

481   "A letter from my friend." Journal, 8-10-1837. Frothingham, 33. The five citations that follow are from the same source: 39 ("gravies"), 113 ("aristocracy"), 109 ("universal"; 5-1-1849), 102 ("give away"; Smith, from Peterboro, N.Y., to Rev. Theodore S. Wright, Rev. Charles B. Ray, and Dr. J. McCune Smith, 8-1-1846), 104 ("receive the list").

482   "*I expect nothing.*" Brown, from Peterboro, N.Y., to F. B. Sanborn, 2-24-1858. Sanborn, opposite 445.

482   "Sometimes . . . quite disheartening." Brown, from Springfield, Mass., to his wife, 11-29-1846. Ruchames, 57.

482   "Father broke down completely." Sanborn, 44.

482   "Discredit, & sore afflictions." Brown, from Springfield, Mass., to his wife, 3-7-1844 [for 1847?]. Ruchames, 59.

482   "*All things considered.*" Brown, from Springfield, Mass., to his father, 1-10-1849. Same, 67.

482   "Reminds one of Omnipotence." Oates, 66.

483   Brown writes from London. Brown, to Simon Perkins, 10-1849. Ruchames, 70.

483   "My bones to rest there." Brown, from Springfield, Mass., to his children, 12-4-1850. Same, 74.

483   "In the same dreadful condition." Brown, from Springfield, Mass., to his wife, 1-17-1851. Ruchames, 75. The citation that follows is from the same source, same page.

483–84   "You must collect together." "Words of Advice . . ." Ruchames, 76–77.

484   "All the lectures we have had." Brown, from Springfield, Mass., to his wife, 11-28-1850. Same, 72.

485 "I told you." Testimony of Salmon Brown, who was present. Oates, 134.

485 "I did God service." Same, 147.

485 "Most truly a Christian." 4-11 through 4-14-1859. Frothingham, 237–38.

486 "My gifts to Brown." Peterboro, 8-15-1867. Same, 257.

486 "I am broken up." Smith, from Peterboro, N.Y., to William B. Astor, 4-6-1848, quoting Astor at a last interview. Porter, II 1259.

486 "Many years beyond the age." Testimony of Joseph G. Cogswell. Jaques, 427.

486 "But three children to inherit." 12-1-1838. Nevins, *Hone*, I 374.

486 "The sole occupant of a . . . mansion." Porter, II 1037–38.

486 "Fat German, Dolly Astor." Same, 1040.

487 "Finest place on the North river." 5-29-1840. Tuckerman, II 29.

487 "Recreant to the Republican Spirit." Portland (Me.) *Transcript.* Quoted in Diamond, 41.

487 Astor's fortune. See Myers, G., I 195; Diamond, 28–29.

487 Whitman remembers Astor. In New Orleans *Daily Crescent;* quoted in Diamond, 24.

487–88 "A rich man has the advantage." Description of Astor's coffin in the *New-York Organ and Temperance Safeguard.* Quoted in Diamond, 33–34.

488 Hone describes Astor's funeral. 4-1-1848. Nevins, *Hone*, II 848.

488 Irving's visits with Astor. Williams, *Sunnyside and Spain*, 14, 16, 36, 39.

488 "Our old friend Mr Astor." Brevoort to Irving, 12-28-1842. Hellman, *Letters to Irving*, II 125.

488 "Astor still holds out." Brevoort to Irving, 10-18-1843. Same, 133.

488–89 Hone dines with Astor. 10-9-1844. Nevins, *Hone*, II 717. The citation that follows is from the same source, same page.

489 "A drive . . . on the 3^d Avenue." Porter, II 1119. The three citations to the conclusion of the chapter are from the same source: 1120.

DREGS

491 Epigraph. 8-1859. PMI, IV 306.

492 "Astor goes to the tomb." Cooper, II 588.

492 Irving as executor. STW, II 210; Porter, II 1055.

493 "Take his ease." PMI, IV 48. The citation that follows is from the same source, same page.

493 We have seen. Pages 12–15 in the present work.

493 "Better off than most old bachelors." Irving, from Sunnyside, to J. K. Paulding, 12-24-1855. PMI, IV 201–2.

493 "Four blessed nieces." Irving, from Sunnyside, to Mrs. John P. Kennedy, late in 1853. Same, 168.

493 "Not without foreboding." PMI, IV 300.

493 "I have no other existence." 9-1855. Same, 196.

494 "I shall not then have written . . . in vain." "The Christmas Dinner." Irving, *The Sketch Book*, 191.

494 "A being of flesh and blood." William H. Prescott, from Boston, to Irving, 1-3-1856. PMI, IV 204.

494 "I was up late and early." George Bancroft to Irving, 5-30-1855. Same, 194.

494 "Afraid that something will happen to me." 2-23-1856. Same, 209.

494   "The saddest possible fate." PMI, IV 104.

495   "Willing to die the next moment." The remark was made in 1849. Same, 64.

495   "Not poppy, nor mandragora." *Othello*, III iii. Irving "stood it very well during the day, but began to have great dread of the night. On parting with him, one night, he repeated most feelingly the passage from Othello . . ." 11-1858. PMI, IV 262.

495   "All sail set." 10-1858. Same, 255.

495   "Will this never . . . end?" 6-28-1859. STW, II 239.

495   "Shutting up my doors and windows." To George William Curtis, 1858. PMI, IV 333.

495   "You should write one more book." Theodore Tilton was the visitor, 11-7-1859. Same, 322–23.

495–96   Sunset over Sunnyside. PMI, IV 326–27; Kime, 239.

496–97   Irving's funeral. *Irvingiana*, xxii–xxvi. PMI, IV 328–31.

497   "A retreat, whither I might steal." "The Legend of Sleepy Hollow." Irving, *The Sketch Book*, 272.

497   "His fearful death agony." "Annals of Harper's Ferry," 25. Cited in Villard, 443.

497–98   *"Kill them, Kill them."* Oates, 295.

498   "This *is* a beautiful country." Villard, 555.

Full Titles of Sources

The list comprises only those books and articles from which citations have been taken or to which the notes refer directly.

Abernethy, Thomas Perkins, *The Burr Conspiracy* (New York, 1954).

Adams, Charles Francis, *Letters of Mrs. Adams, the Wife of John Adams* . . . (Boston, 1840).

Adams, Charles Francis (ed.), *The Works of John Adams* . . . , 10 vols. (Boston, 1856).

Adams, Henry, *History of the United States of America* . . . , 9 vols. (New York, 1891–96; reprint 1962).

Aderman. Professor Ralph M. Aderman of the University of Wisconsin at Milwaukee is editing the letters of Irving for *The Complete Works of Washington Irving*, sponsored by the Center for Editions of American Authors (Madison and Boston, 1969–   ). He has kindly allowed me to examine typescript of letters not yet published as of 1979. Citations from those unpublished letters, which appear in my chapter on Irving in Spain, are so indicated.

Alexander, Holmes, *The American Talleyrand: The Career and Contemporaries of Martin Van Buren, Eighth President* (New York, 1935).

Anderson, Osborne P., *A Voice from Harper's Ferry* . . . (Boston, 1861).

Aronson, Theo, *Royal Vendetta: The Crown of Spain 1829–1965* (Indianapolis, 1966).

[Ballantyne, Alexander], *Reply to Mr Lockhart's Pamphlet* . . . (London, 1839).

Beavan, Arthur H., *James and Horace Smith* . . . (London, 1899).

Beirne, Francis F., *Shout Treason: The Trial of Aaron Burr* (New York, 1959).

Beveridge, Albert J., *The Life of John Marshall*, 4 vols. (Boston, 1916, 1919).

Biddle, Alexander (compiler), *Old Family Letters* . . . Series A (Philadelphia, 1892).

Biddle, Charles, *Autobiography* . . . *1745–1821* (Philadelphia, 1883).

Bigland, Eileen, *Mary Shelley* (London, 1959).

Bixby, William K., *The Private Journal of Aaron Burr* . . . , 2 vols. (Rochester, N.Y., 1903).

Blennerhassett-Adams, Therese, "The True Story of Harman Blennerhassett," *Century Magazine* [7-1901], 351–56.

Booth, Mary L., *History of the City of New York* (New York, 1880).

Bowers, Claude G., *The Spanish Adventures of Washington Irving* (Boston, 1940).

Boyer, Richard O., *The Legend of John Brown, A Biography and a History* (New York, 1973).

Bradbury, John, *Travels in the Interior of America, in the Years 1809, 1810, and 1811 . . .*, Second Edition (London, 1819). Vol. V in Thwaites, Reuben Gold (ed.), *Early Western Travels 1748–1846* (Cleveland, 1904).

Bremer, Fredrika, *The Homes of the New World: Impressions of America*, 3 vols. (London, 1853).

Brown, Ford K., *The Life of William Godwin* (London, 1926).

Bryant, William Cullen, *A Discourse on the Life, Character and Genius of Washington Irving* (New York, 1860).

Buchan, John, *Sir Walter Scott* (London, 1932).

Byron, Lord (George Gordon), *Works. Letters and Journals*, ed. Rowland E. Prothero, 6 vols. (London, 1898–1901).

Byron, Lord (George Gordon), *Works. Poetry*, ed. Ernest Hartley Coleridge, 7 vols. (London, 1898–1904).

Cameron, Kenneth Neill (ed.), *Romantic Rebels: Essays on Shelley and His Circle* (Cambridge, Mass., 1973).

Canby, Henry Seidel, *Classic Americans* (New York, 1931).

Cappon, Lester J. (ed.), *The Adams-Jefferson Letters*, 2 vols. (Chapel Hill, N.C., 1959).

Chittenden, Hiram Martin, *The American Fur Trade of the Far West . . .*, 3 vols. (New York, 1902).

Clairmont, Claire, *The Journals of Claire Clairmont*, ed. Marion Kingston Stocking (Cambridge, Mass., 1968).

Clark, Daniel, *Proofs of the Corruption of Gen. James Wilkinson . . .* (Philadelphia, 1809).

Clarke, H. Butler, *Modern Spain: 1815–1898* (Cambridge, Eng., 1906).

Cockburn, Henry, *Memorials of His Time* (Edinburgh, 1856).

Coleman, William, *A Collection of the Facts and Documents, relative to the Death of Major-General Alexander Hamilton . . .* (1804; reprint Boston, 1904).

Coombs, J. J., *The Trial of Aaron Burr for High Treason . . .* (Washington, D.C., 1864).

Cooper, James Fenimore (ed.), *Correspondence of James Fenimore-Cooper*, 2 vols. (New Haven, 1922).

Cunningham, Allan, *The Life of Sir David Wilkie*, 3 vols. (London, 1843).

Dalgleish, William, "Memoirs of . . . Butler to Sir Walter Scott" [ed. G. E. Mitton], *Cornhill Magazine*, New Series LXX, LXXI (6, 7, 8-1931).

Davis, Matthew L., *Memoirs of Aaron Burr . . .*, 2 vols. (New York, 1836).

Davis, Matthew L. (ed.), *The Private Journal of Aaron Burr . . .*, 2 vols. (New York, 1838).

Dawson, Flora, "The Author and the Divine: or, Washington Irving and the Rev. Charles Simeon," in Vol. II of *Princes, Public Men, and Pretty Women . . .*, 133–42 (London, 1864).

DeVoto, Bernard, *Across the Wide Missouri* (New York, 1947).

Diamond, Sigmund, *The Reputation of the American Businessman* (Cambridge, Mass., 1955).

Dowden, Edward, *The Life of Percy Bysshe Shelley*, 2 vols. (London, 1886).

Duncan, William Cary, *The Amazing Madame Jumel* (New York, 1935).

Dunlap, William, *Diary of William Dunlap [1766–1839] . . .*, 3 vols. (New York, 1931).

Dwight, S. E., *The Life of President* [Jonathan] *Edwards* (New York, 1830).

Ellsworth, Henry Leavitt, *Washington Irving on the Prairie: or, A Narrative of a Tour of the Southwest in the Year 1832*, ed. Stanley T. Williams and Barbara D. Simison (New York, 1937).

Familiar Letters of Sir Walter Scott [David Douglas, ed.], 2 vols. (Boston, 1894).

Fisher, George P., *Life of Benjamin Silliman, M.D., LL.D.*, 2 vols. (New York, 1866).

Fisher, Josephine, "The Journal of Esther Burr," *The New England Quarterly*, III ii [4-1930], 297–315.

Fitzpatrick, John C. (ed.), *The Writings of George Washington*, 39 vols. (Washington, D.C., 1931–44).

Flexner, Eleanor, *Mary Wollstonecraft* (New York, 1972).

Ford, Paul Leicester, *The Writings of Thomas Jefferson*, 10 vols. (New York, 1892–99).

Ford, Worthington Chauncey, "Some Papers of Aaron Burr," *Proceedings of the American Antiquarian Society*, XXIX [4-9-1919] (Worcester, Mass., 1920), 43–128.

Foster, Emily, *The Journal of Emily Foster*, ed. Stanley T. Williams and Leonard B. Beach (New York, 1938).

Franchere, Gabriel, *Narrative of a Voyage to the Northwest Coast of America* . . . (New York, 1854). Vol. VI in Thwaites, Reuben Gold (ed.), *Early Western Travels 1748–1846* (Cleveland, 1904).

Frothingham, Octavius Brooks, *Gerrit Smith* (New York, 1878).

Fyfe, W. T., *Edinburgh under Sir Walter Scott* (London, 1906).

[Gillies, Robert Pearse], *Recollections of Sir Walter Scott, Bart.* (London, 1837).

Godwin, William, *The Elopement of Percy Bysshe Shelley and Mary Wollstonecraft Godwin* [Godwin's letter of 1814 to John Taylor, privately printed], 1911.

Godwin, William, *An Enquiry Concerning Political Justice* . . . 2 vols. (Dublin, 1793).

Gribble, Francis, *The Tragedy of Isabella II* (Boston, 1913).

Grierson, H. J. C. (ed.), *The Letters of Sir Walter Scott*, 12 vols. (London, 1932–37).

Grylls, R. Glynn, *Mary Shelley: A Biography* (London, 1938).

Hague, William, *Life Notes: or, Fifty Years' Outlook* (Boston, 1888).

Harbert, Earl N., "Washington Irving's *Conquest of Granada*: A Spanish Experiment That Failed," *Clio*, III iii [6-1974], 305–13.

Harrison, Gabriel, *John Howard Payne* . . . *His Life and Writings* (Philadelphia, 1885).

Hedges, William L., *Washington Irving: An American Study, 1802–1832* (Baltimore, 1965).

Hellman, George S. (ed.), *The Letters of Henry Brevoort to Washington Irving* . . . , 2 vols. (New York, 1916).

Hellman, George S. (ed.), *The Letters of Washington Irving to Henry Brevoort*, 2 vols. (New York, 1915).

Hellman, George S., *Washington Irving Esquire: Ambassador At Large from the New World to the Old* (New York, 1925).

Hemstreet, Charles, *When Old New York Was Young* (New York, 1902).

Hinton, Richard J., *John Brown and His Men* . . . (New York, 1894).

Hogg, Thomas Jefferson, *The Life of Percy Bysshe Shelley*, 2 vols. (London, 1858).

Holmes, Richard, *Shelley: The Pursuit* (New York, 1974).

Howarth, R. G. (ed.), *Letters of Lord Byron* (London, 1962).

Howe, Julia Ward, *Reminiscences 1819–1899* (Boston, 1900).

Howe, M. A. DeWolfe, *The Life and Letters of George Bancroft*, 2 vols. (New York, 1908).

Hunt, Wilson Price, "Diary Narrating His Overland Trip Westward to Astoria in 1811–12," in *The Discovery of the Oregon Trail: Robert Stuart's Narratives . . .* , ed. Philip Ashton Rollins (New York, 1935), 281–308.

Inglis, Henry D., *Spain in 1830*, 2 vols. (London, 1831).

Irving, Pierre M., "Holograph Journal Describing the Last Days in the Life of Washington Irving, February 28–November 30, 1859"; transcribed by Wayne R. Kime.

Irving, Pierre M., *The Life and Letters of Washington Irving*, 4 vols. (New York, 1863–64).

Irving, Washington.

  I have cited from the following volumes in the ongoing *Complete Works of Washington Irving:*

  > *Astoria, or Anecdotes of an Enterprize Beyond the Rocky Mountains*, ed. Richard Dilworth Rust (Boston, 1976);
  > *Bracebridge Hall, or The Humourists . . .* ed. Herbert F. Smith (Boston, 1977);
  > *Journals and Notebooks, Vol. I, 1803–1806*, ed. Nathalia Wright (Madison, Wis., 1969);
  > *Journals and Notebooks, Vol. III, 1819–1827*, ed. Walter A. Reichart (Madison, Wis., 1970);
  > *Letters of Jonathan Oldstyle, Gent. / Salmagundi; or The Whimwhams and Opinions of Launcelot Langstaff, Esq. & Others*, ed.
  > *Letters. Volume I 1802–1823*, ed. Ralph M. Aderman, Herbert L. Bruce I. Granger and Martha Hartzog (Boston, 1977).
  > Kleinfield, and Jenifer S. Banks (Boston, 1978);
  > *The Sketch Book of Geoffrey Crayon, Gent.*, ed. Haskell Springer (Boston, 1978).

  Citations from Irving's works not at the time available in the edition above I have taken from *The Works . . .* , Author's Revised Edition (New York, 1861). Such citations have been identified by volume title and number:

  > *The Alhambra.* Irving, *Works*, XV.

  In addition, I have cited from the following works by Irving:

  > *Notes While Preparing Sketch Book &c. 1817 . . .* , ed. Stanley T. Williams (New Haven, 1927);
  > *Spanish Papers and Other Miscellanies, Hitherto Unpublished or Uncollected*, ed. Pierre M. Irving, 2 vols. (New York, 1866);
  > *Tour in Scotland 1817 . . .* , ed. Stanley T. Williams (New Haven, 1927).

Irvingiana: A Memorial of Washington Irving (New York, 1860).

Jaques, David Ralph, "John Jacob Astor," in *Lives of American Merchants*, ed. Freeman Hunt (New York, 1858), II 387–439.

Jeffrey, Francis, *Contributions to the Edinburgh Review* (New York, 1860).

Johnson, Edgar, *Charles Dickens: His Tragedy and Triumph*, 2 vols. (New York, 1952).

Johnson, Edgar, *Sir Walter Scott: The Great Unknown*, 2 vols. (New York, 1970).

Jones, Frederick L. (ed.), *Maria Gisborne & Edward E. Williams . . . Their Journals and Letters* (Norman, Okla., 1951).

Keith, Christina, *The Author of Waverley . . .* (New York, 1966).

Kime, Wayne R., *Pierre M. Irving and Washington Irving: A Collaboration in Life and Letters* (Waterloo, Ont., 1977).

Lamb, Mrs. Martha J., *History of the City of New York: Its Origin, Rise and Progress*, 2 vols. (New York, 1877).

Landström, Björn, *Columbus* . . . (New York, 1966).

Latrobe, Charles Joseph, *The Rambler in North America*, 2 vols. (London, 1836).

Leary, Lewis, *Washington Irving* (Minneapolis, 1963).

Leslie, Charles Robert, *Autobiographical Recollections* (Boston, 1860).

Lipscomb, Andrew A., and Albert Ellery Bergh (eds.), *The Writings of Thomas Jefferson*, 20 vols. (Washington, D.C., 1903).

Lochhead, Marion, *John Gibson Lockhart* (London, 1954).

Lockhart, John Gibson, *Memoirs of the Life of Sir Walter Scott, Bart.*, 7 vols. (Edinburgh, 1837–38).

Lodge, Henry Cabot (ed.), *The Works of Alexander Hamilton*, 9 vols. (New York, 1885–86).

Longfellow, Samuel, *Life of Henry Wadsworth Longfellow* . . . , 3 vols. (Boston, 1899).

Lucas, E. V., *The Letters of Charles Lamb* . . . , 3 vols. (London, 1935).

Luquer, Thatcher T. Payne, "Correspondence of Washington Irving and John Howard Payne, 1821–1828," *Scribner's Magazine*, XLVIII [10, 11-1910], 461–82, 597–616.

McCaleb, Walter Flavius, *The Aaron Burr Conspiracy, A History largely from original and hitherto unused sources* (New York, 1903).

McClary, Ben Harris (ed.), *Washington Irving and the House of Murray* (Knoxville, 1969).

McDermott, John Francis (ed.), *The Western Journals of Washington Irving* (Norman, Okla., 1944).

[Mackenzie, Alexander Slidell], *A Year in Spain*, 2 vols. (London, 1831).

Marchand, Leslie A., *Byron: A Biography*, 3 vols. (New York, 1957).

Marchand, Leslie A. (ed.), *Byron's Letters and Journals*, 6 vols. to 1819 (Cambridge, Mass., 1973–76).

Marshall, Mrs. Julian, *The Life & Letters of Mary Wollstonecraft Shelley*, 2 vols. (London, 1889).

Medwin, Thomas, *The Life of Percy Bysshe Shelley*, ed. H. Buxton Forman (London, 1913).

Mitchell, Broadus, *Alexander Hamilton*, 2 vols. (New York, 1957, 1962).

Mitchell, Donald G., *Works*, 15 vols. (New York, 1907).

Modern Traveller, The . . . : *Spain and Portugal*, 2 vols. (London, 1826).

Moore, Thomas, *Memoirs, Journal, and Correspondence*, ed. Lord John Russell, 8 vols. (Boston, 1853–56).

Morison, Samuel Eliot, *Admiral of the Ocean Sea: A Life of Christopher Columbus*, 2 vols. (Boston, 1942).

Morris, Anne Cary (ed.), *The Diary and Letters of Gouverneur Morris*, 2 vols. (New York, 1888).

Morris, Richard B. (ed.), *Alexander Hamilton and the Founding of the Nation* (New York, 1957).

Mott, Frank Luther, *A History of American Magazines, 1741–1850* (Cambridge, Mass., 1957).

Myers, Andrew Breen, "Washington Irving's Madrid Journal 1827–1828 and Related Letters," *Bulletin of the New York Public Library* [1958], LXII, 217–27, 300–311, 407–19, 463–71.

Myers, Gustavus, *History of the Great American Fortunes*, 3 vols. (Chicago, 1907–10).

Nelson, Truman, *The Old Man: John Brown at Harper's Ferry* (New York, 1973).

Nevins, Allan (ed.), *The Diary of John Quincy Adams: 1794–1845* . . . (New York, 1928).

Nevins, Allan (ed.), *The Diary of Philip Hone: 1828–1851*, 2 vols. (New York, 1927).

Oates, Stephen B., *To Purge This Land with Blood: A Biography of John Brown* (New York, 1970).

Osterweis, Rollin G., *Rebecca Gratz, A Study in Charm* (New York, 1935).

Overmyer, Grace, *America's First Hamlet* (New York, 1957).

Padover, Saul K., *The Complete Jefferson* . . . (New York, 1943).

Parkinson, Roger, *A Day's March Nearer Home* (New York, 1974).

Parmet, Herbert S., and Marie B. Hecht, *Aaron Burr: Portrait of an Ambitious Man* (New York, 1967).

Parton, James, *Life of Andrew Jackson*, 3 vols. (New York, 1860).

Parton, James, *The Life and Times of Aaron Burr* . . . , Enlarged Edition, 2 vols. (Boston, 1864).

Paul, C. Kegan, *William Godwin: His Friends and Contemporaries*, 2 vols. (London, 1876).

Peacock, Thomas Love, "Memoirs of Percy Bysshe Shelley," in *Essays, Memoirs, Letters & Unfinished Novels*. Vol. VIII of *The Works* (London, 1934).

Penney, Clara Louisa, *Washington Irving Diary, Spain 1828–1829* (New York, 1926).

Phillips, Paul Chrisler (with concluding chapters by J. W. Smurr), *The Fur Trade*, 2 vols. (Norman, Okla., 1961).

PMI. Irving, Pierre M., *The Life and Letters of Washington Irving*, 4 vols. (New York, 1863–64).

Pochmann, Henry A., *Washington Irving: Representative Selections, with Introduction, Bibliography, and Notes* (New York, 1934).

Pope-Hennessy, Una, *The Laird of Abbotsford* . . . (London, 1932).

Porter, Kenneth Wiggins, *John Jacob Astor, Business Man*, 2 vols. (Cambridge, Mass., 1931).

Pourtalès, Count de, *On the Western Tour with Washington Irving. The Journal and Letters of Count de Pourtalès*, ed. George F. Spaulding, tr. Seymour Feiler (Norman, Okla., 1968).

Prescott, William H., *History of the Reign of Ferdinand and Isabella, the Catholic*, 3 vols. (Boston, 1838).

Priestley, J. B., *The Prince of Pleasure and His Regency 1811–20* (New York, 1969).

Quayle, Eric, *The Ruin of Sir Walter Scott* (London, 1968).

Quennell, Peter, *Byron, A Self-Portrait. Letters and Diaries 1798 to 1824*, 2 vols. (London, 1950).

"Recollections of Washington Irving," by one of his friends. *The Continental Monthly* [6-1862], 689–700.

Reichart, Walter A., *Washington Irving and Germany* (Ann Arbor, 1957).

Robertson, David, *Reports of the Trials of Colonel Aaron Burr* . . . *for Treason* . . . 2 vols. (Philadelphia, 1808).

Robinson, Henry Crabb, *Diary, Reminiscences, and Correspondence* . . . , ed. Thomas Sadler, 3 vols. (London, 1869).

Romance of Mary W. Shelley, John Howard Payne, and Washington Irving, The (Boston, 1907).

Ross, Alexander, *Adventures of the First Settlers on the Oregon or Columbia River: Being a Narrative of the Expedition Fitted Out by John Jacob Astor*

. . . (London, 1849). Vol. VII in Thwaites, Reuben Gold (ed.), *Early Western Travels 1748–1846* (Cleveland, 1904).

Ruchames, Louis (ed.), *A John Brown Reader* . . . (New York, 1959).

Safford, William H. (ed.), *The Blennerhassett Papers* . . . (Cincinnati, 1864).

Sanborn, F. B., *The Life and Letters of John Brown* . . . (Boston, 1885).

Schachner, Nathan, *Aaron Burr: A Biography* (New York, 1937).

Schneider, Norris F., *Blennerhassett Island and the Burr Conspiracy* (Zanesville, Ohio, 1938).

Scott, Sir Walter, *Journal*, ed. W. E. K. Anderson, as *The Journal of Sir Walter Scott* (Oxford, 1972).

Scott, Sir Walter, *Works*, ed. Andrew Lang (Boston, 1892).

Scott, Winfield, *Memoirs of Lieut.-General Scott, LL.D.* . . . (New York, 1864).

Shelley, Mary, *Frankenstein or The Modern Prometheus*, ed. M. K. Joseph (London, 1969).

Shelley, Mary, "History of a Six Weeks' Tour . . ." in Vol. II of *Essays, Letters from Abroad* . . . , by Percy Bysshe Shelley, 2 vols. (London, 1840).

Shelley, Mary, *The Letters of Mary W. Shelley*, ed. Frederick L. Jones, 2 vols. (Norman, Okla., 1944).

Shelley, Mary, *Mary Shelley's Journal*, ed. Frederick L. Jones (Norman, Okla., 1947).

Shelley, Mary, *Rambles in Germany and Italy, in 1840, 1842, and 1843*, 2 vols. (London, 1844).

Shelley, Percy Bysshe, *Cambridge Edition: The Poetical Works* (Boston, 1975).

Shelley, Percy Bysshe, *The Letters of Percy Bysshe Shelley*, ed. Frederick L. Jones, 2 vols. (Oxford, 1964).

Shelley, Percy Bysshe, *The Poetical Works* . . . , ed. Mrs. Shelley, 4 vols. (London, 1839).

Smiles, Samuel, *A Publisher and His Friends: Memoir and Correspondence of the Late John Murray* . . . , 2 vols. (London, 1891).

Smith, Thomas E. V., *The City of New York in the Year of Washington's Inauguration 1789* (Riverside, Conn., 1972; facsimile of privately printed edition of 1889).

Southey, Charles Cuthbert, *The Life & Correspondence of the late Robert Southey*, 6 vols. (London, 1849–50).

STW. Williams, Stanley T., *The Life of Washington Irving*, 2 vols. (New York, 1935).

Syrett, Harold C., and Jean G. Cooke, *Interview in Weehawken: The Burr-Hamilton Duel as Told in the Original Documents* (Middletown, Conn., 1960).

Thwaites, Reuben Gold (ed.), *Original Journals of the Lewis and Clark Expedition 1804–1806*, 7 vols. (New York, first published 1904–5; reprint, 1959).

Todd, Charles Burr, *The True Aaron Burr* (New York, 1902).

Tomalin, Claire, *The Life and Death of Mary Wollstonecraft* (New York, 1974).

Trelawny, E. J., *Recollections of the Last Days of Shelley* . . . (Boston, 1858).

Trent, William P., and George S. Hellman (eds.), *The Journals of Washington Irving*, 3 vols. (Boston, 1919).

Tuckerman, Bayard (ed.), *The Diary of Philip Hone 1828–1851*, 2 vols. (New York, 1889).

Villard, Oswald Garrison, *John Brown 1800–1859: A Biography Fifty Years After* (Boston, 1910).

Wagenknecht, Edward, *Washington Irving: Moderation Displayed* (New York, 1962).

Wandell, Samuel H., and Meade Minnigerode, *Aaron Burr: A Biography Com-*

piled from Rare, and in Many Cases Unpublished, Sources, 2 vols. (New York, 1925).

Wardle, Ralph W. (ed.), *Godwin & Mary: Letters of William Godwin and Mary Wollstonecraft* (Lawrence, Kans., 1966).

Webb, Richard D., *The Life and Letters of Captain John Brown* . . . (London, 1861).

White, Newman Ivey, *Shelley*, 2 vols. (New York, 1940).

Wilkinson, James, *Memoirs of My Own Times*, 3 vols. (Philadelphia, 1816).

Williams, Stanley T. (ed.), *Letters from Sunnyside and Spain by Washington Irving* (New Haven, 1928).

Williams, Stanley T., *The Life of Washington Irving*, 2 vols. (New York, 1935).

Williams, Stanley T., *The Spanish Background of American Literature*, 2 vols. (New Haven, 1955).

Williams, Stanley T. (ed.), *Washington Irving and the Storrows: Letters from England and the Continent. 1821–1828* (Cambridge, Mass., 1933).

Williams, Stanley T., "Washington Irving's Religion," *Yale Review* [1-1926], 414–16.

Williamson, Jefferson, *The American Hotel: An Anecdotal History* (New York, 1930).

Wilson, James Grant, *The Life and Letters of Fitz-Greene Halleck* (New York, 1869).

Wilson, James Grant, *Thackeray in the United States: 1852–3, 1855–6* (New York, 1904).

Wollstonecraft, Mary, *Letters to Imlay* (London, 1879).

Wollstonecraft, Mary, *A Vindication of the Rights of Women* . . . , New Edition (London, 1891).

Woodcock, George, *William Godwin* . . . (London, 1946).

Yarborough, Minnie C., "Rambles with Washington Irving: Quotations from an Unpublished Autobiography of William C. Preston," *The South Atlantic Quarterly* [10-1930], XXIX 423–39.

INDEX

ACKNOWLEDGMENTS

Stanley T. Williams' superb biography *The Life of Washington Irving* (1935) lies at the very heart of this work; without it, I could not have proceeded far. The list of sources itemizes my indebtedness to other scholars whose books and articles I have consulted. Especially useful as points of departure were Stephen B. Oates's *To Purge This Land with Blood: A Biography of John Brown*, Herbert S. Parmet and Marie B. Hecht's *Aaron Burr: Portrait of an Ambitious Man*, Edgar Johnson's *Sir Walter Scott: The Great Unknown*, Eileen Bigland's *Mary Shelley*, and Kenneth Wiggins Porter's *John Jacob Astor, Business Man*. My personal obligations include, at the minimum, kindnesses from the Trustees of Concord Academy, as well as from the staffs of the Boston Athenaeum and the American Antiquarian Society, from Mrs. Wm. Henry Moss and the Concord (Massachusetts) Free Public Library, and from the Boston and New York Public Libraries. For help and encouragement I am grateful to John Cushman, Thomas McFarland, Justin Kaplan, Nancy Myers, Nancy Gleason, Donald Cantor, Thomas A. West, Mary Jane Alexander, Ralph M. Aderman, Lewis Leary, Wayne R. Kime, and—especially—to Andrew B. Myers, Walter A. Reichart, and Herman Gollob. Errors, inevitable in a story so sprawling, are all my own.

Philip McFarland

Philip McFarland lives in Lexington, Massachusetts, with his wife and two sons, and teaches English at Concord Academy.